PRINCE AND THE *PURPLE RAIN* ERA STUDIO SESSIONS

PRINCE AND THE *PURPLE RAIN* ERA STUDIO SESSIONS

1983 AND 1984

Duane Tudahl

ROWMAN & LITTLEFIELD
Lanham • Boulder • New York • London

Published by Rowman & Littlefield
A wholly owned subsidiary of The Rowman & Littlefield Publishing Group, Inc.
4501 Forbes Boulevard, Suite 200, Lanham, Maryland 20706
www.rowman.com

Unit A, Whitacre Mews, 26-34 Stannary Street, London SE11 4AB

British Library Cataloguing in Publication Information Available

Library of Congress Cataloging-in-Publication Data

Names: Tudahl, Duane.
Title: Prince and the Purple rain era studio sessions : 1983 and 1984 / Duane
 Tudahl.
Description: Lanham : Rowman & Littlefield, [2017] | Includes bibliographical
 references and index.
Identifiers: LCCN 2017015244 (print) | LCCN 2017016761 (ebook) | ISBN
 9781538105504 (electronic) | ISBN 9781538105498 (hardback : alk. paper)
Subjects: LCSH: Prince—Criticism and interpretation. | Rock music—United
 States—1981–1990—History and criticism. | Prince—Chronology. | Prince.
 Purple rain.
Classification: LCC ML420.P974 (ebook) | LCC ML420.P974 T83 2017 (print) |
 DDC 781.66092—dc23
LC record available at https://lccn.loc.gov/2017015244

∞™ The paper used in this publication meets the minimum requirements of
American National Standard for Information Sciences—Permanence of Paper
for Printed Library Materials, ANSI/NISO Z39.48-1992.

Printed in the United States of America

CONTENTS

CONTENTS

FOREWORD

There are many things about Prince that interest me, some of which were more powerful during his life, some of which were more powerful just after his death, and some of which are more powerful now, a year or so after his death. I could make a long list: his fashion sense, his sense of humor, his importance as a central cultural figure, his relationship to other stars, his ability to inspire artists in every genre, and so on. But one thing has remained consistent, no matter when I've thought about it, and that's my interest in Prince's studio process.

In 2016 I wrote a book called *Something to Food About*, where I talked about the creative lives of chefs, and that was a backdoor way into some of the issues of creativity that are always on my mind: when an idea starts, how much it has to be refined, how many collaborators are useful for perfecting it and how many run the risk of jeopardizing it, when other creative professionals know that they have hit the sweet spot. That book was fascinating for many reasons, but one of the main reasons was that it reminded me that I have an odd aversion to asking those same questions of musicians. I don't know if it's a form of superstition or a form of competitiveness, but it was somehow safer for me to explore those questions when it came to chefs—and I noticed that the same thing was true of comedians, and painters, and authors. I think I agreed in some ways with the people who warned that it can be tricky to know too much about an artist's process, that it can turn a beautiful thing into a sausage factory, where you see the meat paste before it's squeezed into the casing.

But Prince has a special status. Learning about his process isn't a sausage factory. It's a dream factory. (That's an inside joke—it's the original name of the sprawling album that eventually became *Sign o' the Times*). As long as I can remember, I've been preoccupied with the minutiae of Prince's recording sessions. I've wondered, guessed, and researched, trying to figure out how much he cooked up himself, how much others brought to the table, how long songs hibernated before they woke up, and which songs magically took flight immediately. (I know I mixed a bunch of metaphors there. I don't care. This is a piece about Prince's art, not a rhetoric lesson.)

Take *Purple Rain*. No, don't take *Purple Rain*. Leave it for me. I don't know what I'd do without it. Since I first heard "When Doves Cry"—a song that cemented what was already a serious Prince obsession—as a teenager, I have obsessed about exactly how those songs came together. But take the details of *Purple Rain*. It's a fascinating record, partly a live album recorded at First Avenue, partly Prince's attempt to capture the energy of the mid-eighties arena rock that was dominating the charts, and partly a further exploration of his increasingly experimental funk-rock. I teach a class at the Clive Davis Institute of Recorded Music at NYU. I've done a curriculum based on seventies funk music in general. I've done a curriculum based on Michael Jackson's *Thriller*. I've even done a course on Prince. But *Purple Rain* is the great whitish-purplish whale, as far as an album like that is concerned. I'd love to teach a class on it, with all the intricate details.

Which isn't to say that I could have been the one to collect all those details. That's where Duane Tudahl comes in. He's tireless where other people would be exhausted. He's comprehensive where other people would be uncomprehending. He has personally brought together hundreds of hours of interviews with all the people involved in the making of that record. He's also been given access to material from two journalists and archivists associated with the Prince sound, Alan Freed and Per Nilsen. And maybe more amazingly, he's gotten hold of the daily studio work orders from studios so that he can piece together the massive puzzle of how the record came together.

I don't want to ruin any surprises. You should read this book. But as you read it, you should marvel at all the things it's not. That's a strange thing to say, but I want to say it again. Think of all the things this book is not. There are wonderful books about Prince that are preoccupied with his cultural significance, or the meaning of his music, or the way he changed sexuality for our generation, or any of the other things I mentioned in the first paragraph. I have taught some of them in my class. I have written introductions for some of them. I won't mention them here. That would be churlish. But there are no other books that do this kind of deep dive into the primary source material for an album and reward that kind of diving in incredible ways. Duane has said that he hopes this is the first of many books that handle Prince's catalog in this way, that go through his recordings one by one and try to mine out of the studio logs and musician recollections a fuller picture of what's there. I hope that's true. I hope that when I am an old man with a long beard I can look down my Prince bookshelf and see, next to the other books I've taught, next to the other books I've written intros for, Duane's whole series, paralleling Prince's entire body of work. But don't take my word for it. Take James Brown's word for it: Get up and take the book off the shelf, get into it, and get involved.

—*Ahmir "Questlove" Thompson*

PREFACE

The music I make a lot of the time is reflective of the life I am leading. —*Prince*[1]

Some musicians are forever linked with a specific recording studio: The Beatles at Abbey Road, Elvis at Sun Records, and Hendrix at New York City's Record Plant. Often the studio helped define and shape the musicians, exposing them to a vibe that brought out something timeless. Fleetwood Mac could have recorded *Rumours* anywhere, but the Record Plant in Sausalito, California, provided the womblike atmosphere that helped nourish their album of self-reflection. Recording at Big Pink in Upstate New York literally changed the direction of Bob Dylan's career, just as time at Los Angeles's Sunset Sound changed the career of another Minnesota son. To most people, Prince is forever bonded with Paisley Park, but before Paisley Park, the biggest albums of his career were recorded at Sunset Sound Studios. In fact, his success from those sessions gave him the financial strength necessary to build Paisley Park just outside Minneapolis, a studio patterned after elements from Sunset Sound.

This is an unprecedented look into Prince's time in the recording studio at the peak of his career. These are the stories behind the songs he released and a revealing look at what he kept hidden from the world. This is his trip from cult artist to one of the biggest stars in the world, told through the music he created along the way.

Tragically, with Prince's passing in April 2016 the focus on his career has shifted from the promise of what was to come to the story of what he accomplished. The objective of this book isn't to simply list *what*, *where*, and *when* his music was recorded during 1983 and 1984. The bigger goal is to explain *why*, and hopefully give his music from this era some much-needed perspective by placing it into the context of his life. Any events that take place outside of the studio help weave a larger tapestry of these two years, reflecting light back to his songs, because at the end of the day the music will be what is remembered, and, like all great art, it lasts longer than the artist. The music makes the musician immortal.

This book is based on the memories of those who were there with him on this journey.

I've personally conducted several hundred hours of interviews with the band members, singers, and anyone else associated with these sessions, including the studio engineers who spent weeks alone with him watching his creative process. In addition to this, I've been given access to more than seventy-five hours of interviews conducted by Alan Freed for Per Nilsen and *Uptown* magazine. I've also gathered hundreds of published quotes by practically everyone around Prince during this period; I've allowed their own words to tell the tale and corroborated their stories with hundreds of documents, including daily studio work orders from Sunset Sound Studios, information from the Warner Bros. vault, and various other sources that verified the specific dates and times, to put this epic puzzle together piece by piece. Any date marked with a * is confirmed by the Sunset Sound documentation. This book is not flawless, but it is the most detailed record available of what transpired in the studios.

"[The recording studio] is *his* space," explains Susannah Melvoin, who was one of the few people permitted behind the closed door. "He's never going to go into your space and he'd rarely invite you into his, but his space is the only thing that matters when it comes to his prowess and his ego and his ability." I hope that telling the story through the words of those who were in the room with him gives this a more panoramic perspective. Of course, since the events chronicled occurred more than three decades ago, there will be a fair share of *Rashomon*-like recollections, but I've tried to place everyone's memories in the proper context, and when there were major discrepancies, I've presented both sides, generally favoring those that occurred closest to the actual events. Even Prince himself contradicted many of his own stories in his quest to keep the mystery alive. His cat-and-mouse games with reporters were entertaining, but trying to figure out what was truth and what was hype is difficult. My journey as a funk archivist has been frustratingly fun, and the human rewards have been more than I imagined. The people I've worked with on this book were all open, honest, and helpful and have unearthed information never before published. I've detailed more about everyone involved in the acknowledgements of this book.

There are no hidden agendas in this manuscript. My goal was to tell the story of Prince's incredible rise from critical darling to superstar, but I wanted to do it in a way that hadn't been attempted, so the story is told by documenting his time in the studio as a fly on the wall whenever possible. The more than 220 studio dates for this book include music that ended up on *Purple Rain*, *Around the World in a Day*, and multiple B-sides, along with various albums he'd release in the years that followed. These sessions from the two-year period of 1983–1984 would also yield music for Apollonia 6, the Time, the Family, Sheila E., the Bangles, Sheena Easton, Jill Jones, and Stevie Nicks, as well as numerous unreleased tracks. Each of these songs has a story, and the people who were involved deserve to be recognized. "I have seen Prince write songs right before my eyes. Great songs," remembered his drummer Bobby Z. "He just has the gift. He's a true visionary, and long after people forget about all the other stuff, they'll come back to the music and realize what a genius he is."[2]

Unlike other behind-the-scenes books about studio sessions involving famous musicians, when it comes to Prince it is important to also include as many details as possible about his more than one hundred live performances and countless rehearsals and sound checks during this two-year period, which in turn inspired what was being recorded in the studio. "Prince was always recording," explains his bass player Mark Brown (aka Brown Mark). "Didn't matter where we were. Our performances, our rehearsals, everything was always being recorded. This guy has archives of stuff."

"An idea might jump into his head, and if it's an idea that sticks, he might throw it in the middle of a song onstage," detailed sax player Eric Leeds. "The rest of the band might go, 'That's something we never heard before!' He wants a document of it right there, so he can say, 'Okay, I know it's there, when I need to refer to that, it's there on that night and I'll check it out later, and it will be the center frame to write a new song.' Very much the way James Brown used to work."[3]

This book has been more than twenty years in the making, and along the way many of those being interviewed have asked me if Prince was involved in the book or if I'd interviewed him. Obviously, any insights he'd have would be helpful, so I've tried to include as many quotes by him as possible, but I avoided seeking his thoughts on this project because I am not sure how he would have felt about some of his secrets being revealed. I can imagine his voice saying, "Ignore that man behind the curtain," so I never contacted Prince or Paisley Park about an interview for this book. My suspicions were confirmed in November of 2013, when Prince was asked the following on Twitter: "Ever thought about showing your work process in the studio? Rehearsal is one thing, but how songs were made would be amazing."

His response was enlightening: "**No. It's 2 sacred.**"[4]

What is covered in this book isn't sacred, but it is a glimpse behind the scenes at how a genius created his art and how events and the people closest to him shaped his music. I don't want to pull the curtain back and completely expose the wizard. Instead, I'd like to think of this as just looking over his shoulder, marveling at his craft. The stories behind these songs overflow with struggles, frustrations, fights, love and lust (they both have four letters, but they're entirely different words), and emotional breakups, but also the joys and optimism of the times. In the end, the result is one of the most prolific periods for any artist and a high-water mark for Prince when it comes to the public's reaction to his music. Obviously there is no way I can re-create the period exactly, but I can get rid of some of the mystery behind the birth of many of his songs. I hope the trade-off for shining light on some of the dark corners of this story is that this book brings these studio sessions alive for you. Do yourself a favor: Turn down the lights and play the vocal version of "God" (B-side of "Purple Rain") and imagine Prince recording the piano and vocal in one take, then closing the lid and walking out of the studio without saying a word. I hope reading this book makes you go back and listen to the 12-inch of "America" and visualize the entire Revolution smiling at each other while stepping forward and adding their parts to the twenty-minute jam. I hope it makes you seek out *The Family* album, which Eric Leeds considered "as much a Prince album as anything else he's done."[5] I hope it inspires you to purchase these tracks or at least blow the dust off your Prince collection and listen to lost classics like "She's Always in My Hair," knowing that he recorded it alone in the studio during a single session.

Find the classic Warner Bros. records from this period and play them while you read.

Because of Prince's passing, it is practically impossible to listen to his music without looking through the prism of his absence. Prince touched many of us individually and his music spoke to us in our core, so his loss is extremely intimate and, unfortunately, we will rarely have the chance to share the excitement of hearing it again with crowds of other fans. As personal as it is, his music should be celebrated, and the joy it creates should be shared. Perhaps understanding his passion, his urgency, and his reasons for recording his songs will help you emotionally reconnect with the music and let you experience the goose bumps of hearing it all for the first time once again.

I want this book to create images for each of these songs that are a part of the soundtrack to your life, and hopefully open the eyes of young musicians who want to understand how it was done by someone who'd mastered the studio. It was achieved by his hard work and dedication, and by surrounding himself with people who inspired him and supported his dream. Prince has gone on record many times about not being interested in reflecting on his past. In 2014 he told *Mojo* magazine, **"I don't need to look back. I know what happened."**[6]

Hopefully after reading this, you'll know a little bit more about what happened, and why it was important.

Dig if you will . . .

JANUARY 1983

My name at birth was Prince Rogers Nelson.—Prince[1]

Fast-forward twenty-four years. Prince was at a crossroads.

SATURDAY, JANUARY 1, 1983

Prince was on what was supposed to be the biggest tour of his career, promoting his *1999* album, but morale was collapsing, his band was splintering, and he was barely speaking with some of the musicians in the other groups on the tour. Sales of his recent double album had already peaked and stalled at number 23 on the *Billboard* 200. The title track hadn't been the major hit that was anticipated, heading back down the charts after cresting at number 44. At the beginning of 1983 the track fell to number 65, and it would vanish from the top 100 before the end of the month. Two other albums he'd written and produced, the Time's *What Time Is It?* and the debut album from Vanity 6, were both sinking back down the charts as well, with the former dropping out of the top 100 completely. So far the tour was financially successful, but record sales were indicating that *1999* was not going to be Prince's breakout release. But I'm getting ahead of the story.

The dawn of 1983 found Prince in a difficult spot. He was a cult performer with a very dedicated audience, but he wasn't selling like Warner Bros. wanted. In October 1982 Prince released *1999* (his fifth album in five years) to critical praise, but by this time critical praise alone wasn't going to carry him much further, even

1

with the full backing of the label. Considered by most to be a talented enigma, Prince's appeal to the masses was more about the undelivered promise of something huge, but he hadn't fully tipped the scale from cult performer to mainstream success. Warner Bros. took a huge risk on Prince by putting out a double album of new music, and so far the gamble hadn't completely paid off and—even though his current tour was getting incredible reviews—prospects didn't look great. Alan Leeds, who would oversee the final weeks of the *1999* tour, described it well: "He had his little cult, but it wasn't substantial. It wasn't sizeable."[2]

Although it was never officially called the "Triple Threat Tour," the nickname was used by some for the 1982–1983 American tour featuring Prince, the Time, and Vanity 6. Few in the general public knew that Prince was the puppet master behind all three bands, dictating their style and, although uncredited, writing the vast majority of their music. The irony of this is that he had essentially created his own competition, causing incestuous rivalries within the groups. His method for building his protégé projects can be viewed as if he were creating a play that he wrote, directed, and cast with friends and those in his circle. Each person had a role to play and as long as each remained in character and in costume, the play continued. The Time was what Prince would sound like if he were a rock/funk band and Vanity 6 was what Prince would sound like if he were a female trio. "All the different bands he has created have been sides of his personality," explained keyboardist Lisa Coleman. "Vanity 6 would be the sexy girl, Morris Day would be the comedy guy, and then Prince was the rock star."[3]

Prince was the king of his world, but at the beginning of January 1983, he was still a big fish in a small pond. His influence on the bands was definite and his decisions were final, despite protests by members of Vanity 6 or the Time. "It created a tension between us," confided Time front man Morris Day, "and there used to be some arguments before going on stage about things that I would do that were conflicting with things that Prince would do. I was told not to do certain dances."[4]

"I think those days took a toll on everyone in the Time because it was just a lot of pressure," explained Jesse Johnson a few years later. "If you did a dance that he didn't like or a dance that the audience dug, he didn't particular[ly] like that. He would stop us from doing certain dances, from wearing certain clothes, because he just never wanted there to be any room to upstage him."[5]

But the Time did upstage him on many nights. Prince was responsible for most of the music the Time was performing, but because they had found a way to add their collective personality to the show, at this point in the tour Prince found himself playing catch up to his creation. "There were times Prince would be pissed they were so good," declares lighting director LeRoy "Roy" Bennett. "Oh yeah, they gave him a run for his money."

Prince was treated as the boss to those around him, but his influence in the music industry didn't reflect that. At the time, Prince, his managers, and the executives at Warner Bros. seemed to be the only people who envisioned his full promise. "We believe Prince has much greater name value than the number of records he's sold," proclaimed Bob Cavallo, part of Prince's management team of Cavallo, Ruffalo & Fargnoli. "In the beginning, Warner Bros. Pictures discounted his name value, but there's something about Prince that piques people's interest a little more than some other artists. People don't know a lot about him; he's a little mysterioso and he has a controversial image."[6]

The year 1983 would see Prince the cult musician become Prince the world-wide superstar, but right now the future was still uncertain. Although reviews of his album had been mostly favorable, there were many who didn't see his potential. Pamela Littlejohn, the music critic for the *Los Angeles Sentinel*, gave the album only two stars, noting: "People who are not into Prince and his ilk cannot understand this one. . . . A little of it goes a long way . . . but for those in the Prince cult—this is standard fare."[7]

If Prince was going to succeed, he needed a hit. With a legacy of four Prince albums, two Time albums, and one Vanity 6 album behind him, he had the attention of many but not the respect he probably knew he deserved for his dedication to his craft and his work ethic. "He is the hardest working guy that I've ever dealt with," said James Harris III, a keyboard player for the Time who was more commonly known as Jimmy Jam. "He would literally come to our practices for five or six hours, then he'd go to his own band practice and work with them for five or six hours, then he'd go to the studio and work all night. He's right up there to me with the greats of all time. He's also the type of musician that would be great no matter what era he grew up in. He would have been great in the jazz era with Miles Davis, and in the sixties with Sly and Jimi Hendrix and so on."[8]

"What we took away from him is his vision and his ability to basically think anything is possible," explained Monte Moir, the other keyboard player for the Time. "He would say, 'Oh, we're going to do this,' and we're like, 'Huh? What?' And we would do it. He would somehow make it happen."[9]

Because Prince was sick, his December 28, 1982, concert at Lake Charles Civic Center had been postponed, and he was very run down as the year ended. Three more shows were performed on the remaining days of the year, but the new year was starting off with a limp instead of a sprint. He wrapped up 1982 with a show at Reunion Arena in Dallas, Texas, and tickets for a proposed second night in Dallas on January 1 were printed, but it appears they never went on sale. Two shows remained, including one at the Summit in Houston scheduled for the following night and another in Lake Charles, Louisiana.

SUNDAY, JANUARY 2, 1983

Venue: The Summit (Houston, Texas)
Capacity: 17,500 (approximately 11,426 tickets sold based on two-show average)

MONDAY, JANUARY 3, 1983

Venue: Lake Charles Civic Center (Lake Charles, Louisiana)
Capacity: 5,230 (sold out)

The first leg of the tour was originally scheduled to have wrapped on January 2, but a final night was arranged to reschedule a performance that had been canceled the previous week. Additional European dates were planned for the last half of January, and although two of the dates (in England and the Netherlands) were booked, the shows were postponed until mid-April and ultimately canceled.

With the tour scheduled to resume on February 1, everyone was looking forward to some downtime—everyone except Prince, who decided that this wasn't a time to step back but instead a chance to regroup and refocus. **"When we first went out behind *1999*, the Time, who were opening for us, beat us up every night,"** reflected Prince. **"They would laugh about it; it was a joke to them. Our show wasn't together. I had to stop the tour and get things tightened up."**[10]

FRIDAY, JANUARY 7, 1983*

"Little Red Corvette" (overdubs and mix of 12-inch)
Sunset Sound, Studio 2 | 6:30 p.m.–6:30 a.m.

Producer: Prince | Artist: Prince | Engineer: Prince | Assistant Engineer: Bill Jackson (Peggy McCreary scratched out)

That song was a real life incident. A girl in a little red corvette. —Prince[11]

Although the title track from *1999* was a minor hit on the *Billboard* charts, it was doing well on the Soul charts (number 4) and the Disco/Club charts (number 1), so Warner Bros. wanted Prince to build on this success. During this short break in the *1999* tour, he traveled back to Sunset Sound Studios in Los Angeles to create the 12-inch for his next single, "Little Red Corvette." It was originally recorded on May 20, 1982, in Prince's basement studio in Chanhassen, Minnesota, and was the first song he recorded on his new Ampex MM1200 24-track recorder. Shortly afterward, Prince edited the actual 2-inch master copy of the tape to create the album version. He had Don Batts, his Minneapolis engineer, place all the pieces in a box and ship it to Sunset Sound. During this period, Prince's primary engineer in Los Angeles was Sunset Sound staff member Peggy "Peggy Mac" Mc-Creary, and the bulk of the editing was done by her boyfriend, fellow staff member David "the blade" Leonard. They had reconstructed the album version of the song during the original Sunset Sound sessions while compiling the *1999* album on August 11 and 12, 1982, but the long version was still incomplete. Prince had cut the 2-inch tape into eight or nine pieces, and it arrived in eight or nine pieces. Usually editing like that was done on the 2-track version, so this made the task of putting it back together even more difficult, but they'd done it.

With McCreary unavailable for the session, staff engineer Bill Jackson was given the task of reconstructing the additional three minutes and twenty seconds from the box of scraps. No cassette copies were made of the mixed version for Prince to review outside the studio, probably because he didn't feel the session was complete. "We put like one part on but I don't remember what it was," recalls Jackson. "He mixed it himself. We were plugging in a lot of delays, compressors and harmonizers. He just asked me to do something if he needed something like an EQ [equalization] or putting delays on it. I was just running the tape machine and I remember this because it was one of the only days that we stayed up so late mixing something."

The session lasted until 6:30 the following morning. No cassette copies were made of the mixed version, probably because Prince didn't feel the session was complete.

Status: The extended version of "Little Red Corvette" (8:22) was also known as the "Dance Mix" and "Dance Remix." It was only released for purchase in Germany, Belgium, and possibly a few other locations. A promo version was released in the United States.

It should be noted that Bill Jackson and others are listed as "assistant engineer" on the official documents, but the reality was that they were actually full engineers. "I think finally on [the 1999 album] Prince said, 'Well I'm giving you engineering credits,' remembers McCreary, who'd worked with Prince since 1981, 'and I'm like, 'Well great!' But I was, together with [Prince], engineering. There was nobody else in the room, and nobody else touched any tape. He and I both did the board, I did the setup and the recording of all of the mics, although he sat at the board. It's kind of the way he was with his band; he never let you sit there in the sense that you were totally in charge."
The terms engineer *and* assistant engineer *are both used in the text.*

SATURDAY, JANUARY 8, 1983*

"Little Red Corvette" (mix for 12-inch)
Sunset Sound, Studio 2 | 2:00 p.m.–7:30 p.m.
Producer: Prince | *Artist:* Prince | *Engineer:* David Leonard

> *I bought this vintage pink Mercury at a car auction. It was so bitching-looking that Prince used to borrow it and dent it, which I'd make him feel bad about. He slept in it one time and came up with "Little Red Corvette" . . . even though it was a pink Mercury.* —Lisa Coleman[12]

Less than eight hours after the previous session ended, Prince was back in Studio 2, this time with engineer David Leonard: "When I would edit for him, first of all, every song that we ever recorded was a full reel of tape, like 12–15 minutes long, and everything that came out on the record was edited down to the short, radio versions, but all the originals are long. So the dance versions, the long versions, are the actual originals. They're the full-length versions, and then everything on the record was cut down."[13]

Prince had Leonard create a cassette (TDK C-60) of the mix. After five and a half hours the session ended, giving Prince the chance to have a weekend night out in Los Angeles.

MONDAY, JANUARY 10, 1983*

"**Gigolos Get Lonely Too**" [listed as "A Gigolo Gets Lonely Too"] (edit for single release)
Sunset Sound, Studio 2 | 7:00 p.m.–8:00 p.m. (booked 6:00 p.m.–open)
Producer: Morris Day is listed, but Prince oversaw the session | *Artist:* the Time | *Engineer:* Morris Day | *Assistant Engineer:* David Leonard (Bill Jackson scratched out)

Jesse and Morris and Jerome and Jimmy and Terry had the makings of one of the greatest R&B bands in history. I could be a little pretentious in saying that, but it's truly the way I feel. There's no one that could wreck a house like they could. —Prince[14]

As Prince's career grew and the variety of his music expanded, Prince needed an outlet for his R&B music, so in 1981 he put together the Time. The group was created when Prince wanted to record "Partyup," a track written by Morris Day, who was a childhood friend and the drummer for his early band Grand Central. According to Day, "He was like, 'I can either give you some money, or I'll help you put a band together.' So I said, 'I'll take the band.'"[15]

Prince had attempted a side project called the Rebels in 1979, but nothing was released from those sessions and the project quietly died. For the Time, Prince worked behind the scenes as the invisible partner who dictated the direction, the look, and the sound for the band. Day was initially going to be the drummer and Alexander O'Neal was going to be the singer, but when an agreement over money couldn't be reached, Prince moved Morris from behind the drums to be the front man for the band, despite Day's almost complete lack of experience as a lead singer. "Interestingly enough, we used to call Morris 'Morris "Too Hot" Day,' because Morris would come out from behind the drums and sing ['Too Hot' by Kool and the Gang]," remembered Jimmy Jam, who was familiar with Day before they worked together in the Time. "So we figured if Morris could sing that tune, which was kind of a tough tune to sing, he could definitely cut it as a singer. And he always had a lot of personality and stuff anyway. Even in his drum playing he had a lot of personality. So that's kind of how everything came together."[16]

Work on the Time's debut album was a stripped-down affair, with Prince recording many of their songs on used tape to keep costs down. The Time seemed to be designed to fill Prince's needs, and not necessarily Day's, because it gave Prince a chance to release more than the allotted one album per year he was doing for Warner Bros.

"It was a business favor," explained Time drummer Jellybean Johnson, "but also I think we brought out the black side of him. I really believe it. He had the best of both worlds. Because we were his credibility in the black world. I believe we were the funky, cool, ghetto, gangster part that he always wanted to be. That's what we were. We were his alter ego like that. 'Cause he always wanted to be like that. But he couldn't."[17]

"It was Morris playing drums and me on the bass," detailed Prince in an interview with *Ebony* magazine. **"That's how we would make the basic track. Naked. Just like that, and nobody would know. And then when you put the keys on it and the guitar, then that's what the Time was. And it was perfect."**[18]

With the recording part of the project complete, Prince and Morris began looking for band members and found Jesse Johnson (no relation to Jellybean Johnson), a guitarist from Rock Island, Illinois. On March 8, 1981, Jesse Johnson got his first introduction to Prince:

> Rock Island's really tiny and there was no Black radio there, so I didn't know who [Prince] was. I went to the show at First Avenue and saw him for the first time. I was like, "Oh. Okay, cool." Then the next day we met and I said, "Yo, you really dig Hendrix." He said, "I never watch him." I said, "Aww, you lying mother fucker!" Morris was standing behind him, [signaling] "No, no, no!" Prince kind of fell on the floor and just started laughing. He was just dying. He was cracking up [because] everybody else in the room knew who he was and they were acting different from how they were acting before he got there. So I figured he must have been a big shot or something. Then he said, "Morris said you could really play," and I said, "Well, you want me to plug in and play?" He was like, "No. I like your look. You have a cool look." So that was it.[19]

"The first name of the band was the Nerve and that's what was on the sleeve when we did the test album," revealed Day. "So [the Time] didn't come about until weeks after the album was finished."[20]

"At first we were going to be a black version of Hall & Oates," Johnson eventually added. "But then Prince had another idea."[21]

Day explained, "What we were trying to do, and Prince was masterminding the whole situation, was come up with a name and sayings that you'd have to say every day[,] like[,] 'What time is it?' He came up with 'the Time,' which I thought was pretty clever."[22]

"Prince put a lot of grooming into Morris and [me] personally," emphasized Johnson. "He taught us how to handle that front line. Prince is a stickler for detail. You weren't going to get up there and be an embarrassment to him in any way, shape or form if he could help it. He went out of his way to teach us how to represent properly."[23]

The Time would eventually become a collection of seven performers, almost all of them musicians from multiple local bands. "We were really rival bands back in Northside Minneapolis," reflected Day. "We were all fighting for the same gigs, and the name of my band was Grand Central [with Prince], and Jimmy Jam, Terry Lewis, Jellybean, and Monte had their band, Flyte Tyme, and when I got the record deal . . . Prince said, 'Who we going to get for a band?' and I was like . . . 'Flyte Tyme.'"[24]

Jimmy Jam agreed with the basic premise of this timeline, but maintained a very important distinction: "We were not put together by Prince. We were already a band and had been for quite a while. We actually used to compete with Prince's band, Grand Central, in the early Minneapolis days when we were called Flyte Tyme. That was sort of the origin of everything."[25] Bassist Terry Lewis put it more bluntly: "Prince didn't make us; we were already made. He just gave us an incredible opportunity. Everything fell in line . . . and it was scary."[26]

Although the lineup of the Time consisted of two-thirds Flyte Tyme and one-third Prince's input, Prince maintained control of the band. But simply being around the band influenced Prince as well. McCreary recalls that "around the Time, he was a little more 'street' but he was always the same guy, but you could always tell he was running the show."

Jimmy Jam detailed to Prince biographer Dave Hill that the six original members of the band (Morris Day, Jesse Johnson, Monte Moir, Terry Lewis, Jimmy Jam, and Jellybean Johnson) were assembled and the plan was explained: "Prince more or less said, 'We've done the album, and you're the group.' We did our first gig a few weeks later."[27]

The final member of the band, Jerome Benton, was added soon afterward. "I wasn't in the group as a musician," he said. "I was around and helping things move along and move forward, and eventually became one of the personnel in the group. My role at first was a roadie."[28]

"Jerome was always around. He had a great personality," explained Day. "We had just cut the first album and were rehearsing to go on tour, and there's a part in [the song] 'Cool' where I say[,] 'Somebody bring me a mirror[,]' and we were rehearsing in this dusty little rehearsal hall and Jerome ran into the bathroom and grabbed the mirror off the wall and brought it out and we all just looked at each other like, 'That's got to stay! That's got to be in the show.' From that point on Jerome was in the band."[29]

Publicly, Day was seen as the leader and the public face of the band; he was thought of as the mastermind behind their attitude, which reflected fun and swagger. "The image was 'cool,'" according to Day. "That's the key word. That's what we built the Time around. Cool is an attitude, a self-respect thing."[30]

But privately their self-respect was taking a beating because the public image and the reality were very different things.

Over the next two years, Prince continued to oversee practically every detail of the band, nurturing their image, writing the bulk of the music for their second album, and maintaining final say in practically all of the creative decisions.

Such firm control frustrated members of the Time, who felt he didn't allow them the chance to shine in the studio. "Working with the Time, you had Prince, one of the most creative people in the history of creativity," recalled Jam. "You had Morris Day, who is infinitely talented. And back then, you had like six songs per album. There wasn't a lot of room left for creativity."[31]

Day was also feeling stifled: "He masterminded all of the early concepts and stuff, and I didn't mind because the cat is a genius, you know, no one can take that from him. As things progressed, when there were opportunities for us to do more writing, I know that's when he started to really put his thumb down. So after a while when we all were writing and really starting to feel the creative juices . . . that's when he started to really crack down on us and control us."[32]

This began to slowly drive a wedge between Prince and the Time. Jam was philosophical about why he felt Prince didn't give the band their proper respect: "Prince's thinking is just on a different level than most people's. And people who expect a lot of themselves expect a lot of others. When you think a lot of yourself, you start to believe other people should be thinking of themselves along the same lines. And when they're not, you might say, 'Hey, stupid, why aren't you doing anything?' You end up alienating them."[33]

To compensate, the Time channeled all their energy into their live shows and became incredible performers, so Prince enlisted them as the opening act for his *Controversy* tour, as he would again for the *1999* tour. Drummer Jellybean Johnson later insisted that Prince's plan was backfiring: "He made music and he told us what to play and we came in and played, a lot of times better than what he had. And in concert it went over better than what it did on record, and after a while he resented that shit. He resented it!"[34]

"They were really good," noted Prince's keyboard player, Matt Fink. "They were so tight and would put on such a great show that Prince in some respects thought that they were showing us up . . . I think. They were that good. Back then, the audience would go wild for them and we'd go on stage and Prince would feel that we weren't garnering the same response, so I think that hurt him."

In 1986, during an interview with WHYT's the Electrifying Mojo, Prince agreed: **"They were, to be perfectly honest, the only band that I was afraid of. And, they were turning into like . . . Godzilla."**[35]

"[The Time] rehearsed eight to ten hours a day," explained Jellybean Johnson. "It was really less a job, but we had fun, 'cause we loved being around each other, we loved whenever we would go out and hang. The Time was really like a family back then, the personalities that we had, everybody was into each other and everybody looked out for each other. It was cool."[36]

"With the Time, we were always good buddies as far as the band and so we were just hanging," explained Moir. "We were a bunch of young kids just having a good old time and I think he didn't like that."[37]

The relationships inside the Time were solid, but the band's increasing success grew to frustrate Prince in a way he may not have anticipated, according to Jellybean Johnson: "It was a very positive competition as far as us playing well. After a while I think it was for him, too, because he knew if he didn't play his best, he'd get his ass whooped. He knew that. We were just as hungry as he was."

The Time was scheduled to continue on the *1999* tour when it resumed rehearsals in late January, but a month earlier, on December 16, the underlying conflict had come to a boil. "I remember in Nashville something went down," recalls lighting director Roy Bennett. "There was a big fight during sound check, with Prince riding them pretty hard."

According to Moir, Prince justified his overbearing behavior with Day because "he felt that the only way to get people to do what you wanted them to was to put yourself up here and scream at 'em. Morris said to him, 'Why? We're all friends. I don't need to yell at anyone. All we've gotta do is talk about it.'"[38] Like many situations involving Prince's control, Moir added, "When push came to shove, it was still down to Prince."[39]

Prince expanded on the authority he had over his music: **"My way usually is the best way. I strive for perfection, and sometimes I'm a little bull-headed in my ways."**[40] Despite the tension growing between the two bands, Prince's goal was to make them a huge success, and during today's session he worked on their next single. "Gigolos Get Lonely Too" had been released on *What Time Is It?* several months earlier and was slated to be the third single (after "777-9311" b/w "Grace," which was released on July 30, 1982, and peaked at number 88 on the *Billboard* Pop chart and number 2 on the Black Singles chart, and "The Walk" b/w "OnedayI'mgonnabesomebody," which didn't break the Top 100 on the *Billboard* Pop chart). Prince was working hard to place all three bands on the charts at the same time with one of his songs, so this week he spent his time in the studio getting the tracks ready. Prince's future tour manager Alan Leeds summed it up fairly simply: "I think to him the gratification of being able to come home at the end of the day and hold up the charts and see what the Time record was doing, what Vanity 6 was doing . . . he knew, Warner's knew, his banker knew, they all knew."[41]

During this brief session, "Gigolos Get Lonely Too" was edited for a 7-inch single. A C-60 cassette was made of the edit and given to Prince for review.

It is uncertain whether Prince attended this session. On occasion, he'd conduct edits remotely, giving the engineer the information over the phone. Morris was listed as the producer and he signed the work order; it is unclear whether Day signed because he was supervising or because Prince wanted to keep up the appearance that he was not responsible for pulling the strings for the Time, and this was reflected as much as possible on both the private documents and the released albums. "I think that to not put his name on the records allowed people to look at the Time and take them seriously as a band," continued Leeds. "Whereas, had [Prince's] name been on it, I think that people would have been less prone to take the Time seriously, particularly not having seen the act when the record first came out."[42]

The original recording of "Gigolos Get Lonely Too" featured Day on drums and Jesse Johnson on guitar, with Prince playing everything else. "I had some control," Day would later reflect about the early albums. "But not as much as I needed."[43]

Status: The edit of "Gigolos Get Lonely Too" (3:45) was released on March 9, 1983, with "I Don't Wanna Leave You" as the B-side. It did not enter the Top 100 chart and peaked at number 77 on the Black Singles chart. A mono mix was also released as the B-side and as a promo single, most likely intended for AM radio stations.

Although it is generally spelled Flyte Tyme, multiple documents from that time period reveal that the band was probably referred to as Flyt Tyme, at least for a short period. Flyte Tyme is the name (and proper spelling) of Jimmy Jam and Terry Lewis's company. For the sake of clarity, I've listed the group as Flyte Tyme despite the likelihood that it was actually named Flyt Tyme.

THURSDAY, JANUARY 13, 1983*

"Little Red Corvette" (edits for 12-inch)
"Drive Me Wild" (12-inch and probable edit)
Sunset Sound, Studio 2 | 9:00 p.m.–6:00 a.m. (booked 9:00 p.m.–open)
Producer: Prince | *Artist:* Prince (listed, but Vanity 6 was also involved on "Drive Me Wild") | *Engineer:* Prince | *Assistant Engineers:* David Leonard and "Peggy Mac" McCreary

[Prince] didn't sleep much, he just ate, slept, and drank music every day. I'm sure he probably wasted no time with watching television or doing much else other than taking in a movie occasionally and reading a little or listening to music, which was a big part of what he did. He would listen to other artists for inspiration as well. I know there were times when he was probably going for stretches of getting maybe four or five hours of sleep a night and that was it.—Matt Fink[44]

Like that of the Time, the history of Vanity 6 showcases Prince's desire to create an outlet for his pop music. Prince had been trying to establish an all-girl group as early as 1981 and enlisted his then-girlfriend Susan Moonsie and her sister Loreen, along with Jamie Shoop, who worked for Cavallo, Ruffalo & Fargnoli as Prince's manager, to dress in lingerie and sing in a girl group called the Hookers. The project gained focus when Prince met and was smitten with actress/model Denise Matthews at the 9th Annual American Music Awards on January 25, 1982: "I didn't go home with him right away. He called me, we dated—it was all very romantic. He didn't even know I wanted to sing until he heard me one day. Then he helped me put a group together."[45]

Prince originally suggested she call herself Vagina, but eventually they agreed on Vanity. "You'll have to ask Prince why he named me Vanity," she said, "but I think the main reason is when he looks in the mirror, he sees me."[46]

In February 1982 Prince invited Matthews to join him on the *Controversy* tour, not as a performer but as his girlfriend. Because the concept for the Hookers hadn't been completely fleshed out, their lineup was still in flux. After the sound check for one of the last shows on the tour, Brenda Bennett, the wife of lighting director Roy Bennett, was working backstage and began singing along to a Stevie Nicks track. "I didn't notice that [Prince] was paying attention," she says. "He turned [the tape] off, and looked at me and said, 'You could be the other Hooker!' I looked at him and said, 'What are you talking about?' He then decided to get me involved in the group. I turned to Prince and asked, 'Does it have to be the Hookers?'"

Performing in a band wasn't a stretch for Bennett. Born in Scotland, she had grown up in a family of musicians and had been a singer as well. In 1973 she sang backup for Ken Lyon and the Tombstone Blues Band and on their only album, *Ken Lyon and Tombstone*, on CBS records. Jamie Shoop decided not to join the group, which Prince named Vanity 6, with Denise/Vanity as the front woman and Brenda Bennett and Susan Moonsie as the background singers. "Prince was looking to create a 1980s version of the Supremes," explains Bennett. "All of the girls wearing sexy lingerie and singing the same type of music that he did."

"I was the den mother to everyone," she continues. "Prince told me to baby-sit the girls and mold them so they could rely on me to show them the ropes. Susan was like a sponge when it came to the singing and entertaining. She picked up everything so quickly." Bennett's husband remembers that the hierarchy in Vanity 6 also caused problems within the group: "There was quite often friction between Vanity and Brenda. It was personalities. It was based on the fact that a lot of times Brenda was the person that was set up to babysit Vanity as far as making sure she could sing, and vocal stuff, and in rehearsals making Brenda responsible for that, which was very difficult, because Vanity saw herself as the one in charge. So you've got Prince telling Brenda, 'You're responsible for her singing,' and Vanity saying, 'Well, it's my band.' So it was hard."

Once again, the true leader of the band was Prince.

Prince was able to get Vanity 6 signed to Warner Bros. based on an album he quickly put together. It was released on August 11, 1982, and they rehearsed a brief five-song set that involved dressing up in very revealing lingerie and singing in front of a curtain with the Time—hidden from the audience—performing the album's music. The Time, unhappy about doing double duty during the shows, made very little extra money for their nightly performance, which created more tension behind the scenes, as explained by Jellybean Johnson: "Vanity, Susan and Brenda, they were really nice to me. They treated me nice. And for the most part, they were nice to most of the guys in the Time; it was just the principle, you know, come on, man. That was the whole thing, he didn't want to pay for a band. He wanted to have us. And that's another way to keep us under control and quiet. I'm sure that was the thinking behind that. And management was backing him 100 percent. That's what it was about."[47]

Many of the reviews for Vanity 6 focused on what they were wearing and how they danced. The *Louisville Courier-Journal* reported that "the women gyrated around the stage, much to the delight of the males in the crowd," but some of the reviews were not always flattering. The *Hartford Courant* reported that "no one yelled encore when they were through." A Baltimore paper referred to them as a "pointless novelty,"[48] and the *Pittsburgh Press* reported, "Vanity stinks."[49]

Within the inner circle there were mixed emotions. There were those inside Prince's band who dismissed them, but the feeling wasn't unanimous, according to Alan Leeds: "They were three girls who took what they were doing seriously enough to spend an awful lot of time and energy trying to figure out how to best entertain their audience, and their motives were pure and they worked real hard, so I have a little problem dismissing them as strippers, because the reality is, compared to what's going on today in rap, they were pretty safe."

Both the Vanity 6 and the Time albums list Jamie Starr as the producer, but Jamie Starr was a pseudonym for Prince. At the time, Prince demanded that a fictional backstory about Starr was to be maintained to the press. "Jamie Starr is an engineer," insisted Morris Day during a 1983 interview, "the co-producer of our record. Of course he's real."[50] Prince always enjoyed confusing people when it came to how his music was created. Selling misdirection and intrigue was his way of managing what people thought about him. He was a smart self-promoter and worked very hard at his public relations—and even harder to look like he wasn't working on it at all. "I don't know his reasoning behind it," explained Jellybean Johnson. "It worked, obviously. At least for him, and that's how he wanted it. He could've very easily came out and said, 'Yeah I did the shit.' But he didn't want to do that. . . . He had a picture of Jamie Starr, him and Morris and shit, at the soundboard. It was hilarious."[51]

Many of the tracks from these protégé albums were recorded at Sunset Sound, which gave Peggy McCreary an unparalleled perspective on the Jamie Starr legend: "The Time was a lot of [Prince]; so was Vanity 6. Prince would do most of the stuff and then bring in someone for one part. He'd sing most of the lyrics and then just have whoever replace it, but it was him, it was his genius. He'd always put Jamie Starr's name on it, but that was all a game."

Work continued on the prospective singles for Prince and Vanity 6. "Drive Me Wild" was the fourth release from their record; it had previously been the B-side to "Nasty Girl," but Prince felt confident enough in it to put it out as a single. The album version of "Drive Me Wild" was only 2:33, so during this session Prince worked on the additional five minutes necessary to expand the track. At the time, there were no computers to help the engineer audition an edit; everything was done to the actual tape. David Leonard once again did the physical cutting, but he was very open about his respect for Prince's ear:

> He'd tell me "Cut to this chorus," and point and show me, then I'd mark it on the downbeat and put it together, then he'd say, "No, make that come in later," so I'd go back and take like a half-inch piece of tape off of the verse before, then stick it on there, and then he'd say "Oh no, that's too much, cut that in half," so then I'd go back and get a half-inch piece of tape and edit it into a quarter-inch piece of tape, and then he'd say "Okay, cut that in half again," so now I'm cutting like eighth-inch slivers of tape, and he could always tell if I did or didn't do it. His timing was amazing.[52]

The origin of this track can be traced to before Vanity 6 was formed. Prince originally recorded this in 1981, when the name of the band was still the Hookers. According to Susan Moonsie, the inspiration for the lyrics supposedly came when she met Prince in a Minneapolis club: "He was just standing there drinking orange juice and we started talking. I told him that I wrote songs, then gave him a sample of my lyrics: 'I'm a brand new convertible child, I've never been driven, you're the first. Come on baby: drive me wild.'"[53]

"I am not on this track," remembers Bennett. "This was basically the same way Susan did it. She did very well for someone without experience. There was something very natural about her."

Prince and Susan Moonsie became a couple soon after they met, and remained close during the early stages of the Hookers/Vanity 6. Their relationship would be complicated and eventually compromised by the strong presence of Vanity. "As he began to get successful there were a lot of women," explained longtime engineer Susan Rogers. "Susan [Moonsie] at a young age was smart enough to know, this was a man you're not going to keep for yourself. . . . But she's a gracious woman and she stayed around."[54] A great deal of behind-the-scenes drama was created based on who was receiving Prince's affections, much of which would influence his music.

An edited version of "Little Red Corvette (Dance Remix)" was created during this session. The main differences between the edited version of the Dance Remix and the album version can be found at the beginning and end of the tracks.

Status: Once the extended version of Vanity 6's "Drive Me Wild" (7:04) was completed, it was edited down (2:20) and released with an edit of "3 × 2 = 6" (3:46) as the B-side. It is unclear when the edits on "3 × 2 = 6" were done. The extended version of "Drive Me Wild" was released only in the United States and failed to chart, while the "Little Red Corvette (Dance Remix edit)" (4:33) only found its way to a US promo 7-inch.

FRIDAY, JANUARY 14, 1983*

"Drive Me Wild" (overdubs, mixes, and copies for 12-inch)
"Little Red Corvette" (overdubs, mixes, and copies for 12-inch)
Sunset Sound, Studio 2 | 9:00 p.m.–5:45 a.m. (booked 4:00 p.m.–open)
Producer: Prince | *Artist:* Prince (listed, but Vanity 6 was also involved on
"Drive Me Wild") | *Engineer:* Prince | *Assistant Engineer:* David Leonard

*[Prince's] recording technique was unorthodox. He would
record everything way too loud. It makes everything sound really frantic, so it always sounds louder than it really is. There
would always be an edge to his recordings. There's not a recording we do where there's not something we learned from the way
he worked.* —Jimmy Jam[55]

Additional overdubs were done to complete the 12-inch versions of "Drive
Me Wild" and "Little Red Corvette." The style of some of the guitar work on
"Drive Me Wild," specifically around 4:40 and 5:05, would be revisited later in
the summer when Prince recorded "Computer Blue."

A quick mix was created, a tape was made for reference, and the session was
complete. "Prince didn't like my mixes," recalls McCreary. "It was usually at
the end of the night and you are exhausted, and you just want to go home and
go to sleep and he'd say, 'Mix it.' I'm thinking, 'Excuse me? It's 11:30 at night,
or later, and I want to go home,' so some of them could have probably been
better."

It would be the last studio session at Sunset Sound for more than two
months. The remainder of January would be spent adjusting his live show,
which was scheduled to start in February, as well as taping various music videos
for himself, Vanity 6, and the Time.

EARLY-MID JANUARY, 1983 (ESTIMATE)

"Wonderful Ass" (basic tracking and overdubs)
Kiowa Trail home studio (Chanhassen, Minnesota)
Producer: Prince | *Artist:* Prince | *Engineer:* Don Batts

Prince told me himself that that was written for Vanity.
—Susan Rogers[56]

When Prince wasn't recording at Sunset Sound, he was working from home in Chanhassen, Minnesota. This was the third home Prince had set up like a recording studio. When Prince moved from a rented house on the north arm of Lake Minnetonka in Wayzata, Minnesota, to this house, he had Don Batts set up everything in a finished family room in the basement.

"He had big Westlake monitors mounted up on the wall," Matt Fink described to author Jake Brown. "And there was an isolation room, so he'd had some construction done on that particular home studio to make it more viable as an acoustic-engineered room. He had a drum set and every keyboard of the day—the Oberheim and the Omni, which [the Omni] was a very integral keyboard used on *1999*. He didn't use it much on *Purple Rain*, but was really using the Oberheims quite a bit on the *Purple Rain* album."[57]

The two rooms—one for the control room and one for overdubs—were small, but Prince got huge results from the setup. In May of the previous year, during the first night the studio was operational, Prince recorded the bulk of "Little Red Corvette."

In many ways, music can be seen as Prince's primary language, and it is a bond that he shared with those around him. **"Musicians, when they really communicate, don't have to talk. They just play."**[58] It was also fairly common for Prince to use music to express his feelings to those around him, especially those close to him or those he wanted to add to his inner circle. "Wonderful Ass" is an example of his writing something to someone near to his heart.

Prince and Vanity were going through a tough time, fluctuating between staying a couple and seeing others. At the time, Vanity and Jill Jones were both living in Prince's home. "We all kind of lived together for a little, brief moment, trying to be harmonious," recalls singer Jones, who sang background vocals on this track as well as uncredited background vocals for Vanity 6 during the tour, "and it didn't really go so well."

"On that tour, he was dating Vanity again because they knew they were going to do the *Purple Rain* stuff," she continues, "and he told me, 'I've got to date her to solidify all the contracts or whatever.' And then he would write her songs like 'Wonderful Ass.'"

"Vanity has an ass that don't make no sense, I'm telling you," recalled Jellybean Johnson fondly. "It'd make you leave all your homes. Back then, especially, because she was already beautiful. But that butt she had! Oh my God. And she was turning, wiggling, every night. It was all over."[59]

Jones and Prince worked on the song together in Prince's studio, with both of them adding to the list of rhyming words on the lyric sheet. "It's not a novel idea to rhyme a bunch of words. We were sitting there and coming up with rhymes. 'My sensibilities you aggravate.' Because on one hand I'm thinking it's about Vanity's butt, and she does aggravate you. So, there was a little bit of that and also, we all lived together, so I think I could have commented about her wonderful ass too. (*laughs*)"

But was there only one inspiration for "Wonderful Ass" and the various tracks Prince wrote over the years? Jones gives her thoughts on that:

> I don't think Prince was that literal in his song writing. I think it's a bit of an insult to any creative person or a writer to think that inspiration is that linear. I think that we do get inspired by all sorts of stuff. Vanity took it; she owned it. She played it and announced that this song belonged to her, but I also don't think that that's how you write songs. And I think that there could've been many things that could have inspired him. We went to see so many movies, *Frances*, all these other things. *Flashdance*. There were so many things that play into what works in decision making.

"Wonderful Ass" isn't a classic love song by any stretch of the imagination. It is more of a playful song with lyrics written as a compliment unique to Vanity, and it is obvious that it was a track Prince enjoyed recording. The lyrics aren't to be taken too seriously, with Prince describing the differences between himself and his partner, but being distracted by her ass, and even repeating the phrase "You're so wonderful" before revealing that the wonderful part of her is that she's "got a wonderful ass."[60]

Some of the language in the song, although tame in retrospect, was considered slightly racy, but as he often did, Prince performed it with a wink and a smile. Considering his history of vulgar lyrics, it is easy to confuse the man and his art. Engineers like Susan Rogers were constantly put on the hot seat regarding this:

> People asked me: "How can you work for that nasty man?" And I have never worked for anybody with more respect for women. There was an aspect of Prince's character, which was a mysterious mythological figure who doesn't speak much and is half man/half woman. Then there is another aspect, which is very much close to the Morris Day/Time-figure, a wisecracking guy who makes lewd jokes about women. The "Prince" character that he created for himself is much more rude than I think he is himself, because I never, ever, ever received anything but respect from him and I really must say that for the record.[61]

By the time Rogers joined the Prince camp in the summer of 1983, the song was sitting on the shelf, and she had doubts about what was planned for the track. "I don't think he ever intended to release that. It was more like a song that was fun to write and sing."[62]

The tune is a solo venture featuring keyboards over a Linn drum pattern and appears to contain no outside help, at least for the basic recording. Although those around him didn't imagine him placing it on a Prince album, it is possible that, based on the humor in the track, it might have been considered for the Time. Prince even ended the song with an impression of Morris Day, saying, "You know I like yo' ass."[63]

Status: This early version of "Wonderful Ass" (6:08) remains unreleased, but it was revisited in September 1984 with the help of Wendy Melvoin and Lisa Coleman. The updated "Wonderful Ass" (6:24) was included on the *Purple Rain Deluxe* (Expanded Edition) CD set in 2017.

The track was considered for the *Apollonia 6* album as well as the unreleased 1998 Prince and the Revolution album *Roadhouse Garden.*

It is possible that this song was already recorded in mid-November 1982. Jill Jones remembers that after a concert in Louisiana, she and Prince traveled home to Minneapolis and worked on this in his home studio. That session could have either followed a performance in New Orleans, Louisiana, on November 14, 1982, or after his show on January 3, 1983, in Lake Charles, Louisiana.

The Time and Vanity 6 continued to rest during this period, so Prince focused his energy on his own band, because the structure was changing. Prince's band consisted of Lisa Coleman and Matt "Dr. Fink" Fink on keyboards, Bobby "Bobby Z" Rivkin on drums, Mark "Brown Mark" Brown on bass, and Dez Dickerson on lead guitar. The core of this band had gone unchanged since Brown Mark was added in 1981 (replacing Prince's childhood best friend, André Cymone), but during this tour seeds of discontent were growing in Dickerson.

In 1978 Prince and his managers were looking for a guitar player but were having no luck. Although Dickerson had always planned to be a solo artist, he hadn't found his path yet. He played guitar in several bands, and when he heard that a local musician who had a record contract with a major label was looking for a guitarist, he assumed it was Prince, put his quest for a solo career on hold, and jumped at the chance. During the local audition at Del's Tire Mart, Dickerson jammed with Prince's band for fifteen minutes. He later recalled:

I just went in and just kind of played rhythm and tried to get a feel for what André and Prince and the other guys were doing. And when Prince would give me the nod and have me solo, I'd solo, say what I wanted to say, play my best stuff, and then go right back into playing rhythm and not overstate it, and it turned out that's what made the difference. He had auditioned over one hundred guys on both the East Coast and the West Coast and every single one of them tried to blow him away. I was the only guy that actually tried to fit in.[64]

A shorthand developed very quickly between Dickerson and Prince: "Originally, Prince wanted to be a black version of The Rolling Stones. His Mick to my Keith."[65] Prince relied on Dickerson to write lyrics to songs like "Cool" and to add his signature guitar work to his breakthrough hit, "Little Red Corvette." It was a solid musical collaboration and a trusting and tight friendship. "I've never laughed as much in my life as I did when I was in that band," recalled Dickerson, "until the last year; then it got real serious."[66]

"By *1999* things had changed on a number of levels, particularly live," Dickerson detailed to *No. 1* magazine:

It was becoming Prince and his band. The philosophies were changing, he was doing brasher things—going out on a limb lyrically. His image was becoming more flamboyant too. The raincoat went from plain grey to purple—that's how the purple thing started. It smacked of a movement and I didn't want to be involved with a movement.[67]

We argued many times during the tour but they were not arguments in the negative sense, more like debates. We argued about the songs we should be doing, how to present them. From the beginning, of course, it had been clear it was Prince's project—he always had the last word—but obviously as it got bigger, it got more out of control. No one's ever been able to say no to Prince, to tell him not to do something—even now they can't. They could advise him but he'd still have the final say.[68]

During this period, Dickerson had a spiritual revelation and started feeling that the direction and the message Prince was pushing weren't compatible with his faith: "There were a couple of songs on the *Dirty Mind* LP that went too far. One of them was 'Sister.' I had a very hard time doing that one. Sometimes onstage I'd just mouth the words so that at the end of the day I could say 'Okay, I played it but I didn't write it and I didn't sing it.' I kept my conscience clear."[69] But his charade wasn't working, and the heavy sexuality was weighing heavily on Dez: "I would look out in the audience and see somebody with their eight or nine-year-old and I'd think about the things we were singing about and the things we were doing on stage and I'm thinking, now would I want my nine-year-old daughter out seeing someone else do this? No, I wouldn't. I wouldn't. That was kind of the deal breaker for me."[70]

While Dickerson maintained his friendship with Prince, he started distancing himself from him professionally. Prince was well known for holding three- to four-hour sound checks, and Dez grew tired of them and wanted out: "I came from a background where I was always the guy cracking the whip on the rest of the band to try to drag everybody else along: Come on, we gotta get better, we gotta work harder. This was the first time I had been in a situation where there was actually somebody who was more of a maniac than I was and it had reached a point where we worked so hard at it that it stopped being fun after a few years."[71]

Dickerson asked Prince if he could simply show up, get a feel for the hall, make sure his guitar and monitor worked, and then leave. Prince agreed, conducting most of the extended sound checks without his lead guitar player. In retrospect, even Dickerson conceded to author Dave Hill that he was responsible for his own problems within the band: "I didn't feel comfortable with myself anymore. Because of that, I became very difficult to be around. I was pretty moody. Later, I realized that was just a by-product of not being very happy with what was happening, and where we were going; and at the same time feeling there wasn't a whole lot I could do to have any impact on it. I dealt with it by . . . being a jerk. I guess if I'd been him, I would probably have fired me."[72]

Prince decided to continue the tour with Dickerson as the lead guitarist, but his days in the band were numbered. Luckily for Prince, Dickerson's eventual replacement was already part of the band's extended family: His keyboard player, Lisa Coleman, had introduced Prince to her childhood friend Wendy Melvoin, and Prince took a quick liking to her talents, using her on a few studio sessions during the previous year. He took extra notice of her guitar playing when he overheard it coming from Coleman's hotel room during the Christmas holiday in New York. "I was actually out on the *1999* tour," detailed Melvoin, "but not formally. It was kind of like my 'prep work' as Prince put it. I did a little bit of vocal work on the *1999* record, but it wasn't until right after that he found out I played the guitar."[73]

Coleman remembered:

Wendy was in my hotel room playing [an acoustic] guitar, and Prince heard the guitar coming from behind my door and knocked on the door and was like, "Who's playing guitar in there?" He thought it was really good. And I said, "It's Wendy," and he came in and said, "Play something," and she just strummed this large beautiful chord and he was like, "Huh? How did you do that?"[74]

Prince asked Melvoin to join the band during a run through of "Controversy" and she knocked it out of the park. "The 'Funky Little Wendy' side of her came out and it was just over," Coleman joyfully recalled. "Prince began a love affair with her playing."[75] Melvoin was hired for three hundred dollars a week. Although she didn't play during the concerts, she spent time jamming with Prince and the other members of his band, and bonds began to grow.

"That first time Wendy jammed with us at sound check on 'Controversy' . . . [i]t's like when you'd hear the Beatles talking about when they found Ringo," reflected Bobby Z in 2016. "You just knew that was the future."[76]

Dickerson would continue until the end of the tour, but it was obvious to everyone that Melvoin was in the wings waiting to play.

Prince regrouped the bands near the end of the month to restructure the shows. Prince removed "Automatic," while "Sexuality" and "Let's Pretend We're Married" were added to the set on occasion.

During the first leg of the tour, "Little Red Corvette" was played sporadically, often as the third track of the show, but by early December it had been removed from the set list completely. With its release as a single, it was added back into the set, but much later in the show. In addition to shuffling the songs for the concert, it was also decided to produce a music video to reflect the growing attention other artists were getting on MTV. "We were on tour when 'Little Red Corvette' started doing well on radio," explained Lisa Coleman. "So we squeezed in a video."[77]

Music videos were just starting to explode during this period, and contemporaries such as Michael Jackson were creating visually stunning short films that were gaining attention. Over the last three years Prince had created six videos, but they were simply variations of performances. He would continue this trend—not breaking any new ground with the videos for his latest album—but even just playing with the band was different than with other performers. Even Time member Monte Moir recognized this: "He has an aura about him, and when he walks in the room you feel it, and if he walks onstage—when he used to come up and jam with us or something—and it's like the whole stage lifts up about a foot and a half because there's something going on with him that's not the normal human being walking around. He's one of the few people I'd say is truly a genius."[78]

A video was also created for the recently recorded extended version of Vanity 6's "Drive Me Wild." It showcased Susan Moonsie singing and dancing during an onstage party scene made up of many people on the tour, including Prince's lighting director, Roy Bennett, who was not teamed with his wife but instead cast as Moonsie's partner. The video also featured Prince's most iconic bodyguard Chick "Big Chick" Huntsberry dressed as a fairy godfather who granted wishes with his magic wand.

FEBRUARY 1983

TUESDAY, FEBRUARY 1, 1983

Venue: Lakeland Civic Center (Lakeland, Florida)
Capacity: 10,000 (9,500 tickets sold)

The second leg of Prince's *1999* tour began in Lakeland, Florida. The venues on this half of the tour hadn't changed much: he was still playing in theaters of the same size—and, in many cases, the exact same locations he'd been playing since 1980. Despite a push to promote his album, including a recently aired lip-synced performance of "1999" on the syndicated television show *Solid Gold*, the expected growth in crowd size hadn't materialized. The album was moving down the charts and there was concern that perhaps Prince's popularity had peaked.

WEDNESDAY, FEBRUARY 2, 1983

Venue: Savannah Civic Center (Savannah, Georgia)
Capacity: 8,000 (possibly limited to lower number; attendance unknown)

While Prince was touring, he worked hard to make his life on the road an extension of how it was at home. Often musicians wear costumes or clothes just for the show; Prince wore similar clothes both on and off the stage. "I've never really seen him wearing a T-shirt and shorts," remembers tour manager Murielle Hamilton. She also recalls that despite the problems, he seemed very happy with most of the people who surrounded him on the tour: "He knew many of these people for a long time. He had grown up with some of them, and so I think in that sense, he liked that level of comfort. They might be annoying, but they were known quantities."

THURSDAY, FEBRUARY 3, 1983

Venue: Augusta–Richmond County Civic Center (Augusta, Georgia)
Capacity: 9,000 (possibly limited to lower number; attendance unknown)

FRIDAY, FEBRUARY 4, 1983

Venue: Greensboro Coliseum (Greensboro, North Carolina)
Capacity: 15,900 (possibly limited to lower number; attendance unknown)

SATURDAY, FEBRUARY 5, 1983

Venue: Richmond Coliseum (Richmond, Virginia)
Capacity: 12,500 (possibly limited to lower number; attendance unknown)

At this point in the tour, "1999" was still ending the encore and "Little Red Corvette" wasn't a showstopper yet.

SUNDAY, FEBRUARY 6, 1983

Venue: Roanoke Civic Center (Roanoke, Virginia)
Capacity: 9,828 (5,115 tickets sold)

Only half of the seats for this show were sold. While on the road, the Time, as a live act, was gaining strength. "Prince created the Frankenstein monster," remembered Morris Day. "It was little when it hatched. It was nothing to fear. Then the shit grew and grew right before his eyes, and we started to come into our own. It got ugly for him some nights. He had to come behind us, and we only had 30 minutes to perform. But it was a dangerous 30 minutes."[1]

"We couldn't wait to get to the next show," Jellybean Johnson proudly proclaimed. "Let's whoop his ass some more. That's satisfaction."[2]

Jesse Johnson remembered:

We used to laugh about it. He'd come in the dressing room some nights, every night practically, and have these big talks with Morris and say, "Don't you guys go out there and do this" and we'd go "Oh, okay. You got it. Cool!" And then, he'd leave and we'd go out and do it anyway and just get in trouble and get docked because it got to the point where we couldn't take that stuff anymore, so we just started getting in trouble just going hey, whatever is going to happen, you know, because it had got to a point that it was utterly ridiculous."[3]

Brown Mark remembered talking to Prince about the Time's strength: "I used to have conversations with [Prince] every night. I'd be like, 'These cats are burning it up. They are burning up the stage dude'; he's like, 'They don't got nothing on us, you watch. You watch.'"[4]

"There was to be only one headliner," explained Day in 1984. "So Prince was it."[5]

Prince was originally scheduled to fly back to Minneapolis during a three-day break from the tour, but instead he traveled to Los Angeles.

TUESDAY, FEBRUARY 8, 1983

"Stand Back" (overdubs)
Studio 55 (Los Angeles, California)
Producer: Jimmy Iovine | *Artist:* Stevie Nicks | *Engineer:* Shelly Yakus

[Prince] spoiled me for every band I've ever had because nobody can exactly re-create—not even with two piano players—what Prince did all by his little self.—Stevie Nicks[6]

"Stand Back" was a direct result of Stevie Nicks's January 29 wedding. "I'm driving to my honeymoon night in Santa Barbara from L.A., and 'Little Red Corvette' comes on," Nicks remembered. "We're like, 'Oh my God, it's Prince!' So I start singing all these words, and I'm like, 'Pull over, we have to get a cassette player! And we have to record this!' I'm writing in the car—here we are, newlyweds, and we get to our hotel and we're setting up the tape recorder and I've made up my whole new melody to [the song]."[7]

When she returned to Los Angeles, she requested and was given Prince's private phone number ("I'm Stevie Nicks, I can get it."[8]), called him, and hummed it to him. "I told him: 'I'm recording this song and I wrote it to "Little Red Corvette" and I'm giving you 50 percent of it and I want to know if you'd like to come play on it on one of the next three nights.' He was there in an hour."[9]

"When I got there, her and Jimmy Iovine couldn't figure out how to work the drum machine," added Prince, **"because people were using live drums at that point . . . so I went down there and programmed it for them and pretty much played most of the song there in about twenty or thirty minutes."[10]**

"He came in, listened to the song—you know, very cool, very quiet," detailed Nicks. "And I said, 'Do you hate it?' and he said, 'No, it's okay, it's cool,' and they set up an OB-8 for him and he played the 'doo-doo-doo-doo-doo,' the 1/16-note thing, and then, he did it like one time. And then he went to the middle part where it goes 'deedat-deedat-deedat-deedat.'"[11]

Nicks would later add that Prince "walked over to the synthesizers that were set up, was absolutely brilliant for about twenty-five minutes, and then left."[12]

Prince supposedly also added several tracks. Ultimately they didn't use everything he played, but his synth part can be heard prominently in the final mix. Nicks's 1991 *Timespace* tour book summed up the way the song came together: "It never belonged to me, it has always belonged to the world and to Prince, who inspired the entire song."[13]

"If you really listen carefully, you can sing 'Stand Back' along to 'Little Red Corvette,' and you can sing 'Little Red Corvette' along to 'Stand Back,'" she said. "So, I gave him half of the song for that inspiration."[14]

Status: "Stand Back" (4:47) was released in May 1983 by Stevie Nicks on *The Wild Heart.* The single (4:18) landing at number 5 on the *Billboard* Hot 100 and number 2 on the *Billboard* Top Tracks. This was Prince's highest-charting song on the *Billboard* Hot 100 to date.

There have been reports (including Nicks's personal recollection on several occasions) that Prince's part of the track was recorded at Sunset Sound. According to the official accounts, it was most likely recorded at Studio 55 on Melrose Avenue in Los Angeles, California.

WEDNESDAY, FEBRUARY 9, 1983

"Little Red Corvette" was released as a single, featuring the album track "All the Critics Love U in New York" as a B-side. The song would reach number 6 on the *Billboard* Hot 100 charts in the United States on May 21, 1983.

THURSDAY, FEBRUARY 10, 1983

Venue: Providence Civic Center (Providence, Rhode Island)
Capacity: 13,300 (possibly limited to lower number; attendance unknown)

FRIDAY, FEBRUARY 11, 1983

Venue: Hartford Civic Center (Hartford, Connecticut)
Capacity: 16,200 (possibly limited to lower number; attendance unknown)

A show originally scheduled for February 12 in Norfolk, Virginia, was postponed until March 8 due to inclement weather.

After peaking and declining, Prince's album was once again shifting. The release of "Little Red Corvette" and the subsequent airplay was giving *1999* a much-needed boost. The new attention was also having an effect on the size of his audience. Prince was no longer just getting critical praise; there was a buzz on the street.

Change was in the air, and these were the last days of Prince's life under the radar.

SUNDAY, FEBRUARY 13, 1983

Venue: DC Armory Starplex (Washington, DC)
Capacity: 10,000 (attendance unknown; since there were two shows it seems unlikely capacity was limited)

MONDAY, FEBRUARY 14, 1983

Venue: DC Armory (Washington, DC)
Capacity: 10,000 (attendance unknown; since there were two shows it
   seems unlikely capacity was limited)

Ticket demand for Prince's February 13 DC show was so great that a second show had been added. While this was an anomaly for the 1983 leg of the tour, it foreshadowed his increasing popularity. "The crowds were nuts and every one of his shows were so incredible. It felt like he was huge," says Murielle Hamilton. "Some other people might have been content to just have a great show, but he pushed it on every level. I mean the costumes, the makeup, the choreography, the everything. When you saw one of those shows, it was obvious that he was just a massive star. I think he always knew he was a massive star." The shows were getting stronger and stronger, which pushed the Time to perform at a higher level, fostering an even deeper sense of competition.

"To a point it was real positive," explained Monte Moir. "On our side it was 'Let's kick his ass tonight!' But after a while, it became unhealthy."[15]

Part of the reason it was becoming unhealthy was that no matter how much success the Time was getting from their audiences, the fact that they were secretly controlled by Prince haunted some of the band members. Jesse Johnson remembered: "It's hard to put into words because in the movie [*Purple Rain*], both groups are acting as if they are their own entity, but in real life, all the groups are under Prince's control. If you look at it on a business document, we were another one of Prince's bands. We were the first and highly successful, but never the less, it was almost like the more success you had, I don't really think it mattered because at the end of the day, it was somebody else's thing."[16]

Jellybean Johnson agreed: "It would have been one thing if we were a collection of guys who weren't talented, but we had some super talented guys in that band. So any time you got that much talent in one band, even though we loved each other and we loved playing together, everybody's looking down the road and looking at each other. And that's what it was, and we knew, even though it was hard to think about, that there was no future there if we continued to stay there and be under his wing like that. We knew that."[17]

"We were angry, because we were so broke," explained Jesse Johnson. "We were all pretty pissed, and that energy came out in our show. We were out for blood."[18]

TUESDAY, FEBRUARY 15, 1983

Venue: Carmichael Auditorium (Chapel Hill, North Carolina)
Capacity: 10,200 (possibly limited to lower number; attendance unknown)

> *You have to realize, we're some kids from the street. The original Time was just some ghetto kids from the street. We're like a gang. And Prince's band, they couldn't compare to us with that. And he knew it. And deep down, Prince wants to be one of us and he couldn't, because he was Prince.* —Jellybean Johnson[19]

Jimmy Jam has also referred to Prince as a "silent partner" in the Time, so from the first meeting of the band he was a key part of their inner circle. During the previous year's *Controversy* tour and the early dates of the *1999* tour, Prince would join the Time on their bus for stretches of the travel. In many ways Prince actively kept the bands apart and could straddle both because he was the boss. He was very proud of his band, but the Time was like an exclusive club he could drop in on at any time.

"We kind of became sort of like an alter ego for him. A chance to be very funky, to collaborate on very funky tunes, and he enjoyed when we would rehearse and stuff," explained Jam. "He would rather come to our rehearsals and jam with us than he would with his own band. And a lot of his groove ideas came from jamming with us."[20]

The tension was beginning to take a toll on all three groups on the tour. The Time wasn't happy with Prince, Prince wasn't happy with the Time, and Vanity 6 was erupting with internal conflicts. According to Brenda Bennett, a performance error created backstage drama for Vanity 6:

I blanked right on stage in front of all these people, [during "If A Girl Answers (Don't Hang Up)"] and forgot my part, so I ad-libbed and it threw Vanity off so much that we fought after the show. Vanity wanted to stab me about this, and she got a copy of the tape from the soundman and played that part, stopped the tape, rewound it and played that part of the tape over and over. She just kept rubbing it in. The Time were in the other side of our dressing room and they were taking bets about who was going to walk out of there alive.

WEDNESDAY, FEBRUARY 16, 1983

Venue: Macon Coliseum (Macon, Georgia)
Capacity: 10,200 (possibly limited to lower number; attendance unknown)

A show scheduled for the following night in Columbus, Ohio, was rescheduled to March 9 for unknown reasons.

FRIDAY, FEBRUARY 18, 1983

Venue: Tallahassee–Leon County Civic Center (Tallahassee, Florida)
Capacity: 9,975 (sold out)

SATURDAY, FEBRUARY 19, 1983

Venue: Jacksonville Veteran's Memorial Coliseum (Jacksonville, Florida)
Capacity: 11,628 (sold out)

SUNDAY, FEBRUARY 20, 1983

Venue: Mobile Municipal Auditorium (Mobile, Alabama)
Capacity: 12,000 (possibly limited to lower number; attendance unknown)

TUESDAY, FEBRUARY 22, 1983

Venue: Greenville Memorial Auditorium (Greenville, South Carolina)
Capacity: 12,600 (possibly limited to lower number; attendance unknown)

THURSDAY, FEBRUARY 24, 1983

Venue: Buffalo Memorial Auditorium (Buffalo, New York)
Capacity: 14,300 (possibly limited to lower number; attendance unknown)

FRIDAY, FEBRUARY 25, 1983

Venue: Michigan State University Auditorium (East Lansing, Michigan)
Capacity: 3,600 (attendance unknown)

SATURDAY, FEBRUARY 26, 1983

Venue: Toledo Sports Arena (Toledo, Ohio)
Capacity: 7,500 (attendance unknown)

SUNDAY, FEBRUARY 27, 1983

Venue: Crisler Arena (Ann Arbor, Michigan)
Capacity: 13,700 (possibly limited to lower number; attendance unknown)

This was originally planned as a day off, but a concert was scheduled to fill in the date. The fact that it was only an hour away from the previous night's show made it an easy slot to fill.

MONDAY, FEBRUARY 28, 1983

Venue: Pittsburgh Civic Arena (Pittsburgh, Pennsylvania)
Capacity: 16,000 (12,860 tickets sold)

MARCH 1983

We could see we were at a turning point.—Dez Dickerson[1]

Rolling Stone magazine had just voted Prince the "Artist of 1982" for his *1999* album. The readers' choice had been Bruce Springsteen, but the tide was turning, and it wasn't only critics who were recognizing Prince's work. "Prior to [the *1999* album], MTV never had urban artists on," detailed Dez Dickerson. "It was at the point when Michael Jackson's 'Beat It' was on and we were on with the whole '1999'/'Little Red Corvette' thing and all that changed. . . . Because of this perfect storm, the songs had a sort of a runway to land on in the public perception that no Prince record before that had had."[2]

"When 'Little Red Corvette' became a big pop smash, we started seeing a lot more white people," added Jellybean Johnson. "There was always some mix before, but it was basically black. When 'Little Red Corvette' hit, there was a lot of white people, I can tell you right now."[3]

TUESDAY, MARCH 1, 1983

"Katrina's Paper Dolls" (basic tracking)
Universal Recording Corporation (Chicago, Illinois)
Producer: Prince | *Artist:* Prince | *Engineer:* Prince (assumed)

I remember that Susan, at one point, played me "Katrina's Paper Dolls," and I thought it was such an amazing song and so haunting and poignant.—Murielle Hamilton

One of the largely unreported stories during the *1999* tour was Prince's habit of recording wherever and whenever he could. "He would just go to a studio locally, and he could play every instrument, so somebody rented out whatever he was going to need in advance and booked an engineer," recalls Murielle Hamilton, who was his tour manager during this part of the schedule. "He would just go and record for five or six hours and so there's a million tapes out there that no one has ever even heard. He was really just an absolute workaholic."

Work on "Katrina's Paper Dolls" might have included additional help from others during this session. "It was a song we wrote with my sister, Cole Ynda," Lisa Coleman posted on wendyandlisa.com. "We did it to 'try out' some gear or something. I don't know what Prince was thinking at the time. He just gave us some studio time at this place and asked us to go record something."[4] Several versions are rumored to exist, including an experimental demo (14:08) consisting of piano and layers of voices from Cole Ynda, a condensed and embellished version of the demo (2:31) with Prince sharing vocals with Cole as well as a recording that features only Prince's vocals (3:30). It is unclear which version of the track was recorded on this date.

"Katrina" was Vanity's middle name and it has been rumored that the track was recorded with her in mind, although this has not been confirmed and no documentation exists of Vanity's vocals being added to the song. It is unclear whether the song was intended to reflect his thoughts about her or if her name simply sounded appealing and inspired the number.

Status: "Katrina's Paper Dolls" (3:30) was included on the *Purple Rain Deluxe* (Expanded Edition) CD set in 2017. The song was also reworked (4:23) in late 1986.

Prince suggested that "Katrina's Paper Dolls" be considered for a spot on *Crystal Ball II*, and requested that those who attended his *Celebration* event in 2000 vote on the potential track list. *Crystal Ball II* was never released.

Prince did not restrict his writing and recording to the studio. His focus was fairly obsessive when it came to music. "He was pretty serious and committed," explains Hamilton:

He really wanted it to be right, and he was often either rehearsing a specific song where he hadn't been happy with the way it went the night before and he wanted to clean something up during the sound check, or sometimes he would just play and maybe try something new, a song, at the sound check, or even in the show, and that would be the first and last time you'd hear it. He'd just try it out and he'd be like, "Whatever." He always had some sort of melody in his head. It was never ending.

In addition to his concerts, rehearsals, sound checks, and time in random studios, there were several occasions when he'd also seek out other ways of crafting his skills. According to Hamilton:

He liked to jam and play with other musicians. After the show, we'd go to clubs and often they'd just have a live band, and he would sit in with the band, and he'd sort of take over for the drummer and move on to the bass player. You should have seen him in those clubs late at night, he was just totally ripping it on the drums. Other instruments, too. I don't really know how it worked out, if the band was told in advance Prince was going to come in and he wants to sit in, but it was very fluid, where he would just sort of ease in and take one stick as the drummer is getting up and moving, and hands him the other stick, without missing a beat, and all of a sudden it's [Prince] playing, and I've seen him play at least five or six different instruments, and the saxophone, too. You noticed he just plugged into the socket of the universe and it blew through him, and that was it. He became an instrument.

WEDNESDAY, MARCH 2, 1983

Venue: Peoria Civic Center (Peoria, Illinois)
Capacity: 11,400 (possibly limited to lower number; attendance unknown)

THURSDAY, MARCH 3, 1983

Venue: Hara Arena (Trotwood, Ohio)
Capacity: 8,000 (possibly limited to lower number; attendance unknown)

SATURDAY, MARCH 5, 1983

Venue: Baltimore Civic Center (Baltimore, Maryland)
Capacity: 12,447 (sold out)

SUNDAY, MARCH 6, 1983

Venue: Wicomico Youth and Civic Center (Salisbury, Maryland)
Capacity: 5,130 (attendance unknown)

TUESDAY, MARCH 8, 1983

Venue: Norfolk Scope (Norfolk, Virginia)
Capacity: 13,800 (possibly limited to lower number; attendance unknown)

Prince's growing popularity allowed them to revisit Virginia for the fourth time on this tour. Three of the concerts were within the previous several weeks. This show was a reschedule of his canceled February 12 performance.

The rivalry between Prince and the Time had been brewing during their two tours, and now with Prince's increased popularity, Morris and his band pushed even harder to win over the growing audience. "As far as the crew was concerned, we were having a great time!" exclaims Roy Bennett. "The audience was reaping all the rewards from the frustration between the two groups."

WEDNESDAY, MARCH 9, 1983

Venue: Columbus Municipal Auditorium (Columbus, Georgia)
Capacity: 5,200 (sold out)

THURSDAY, MARCH 10, 1983

Venue: Monroe Civic Center (Monroe, Louisiana)
Capacity: 9,000 (possibly limited to lower number; attendance unknown)

FRIDAY, MARCH 11, 1983

Venue: Von Braun Civic Center (Huntsville, Alabama)
Capacity: 10,106 (possibly limited to 8,738; attendance unknown)

SATURDAY, MARCH 12, 1983

Venue: Knoxville Civic Auditorium (Knoxville, Tennessee)
Capacity: 10,000 (possibly limited to lower number; attendance unknown)

SUNDAY, MARCH 13, 1983

Venue: Wings Stadium (Kalamazoo, Michigan)
Capacity: 7,549 (possibly limited to lower number; attendance unknown)

With his new popularity, which was largely a reflection of his place on the charts, Prince placed songs like "Little Red Corvette" toward the end of the set, usually just before the encores. The new crowds and his growing base of white fans were proof to many that he was expanding his audience, as Jellybean Johnson explains: "He could do both 'Little Red Corvette' and all that pop shit. He could do it and have the white folks and stuff. And that's what he wanted. And that's the reason when he made *Purple Rain*, he exploded. Because he had everybody."[5]

MONDAY, MARCH 14, 1983 (ESTIMATE)

"Strange Relationship" (basic tracking and overdubs)
Kiowa Trail home studio (Chanhassen, Minnesota)
Producer: Prince | *Artist:* Prince | *Engineer:* Don Batts

*He kept taking that out every once in a while and jamming
with it, instead of putting it out, but he finally put it out. How
it changed, I don't remember much.*—Matt Fink

Unlike his studio time in Los Angeles, in Minneapolis Prince had the ability to record whenever the urge struck without leaving his home. Almost every day Prince would be in his studio, so Don Batts would leave the tape on the machine, ready to go when inspiration struck. When Batts arrived in the morning he'd sometimes see a pile of tapes with no labels, so he'd have to listen to them and label them for filing. He was also on call 24/7 in case Prince had a technical question in the middle of the night.

"Strange Relationship" was a track he'd revisit over the next few years, but when it was originally conceived, it was another track inspired by Vanity. The song was different in tone than numbers like "Wonderful Ass" because it lacked their humor.

When he was finished with the session, he dubbed it to a cassette for Vanity. "I remember him giving her 'Wonderful Ass' and 'Strange Relationship,'" remembers singer Jill Jones:

She had her little beat box and her cassettes. He gave out cassettes then. She'd play it before the show, while me, Susan, and all of us are getting dressed. It wasn't discreet. It was just a strange relationship. It was really true that he didn't want to see her happy and he didn't want to see her sad. Because she started dating other people . . . and he got pissed. She was like, "I'm moving away from him. Fuck him. I'm really famous. People love me." So she was getting something and that was the only thing he had to yank her back in.

Status: "Strange Relationship" was revisited and rerecorded more than once before a version (4:04) was released on his *Sign o' the Times* album in 1987. Although multiple sources indicate that Prince worked on "Strange Relationship" on this date, he may have begun the initial tracking during an earlier undocumented session.

TUESDAY, MARCH 15, 1983

Venue: Met Center (Bloomington, Minnesota)
Capacity: 13,729 (sold out)

WEDNESDAY, MARCH 16, 1983 (AFTER-MIDNIGHT SHOW)

Venue: Registry Hotel (Bloomington, Minnesota)
Capacity: unknown

Prince's star was on the rise when he returned home for a brief victory lap. By this time "Little Red Corvette" was a Top 40 hit (number 37 this week, on its way to number 6), which buoyed the album, bouncing it back up the charts as well. While everything was looking well from the outside, deep cracks had formed in the band, and Dickerson was uncomfortable singing some of the more overtly sexual songs because of his religious beliefs. "It was certainly a major factor," he remembered, "in that I became increasingly uncomfortable with the influence we were having on young people and youth culture in general."[6]

Now that they were playing to their hometown—and all the families and friends who'd be attending—Dickerson decided to discuss his new distaste for some of the songs they were playing and wanted to request that Prince eliminate some of the more sexually explicit songs. He asked the band to support his views in the conversation with Prince, which he was planning to have during the show's sound check, and the band reluctantly agreed to have his back. Matt Fink recalls that it didn't go as planned:

> When the time came for the vote to happen, Dez told Prince about this and that the band was supporting him, but everyone clammed up . . . everybody. And then he came to me, it was my turn to vote and I said, "It is Prince's show." . . . I was scared! You know what Dez did? He picked up a drum stool that was sitting there and came after me and chased me off the stage with it. He threatened to hit me with it and he came after me. He took all his frustration and came after me because I was the last guy and I said . . . maybe this wasn't such a good idea. It was like two days before we are talking again.

A 2:00 a.m. after-party was held at the Registry Hotel. Stevie Nicks, who'd been watching the earlier show from the side of the stage, mingled with the families and friends. A short jam session was held that included members of Vanity 6, the Time, and Prince's band, with Prince sitting in on drums.

Prince spent his time in Minneapolis discussing a potential movie with his management and meeting with William Blinn about writing the script. Prince told him he wanted "a picture that people would think of as 'weird' but couldn't get away from. He's got something he wants to communicate. I don't know if it's something you could write down. It's an attitude more than anything else."[7]

THURSDAY, MARCH 17, 1983

Venue: Metro Center (Rockford, Illinois)
Capacity: 10,000 (possibly limited to lower number; attendance unknown)

FRIDAY, MARCH 18, 1983

Venue: Omaha Civic Auditorium Arena (Omaha, Nebraska)
Capacity: 9,600 (sold out)

SATURDAY, MARCH 19, 1983

Venue: Municipal Auditorium (Kansas City, Missouri)
Capacity: 9,330 (sold out)

MONDAY, MARCH 21, 1983

Venue: Radio City Music Hall (New York, New York)
Capacity: 5,882 (sold out)

You've got to let people do what they do to get some of that go-
ing, and he had such a vice grip on everything that it just kind
of squashed people's ability to do too much.—Monte Moir[8]

Roy Bennett recalls how the tension continued to spill over after one of the New York shows:

> I remember Brenda and Vanity getting in a huge fight, and Prince saying, "Don't you have any control over your wife?" I pretended to hold a remote control and said, "I guess my batteries have gone dead!" Brenda apparently had Vanity up against the wall by the throat. Brenda was one of those women who grew up between two brothers. She wasn't like that all the time, but she could be very tough. It was basically Vanity trying to blame Brenda for something. There was constant friction between them.

Part of the reason for the growing frustration was that many of the band members felt they weren't being paid properly. "I was only getting $250 a week, and I had a hit song out," Vanity complained in a 2013 radio interview. "I was [performing for] thousands, hundreds of thousands of people a month, but I wasn't getting paid for any concert tours, nothing. So Prince was taking all that money and I thought, 'You know what? This is adding up to nothing! I'm living in a hotel. I didn't even have an apartment.'"[9]

To compensate for this, Prince would occasionally treat Vanity 6 to something nice. "He would really do sweet stuff at times," recalls Hamilton, who had started out on the current tour managing Vanity 6 before she was promoted to Prince's tour manager. "When I was still with Vanity 6, he went out somewhere and he bought us all robes. Four of the same dressing gowns in four different colors. A different color for each one of us. It was very sweet."

As usual, the financial situation frustrated members of the Time, but as an added insult, they were sometimes taken off the bill, generally in the major cities like New York and Los Angeles. They still performed, but only as the backing band for Vanity 6 and always hidden behind the pink curtain. "He made us play for them and wouldn't let the Time play," complained Jellybean Johnson. "Do you know what it's like to have a major star—Quincy Jones, Sting—coming to see us, and we don't play?"[10]

"After a while, it was like, 'You guys can't do New York, you can't do L.A.' There were a lot of issues starting to brew behind the scenes," recalled Day.[11]

"His real knack is trying to discourage people, and keep them from being confident," Jesse Johnson explained in 1988. "He used to tell us that people wouldn't know us if we walked down the street. He likes to tell you stuff like that, because of course if you got people believing that, they're always going to be there, accepting that small paycheck and feeling happy."[12]

"We were all loyal to Prince," reflected Jellybean. "He may not think so, but we were. That's the thing, so after bumping your head so much against the wall, you just have to protect your interests."[13]

With no financial incentive from ticket sales and no publishing money coming in from songwriting for the Time, Jimmy Jam recognized what he and Terry Lewis needed to do:

> The writing was on the wall, for better or worse, that we were not going to be writing for a Time album, which we accepted. Once again, I don't have a problem. The songs that we were getting were great songs, the albums were great albums. But it didn't mean that we felt like we weren't talented in our own right as writers. We just wanted the opportunity to try to do it. Our whole thing was, let's see if we can do it on our own. We have the cachet of being members of the Time and that's a great thing. Let's walk in and see if we can get some gigs going, so that is kind of what happened.[14]

There were no shows scheduled for the next two days following the Radio City concert, giving the tour a chance to travel from New York to San Antonio, Texas. To fill the time, Jam and Lewis were booked to produce a recording session in Atlanta, Georgia. It was a decision that would change the direction of their careers, but not in the way they had planned.

THURSDAY, MARCH 24, 1983

Venue: San Antonio Convention Center Arena (San Antonio, Texas)
Capacity: 16,573 (possibly limited to lower number; attendance unknown)

It's probably the saddest day of my life. —Jimmy Jam[15]

Jam and Lewis had flown to Atlanta to produce for the S.O.S. Band record and had planned to fly to San Antonio on the day of the show. "We get to the airport and it starts snowing," recalled Jam. "Well, we didn't think that was any big thing, being from Minnesota, and we were like, 'What's a little snow?' It really snowed less than an inch. It had to be literally half an inch of snow, but the airport shut down. It was like a nightmare and it was just a helpless feeling."[16]

Jam and Lewis were able to call and alert Prince about their dilemma. Although he hadn't joined the tour yet, Alan Leeds could understand why Prince would be upset: "They can blame it on the snowstorm, but the reality is you never take the last plane out. It's the first thing you learn in the tour business, is never schedule the last flight, always take the one before it. So when it goes south you've got a shot to make the gig. You just don't do that. And to do that was a 'fuck you' in the face of Prince and his management and the other guys in the band."[17]

Prince gathered everyone in the dressing room and explained the situation, and it was decided to continue with the band playing backup for Vanity 6 as well as doing their own set. "Prince was on me, because Terry and Jimmy are my boys," remembered Jellybean Johnson. "And I couldn't say nothing; Morris, all of us knew they were going and we knew there was no way in hell that they would miss a gig, they would be back in time. But in Atlanta, if it gets half an inch of snow, they close down. No more airplanes, nothing. So what can you do?"[18]

Lisa Coleman and Prince were tasked with playing keyboard and bass from behind the curtain, while Jill Jones stood in Jimmy's place and Jerome took Terry's spot on the stage.

Guitarist Jesse Johnson remembered the humor behind the scenes: "Morris and I were dying onstage. We were laughing our butts off the whole time. There was a part of the song where Morris would go, 'Terry,' but there was no Terry."[19]

"It was the funniest show," agrees Jones. "I knew these two chords because I had seen them play them. Prince was not happy. There was trouble in River City!"

Despite the backstage drama, the reviews were very positive. The *San Antonio Express News* enjoyed Prince's show, but proclaimed that the Time "stole the heart of this San Antonio crowd" and "played on the emotions of the fans and wiped them out with an unforgettable encore featuring 'The Walk.'"[20]

Prince seemed to be over the entire event when Jimmy and Terry rejoined the tour for the remaining dates, according to Jam: "Prince thought we'd gone to Atlanta to see some girls. So when we saw him, he just said, 'That's what you get.' He and management fined us for missing the gig, which was kind of laughable. I think they fined us $2,000, but we were making only $170 a week, so I don't know where they thought they were going to get that money from!"[21]

FRIDAY, MARCH 25, 1983

Venue: Lloyd Noble Center (Norman, Oklahoma)
Capacity: 12,540 (possibly limited to lower number; attendance unknown)

After this show, the tour headed to Los Angeles for a few days of rest and recording at Sunset Sound before the concert at the Universal Amphitheatre on March 28. Wendy Melvoin's position as the potential replacement for Dickerson was becoming more and more obvious as her connection with Prince grew. "We have a lot of fun together," she said in 1986. "When I first joined the band, Lisa and I convinced him to come to Los Angeles to stay with my sister Susannah, Lisa, me and our three Persian cats. Susannah and Lisa and I all slept on the fold-out couch and we put him in my bedroom. We'd go out in my old beat-up Mustang and get ice cream and drive around. It was like having a pajama party."[22]

"We'd go to the grocery store together late at night," Wendy later reflected on how relaxed Prince was with them. "One time, he grabbed a massive bag of grapes that the guys were getting ready to display. There was something cute and naive about it—'You don't need that many!'—but he bought them."[23]

At the same time as his relationship with Wendy was growing, his relationship with the Time was being stretched thinner and thinner. But there was a tour to complete, and while Prince had the reins, he was still going to make the calls.

SATURDAY, MARCH 26, 1983*

"**Jungle Love**" (basic tracking and overdubs)
Sunset Sound, Studio 2 | 3:30 p.m.–2:00 a.m. (booked 3:00 p.m.–open)
Producer: Morris Day (Prince scratched out) | *Artist:* the Time (Prince scratched out) | *Engineer:* (Prince scratched out) | *Assistant Engineer:* "Peggy Mac" McCreary

> *I played tapes of my songs for him, and Prince would literally start laughing. He'd call Morris over and be like, "Listen to this, listen to this," and they both laughed. When I brought him the music for "Jungle Love," he wasn't laughing anymore.—* Jesse Johnson[24]

"Sometimes it was disastrous," recalls Peggy McCreary:

> I remember one day he came in with a bandana tied around his knee and no shirt and ripped red pants and he had a bandana tied around his head and he had an attitude. He just sat down at the drums and told me to put up clean tape, and I

thought that we would be mixing and I'm madly flying around trying to put up clean tape to record. The rest of the Time were there and they were playing, and they had a groove going and they'd be ready to record and Prince would say, "Roll it" and I wasn't ready, and he would just be in the mood to make fun of you: "Is that your L.A. kick drum? Ooohhh, that's a good one." Just mocking you, and it just went on and on, sometimes all day long. You always had your guard up because you never knew when you were going to be zapped.

The song they were tracking on this date was "Jungle Love," which was originally recorded in Minneapolis by Jesse Johnson. The journey from demo to a song by the Time was a long one, slowed by Prince's control over the band. Prince was always looking for new material and new inspiration, but at the same time discouraged those around him from direct participation. Taking a page from Jam and Lewis, Johnson put aside money he'd been earning from this tour and purchased a Tascam reel-to-reel 8-track recorder. One of the tracks he created became the basis for "Jungle Love."

The session included Jimmy Jam, Morris Day, Terry Lewis, and Jesse Johnson, who witnessed Prince's anger, which on this day was aimed at McCreary. "I remember the guys looking at me like, 'I'm just glad it wasn't me he was doing this to," insists McCreary:

> But they didn't stick up for you because they were just glad that it wasn't them that day. He was on me all day long. He had his shirt off, his pants unbuttoned a few buttons, and he had this attitude that would kill you. I don't know why, but he was cocky that day and I don't work well under that kind of criticism. Jesse always had those puppy dog eyes, like, "I'm just glad it's not us." Everyone was just walking around on pins and needles. He was in one of those moods to rip someone a new butthole and it was me that day.

"I loved Peggy Mac!" exclaims Jesse Johnson. "Her and Prince were always about to kill each other, but she got such a great sound on everything. She was one of the best engineers I've ever worked with in my life. She was so great. She'd set up that drum kit and have that shit so killin'."

McCreary adds her memory of sessions like this one:

> I remember something went wrong one day and I had accidentally erased something and he wasn't talking to me, and I finally asked him if he wanted someone else on this, and he just looked at me and said, "You're here aren't you?" and he just walked away. There was never any encouragement, never a pat on the back, but then he'd write you a song or do something like that. He wasn't very person-

able. I remember once I made a mistake and he turned around to me and said, "It's a good thing you're cute." That was about as close as I ever got to a real compliment about my work.

"I saw him do that to others on other days," McCreary continues, "and everybody just immediately stepped aside, thinking, 'Oh, don't make one wrong move,' and if you made one wrong move he was on you like a ton of bricks. Very unforgiving. He didn't appreciate mistakes. Nobody does, but mistakes happen. It's just human error."

Overdubs took place after the 10:00 p.m. dinner break, with Jesse Johnson using Prince's Hohner Telecaster to play rhythm guitar. It was likely that during this session Johnson added his solo using a pink G&L prototype and his 1979 Marshall JCM 800 amp. After the session, Johnson and Foster Sylvers (producer, songwriter, and member of the Sylvers) went to another studio and recorded guitar on "Dead Giveaway" for Shalamar. "Dead Giveaway" would be released in July, and Jesse's rhythm guitar work on the track would go uncredited.

A rough mix of "Jungle Love" was completed by 2:00 a.m. and a single C-60 cassette was made of the session.

Status: "Jungle Love" (5:26) was eventually placed on the Time's *Ice Cream Castle* album. An edited single (3:26) was released on December 12, 1984, in the United States and rose to number 20 on the *Billboard* Hot 100 Singles chart, as well as number 6 on the *Billboard* Black Singles chart and number 9 on the *Billboard* Dance/Disco Top 80 chart.

The song would also be featured in the *Purple Rain* movie, but the version used in the movie was from a live performance recorded on October 4, 1983.

SUNDAY MARCH 27, 1983*

"Cloreen Bacon Skin" (basic tracking and overdubs)
"My Summertime Thang" (basic tracking and overdubs)
Sunset Sound, Studio 2 | 3:00 p.m.–11:00 p.m. (booked from 4:00 p.m.–open)
Producer: Morris Day (Prince crossed out) | *Artist:* the Time (Prince crossed out) | *Engineer:* (Prince crossed out) | *Assistant Engineer:* "Peggy Mac" McCreary

There is a track called baconskin that thumps [for] 15
minutes. SICK.—Prince[25]

Prince relied on Morris Day's drum skills for many studio tracks for the Time, and because Day was always in the pocket, it was easy for Prince to jam with him as he looked for the next song. "What people don't know about Morris is that he is one of the best drummers that you've ever seen," declared band member Terry Lewis. "And one of the funniest cats of all time. Just a natural."[26] On occasions like today's sessions, Prince would tap into Morris's funk and sense of humor to help unlock their next song. "Cloreen Bacon Skin" was the ad-libbed jam that was recorded during this session.

"They had been up for a long time," explained future engineer Susan Rogers. "The song starts and then all of a sudden Morris loses the groove and Prince turns around to see what has happened and Morris's headphones have fallen off, so you can hear at the beginning of the tape talking and laughing between the two of them, and then they went ahead and finished the song."[27]

"Everything U hear is impromptu," according to the album's liner notes. "No lyrics or music, even the title was made up a split second be4 U hear it."[28] This may also be the only song that he mentions his half-brother, Alfred, by name. It is likely that Prince still had the previous night's recording of "Jungle Love" in his head, because he sings, "We're going to go to the jungle one time"[29] during the track. Songs like this were done in a character created by Prince and Day. The voice was often considered to be the mythical producer Jamie Starr, but when Prince took the lead vocal for a song by the Time, he was channeling someone else altogether. "It's funny," reminisced Rogers, "when Prince would do that funny voice—that was him imitating men of his father's generation, you know barber shop guys. 'Cloreen Bacon Skin' was the same kind of a voice and same kind of . . . 'Why do you want to fuck with me, I'm too old!' He was doing his dad."[30]

The song appears to have never been seriously considered for placement on an album by Prince (although there was some evidence that it was a potential B-side for the Time), but it was a great exercise to help flesh out ideas. In fact, elements of this track can be found on many songs, including "Tricky," "Chocolate," "Do Yourself a Favor," "The Bird," and "Irresistible Bitch."

The other track recorded on this date was "My Summertime Thang," which involved Jam and Lewis playing along with Prince and Day. The song includes a riff that sounds like it was inspired by Vanity 6's "If a Girl Answers (Don't Hang Up)." It was never a favorite of Prince's, and once recorded it sat in the vault for years before its inclusion on the Time's 1990 reunion album, *Pandemonium*.

Between 1983 and 1989, Prince would forget his original reaction to the track, as Rogers details: "He pulled that one out three times and the third time he said: 'Can you do me a favor? Take a pen and write on this box "WEAK" and remind me if I ever ask to hear it again don't ever pull it out of the closet.' So I wrote 'WEAK' with big letters and I circled it. And it was after I'd left him that I was amazed to see that he had used it on the *Pandemonium* album."[31]

Jimmy Jam was much more fond of the track and wanted to resurrect it during the *Pandemonium* sessions:

> We always loved the song, so that was one of the ones we asked Prince for. We said, "Hey Prince, 'My Summertime Thang,' can we have that? That was our song from back in the day." And he said, "Yeah, you can have it. But I changed the words. It's called 'The Latest Fashion' now." And we're like, "No, no, no, no." So that was sort of a compromise. He wanted it as "The Latest Fashion" because it worked in [*Graffiti Bridge*] for the scene. But we wanted it as "My Summertime Thang" because that's what it was back when we had it.[32]

Prince was still in control of the Time, but band members were hungry for other ways to express their talent. "This was a super creative time in our lives," explained Day. "We were all writing, submitting stuff. By the time we got to write songs we had turned down so many gigs and so much money from people who wanted us to write and produce for them. . . . But we were unable to."[33]

While the band was on the road, Prince worked to maintain the integrity of the group, but as they learned more about the industry and the process of creating music, his hold on them grew weaker. "I can't lie and say I didn't pick up stuff from him. I learned how to be funky because of Prince," admitted Jellybean Johnson. "A lot of my funk came from being around him, because he's such a funky cat. But at the same time it's hard, because he's not an easy guy to be close to. So it's like he's begrudgingly letting you learn shit from him, but he really don't want you to learn it. But you can't help but learn something from him if you're around him enough."[34]

In retrospect, many in the band felt they had gone about as far as they could go under Prince's strict hand, and their rivalries were no longer just below the surface. "Morris was clairvoyant," remembered Jimmy Jam. "When we were selling out shows and kicking Prince's ass in concert, Morris had a meeting and told us [the group] isn't going to last forever. He told us that everybody needed to figure out individually what [they were] going to do next. That's a tough thing to hear when you're at the top. But that's when [Terry and I] began songwriting and producing for others."[35]

Despite their differences, some of the members look back with great respect for Prince. "He was a wonderful mentor for us," Jam reflected in 2011, "and the reason that we're here today is because of him giving us the break of putting us on the map with him."[36]

The reality was that Prince had changed from mentor into tormentor, and his absolute authority would soon destroy the Time.

Status: "Cloreen Bacon Skin" (15:37) was released in 1998 on Prince's *Crystal Ball* CD set. In 1990 "The Latest Fashion" (4:01) was released on Prince's *Graffiti Bridge* album and "My Summertime Thang" (6:54 with 19-second intro and 4:26 extended section) was released on the Time's *Pandemonium* album. Alternate versions of "The Latest Fashion" (4:07) and "My Summertime Thang" (7:14, with a 4:26 extended section) were rerecorded for the Time's unreleased album *Corporate World.*

According to the booklet for Crystal Ball, *"Cloreen Bacon Skin" was recorded during the sessions for the Time's second album,* What Time Is It? *but today's session (March 27, 1983) is based on the work order from Sunset Sound as well as archival information from the vault at Warner Bros., so the album notes are probably incorrect.*

The new enthusiasm on the charts and the crossover crowds at the concerts boosted Prince's confidence regarding making a movie that loosely followed his story. **"I really wanted to chronicle the life I was living at the time,"** Prince told Larry King in 1999, **"which was in an area that had a lot of great talent and a lot of rivalries. So I wanted to chronicle that vibe of my life."**[37]

"When he came to us with this idea about a movie, we were all excited," remembered Brown Mark. "We knew Elvis Presley used to do it. We knew the Beatles did it. And we were all excited to see what happens. And he had this great idea, this great script; next thing I know, he went to Hollywood and came back and we were doing the movie. It was a pretty exciting time period."[38]

Matt Fink recalls the moment he learned Prince's thoughts about the film: "He came to me at the end of the *1999* tour, he sat me down at lunch one day and told me about his plans to do a movie and all that. And I was astounded. I said, 'Really? We're going to do a movie?' He goes, 'Yeah.' At first I couldn't believe it. I thought, he's got to be whacked. (*laughs*)"

Fink had grown up with a background in theater and dance, and had been raised by two seasoned actors, so the idea of acting in a movie sat well with him. The biggest missing details were the songs. "The music wasn't even in the works yet," he would later recall. "Maybe one or two songs, but that was it."[39]

With his highest-charting song still selling, it would have been easy to simply use that track in the movie, which would help sell more copies of the album. It was an audience-tested success and would be a way to play it safe by guaranteeing public interest in the music. Prince decided against that path.

Prince was asked to re-sign with Cavallo, Ruffalo & Fargnoli, but according to Bob Cavallo, Prince added one big stipulation before he'd sign: "Steve calls me and he says: You're not going to believe this; he doesn't want to sign it unless you get him a major motion picture, and it can't be some drug dealer, or jeweler, or some friend of Cavallo. It's got to be a major studio. So that his name is above the title."

"Prince wanted to make a movie," confirmed Fargnoli, "so we got together and proceeded as if everybody in the world thought that was a good idea."[40]

By this time William Blinn had been hired as a writer and Prince granted him access, so he spent time with the band, learning everyone's personalities and some of Prince's vulnerabilities. "It's hard to have that much power and have close friends," Blinn said. "It's tough for him."[41]

"It was as if he were sorting out his own mystery," he added. "An honest quest to figure himself out. He saved all the money on shrinks and put it in the movie."[42]

Although the script would be rewritten, Blinn's draft was the script that was being circulated to generate interest in the project.

Many people who were around Prince during this period suggested that he'd been working on the ideas for his movie and writing them down in a purple notebook. "It's nonsense. There was no purple notebook that I saw," explains Purple Rain *director and writer Albert Magnoli. "Years later, after the movie was in the theater, I kept on hearing about this purple notebook. And I said to Prince, 'What purple notebook?' and he says, 'I used to walk around with a purple notebook and I took notes; everybody assumed I was writing a movie and I never told them I wasn't.'"*

MONDAY, MARCH 28, 1983

Venue: Universal Amphitheatre (Universal City, California)
Capacity: 6,189 (sold out)

Prince's newest peak in popularity created a buzz in the industry, and celebrities showed up for the performance. Perhaps hoping to avoid being outshined, Prince had the Time dropped from the show once again. "We worked our asses off," stressed Jesse Johnson. "For five months before a tour, we'd rehearse every day. In some cities we kicked Prince's ass so badly he even came into our dressing room and told us. It was like a grudge match every night."[43]

Monte Moir agreed: "Some of the reviews were starting to say that we were doing better shows and he hated that. So it was like, he'd started this thing, and it had got to be bigger and bigger. He liked it, but he hated it. He'd done something good, but now he wanted to tear it apart."[44]

"Everybody knows back in the day especially New York and L.A. were the top markets," Jellybean Johnson revealed in 1995. "We were huge in those markets. But the only time we got to officially play there as the Time was during the *Controversy* tour the first year. The second year, only him and Vanity 6 played. We saw we weren't on the schedule, we were pissed. We took it very personal, especially when you're in the dressing room and you're backstage and every major celebrity you can think of is at this show. Every major movie star, every major athlete because it's L.A. Magic, Quincy, Bruce Springsteen, everybody's back in this area, that you had grew up watching. And you are behind a fucking pink curtain."

"He didn't give us [an explanation]," said Johnson. "He didn't have to. He's the boss."[45]

His show featured the live premiere of "Moonbeam Levels," an unreleased track recorded the previous summer. "'Moonbeam Levels' is one of the greatest songs he has ever written," reflected engineer Susan Rogers. "He considered putting it on just about every album that I know of, that I've worked with him on, including *Purple Rain*, *Around the World in a Day*, *Sign o' the Times* and *Parade*. I think 'Moonbeam' is probably as honest a lyric that he has ever written."[46]

"Moonbeam Levels" (4:06) would be released in 2016 on the posthumous *4Ever* collection.

TUESDAY, MARCH 29, 1983

Venue: San Diego Sports Arena (San Diego, California)
Capacity: 14,941 (possibly limited to lower number; attendance unknown)

The stress of the tour was proving too much for tour manager Murielle Hamilton, who decided that she'd had enough:

> It was a pain in the ass. I quit in San Diego, because we were so close to L.A., where I lived, and I was so sick and tired of dealing with politics within the band. I said [to Prince], "I'm really sorry but I have to go," and he said, "Okay." Tour managers are replaceable, and Alan Leeds was around and I thought: It's perfect, he can replace me. I can go home and be done with this. Prince was always very nice to me, so he was not the problem. I was supposed to keep the band issues out of his hair. At the time, there were maybe six dates left or something, that I just didn't have it in me. I wanted to go home.

Although it was her last gig in the music industry, Hamilton maintained a close relationship with the members of Vanity 6, and decades later still considers them close friends.

"The tour had been out for a couple of months," recalled Alan Leeds. "And the word had spread that this was a tough tour to work on. The artist was impossible. The management was demanding. . . . In the tour industry *1999* had become renowned for being 'Oh, *that* tour . . . the tour from hell.' So [production manager Tom Marzullo] says to me, 'Would you be interested in going over there?' and I'm like . . . 'Yeah, why not?' That's just how I am. Sounds like an adventure."[47]

Leeds, who'd previously worked as tour manager for James Brown, was wrapping up his work on the American leg of Kiss's *Creatures of the Night*/10th Anniversary tour when he joined the *1999* tour: "I met them in San Diego. [Steven Fargnoli] introduced me around and sternly warned me to tread lightly until Prince signaled his comfort with having me around. 'He takes a minute to warm up to strangers,' was Steven's memorable understatement. I made a point to befriend the band and bodyguard Chick Huntsberry, who seconded Steve's warning not to bum-rush Prince."[48]

Leeds instantly noticed part of the cause of the reported tension: "It was obviously a tour split into cliques. My responsibilities were Prince and his band. The support acts, the Time and Vanity 6, had their own staffs and agendas. Jimmy Jam and Terry Lewis had famously clashed with Prince over missing a gig, and the Time's morale was forever ruined."[49]

Leeds recalled:

> You had guys who were unhappy, and they weren't even always able to understand why they were so unhappy, because after all, they were remarkably successful and deserved the success, because certainly, at least onstage, they held their

own—I mean, *they* did it. They got up there and sang and played. So there was disharmony within the band, the frustrations of not being able to have more say-so in what was written and played on the albums. So I think that in order to justify to themselves, they started to conjure up a bad guy. They had to have somewhere they could point and say "This is the reason."

The month that I was there was in fact the most tumultuous month, when all the shit was hitting the fan, and despite all of that, I mean the reality is this was a Prince tour and he was the guy who was breaking wide open, "1999" had hit, "Little Red Corvette" was blowing up, and I gotta tell you something, this was his house."[50]

"[Prince] sensed, correctly, that fostering a competitive environment would motivate both bands when on tour together and, at times, keep things interesting for himself as well," according to Leeds.[51] While the competition was great for the audience, it was causing more rifts in the bands. The mutual admiration and respect the Time and Prince enjoyed was being tested, and was failing. "There was an intense rivalry that I'm sure began as a mutual admiration," observed Leeds. "And at some point the rivalry surpassed the admiration."[52]

WEDNESDAY, MARCH 30, 1983

Venue: Veterans Memorial Coliseum (Phoenix, Arizona)
Capacity: 12,221 (9,223 tickets sold)

THURSDAY, MARCH 31, 1983* (DAY)

"Cloreen Bacon Skin" (mix)
Sunset Sound, Studio 1, 1:00 p.m.–2:45 p.m. (booked 1:00 p.m.–6:00 p.m.)
Producer: Morris Day listed, but Prince oversaw the session | *Artist:* the Time | *Engineer:* Prince and/"Peggy Mac" McCreary

I'm a musician. And I am music.—Prince[53]

"I saw a bit of an interview with [Prince] and I heard him make the statement, talking about himself, where he said, 'I am music.' And I have to agree with that," affirmed Morris Day. "I think he's just invested himself to the degree where that's just who he is. He's incredible. Sometimes I had to look at him, shake him up a little bit, and say, 'Are you the same cat I grew up with?' Because it's pretty amazing to see him do his thing."[54]

Prince was back in the Los Angeles area for a show in Long Beach, and as usual, he couldn't stay away from the studio, so Sunset Sound scheduled a rare session for him in Studio 1. Prince wanted to do some additional work on "Cloreen Bacon Skin" for some reason—perhaps to allow Warner Bros. to listen to it for consideration as a potential B-side for the Time's next single. Prince's usual rooms, Studios 2 and 3, were no longer being held for him, so Sunset Sound offered him the only room that was available. The session ended early so Prince could get to the sound check for his show that evening.

One cassette was made of the mix. Although Day was listed as the producer, it is unclear if he attended the mix.

THURSDAY, MARCH 31, 1983 (EVENING)

Venue: Long Beach Arena (Long Beach, California)
Capacity: 13,574 (sold out)

We wore his ass out in Long Beach.—Jellybean Johnson[55]

Prince, the Time, and Vanity 6 were all on the bill for this show. Because of the proximity of Long Beach to Los Angeles, it was a chance for the Time to perform for the local crowds.

APRIL 1983

FRIDAY, APRIL 1, 1983

Venue: Oakland–Alameda County Coliseum (Oakland, California)
Capacity: 14,340 (possibly limited to lower number; attendance unknown)

SATURDAY, APRIL 2, 1983

Venue: Selland Arena–Fresno Convention Center (Fresno, California)
Capacity: 11,300 (possibly limited to lower number; attendance unknown)

SUNDAY, APRIL 3, 1983

Venue: Oakland–Alameda County Coliseum (Oakland, California)
Capacity: 14,340 (possibly limited to lower number; attendance unknown)

Because of Prince's newfound popularity, it was decided to extend the tour for another week, and Easter Sunday found the band heading back to Oakland for a second show, where they were introduced to the woman who would become Prince's drummer: Sheila E. Prince had met her years earlier, but it is doubtful that anyone in the room could conceive how their relationship would change his music and his focus.

MONDAY, APRIL 4, 1983

Once again Prince played in the Los Angeles area, but this time it was only lip-syncing "Little Red Corvette" at the KTLA Studios for the television show *Solid Gold*. He had previously performed "1999" on the program in December. The episode would eventually air on May 14.

TUESDAY, APRIL 5, 1983

Venue: Denver Auditorium Arena (Denver, Colorado)
Capacity: 5,790 (sold out)

THURSDAY, APRIL 7, 1983

Venue: Mecca Arena (Milwaukee, Wisconsin)
Capacity: 9,532 (sold out)

FRIDAY, APRIL 8, 1983

Venue: Joe Louis Arena (Detroit, Michigan)
Capacity: 21,672 (sold out)

> *Detroit . . . was always our biggest market because they really discovered us and took to us right away. The fact was we were different.*—Jimmy Jam[1]

Because Detroit had adopted the Time in many ways, it is odd that Prince decided to promote the concert without advertising that the Time would also be on the bill. Perhaps it was all part of the rivalry between them, and he was hoping to show everyone that he could sell out Joe Louis Arena without anyone's help—and he did it. In a lucky twist for the audience, the Time did open the concert. "The last month of that tour was very uncomfortable," remembered Alan Leeds. "The vibes on the road were very bad. And there were a couple of gigs the Time did not play, and a couple of the guys were very outspoken about how they were left off of those gigs, one of which is supposedly the Detroit show on April 8. Because they were not advertised for that show, it is often thought that they didn't appear, when in reality they did play the show, even though they weren't advertised."[2]

SATURDAY, APRIL 9, 1983

Venue: Richfield Coliseum (Richfield, Ohio)
Capacity: 17,500 (possibly limited to lower number; attendance unknown)

Prince advertised the Time and Vanity 6 as opening acts once again, and both performed as scheduled.

SUNDAY, APRIL 10, 1983

Venue: UIC Pavilion (Chicago, Illinois)
Capacity: 10,638 (sold out)

> *The 1999 tour was huge. It was a hugely successful tour, but I can't go on without saying that the Time kicked his ass in almost every city we played in. But that's just me, and you'd have to get other people's opinions on that.*—Jimmy Jam[3]

Practically everyone on the tour saw firsthand the intense rivalry between Prince and the Time. "It was meant to be stiff competition because he kind of created the Time to be just that," explained Dez Dickerson. "But I think as far as Prince's expectation, I think they went above and beyond it to the point where it was kind of like the Frankenstein monster thing. Whoa! This was as successful as we expected it to be and there were some aspects of it that he didn't expect, but we wanted them to go out every night and beat it up so badly so that we could not ever phone it in."[4]

Unlike the previous year's tour to promote his 1981 album *Controversy*, which concluded with an epic food fight involving members of the Time snatched from the stage in mid-performance, the *1999* tour finished on a more anticlimactic note. A private after-party at Park West ended early when police arrived because a permit was never secured. Members of all three groups (as well as the crew and anyone else who was hoping to enjoy the party) escaped through a side door onto the very crowded tour bus.

By any measure, the *1999* tour was a commercial and critical success, grossing $10 million and becoming one of the biggest moneymaking tours of the year. A rarely discussed financial benefit of the tour was that Prince also made large donations to various charities. At the time, Prince's philanthropic work didn't get the press it deserved, but he quietly gave to several charities, and live concerts were common vehicles for his goodwill. This was a trend that would continue through his entire career.

Prince flew to Minneapolis to continue creating the framework for his movie, which at this point was called *Dreams*. After the tour, Dez Dickerson stayed in Los Angeles, talking to various record companies in an attempt to get his solo career off the ground. He was still a part of the planned movie project, but as the story was being developed, Prince asked him to fly back to Minneapolis for a face-to-face talk about their future.

According to Dickerson, "[Prince] said 'We're at a crossroads with this film, we're making a big investment. I need you to either bail now or make a three-year commitment to stay with the program. If you do the solo thing, that's cool. I'll help you do it, my people will manage you and the whole bit.' I thought and prayed about it, and decided I couldn't commit to another three years. I was genuinely unhappy by that time."[5]

The movie script was retooled after he opted out, and his supporting role was reduced to a cameo.

While the script for the movie was in flux, Prince's band began to gel, with Wendy Melvoin being offered the open position in the group. "It was just very obvious that Dez was unhappy," according to Bobby Z, "and Wendy was just at the absolute right place at the right time and was Lisa's best friend. She brought so much to the group, and her personality brought so much to balance the band out and make it the band it became. It couldn't have become the Revolution with Dez. It needed her to bring out that extra oomph!"[6]

Although there was still a little unfinished business, the ultimate decision had been made. Dez Dickerson was out. Wendy Melvoin was in. The Revolution was born.

TUESDAY, APRIL 12, 1983 (ESTIMATE)

"The Bird" (basic tracking)
Kiowa Trail home studio (Chanhassen, Minnesota)
Producer: Prince | *Artist:* the Time | *Engineer:* Prince | *Assistant Engineer:* Don Batts

> *I wrote a 4-track version on the* 1999 *tour. Prince kinda liked the hook, he threw the rest of what I did in the trash can as he commenced to write and performed a straight heater.*
> —Jesse Johnson[7]

A day after he arrived home from Chicago, Prince spent part of the afternoon in his basement recording a new song called "The Bird," written by Jesse Johnson for the Time. That evening, after Morris Day added his vocals, Johnson was called over to Prince's house and was blown away once he heard where Prince took the track. In 2014 Johnson posted a story on his Facebook page about the recording on that night, and how Prince's tape machine broke down and Johnson was asked to rewind it by hand:

> Morris is laughing his ass off, and 'course I'm like "Man fuck that, you better call Don Batts [his tech] to fix that shit!" Prince is now cracking up. We have to finish the song, so I go "WTF" and start rewinding the machine by hand. P could see what I was doing, so I had a drum stick on the reel where the holes are rewinding the machine, by the time Prince sees what I'm doing, he yells "what the f**k are you doing Jesse?" "Rewinding this raggedy ass machine," I said, as he jumps up to come look at the tape to see if I damaged it in any way he sort of trips over Morris who has this long ass Q-tip type things that are made for sticking in a solution and cleaning your tape heads, so before he could reach me he's yelling at Morris to stop using his tape head cleaners to clean his ears! Now I'm on the floor, because Morris would always do that and Prince had told him a thousand times before not to! Needless to say we got the track finished and the rest is history.[8]

Day's vocals were added very quickly, but his singing lacked intensity. Prince tried to add some of the fun and energy—with spoken comments like, "Hey, Morris, find out if you've got any fine girlfriends," at 4:49 in the song, wolf-whistling, and using a longer keyboard riff of "The Star-Spangled Banner" during the "Fellas, what's the word?" section at 5:30—but overall, the experiment wasn't a success.

Status: The studio version of "The Bird" (6:29) was considered for placement on the next album by the Time, but was ultimately replaced by a live version recorded at First Avenue on October 4, 1983. The studio version remains unreleased.

Although Jesse has publicly explained that he went to Prince's house on a Wednesday night, it is possible that he got there late on a Tuesday night and the session drifted into the next day. The date of this session hasn't been verified, so the placement here is speculation based on descriptions and recollections of those involved.

THURSDAY, APRIL 14, 1983*

"**My Summertime Thang**" (mix)
Untitled song ["Chili Sauce"] (basic tracking and overdubs)
Sunset Sound, Studio 2 | 8:00 p.m.–5:00 a.m. (booked 8:00 p.m.–open)
Producer: Prince, although Morris Day was listed and Prince was crossed out | *Artist:* the Time (Prince crossed out) | *Engineer:* Prince | *Assistant Engineer:* "Peggy Mac" McCreary

> *Okay, I'm going to explain it like this. If you are playing funk and you want to up the ante of the groove, you would say . . . "CHILI SAUCE" and the groove will take a subtle yet massive change. . . . [H]opefully the result is even funkier.*
> —Wendy Melvoin[9]

One of the hallmarks of Prince's career was that when a new challenge truly intrigued him, everything else would become secondary. Once he got the bug to create a movie, the planned dates for a European leg of the tour were canceled and the tour was officially over. Prince committed to focusing on the pending movie as well as any music that could be used for that project. The first date back at Sunset Sound involved work on a new track for the Time.

"In the studio for the Time album, the band was there most of the time. They played on a lot of the stuff, but [Prince] would be the leader of what was going on," recalls Peggy McCreary. "Sometimes he would jump on the drums and then jump on another instrument and then he'd tell Morris to jump on the drums. They weren't always there, but they were around a lot. I mean Jimmy Jam, for example, couldn't figure out what I was doing there. It was funny because he'd be like, 'Man, you're really good,' even though at the time I'm not sure if he even knew what I was doing."

"The studio experience overall couldn't have been a better learning opportunity because he was very unorthodox, but it was very spontaneous," recalled Jam. "Prince was always the most prolific, always the quickest and he was totally self-contained. He could engineer, write it, play it, he could do pretty much everything and do it efficiently. It was a great lesson to me, and valuable lesson, on how to record. His attitude towards music was 'You've got to make visual records.' The record has got to put you in a place where you visualize something."[10]

"My Summertime Thang" is listed on the work order, so additional overdubs or a mix probably took place. Prince purchased a 2-inch tape, so it is likely he started recording a new, as-yet-untitled track—probably "Chili Sauce"—as well.

As he did much of the time, Prince started with a drum pattern: **"I've had this Roger Linn drum machine since 1981. It's one of the first drum machines ever created. It takes me five seconds to put together a beat on this thing."**[11] Prince began working on the song at 9:30 p.m. and had the basic tracks to tape by midnight. The next five hours were spent overdubbing the new track. Prince decided to add strings, and a viola player, Ilene "Novi" Novog, was recruited for the late session. Novog remembers, "He was really good to work with, very professional and a workaholic. When I first got a call, I was exhausted and it was about 12:30 at night and I didn't really know them, and I thought he was going to be a little brat. I knew '1999' and I loved the song, and then I got called in for something for the Time called 'Chili Sauce.' He sat down and played the piano and he was very nice."

It is unclear whether any dialogue was placed on the track on this date, but it is unlikely because the name of the song wasn't listed on the paperwork. One C-60 cassette was created of the track, and the session was over at 5:00 a.m.

It was very common for Prince's sessions to last much later than those of most other musicians. McCreary explains: "People say that you have to do a lot of drugs to be able to stay up that late, and I tell them, 'No. If you did a lot of drugs, you wouldn't be able to stay up like that.'"

Status: "Chili Sauce" (5:47) was released on the Time's *Ice Cream Castle* album the following year.

FRIDAY, APRIL 15, 1983*

> **"Proposition 17"** [working title for "Chili Sauce"] (overdubs)
> Sunset Sound, Studio 2 | 9:00 p.m.–4:45 a.m. (booked from 4:00 p.m.–
>   open)
> *Producer:* Morris Day is listed, but Prince oversaw the session | *Artist:* the
>   Time | *Engineers:* "Peggy Mac" McCreary and Richard McKernan

> *We always have fun with taking words and doing something a little different with them, like "chili sauce." Morris's daughter walked into rehearsal one day and said, "chili sauce," and chili sauce was born.* —Jimmy Jam[12]

Prince arrived a few hours late for the session, but once he did, work resumed on "Chili Sauce," which at this point was named "Proposition 17." The title becomes more obvious when you count how many times Day propositions the woman he is trying to seduce in the song. The detail and layers of sound effects add to the humor of his seduction, setting up the scene in a public restaurant. "He loved the sound effects we had and would sometimes just pop on the sound effects LP and just listen to stuff like 'body falls' and 'restaurant' sounds," remembers McCreary. "If you listen to some songs you'll hear 'restaurant walla' and 'baby crying' and [Prince's song] 'Lady Cab Driver' had traffic."

"I always spend a lot of time and energy thinking about and seeking out those little touches," Prince explained to *Guitar World* magazine. **"Attention to detail makes the difference between a good song and a great song. And I meticulously try to put the right sound in the right place, even sounds that you would only notice if I left them out. Sometimes I hear a melody in my head, and it seems like the first color in a painting. And then you can build the rest of the song with other added sounds."[13]**

This was a transition day and a test day for a new engineer. Normally Prince's sessions were engineered by Peggy McCreary, but she wasn't available for the next few days, so another engineer was needed. Prince had recently noticed staff engineer Richard McKernan, thanks to an event in the Sunset Sound parking lot, as McKernan explains:

> One day I was just sitting in the front window waiting for Prince, and [a number of fans] were all by the front of the cars, and then in came Prince. He got out of the car and he was putting on his coat, and I saw [the large group of fans] and I just stood between him and them. He turned around and he was just pale and he ran in. The next thing I knew, Peggy came out and said, "Boy he really appreciated that." And so by the end of the day he called me back there and he said, "You want to work with me?" And I said, "Sure," and Peggy was really happy because she could go on vacation.

SATURDAY, APRIL 16, 1983*

"Proposition 17" [working title for "Chili Sauce"] (overdubs)
"If the Kid Can't Make You Come" [listed as "If the Boy Can't Make You Come"] (basic tracking and overdubs)
Sunset Sound, Studio 2 | 4:00 p.m.–11:00 p.m. (and 5 additional hours on hold)
Producer: Morris Day is listed, but Prince oversaw the session | *Artist:* the Time | *Engineer:* Prince | *Assistant Engineer:* not listed but probably Richard McKernan

> *It was Morris' idea to be as sick as he was. That was his personality. We both like Don King and got a lot of stuff off him, because he's outrageous and thinks everything's so exciting—even when it isn't.*—Prince[14]

Additional work was done for these tracks for the Time. Once again, Day was listed as the producer, but Prince was always in control. "Morris was never in the studio alone with me," according to McKernan:

> When we were working with Morris, it was pretty much just to do some vocals. I don't remember him having too much to do with the production of it. Prince would put songs together and my perspective of it was, Prince would get to a point and say, "Well, okay, I'll give this one to Morris." I always got the feeling

that he was thinking, "Well, I don't want this song on my album, so I'll put it on his album." I don't know if that's what he was thinking, but it always seemed like that.

Their guitar player, Jesse, was there. Jesse was the only other musician who Prince would actually call in. There were people that would float in and out, but Jesse was the only musician that added anything. I never did any drums with Morris. Morris would come in and fool around with the drums, but it wasn't anything that got to tape.

Jesse Johnson supposedly also played drums on the song.

McKernan continues:

[Prince] had one of those old Linn drum machines, and you'd have everything set up and usually on drums, he'd tell you the day before what he'd be recording. We'd get the drums down there and mic it up and have somebody play it and he'd show up and then there would be a bass set up and a keyboard set up. And you'd get the things to that point and he'd stop before doing a vocal and he'd say, "Tomorrow we're going to do vocals," or sometimes the vocal mic was already set up in the room to the side. If he'd been in there for a bunch of days in a row, everything would be set up.

Work on the tracks occurred from 4:00 p.m. until 11:00 p.m., when Prince ended the session and left. The engineer was on hold for another five hours before they received word that Prince was not returning. Fellow engineer Bill Jackson recalls how the engineers were occasionally left hanging: "You had to wait there until someone called and said that he wasn't going to come back . . . unless he just absolutely said, 'Nope, I'm going home,' and then you went home and waited for the phone to ring. (*laughs*)"

Status: "If the Kid Can't Make You Come" (9:13) was eventually edited down (7:33) for release on the Time's *Ice Cream Castle* album.

There was often a difference between what was written on the Sunset Sound work orders and what was actually recorded. McKernan explains his view on this: "The work orders were just enough to get by because the record companies wanted certain information to be kept up on. . . . Some people wanted every little thing on there. At Sunset, there was so much work going through that they kept it accurate by projects."

SUNDAY, APRIL 17, 1983*

"Proposition 17" [working title for "Chili Sauce"] (overdubs)
"If the Kid Can't Make You Come" [listed as "If the Boy Can't Make You Come"] (overdubs)
"My Summertime Thang" [listed as "My Summertime Thing"] (overdubs)
"Chocolate" (basic tracking and overdubs)
Sunset Sound, Studio 2 | 5:00 p.m.–10:00 a.m. (booked from 4:00 p.m.–open)
Producer: Prince, although Morris Day was listed and Prince was crossed out | *Artist:* the Time (Prince crossed out) | *Engineer:* Prince | *Assistant Engineer:* Richard McKernan

> *I like to go with my intuition. Something hits me and I need to get the track down before I can move on. It's like there's another person inside me, talking to me.* —Prince[15]

During this seventeen-hour session, Prince and Day worked on several songs that involved Day using his techniques to seduce a woman. The woman in question was Sharon Hughes, who probably added her parts for most of these songs on this date. Prince also recorded some of his vocals during this session. McKernan remembers:

> On vocals [for Prince], you'd set him up and stay there for a while to make sure he is fine, and then you'd just give him the controls to the tape machine for punch ins and other stuff. He'd just want you to leave the room. The mic would be set up just over the board and he'd sit there. There were a couple of songs we did where the girls came in and we'd put a piano stool behind the console, and Prince and Wendy and Lisa would do the same thing with background vocals. They usually did it to harmonize the one track and then we'd double it and do the other track.

Prince played the confused maître d' (or waiter) on "Chocolate," "My Summertime Thang," and "Proposition 17." Songs like these three brought out Prince's playful side, and he and Day had a great time just goofing off during the spoken parts. "**[Comedians] have had a great deal of effect on my music**," explained Prince. "**It was always a challenge to be funny in music. It was always a challenge to have some sort of humor for a song and to make somebody feel good. That's the biggest challenge.**"[16]

"He's brilliant. Enigmatic, strong, aesthetically pleasing, sensual, intellectual, philosophical, more than musical," described Wendy Melvoin. "If he feels comfortable with you, he'll crack you up."[17]

"One of my fondest memories was his sense of humor," reflected Brown Mark. "He was the kind of person, if Hollywood had tapped into it more, could really do that type of thing. He could have done some great comedy films with the likes of Eddie Murphy and such. He really had great comic timing, he was one of the funniest guys I ever met."[18]

"Prince had a great sense of humor and he was a practical joker,"[19] agreed Fink. Prince's use of practical jokes can be found in the song "If the Kid Can't Make You Come," not only in some very funny dialogue between Prince and Day but in the title as well. Day, his rival in *Purple Rain*, sings about sexual satisfaction only coming from "the Kid." The phrase is also repeated at the end of "Chili Sauce," and an early version of the script also included the phrase "Baby, if the Kid can't make you come, nobody can." Prince's nickname among his managers was "the Kid," and his character in *Purple Rain* would share that name after the song was recorded. It was likely that Day eventually recognized this, and although the song is played live by Morris Day and the Time, it isn't part of their usual concert set list.

The song that was created during this session, "Chocolate," was a funk workout built around a steady drumbeat and a repetitive bass lick built up with guitar and keyboards. "'Chocolate' is James Brown," according to Jellybean Johnson. "That's some great shit, that's just hard-core James sound. I loved it."[20]

It is rumored that Day played drums on this track, as well as on "My Summertime Thang." All of today's songs were interlinked by similar themes, phrases, and attitudes, so it was obvious that some would probably not be placed on the Time's next album, which wouldn't be assembled until after the movie was complete. Because of this, all of these tracks would sit on the shelf for almost a year. "My Summertime Thang" and "Chocolate" would be revisited on a future Time album.

Jimmy Jam and Terry Lewis continued to hide the fact that they had been producing an outside band when they missed the concert in March, but with their new recognition came the inevitable exposure in the press. "We knew there was a picture of us in *Billboard* magazine working with the S.O.S. Band," according to Jam. "We were trying to hide every *Billboard* magazine we could find. Every time the manager would try to give it to him, like, "Oh Prince, here is the new *Billboard*," we would snatch it. We were thinking, 'Oh, he'll never see it,' and of course, he finally did."[21]

Despite the humorously light tone of these tracks, according to Jellybean Johnson, Prince was not happy: "The fallout from Jimmy and Terry was about to happen. It hadn't happened yet, but it was real close, so the tension was a big, big cloud over everybody. It was an uneasy time."[22]

Status: The only new track, "Chocolate" (5:50), did not make it onto the *Ice Cream Castle* album, but it was eventually included on *Pandemonium* in 1990. The single was released on October 1, 1990, and peaked at number 44 on the *Billboard* R&B Singles chart.

An early edit of the demo faded out after the phrase "you gotta step on the gas, we gotta get the hell out of here, come on,"[23] at approximately 5:15 of the track.

Once it was decided not to include the track on *Ice Cream Castle,* the song was almost recorded by another artist, according to Peggy: "'Chocolate' was something that he may have been working on for the Time, but when Eddie [Murphy] asked him for a song, he offered it to him. From what I remember, Eddie turned him down. That was probably a very sore spot with him. I knew because of pride, he'd try to get that sucker out there some way."

According to Dez Dickerson's 2003 autobiography My Time with Prince, *the nickname "the Kid" came from Dickerson. Prince's managers also referred to him by this nickname, which Albert Magnoli noticed as he was working on the script for* Purple Rain: *"Cavallo, Ruffalo & Fargnoli never referred to Prince as 'Prince.' They always said 'the Kid.' So I go, 'Why don't you call him by his name?' They go, 'We hate the name. We call him the Kid.' They would call him 'the Kid' to his face. When they were together they always called him the Kid, and I noticed other musicians were calling him the Kid, so obviously he knew."*

It should also be noted that it was likely the April 2, 1983, edition of Cashbox *magazine and not* Billboard *magazine that Jam and Lewis were hiding from Prince, because* Cashbox *contained the photo of Jam and Lewis working with the S.O.S. Band that Jam described.*

MONDAY, APRIL 18, 1983*

"Proposition 17" [working title for "Chili Sauce"]
Sunset Sound, Studio 2 | 7:00 p.m.–6:00 a.m.
Producer: Prince, although Morris Day was listed and Prince was crossed out | *Artist:* the Time | *Engineer:* Prince | *Assistant Engineer:* "Peggy Mac" McCreary

Was there tension? That was Prince's sessions. There was always something going on.—Peggy McCreary

Today's session was scheduled to begin at 7:00 p.m., but was delayed for a band meeting between Prince and various members of the Time. He'd been upset for a while about Jimmy Jam and Terry Lewis missing the San Antonio gig on March 24, and he was convinced they were cashing in on the Minneapolis sound by producing bands outside of Prince's range of influence. "He felt that we would be giving away the Time sound," recalled Jam. "We never felt that way. We felt like the songs we were doing didn't have anything to do with the way the Time sounded. We actually even got accused of doing a song that we didn't do that Leon [Sylvers] produced that was influenced by the Time, which was a Whispers single called 'Keep On Loving Me.' And Prince swore we did that record, and I said, 'We weren't even around. We didn't have a thing to do with that record.' He truly believed that what we were doing outside of the Time was a conflict of interest."[24]

Prince knew that the upcoming *Purple Rain* project had the potential to bring huge success to everyone attached to it, and the idea of diluting his sound may have bothered him, so he decided to lay down the law. Prince, Jesse Johnson, Morris Day, Terry Lewis, and Jimmy Jam were present for the meeting. "Studio 2 had a little room off of it that was really small." Johnson explained in 2011. "I mean, you could stretch your arms out in it and almost touch both sides of it. So Prince, Morris, and myself were in the room, and then Terry and Jimmy came in and we closed the door, so no one else was in that room and those five people know what happened in that room."[25]

It was at this gathering that Jam and Lewis were fired.

"Prince did all the talking," reflected Terry Lewis. "That's all I know."[26]

There are two very different accounts of what went down. **"I'm playing the bad guy, but I didn't fire Jimmy and Terry,"** Prince told *Rolling Stone* magazine in 1990. **"Morris asked me what I would do in his situation. You got to remember, it was his band."**[27]

"He absolutely fired them," said Day. "He didn't ask me anything. I was very upset. [What Prince said was] totally misleading. I never made the call for them to be fired from the group."[28] In another interview, Day expanded on his thought: "There wasn't much to say, because basically, we were part of his production company. He was calling the shots. So it was just something that I kind of had to live with, regardless of how I felt."[29]

Johnson agreed with Morris' version of the story:

We [Morris and Jesse] didn't tell them shit. We just sat there and listened to Prince. The Time was Prince's thing. All those groups were Prince's groups.

[Afterward] Prince said to me . . . no one was in the room except for him and I, and he said, "You'll see, you'll never hear from those guys again." He was very, very, very wrong about that and when they won their Grammy for Producer of the Year, I remember calling his house and leaving him a message saying, "I thought you said we wouldn't hear from them again."[30]

In 1996 Jimmy Jam commented publicly on this during a benefit show: "[Prince] just took his six-inch pumps and kicked us out the door."[31]

After the meeting there was a brief break, and the remainder of the recording session was spent on overdubs for "Chili Sauce" (which was still referred to as "Proposition 17" at this point), starting at 10:00 p.m. and wrapping at 6:00 a.m. the following day.

Few knew it, but the firing of Jimmy Jam and Terry Lewis was the beginning of the end for the Time.

"When we started switching musicians," reflected Day, "it wasn't my favorite band anymore, I wasn't happy from that day."[32] According to Alan Leeds, "Morris was not happy with what Prince had done: 'It's my band, but I have no voice in this.' Of course, the hypocrisy was, it never really was his band."[33]

The entire situation was summed up best by Jerome Benton, who felt it extremely hard because he was Terry's brother: "Terry and Jimmy were 'released of their duties.' They were fired by Prince . . . out of Morris's band. How could Prince fire a band member? I guess because he was in charge."[34]

The irony about this firing and the eventual disintegration of the band was that Jimmy Jam and Terry Lewis each achieved an unexpected level of success once outside of Prince's long shadow—at least unexpected by Prince. "All this shit is just so childish when you look back on it," Jellybean Johnson sharply explained in 2013. "Every guy in the Time, with the exception of Jerome—and Jerome had his own record deal—every guy in the Time had a Top 10 hit. Every one! Monte, Jesse, Jimmy and Terry sold over 100 million records. All of us had Top Ten, Top Five records. Prince could have had all of us. Didn't want to pay us; didn't want to do it."[35]

By a strange coincidence, Jam and Lewis spent the rest of that evening in a recording studio with the S.O.S. Band finishing the tracks that they created in Atlanta. The songs ("Tell Me If You Still Care" and "Just Be Good to Me") ended up being their first major hits as producers, allowing them to establish their careers outside of Prince's shadow.

WEDNESDAY APRIL 20, 1983*

"Velvet Kitty Cat" (basic tracking)
"My Love Belongs to You" (basic tracking)
"If the Kid Can't Make You Come" (overdubs)
Sunset Sound, Studio 3 | 3:30 p.m.–1:30 a.m. (booked 7:00 p.m.–open)
Producer: Morris Day is listed, but Prince oversaw the session | *Artist:* the
Time | *Engineer:* Prince | *Assistant Engineer:* "Peggy Mac" McCreary

*We were never allowed to say anything because it was like the
Mafia. We were sworn to secrecy.*—Peggy Mac

For today's session, Prince switched from Studio 2 to the much more private
Studio 3.

"The recording console was basically a clone in every room back then,"
explains Sunset Sound owner Paul Camarata. "But the recording rooms were
totally different. Every room has its own flavor. One was low ceiling, one was
high ceiling. One was more of a traditional square, and one was more of a rect-
angle, and they all sounded different. Studio 3's control room was much bigger.
Also, Studio 3 had much more capability in the isolation booths. It had multiple
isolation booths. Studio 2 at the time only had one isolation booth."

Prince recorded two tracks on this date. The most complete would be "Velvet Kitty Cat," a throwaway song that many thought was recorded for the Time,
but was in fact created for Vanity 6. The title was a not-so-subtle reference to a
velvety smooth vagina, but the song's lyrics reflected none of that sexuality. In
fact, the words—which included phrases like "She's man's best friend, furry,
cuddly and fat / Take a swing, you're up to bat, my velvet kitty cat"[36]—are silly,
even for Prince's side projects. Considering that this is the era during which
Prince wrote some of his most timeless material, it is obvious why this song
didn't see the light of day during his lifetime. This also may be the only time
Prince tried using the Roland TR-606 Drumatix instead of the LM-1 Linn
drums.

"My Love Belongs to You" is a seven-minute song that is a much stronger
example of what Prince could do in the studio. It is a funky synth riff that has
various guitar parts played on top of the keyboards. It is unclear whether lyrics
for this track were ever completed, because as of the end of this session, it remained an instrumental and was given its title before any vocals could be added.

There are no future references to this song in Prince's studio documents, nor in the Warner Bros. vault.

Additional work was done on "If the Kid Can't Make You Come," although it is unclear what was recorded.

Status: "Velvet Kitty Cat" (2:43) was originally intended for Vanity 6 but was also offered to Apollonia 6. It is possible that Susan Moonsie eventually recorded the vocals for the track, but if those sessions took place, they were likely completed in Minneapolis. A version with Prince's vocals was released in 2017 on the *Purple Rain Deluxe* (Expanded Edition) CD package.

"Velvet Kitty Cat" (2:28) was rerecorded by Prince in April 1985 as a rockabilly song with several lyrical differences.

To date, "My Love Belongs to You" (7:08) remains unreleased.

THURSDAY, APRIL 21, 1983*

> **"Chocolate"** (overdubs and vocals, probably Prince, Jill Jones, Wendy Melvoin, and Lisa Coleman)
> Sunset Sound, Studio 3 | 1:30 p.m.–1:30 a.m. (booked 1:00 p.m.–open)
> *Producer:* Morris Day is listed, but Prince oversaw the session | *Artist:* the Time | *Engineer:* Prince | *Assistant Engineers:* "Peggy Mac" McCreary and probably Richard McKernan

> *It was fun. [Prince was] very quiet and very much to himself. But after a time working with him, you knew he appreciated you. The common thing was that people had no idea where he was coming from because he never shows too much emotion or thankfulness or anything like that.*—Richard McKernan

Additional overdub work was done on "Chocolate," including vocals, probably from Jill Jones, Wendy Melvoin, and Lisa Coleman as well as Prince. As with most of the songs, Prince wrote the music and the bulk of the lyrics, which featured the familiar theme of Morris Day once again trying—and failing—to seduce a woman, and complaining that his date had turned him down after she'd ordered eighteen jumbo shrimp for dinner. "Morris might have had some things to do with lyrics," observes McKernan, "but my recollection is that if he had any input, it was very minute. Most of that stuff were all Prince's ideas. Morris might want something to be changed, but 99 percent was all Prince." Because of the late hours, Prince was going through multiple engineers, often burning through them fairly quickly. **"There will be times when I've been working in the studio for twenty hours and I'll be falling asleep in the chair, but I'll still be able to tell the engineer what cut I want to make,"** recalled Prince. **"I use engineers in shifts a lot of the time because when I start something, I like to go all the way through. There are very few musicians who will stay awake that long."**[37]

McKernan corroborates Prince's story:

I left shortly after [these sessions] because you put so many hours in and with Prince, because he wasn't consistent, we'd leave at 2:00 a.m. and he'd say, "Let's start at 10" and you'd get there at 10 and he'd call you and say, "Well, I'm not going to be there until 12," and then you'd stay until 12 and he'd be another hour. And then he'd finally get there, then how many hours doing some stuff, and he'd say, "I'll be right back; I'm going to the movies and I'll be back at 9," and then 9 o'clock would come around, and then 10, and then he'd call and say, "I'll be there in an hour." After putting in a lot of hours, the last place you want to be is there. It was fine if you were in a production state, but just to sit around and vegetate in the studio can really wear you down, and I just couldn't take it anymore.

Despite the late hours, McKernan reflects fondly about Prince's skills in the studio: "My impression of him as a musician? Fabulous. I mean he's real street. A real streetwise musician. He really conveys an attitude on the records. Ask any songwriter and they usually have a couple of hits, but they are writing the same song over and over, and I never heard that with Prince. And you can see that from his history, from the early days to now the gamut that he's run. That is where my appreciation comes in."

It is probable that overdubs were done on multiple tracks during this session, which ended with four cassettes being made (two C-60 and two C-90 tapes).

FRIDAY, APRIL 22, 1983*

"Chocolate" (vocal overdubs with Morris Day)
Sunset Sound, Studio 3 | 1:30 p.m.–1:00 a.m. (booked 1:00 p.m.–open)
Producer: Morris Day is listed, but Prince oversaw the session | *Artist:* the Time | *Engineer:* Prince | *Assistant Engineer:* "Peggy Mac" McCreary

*Sometimes it is a curse, but it's also a blessing. It's a gift
that I am completely grateful for. That's why I keep [mak-
ing music], because I don't want to be ungrateful for the
gift.*—Prince[38]

Earlier in the week, Prince had recorded the vocal guide track for "Chocolate"
using his old man/dad voice, and during this session Day recorded his vocals,
copying Prince practically verbatim, peppering it with his signature *woo-ha*
laugh.

In 1989, when the Time reunited with all the original members, Prince insisted on placing the song on their *Pandemonium* album, although some of the
band members were unhappy about its inclusion because they felt the song was
too old and wasn't very strong. In the end, Prince miscalculated, and it had only
moderate success on the R&B charts.

Matt Fink recalled that this happened a lot, and no matter what, Prince was
always the final say: "Any time you worked with Prince, it wasn't about being
able to control the situation, so if you were going to complain, you just had to
go, 'Okay, well this is what he's going to do,' and go with it, and let it be, or you
could voice your opinion, which rarely was taken into consideration. You could
say, 'Hey I don't think this is working,' or 'This isn't right,' or 'This doesn't feel
good. Do you think you can change it?' Usually he would make his decisions
and that would stick, whether you like it or not."[39]

Prince was heading to Minneapolis and had his music packed up for the
trip, which implied he was going to be away for an extended period. "It would
vary," explains Sunset Sound's general manager, Craig Hubler. "If he was going to come back in a couple of weeks and not do any recording [at home], he
would leave them here. He often had big flight cases, where all the tapes would
be packed in."

Prince usually headed to Minnesota in mid-to-late spring. "I think it was
something about the weather," reflects Paul Camarata. "He didn't want to be
out there in the winter. When he wasn't here, it was usually late summer or fall,
but he was always out here in the winter and the spring because Minneapolis is
a very harsh place. We didn't see him much in the summer."

Almost like clockwork, Prince did not return to Sunset Sound for several
months.

*Hubler reveals that not every tape shipment went smoothly: "One time, we got
a big flight case from Minneapolis with these big master padlocks on them, and*

nobody sent the keys. We couldn't get into the thing. We had to get a locksmith to saw off the locks, just to get to the tapes."

Prince supposedly attended a concert featuring George Clinton & the P-Funk All Stars on either April 23 or 24 at the Beverly Theatre in Los Angeles.

SATURDAY, APRIL 30, 1983

"Sex Shooter" (basic tracking/overdubs)
"Promise 2 B True" (basic tracking)
Kiowa Trail home studio (Chanhassen, Minnesota)
Producer: Prince | *Artist:* Vanity 6 | *Engineer:* Don Batts

"Sex Shooter" was a definite. It was going to be in the movie.
—Brenda Bennett

Prince had been ignoring Vanity 6 during this time, so when he returned to Minneapolis, he quickly began producing another batch of songs for the group. "Sex Shooter" was one of the first tracks for the project. Prince had his Minneapolis engineer Don Batts record Vanity's vocals.

Over the previous two years, Batts had been involved in practically every track recorded at Prince's home, which included songs from Vanity 6's album as well as the Time's first album. Because of this, he was very familiar with what Prince wanted from a vocal performance.

"I remember phone calls in the middle of the night to record at his house," explains Brenda Bennett. "But he would also call me up to watch TV with him, and sometimes we wouldn't even talk. Sometimes it would be to talk about the movie. You didn't know what he'd want: TV, a drive, or he'd often just want to record in the studio. We recorded a lot of the Vanity 6 second album, but the only carryover [to the *Apollonia 6* album] was "Sex Shooter." "G-Spot," "Vibrator," and "Moral Majority" were all part of the planned, but never finished album."

Prince also recorded a track, supposedly for Vanity 6, called "Promise 2 B True" (or possibly "Promise to Be True"). The lyrics were about a lover who was apologizing for his/her infidelity and included the singer lamenting, "I know I messed up, and I promise to be true the next time." The song itself has been described as a melodic cross between new wave, arena rock, and dance music, consisting of a distorted guitar placed over a Linn drum loop.

It is unclear if Vanity recorded vocals for the song.

It is also likely that Prince worked on "Velvet Kitty Cat" during this period, perhaps adding Susan Moonsie's vocals to the track, but no documentation exists to verify the exact date.

Status: The version of "Sex Shooter" (7:04) containing Vanity's vocals was edited down (5:05), but neither version was ever released. It was rerecorded with Apollonia's vocals in October 1983 and included in the movie and on the *Apollonia 6* album.

"Promise 2 B True" was revisited by Dez Dickerson in May 1983 and Bonnie Raitt also worked on the track in early 1987; both versions remain unreleased.

MAY 1983

I was on the cover of Rolling Stone *with Vanity, when I didn't even do an interview, when I wouldn't talk to them. Once you've done something like that it's like, okay, what's the next thing?*—Prince[1]

Rolling Stone magazine featured Prince on the cover of its April 28 issue. The power of his celebrity was growing, and it wasn't just the critics who were noticing. The tour was a major success and very soon his *1999* double album would be certified Platinum with over one million records sold. His next focus was the movie (still called *Dreams*), which so far had neither a shootable script nor an album with any finished songs, so Prince began working on potential tracks for the upcoming film and side projects. The first task was solidifying the Revolution, and with the addition of Wendy Melvoin all the members were now in place. "I was this kid, just out of high school," reflected Melvoin. "I had no real performing experience."[2] Prince took her under his wing, giving her his attention and encouragement.

"Once she was finally hired into Prince's band, it was like a dream for me," Lisa would expand in a 2009 interview with *Out* magazine. "I had fallen in love with Wendy, my childhood friend, and suddenly we were looking at each other differently, but I had to leave on the road all the time. It was always just torture."[3] Having her in the Revolution meant less time apart, and translated into a faster form of musical communication within the band.

"It wasn't the greatest bunch of musicians in the world. I mean, I've played with some dynamite cats, but being a dynamite musician can never take the place of being a team," explains bassist Brown Mark. "Playing with people you jam with and that you grew to love as family, because that's what we were. If one person had a problem, everybody had a problem. Wendy was the youngest, but I was one of the babies in the group and Lisa always, always looked after me. Always watched my back."

As the band grew closer, their trust translated to music, and Prince relied on them in a way that he'd never done in his career. In a future interview with *Rolling Stone*, Prince described each of the members of the Revolution:

> **Bobby Z was the first one to join. He's my best friend. Though he's not such a spectacular drummer, he watches me like no other drummer would. Sometimes, a real great drummer, like Morris [Day], will be more concerned with the lick he is doing as opposed to how I am going to break it down. Mark Brown's just the best bass player I know, period. I wouldn't have anybody else. If he didn't play with me, I'd eliminate bass from my music. Same goes for Matt. He's more or less a technician. He can read and write like a whiz, and is one of the fastest in the world. And Wendy makes me seem all right in the eyes of people watching. She keeps a smile on her face. When I sneer, she smiles. It's not premeditated, she just does it. It's a good contrast. Lisa is like my sister. She'll play what the average person won't. She'll press two notes with one finger so the chord is a lot larger and things like that. She's more abstract. She's into Joni Mitchell, too.[4]**

"The guys in the early days [André Cymone and Dez Dickerson] made it very clear to Prince that they had solo careers," reflected Bobby Z. "Prince was frustrated by that, and it wasn't until Wendy joined—until his dream of a Fleetwood Mac–style band came true—that it really became the band he wanted it to be."[5]

"That whole period was like boot camp," recalled Matt Fink. "He knew this was a major deal for him, and he certainly felt a lot of pressure to pull it off. He made it very clear to all of us that we had to be disciplined in our work and dedicated to what we were doing. He just worked non-stop: he never slept."[6]

Prince's studio sessions during the next few months of 1983 are difficult to date, but whenever possible they have been placed into the proper month to give them some context.

SUNDAY, MAY 1, 1983

"Moral Majority" (basic tracking/overdubs)
Kiowa Trail home studio (Chanhassen, Minnesota)
Producer: Prince | *Artist:* Vanity 6 | *Engineer:* Don Batts

> *[In] the home on Kiowa Trail, the studio was just a bedroom. So there wasn't much room. There were keyboards on the side, perpendicular to the console and that was very convenient because he could stand right behind the console and he can play electric guitar direct from the amp in the other room, but there was no room for a drum kit in that room. It was just a control room, because it was like a suburban home and it was a fairly small additional bedroom.*
> —Susan Rogers

During this time period, a group of conservative citizens known as the Moral Majority were actively campaigning against anything in entertainment they felt was immoral. It is unclear whether they ever targeted Vanity 6, but Prince decided to comment about them with a track that name-checked their organization. The song was very up-tempo and had a chorus that repeated the title, which continued a theme of his early political works such as "Controversy."

To get the proper echo on the background vocals, Prince had the mic positioned down the hall from the room that contained his equipment. Vanity 6 member Brenda Bennett and her husband, LeRoy ("Roy"), were asked to work on the track. "[Prince] had a mic set up in his bathroom and he had me screaming, 'Moral Majority!'" explains Roy Bennett. "And I remember at one point we were all in there. I did that for a while, and Jamie [Shoop] and Susan [Moonsie] and Vanity came in, and I sat down on his toilet. We were in there doing the vocal part, more of that yelling, 'Moral Majority,' and I remember sitting down, and sitting on the handle of the toilet, right in the middle of the session. It gave away where we were."

Status: "Moral Majority" (6:13) was eventually shelved when the second Vanity 6 album was abandoned. It remains unreleased.

MAY 1983 (DATE UNCERTAIN)

"Modernaire" (basic tracking)
Kiowa Trail home studio (Chanhassen, Minnesota)
Producer: Prince | *Artist:* Dez Dickerson | *Engineer:* Don Batts (assumed)

["Modernaire"] was written during my transition into the solo thing. At first, I felt it strayed too far from my more aggressive rock sensibilities, but I grew to like it more over time.—Dez Dickerson[7]

Dez Dickerson had left to pursue a solo career, but Prince had made a deal with him to keep him involved in the movie. To showcase Dickerson and his band, he recorded a new track called "Modernaire," which was a word used to describe "someone who is not just ahead of the curve, but around it already,"[8] according to Dickerson. The track is comprised of Linn LM-1 drum effects, keyboard, synth bass, and a simple repeated guitar riff. Like all the songs recorded in his basement studio, practically everything was done by Prince. Jill Jones was brought in to recite act 2, scene 2 of Shakespeare's *Romeo and Juliet*, which was layered in backward for texture.

Surprisingly, the number doesn't feature a strong lead guitar part. In fact, most of the sections that could have featured Dickerson's guitar work were actually played on keyboard. The extended version of the track features a solo that sounds like it is played on the guitar but is drastically processed to sound like a keyboard.

Status: "Modernaire" (8:15) was edited down (4:02) and released in 2005 on *Dez Dickerson: A Retrospective*. The edited version debuted in *Purple Rain* (at 25:08, just after "Take Me with U"), where it is performed onstage by Dickerson and his band, the Modernaires. The longer version remains unreleased.

It is possible that this song may have been performed by Dickerson during his show at First Avenue at the end of August. Prince would recycle the section from Romeo and Juliet *during the 1988/89* Lovesexy *tour intermission.*

MAY 1983 (DATE UNCERTAIN)

"**Modernaire**" (Dez Dickerson vocals/possible guitar)
"**Promise 2 B True**" (Dez Dickerson vocals/possible guitar)
Kiowa Trail home studio (Chanhassen, Minnesota)
Producer: Prince | *Artist:* Dez Dickerson | *Assistant Engineer:* Don Batts
(assumed)

[Modernaire] was originally supposed to be on the soundtrack album. There was supposed to be a true soundtrack album with all the music from the film on the album, but after the principal filming, Prince kept writing stuff. And they kept adding more music, so it ended up being a Prince album and not a soundtrack album.—Dez Dickerson[9]

Prince would eventually create a soundtrack-like album with a variety of acts for the *Purple Rain* sequel, *Graffiti Bridge,* but talk of a multiartist soundtrack album for *Purple Rain* didn't go much further than the initial conversation. According to Bobby Z, "There was debate whether it was going to be a [more conventional] soundtrack to the film—which included the Time and Apollonia 6 songs—but he said, 'No, I want it to be Prince and the Revolution.' So it's not really a soundtrack; it's a Prince and the Revolution record that happened to be for a movie."[10]

With Dickerson in town to perform with Prince at the 3rd Annual Minnesota Music Awards, it is likely that he recorded his vocals on "Modernaire." Prince also requested that the engineer pull an unreleased Vanity 6 track, "Promise 2 B True," out of the vault for consideration as well. It is likely that Dickerson added guitar and his vocals to the song.

Status: Dickerson's version of "Promise 2 B True" was shelved and remains unreleased.

SUNDAY, MAY 15, 1983 (ESTIMATE)

"**Possessed**" (basic tracking)
Kiowa Trail home studio (Chanhassen, Minnesota)
Producer: Prince | *Artist:* Prince | *Engineer:* Don Batts (assumed)

He took the best bits of Beethoven and the Beatles and James Brown. He was able to ride that edge of uniqueness, and [it was] so brilliant the way everything was presented to you every day. You were just kind of shocked. Everything was so effortless to him.—Bobby Z Rivkin[11]

"Possessed" is a track that had been around for a while. Prince had debuted part of it on December 10, 1982, in Chicago during the *1999* tour. He eventually played the entire track on March 21, 1983, at Radio City Music Hall in New York City, but getting a proper version of it on tape was difficult, even when Prince set aside studio time for it and he'd take several passes at it before he was happy.

It is likely that Prince recorded all of the instruments on this song.

Prince's influence on this track was James Brown, and he dedicated the song to him on the *Prince and the Revolution: Live!* concert tape, released in 1985.

Status: Today's version of "Possessed" (8:46) remains unreleased. Additional work would be done on the track, and it would be revisited multiple times before it was completely rerecorded the following year. The 1984 version of "Possessed" (7:56) was released in 2017 on the *Purple Rain Deluxe* (Expanded Edition) CD set.

MONDAY, MAY 16, 1983

Venue: Carlton Celebrity Room (Bloomington, Minnesota)
3rd Annual Minnesota Music Awards

On May 16th, I would appear onstage with Prince in our hometown for the last time. It was the Minnesota Music Awards and I joined the band for one song.—Dez Dickerson[12]

Prince was honored with six awards, including Male Vocalist of the Year, Producer of the Year, Musician of the Year, Band of the Year, and Best Producer. His *1999* album won Album of the Year, and "Little Red Corvette" won EP/45 of the Year. The Time also won for Best R&B/Soul/Ethnic.

Prince and his band were joined by Morris Day, Jesse Johnson, and Vanity 6 for a performance of "D.M.S.R.," which at the time was a promo single in the

United Kingdom and was likely being considered for release in North America. On a more historic note, this was the final time Prince shared the stage with two people who were very close to him: former lead guitarist Dez Dickerson and Vanity, who would leave later in the summer.

MONDAY, MAY 16, 1983

Venue: First Avenue (Minneapolis, Minnesota)

Prince celebrated his awards by playing a brief set that included "Cloreen Bacon Skin," with Jah Wobble, the original bass player for Public Image Ltd. Prince supposedly grabbed Wobble's bass, licked the E string, and said, "Nice and greasy; just the way I like it."

TUESDAY, MAY 24, 1983 (ESTIMATE)

"Possessed" (overdubs)
Kiowa Trail home studio (Chanhassen, Minnesota)
Producer: Prince | *Artist:* Prince | *Engineer:* Don Batts (assumed)

> *Prince could walk into a studio and play full, difficult parts in one take that were just streaming from his soul. It was an incredible thing to watch. He got to that level. I just don't know too many people that obtain that really.*—Matt Fink[13]

Additional overdubs were reportedly done on this date. The track would eventually contain background vocals by Jill Jones, but it is unclear if that was done on this date or at another time.

MAY 1983 (DATE UNCERTAIN)

"G-Spot"
Kiowa Trail home studio (Chanhassen, Minnesota)
Producer: Prince | *Artist:* Prince/Revolution | *Engineer:* Don Batts

"G-Spot" we used to jam on all the time.—Bobby Z[14]

Prince had a lot of music to create for the upcoming movie, and every track that was recorded had the potential to be either in the film or on one of the upcoming albums he was overseeing. He would be crafting the soundtrack album, but there would also be releases by the Time, Vanity 6, and maybe even some of the other performers he was grooming. "This was a very confusing period," explains engineer Peggy McCreary, "because there were times that we were laying down tracks for the Time, Prince, and the Vanity 6 album all very close together. I really remember just being so damn tired, so a lot of it just seems like I was in a fog."

Prince worked on this in his home studio, and during the recording he tried something different. "When he was laying the track for 'G-Spot,' he went and got a saxophone," remembers Jill Jones.

> He got the sax out and he already knew the parts that he wanted. I can remember because I was like, "What the hell?" Didn't matter. I'm like the perfect cheer-leader for that dude. It's great, you want to do brain surgery later? You can do it! You can do it! Come on, it's a couple of little knives, you can do it. (*laughs*) But there he was, and he didn't stop until he got it the way he wanted it. The basic riff was Prince on a saxophone and it was almost as big as he was.

Prince's attempt on the sax was quickly replaced with keyboards, which would eventually be replaced by a more elaborate horn section featuring saxophone by Bob Minzer, Chris Hunter, and Roger Rosenberg; Jon Faddis and Randy Brecker on trumpet; and Jim Pugh on trombone.

"G-Spot" was a groove Prince had the band work on many times. As Bobby Z recalled, "'G-Spot' was almost a Time riff, where it was like a song for the Time or something. It had that synth thing and that lick. It was just the one tune that he loved jammin' on."[15] The band circled around the main riff, with Prince adding some spontaneous lyrics as if he were James Brown telling Maceo Parker to "blow your horn" and throwing a shout out to JB's "Mother Popcorn." Although the band may have rehearsed the track, it is unclear whether any of the Revolution actually played on it in the studio. Prince often recorded overnight after the band had left, and because he could do it all himself, he did many of his songs on his own: **"When it was three o'clock in the morning, and I'd try to get Bobby Z to come out to the studio, sometimes he'd come, sometimes he wouldn't."**[16]

The rest of the lyrics were based on a chat between Prince and Jill Jones regarding the female erogenous area called the G-spot (or Gräfenberg spot), which had been getting a lot of press at the time. Jones recalls, "I was reading a magazine about G-spots and had a conversation with him about it. He walked away with that info and he came back with the song."

Originally Prince sang his own lyrics, but as with many of his songs, it was offered to other performers. Vanity added her voice to the song, and it was scheduled to be included on Vanity 6's second album. It was eventually placed after "Vibrator," an unreleased Vanity 6 track that featured a segue into "G-Spot." Once it was decided that the song wasn't going to be released by Vanity 6, Jones was brought in to add her lead vocals to the song. She says, "He had a guide vocal on that. It wasn't like, 'You sing this or you sing that'; he wasn't like that with me. Occasionally it was, 'You go higher,' but he was very easy to work with. Laughing at certain things that he'd do or that someone else would do, and he'd say, 'I'm keeping that,' so recording 'G-spot' was a lot of fun."

The idea of releasing an album by Jones was discussed, so she relocated from Los Angeles to Minneapolis. "I didn't know if I was going to get an album to work on," she remembers. "I guess that was the premise."

Status: "G-Spot" (4:30) was released in 1987 on Jill Jones's only Paisley Park record. A single edit version (4:02) and a remix (6:23) were also released. The song was rehearsed with the Revolution during the summer of 1983, and was included in Albert Magnoli's early drafts of the *Purple Rain* script but removed before shooting began in November. It was also one of the tracks slated for the benefit show that Prince would perform in August. Ultimately, it wouldn't be included in the film and wasn't ever performed live.

"G-Spot" was recorded before Prince's longtime engineer Susan Rogers worked with him, but she recalled a funny remnant that was possibly from the session: "Downstairs in his home was a little utility room and there was a little cartoon book sitting on top of his washing machine called Looking for the G-Spot *or* Where Is the G-Spot? *I got the impression that this was something that somebody had given him and which had then inspired him to write the song."*[17]

JUNE 1983

We were all in acting, dance and speech classes, wardrobe fittings, and rehearsals for our acting scenes. It was a flurry of activity from morning 'til night with very little time off. On top of the work we were doing for the film, everyone—the Time, Vanity 6 and Prince—was in the studio recording our next albums, all to be released at the same time the Purple Rain *film would be coming out.*—Brenda Bennett[1]

Prince's twenty-fifth birthday on June 7, the start of the summer, and the new focus on his next project helped create an optimistic mood for most of the performers, with one large exception. The firing of Jimmy Jam and Terry Lewis from the Time devastated the entire band, and Morris Day's frustration about his lack of control was festering. "Morris was pretty upset," explained Jellybean Johnson. "He did everything in his power to get the guys back in the band, but Prince wasn't having it; Prince had decided that they weren't going to be in it."[2] Morris showed little interest in the work necessary to make the movie, in both the rehearsal for his band and the prep being done by the actors during the summer: "I started going to acting class and dancing class and all sorts of silly stuff. I got kicked out of acting class, because I kept clowning around and the guys said I was disrupting it for everybody."[3]

According to Jesse Johnson, "Morris took it harder than any of us. It was his band and somebody else was doing the dismissing."[4] Despite having helped create the band, Day was powerless as he watched it fall apart.

With two gone, the remaining members began strapping on their parachutes. "About a month or so later I decided that I didn't want to be around because there was too much stuff I didn't want to be around," explained Time keyboardist Monte Moir, who left after attending one rehearsal for the movie. "I was not happy about being there at the time."[5]

Drummer Jellybean Johnson agreed:

I left for a while because I was pissed and I was just disillusioned. I was just really mad and upset at him. How could he do that, after we spent two years and made him a ton of money? Ungrateful shit. I knew from the groundwork we had put out in those two years that he stood a chance to make a ton of money. And here it was, we were about to be left out of it. So it just got to me, and after a while, I thought about it, and I hadn't worked a job in about [three or four] years. I had quit college to be in this shit. I was having my first child. Jesse said, "C'mon let's do this thing." I needed the money, so I went back. It's one of the hardest things I ever did, was to go back and have to put your tail between your legs and reconsider.[6]

With three of the seven members gone, the positions needed to be filled, and word went out to a variety of musicians in the Minneapolis area. Twin Cities keyboard player Paul Peterson, a member of the very well-known Peterson music family, explained how he was told: "I had just graduated in June from Holy Angels [Academy of the Holy Angels, a private coed Catholic school in Richfield, Minnesota], and I was hanging out with my best friend Brett Ward up in Breezy Point, and I got a phone call from my brother-in-law that says, 'Get down here, you have an audition with the Time.' I'm like, 'Huh? Leave my vacation?' (*laughs*) So I did exactly that."[7] A tape was sent to help him rehearse, but it didn't arrive until the night before the audition.

He recalls:

I was nervous. I went and did the best I could, based on all the training I got from my family and all the gigs I had done prior to that. I guess it turned out okay. I wish I could remember the exact number [of songs I played], but, it felt like a million songs.

The first time I met Prince was at the first callback—my second audition [with the Time]. He wasn't at the first one. I was nervous. He was this big rock star. He walked into the room and I think we were picking out swatches for the material we were going use for the suits in the movie. I had picked out a beautiful black pinstriped suit and he said "No, you've got to stand out." Then he picked out an orange one for me. I said "I'm not wearing that." He said "Yes, you are."[8]

Prince also played a trick on Peterson that would eventually show up in *Under the Cherry Moon*: "I don't know whether I was the first person or whatever, but I'll never forget it. He wrote down the words, 'Wreck. A. Stow.' And he asked me to say that out loud. I was scared to death and I said, 'Wreck Uh Stow.' He said, 'What is it?' 'I don't know.' 'Say it again.' 'Wreck Uh Stow.' 'What is it?' 'I don't know.' 'Where do you buy your records?' 'Record store.' Oh, ha, ha ha. So that was his breaking the ice with me. That was my first encounter with him."[9]

Prince also tried to exert his influence when he asked new member Mark Cardenas to wear blackface. Cardenas was shocked; he looked at Prince and replied, "'I'm not going to do blackface. Nope.' I just said, 'I'm not going to do that.'" Luckily for everyone, Prince agreed.

Once the new members (Peterson, Cardenas, and Rocky Harris) began rehearsing with the Time, Jesse Johnson would oversee many of the rehearsals because Day often did not participate, and when he did he displayed very little interest in the replacements. According to Johnson, "[Morris] used to just come in and say, 'Jesse, have 'em play something,' and somebody would play something and he'd say . . . , 'Jesse, come here. Go tell them to never play that note again.' And I'd go back there and say, 'Morris said don't ever play that note again in front of Morris.' And that's the truth."[10]

"Morris was very standoffish to the new guys in the band," remembers Cardenas. "He occasionally came to rehearsal, most of my dealings were with Jesse Johnson and Jellybean and Jerome."

Peterson recalled: "From the minute I got the gig it was like, Okay, well, here it is and how you act, how you walk, how you talk, what the shtick is—because there was a shtick. We didn't call it shtick, but it was shtick. I'm telling you, it was like you had to have this attitude, man. You could not be the little, tiny white kid from Richfield. You needed to be cool."[11]

"Paul, I liked from day one," remembered Jellybean Johnson, "because he was only eighteen years old. He was just a kid, he was sweet, the way he didn't know shit about grabbing his dick. We knew we were going to have to teach him all of that stuff, but he looked like he was ready to learn, and he was a Peterson so he had enormous talent."[12]

Despite his acceptance by Jellybean Johnson, Peterson could feel the tension, and he understood why the new members weren't all embraced immediately: "They just lost their brothers. They just lost Jimmy Jam, Terry Lewis, and Monte Moir, and they weren't happy, so we were trying to fill those shoes. Looking back on it now I can see where their discontent was. I could've been the most talented keyboard player on planet earth and they still would've been bummed that their bros were gone, but it was school, and they really, in a short amount of time, gave great direction. Long hours in the studio and/or just cussing us out was really what it was. They cussed us out a lot. (*laughs*)"[13]

"He must have been Prince's choice," reflected Jellybean Johnson, "because Jesse really rode Paul."[14]

During a conversation with Donnie Simpson, Day revealed how he felt during this period: "That's when it started getting strange for me, and it didn't have the same vibe. I knew that was the beginning of the end because I was used to looking back and seeing familiar faces with people like my brothers, and I knew what to expect. When we started to get the new members, it was just too different."[15]

The Time was falling apart. Prince was still in charge, but as he tightened his grip the players felt more powerless, despite the huge boost that the movie could potentially give the band. This disconnect was a reason the Time was privately being referred to as "Part Time," "Half Time," or "Time Out."

The outlook didn't look good, according to Cardenas: "I got a sense that the Time was over."

TUESDAY, JUNE 21, 1983

"I Would Die 4 U" (rehearsal)
The Warehouse (St. Louis Park, Minnesota)

We would average six or seven 90-minute cassettes every rehearsal day. Imagine the stuff that's in the vault.—Robert "Cubby" Colby[16]

Prince was looking for songs to consider for the upcoming film and soundtrack, so he had the band rehearse "I Would Die 4 U" on this date. The song had been written more than a year earlier and was previously worked on during a sound check on February 15, 1982, in San Francisco, California, but this was likely the first time it was played with the full Revolution now that Wendy Melvoin had replaced Dez Dickerson. Prince decided to add some complexity to the track and asked for help from Matt Fink: "At first he wanted me to play the bassline on 'I Would Die 4 U' manually. So we tried it during rehearsal first, which I could pull it off, but it was not easy. And sometimes I would get off rhythm a little bit because you had to be so spot on, and you had to play it with two hands! So Prince says, 'Well, Matt, why can't you play it with one hand and play the chords with the other hand?' And I said, 'You try it.' But neither one of us could do it."[17]

It was decided to sequence some of the keyboards, so Don Batts created a cutting-edge system that could be triggered by Bobby Z during the live performance. "He had a really good backline tech back then, Don Batts," remembered Robert "Cubby" Colby, who was also an audio tech/mixer for Prince for years. "When Prince had the Revolution, it was he and Don. Prince had learned all this engineering technique and learned a lot from Don and [other] recording engineers."[18]

"Don Batts was a genius," agreed Bobby Z.[19]

According to *Purple Rain* director Albert Magnoli, the original inspiration for the track may have come from something that happened to Prince when he was younger: "Prince told me that his father had said one time, 'I would die for you.' I think that he mentioned that to me; it was in the song, and somehow I knew that this was something they had visited a long time ago." The line would be repeated by the Kid's father in the film.

Status: This rehearsal has not been released. "I Would Die 4 U" was linked with "Baby I'm a Star," and they both debuted during Prince's August 3, 1983, show at First Avenue. The basic tracks recorded on that evening required overdubs and editing before the completed track (2:49) was placed on the *Purple Rain* album.

TUESDAY, JUNE 28, 1983*

"Chocolate" (24-track transfer)
Sunset Sound, Studio 2 | 11:30 a.m.–1:30 p.m. (booked 11:30 a.m.–1:30 p.m.)
Producer: Prince | *Artist:* Prince | *Engineer:* "Peggy Mac" McCreary

I think artists absorb stuff and it just becomes part of their computer base, to coin a phrase. How it comes out is maybe even randomly writing a new song that may have an influence that's quite obvious from a Little Richard or James Brown or in Prince's case Santana or Sly Stone, but you don't necessarily think that as you're writing. In other words, as the music is coming out and you're playing or writing a song, you're not consciously saying, "This will be my Sly Stone song" or "This will be my Beatles song" or "This will be my James Brown song." It's just the song you feel at that moment, and the input that you're drawing from is all of those influences that you've absorbed all your life of listening.—Alan Leeds[20]

This was the only official work on Prince's music done at Sunset Sound until mid-August. It was a 24-track transfer session of the song "Chocolate." A transfer like this simply means that a copy of the tape was made. Since Prince was in Minneapolis preparing for the film, this tape was sent to him, probably for consideration in the movie.

WEDNESDAY, JUNE 29, 1983

Venue: Prom Center (Saint Paul, Minnesota)
2nd Minnesota Black Music Awards

Once again, Prince was honored in his hometown, this time as Musician of the Year. He gathered his band to perform "D.M.S.R." and "1999." This was the first time they performed without Dickerson, but curiously, Wendy Melvoin wasn't included.

JULY 1983

During the summer, Prince was scheduled to meet with Albert Magnoli to discuss the possibility of directing the movie. Magnoli had recently graduated from film school at the University of Southern California, and while he was young and energetic and had experience as an editor, he'd never directed a feature-length film, so the risk was high. In addition, Magnoli's knowledge of Prince was limited, so before he traveled to Minneapolis for a meeting, he asked Cavallo, Ruffalo & Fargnoli for every video they had on Prince, including concert footage and music videos, and Magnoli immersed himself. While watching the tapes, he noticed a trend: "I began to realize: Oh, Prince is jumping from one era to another within a year, which is rare. Okay, the next jump is going to be even larger, because that's what the film will do. That's what I'm thinking. I got on the plane to Minneapolis the next day."

The director's insight into Prince expanded during an unexpected first encounter while Magnoli was sitting in the hotel lobby in Minneapolis waiting for their initial meeting:

> There was a big moment for me to see Prince when he didn't know I was in the room. So he comes out of the elevator, and its precisely twelve midnight, and he walks across, right in front of me, right to left, because he's looking toward the door and that's where his manager is. He doesn't know I am sitting off to the side. So I was able to observe him for the whole length of that walk and I was able to absorb from that an enormous amount of vulnerability, and an enormous amount of pain. And that's when I came up with the whole idea of this conflict between father and son and that the father had stopped writing and was burying his music and was even saying that he doesn't even write anymore.

When Magnoli was asked about his thoughts on the movie, he told Prince that he felt the original script "sucked" and proceeded to pitch his own version of the movie. Prince agreed and granted the young filmmaker access to his band, his personal life, and his archive of music to help shape the project. Magnoli recalls:

> He had this little studio in the basement of his suburban home at the time, and he essentially had a hundred songs, or whatever the number was, that he had written and produced, created and done either by himself or with other people in the group or whatever. Very little of it was the Revolution; most of it was music he had prior to that, and we started listening to songs, and I liked what I heard, and I immediately said to him, "We're not going to be able to sit here and listen to a hundred songs, obviously."

Prince gave him a copy of the songs as well as the lyric sheets to help him determine which ones would be needed for the movie and the album: "We had agreed that it can't be a double album, that it was going to be a twelve-song album from him, maybe four, five, or six songs, whatever the number was from Morris Day and the Time, and there might be a miscellaneous band or two after that. We're essentially talking about one twelve-song album, kind of a *Purple Rain* soundtrack musical, whatever, but it wasn't going to be a double album thing."

In essence, the movie didn't have any specific music attached, so the album existed only as a concept. The actual tracks that would wind up on the album would be decided almost entirely based on what was in the film, and the film couldn't be fully fleshed out without the music. It was the classic "chicken or the egg" situation because the music would shape the narrative and support the story, but the music had to be compelling enough for the album to stand on its own.

Magnoli says, "I was able to go back to L.A. at the time and listen to all the music, read all the lyrics, and then based on that, when I began writing the screenplay, I was able to visualize and write the music and select the song necessary for the emotional underpinning at that moment in the script."

The plan was for Magnoli to finish his current project, then come back to Minneapolis in August to interview everybody around Prince and finish writing the script based on what he absorbed.

TUESDAY, JULY 12, 1983

"Baby I'm a Star" (likely a rehearsal)
The Warehouse (St. Louis Park, Minnesota)
Producer: Prince | *Artist:* Prince and the Revolution | *Engineer:* unknown

I feel that music is a blessing. I don't feel like I'm working. So when I'm not "working," I'm thinking about it, so music takes up a good portion of the time.—Prince[1]

The version of "Baby I'm a Star" that was eventually released was radically different when it was demoed by Prince during the summer of 1981. It contains almost all the same lyrics, but it includes a much sparser layering of keyboards, piano, and vocal overdubs. Don Batts recalled how the elements existed, but in a very different form: "That was absolutely magic. It was really from the heart. He was playing at his peak, almost sort of like Stevie Wonder. It was an incredible rocking tune and I still consider it far superior. I think they overdid it later on *Purple Rain*."[2]

An updated version of the song was worked on today. It is unclear if it was a rehearsal or a new recording.

Status: The 1981 demo of "Baby I'm a Star" (3:56) and the updated version both remain unreleased.

"Baby I'm a Star" was listed on a Sunset Sound work order from December 7, 1981, but it is unclear if they actually worked on it during that session as the title was scratched out.

JULY 1983 (DATE UNCERTAIN)

"Electric Intercourse" (basic tracking)
Kiowa Trail home studio (Chanhassen, Minnesota)
Producer: Prince | *Artist:* Prince | *Engineer:* unknown

["Electric Intercourse"] is the kind of song when little girls love Prince. It's like "Do Me, Baby" or something like that but a little more risqué. It was successful when we played it live, but in the studio it wasn't quite as dynamic.—Lisa Coleman[3]

Prince was focused on creating music that told a story for the upcoming film, and he spent a day in his home studio working on what was scheduled to be the emotional ballad for the scenes with Vanity. The song was given to the Revolution to rehearse for an upcoming benefit show at First Avenue, and in the live context the song came alive.

Over the next few months, the movie that was being planned would morph into a film with a very different tone. In August, Magnoli's script for *Purple Rain* included "G-Spot" and "Electric Intercourse" in the section after Morris and Vanity were enjoying a drink together at First Avenue. Eventually Vanity's part was recast and renamed and given to Apollonia Kotero, "G-Spot" was removed from the film and soundtrack, and "Electric Intercourse" was replaced by "The Beautiful Ones." "It was a good song," reflected drummer Bobby Z, "but I think 'The Beautiful Ones' was written late and it was a better one, without a doubt."[4]

Status: "Electric Intercourse" (4:57) was included on the *Purple Rain Deluxe* (Expanded Edition) CD set in 2017. The track was considered for a spot on the unreleased *Crystal Ball II* set in 2000.

SUMMER 1983 (DATE UNCERTAIN)

"Vibrator" (basic tracking/overdubs)
Kiowa Trail home studio (Chanhassen, Minnesota)
Producer: Prince | *Artists:* Vanity 6 | *Engineer:* Don Batts (assumed)

> *I remember being at the house and I remember when Denise [Vanity] had this massager that she used, and it was for her back, because she had a bad back, and it sounded like a lawn mower.* —Jill Jones

One of the hallmarks of the *Vanity 6* album was the humorous skit during "If a Girl Answers (Don't Hang Up)," and Prince decided to continue in that direction with a song called "Vibrator," which was about a vibrating personal massager. The lyrics repeatedly explained that her lover's services were no longer necessary because her vibrator "makes me feel so good."[5] "Oh my God. (*laughs*) It was definitely for the second Vanity 6 album," recalls Brenda Bennett upon hearing the track again. "You can hear in her performance that she had really improved, but as far as I could tell, there was no way he would release it . . . and he hasn't! That is Jill and Vanity at the end of the song."

"They went in the studio and I think Susan [Moonsie] was there, and I remember just laughing," recalls Jill Jones. "How crazy is that? I had forgotten about that. That was when we were all getting along! That was at Prince's house in Minneapolis. It was right before the *Purple Rain* stuff started going, because [Vanity] hadn't left yet. We were all in the studio together, and it was easy to work because you could do your part and then go upstairs and make tea."

Prince once again played a similar character as he had on "If a Girl Answers" during the four-minute comedic section, which concludes with Vanity achieving an orgasm at the end of the song. Jones recalls her reaction when that section was taped: "After I recorded my part I ended up leaving the studio and went upstairs, and she went down there and then that thing just (makes loud grinding noise). As I remembered it was like a lawn mower (*laughs*) and she alluded [to me] that they did this experimentation thing. Anything for art! I was watching TV and it was really loud and it didn't take a genius! There were a lot of things that went on like that in the studio for sure. For sure!"

Status: "Vibrator" (7:10) remains unreleased, although Vanity's moaning was eventually used on the song "Orgasm" for Prince's *Come* album as well as on "7" from the Madhouse album *8* and on "21" from the unreleased Madhouse album *24*. Prince would later spend time at Sunset Sound reviewing "Vibrator," but it is unclear whether the session contained any additional overdubs.

Other tracks that are difficult to confirm being recorded in Minneapolis during the summer of 1983 include "Electrocution," and "Money." No additional information is available about either of these songs.

SATURDAY, JULY 16, 1983

Untitled song (with Stevie Nicks)
Kiowa Trail home studio (Chanhassen, Minnesota)
Producer: Prince | *Artist:* Prince and Stevie Nicks | *Engineer:* Don Batts
(assumed)

Q: So you can go into a session and not even have the full picture in mind, lay down the bass line, and then build around that?
*A: **I could. I've done it before, yes.**—*Prince[6]

Five months earlier, Prince had worked with Stevie Nicks on "Stand Back," which was currently a *Billboard* Top 15 hit and still climbing the charts. When her tour brought her to the Twin Cities, Prince invited Nicks to spend the evening with him at his home, hoping to create another track with her:

> Prince came and got me right after the show. I'm still in my chiffon stage outfit and he's in his purple stage outfit. We get in his purple Camaro and bomb out onto the freeway at 100 mph. I'm terrified, but kind of excited, too: "Shit, we're going to get pulled over!" So we get to his purple house and he has a studio downstairs and we try to write a song together. But I've just done a show and I'm tired, so I go upstairs and sleep on the floor of his purple kitchen. In the morning he wakes me up and I have some coffee and I sing a little part on the song. But I've got to be at the airport by 2 p.m. to take-off and you do not miss that plane. We get into the purple Camaro again, Prince bombs it down the freeway and right out onto the tarmac alongside our private jet. He comes around to open my door and we hug goodbye, but we both look like crazy people. I get on the plane and the rest of the band are like (drums fingers, rolls eyes). I'm like, "What? Nothing happened."[7]

Status: The title of the song is unknown and it appears to remain unreleased.

Nicks's interview indicates that it was a Fleetwood Mac tour, but if this date is accurate, she was on a solo tour for her album The Wild Heart *and played at the Met Center in Bloomington, Minnesota, on July 15, 1983.*

A large portion of the summer was spent re-creating the Time as the powerhouse group from the last tour, but a lot of work was going into blending the new members with the old. On the other hand, Prince had been rehearsing the Revolution (with Wendy Melvoin replacing Dez Dickerson), and it was going very well. "The idea of integration is important to Prince, to me and the rest of the band too," revealed Lisa Coleman. "It's just good fate that it's worked out as well as it has the perfect couple of black people, the perfect couple of white people, couple of girls, couple of Jews. Whatever. He's chosen the people in his band because of their musical abilities, but it does help to have two female musicians who are competent."[8]

"The Revolution I feel, chemistry wise, was one of the best groups [that played] with Prince," reflected Matt Fink, who'd played keyboards in several bands with Prince. "I also felt [it worked] looks wise; the fact that there were two women, it was like the configuration of Fleetwood Mac."[9]

Prince was spending a lot of time with the Revolution in the studio, finding out their limits and, like he does with almost everyone around him, pushing their limits, as Peggy McCreary remembers, during rehearsals and studio time: "When I knew Wendy, she was so freaked out to solo. Prince used to joke with her 'Are you going to solo? Are you going to solo?' You just felt for her because it was so hard, but then once she got that under her belt, she just flew!"

SUMMER 1983 (DATE UNKNOWN)

"**Purple Rain**" (writing and rehearsal)
The Warehouse (St. Louis Park, Minnesota)
Producer: Prince | *Artist:* Prince and the Revolution | *Engineer:* unknown

> *Q: Was ("Purple Rain") written in 1979?*
> *A: **This is yet another fiction based melodrama.**—Prince[10]*

Prince was aiming in a different direction than he ever had before: epic, guitar-based rock music. "Given the crossover that began with [the success of] 'Little Red Corvette,' and a couple of others off the previous album, it had finally begun to deliver him a large white audience, or if not large, at least a growing white audience," detailed Alan Leeds. "And it was only logical to not want to ignore that new audience when you make your next record. And certainly the economics of the film industry do not allow for an R&B movie. The expense of film and the need to recoup dictates that you have as wide an appeal as possible, and it just makes sense that he went into it saying, 'I've got to make some pop music, because it's going to be in a movie.'"[11]

Rumors of the origin of the title track to *Purple Rain* have circulated for a long time, but there isn't anyone involved with the creation of the track who traces it back before 1982–1983. According to those around Prince, the history of the actual track has several influences. Dez Dickerson feels that his own rock-and-roll history had some sway in creating the song: "Prince is a great guitarist in his own right, so I don't know if he wouldn't have written that kind of stuff without me around, but I'm glad I had the chance to influence his sound somewhat."[12]

Fink explains how he believes the influence should be shared, based on a conversation that he had with Prince while on the *1999* tour in 1982–1983: "We were out on tour and Bob Seger was shadowing us wherever we went and he said, 'I don't understand the appeal of that stuff.' I said that it was like country rock. It was white music. 'You just need to write a white tune. You should write a ballad like Bob Seger writes, you'll cross right over.' And he did! He took my advice. I really think that he listened to me at times like that."

In the movie *Purple Rain*, the music for the title track was written by Melvoin and Coleman, with Prince adding his own lyrics. The reality is a little different. Melvoin shed some light regarding the song's origin: "In answer to everyone's question: Did Wendy and Lisa write 'Purple Rain'? The answer is no. But . . . did we help? Yes, we did."[13]

Prince himself felt like an inspiration for the song came from outside the band, specifically from "Faithfully," a Top 20 single from Journey's 1983 album *Frontiers*, so he reached out to the writer of the song, Jonathan Cain, to discuss it with him. "I want to play something for you, and I want you to check it out. The chord changes are close to 'Faithfully,' and I don't want you to sue me," Prince supposedly told Cain during the phone call. "I thought it was an amazing tune, and I told him, 'Man, I'm just super-flattered that you even called. It shows you're that classy of a guy. Good luck with the song. I know it's going to be a hit.'"[14]

"Prince felt, I guess, it was obvious enough that he was worried we were going to sue him," remembered Journey guitarist Neal Schon. "We all talked about it and everybody said, 'Nah, it's the highest form of flattery. Let it go.'"[15]

Although the chord progression was reportedly first played during the sound check before the show in Cincinnati, Ohio, on December 12, 1982, it wasn't worked on in great detail until the summer of 1983, when it was brought back out to the band at the warehouse. "Prince came to us with the chords for the song during rehearsal," recalled Fink. "He had the song, but the arrangement wasn't quite finalized yet and I don't think the lyrics were finished. So when he brought it to us, he just said, 'Play what you feel.'"[16]

"We were seriously camped out in a warehouse working out these songs, and we would really write them as a band and we were so tight by that time, and Wendy fit in so well and added such a beautiful color in her guitar playing and her funk abilities," Coleman explained in 2009. "She had the perfect combination of groove and nice beautiful chords, which is really indicative of that record, *Purple Rain*. The song itself, the opening chords, are Wendy with her beautiful big chords, like a chorus effect on it."[17]

"I started playing this chord," described Melvoin as she played the opening note. "And then we tried to change the chord, and Prince's chords at the time were much more simple then. We kept all those suspended chords in there and then I put the 9 in there."[18]

"It was the perfect song for that band," declared Coleman. "It just kind of called everybody into almost like their perfect role. It summed up kind of what the band was at that time."[19]

In 2011 Prince released a statement opening up about how much the Revolution was in sync during that period, specifically his drummer and longtime friend Bobby Z: **"Nobody plays drums on the song 'Purple Rain' like Bobby. Never flashy or loud, he plays like a slow burn love song. Bobby's way of playing made each live rendition of the song better than the last."**[20]

But it wasn't just Bobby Z who was hitting on all cylinders. Prince was continually open to suggestions from the band, and when Fink came up with a signature part of the song, Prince quickly incorporated it into the emotional climax:

> The line at the end where [Prince] sings the falsetto way up high that has no lyric, that was a keyboard line I was playing when we were learning the song, and he incorporated that into the end of the song. That was something he took from something I came up with. Not a big deal. I'm not mad about that because he gave us artist royalties for that record for the contributions we made, even though he didn't say that I contributed to that with a little writing or something, but he knew everybody was involved and had their own parts that they came up with.

According to Melvoin, the emotional connection with the song shared by the band members was contagious and resonated with a woman who happened to witness its birth: "By the end of the day, it was pretty much solid. I remembered this woman walked in with her bicycle. She was like a bag lady. She sat down on a chair in front of us while we were playing. Really quiet, very demure, really sweet. And she just started crying while we played 'Purple Rain.' She was bawling."[21]

"You listen to the influences of that song. That song could have been done by a country artist," says Fink. "It's like very mainstream, midwestern United States rock and roll. There's no funk in that thing at all. (*laughs*) There's not R&B in that song, it's just straight ahead anthemic rock and roll."[22]

Melvoin nailed it when she explained that "Purple Rain" is "one of those undeniable BIC lighter songs."[23]

There is an alternate history of the track that involves Stevie Nicks. Nicks and Prince had recorded together earlier in the year, and according to Nicks, Prince gave her a tape and asked her to write the lyrics. "I've still got it [the demo cassette]—with the whole instrumental track and a little bit of Prince singing, 'Can't get over that feeling,' or something," she said. "I told him, 'Prince,

I've listened to this a hundred times but I wouldn't know where to start. It's a movie, it's epic."[24]

It is possible that Prince gave her the cassette containing this early version either during their recent July 16, 1983, session or as early as February 8, 1983, during their time recording "Stand Back."

But what is the song about? **"Once [my songs] are on that record they are yours to make what you want of them,"** explained Prince. **"I don't want to spoil the process by explaining what I think they are about."**[25]

"Prince never talked about what *any* song was about," revealed Melvoin. "It never came out of his mouth: 'Ladies and gentlemen, this next song is about my mother' or whatever. He never suggested it, never talked that way to a friend. It was all weird parables, and you just took it for what it was."[26]

Despite the song's origin or meaning, the reality is that on "Purple Rain"—arguably Prince's most iconic song—he brought the basic idea to his band, but it wouldn't be the same track without the help of the Revolution. In the credits for the song, every member of the Revolution is recognized as performing on the track. At the end of the day, a song like "Purple Rain" not only profiles Prince's skills but should remind the listener that the Revolution was a great band.

"Purple Rain" would define Prince to many people and would become his "Stairway to Heaven." It would grow into one of the most recognizable songs of the 1980s, if not in all of rock history, and would be performed by Prince on practically every tour (at almost every regular show) for the rest of his career. Decades later, the song does not seem dated. Prince explained this to CNN in 2004: **"One of the reasons for that is that I never wanted to fit in with my music. Whatever the trend was, I usually went the opposite direction."**[27]

Status: The ten-minute demo/rehearsal of "Purple Rain" remains unreleased, as does the version from the December 12, 1982, sound check in Cincinnati, Ohio. The rendition of "Purple Rain" that was on the soundtrack album (8:41) was based on a live performance from August 3, 1983, and included a great deal of overdubs added in the weeks following the concert.

On September 26, 1984, the track was released as the third single from the soundtrack album in the United States (it was released on September 10, 1984, in the UK), and it peaked at number 2 on the US *Billboard* Hot 100 chart and number 4 on the *Billboard* Black Singles chart. Various official edits of "Purple Rain" were released, including two 7-inch edits (4:02 and 4:30), a 7-inch promo long radio edit (5:37), a 12-inch "Long Version" (7:05), and a 7-inch promo radio edit (4:19).

The only post-1983 Prince tour that didn't feature "Purple Rain" was the 1995 Ultimate Live Experience Tour, but that was because that tour featured none of his hits. In fact, "Purple Rain" was not played even once during his shows in 1994 and 1995.

"Purple Haze" has been listed as an inspiration for the title, and the phrase "purple rain" can also be found in songs from America ("Ventura Highway") and Stevie Wonder ("Purple Rain Drops," the B-side of "Uptight"). Prince's father supposedly composed a track called "Purple Shades" several years earlier, and Prince himself had composed a track called "Purple Music."

"Purple Rain" would be the closing track Prince played during his final full concert in Atlanta, Georgia, on April 14, 2016, the week before his death.

LATE JULY 1983

"Darling Nikki" (basic tracking)
Kiowa Trail home studio (Chanhassen, Minnesota)
Producer: Prince | *Artist:* Prince | *Engineer:* Prince | *Assistant Engineer:* Don Batts

When I was making sexy tunes, that wasn't all I was doing. Back then, the sexiest thing on TV was **Dynasty,** *and if you watch it now, it's like* **The Brady Bunch.** *My song "Darling Nikki" was considered porn because I said the word "masturbate." Tipper Gore got so mad. It's so funny now.*—Prince[28]

Music was being created at the warehouse in St. Louis Park, but Prince was still doing the actual recording at home in his basement. In fact, the album's liner notes teased that "Darling Nikki" was "recorded at a place very close 2 where u live." During this session, Prince began work on a song that would bring him a great deal of attention not only from fans but also from the censors. "Every generation likes to shock," reflected Alan Leeds, "and Prince has made a career out of a teenager's quest to shock people. But it's who he is."[29]

"He takes irreconcilable opposites like pleasures and politics or sex and love and merges them in a music style that is in itself a wonder of blending," revealed Brown Mark. "His mom had this wild collection of porno novels and when his dad split, he left Prince a piano. For him, sex and music are very natural mixtures."[30]

When Prince recorded at home, there were very few tasks the engineer had to do to facilitate the session, so he'd often assumed the position of his own engineer. Everything was already in place because of Don Batts. The instruments were patched in and ready, and Batts would leave tape on the machine, which meant that Prince only had to press the record and play buttons.

Seemingly inspired by a riff from Vanity 6's "3 $\times$ 2 = 6" that progressed down the musical scale, "Darling Nikki" was a very sparse tune, relying largely on Prince's live drums and keyboards, with a few guitar accents added to the mix. The guitar avoided overpowering the song until the end, when the sounds started erupting and all the instruments came together in an angry orgasmic fury. The drums were embellished by the Linn, and the rapid beats were created when Batts showed Prince how to play the pattern with his fingers.

Once all the elements were added, the vocals were recorded. As with the song itself, the vocals go from calm, almost passive, to passionate screaming, and a plea for Nikki to come back to him, based around the sensual pattern of the peaks and valleys of lovemaking. As the song rises and falls, increasing the sexual tension, it is easy to imagine his pain in the plea for her to return, as if someone close to his heart was threatening to leave him. "Sometimes when he's alone, especially, he can reach these places that are just unbelievable," recalled Coleman. "He's an impressive screamer."[31]

"Only a few people that can scream like that," added Melvoin.[32]

The screaming and pleading vocals were a very effective counter to the sparse sections of the song and were probably the reason Prince referred to the track as **"the coldest song ever written."**[33] Because he worked alone on many of his home sessions, Prince would have to press "record" and then walk over to the drum kit, and then, when he was finished, walk back to stop recording.

"That's how it was back then," according to Coleman:

I'm not kidding. He'd start with the drums, but he'd already have the song in his head. . . . And he'd go and press "record" on the machine and then run over to the drums and you'd hear him jumpin' over things and trippin' over wires, he'd sit down on the drums, and then count himself off, tick, tick, tick. And then he'd play and sometimes he'd have lyrics written down on a piece of notebook paper and so he'd try to sing it in his head and sometimes you'd hear him kind of grunting and singing a little bit of the song on the drum track. And then he'd imagine in his head like . . . he told me this, like you have to kick the bass player's ass. Like when you're playing the drums, kick the other guy's ass. Put things in there that's going to make the other guy . . . which was all him, you know . . . do something unexpected or try to keep up. So it was so cool because then the drum track would be down and then he'd go and get the bass and play the bass and then that weird drum lick would come up and then he'd go, "Oh," and then try to kick the guitar player's ass, etcetera, etcetera.[34]

"When I first moved out there," Coleman continued, "I stayed in his house for a while and we'd just be in the studio all the time, and sometimes I'd be the one punching him in or whatever. That was a lot of good stuff."[35]

After he was done recording "Darling Nikki," Prince's altered voice was captured by the mics on the drum kit. He was in a playful mood and he revisited a familiar character he's used in many songs ("Cloreen Bacon Skin" and "Chocolate," among others) and this person was so unhappy with Prince's performance that he was firing him. The character he is playing is his imaginary manager, Jamie Starr. The reason it was recorded was because of the walk back to the deck to stop the tape.

"[Prince] gets over with everyone because he fills everyone's illusions," Miles Davis explained in his 1990 autobiography. "He's got that raunchy thing, almost like a pimp and a bitch all wrapped up in one image, that transvestite thing. But when he's singing that funky X-rated shit that he does about sex and women, he's doing it in a high-pitched voice, in almost a girl's voice. If I said 'Fuck you' to somebody, they would be ready to call the police. But if Prince says it in that girl-like voice he uses, then everyone says it's cute."[36]

Not everyone thought it was cute. Tipper Gore, wife of Democratic senator (and future vice president) Al Gore, heard the lyrics and was inspired to create a watchdog group called the Parents Music Resource Center (PMRC). The PMRC noted that the lyrics were pornographic and listed the song (as well as the Prince-penned "Sugar Walls") as part of the "Filthy 15." *Purple Rain* would be one of the first albums to have an official warning label that read: "Parental Advisory: Explicit Lyrics."

It seemed that Prince wanted to disturb the Moral Majority and those he felt might censor him, so he pushed the envelope of what was acceptable, but the definition of what was shocking changed over time, and what was once the vanguard of rude behavior became much more mainstream. In 2004 Prince put the entire controversy in context: **"If you take the words to 'Darling Nikki,' which I got into a little bit of hot water about back in '84, if you take those lyrics and read them now, it's a little different than say the president of the RIAA [Recording Industry Association of America] reading the lyrics to one of these current hip-hop songs at a congressional hearing."**[37]

"It is so funny because he doesn't talk like that," reveals Peggy McCreary. "You'd think that someone that explicit would be rude, but he never was like that. He was never sexually rude. At least not to me he wasn't."

At this point in the film's development, Vanity was still the female lead, so the song fit well into the film, according to director Albert Magnoli: "Vanity is dangerous. She has a dangerous sexuality. I hear 'Darling Nikki,' and I immediately knew that ultimately, I just sensed that this is going to become very controversial. And I knew it was extremely dark compared to all the other things. And I knew narratively I was going to be in a very dark place with these characters anyway, because now they're going to start to betray each other."

Status: By the end of the session, "Darling Nikki" (4:00) didn't include the extended blend of sound effects and backward vocals that followed on the version released on the *Purple Rain* album (4:15). At this point the track contained an additional middle breakdown that would ultimately be removed.

LATE JULY 1983 (ONE DAY AFTER RECORDING "DARLING NIKKI")

"Darling Nikki" (playback)
Kiowa Trail home studio (Chanhassen, Minnesota)
Producer: Prince | *Artist:* Prince | *Engineers:* Don Batts and Susan Rogers

> *"Darling Nikki" was done by Prince at home by himself. It was a combination of real drums and the Linn. I went there the next day and heard it, and he showed me how he did it.*—
> Bobby Z[38]

"Darling Nikki" was the last track recorded by Prince's longtime home engineer Don Batts, who left because of a dispute with Prince: "There were some broken promises to me from Prince's management: bonuses and things I was supposed to get that never materialized. And my salary was being cut. I was pretty much putting my heart and soul into the job. I hadn't had a day off in years. I asked Prince for help but he wasn't taking care of me any longer. He really wasn't listening anymore."[39]

Batts recalled that there were more than eighty songs on the shelf waiting to be placed on a project. During the transition period Prince brought in Susan Rogers, who would remain his engineer for the next five years. Although trained as a maintenance technician, Rogers was already very familiar with Prince's music: "He was my favorite artist in the world. If someone had asked me in early 1983, 'What would be your dream, if you were to write down on a piece of paper your fondest wish and hope?' I would have written down 'to work for Prince.' And that actually happened . . . the dream literally came true. I was so lucky and I cherished every moment."[40]

When Batts played the half-inch recording of "Darling Nikki" to show Rogers what Prince had been working on the previous night, she was floored: "I just couldn't believe it. I thought I was hearing the greatest thing I had ever heard in my life. I was just astonished. The song was amazing and I thought: 'Wow, that's what he is capable of doing. This Soundcraft, this old 3B console and this MM1100, these few little pieces of gear—this guy can do anything!' So, needless to say, I was really, really excited to get going."[41]

Her first task was to update his studio to more closely reflect the setup at Sunset Sound, which consisted of a system designed by Frank De Medio. De Medio would eventually build the system in Studio B at Paisley Park, but for now, Prince decided to purchase an API console, which was similar—but not identical—to the one at Sunset Sound. To make room for his new board, he needed his Soundcraft board removed, and during this process he also wanted his tape machine repaired and a quick overhaul of his entire system. This was normally something Batts would oversee, but with him on his way out, the job went to Rogers:

> He didn't have anyone on his staff who was qualified and who had the background to get the studio up and running, so I was given the directive to prepare the studio and do it quickly, because he was upstairs raring to go and had all this music, and he needed his tape machine fixed and he had a new console . . . and so the old console came out of his old studio and I installed the new one. Typically, this would be a three- or four-person job, but I was in Minneapolis all by myself. That's okay. I got it all done, got the new console installed, tackled the tape machine next. He had an Ampex 1100, I think it was, got it repaired, got it pulling tape, got the whole studio up and running. Fixed some things and I was ready to roll.[42]

During the several days Rogers pieced together the new elements for Prince's basement studio, he was upstairs working with Susan Moonsie and Brenda Bennett (two-thirds of Vanity 6 and eventually Apollonia 6) on music for *Purple Rain*.

There is some confusion about whether Prince owned an MM1100 or an MM1200. The 1200 is an update of the 1100, but they are very similar.

LATE JULY 1983 (SEVERAL DAYS AFTER RECORDING "DARLING NIKKI")

Session canceled
Kiowa Trail home studio (Chanhassen, Minnesota)
Producer: Prince | *Artist:* Prince | *Engineer:* Susan Rogers

> *That evening at about seven o'clock I got a phone call, and a voice, I think it was Prince's, says: "Is it ready?" He didn't even introduce himself. And I said: "Yes, it is." And he said: "Can you come here right away?" And I said: "I'll be right there."*—Susan Rogers[43]

Susan Rogers drove to Prince's house, entered through the back door, and waited for him in his studio. Upstairs, she heard Prince's voice, as well as various other females talking, laughing, and dancing:

> I waited, and I waited, and I waited. . . . Four hours went by and I thought: "Come on, he must know that I am here." Suddenly I heard little feet on the stairs and he came running down the stairs and he stuck his head around the corner and said, "We're not going to work tonight, that's all. Bye." And I was so astonished, I thought: "Damn it, I just moved two thousand miles and I at least want to meet this guy." So I went after him and he was running up the stairs and I stuck my head around the corner and I said, "Prince." He stopped and turned around and I stuck my right hand out and I said, "I'm Susan Rogers." Then he kind of smiled and said, "Oh, nice to meet you." And we shook hands and he took off and ran up the stairs. I thought: "All right, at least we are properly introduced." That was all that night.[44]

LATE JULY 1983

Session canceled
Kiowa Trail home studio (Chanhassen, Minnesota)
Producer: Prince | *Engineer:* Susan Rogers

> *The next day he, or someone, called me and told me to go the studio. So I did, and this time he didn't keep me waiting, he came right down.* —Susan Rogers[45]

When Prince arrived in the studio, it was immediately apparent that he wasn't happy with the design of the new console, specifically the placement of the equalizers as Rogers recalled:

> The equalizers were way up near the meter bridge, and he preferred the one at Sunset Sound where they were right above the faders. So he instructed me to pull that console out of his home studio and put the Soundcraft back in.
>
> I felt unhappy for him because I could see that he was anxious to record and he was very disappointed that this wasn't what he wanted. And I tried to convince him that [the equalizers] weren't that far away. All he had to do was to lean an inch forward in his chair and he could reach it. But he just said, "I can't work on this. Get it out of here and get the other one back in. Hurry."[46]

Rogers called Prince's manager, Steve Fargnoli, and explained the situation: "They flipped out and said I had to do everything I could to persuade him. He had to keep it, because they had just paid twenty-five thousand dollars for that board. I said, 'I just went to work with that guy, I'm not going to persuade him to do anything.'"[47]

Prince won. That day the API came out, and the Soundcraft was reinstalled into his home studio.

No recording took place on this date.

LATE JULY 1983 (SEVERAL DAYS AFTER RECORDING "DARLING NIKKI")

"Darling Nikki" (Prince vocal overdubs)
Kiowa Trail home studio
Producer: Prince | *Artist:* Prince | *Engineer:* Susan Rogers

> *There were a couple of songs on the [Purple Rain] album he did by himself. I think "Darling Nikki" was by himself. It was all him, which you can kind of tell because it's got that fierce, like, ridiculously crazy quality.* —Lisa Coleman[48]

Susan Rogers would turn out to be one of Prince's most notable engineers. She had a lot of the technical qualifications he wanted in an engineer, but the main hurdle was that Rogers wasn't an engineer. She was a maintenance technician whose skills involved putting together a studio, not running the session. In other words, she knew how to build the plane, but had never flown it. Tonight, she'd get to take it for a test-flight.

As soon as the previous system was reinstalled, Prince arrived, ready to record.

"He asked me to set up the vocal mic," recalled Rogers. "I got it all ready to go and I said, 'Okay, it's ready. Who is going to engineer it?' And he looked at me like I was nuts and said, 'You.' I thought: 'Oh my God, he asked for a technician and he doesn't realize that I'm not an engineer.' But that's what I wanted to be anyway, and I wasn't going to tell him the difference."[49]

The main vocals had been recorded during the earlier session with Don Batts, but Prince wanted Rogers to help him to record a few additional vocal parts, as she explains: "I set up the vocal mic and then I left. So he could have done vocals on that one, he could have finished up some other things, or he could have just wanted to do vocals on something else. I'm just not sure." The final version of "Darling Nikki" contains no harmony or background vocals, so if he recorded any, they were deemed unnecessary.

"I was stunned at 'Darling Nikki,'" remembered Rogers. "He asserts his dominance simply by allowing the woman to be dominant. Allowing her to be the antagonist and for himself to be the protagonist, he's able to show a lot of strength there. What I find interesting about it is that it is not the power of conquest; it's the joy of being conquered. If you recall the lyrics on that song, she is the seductress, not him."[50]

Others in the band were equally impressed. "I loved it when I first heard it," remembers Matt Fink.

I liked that one a lot. You know . . . controversial. I thought, this is the usual, let's go overboard on the sex stuff, but my sensibility all along was this is scary, you are treading some dangerous water with all this sexuality but that was his vision. I personally always felt that the song inside was great. I thought this is really different, I thought this is breaking new ground. I said it could hurt you commercially with record sales. I was always worried about that part of it—losing people because of it—but he didn't care. I would make those comments and it would go in one ear and out the other.

In 2004, when asked about his reflections on the blatant sexuality in some of his music, Prince explained his thoughts to CNN: "**I don't have regrets like** that when it comes to music. As you grow and as you evolve you learn more about yourself, you learn more about the people around you. You start to see yourself as a part of the whole universe and all that changes, so I think I've done the best that I could with what I had to work with at the time."[51]

The Soundcraft board would ultimately be replaced again when he upgraded his studio the following year, but the console that was removed ended up staying in the Prince family when it was sold to Time guitarist Jesse Johnson: "Prince sold me his Soundcraft recording board for $23,000. He used that same board to record 1999, What Time Is It? *and* Purple Rain. *I went to the Civic Center where he was doing dress rehearsals for the* Purple Rain *tour [October 1984] and gave him a check. That's how I was able to finish [my] studio."[52]*

AUGUST 1983

*There is a link between the storyline and Prince's own profes-
sional struggle.*—Albert Magnoli

Like his character in *Purple Rain*, Prince had always been a highly motivated
artist. The epic nature of a movie brought out the strengths in him, and he
searched deep inside to make this his most personal project, working harder
than ever. "He is demanding of himself and everyone who works around him,"
explained his manager, Steve Fargnoli. "You always have to be on your toes. He
doesn't play by the rules."[1]

Albert Magnoli was now back in Minneapolis working on his rewrite of the
script. Although the script was in flux and the characters were evolving, the main
concept of the movie hadn't changed much. It was still about a misunderstood
artist who didn't play by society's rules, struggling to prove himself to the world,
and the rewrites began focusing on making everything more realistic and making
Prince's character more vulnerable. His weakness is exposed through the relationships of those around him, so continued focus was placed on both his enemies
and those he allowed into his inner circle. According to Magnoli, "My research
was for me to sit down and say, 'Okay, I have a scene I'm developing between
you, Wendy, Lisa, and Prince, and you're very angry at him. And you're in the
dressing room and you're about to go on and you want to know if he hears your
music. Give me what you feel like?' And they start, 'Oh well, yeah that happens
all the time!' So, all of their shit comes up because they've been in that with him."

"I had no idea what the movie was going to be," Wendy Melvoin explained
to Jon Bream in 2004. "Al and Prince were writing it as they were going. During

---

that whole summer, people were called in and asked, 'What is your relationship with Prince? How would you see a situation arise?' Blah, blah, blah. Then 10 days later, there would be some pages [of script]."[2]

According to Magnoli, those in the camp were very open about their issues with Prince: "Wendy and Lisa didn't mind revealing the shadows. They were quite vocal about it and I instigated that conversation. What I did was simply understand that this is an opportunity for me to create a scene that would have poignancy and move not only themselves, but the audience."

As the script got tighter, Prince demanded that the bands get tighter as well, and he has always been a hard taskmaster to his bands. He was known for drilling his songs into the band members, but this time the stakes were higher because it was expected that many of the tracks could be used as blueprints for his next album: the soundtrack to his planned movie. "The film was paramount and the music secondary—or, not secondary, but supportive to the film," recognized Alan Leeds. "And by definition the film dictated a certain kind of music that had that wide appeal, and would appeal to a larger demographic. So I don't think it was a concerted effort to either go too white or away from black, as much as it was just the logical music at that time in his career."[3]

The movie would likely succeed or fail based on the music, so it had to connect with the audience on an emotional level he'd never attempted. Prince made a bold move and, borrowing a page from the script, he decided to premiere several of the potential tracks onstage at First Avenue to a hometown crowd. At that point, full funding for the movie wasn't secured, so there was no guarantee the film would be made in spite of the months of planning. If the new music disappointed the crowd, it might be a blow that would scare away any potential investors, but Prince decided to trust his instincts, and for the last several weeks he had been preparing for the most important concert of his career.

"Of course, there was the skepticism in the back of your mind that [the movie] would actually happen," said Matt Fink. "But knowing Prince, and how hard he works at those kind of things, I thought if anybody could pull it off, he could."[4]

WEDNESDAY, AUGUST 3, 1983

"Let's Go Crazy" (live)
"When You Were Mine" (live)
"A Case of You" (live)
"Computer Blue" (live)

"**Delirious**" (live)
"**Electric Intercourse**" (live)
"**Automatic**" (live)
"**I Would Die 4 U**" (live)
"**Baby I'm a Star**" (live)
"**Little Red Corvette**" (live)
"**Purple Rain**" (live)
"**D.M.S.R.**" (live)
Venue: First Avenue (Minneapolis, Minnesota)
Capacity: 1,558 (sold out)
Artist: Prince and the Revolution | *Engineers:* David "David Z" Rivkin and
   David Leonard

We were at a very good place musically.—Prince[5]

All of the summer's rehearsals would be put to the test on this evening, as the Revolution debuted to a sold-out hometown crowd at First Avenue. Technically, the Revolution wasn't actually introduced by name. For now, it was just Prince and his band. This concert was one of his greatest shows . . . but even more so when viewed in retrospect. Few in the audience understood that they were witnessing a historic event featuring a blend of five familiar tracks, one cover of a Joni Mitchell piece, and the official premiere of six original songs that would change the course of Prince's career.

"We were so well rehearsed that any opening night jitters melted away after the first song was played," reflected Fink. "I think Wendy was more excited than nervous."[6]

The pressure was on nineteen-year-old Wendy Melvoin because of the position she was filling: the spotlight formerly held by the iconic Dez Dickerson, Prince's longtime guitarist. "I was a nervous wreck," she remembered. "We had massive amounts of rehearsal so I was well prepared musically. But I felt like I had to fill Dez's shoes. People would be looking at me, 'Who's this young white chick that replaced this cool crazy-looking black guy on guitar?'"[7]

In many ways, Melvoin wasn't actually replacing Dickerson, because Prince adopted almost all the lead guitar work for this show, with the exception of Dickerson's solo from "Little Red Corvette," which became hers. Melvoin's role in the band was rhythm guitar with the occasional solo, while Prince performed much of the lead guitar work. Except during his 1986 tour, this would remain the case for most of Prince's career.

This concert began like the album, the movie, and the eventual tour: with the opening notes from the as yet unreleased "Let's Go Crazy." Prince was likely already imagining how this would appear in the upcoming film as he was first revealed in silhouette, playing the role of the traveling minister preaching to his congregation: "Dearly beloved, we are gathered here today to get through this thing called life . . ."[8] over the sounds of a church organ. The first spotlight shined on Melvoin, introducing her immediately to the crowd—and letting the audience know that this was a new band.

Prince was obviously enjoying himself as he assumed the position of guitar god by taking the first solo of the night. This was his band, and Prince was not going to be confused as just a band member. He owned it and controlled everyone in the room. Dipping briefly into his previous catalog, the band performed the rocker "When You Were Mine" (from his 1980 *Dirty Mind* album) followed by the only cover of the night, Joni Mitchell's "A Case of You," which carried an emotional connection for Prince: "**['A Case of You'] is one of my favorite songs 2 sing because the melody is so heartbreaking. The lyrics read as tho the writer is extremely enamored with the subject and yet the melody sounds as if they are about 2 break up. . . . [The record] has such a haunting feel that it would make even the hardest thug shed tears.**"[9]

Prince was a longtime fan of Mitchell's music. The credits for his *Dirty Mind* album thanked "Joni," her name was featured on the back cover of 1981's *Controversy*, and his songs have been peppered with references as far back as his second album, when he borrowed a line from Mitchell's song "Coyote" (a track from her 1976 album *Herjira*) and used it in the title of "When We're Dancing Close and Slow." He would eventually include elements influenced by Mitchell in songs like "Kiss" (from 1986's *Parade* album), "Others Here with Us" (a 1985 outtake), "The Ballad of Dorothy Parker" (from 1987's *Sign o' the Times* album), "The Sacrifice of Victor" (from 1992's symbol album), "The Circle of Amour" (from his 1998 *The Truth* album), and many others.

Although she wasn't as familiar with his work, Mitchell knew that Prince was a longtime fan:

> Prince attended one of my concerts in Minnesota. I remember seeing him sitting in the front row when he was very young. He must have been about 15. He was in an aisle seat and he had unusually big eyes. He watched the whole show with his collar up, looking side to side. You couldn't miss him—he was a little Princeling. (*laughs*) Prince used to write me fan mail with all of the U's and hearts that way that he writes. And the office took it as mail from the lunatic fringe and just tossed it! (*laughs*)[10]

During the debut of "Computer Blue," Melvoin shared the first guitar solo with Prince, but for the most part Prince dominated the stage, completely in his element, proud of the new band, new music, and new direction. The next eight songs bridged the recent past and the future, with four new songs ("Electric Intercourse," "I Would Die 4 U," "Baby I'm a Star," and "Purple Rain") and four songs ("Delirious," "Automatic," "Little Red Corvette," and "D.M.S.R.") from *1999*, which was still in the top 10 on the album charts.

What stood out is Prince's control of the stage, confident even when presenting untested songs to the hometown crowd. While he was backed by a very strong, tight, and well-rehearsed band, his onstage interaction with them was sparse, and the individual moments he granted to the band were infrequent—but two of them would become a tradition in their live shows, including Melvoin's time in the spotlight at the start of "Purple Rain" and Fink's iconic solo in "Baby I'm a Star." "I came up with that solo live at the First Avenue gig," revealed Fink. "'Baby I'm a Star' sounds like this big grinding orchestra with all these cool interludes and that James Brown energy. And hearing Prince [shout out] my name on the song meant a lot to me. He was basically saying, 'Here's my go-to guy . . . the Doctor!'"[11]

As a way for Prince to give something back, this evening's concert raised twenty-three thousand dollars for the Minnesota Dance Theater (MDT), and Loyce Holton, the artistic director for the MDT, was present to witness the performance. "[Loyce] had trained everyone how to dance for the film," explained Alan Leeds, "so Prince wanted to return the favor."[12]

During a break between "Little Red Corvette" and "Purple Rain," Holton was brought onstage for a hug from Prince and a moment when she declared her gratitude to him: "We don't have a Prince in Minnesota. We have a king."

The final songs of the night took the crowd in two very different directions. "Purple Rain" was a more personal track about reflection and love, while "D.M.S.R." found Prince back in his black leggings, heels, and what appeared at first glance to have been tight black underwear—reminding the crowd that he was still outrageous and unwilling to compromise, and wanted everyone to have fun. It was a great track on which to end the show because it left everyone in a party mood, unlike the vibe from the debut performance of "Purple Rain."

Bobby Z's brother David (aka "David Z") oversaw the recording of the concert and noticed the crowd's quiet reaction: "The audience was stunned because they had never heard that song before. If you haven't heard that song before there wasn't applause. I think that Prince's music is the type of music that takes you a little bit of time to get used to it, not right away. And then you can't live without it. Whereas there's a lot of songs that the minute you hear it, it sounds like a hit, then two weeks later you are done with it. He would just have that ability to get under your skin. He was brilliant that way."

If the initial reaction to the opening chords of "Purple Rain" was subdued, it was the last time the song was played publicly without causing an extreme emotional reaction. Several issues made it confusing to the crowd. The first was obvious: Prince wasn't onstage as the opening chords were played, so the crowd was listening to an unfamiliar song performed by Melvoin, a guitar player they'd never seen before. As the track went on, the reaction changed and the crowd began to recognize the passionate power behind the song. Once it was featured in the movie, the song would be forever linked with the summit of his success as well, and it would remain one of the most emotional connections he'd have with his fans.

At this time in 1983 Prince was peaking, and he was connecting with his audience in a personal way, delivering on the promise of his potential, confirming what the critics had been saying for several years, and giving what is considered by many to be the performance of his lifetime. This evening's show played a large part in the Prince mythology, making the music performed—as well as the actual club—more famous than anyone realized. What most people didn't know was that this evening's music was not just a snapshot of where Prince was musically at that moment, but a blueprint for the soundtrack album to the movie that was still being written. The new songs that made it to the album stayed in the order in which they were performed. They were shuffled slightly for the finale of the film, but the concert helped shape the structure of the music planned for the movie.

One of the people in attendance was Magnoli, who was back in town working on the script, narrowing down the list of possible tracks for the project, and visiting potential locations for the film. He was taken by Prince's stage presence and by the emotions brought out in "Purple Rain": "I wanted to shoot there, so I was looking at everything, and then he started playing that song, and I stopped and went, 'Whoa.' He finished playing, and I said, 'That's the song.' And so I went up to him after the set, and I said, 'That song that you did, that one up there, that could be *the* song,' and he said, 'Wow. Okay,' because he himself hadn't even thought of it. I asked what's the name of it and he said, 'Purple Rain,' and I said, 'Okay,' and he said, 'Can we call the movie *Purple Rain?*' And I said, 'Yeah, that's the name of the movie.'"

Dreams was now *Purple Rain*.

Prince would perform many of these songs for the rest of his career, through numerous versions of his band, but the bottom line is that for the premiere of "Purple Rain" there were only five people Prince trusted enough to stand with him on that stage to play the song: Wendy Melvoin, Lisa Coleman, Mark Brown, Bobby Rivkin, and Matt Fink, and there is nothing that can take that away from them. They would become Mount Rushmore for many Prince fans and were there when rock-and-roll history was made. Their contributions will never be forgotten. Prince knew how much of a game changer these tracks could be, and he wanted to capture the energy of the show on tape.

A mobile recording truck containing an Ampex tape deck and an API console was quickly rented from New York's Record Plant, and David Leonard and David Z were brought in to oversee the recording. "The intention of the recording was to use some of the songs on the album," explained Susan Rogers, "specifically 'I Would Die 4 U' and 'Baby I'm a Star.' I think he wanted to see what he could get, he wanted to see his band work out. He wanted to get as much as possible that he could use."[13]

"We recorded the concert. And it was amazing," says David Z. "[Prince] drove up to the truck and rolled down his window and said, 'How did it go?' 'It sounded great.' And just then a girl stepped off of the curb with the trench coat on, and she opened it and she was naked underneath. He looked at her and he goes, 'No, no, don't do that.' Rolls up his window and drives away. That was our conversation."

Status: Of the six new tracks, only three of them made it onto the album based on this performance. "I Would Die 4 U"/"Baby I'm a Star" (7:03) and "Purple Rain" (13:05) were taken into the studio for overdubs and editing, and were eventually released on the *Purple Rain* soundtrack (2:49, 4:25, and 8:42, respectively) and featured in the movie. An edit of "Baby I'm a Star" (2:46) was also released.

"Computer Blue" (6:28) and "Let's Go Crazy" (5:17) were rerecorded from scratch later that week, while this live version of "Electric Intercourse" (5:23) and the remainder of the concert remain unreleased.

THURSDAY, AUGUST 4, 1983

All tracks from previous night's concert (reviewed)
Kiowa Trail home studio (Chanhassen, Minnesota)
Producer: Prince | *Artist:* Prince and the Revolution | *Engineer:* David Leonard

> Purple Rain *started when we recorded the tracks of the live*
> *show at First Avenue.* —David Leonard[14]

Prince reviewed the previous night's concert to decide which of the new songs worked in a live context, and which would be best rerecorded in the studio. At the time, four tracks ("I Would Die 4 U," "Baby I'm a Star," "Purple Rain," and "Electric Intercourse") were deemed worthy of additional polish. "Computer Blue" and "Let's Go Crazy" were decided to be inferior, so the live versions were shelved.

It is unclear if any overdubs were recorded after listening to the show.

David Leonard engineered some of the studio sessions over the next week. Because he was based in Los Angeles, he couldn't continue as Prince's Minneapolis engineer. Instead, he helped with the transition for Susan Rogers, who had impressed Prince enough to ask her to relocate to the Twin Cities: "I was just packing my bags. August 3 is my birthday, and I'd been hired by Prince and I was in Los Angeles saying goodbye to my friends and getting ready to head up to Minneapolis."

SATURDAY, AUGUST 6, 1983

No music recorded
The Warehouse (St. Louis Park, Minnesota)
Engineer: David Leonard

> *I was hired on a full-time basis to do whatever it was he needed*
> *done technically, whether it was record in the studio or in a*
> *mobile truck or assisting videos or assisting moviemaking.*
> *Whatever he needed done, I was there twenty-four hours a day,*
> *seven days a week.* —Susan Rogers[15]

Prince's ideas came very quickly, and he didn't like anything slowing down the process. At the same time, he was expanding his sound, but he wanted to include additional people in the recording sessions. Because of the limited size of his one-room basement studio, there was no way to record the entire band, so it was decided to convert the rehearsal space at the St. Louis Park warehouse into a recording studio as well. This gave him the ability to work out the parts of a song, and then immediately get it to tape while everyone was hot. Many artists work on demos in their home studios, then eventually attempt to re-create them in another studio with a new engineer and producer. Prince would be able to bypass that entire process, but first he had to have the studio assembled in the warehouse. He asked Susan Rogers, Rick "Hawkeye" Henriksen, and David Leonard to create this for him. At first, Leonard thought he might have a solution, which involved the API console that had been removed from Prince's home studio: "It was still sitting in the crate—presumably waiting to be returned. So I decided to use that, and told him I needed to set up that night and we could do it the next day. So we took that API console out of the crate and set it up on road cases."[16]

They had the console but not the speakers. Rogers continues the story: "I phoned around town and ended up phoning MPR [Minnesota Public Radio], a radio station in St. Paul which had speakers that they'd let us borrow, because we needed big, self-contained monitors. So Hawkeye and I and David took a van to St. Paul and picked up these big speakers and brought them back. We wired up the studio as quickly as we could at the warehouse. There was a smaller office room near the front, and that's where we put the console."

A carpet was placed under the mixing board so it wasn't sitting on a bare floor, and it was ready to go. The setup wasn't optimal by any standard, but, as Leonard explained, they found a way: "The band had a PA blasting and I was in the corner of a warehouse, so I had to use headphones to record."[17]

It wasn't ideal, but the results were legendary.

SUNDAY AUGUST 7, 1983

"**Let's Go Crazy**" (basic tracking and overdubs)
The Warehouse (St. Louis Park, Minnesota)
Producer: Prince | *Artist:* Prince | *Engineers:* David Leonard, Susan Rogers

My original draft of "Let's Go Crazy" was much different from the version that wound up being released. As I wrote it, "Let's Go Crazy" was about God and the de-elevation of sin. But the problem was that religion as a subject is taboo in pop music.—Prince[18]

Albert Magnoli was still writing the most recent draft of the script. In the previous version, the movie opened without a music scene. Once Magnoli heard the song and saw it performed at the First Avenue show, he knew he had the ideal spot for the track: "I love the song. And so to me it was the perfect song to open. And the interesting story about that is that the song was only three minutes long, so when I designed the montage in the opening it was seven minutes. So I had to go to Prince and he had to elongate it. He basically punched into the middle, added a new middle, which brought it to its length."

Prince had been able to record rehearsals in the past, but only on a bare-bones system that fed the sounds to a cassette recorder. Now, for the first time, he could create multitrack recordings of band rehearsals and document how a song was written. Within a short time, he wasn't just recording the rehearsals, he was recording everything. Leonard remembered how rapidly the warehouse morphed from rehearsal hall to recording studio: "On the weekend I recorded 'Let's Go Crazy,' Prince wanted me to go to the warehouse where he rehearsed, and he had the full-on production rehearsal with lights and sound, and they were working on that song and wanted to record it. It's almost like it was supposed to be done the night of the [August 3, 1983] show, but we were recording it after the fact."[19]

Just as Prince was concerned about "Purple Rain" being similar to a song by Journey, he was equally cautious about the song's similarity to one written and produced by his former bass player, André Cymone: "I had a song called 'Let's Get Crazy' with Evelyn 'Champagne' King and he called and said, 'I got a song 'Let's Go Crazy.' I don't want you to think I took it from you.'"[20] Other than the similar titles, the songs had very little in common. "Let's Go Crazy" dates to earlier in the summer, starting with a jam session, according to Prince's bass player Brown Mark: "He's probably got tons of different versions of it, where we would just be in the rehearsal hall just jamming on it, and the tapes would be rolling, and then he takes it and creates the song from it. He would get in the studio and he would replay parts here and there, but for the most part everything stayed the same, the live energy was there."

"He taught it to us in rehearsal one day," Matt Fink recalled about the first time he heard the track. "He taught that organ intro to me on the Oberheim, and I played that live for the recording. It was a Farfisa organ sound, like an old garage band organ, an old-style box organ, it was very similar tonally to that."[21]

"I thought it was kind of silly," reflected Coleman. "The more we played it, the more it developed into a sparkly, tough song. It's sort of Disneyland, but it's talking about life before death. The band added just the right attitude."[22]

Sections of the song can also be traced back to much earlier work. Prince's "Let's Go Crazy" solo bears a strong resemblance to the solo in his live performances of "Why You Wanna Treat Me So Bad" from as early as the 1981 tour.

In addition, the wrap-up of "Let's Go Crazy" can be found on many old blues songs as well as on Van Halen's "Ice Cream Man" (from their 1977 debut album).

Regardless of where the song began, the Revolution had been rehearsing "Let's Go Crazy" for most of the summer, and had performed it live earlier in the week, so they had it down tight. The band ran through the track a few times to check recording levels and to verify that the newly installed equipment was operating properly. Leonard explained in more detail about how everything was recorded: "The drums on that song were two sets of LM-1 Linn drums that Prince had Bobby playing pads on the triggers that were triggering the Linn drums. For the guitars, we mic'd the stacks. The band had rehearsed it, so we just rolled tape and went. It wasn't more than one or two takes, and it was done. It was my favorite song I recorded with him because I recorded it on a shoe-string on a console with a pair of headphones. He had some amazing material."[23]

After the initial recording, Prince had the band add a few overdubs, including background vocals and Matt Fink's solo. "At first I tried to do something melodic," Fink said, "but because the song was called 'Let's Go Crazy,' I thought I should do something that was out there. I just started randomly smacking the piano not really intending to play anything. And Prince loved it. I wish that the long version could have been on the actual *Purple Rain* album."[24]

In 1983 Prince didn't have a system that allowed programming of a precise section that was to be recorded, so the engineer was responsible for punching it in. This meant the engineer literally had to start recording at a certain spot on the tape and stop the machine at a specific later spot, which requires extreme precision, as Fink explained: "The punching-in process has to be done by a really good engineer, because if the engineer screws up then you lose that take completely and you've got to start over because it erased something in there accidentally, or you just have to punch in and fix a bigger spot because he didn't get you out in time, or he got you in too soon. Whatever reasoning, if you don't have a good engineer punching you in and out, you're in trouble."[25]

Leonard flew back to Los Angeles after the main part of the song was recorded, leaving Rogers alone in the studio with Prince, who wanted to overdub some of his guitar work. The session was Rogers's first time fully in charge of engineering Prince's music, and she reveals that it didn't go as smoothly as she hoped:

> I was operating the remote and Prince was playing [the guitar solo on "Let's Go Crazy"], and he made a mistake and he told me to roll back. So I rolled back to the top of the solo and the tape was playing and I'm watching Prince play guitar. Now bear in mind that I was a maintenance tech, so I knew all of the equipment like the back of my hand. I wasn't a recording engineer. So he's playing the guitar solo and

the tape machine is rolling, but it's not in "record," and I thought to myself, "He's probably going to be mad at me if I don't record this." So I reached over and—*dink!*—pressed record, and he reached over and went—*dink!*—and stopped the tape. And he said, "Who cued you?" I said, "Well, you were playing so I thought you wanted me to record it." He said, "Roll back, I'm going to play along. Watch me for a cue and then punch in." I was thinking: "Wow, I'm not fired!" So I rolled back and he played the solo. I watched him and he would raise his head up and as he would start to put his head down—that meant "now," so I'd punch in. So that was my first time punching in with him. I survived, and eventually we developed that understanding of each other to where he'd make a mistake and he wouldn't have to tell me; I'd just know based on his expression. I'd watch him. I'd never watch my hands. It was like being a player. You watch your artist and your artist is going to play along and there is going to be something in his face or body language that tells you that he's ready now and you wait until the appropriate place in the bar, or just go to the head of the bar where there is an appropriate pickup, and the two of us worked very seamlessly together. So we developed that kind of working relationship.

A rough half-inch mix was done at the end of the night.

"My first impression was that this guy is extremely intelligent, extremely creative and I was so happy and delighted with the fact that he was at the beginning of his career," recalled Rogers. "You would sense that this guy was at the beginning of something great."[26]

Status: The full version of "Let's Go Crazy" (7:35) was released as an "extended version" on the 12-inch single and was featured in the movie. Prince enjoyed Fink's solo so much that the film features him personally playing the part that he created. Eventually the track was edited down (4:39) and placed as the opening song for the soundtrack album. It was modified again (3:46) for the single release, and on July 18, 1984, it became Prince's second number 1 song.

According to the handwritten lyric sheet, the song's original title was "Let's Get Crazy."

MONDAY, AUGUST 8, 1983

"Computer Blue" (basic tracking)
The Warehouse (St. Louis Park, Minnesota)
Producer: Prince | *Artist:* Prince and the Revolution | *Engineer:* Susan Rogers

The next day [after "Let's Go Crazy"] we did "Computer Blue"
the same way, with the band, and everybody was very happy
and very excited about it. —Susan Rogers[27]

Now that Prince had a way to record the band properly, he started doing it more aggressively. "At this time he wasn't doing much at home," maintained Rogers. "He was really happy working at the warehouse. As much as he had enjoyed recording at home before, he was now happy to have all his instruments there; nothing had to be carried back and forth, his band members were there if he needed them. He had a good setup."[28]

Another track Prince wanted to rerecord from the August 3 benefit show was "Computer Blue," so he gathered the band to retrack the tune from scratch. Bobby Z emphasized that regardless of the primitive setup, it inspired the music that they recorded: "What Prince was doing with the warehouse was totally unique. He put this board right in the middle of this very echoey place, and rolled tape without giving the technical aspects of it any real thought. There was never any proper separation between the board and the instruments. If it sounded okay, that other stuff just didn't matter to him. He believes in spontaneity and getting good performances, not whether a mic is placed properly or not."[29]

"Computer Blue" was conceived earlier in the year, and like many of the other recent tracks, it had started in a jam session. "I inspired that song," asserts keyboardist Matt Fink. "It was from a jam at a rehearsal. Before the rehearsal started, I started playing the bass part on my own, against the groove. Bobby had the groove going, and for all intents and purposes everyone should have had a writing credit on that, if you want to get down to brass tacks, but it was inspired by my keyboard bassline. He liked it right away and he said, 'Let's turn that into something.'" In 2009 Fink would expand more on the process: "We recorded a rough version of it and he took it into the studio and just incorporated it all and made it fly that way. Lisa and Wendy came in and they did some of the stuff on it. Prince borrowed the bridge/portal section from his own father who had given him some music over the years to play around with. So that particular song was a real mixture of different people and influences."[30]

"[My father] co-wrote 'Computer Blue.' . . . He's full of ideas," according to Prince. **"It'd be wonderful to put out an album on him, but he's a little bit crazier than I am."**[31]

Susan Rogers remembers John L. Nelson's contribution to the songwriting slightly differently:

This was the time when he first was beginning to bring his father into his life, so his dad was around a lot. His father was in his late sixties by this time, and they were trying to develop a relationship. Prince had a lot of respect for his father. I was told that Prince gave his father songwriting credit on many of his songs. This was the way he helped his father financially. I don't believe that it's true that John Nelson wrote that little part of "Computer Blue," that beautiful part, because what I have heard of John Nelson's piano playing—and I have recorded him some—it's quite a bit different, although he may have taken up a musical theme that Prince inverted and turned it inside out and put to his own music. So Prince gave his dad songwriting credit to help his dad financially.[32]

Ultimately, songwriting credit for the song was shared between Prince, John L. Nelson, Wendy Melvoin, and Lisa Coleman. Because the track was based on Fink's original riff, he disagrees with this decision: "That kind of bothered me, because I thought that it should have just been a split between me, Prince, and his dad, and that's it because I don't know what they contributed. They always thought it was funny too. They always thought that was a weird call."

In 1998 Melvoin elaborated on their input to *Bam* magazine, verifying that even she was confused about this issue: "For 'Computer Blue,' we just contributed a keyboard line. That's writing? You just never knew what [credit] he would give you."[33]

"Sometimes it is a little complicated," cautioned Alan Leeds:

Maybe you're rehearsing a riff, maybe Prince will start a song, and you're just jamming, and somebody will devise a keyboard lick, or a horn lick, and there's a thin line between what's an arrangement and what's a composition. I won't go into it in any more detail than that, but there's a gray area. Whenever—to my knowledge, anyway, ten years working for him—whenever there was a question . . . somebody said, "Hey, man, make sure I get a piece . . . I wrote that lick," whenever anything was ever questioned, or questionable, Prince always gave. He never argued, because the last thing in the world he wanted to have was a musician who was (a) unhappy or (b) felt manipulated or cheated.[34]

Fink would later partially concede that "Prince really was the main lyricist and melody maker for the songs and I'm pretty sure very rarely took or did not take any lyrical content from people. He was really the main guy on that."[35]

The track was expanded from the benefit show's six-and-a-half-minute song to a jam that lasted more than fourteen minutes. The result was a loose exercise with Prince's guitar and guitar effects over most of it. When the version from this session was completed, Prince ended the song with more than two minutes of feedback and noise, but it is unlikely that was considered part of the song.

It is possible that additional overdubs were done on "Computer Blue" before this version was shipped to Sunset Sound in Los Angeles.

Status: "Computer Blue" (14:02) was edited several times (11:44, 10:40, 7:30, and possibly more), but the version recorded today was deemed incomplete. The following week, Prince and the Revolution would gather in Los Angeles and complete the track. A drastically edited version (4:00) was eventually released on the *Purple Rain* soundtrack. The longer versions remained unreleased during his lifetime, but a version of it renamed "Computer Blue ('Hallway Speech' Version)" (12:19) was eventually placed on the *Purple Rain Deluxe* (Expanded Edition) CD set in 2017.

During this period, Vanity wasn't happy with her place in the Prince camp. The summer had been spent recording new music and in rehearsals preparing for the upcoming movie, but her romance with Prince had soured and she didn't feel she was being compensated properly for all her work. Her name didn't appear on the guest list for the August 3 benefit show (although she was reportedly in attendance), and there is no documentation of any additional tracks recorded with her in August.

Magnoli recalls:

Vanity was in the development when I was there in August. So she was going to be in the movie, and was going to be in Vanity 6. In the first two weeks I was there in August, there was tension in real life between Vanity and Prince. She was a very independent woman in an extremely male-oriented world called Minneapolis. And she was a tough girl, and they were having their issues. I was writing it with her in mind, and then she came to me one day, and said, "I have a dilemma." "Okay, Vanity, what's the dilemma?" And she said, "Martin Scorsese talked to my agent, and he wants me to play Mary Magdalene in his movie." So she says to me, "What should I do?" And I said, "This is my first picture. It's a musical. Martin Scorsese? Okay, I don't want to steer you wrong here, but gee whiz, that's a great opportunity, I can't be dishonest." I said, "This is going to be a hard one. What do you want to do?" And she said, "I don't know, but I'm leaning toward doing Mary Magdalene." And within forty-eight hours, she was out.

After a failed negotiation with Prince's management for more money, she chose to accept the role in Scorsese's *The Last Temptation of Christ*.

"[*Purple Rain*] was Prince's dream," Vanity explained at the time. "He was bringing in everybody for very little money. You've got to pay people. You've got to be fair."[36] In 2013 she expanded on her reasons: "Prince wanted to pay me five thousand dollars for the entire film. That's ridiculous. Yeah, five thousand dollars—I'm like outta here. That's the best you can do? Bye!"[37]

"Vanity wanted more money," agrees bandmate Brenda Bennett. "Vanity wanted much more money to do *Purple Rain*. The script was basically finalized and, unbeknownst to us, she had gotten an agent and an accounting firm. Her lawyers got her out of it because she wanted out. She wanted in on her terms, but Prince never called her back after she left."

Unfortunately for Vanity, the Scorsese project was delayed and scheduling conflicts kept her out of that movie as well. Vanity bounced back and was hired to act in *The Last Dragon* for a reported three hundred thousand dollars. "Most people probably would think that is why I left, but that's not why I went solo. Prince discovered me; he discovered all of us. He's a great person—a brilliant kid. But I had planned to go solo all along," she explained in 1984. "If you're a very independent person, like I am, you don't base your career on what happens in your relationship with a man. I'm a career-oriented person, and I go with my career. As far as I'm concerned, your career is there for life; a man sometimes isn't. You don't know how long love is going to last. Other women might feel differently, and sure, I'd love to have babies and all that stuff one day. But right now, my career is the most important thing in my life."[38]

With Vanity gone, there was a new role to fill in the movie, in Vanity 6, and, to some extent, in Prince's heart. "I think that Prince and Vanity were a lot alike," remembers Peggy McCreary. "She was a female Prince. I think he was hurt when they broke up."

"In his personal life, I think Prince was disappointed that Vanity had left," added Rogers. "Things weren't going along as well as he would have liked it, but he was beginning to realize that people are the tools he needed to get his work done. He was very, very happy with Wendy Melvoin, delighted to get Wendy in the band. Anyway, he had the band he wanted, he was beginning to get the equipment that he wanted, and he could record whatever he wanted to."[39]

"In our world Vanity was famous, and we thought it was like a big common grab on the audience to want to see the movie to see Vanity and Prince in love or fighting," explains Bob Cavallo. "So yes, I thought it was a big loss."

With Vanity gone, the hunt for a replacement was on. Until then, Prince focused on his music.

AUGUST 1983 (DATE UNKNOWN)

> **"Possessed"** (attempt at basic tracking)
> The Warehouse (St. Louis Park, Minnesota)
> *Producer:* Prince | *Artist:* Prince and the Revolution | *Engineer:* Susan Rogers

> *I think I'm only a conductor of whatever electricity comes*
> *from the world, or wherever we all come from. To me, the*
> *ultimate responsibility is the hardest one—the responsibil-*
> *ity to be true to myself.* —Prince[40]

The vibe from working with the Revolution on many of the recent tracks was infectious, and the sound that Prince had been achieving while using them was thicker and more intense. The band had been playing "Possessed" in concert during the last tour, so they were very familiar with jamming on it. Prince decided to make another attempt at recording the track, this time using the entire band to see how it would evolve.

"There is a funny story about 'Possessed,'" recalled Susan Rogers:

> For one reason or another we had difficult times recording that. He tended to avoid it. It was during a hot day and the air conditioning was going on full power, and the band was attempting to cut "Possessed" and they were rehearsing it. And for some strange reason, they kept blowing fuses, the whole building was shut down. It was odd because we had been in the same situation before and had never blown the fuses when we had the whole band going. We couldn't figure out why we were drawing so much current; maybe it was because of the air conditioning. Somebody made a joke that it was because of the nature of the song, that it was the devil shutting us down, and we all laughed about that until the fuses kept blowing and kept blowing until Prince said, "I'm not doing this song, it is not meant to be." He was so superstitious that way, and he just stopped. He moved on to something else, and had that song cut another time.[41]

Status: Although work on "Possessed" from this session was aborted, it is likely that a full version was attempted once again at the St. Louis Warehouse. The exact date of that session is unknown. The song was ultimately rerecorded on March 17, 1984, with an updated arrangement and new lyrics. An instrumental rendition of the 1984 version can be heard in the *Purple Rain* movie during the scene when Apollonia and Morris Day are having a drink at First Avenue.

AUGUST 1983 (DATE UNKNOWN)

"17 Days"
The Warehouse (St. Louis Park, Minnesota) and Kiowa Trail home studio
(Chanhassen, Minnesota)
Producer: Prince | *Artist:* Prince and the Revolution | *Engineer:* Susan Rogers

> *We all had writing credit on that: Me and Lisa, Wendy and*
> *Prince. That was recorded at the warehouse. I just remember*
> *that groove and I remember all of us coming up with our own*
> *parts on it.*—Matt Fink

Before Prince left for Los Angeles, he and the Revolution continued working on potential tracks for the *Purple Rain* project, including songs for the Time and Vanity 6. "['17 Days'] came out of a *Purple Rain* rehearsal," recalled Melvoin. "Me and Lisa started playing a riff, and Prince started singing that melody."[42]

"I think we were being really playful because we started doing like a reggae groove and we were twisting things around," remembered Lisa. "It's like musicians, we used to bust each other's chops all the time doing polyrhythms, this feel against that feel, [and it] ended up being cool. He was like, 'Hey, I kinda like this.'"[43]

Although the Revolution recorded the track, the lead vocals were performed by Brenda Bennett of Vanity 6. "We rehearsed it with the band at the warehouse with Brenda singing lead," recalled Rogers. "That was intended for Brenda; it never came out that way, but we did record it live with the whole band at the warehouse."[44]

Additional parts, including Bennett's spoken section, were recorded at Prince's home studio. "When I heard it," says Bennett, "I remembered sitting down with a piece of paper and combining some of what Prince wrote with what I wrote. We laughed and joked about speaking in a 'sexy alien monotone.'"

Bennett phoned her husband, Roy, to talk about the song. He remembers, "I was back at home in Rhode Island and she called me, and was all excited about a new song that she'd recorded with Prince, '17 Days.' They were doing rehearsals, and suddenly a jam session came and they started playing that, and it was great. It ended up where Brenda started singing. She sang the vocals on it in the studio."

Brenda confirmed that this was one of her favorite tracks: "Love, love, love the song. I have a recording of it when I did the song for the second

Vanity 6 album. I wish that one had come to fruition."[45] Prince decided that he wasn't satisfied with the results of the first attempt and shelved it for a few months.

Status: This version of "17 Days" remains unreleased. It was rerecorded the following year from scratch and placed on the B-side for "When Doves Cry." Despite putting this early version on the shelf, Prince must have ultimately enjoyed this song a great deal because in 2004 he added a snippet of the rerecorded single to his song "Musicology."

The lyrics were partially inspired by Prince's song "How Come U Don't Call Me Anymore" (the B-side for "1999"), which included a callback (pun intended) to him begging for his lover to pick up the phone.

It is likely that the song was crafted with Bennett in mind, as the lyrics include references to "two cigarettes" and she was a smoker at the time. She can even be seen on the cover of the Apollonia 6 *album with a cigarette in her hand.*

It is also possible that the track was recorded in October 1983.

MONDAY, AUGUST 15, 1983*

"Computer Blue" (overdubs)
"Purple Rain" (overdubs and adding twenty-four tracks, string overdub)
Sunset Sound, Studio 3 | 12:30 p.m.–2:00 a.m. (booked noon–open)
Producer: Prince | *Artist:* Prince | *Engineer:* Prince | *Assistant Engineers:* "Peggy Mac" McCreary and David Leonard

> *My favorite track will always be "Purple Rain." The opening chords to the final sustain. It captivates me and I feel like it was part of history.* —Bobby Z[46]

The script was being rewritten and there was pressure to complete the new music, so Prince returned to Los Angeles committed to finishing the songs. The full financing for the film had yet to be locked in, but they were hoping to begin shooting at the end of October. Other music that was to be used for incidental purposes could be created after the shooting was finished, but any band performances had to be completed much earlier because they would have to be rehearsed, choreographed, lit, and blocked before they were filmed. Once the "live" performances were shot, there could be very little alteration to the music.

Prince was back in Studio 3 at Sunset Sound with his main engineer at the time, Peggy McCreary. Studio 3 was Sunset Sound's largest room and gave Prince the ability to record more with the Revolution. According to Sunset Sound owner Paul Camarata, Studio 3 is also very segregated from the main building and contains its own entrance and exit: "It has its own bathroom and its own lounge, so you could go in there, and Prince was a pretty private guy. Somewhat shy . . . although he would come out and commingle on the basketball court. Other than that, he was holed up in the room. He always had an array of people coming over, mostly good-looking women. It was pretty amazing."

Not completely satisfied with the results from the Minneapolis recording of "Computer Blue," Prince felt, for the first time, that the twenty-four individual tracks weren't enough to replicate what he heard in his head, and he had to make the choice of either compromising or accommodating his vision. He decided to double the number of tracks available from twenty-four to forty-eight and told McCreary to take care of this:

> All of a sudden he wanted to add things like strings and I said, "Excuse me. We only have twenty-four tracks. We don't have enough room." And he just said, "Make some more." That's just the way he worked. So then I had to hook up two machines, which was a lot of equipment, which wasn't the way he was used to working, and it doesn't always happen as fast as he was used to and liked. So David [Leonard] lent a hand because I couldn't handle it all myself. David and I started working together as a team on this stuff.

According to the studio notes, a fresh tape was used for the new recording, but instead of being for an all-new version of the song, it was used for the second deck (an Ampex MM1200) to provide the additional twenty-four tracks. Sunset Sound supplied a Q-Lock tape machine synchronizer to link up the two decks. The additional machine would be used for the next several months. Prince was pushing the limits of equipment as well as those in everyone around him, especially his engineers, remembers McCreary: "Some of the songs were so long and he couldn't quit. He just kept going and going and going. And that was so hard, because then you had to overdub them. A long song meant a long day and that is how he would wear you down. He needs his sleep, but only after a certain point."[47]

The basic parts of the track were kept intact, but Prince began making changes to the song starting around the five-minute mark.

Toward the end of the session, Prince decided to add strings to the live version of "Purple Rain" using the Oberheim keyboard performed during the concert as a guide track. Novi Novog was brought in to play violin and viola, and Suzie Katayama and Lisa Coleman's brother David were invited to play cello. David Coleman remembers:

Out of the blue, my sister calls me from Sunset Sound and said that they were doing some strings for a Prince song right now with Novi and Suzie and we think a third string player would groove better. It fills it in and the chemistry is important. I said, "Okay," and that I would be down there in four hours, so I washed up really quickly and practiced the cello because I'd been doing all percussion and I was only playing cello once in a while. So I ran through some scales and ran right down to the studio.

I walked into the control booth and [Prince] said, "Hi David. Do something!" He got up from the console and I sat in his seat and they played me the track and that was it. I went in and joined Suzie and Novi and we started from there. Suzie used to call my cello playing "rock-and-roll cello." She could play circles around me, but we grooved together. The three of us playing had good chemistry and we just sounded good together.

In a show of trust for those around him, Prince relied on Lisa Coleman to guide the string overdubs. "What would happen was Lisa would come in and she'd do some things on the piano so we'd learn our parts by ear," recalled David. "So we'd go through the song and punch in our string parts. Prince was sitting next to [Lisa] and they'd decide, but I think that Lisa was taking the lead when it came to the string arrangements."

McCreary recalled the change in Prince's mood as he watched her take charge: "It was neat to see Prince relaxing for once and not having to do it all himself."[48]

A rough mixdown was created and one C-60 cassette was made of the session.

TUESDAY, AUGUST 16, 1983*

"Computer Blue" (overdubs)
Sunset Sound, Studio 3 | 3:00 p.m.–4:30 a.m. (booked noon–open)
Producer: Prince | *Artist:* Prince | *Engineer:* Prince | *Assistant Engineers:*
   "Peggy Mac" McCreary and David Leonard

It took two engineers to do this stuff. It was just wild to watch him work. —Peggy McCreary

If "Purple Rain" was the "Stairway to Heaven" of the album, "Computer Blue" was becoming its "Bohemian Rhapsody." Building on the fourteen-minute version recorded in Minneapolis, the Sunset Sound sessions included suitelike portions, many telling stories of seduction and trust.

The session was scheduled to start at noon but was delayed until 3:00 p.m., and mostly consisted of two spurts of overdubs to "Computer Blue," the first from 3:00 p.m. to 8:30 p.m. and the second from 9:30 p.m. to 4:30 a.m. The technical tasks for this song were getting more and more complicated, and ultimately Prince realized he had to continue having a team of two engineers (very often McCreary and Leonard) running the sessions together. "I triggered synths off of hi-hats and stuff like that," Leonard told author Jake Brown. "I remember gating stuff and triggering stuff. It was cool."[49]

Prince was starting to delegate parts to others, but only as long as they added to his vision. If not, he'd continue to do the parts himself. "He's the boss," according to Leonard. "But when he calls upon them for ideas they definitely come up with something. He'll give somebody parts of a song or cassettes to figure out parts."[50]

A rough mix was created of the day's work and two C-60 cassette tapes were made of the session.

WEDNESDAY, AUGUST 17, 1983*

"Computer Blue" (overdubs)
Sunset Sound, Studio 3 | 3:00 p.m.–1:00 a.m. (booked noon–open)
Producer: Prince | *Artist:* Prince | *Engineer:* Prince | *Assistant Engineers:*
"Peggy Mac" McCreary and David Leonard

When Prince and the Revolution came out in the early Eighties, you felt there was a change happening. You felt that with The Beatles. Someone will find that new thing, grab it, and that starts it. —Wendy Melvoin[51]

During this time, Prince was very open to influences and inspired by other artists. The cold isolation of "Computer Blue" can be traced to musicians like

Ultravox and Gary Numan. "All sorts of bands from that era, like the Cocteau Twins, were a big, big influence," explained singer Jill Jones. "Roxy Music, Gary Numan. He would listen to them, whether it be to study, to understand the rhythms. He would go to sleep listening to these records and you'd wake up to them."[52]

Listening to "Computer Blue," it is easy to hear Prince's interest in Gary Numan. In fact, Numan's style can be heard near the end of "Purple Rain," which can be directly attributed to the last thirty seconds of Numan's song "I Die You Die" (from his 1980 album *Telekon*). His impact can also be heard on earlier Prince tracks like "Let's Pretend We're Married." Numan's press releases often quote Prince's praise for him: "**There are still people trying to work out what a genius Gary Numan is.**"[53]

In 2009 Lisa Coleman and Wendy Melvoin described how they would find influences for Prince, both on purpose and accidentally. "We would hang out and play records for each other," offered Coleman. "Have you heard this thing and have you heard that?"

"It was fantastic," interrupted Melvoin. "Those were the days."

"And it was like as if you were in your college dorm or something . . .," observed Coleman.

Melvoin agreed: "We were in our college years for sure together."[54]

Three rounds of overdubs occurred during this session. From 3:00 p.m. to 6:00 p.m., from 7:00 p.m. to 9:00 p.m., and finally from 11:30 p.m. to 1:00 a.m. No mixdown was logged and no cassette tapes were made of today's recording, so it is likely Prince felt he wasn't finished and that work would continue the following day.

During the evening break, Prince probably went to see Peter Gabriel play at the Greek Theatre, where he heard David Tickle, who mixed the sound during the concert. Prince was impressed enough to hire him to do the same for the *Purple Rain* tour.

Eventually Gary Numan would return the compliment by recording a version of Prince's "U Got the Look." Prince would also sample Numan's "Remember I Was Vapour" (also from Telekon*) in his original 1988 version of "Rave Un2 the Joy Fantastic."*

On August 17, 1983, "Delirious" (backed with "Horny Toad") was released as a single, the third track from Prince's *1999* album. It would stay in the *Billboard* Top 100 for eighteen weeks, peaking at number 8 on October 29, 1983.

THURSDAY, AUGUST 18, 1983*

"Computer Blue" (string and vocal overdubs)
"Baby I'm a Star" (string overdubs)
"Purple Rain" (string and vocal overdubs)
Sunset Sound, Studio 3 | 3:00 p.m.–5:00 a.m. (booked noon–open)
Producer: Prince | *Artist:* Prince | *Engineer:* Prince | *Assistant Engineers:*
"Peggy Mac" McCreary and David Leonard

The question is always, "What needs to be here right now?" It's not about what's hittin'. What sound needs to be here at this moment? It's all about trust, and keeping the channel clear.—Prince[55]

From 3:00 p.m. to 6:00 p.m., Prince recorded additional spoken parts for the extended version of "Computer Blue." In one of them, commonly referred to as the "hallway speech" by Prince fans, Prince tells the story of a man who lived alone in a house and while escorting a woman to his bedroom, he named the hallways after emotions, including lust, fear, insecurity, hate, and pain. His vocal delivery is reminiscent of the spoken-word section of Ebn-Ozn's July 1983 song "AEIOU sometimes Y." The Ebn-Ozn track was getting airplay on MTV and was being hyped as the first song to be completely recorded on a computer, which might have grabbed Prince's attention. Again, he seemed to be pulling influences from anywhere he could, no matter how minor, to create a new sound.

He recruited Bobby Z to scream, "It's hell, Computer Blue!" to the track. Prince also recorded other members of the Revolution to embellish that scream; they can be heard on the opposite track when listening on headphones. Prince mapped out multiple pages of dialogue for members of the band to recite and chant, most of which was not used in the final album version, including sections of Melvoin and Coleman coldly castigating the computer for being narrow-minded and chauvinistic and for "falling in love too fast, in heat too soon."[56]

The most famous of today's vocal overdubs involved the opening dialogue between Melvoin and Coleman regarding the temperature of the water:

Lisa: "Wendy?"
Wendy: "Yes, Lisa."
Lisa: "Is the water warm enough?"

Wendy: "Yes, Lisa."
Lisa: "Shall we begin?"
Wendy: "Yes, Lisa."[57]

Coleman described how innocently it took place: "Prince handed us a piece of paper and said, 'Will you guys go out there and say this?' I didn't think twice. Honestly, I hate to say that it doesn't mean anything. Is it tea? Is it a bathtub? Whatever you want to think. It was just us being cheeky."[58]

"We didn't even think it was this weird psychosexual lesbian thing," insisted Melvoin. "I had no idea."[59]

The recording took only a few minutes, but the effect created years of confusion among fans, largely because of speculation about (and eventual confirmation of) the long-term relationship between Melvoin and Coleman.

"[Our relationship] was never meant to be a secret," emphasized Coleman in 2009. "We were just who we were. She was my girlfriend, and that lasted until just about six years ago. We were married for 20 years. I mean, not married, but together."[60]

In the April 2009 issue of *Out* magazine, Melvoin and Coleman gave a frank interview regarding this topic.

Wendy: "[Prince] was incredibly conscious of it. Look at the way he looked during *Dirty Mind* and *Controversy* and *1999*. He was so androgynous. He didn't care if you were [paraphrasing Prince's 'Uptown' lyric] 'black, white, straight, gay, Puerto Rican, just a freakin'.'" That guy wanted fans. So any way he could get them—and a more interesting way he could do it—appealed to him. The Sly and the Family Stone mentality, that whole black/white/freaky thing on stage appealed to him."

Lisa: "I'll give you an example. We had a photo shoot for the *Purple Rain* poster. We were all in our different positions and he at one point walked over to me and Wendy and lifted my arm up and put my hand around Wendy's waist and said, 'There.' And that is the poster. That's how precise he was about how he wanted the image of the band to be. He wanted it to be way more obvious. We weren't just the two girls in the band. We were the gay girls in the band. It was very calculated."[61]

From 6:30 p.m. until 2:30 a.m., string overdubs were completed for "Baby I'm a Star" and "Computer Blue" as well as a few additional parts of "Purple Rain." Prince used the same performers from earlier in the week: Novi Novog, Suzie Katayama, and David Coleman. "You can't get around nepotism in Hollywood, man!" laughs Coleman. "I was very lucky."

"Prince was all smiles. If we made a mistake, he'd make a face. There was something about Prince. He'd make you laugh. 'Oh that was a little weird,' and he'd twitch and we'd just laugh. He was a funny man when I worked for him. He moved so fast. It was like doing three songs in one day. Prince was someone who it just seemed to come right out and it was like a printing press."

"When we were recording we got to experiment, and a lot of times he'd take the first take," explained Novog, "even though there may be mistakes. He'd say, 'No'; he wants the feeling. There was something about the first emotion that he wanted or your first impression of the song that he wanted. Because in that era, everybody was kind of doing the sterile music where you'd do twenty takes of one thing, and he didn't work like that."[62]

Prince and Lisa Coleman are listed on the album as arranging the strings, but much of it was done once again by Coleman herself with Prince observing.

The session ended after two and a half hours of mixing the songs. "He loved to just grab the EQ knobs and just add some excitement here and there, and he never worried about what he was doing," observed Susan Rogers.[63] The methods changed a bit during *Purple Rain*, but years later Prince acknowledged to *Keyboard* magazine how little care he put into mixing some of his biggest hits from this era: **"My mixes have always been terrible. All of them. Listen to anything. '1999,' 'Darling Nikki,' 'Purple Rain.' They're all that way."**[64]

A single cassette was created for Prince to review and evaluate.

FRIDAY, AUGUST 19, 1983*

"Computer Blue" (overdubs)
Sunset Sound, Studio 3 | 3:00 p.m.–4:00 a.m. (booked noon–open)
Producer: Prince | *Artist:* Prince | *Engineer:* Prince | *Assistant Engineers:* "Peggy Mac" McCreary and David Leonard

> *When I write an arrangement, I always picture a blind person listening to the song. And I choose chords and sounds and percussion instruments, which would help clarify the feel of the song to a blind person. . . . But with everything I do, I try to keep that blind person in mind.* —Prince[65]

Apparently Prince wasn't completely happy with the version of "Computer Blue" from the previous day, and now that he had a total of forty-eight tracks to fill, he continued with the overdubs. From 3:30 p.m. to 6:30 p.m. and from 11:30 p.m. to 4:00 a.m., Prince made additional changes to the song.

It is unclear what happened during the five-hour gap in recording, but it is likely that he attended either a concert or a meeting for the upcoming movie.

A single cassette was made at the end of the session.

SATURDAY, AUGUST 20, 1983

Venue: Beverly Theatre (Beverly Hills, California)

> *James Brown played a big influence in my style. When I was about ten years old, my stepdad put me on stage with him, and I danced a little bit until the bodyguard took me off. The reason I liked James Brown so much is that, on my way out, I saw some of the finest dancing girls I ever seen in my life. And I think, in that respect, he influenced me by his control over his group.* —Prince[66]

Prince took the night off to attend a concert that featured B.B. King and James Brown. During Brown's performance, Michael Jackson was invited onstage to perform "It's a Man's Man's Man's World." The band started playing "There Was a Time," and very quickly Jackson told Brown that Prince was in the audience; Brown called him up, asking him to jam with the two of them. One of Prince's bodyguards, Chick Huntsberry, carried him up to the stage. Prince hugged Brown and borrowed a guitar from the band. After a quick jam, a few dance moves (including Prince's James Brown–influenced routine with the microphone, which Brown was unfortunately too busy to witness), and a brief attempt to get the band and crowd to follow his lead, Prince left without a good-bye to the Godfather of Soul, falling into the audience as he attempted to lean over the crowd using a prop light post that wasn't securely fastened to the stage. "Prince played some guitar but I think he was a little nervous," Brown wrote in his 1986 autobiography. "Michael fit into my thing a little better since he had been studying me for years. But later Prince studied and he got into it real good. When I was in California later, he came to a show and lay on the floor backstage and watched my feet. Afterward, he asked me if I had roller-skates on my shoes."[67]

Only James Brown had the power to unite Prince and Michael Jackson in concert, and it is a shame that nothing came of the three of them onstage together.

Jackson and Prince shared a common interest in James Brown, but they also shared a mutual respect for each other. Jackson had attended Prince's March 31, 1983, show in Long Beach, and Prince had grown up a fan of the Jackson 5. They met up several times at various studios and soundstages and were apparently even competitive while playing ping-pong against each other at Sunset Sound. Unfortunately, they never worked together in the studio. Quincy Jones invited Prince to participate on "We Are the World" (which was written by Jackson and Lionel Richie) in 1985, but Prince declined. Jackson also wanted to record a duet with Prince for his 1987 track "Bad" but was turned down again. Years later, Prince explained to Chris Rock why he decided against teaming up on that track: **"The first line in that song was 'Your butt is mine.' Now I'm sayin' . . . who is saying that to whom? 'Cause you sure ain't saying that to me, and I sure ain't sayin' that to you. So right there we got a problem."** [68]

Although Prince made light of the situation, there seemed to be a more obvious reason: Prince wasn't comfortable when he wasn't in control. This is why he chose to leave the stage at the Beverly Theatre. "We had no idea that he was going to be called up, so it's not like he was prepared for the stage, even though he looked like he was," remembered Jill Jones, who, along with Bobby Z, attended the show with Prince. "It was very, very choreographed and structured how [James Brown] wanted to be, and [Prince] just kind of choked in a really weird way."[69]

The media often played up the rivalry between Prince and Michael Jackson, claiming that Prince's main objective was to overtake Jackson, but those closest to Prince had a slightly different outlook. "Michael wasn't the biggest priority to kill—it was everybody," Wendy Melvoin explained to author Alan Light. According to Lisa Coleman, "It was Prince against the world."[70]

Status: When the James Brown show was released on DVD (as *James Brown with B.B. King—Live at The Beverly Theatre 1983*), Prince was conspicuously absent, probably because he didn't feel confident enough about his performance and refused to give his permission. Michael Jackson's appearance was included and was promoted on the cover.

SUNDAY, AUGUST 21, 1983*

"Computer Blue" (overdubs)
Sunset Sound, Studio 3 | 1:00 p.m.–4:30 a.m. (booked noon–open)
Producer: Prince | *Artist:* Prince | *Engineer:* Prince | *Assistant Engineers:* "Peggy Mac" McCreary and David Leonard

This was a great song. It just took forever.—Peggy McCreary

Prince went back into the environment he could control and worked to tame "Computer Blue," a song that was an anomaly for Prince. He was creating something special with this song, and continued to put more and more effort into crafting the sound, but it was taking much longer than expected. Working on a track over the course of multiple days was something he didn't often do, and this may have been the most time he'd ever spent on an individual song. Over the course of his career, some of his engineers felt Prince seemed more concerned about the creation of the song than he did about "producing" it after the music was put on tape. "My vibe about Prince is he's so 'song-centric,'" explains David Knight, who would later be his engineer. "You have to remember that a lot of his stuff was crafted in six hours. The time that he first started writing the song to the rough mix and it never got looked at again, that's not production, that's not a lot of crafting, that's writing the song and capturing these elements the way I want to and not a lot of second-guessing. It's him capturing an essence and getting it onto tape and turning the page on the next one."

Although Prince was working on creating a new sound, his solo in one of the extended versions of "Computer Blue" sounds similar to the solo in the extended version of the Vanity 6 song "Drive Me Wild," specifically around 4:40 and 5:01. **"They don't *all* sound different. There's a couple times I copied myself,"** admitted Prince in a 1986 interview with WHYT DJ the Electrifying Mojo. **"I try not to do that too much. If I do, then it's usually someone around, Wendy or Lisa, who says, 'Hey, man, I've heard that. Put it away.' And it goes away."**[71]

Almost fourteen hours of overdubbing went into today's session. At the end, a single cassette was made of the song. Prince then took a one-week break from recording at Sunset Sound. It is possible he went back to Minneapolis to record additional tracks and supervise some of the rehearsals for the Time. It is also likely that he attended Dez Dickerson's solo debut at First Avenue on August 28.

MONDAY, AUGUST 29, 1983*

"Computer Blue" (overdubs)
Sunset Sound, Studio 3 | 5:30 p.m.–7:30 a.m. (booked 3:00 p.m.–open)
Producer: Prince | *Artist:* Prince | *Engineer:* Prince | *Assistant Engineers:* "Peggy Mac" McCreary and David Leonard

When you sit down to write something, there should be no guidelines. The main idea is not supposed to be, "How many different ways can we sell it?" That's so far away from the true spirit of what music is. Music starts free, with just a spark of inspiration. —Prince[72]

Today's session was delayed from 3:00 p.m. until 5:30 p.m., when Prince arrived back in Los Angeles after his trip to Minneapolis. After eight and a half hours of additional overdubs and mixing, the session ended the following morning.

An expensive meal from Gourmet Faire was brought in, so it is likely that various people connected to the film/record were in attendance, possibly to listen to the most recent versions of the songs for the soundtrack and to discuss plans for the film. As the studio got busier, Peggy McCreary, who had been recording with Prince since 1981, missed the days when it was just the two of them in the studio:

> He didn't have to be "anybody" with me. We didn't talk a lot, but sometimes he'd talk about his past and about his family, which wasn't a happy subject for him. He wasn't a talker, but he probably talked to me more than he did to most people. If you ask him questions . . . he'd talk. Being with someone for over five years, day and night, you'd find out little tidbits, little windows into who they were. And also, his manager told me some stuff which shed some light into who he was. About how he grew up and didn't have a place to live and how by the time he was twelve he was out on the street, and how he lived in André's [Cymone] basement and his dad would come by every week or so and bring him cake, and that was the kind of food that he ate. It was kind of rough. He was pretty much abandoned until he made it, and then of course everyone showed back up.

Albert Magnoli submitted the first draft of his script today. For the first time, it was officially listed as Purple Rain.

TUESDAY, AUGUST 30, 1983*

"Computer Blue" (overdubs)
Sunset Sound, Studio 3 | 3:30 p.m.–1:15 a.m.
Producer: Prince | *Artist:* Prince | *Engineer:* Prince | *Assistant Engineers:* "Peggy Mac" McCreary and David Leonard

A lot of Prince songs, the first time you hear them you go, "What the heck did I just hear?" Prince's songs were more complex than the average pop songs.—Matt Fink[73]

From 3:30 p.m. until midnight, Prince continued to add overdubs to "Computer Blue." At the end of the session, a quick mix was completed and five cassette copies were created. For Prince to have generated so many cassettes likely means that they were passed to executives at the record company and to those involved with creating—and possibly financing—the movie.

WEDNESDAY, AUGUST 31, 1983*

"Computer Blue" (overdubs)
"I Would Die 4 U" (overdubs)
Sunset Sound, Studio 3 | 10:30 p.m.–1:30 a.m. (booked 10:00 a.m.–open)
Producer: Prince | *Artist:* Prince | *Engineer:* Prince | *Assistant Engineer:* "Peggy Mac" McCreary

Even if the music was coming through me, I was still listening to it as an admirer of the sound, so whatever I heard, be it a lyric or a melody line or a beat or whatever, sometimes just the bassline, I paid attention to it, and I would let that start the song first. Once you get that main thing down, then that's the leader and that's going to tell you what the next instrument is supposed to be.—Prince[74]

The start time of this session was moved from 10:00 a.m. to 7:00 p.m., and it began with a three-hour meeting. This was probably another gathering of executives involved in the upcoming film, which may have turned into a chance to discuss the recently delivered script and reveal all the songs that Prince had been recording. Once the meeting ended, Prince spent three hours adding various overdubs to "I Would Die 4 U."

At the end of the session, one cassette was created for Prince to review.

When August ended, "Computer Blue" was finally complete. Prince could continue working on other tracks, including what many believe are some of the most beautiful songs on the *Purple Rain* album. The unfortunate side effect of squeezing so many strong songs onto the soundtrack was that "Computer Blue" would be edited several times, losing all the incredible layers that were recorded over the last two weeks.

SEPTEMBER 1983

September found the movie in a slight state of chaos. Vanity's abrupt exit had compounded the work that needed to be done to prepare for the movie. Now that the script was finished, one of Albert Magnoli's major tasks was casting the female lead role, as he explains: "Vanity's presence is so freaking strong, she can make the Red Sea part. She was a force of nature." Magnoli recalled one encounter with her at First Avenue in mid-August after she had left the project: "I'm sitting up there in the mezzanine area and I feel this quickening in there. Seconds later, someone comes up to me and says, 'Vanity just came in.' I'm not exaggerating. She has this thing, and she comes in with painted-on clothing, second skin, leather, latex, I don't know what it is, but she looks fantastic, and what surprised me is the attitude, she's tough. So looking for that, I couldn't find it."

Vanity's replacement would have to fill her role in the movie as well as the lead position in Vanity 6. Until then, both the film and the group were in flux.

The Time continued to have problems as well. Jimmy Jam, Terry Lewis, and Monte Moir had been replaced, and the new band was currently rehearsing for the movie and for a potential test show in October. Unfortunately, Morris Day was growing more frustrated at Prince's control over what Day considered his band. Once a powerful performing machine, the band was now struggling just to stay together, and there was resentment overflowing from within the group. "What was going on is, like the way Vanity had one foot out the door, the Time had one foot out the door during the making of *Purple Rain*; so there was a rivalry," according to Magnoli. "The competition between the bands was very real when I got there."

Jesse Johnson was put in the position of getting the Time into shape for the show and the movie. "I rehearsed with the band, but it wasn't the same. Even when Morris was at the rehearsals in body, his heart wasn't in it," he explained. "I knew him long enough that I could tell."[1] When Day was involved in the rehearsals, he often acted completely disconnected from the new members, and instead of learning their names he'd say things like, "Whoever's taking Monte's place, play something."

Paul Peterson, the keyboard player who had replaced Monte Moir, noted how difficult it was to be one of the new guys in a very well-rehearsed band: "When you're in the middle of it, you're trying to do your best to hang on because things are moving so quickly. And I was right in the middle of it, so it meant rehearsal six days a week, 10 hours a day—especially during that time. [Prince] was meticulous and wanted things perfect and right, and the people that he had hired underneath him—Jesse Johnson being the person for that time—he cracked the whip hard on us."[2]

"The attitude of the entire time was you do this, you do this, you do this or you're fired," remarks Mark Cardenas, who had replaced Jimmy Jam. "I don't know if they're just fucking with us as new guys or what. And of course, as the new guys we heard countless stories about when they were new and what they had to do when they were just getting started and all the shit they put up with Prince which gave them license to safely treat us like shit too."

"Prince had promised Morris a certain amount of money when they came off the [1999] tour," revealed Pepé Willie, a longtime friend of both Day and Prince. "And when they came off the tour, it seems like Morris had owed Prince a substantial amount of capital which exceeded the amount which he was supposed to have gotten when he got off the tour in the first place. He felt that Prince had set him up. . . . [S]o it was coming for a while. And I guess that Prince wanted payback for helping Morris, and Morris was going, like, 'Hey man, how long do I have to pay you back? I know I have paid you back already in triple, so how much more do you want from me?'"[3]

Although Prince was in control of the group behind the scenes, the public still thought Day was the leader of the band. The Time had been created as a favor to Day, but it was never an equal partnership; Prince had proven that when he fired two of the band's members. With the control taken completely out of his hands, Day saw his time with the group running out. "The band had changed and it wasn't what it used to be for me," concluded Day. "I could do anything with the old band. I could forget half the lyrics on stage and these guys would know exactly what to do. We had the kind of rapport that always felt good. It always felt right when we hit the stage, no matter what the circumstances."[4] But regardless of Day's opinion of the band, Jesse Johnson worked hard to make sure the Time was tight and ready. Cardenas recalls how much focus Johnson drilled into the band: "It was ridiculous how well we knew the music. We knew them so well by the time we actually played them it was almost impossible to screw up." Johnson even brought in Jimmy Jam to watch the new band rehearse, and Jam approved, supposedly saying to Johnson that they were "stompin'."[5]

But no matter how good the Time got, the hierarchy was always apparent. "On one side of the warehouse was Prince's huge stage," recalled Cardenas. "On the other side was the Time's little club set up. It was a constant reminder of how big Prince was and how little the Time were."[6]

While much of this was going on in Minneapolis, Prince flew to Los Angeles to concentrate on his music.

THURSDAY, SEPTEMBER 1, 1983*

"I Would Die 4 U" (guitar overdubs)
"Baby I'm a Star" (guitar overdubs)
Sunset Sound, Studio 3 | 1:00 p.m.–12:45 a.m. (booked 1:00 p.m.–open)
Producer: Prince | Artist: Prince | Engineer: Prince | Assistant Engineer: "Peggy Mac" McCreary (David Leonard is not listed but was probably present)
Additional 24-track machine (MM1200) billed on this date.

I don't feel sexy when I play guitar—I feel angry. —Prince[7]

These two tracks were connected when they were originally taped during the August 3 benefit show. Prince decided he liked how they functioned together, so he maintained their order and flow for the *Purple Rain* movie and soundtrack album. Because of the way the concert was recorded, the tracks weren't completely clean. The drum machine was isolated, but the cymbals and some other instruments would occasionally leak on the open mics and additional work on all the tracks was necessary. "Everything was sweetened," explained Susan Rogers. "No major reconstructions, just shortening because he played them longer onstage and re-singing the lead vocals to get that leakage off."[8]

The process of "sweetening" means that mistakes made during the performance were either cleaned up by rerecording that section or, sometimes, covered up in the mix by adjusting the audio levels or accentuating another instrument. Although the original performance was recorded on 24-track tape, Prince continued to use the 48-track setup he'd begun in mid-August to work on these songs.

The session started out with eight hours of guitar overdubs. During the August 3 concert, Prince's guitar on "Baby I'm a Star" was supposedly out of tune, so he had to make overdubs based on that same slightly out-of-tune instrument. As usual, Prince played his guitar while standing next to the mixing board, listening to it on headphones with a microphone in front of the speaker in the studio. This was a common practice when he was recording on his own.

After dinner, another two hours and forty-five minutes of overdubs were put to tape. A single cassette copy of the session was created for Prince to review.

FRIDAY, SEPTEMBER 2, 1983*

"**I Would Die 4 U**" (various overdubs including vocals)
"**Baby I'm a Star**" (various overdubs including vocals, presumed)
Sunset Sound, Studio 3 | 4:00 p.m.–2:30 a.m. (booked noon–open)
Producer: Prince | *Artist:* Prince | *Engineer:* Prince | *Assistant Engineer:*
   "Peggy Mac" McCreary (David Leonard is not listed but was probably present)
Additional 24-track machine (MM1200) billed on this date.

> *[Engineers] drive me crazy. It's because they're so technical. Everything just got so esoteric. . . . "We've got to do this a certain way," when you're ready to play. The engineer I use and give credit to on the album, she sets everything up for me, most of the time before I come in. And then I just do what I have to do and split. She puts things together afterward.*—Prince[9]

No matter what time the session was scheduled to begin, the engineer (or assistant engineer, depending on the credit being given) would show up thirty minutes early to make sure the studio was ready to go when Prince arrived. He wasn't fond of waiting for anything, especially for something technical.

Today's session was originally slated for noon, but Prince rescheduled it for 3:00 p.m. and didn't show up until 5:30, leaving engineer Peggy McCreary waiting:

> What would happen is we would leave at 4 or 5 in the morning and he would call with an 11 a.m. or a 2 p.m. start and he would sleep, but I had to get there early to set up, so he'd be rested and I'd be there pumped up on coffee, and he wouldn't show up and I would be waiting. I said to him that "this is killing me" and he would just say, "Well I didn't wake up," and everyone was afraid to wake him up. He'd say, "I tell them to wake me up, but they don't." I'm like, "Right, whatever." So he gave me his number straight into his room or wherever he was and he said just call me when you're here. So that worked out pretty well, but that took quite a few years and I was just fried. He didn't want anyone else there, and he'd keep me waiting and he would come in with an attitude because he kept me waiting so long.

Prince did nine hours of additional overdubs on these tracks, including replacing much of his own lead and background vocals, but they always required a little more effort to match the energy of the live performance. Because the song was still incomplete, Prince didn't work on a mix or make a cassette copy at the end of the session.

The phrase "We are all a star" in "Baby I'm a Star" probably comes from Sly & the Family Stone's "Everybody Is a Star," which had been covered by Prince's first band, Grand Central. The underlying theme is that everyone is a star and we're all important and serve a purpose.

SATURDAY, SEPTEMBER 3, 1983*

"I Would Die 4 U" (overdubs and mix)
"Baby I'm a Star" (overdubs and mix)
Sunset Sound, Studio 3 | 1:30 p.m.–5:00 a.m. (booked 1:00 p.m.–open)
Producer: Prince | *Artist:* Prince | *Engineer:* Prince | *Assistant Engineer:* "Peggy Mac" McCreary
Additional 24-track machine (MM1200) billed on this date.

> *He'll wear you out. Prince'll wring your soul out. He spits out two singles a day and mixes them.*—David Z[10]

Prince continued his overdubbing from the previous day. After three and a half hours he created a mixdown of "I Would Die 4 U" and "Baby I'm a Star." Often his mixes were done very quickly because of the prep work that took place along the way. Susan Rogers explained the process:

> While he was playing, I would be finessing the sound and just getting it . . . because I knew that he wanted to print it to half-inch when we were done, so I would be cleaning things up and sort of getting sound on things as the song was developing. So usually when we were done overdubbing, it was in good shape. We would print it and call it "rough mix," unless we had the energy and he wanted to go ahead and take the time to tweak it the final degree and call it the "master," and then we'd mix it and that would be it. It would be mixed. So it pretty much was mixed as we went along.[11]

As the *Purple Rain* movie moved closer to becoming a reality, Prince probably realized the importance of making these tracks as perfect as possible. During today's session, he decided to spend six hours mixing the two tracks, and once he was happy with the mixes he spent another five hours editing them. Instead of making them shorter overall, the combined songs were extended by an extra minute beyond the original live versions.

At this point in the process, there were still an additional sixteen measures in "I Would Die 4 U" that would ultimately be deleted. Also, "Baby I'm a Star" still contained Prince's spoken intro to the song from the benefit concert: "There's a party in here tonight, somebody clap your hands, come on, everybody rock the house . . . do it."

Two cassette copies were made of the session.

SUNDAY, SEPTEMBER 4, 1983*

"Baby I'm a Star" (vocal overdubs)
Sunset Sound, Studio 3 | 1:30 p.m.–5:00 a.m. (booked 1:00 p.m.–open)
Producer: Prince | *Artist:* Prince | *Engineer:* Prince | *Assistant Engineer:* "Peggy Mac" McCreary
Additional 24-track machine (MM1200) billed on this date.

> *My music wants to do what it wants to do, and I just want to get out of its way.*—Prince[12]

Ten hours of additional vocal work were done in this session. Although it is unclear what was overdubbed, this is probably when the backward message added to the beginning of "Baby I'm a Star" was recorded. This process consists of recording a sound (in this case a voice) on a tape and then playing the tape in reverse—or, more accurately, loading it on to the tape machine backward. A half-inch tape was prepared for this, and Lisa Coleman recorded the following: "So, like, fuck them man. What do they know? All their taste is in their mouth. Really, what the fuck do they know? Come on, baby, let's go . . . crazy!"

This was added to the previous day's mix. It can be heard at 0:17 and again at 4:03 on the released track.

Although what was done during this session has been referred to as "backward masking," technically that phrase refers to a hidden message on an audio recording that is only revealed when played backward. There was no effort to bury today's recording in the mix, so it is not actually backward masking.

MONDAY, SEPTEMBER 5, 1983*

"Baby I'm a Star" (vocal and synth overdubs)
Sunset Sound, Studio 3 | 1:00 p.m.–12:30 a.m. (booked 1:00 p.m.–open)
Producer: Prince | *Artist:* Prince | *Engineer:* Prince | *Assistant Engineer:*
   "Peggy Mac" McCreary

> *Most people in L.A. will get a band, cut all their tracks one*
> *week, and for the next few months do overdubs and vocals.*
> *Then they'll sit down for a month and mix the whole record.*
> *Prince does not do things that way. . . . A lot of times he doesn't*
> *leave until it's done, even if it takes a couple of days.*—Peggy
> McCreary[13]

Prince was apparently still convinced that "Baby I'm a Star" wasn't complete and spent the first seven and a half hours working on replacing his vocals. One of the most recognizable changes was when Prince sang, "Ain't nothing wrong with your ears,"[14] replacing his humorous "Ain't nothing wrong with your big ol' ears."[15] Prince must have felt the phrase wasn't appropriate for the album and the movie, but it found its way back into the live performance of the track as soon as he started touring.

After a dinner break he added another two hours of synth overdubs to replace various parts of the performances of Lisa Coleman and Matt Fink. "I think that he thought he could do it the best," explains Fink, "and that musically he felt like he could get what he wanted because he could do it himself. He would always know what he would like because he knew he could do it. I'd say it was the control aspect. Having complete control. That was one thing Prince always had to have. I know that."

Prince has gone on record saying that being called a "**control freak is a compliment.**"[16] He explained what he credited as the origins of this behavior: "**That whole thing came from my early days, when I was working with a lot of people who weren't exactly designed for their jobs. . . . I had to do a lot, and I had to have control, because a lot of them didn't know exactly what was needed.**"[17]

Childhood best friend and former bandmate André Cymone felt Prince's apparent need to control every situation had much deeper roots: "Prince's dad was a very, very big influence. A lot of the work ethic was instilled by some of the things that he said. 'If you want to be the best, you've got to play. You've got to practice. And when other guys are running around and out on the streets and blah, blah, blah, blah, and getting these girls pregnant and blah, blah, blah . . . you guys need to be practicing.' I remembered all that stuff and I really took that stuff to heart."[18]

"**My father was so hard on me,**" Prince recalled. "**I was never good enough. It was almost like the army when it came to music.**"[19]

Prince was almost always in control, but his first movie was scheduled to start shooting within a few weeks, and he would relinquish more control than he ever had in his entire career.

A single cassette was made of the song at this stage, and the session ended at the unusually early time (at least for Prince) of 12:30 a.m.

TUESDAY, SEPTEMBER 6, 1983*

"**Baby I'm a Star**" (overdubs)
Sunset Sound, Studio 3 | 1:00 p.m.–1:00 a.m. (booked 1:00 p.m.–open)
Producer: Prince | *Artist:* Prince | *Engineer:* Prince | *Assistant Engineer:*
"Peggy Mac" McCreary
Additional 24-track machine (MM1200) billed on this date.

I'll have a color or a line in mind, and I'll keep switching things around until I get what I'm hearing in my head. Then I'll try to bring to earth the color that wants to be with the first color. —Prince[20]

Performers like Michael Jackson took weeks in the studio getting the sound perfect for every track. For the most part, Prince was more immediate in finding his sound, and until this period he generally worked on the music quickly and moved on. "[Prince] taught us perfection is in spontaneity," explained Terry Lewis. "You just do it, and whatever it is, it's perfect! Create, and don't ponder what you created."[21]

But Prince was changing, and it was becoming more common for him to focus on a single song for days. He continued overdubbing parts on "Baby I'm a Star," still looking to replicate the sound he had in his head. It is very easy to imagine how an artist with that much commitment to perfection would want to eliminate any flaws in the music, especially considering that, for the most part, he wasn't a perfectionist at all. "[Prince] was not a perfectionist," explained Susan Rogers. "He wouldn't have had that output if he'd been a perfectionist. What he was was a virtuoso player and a genius with melody, a genius with rhythm, a genius at writing songs. It just poured out of him—he couldn't wait on perfection. The important thing was to have the sound serve the ideas, not the other way around."[22]

According to some of his engineers and bandmates, Prince could get lost in recording music and lose track of time. The people around him were essential for technical reasons, but Prince was very satisfied creating songs by himself. "You were a distraction. You were a necessary evil on a Prince session," reflects Prince's future engineer David Knight. "He needed people to run the console and get the tapes set up and so forth, but you were a necessary evil and you weren't a collaborative or a creative element in the recording of his album. I think if Prince could walk around in his studio with fifty instruments plugged in and ready to go at any point and he had an iPad and he could just go boom, record, this input on this track and mic it at this volume, I don't think he would work with anybody. I think he would work by himself."

In 2009 guitarist Wendy Melvoin shed some light on Prince's work ethic and focus: "He's a guy who doesn't question himself. Even if he fails, he doesn't think too much about it. He is one of the most committed people I've ever met."[23]

Two cassettes were made at the end of the session, but once again he wasn't satisfied.

WEDNESDAY, SEPTEMBER 7, 1983*

"Baby I'm a Star" (vocal overdubs)
Untitled song (basic tracking for "I Am Fine")
Sunset Sound, Studio 3 | 1:00 p.m.–12:30 a.m. (booked 1:30 p.m.–open)
Producer: Prince | *Artist:* Prince | *Engineer:* Prince | *Assistant Engineer:*
"Peggy Mac" McCreary
Additional 24-track machine (MM1200) billed on this date.

> *I just feel I've been extremely lucky to have someone like Prince—himself personally—think that I was good.*—Lisa Coleman[24]

Prince continued working on "Baby I'm a Star." During this session Prince spent the first four hours replacing various vocals. After a dinner break at 6:30 p.m., additional vocals were added, some of which probably included background vocals from Wendy Melvoin, Jill Jones, and Lisa Coleman. Coleman recalled laying down some of the background vocals: "We were adding a couple of parts, and Jill Jones and I were at the mic singing the chorus parts, 'Staaaaaaaar Wooo!'And for some reason, we had an uncontrollable giggle attack. We tried to keep singing, but by the last set of choruses we were crying, fully hysterical. Prince was really annoyed and begged us to get it together on the talk back: 'Come on! STOP IT!' But we couldn't! I think you can hear the difference in the background vocals at the end. It's all Prince because Jill and I ran outside."[25]

"Lisa and I always screwed around," laughs Jones. "We did goof around a lot and sometimes he'd be in the mood for it and sometimes he wouldn't. We really enjoyed working together all the time. We always had a great connection."

Prince was beginning to trust Melvoin and Coleman more and relied on them in ways that exposed his feelings about what they added to his music. "It was just so wonderful," expressed Melvoin, "because we loved doing what we were doing so much and believed in it so much. It was just so wonderful that it was also being loved and being believed in."[26]

"[Wendy] came furthest of anyone I've ever seen at pulling Prince out of his shell," explained Susan Rogers. "He adored her and felt comfortable with her. Everyone else was more or less intimidated by him."[27]

At 10:00 p.m. Prince was struck by inspiration and took a break from "Baby I'm a Star" to focus on a new track. He began this brief detour—possibly with the help of Melvoin and Coleman—by laying down the sounds for a new, untitled song, but this was more experimental and didn't fit the mold of most of his music. In fact, it didn't even have a true beat or rhythm to it, but consisted of a collection of sound effects and vocal chants.

Prince stopped recording at 6:30 in the morning, and a single cassette was made of the session, which presumably included the latest version of "Baby I'm a Star" as well as the new track.

Status: Although it has been previously reported elsewhere that today's song was an instrumental called "I Am Five," it is almost certain to have actually been called "I Am Fine." It achieved fame when it was placed at the end of side one of *Purple Rain* as the coda to "Darling Nikki." Prince's vocals were played backward on this track, but a recording of them was played forward during the *Purple Rain* tour.

THURSDAY, SEPTEMBER 8, 1983*

"I Am Fine" (overdubs)
Sunset Sound, Studio 3 | 3:30 p.m.–1:00 a.m. (booked noon–open)
Producer: Prince | *Artist:* Prince | *Engineer:* Prince | *Assistant Engineer:* "Peggy Mac" McCreary and possibly David Leonard
Additional 24-track machine (MM1200) billed on this date.

> *There's nothing like the feeling after you've done something and play it back and you know that you'll never hear anything like it, and that they'll never figure it out.*—Prince[28]

It appears that there may have been instruments used on this, possibly including drums, but they were eventually removed in the mix, leaving only the sound effects and Prince's vocals, which were recorded over nine hours on this date. His vocals were multilayered to sound like a chanting choir, and sections were played in reverse to give it a haunting, almost spiritual vibe. When played forward, he said: "Hello. How are you? I'm fine 'cause I know that the Lord is coming soon. Coming, coming soon." Once again, it wasn't technically backward masking because usually that means it was masked or hidden on the track. This was a bold, in-your-face backward section that added to the track's ethereal feel.

Under the music bed he'd created, Prince layered some of the same elements from the *Authentic Sound Effects* library that he had placed at the end of the Vanity 6 track "Wet Dream," including wind, thunder, and rain.

In many ways this track was a companion piece for a two-minute song Prince had recorded in 1981 called "The Second Coming," which was played at the start of the show during his *Controversy* tour. This was a pattern he would duplicate when he played a variation of "I Am Fine" during the *Purple Rain* tour.

At the end of the session, "I Am Fine" remained isolated from anything else Prince had recorded. It was placed on the shelf and was not touched until later in the month.

FRIDAY, SEPTEMBER 9, 1983*

"Baby I'm a Star" (overdubs)
Sunset Sound, Studio 3 | 3:30 p.m.–2:00 a.m. (booked 4:00 p.m.–open)
Producer: Prince | *Artist:* Prince | *Engineer:* Prince | *Assistant Engineer:* David Leonard
Additional 24-track machine (MM1200) billed on this date.

In people's minds, it all boils down to "Is Prince getting too big for his britches?" I wish people would understand that I always thought I was bad. I wouldn't have got into the business if I didn't think I was bad.—Prince[29]

After the brief detour on "I Am Fine," Prince came back to "Baby I'm a Star" with fresh ears. It is unclear what he spent ten and a half hours overdubbing during this session, but although time was dwindling away, he continued to push for some form of perfection. Ultimately there were additional instruments that didn't make it into the final version, but this was fairly common during his career. Future Prince guitarist Miko Weaver reflected on this when discussing his time with Prince in the studio: "He'll put down tons of tracks, everything he can think of, then listen back and take what he wants. What ends up on the final mix may be just a fraction of what's on the tape."[30]

No tape copy was made at the end of the session, probably because Prince knew he still wasn't finished with the track.

SATURDAY, SEPTEMBER 10, 1983*

"**Baby I'm a Star**" (various overdubs)
Sunset Sound, Studio 3 | 1:00 p.m.–10:00 p.m. (booked noon–open)
Producer: Prince | *Artist:* Prince | *Engineer:* Prince | *Assistant Engineers:*
David Leonard and "Peggy Mac" McCreary
Additional 24-track machine (MM1200) billed on this date.

*Being in the studio is kind of a boring life. Anybody who's ever
worked [on live events] thinks studios are really boring.—*
Peggy McCreary[31]

It is almost impossible to imagine that being in the studio with Prince was "boring," but when the work gets repetitive it takes a toll. ("He'd work three days straight without sleeping," recalled guitarist Dez Dickerson.)[32] Even though Prince preferred to be alone, he relied on his engineers, specifically Peggy McCreary. "She did everything," recalls Sunset Sound assistant engineer Mike Kloster. "She would get everything down, get it to tape, record everything to tape, get it all coming back and when you sit down to mix, she would set everything up and he would kind of sit there, and she'd get everything set to a good level and say, 'Okay, this is . . . [points at mixing board], if you want more of this . . . [points at another part of the board].' She'd let him do a little final tweaking."

Because of the intricately detailed work needed, what Prince required from his engineers varied, so he had more than one on some sessions. Usually it was David Leonard and Peggy McCreary. McCreary remembers, "It's funny the way [Prince and I] worked; whatever Prince couldn't do, I did. He was great at balancing and he knew exactly what he wanted, and of course there were going to be certain limitations to that. He let David and I take over a lot more with the sessions. He liked to be alone in the studio, and there were times when you were yawning and so tired and he would just look at you and say, 'Just set me up and you can get out of here for a little while,' but he wouldn't let you go home."

"You just couldn't be weak in any way, shape or form," explains engineer and co-producer David Z. "Weakness was for sissies. He'd come down on you like a drill sergeant. He just wouldn't accept it. 'You're tired? Oh, I'll get someone else.' That's the way he wanted it. He once told me that you work better when you're tired, because you don't overthink it, and you just let it come out, so it's much better to work when you're tired."

Because Prince tried not to overthink in the studio, he had to rely on others to think for him when it came to the technical part of recording music, and according to many, this frustrated him. Even Alan Leeds, whose main experience with Prince was in the context of his live shows, witnessed how he treated his studio engineers: "He was unmerciful towards engineers and technicians. He had absolutely no patience with equipment and its limitations. If a tape had to be rewound, he'd pace for thirty seconds and then sarcastically ask an engineer, 'Aren't you ready yet?' While they frantically tried to repair a problem, he might stand over them with arms folded or begin pacing back and forth."[33]

For nine hours, Prince overdubbed additional keyboards and vocals to the track. When it came to vocals, Prince created a technique early on that he trained each of his engineers to follow. David Knight explains:

> He engineered the vocals himself so you had this great big boom mic that you would swing out over the console, it was a Neumann U 47 tube mic, and we would hang it right where he could sit at the desk, put some headphones on himself, and set up the tape machine. We'd show him the patch cord so when you move from track to track, track 16 through 22 that you can record on. He knew how to engage track 22 and move the track cord over, raise the fader, and run his own mix. And so that was when you, as an engineer, would hurry to the lounge get a quick snack and try to sleep and literally just get forty-five minutes or an hour nap, and next thing you know he'd come knocking at the door and say, 'I'm ready,' and you'd throw together a really quick fifteen- or twenty-minute rough mix."

The quick mix from this session was dubbed to a C-60 tape.

SUNDAY, SEPTEMBER 11, 1983*

"Baby I'm a Star" (overdubs)
Sunset Sound, Studio 3 | 2:00 p.m.–12:30 a.m. (booked noon–open)
Producer: Prince | *Artist:* Prince | *Engineer:* Prince | *Assistant Engineer:*
  David Leonard
Additional 24-track machine (MM1200) billed on this date.

*I hear everything in my mind but as I overdub synth parts, I
flip through the presets I like until I find the sound I want for
the next phrase. I listen to what tone goes with what color. I
usually don't change the sounds themselves.* —Prince[34]

Prince arrived late and worked for ten and a half hours on "Baby I'm a Star." Once again, it is difficult to know what Prince was overdubbing because the work had now been going on for eleven days. "When you work for Prince, he was very hands-on," noted David Leonard. "I mean you would just set stuff up and he would go and he has a vision, so he would just ask you to do stuff, and if you tried things, he would like it or not, but pretty much he was driving the boat."[35]

The session ended unusually early for Prince, and no mix was done.

MONDAY, SEPTEMBER 12, 1983*

"Baby I'm a Star" (mix)
"Electric Intercourse" (overdubs and mix)
Sunset Sound, Studio 3 | 6 p.m.–1:30 a.m. (booked 1:00 p.m.–open)
Producer: Prince | Artist: Prince | Engineer: Prince | Assistant Engineers: David Leonard, "Peggy Mac" McCreary and possibly Terry Christian
Additional 24-track machine (MM1200) billed on this date.

I can't leave a good idea unfinished. If I do that, it drives me nuts.—Prince[36]

The session was slated to start at 1:00 p.m. but was pushed until 6:00 p.m. Prince was ready to put a final touch to "Baby I'm a Star" and he spent much of the session mixing it. Overall, "Baby I'm a Star" was the track that demanded the most work, but because it would be the final song in the film, Prince likely wanted it to reflect what he heard in his head. "Prince was and is so dedicated to his craft," explained keyboard player Matt Fink. "More so than any other artist, from what I've read and what I know, Prince is probably at the top as far as the amount of hours that he puts into his craft."[37]

"Electric Intercourse" was also mixed on this date. It is likely that this was for the live recording from August 3 and not the studio version of the track. It is also unclear how much overdubbing, if any, was done with this mix, and there is no indication of any additional work on it during any other session at Sunset Sound, so Prince may have felt the track wasn't working for this project and put it aside until inspiration struck him.

David Leonard, who sat at the board during many of the mix sessions, commented on one of the many tools in Prince's belt when it came to getting the right sound: "During that period, mixing norms for Prince involved having the Lexicon reverb on the drums, which involved setting up a chamber and the Lexicon delay, those were the things that were always plugged up. Sunset Sound had three actual live chambers, echo rooms with mics in them, and they were set off the mixing board, so when you were mixing, you could run anything through them. So anything Prince mixed during that era out of Sunset Sound, which was all of *1999* and *Purple Rain*, generally had a chamber on it, for all those records."[38]

Close inspection reveals that many of the songs during this period (including "Baby I'm a Star" and "Purple Rain") contain a distinct reverb sound on the drums and often on the vocals as well.

The two mixes were recorded to a single cassette tape and the session was over at 1:30 a.m.

Status: The live version of "Electric Intercourse" (5:13) remains unreleased.

Terry Christian's name is written on this date, but it was scratched out, so he may not have been at the session. When asked whether he was there, Christian wasn't sure.

TUESDAY, SEPTEMBER 13, 1983*

"**Purple Rain**" (various overdubs)
Sunset Sound, Studio 3 | 1:00 p.m.–12:30 a.m. (booked 1 p.m.–open)
Producer: Prince | *Artist:* Prince | *Engineer:* Prince | *Assistant Engineer:*
"Peggy Mac" McCreary
Additional 24-track machine (MM1200) billed on this date.

> *I can hear my influence in "Purple Rain" in the harmony, but I don't know if that's coming from him or from Wendy and Lisa, because they've also assimilated some of the modality of the open tunings.* —Joni Mitchell[39]

The fact that Joni Mitchell could hear her influence in Prince's music reveals how much her music inspired him. He expanded on this during a 1985 MTV interview: "**Joni Mitchell . . . taught me a lot about color and sound, and to her, I'm very grateful.**"[40]

Now that he had wrapped up work on "Baby I'm a Star," Prince refocused on the title track. For the first time since mid-August, he began adding overdubs to the song. For seven hours he corrected mistakes he heard in the live mix, including rerecording parts of his own solo, which was probably overdubbed during this session. "Prince knows what he wants," explained McCreary. "Any leader of a band does."[41] Prince was ruthless with anything he felt could be made better, and like he'd done with "Baby I'm a Star" and other songs from the live August benefit show, he replaced parts recorded by the band members with his own. As usual, this was done to expedite the process. **"I have a communication problem sometimes when I'm trying to describe music [to others in the studio],"** he explained.[42]

He had trouble communicating about more than music. "He was very quiet and very shy when he first came into the studio," David Leonard explained to author Jake Brown. "When I first saw him, and then after *1999* and then *Purple Rain*, he was a little more comfortable with me. We never got to be friends, like he wouldn't call you up to go hang or anything. He wasn't very happy or friendly. I don't know . . . he was tortured. I guess that would be the word I'd use. It wasn't that he was unkind, it's just that he was very private and driven."[43]

"He's a real 'to himself' kind of person," agreed Morris Day.[44]

Mike Kloster concurs: "You could talk to him and he would sometimes just ignore you completely. And I don't know if he was just being rude or if it was because he was lost somewhere else. When he got to the studio, he worked the majority of the time there. He would just be working the whole time. He kept it that way and he knew it was a power play. He knew how that could help him and I think that's why he's very good. He's smart and he knows how to manipulate things to put him in the position of power."

That didn't necessarily translate to those outside his circle. "Some of our other clients would avoid booking time here if they knew he was here," explains Sunset Sound general manager Craig Hubler:

We don't know if they felt intimidated by his success, or jealousy, or he was so different that they felt uncomfortable coming here. Some clients used to come up to him in the courtyard, when he was playing basketball, and they complimented him on his work, and he would often just stare at them, not say a word, and just walk away. Sometimes he mumbled, "Thank you," and sometimes he mumbled something else. Most of the time people didn't understand what he said to them. Perhaps they were offended, thought he was rude, but knowing him as long as we have, it mostly was that he was shy. He didn't relate well to people he didn't know.

According to Matt Fink, part of this was planned: "He wanted to keep his whole mystique going. There were times when he just wanted to keep his mystique alive and not talk. He just didn't want to be talking to anybody. That way, it also saves you from over-exposure when you're not talking all the time."[45]

"[Prince] was more open than people gave him credit for," Fink added. "He's also not as introverted as people claim either, because when you get to know him and get to be friends with him, he opens up quite a bit. You're able to speak with him on a regular basis and he also had a very gregarious nature to him."[46]

The ironic thing is that while Prince didn't want everyone around him to know him that well, he expected them to be able to read his mind, which often made it difficult to know what he wanted. "I've seen him have trouble with a lot of people," said David Z. "He's not real communicative with everybody. He somehow just expects things to be perfect, and when they're not he can get mad."[47]

Prince's anger made even those as close as Wendy Melvoin nervous: "At times I was scared of Prince because he had anger stuff. When he was pissed, you wanted to avoid his eyes. His eyes could burn you. There were moments where you were scared of him as a human being; he looked like he was going to fucking kill somebody. And a lot of times that would be me."[48]

For the last four hours of the session, Prince had McCreary bounce the tracks, preparing for the mix the following day. Once this was finished, a cassette copy was made of the session and it wrapped up at 12:30 a.m.

WEDNESDAY, SEPTEMBER 14, 1983*

> **"Purple Rain"** (mix)
> Sunset Sound, Studio 3 | 3:00 p.m.–12:45 a.m. (booked 3:00 p.m.–open)
> *Producer:* Prince | *Artist:* Prince | *Engineer:* Prince | *Assistant Engineers:*
>   "Peggy Mac" McCreary and probably David Leonard
> *Additional 24-track machine (MM1200) billed on this date.*

> *He's truly a genius-level musician. Everything I saw him do as far as his time and playing on "Purple Rain," that was something. I think he always puts himself under musical pressure to make it as genius as he could.* —David Leonard[49]

Prince seemed committed to taking his music to the next level in his career. He wasn't looking for a small jump, but seemed to be wanting a change in direction—

one that built on the large sound of *1999* but added more of a rock element. Relying on his influences, he pushed for a new summit.

Albert Magnoli, who had been in Los Angeles finishing up the script, had various meetings with him during this time. Having spent time studying Prince and his music fairly closely, Magnoli had some insight into the evolution of his sound: "Prince was a hybrid of Sam Cooke, Little Richard, Jimi Hendrix, and James Brown. And not only that, what about Sly & the Family Stone? And what's the thing that's going to make you stand out? Keyboards? I doubt it. Guitar."

"Prince made most of the music for the *Purple Rain* album with the concept of the film in mind," explained Alan Leeds, "and visually, the idea of a rock icon with a guitar, posed with his legs open, has a lot more cinematic impact than a guy standing at a keyboard. So I think just the fact that this guy saw himself as a movie star making a musical, a rock musical, dictated that he made sure he gave himself the vehicles to do his guitar shtick, because it was the role, this is the imagery."[50]

Having the Time as the surrogate for Prince's funky side gave him freedom to head in a more rock-and-roll-oriented direction, which was ultimately good for the movie and good for continuing his crossover appeal.

The Revolution, including drummer Bobby Z, agreed: "'Purple Rain' is just one of those moments, as a band, that you live for. From the first moment of rehearsal, when I heard the strains of it on Prince's piano, to the last time we played it live at the Myth [on May 25, 2013, after Bobby had recovered from his heart attack]. It just really has something about it, the way it crescendos, the way it crashes, and the way the guitar solo takes you to a place where you just feel different about your life. No matter what, when you hear those opening chords of 'Purple Rain,' you just stop time somehow, and just listen."[51]

Prince worked on the mix of "Purple Rain" for almost ten hours, but no cassette copy was made of the evening's mix at the end of the session. A decision was made to complete it the next day.

Magnoli left the following day for Minneapolis to continue preproduction for the movie.

THURSDAY, SEPTEMBER 15, 1983*

"Purple Rain" (mix)
Untitled Song (basic tracking for "Irresistible Bitch")
Sunset Sound, Studio 3 | 1:00 p.m.–12:30 a.m. (booked noon–open)

Producer: Prince | *Artist:* Prince | *Engineer:* Prince | *Assistant Engineer:* "Peggy Mac" McCreary
Additional 24-track machine (MM1200) billed on this date.

Prince often started with drums in a recording situation. They were of paramount importance to him. He'd either come in and lay down a drum track on the machine or walk over to the drum kit and tape the lyrics to the tom-tom so he could sing the song in his head as he was playing. Mind you, he never had a click track going. All the music and arrangements would be worked out in his head and he just played the fills where he thought he'd need them.—Susan Rogers[52]

Prince spent seven and a half hours working on the final mix for "Purple Rain." The calm before the storm was ending and there were more and more distractions, with more obligations, meetings, and visits changing the vibe of his studio work. "There was something about the studio that was like a womb that wrapped around you for protection, and we had Studio 3 pretty much to ourselves," reflects McCreary. "We had a bathroom, we had a kitchen, and we would shut ourselves off from everything. We didn't need to go out and so since Studio 3 was a separate building, nobody came in—nobody dared walk back there—but then eventually people started showing up, the bodyguards etc. And it was different once the business started to grow and the distractions happened. I don't think he was as focused once he started to do the movies."[53]

Despite Prince's schedule and the addition of multiple people in the studio, he was singularly focused on this song. Unlike many musicians who collapse under pressure, Prince seemed to thrive on the challenge. His manager, Steve Fargnoli, explained Prince's mind-set during periods like this: "Where other guys go out and buy cars and buy drugs and buy jets, this kid is not interested in that. He's interested in things that satisfy his creative urge."[54]

And as always, Prince's creative urge involved sharing his newest music in some form.

Prince was working on *Purple Rain* the album and *Purple Rain* the movie, as well as keeping his name in the public eye. The year 1983 was the first since the release of his debut album that Warner Bros. hadn't issued a new collection of his songs, instead they continued to mine tracks from his *1999* album. It had now been a year since that album was unveiled, and a fourth single, "Let's Pretend We're Married," was chosen for release in mid-November. Prince, always looking to get his most recent music out to the public, decided to rerecord "Irresistible Bitch," a track he'd demoed in 1981.

The last ninety minutes were spent laying down the basic tracks for the song. It is unlikely that any vocals were recorded on this date.

"The thing is, you don't know if he already knew the song in his head or if it was unfolding before your eyes," remembers Kloster about sessions like this. "He would start with a drum machine and get a rhythm going, and then the bass."

Although it has been rumored that Morris Day played drums on "Irresistible Bitch," there is no confirmation of the accuracy of that claim. There are two reasons for this rumor. The first is based on Prince's comments in the booklet from his *Crystal Ball* CD. In it he remarked that "**[a] new style of playing derived from this recording style, and several songs were cut in the same vibe—the coolest being 'Irresistible Bitch.' Only Morris and Prince were present on this recording.**"[55] Prince was discussing the track "Cloreen Bacon Skin," but others have inferred that Morris played on "Irresistible Bitch" as well. The second reason is that "Irresistible Bitch" and "Cloreen Bacon Skin" basically share the same beat.

Day was probably in Minneapolis during this period, so it is highly unlikely that he participated during this session.

Status: "Irresistible Bitch" (4:13) was issued as a single on November 16, 1983, as the B-side for the 12-inch of "Let's Pretend We're Married." The original recording (4:32) from 1981 remains unreleased.

Although "Let's Pretend We're Married" was the fourth regular US single release from *1999*, following "1999," "Little Red Corvette," and "Delirious," it was the sixth overall: "D.M.S.R." was released as a promo in the UK and "Automatic" was released in Australia, both before "Let's Pretend We're Married."

FRIDAY, SEPTEMBER 16, 1983*

"**G-Spot**" (overdubs)
"**Irresistible Bitch**" (overdubs)
Sunset Sound, Studio 3 | 4:00 p.m.–4:00 a.m. (booked noon–open)
Producer: Prince | *Artist:* Prince | *Engineer:* Prince | *Assistant Engineer:* "Peggy Mac" McCreary
Additional 24-track machine (MM1200) billed on this date.

[Prince is] a very funky drummer. As a lead guitarist he does all that incredible soloing, but funk is his strong point and he's got that mastered on the drums.—Morris Day[56]

Long sessions were the norm for Prince, and for weeks he'd been burning the candle at both ends. On this date, "G-Spot" was taken out of the vault for some additional overdubbing. It had been recorded during the summer, and Prince was probably trying to decide which track would work best as the B-side for "Let's Pretend We're Married." Whichever song he picked, it would have to complement the highly sexual A-side, which contained the phrase "I sincerely want to fuck the taste out of your mouth."[57]

The choice was between a song that was months old or an even older song that he was rerecording this week. Not surprisingly, he chose his most recent work. Approximately ninety minutes of overdubbing may have been done on "G-Spot," but it was set aside. The track was originally considered for the *Purple Rain* project. "I think 'G-Spot' was supposed to be the shocker," recalled Bobby Z. "And I think that 'Darling Nikki' was written and it was a better one."[58]

After a short dinner break, Prince began finishing the revised version of "Irresistible Bitch." The next nine and a half hours were spent recording the elements for this very sparse song. Prince updated his original track with live drums, giving the new version a driving beat that the demo lacked. "The most impressive thing about working with Prince in the studio was his internal clock," said David Leonard. "It was amazing, his time. For instance, when he was playing drums, I've seen him do so without a click track, and stop playing and just keep singing and then come back in playing drums for a breakdown of a song, then be able to come in and pick up an instrument and time it exactly the same over an eight-bar break or something, that's pretty inhuman—with NO click track."[59]

It is likely that Prince added his vocals during this session, including a spoken section in which he repeated the phrase "I want you" and "irresistible bitch," which was placed in reverse around twenty-five seconds into the track and buried deep in the mix.

Written from a perspective similar to "When You Were Mine" (from 1981's *Dirty Mind*), "Irresistible Bitch" is a lover's lament about how weak he is for the woman he desires. Instead of the sexually aggressive character in "Let's Pretend We're Married," Prince takes a submissive role and allows the woman to dominate him, giving the A- and B-sides of the release a sort of sexual balance. This reversal of control is something Prince had mastered on many of his songs, including "Darling Nikki."

At the end of the session, quick mixes were done and two cassettes were created.

SATURDAY, SEPTEMBER 17, 1983*

> **"Irresistible Bitch"** (Wendy Melvoin and Lisa Coleman vocal overdubs)
> Sunset Sound, Studio 3 | 4:00 p.m.–10:30 p.m. (booked 4:00 p.m.–open)
> *Producer:* Prince | *Artist:* Prince | *Engineer:* Prince | *Assistant Engineers:*
> "Peggy Mac" McCreary and David Leonard
> *Additional 24-track machine (MM1200) billed on this date.*

> *We found each other intellectually and spiritually stimulating.*
> *. . . Both Lisa and I were so supportive of him intellectually*
> *and creatively that I think he responded to it. We were at-*
> *tracted to each other's brains.*—Wendy Melvoin[60]

Prince brought in Wendy Melvoin and Lisa Coleman to add to the background vocals on "Irresistible Bitch." "Lisa and I were really close friends with him," reflected Melvoin in 2012, "so when you are hanging out with your 'buddies' you are sharing music, sharing ideas, sharing philosophies and by that time he wasn't a huge, mega-superstar, so there was much more of a reasonable connection you could have on a daily basis, so we spent a lot of time together, the three of us. And we all had the same likes and dislikes and the humor was very similar and I think he also felt very safe with Lisa and I because we were a couple."[61]

According to those around him, Prince was developing a romantic interest in Wendy's twin sister, Susannah. As with many of his love interests, Prince would soon be including her in his music. Susannah's voice would be added to many of his songs and she would become a muse for a long string of projects.

After five and a half hours of vocal overdubs, a cassette was made and the short session ended at 10:30 p.m.

SUNDAY, SEPTEMBER 18, 1983*

> **"Irresistible Bitch"** (overdubs and mix)
> Unknown track (probably combining "Darling Nikki" with "I Am Fine")
> Sunset Sound, Studio 3 | 1:00 p.m.–10:00 p.m. (booked 1:00 p.m.–open)
> *Producer:* Prince | *Artist:* Prince | *Engineer:* Prince | *Assistant Engineers:*
> "Peggy Mac" McCreary and David Leonard

*I've always written real explicit and I've always said what
was on my mind. When I was young I used to read my
mother's dirty books that she had hidden in her bedroom.
That was after my father left. I always rambled through
her things and when I got sick of reading those, I'd write
my own. Sex was always most interesting to me because it
dealt with human life more than anything. The reproduc-
tive process and the fact that people lose their cool behind it
is enough to write about.*—Prince[62]

This was another short session, putting the finishing touches on "Irresistible
Bitch." After six hours of overdubs and a brief mix, the track was finished.
At 7:00 p.m., Prince began working on a new track, but there are no details
and no title. It is likely that he spent three hours working on parts of "Darling
Nikki" and possibly the section of the track that was recorded days earlier as
"I Am Fine."

A new tape was created, probably preparing to blend "I Am Fine" with the
recording of "Darling Nikki." If this was the case, it made sense for him to have
assembled them both to a fresh tape so the original recordings remained pris-
tine. Eventually, thirty-six seconds would be trimmed from "Darling Nikki,"
but it is unlikely that the edit occurred on this date.

One cassette was made of the day's work, and the session ended long before
midnight for the second night in a row.

MONDAY, SEPTEMBER 19, 1983*

"Darling Nikki" (edit)
Sunset Sound, Studio 3 | 1:00 p.m.–12:30 a.m. (booked 1:00 p.m.–open)
Producer: Prince | *Artist:* Prince | *Engineer:* Prince | *Assistant Engineers:*
  "Peggy Mac" McCreary and David Leonard

*Prince recorded ["Darling Nikki"] in his basement in Minne-
apolis. You can tell the sound of that one is pretty different.*—
David Leonard[63]

Work continued to blend the songs "Darling Nikki" and "I Am Fine" into one
track. Cassette and safety copies were created early in the session, probably

just in case this experiment didn't sound natural. At 4:30 p.m. Prince began overdubbing on the tracks and joined them, creating the combined version that ends the first side of the *Purple Rain* album. Like his 1981 song "Controversy," which had him reciting the Lord's Prayer while singing about human curiosity regarding sex, race, and drugs, "Darling Nikki" now contained a blend of the pure and the profane, something he was turning into an art, according to Susan Rogers: "It was really common for Prince if he went very far in one direction, that was strongly lust, passion based on just carnal lust, he would attempt to balance that statement with a more spiritual statement, and that place where that backwards gospel bit comes on the album is no accident. That's the redemption that follows his journey to hell in Nikki's castle."[64]

"This is his way of asking for forgiveness for having lust in his heart, and doing it in a way that was artistic," explained Rogers. "Great art comes from conflict, and he was conflicted, for sure."[65]

TUESDAY, SEPTEMBER 20, 1983*

"The Beautiful Ones" (basic tracking and mix)
Sunset Sound, Studio 3 | 12:30 p.m.–5:15 a.m. (booked noon–open)
Producer: Prince | *Artist:* Prince | *Engineer:* Prince | *Assistant Engineers:*
   "Peggy Mac" McCreary and David Leonard

> *Q: Why was the track "Electric Intercourse" suddenly deleted from the film and soundtrack?*
> *A: **Once "The Beautiful Ones" was completed, it was always the ballad of choice.***—Prince[66]

Prince was generally someone who recorded all night. It wasn't uncommon for the sun to be coming up as he left the studio, but for the last several evenings he'd ended the shift much earlier than usual. On this evening, that was going to change. For almost two weeks he seemed content not to record anything from scratch, choosing instead to tweak songs that were already written and recorded. For this session Prince was inspired by another muse, Susannah Melvoin, the twin sister of his guitarist. "He was with Susannah at that time," explains Peggy McCreary. "It was kind of written about her, but he had a lot of really gorgeous women around at that time, and so it was about her, but it was also referring to many of the women that were around him at that time. It was a very turbulent time and kind of a scary song, the way he screams, and it has a lot of passion and emotion in that song. I think that he was very much in love with her."

Prince's Minneapolis engineer, Susan Rogers, confirmed this:

> I was told by David Leonard, when he and I were in the control room in Prince's house and we were listening back to a tape of "Beautiful Ones," and David said, "I know who this is about. Susannah." And he told me the story of how Prince loved Wendy, she was a great guitar player and a great personality, but when he met her twin sister Susannah he was absolutely smitten. Prince started sending her flowers every single day. And he sent her flowers delivered to her house every day for almost a year. So I think that David very well could have been right, that "The Beautiful Ones" was written specifically for Susannah.[67]

"He was recording for *Purple Rain*, and he was falling in love with me," reflects Susannah Melvoin. "And I was in the studio constantly with him. This was so funny, but he would send flowers to the house where Wendy and I and Lisa lived every day for a year and a half. It wasn't a day that went by where there wasn't a huge thing of flowers. Now it started to look like a funeral home because there was no way to keep up with the amount of flowers. There'd be dead ones, there'd be live ones, there'd be pretty ones, there'd be ugly ones and it was just, 'Where are we going to put all this stuff?'"

Susannah explained her role in this to writer Matt Thorne: "Some people say I was his muse, and I don't know if that's what it was, but I can say I did inspire a certain kind of writing. There was a part of him that wanted to express himself in a deeper way, and I think our relationship was an opportunity for him to do that at the time. So if that's what being a muse is, that's what it was. I think Wendy and Lisa had the same effect."[68]

Prince himself disagrees with everyone's assessment regarding the inspiration:

> **If they look at it, it's very obvious. "Do you want him or do you want me," that was written for that scene in *Purple Rain* specifically. Where Morris would be sitting with [Apollonia], and there'd be this back and forth. And also, "The beautiful ones you always seem to lose," Vanity had just quit the movie. To then speculate, "Well, he wrote that song about me"? Afterwards you go, "Who are you? Why do you think that you are part of the script that way? And why would you go around saying stuff like that?"**
>
> **It's not about somebody human that I'm looking at right now. It wouldn't have worked if it was. This was literally for that character. And that's why it worked.[69]**

Work had stopped on "Electric Intercourse," which was intended to be the emotional love song for the movie and soundtrack, but it wasn't fitting properly and both the studio and the live versions had been shelved, leaving a void in the movie and the soundtrack. "I heard 'Electric Intercourse,' and obviously it wasn't right for the movie," recalls Magnoli. "It didn't fit into the film the way it needed to. The music that fits into that film, as you see it, is relatively seamless. You never question it. And that's a hard thing to achieve, and the fact that we did it again and again is telling to the amount of work that went in to make all that seamless so that it would fit into the narrative, and [Prince] knew there was a song necessary."

In hindsight it is obvious that "Electric Intercourse" was written for a different *Purple Rain*—one that starred Vanity. Both songs were worthy of release, but once the female lead left the tone of the entire project was altered, and the track seemed drastically out of place. With the song no longer fitting the movie's narrative, Prince set it aside. For "The Beautiful Ones," he sang about getting married, which didn't fit Vanity's movie persona but sounded tailor-made for a different type of character. The role had yet to be cast, and with shooting scheduled to start in a little over a month there was mounting pressure to find the actress.

As the production got closer to filming, Prince also had to start locking in the music to be performed. He had many tracks ready but was still missing the proper power ballad. Revolution drummer Bobby Z made the best observation about this song and about Prince in general when he said, "That's what happens when you give Prince 24 hours by himself."[70]

Fink was equally blown away: "'The Beautiful Ones' is my favorite song on *Purple Rain* because it's orchestrated in such a unique way. Prince created this other world using synthesizers, guitars, pianos, lots of digital delay, and reverb. And the vocals are just ridiculous."[71]

The reaction from within the band was universally positive. Wendy Melvoin explained that "[w]hen [Prince] wrote 'The Beautiful Ones,' we were in L.A., and I remember going . . . you're so totally in tune right now with your creativity. You are so on a roll. I just remember hearing that song and thinking to myself . . . God, you're so good. You are so good at this."[72]

The test for the song was going to be with Magnoli, who would be responsible for determining whether it belonged in the movie in a way that "Electric Intercourse" didn't: "I loved this song because it fits into the movie that's being made."

Prince began laying down the basic tracks at 1:00 p.m. and spent the next four hours recording the drums, keyboards, and piano (on the studio's Steinway), which David Leonard recorded using AKG C414 mics. After that, Prince spent the next ten hours on overdubs including his emotionally powerful vocals. As usual, he had a method of asking the engineer to leave the room while he recorded vocals, according to McCreary:

> I remember setting up a microphone above the mixing board and giving him a pair of headphones so he could monitor what he was singing. He'd run the machine and just sing like crazy. It would be four in the morning and I'd hear this "yeaaaaaaaaahhhhh" and stomping coming from the studio. (*laughs*) He had no tolerance for human weakness and that's basically what it is and there are only so many hours a person can work. . . . He needs his sleep, but only after a certain point. I've read that that is a characteristic of geniuses—they go for long periods of time without sleep and then they go for days with nothing but sleep, and he would definitely do that.

The song wrapped in one session, and after an hour of mixing, "The Beautiful Ones" was put to cassette. Prince left at 5:15 a.m., almost seventeen hours after the session began.

It is easy to imagine how proud he was of his recent accomplishments. Within two months he'd completed seven of the nine tracks for his album. The running times would change, but as of now the music necessary for the film was done and he could focus on songs for the Time and the unnamed female group that would replace Vanity 6. Work would continue in Minneapolis.

Prince wouldn't record in Los Angeles again until late December, after the main filming was complete.

Status: "The Beautiful Ones" (6:07) was ultimately edited (5:14) and released on the *Purple Rain* soundtrack album. It was not released as a single.

It is unclear when Prince actually wrote the track, but it was likely formed in late July/early August 1983, when Susan Rogers recalled hearing it for the first time: "While I was downstairs in his bedroom for a week installing his console and doing his wiring, Prince was just waiting for his studio to be built, and I would hear him on the piano playing over and over again. I heard him play an early version of 'The Beautiful Ones' more than any other song. He was just working it out over and over again. It was a powerful theme for him in his playing. It was really a privilege to hear him play these great songs. He would sit down at the piano and just play."[73]

WEDNESDAY, SEPTEMBER 21, 1983*

"**Computer Blue**" (eventually released as "hallway speech" version)
"**Purple Rain**" (full length)
"**The Beautiful Ones**" (full length)
"**I Would Die 4 U**" (full length)
"**Baby I'm a Star**" (full length)
"**Irresistible Bitch**"
Sunset Sound, Studio 3 | 12:30 p.m.–4:00 p.m.
Producer: Prince | *Artist:* Prince | *Engineer:* Prince | *Assistant Engineer:*
   "Peggy Mac" McCreary

*We spent more time on that record than any other record. . . . We
spent months and months on* Purple Rain.—David Leonard[74]

Prince had spent twenty-four days in a row in the studio without a break. With
the weight of the biggest project in his career riding on the back of a twenty-five-
year-old, one can only imagine the pressure he felt to create something great. It
is easy to forget that Prince spent much of this time alone in the studio, writing,
recording almost all the instruments, singing, and producing the music. No one
else in popular music was doing that and maintaining that level of creativity.

   Seven cassettes were created of this collection of tracks, probably for the
director, the record label, and members of the band. The purpose for this collection is unclear. It is possible that he was gathering the tracks the Revolution
would be performing onstage in the movie, but if that was the case, he didn't
include "Let's Go Crazy" and "Darling Nikki" and there was no reason to include "Irresistible Bitch."

*The following day (September 22) Prince's management sent a letter of intent to
First Avenue offering one hundred thousand dollars for use of the Main Room in
the movie. The dates requested stretched from November 26 to December 20.*

WEDNESDAY, SEPTEMBER 28, 1983*

"**Irresistible Bitch**" (copy made)
Sunset Sound, Studio 1 | 2:30 p.m.–3:00 p.m.
Producer: Prince (probably not in attendance) | *Artist:* Prince | *Engineer:*
   "Peggy Mac" McCreary

He was a genius, and it was an incredible experience to watch him work. He worked constantly and it was really grueling. He'd leave and you'd get maybe a day off, and then you'd be put on another session, because he wasn't doing just his own stuff.—Peggy McCreary

Peggy McCreary made two cassettes of the B-side for Prince's next single, "Irresistible Bitch." He may have dropped by to pick up the cassettes, but he probably didn't attend this brief afternoon session in Studio 1.

With all the music needed for the Revolution's live portion of the movie finished, Prince flew back to Minneapolis, where filming was scheduled to start in a month. October was going to be very busy, with final rehearsals, recasting the female lead, and the script changes that would come with the new character. He would also spend the month working on music for the other artists in the film: the Time, Jill Jones, and the (as-yet-unnamed) girl group replacing Vanity 6.

All the prep work for the year was about to test Prince in a manner he'd never before experienced. If it failed, it could set him back and derail any momentum he had from *1999*, potentially turning his name into a punch line. If it was a success, it would make him a superstar.

Either way, he was entering uncharted waters.

OCTOBER 1983

When Prince came to the rehearsal space, everybody clammed up and shut down and just kind of "Oh, Prince is here" kind of thing. Occasionally, depending on what kind of mood he was in, he would hear us, he would laugh, and then maybe change a couple of parts, and fine-tune a few things. He was excited about the sound. —Mark Cardenas

Likely inspired by the success of Prince's show on August 3, which previewed multiple tracks for the *Purple Rain* album, it was decided to have the Time debut their new tracks that were also premiering in the movie. This would give the band a chance to work out the kinks with the new members replacing Jimmy Jam, Terry Lewis, and Monte Moir, and would also allow director Albert Magnoli the opportunity to observe the band in front of a live audience at First Avenue. "If I am preparing to shoot them in a movie, I need to see them in their own element," Magnoli says. "I got to see Prince in his own element, and if the band is being shot for a motion picture, I need to see how do they act on stage. That's the authenticity that I want to be able to convey."

TUESDAY, OCTOBER 4, 1983

"The Bird" (live in concert by the Time)
"Jungle Love" (live in concert by the Time)
Venue: First Avenue (Minneapolis, Minnesota)
Capacity: 1,558 (attendance unknown)
Artist: The Time | *Engineers:* David Leonard and possibly Susan Rogers and "Peggy Mac" McCreary

[Prince] helped us form the blueprint, but it was getting crazy for me. With every step of success, he became more difficult, and I was getting the brunt of it. We are not hating on him. We are just telling the story. If it sounds ugly, then it was ugly. We are just telling what happened.—Morris Day[1]

The new lineup for the Time performed an eight-song set at First Avenue in Minneapolis, including the premiere of the two tracks planned for the upcoming movie: "The Bird" and "Jungle Love." For the crowd, this was a chance to catch a rare hometown performance by the band, and they weren't let down. The reaction to both songs was overwhelmingly positive, and the concert gave the band the chance to introduce the dance moves to "The Bird" as a rehearsal for their scene in *Purple Rain*. According to Day, the roots of his moves came from his childhood: "It's really a takeoff of the old 'Pterodactyl' from *The Flintstones,* if you remember that. That was more like arms (extends his arms) and flappin' the hands, while 'The Bird' is more like you get the wings going. It's just a modernized version of that with some funk behind it."[2]

The live version of "The Bird" was very similar to the previously recorded studio version, but in concert the band altered the "Star Spangled Banner" riff at 5:21 (which can be heard on the *Ice Cream Castle* album) as Day shouts, "Fellas, what's the word? When you want to get some, what you do?" For some reason the riff was cut in half and can be heard soon after the guitar solo on the album version.

"What's great about the Time is that they are literally the polar opposite of Prince and so that strengthened the thematic area," observes Magnoli. "To me it's the peacock against the black swan, right? Black swan, Prince. Peacock, pretty feathers, Morris Day. And because they are so opposite each other, you have drama."

But this wasn't just part of the script. The tension within the Time as well as between the band and Prince was very real—a powder keg ready to explode. "Morris was really very unhappy and basically non-participating," noted Susan Rogers. "He was going to get the movie over with and then it was obvious that he was out of there. He wasn't communicating with anybody. Everyone else was doing their best to hold their end up, but it was really an unhappy situation. Everyone was looking for a way out. Jellybean, the drummer, was really unhappy and wanted to be with Jimmy and Terry. Jesse wanted it because it was a job, but in the meantime he was doing his own demos and wanted out as quickly as possible. So no one was really happy."[3]

The frustration regarding how much money the Time was making boiled over during the show when Day openly mocked Prince about the fact that he charged twenty-five dollars for a ticket to his August show ("I couldn't afford it so I stayed home"). Day played the part of a revival preacher looking for donations, with "Prince, are you out there? Did you give? You took! Did you give?" It obviously struck a chord because days later, when Prince was teaching the Revolution some of the songs he'd recently recorded, he was still making references to Day's quote. In fact, he would revisit this phrase when creating the Family, the band that would eventually replace the Time after they self-destructed.

By the end of the concert, Day's patience had run out. "I was production manager for that show and at the side of stage when it concluded to escort the band to the dressing room," recalls Alan Leeds. "Instead, Morris unexpectedly bolted to the door behind the stage, which leads into a private garage where his car was parked. He did not utter one word before getting in the car and driving off, still in his stage clothes. Even the band was stunned, looking for him to celebrate the well-received performance."

From outside the venue in the truck, a basic 24-track recording was made of the concert for the two new songs, and the live versions of both tracks were being considered for use on the Time's next album. "Jungle Love" and "The Bird" had already been recorded in the studio, so, as he had done with the songs he and the Revolution had performed live at the benefit show in August, Prince would have to decide which versions of these tracks worked best for the album and the movie.

The music sounded incredible and the performance went very well, but the bigger question was: Could Prince keep the Time together long enough to finish the movie and any remaining tracks for an album, or would Day quit and join Vanity as a former employee?

Status: Tonight's live performance of "The Bird" (7:28) was overdubbed in the studio and an edited version (7:03) was released on the Time's *Ice Cream Castle* album. The thirty-two-second introduction to the song was kept intact for the album but drastically condensed for the movie.

The live rendition of "Jungle Love" (4:10) was not released on the album; the studio version was chosen instead. Like "The Bird," the audio from "Jungle Love" was featured in the movie, with the band lip-synching their performances from this evening.

Nothing else was officially released from this concert, which would be the only show featuring this lineup of the Time. Rocky Harris would be replaced by Jerry Hubbard while the movie was being filmed in November.

Prince would recycle Morris Day's biting phrase on March 3, 1986, during a show at First Avenue when he was upset with Paul Peterson for leaving the Family: "Paul Peterson, you out there? Did you give? You took. Did you give?" followed by the chant, "St. Paul, punk-of-the-month."

WEDNESDAY, OCTOBER 5, 1983

"**The Bird**" (live in concert by the Time)
"**Jungle Love**" (live in concert by the Time)
The Warehouse (St. Louis Park, Minnesota)
Engineer: unknown

It is likely that Prince spent part of the day reviewing the 24-track recording of the previous night's show.

WEDNESDAY, OCTOBER 5, 1983*

"**Purple Rain**"
"**The Beautiful Ones**"
"**I Would Die 4 U**"
Sunset Sound, Studio 1 | 8:00 p.m.–11:30 p.m.
Producer: Prince (not in attendance) | *Artist:* Prince | *Engineer:* "Peggy Mac" McCreary

Two-track copies were created during this brief session in Studio 1. Prince was still in Minneapolis, so he didn't attend the session.

SUNDAY, OCTOBER 9, 1983

> Rehearsal with the Revolution
> The Warehouse (St. Louis Park, Minnesota)

> *Sometimes he would work the song out with the band as he was writing it, and start teaching us the song, and then he would go back in the studio and finish it. Or in other cases, he would just go in and do them, and then present them to us on a tape when it was finished, and I'd say 80% of the time, that's how it was done. After he'd hand us a cassette of the mixed song, [he'd] say "Okay, go learn this" and we'll start rehearsing it.*—Matt Fink[4]

Prince spent the day teaching his band many of the recently recorded songs, including "Darling Nikki" and "The Beautiful Ones," as well as the updated versions of "Let's Go Crazy" and "Computer Blue," which at this point had an ending that was shorter than the released version and included only two repeats of the lead lines just before the final scream. This unreleased edit of the song can be heard in the movie, but the following spring Prince would reconsider the edit and extend it to four repeats of the lead line at the end of the track.

All of these versions would be featured in the performance scenes in the movie. The band was already very familiar with "I Would Die 4 U"/"Baby I'm a Star" and "Purple Rain," as they hadn't changed much since they were performed in August. The rehearsal also included the band jamming on "17 Days" as well as "You Are in My System," a song that had charted in 1983 for the System and for Robert Palmer.

INTRODUCING: APOLLONIA KOTERO

> *[Apollonia is] one of the sweetest people I've ever met.*
> —Prince[5]

With Vanity out of the picture, literally and figuratively, a new actress was needed to fill her role. Casting calls were done in New York and Los Angeles looking for a "beautiful, voluptuous female, between 18 and 21, under 5-foot-4, sexy with an open, ripe look . . . and any ethnic type with an exotic European allure," and the production was swamped with actresses.

Albert Magnoli had his work cut out for him: "I saw hundreds of girls and no one could replace Vanity, and so it was a miracle that at the very end, Apollonia walked in, and she was the direct opposite of Vanity. You had Vanity, gorgeous and dark, and you had [Patricia Kotero], gorgeous and light. And I realized that because they were so opposed to each other, they would work. She looks fantastic, and what surprised me is the attitude; she's tough. Apollonia finally came in so diametrically opposed to her, so I immediately said, 'I'm literally looking at light, when I had been trying to find the dark.'"

The next step was to have Kotero travel to Minneapolis, so Magnoli arranged a meeting between her and Prince: "I called him and said, 'This girl might be the girl. Her name was Patty, Patricia.' I said, 'Why don't you come by and see if she can sing,' because that was a big deal. So I said, 'Prince is going to be by. Take a ride to go to his house, and we'll figure out if you can sing,' and she says, 'Okay.' He walks in, she's nervous, he's nervous, and so they go off together with the bodyguard."

Soon after they left, Prince phoned Magnoli: "He calls and says, 'What do you think?' And I said, 'Listen, can she sing?' And he goes, 'I can make it work.' And I said, 'Okay, if you can make it work, I can make it work.'"

Prince was taken by Patricia's looks and personality and by their immediate chemistry, and she was hired as the female lead. Although she was brought in to replace Vanity, Kotero's personality took the character in a different direction and a name change was in order. The name "Apollonia" can be traced back to Prince's fascination with movies, specifically *The Godfather* and Michael Corleone's first wife, Apollonia Vitelli-Corleone (played by Simonetta Stefanelli). Prince loved classic films and invited those close to him to share in this passion. Prince called Magnoli with the update: "He goes, 'Can we call her Apollonia?' And of course, *The Godfather*, and I said, 'Yeah.' And I go, 'Where's that coming from?' And he said, 'I have no idea, it just came to me,' and so I said, 'Okay, it's Apollonia, what the heck?'"

Prince also ran it by the remaining Vanity 6 members, Brenda Bennett and Susan Moonsie, since they would be performing together. "[She] was the one who looked the best and her reading was very good," remembers Bennett. "Prince was sitting with us and we told him. He had to make a decision and he asked us about the name 'Apollonia.' I liked it."

"She came to rehearsals and saw how we work together," Wendy Melvoin reported in 1984. "Apollonia was genuinely excited. She came to us and said that she thought a lot of us and the band and she really wanted us to accept her."[6]

MID-OCTOBER 1983

> "**Sex Shooter**" (Apollonia vocals, first attempt)
> Kiowa Trail home studio (Chanhassen, Minnesota)
> *Producer:* Prince | *Artist:* Apollonia 6 | *Engineer:* Susan Rogers

> *Apollonia brought a more pure, innocent, and sensual aspect to the movie. It would have been really dark with Vanity.*
> —Albert Magnoli

The first track Apollonia taped with Prince was a rerecording of Vanity 6's "Sex Shooter." Brenda Bennett details how they worked with her initially: "Apollonia will tell you, she had not been a singer before, and we had her copy Vanity's vocals. I think that it was tough for her. She came in wanting to be a partner. David Lee Roth and Apollonia dated, so she knew musicians. She wanted to make a success of this. She was friendly and wanted to try hard and she was very diplomatic. It didn't come easy, but she was much easier to work with than Vanity. She had no preconceived notions about singing, but she was mainly an actress."

With Vanity out of the picture, Prince decided to go in a slightly different direction and discarded "Moral Majority," "Vibrator," and other tracks recorded for Vanity 6's aborted second album, but he was firm about using "Sex Shooter." Because of the different personalities of the actresses and the characters, it was suggested to shift everything from sexual to sensual.

Prince apparently agreed with this assessment and focused on changing the tone with the vocals.

Early in the casting, Apollonia had given Prince a demo tape of her singing, so he knew she had potential, but listening to a tape and laying down vocals for a new track are two very different tasks, as Susan Rogers explained: "She was warming up, in a quiet little voice, with the Beatles' 'When I'm 64,' and that was the preparation for singing 'Sex Shooter.' I realized, 'Oh boy, this one's going to be tough,' because obviously the poor woman was no singer, she was an actress. He was demanding the impossible."[7]

Prince thought the mood would be more relaxed if she were singing without an audience, so he asked Rogers to go upstairs and wait in the living room while he and Apollonia stayed downstairs and recorded her voice, coaxing her to be more assertive and confident. A few weeks later, once Apollonia's vocal abilities and her comfort level grew, she and Prince would revisit the song.

Apollonia wasn't the only one learning what her role in the studio with Prince would be. Susan Rogers was starting to understand what Prince expected of herself as well: "Prince needed an all-around engineer, one who could repair and use his equipment. I had to learn very quickly what sounds he liked, but I was helped by Jesse Johnson, who taught me how Prince liked the kick drum to sound, what reverb he liked on his vocal, what mics he used, etc. By the time Prince came home from Los Angeles, I knew enough to be of great use to him in the studio."[8]

Status: This updated version of "Sex Shooter" (6:52) was released as a 12-inch "Dance Version" and edited (3:02) for release as the 7-inch single. The track was edited (3:40) for placement on the *Apollonia 6* album. The single would peak at number 85 on the *Billboard* Hot 100 singles chart, number 19 on the *Billboard* Black Singles chart, and number 32 on the *Billboard* Hot Dance/ Disco chart, likely helped the song's presence in the *Purple Rain* movie.

It is unclear when Prince made musical changes to the song, but during the summer, additional vocals had been added by Brenda Bennett, Susan Moonsie, and Jill Jones. An instrumental track of the new version was also created for use in the movie.

MONDAY, OCTOBER 24, 1983

"Wednesday" (basic tracking, Prince/Jill Jones vocals)
Kiowa Trail home studio (Chanhassen, Minnesota)
Producer: Prince | *Artist:* Jill Jones | *Engineer:* Susan Rogers

> *["Wednesday"] was a little piano piece that he was playing upstairs for quite a while before it was recorded.*—Susan Rogers[9]

It seemed like every musician in Prince's orbit was getting some sort of music for the movie. Today Prince worked on a tune called "Wednesday" for Jill

Jones. "We recorded it at his house and he had put a guide vocal on it," remembered Rogers, "but it was written into the film as being a piece for Jill. It was written into the story line where she was going to be someone who is madly in love with him."[10]

"It was a really sweet song," reflects Jones. "It was a piano song. We did record that at his house. He mic'd the piano upstairs to downstairs. It had these really dark lyrics, but I loved it. It was very whimsical."

The lyrics touched on how serious Jones's character was about Prince and hints at her possible suicide by threatening if he doesn't return home by Wednesday, "there's no telling what I might do."[11] The lyrics had been altered so Jones sang that she "contemplated your embrace"[12] instead of "contemplated suicide" to mask the number's dark tone.

"[In the movie] it was me at the piano playing and singing, and then they cut it out," remembers Jones. "He said he was really sad about it. I really did not believe him."

Magnoli explains his process regarding that scene: "I shot a portion of it in the movie. I put the camera like an inch off the ground. And was able to track across a very shiny floor right up to her legs and her face playing the piano. Freaking gorgeous, but that's before Prince shows up and says, 'What's cooking?' She's great, great, great—she's beautiful—but where the hell is it going? It was like a different movie."

Status: "Wednesday" (1:41) was shelved and has never been released.

With only a few days left before the start of filming on November 1, Prince was rapidly finalizing as much of the music as possible. The pressure to complete this must have been difficult for him, especially considering that outside of touring and working with the record label, this is the most control over his career he had ever handed to others.

On October 25 Vanity reached out to talk to Prince for the first time in weeks, and after speaking on the phone, they decided to meet up and talk. "In spite of everything, I'll miss and love him," Vanity wrote in her diary. "He showed at First Avenue and said a genuine hello. Come to think of it, we never said 'Goodbye.' I cried of course."[13] After talking, they parted for good. She'd been replaced in the movie and she was already packed and moving out of Minneapolis the following morning, days before the movie was to begin shooting.

SATURDAY, OCTOBER 29, 1983

"Father's Song" (basic tracking)
Kiowa Trail home studio (Chanhassen, Minnesota)
Producer: Prince | *Artist:* Prince | *Engineer:* Susan Rogers

Q: What's your favorite song from Purple Rain?
A: Maybe "Father's Song," which wasn't on the album.
—Alan Leeds[14]

This was the last weekend before shooting was scheduled to start, and once again Prince decided to turn to the piano, this time to revisit a piece of instrumental music he'd incorporated in "Computer Blue" two months earlier. According to Prince, "Father's Song" was written by his father, John L. Nelson. "His father was hanging around during the recording of a lot of the album," remembered Peggy McCreary. "During that time, people came out of the woodwork. He was all of a sudden 'reclaimed' during the *Purple Rain* era by his family. He liked his dad, and that's why that song sort of hit home."

"Prince and his dad had a very deep, important relationship," reflected Lisa Coleman. "His father was a piano player. Prince really looked up to him. Their relationship needed a lot of healing. . . . This song was a healing gesture."[15]

It is likely that this was recorded for the scene in the movie where his father (played by Clarence Williams III) played the track on his piano, which can be seen at 57:24 in the movie. Although the version that was recorded today didn't end up in the film, it was a placeholder and was probably given to Albert Magnoli for rehearsals and storyboarding.

The song is a piano-only track containing no vocals and no overdubs. A copy was made at the end of the session. Prince would eventually add synths to the track, but that probably happened on another date.

Status: The overdubbed version of "Father's Song" (5:22) was included in the *Purple Rain Deluxe* (Expanded Edition) CD set in 2017. The piano-only version of the track (5:15) remains unreleased. "Computer Blue" uses the melody at 2:30 on the released version.

The number was featured in the movie, but the film's version was from a take recorded in 1984.

In 1994 an EP called Father's Song *that contained four of John L. Nelson's compositions was released by Vive Records. None of them contained work by Prince.*

NOVEMBER 1983

Production for *Purple Rain* officially began on November 1, although some exterior shots were reportedly filmed the previous day to beat the pending bad weather. Because the movie would be shooting until just before Christmas, Prince focused most of his energy on the film, leaving little time for studio work. That doesn't mean that none occurred, but very little has been verified.

SUNDAY, NOVEMBER 6, 1983 (ESTIMATE)

"Sex Shooter" (Apollonia vocals, second attempt)
Kiowa Trail home studio (Chanhassen, Minnesota)
Producer: Prince | *Artist:* Apollonia 6 | *Engineer:* Susan Rogers

The character Apollonia plays in Purple Rain *in a way parallels who she really is. She came to Minneapolis as a spunky, giving kid who wanted to learn. She was nice, she was intelligent, she had flair and spunk. She was the new kid on the block, but she fit in.* —Wendy Melvoin[1]

With the movie finally shooting, Apollonia was gaining confidence and finding her voice on the project. "Vocals weren't quite her stuff," recalled Susan Rogers, "but she kept working on it, kept getting better. They were back in on another day and she did the vocals on it, maybe a week or so after the first attempt, because that was right when they started making the movie, and they had weekends off, or at least Sundays off, and they would come in on a Sunday."[2]

Prince would eventually create a track with her that reflected the sound he wanted. He probably realized that because Apollonia was an actress, it made sense to have her act the part of a singer, which revealed the voice of her character. Ultimately even Rogers conceded that Apollonia "had this campy quality to her voice that was perfect."[3]

Brenda Bennett recalled how he worked with new talent: "Prince has a way of extracting from you, sometimes painfully and sometimes without you even knowing it. Creatively, he pulls out your best parts; parts you never even knew you had or could do. He wasn't always nice about it . . . but then . . . it wasn't about being nice. It was about learning how to reach out and grow in a direction you may never have even tried to on your own."[4]

The tune was very catchy, and although the song was originally intended for her predecessor, Apollonia added her own flair that reflected her personality. Vanity's moaning was eliminated and Brenda Bennett recorded some additional background vocals. Ultimately, Apollonia's performance altered the effect of the track, turning it into a more playful pop song.

MONDAY, NOVEMBER 7, 1983

Purple Rain compilation
Kiowa Trail home studio (Chanhassen, Minnesota)
Producer: Prince | *Artist:* Prince and others | *Engineer:* Susan Rogers

Even on the set of Purple Rain *the movie, he was running back and forth to do recordings.* —Susan Rogers[5]

According to sources, a test pressing of *Purple Rain* was created on this date. It included the following tracks: "Let's Go Crazy," "The Beautiful Ones," "Computer Blue," "Darling Nikki," "Wednesday," "Purple Rain," "I Would Die 4 U," "Baby I'm a Star," and "Father's Song."

Although it doesn't make sense to have two versions of "Father's Song" (it was also part of "Computer Blue") and a solo track by Jill Jones, Susan Rogers feels this configuration may be from an actual test pressing: "The reason there would be a song with vocals by Jill Jones on it was it was kind of a soundtrack from the movie. It was intended for singing in the movie. It would've made perfect sense. He was just anxious to get the record done. It was a little premature, but he did this test pressing because he was anxious: 'What's my record going to sound like?'"[6]

This track listing contains all seven of the songs he'd recorded that were intended for the movie, but this configuration might not be complete. There could have been a second disc/cassette that was intended to be part of the collection; this would likely have included "Jungle Love" and "The Bird" and possibly "Modernaire."

EARLY NOVEMBER 1983

"Mia Bocca" (Jill Jones vocal)
Kiowa Trail home studio (Chanhassen, Minnesota)
Producer: Prince | *Artist:* Jill Jones | *Engineer:* Susan Rogers

Jill had a part in Purple Rain *and "Mia Bocca" may have been written specifically for the film. That was written specifically for her; it was never intended for him.*—Susan Rogers[7]

In the first draft of the script for *Purple Rain* (when it was called *Dreams*), the only track listed was "Mia Bocca," which was originally recorded in 1982 or possibly early 1983. Prince had written and recorded it largely on his own, but the inspiration and some of the lyrics came from Jill Jones, who regrets not pushing for a cowriter credit. "We were writing and I seem to have lost all my sensibilities," recalls Jones, "because I remember working on that with him and I didn't even deal with publishing and considering my family's background [Jill is related to Berry Gordy, the former head of Motown Records], I am like a total asshole for not doing something."

When asked if she participated in the writing of the track, she replied, "Definitely! Mainly he was the leader of it, but a small percentage of it would have been nice! It was about my mouth. It came down to that. I was a little shy with some of those things. And I think that he made those things to go with that. Because the truth of the matter was that I had only been with one person before I met him. Like two times. It was pretty new to me. It's a wonder I'm not in a nunnery! (*laughs*)"

Prince and Jones struggled with some of the lines while recording the vocals, and because the title and parts of the lyrics were in Italian, they reached
out to anyone local who might be able to translate for them. "We called a lot
of Italian restaurants to work on our Italian," Jones laughs. "In Minneapolis!
We found out that in Minneapolis it was broken Spanglish they were giving
us. All their verbs were wrong! And all my friends in Europe are like, 'You
aren't dealing with people that are Italian!' The busboy who gave us the
translation probably gave us half Italian and half Spanish. I learned all about
that song when I finally went to Italy: 'You've gotta the verba backwards!'
(*laughs*)"

Status: It is likely that additional work was done on the vocals for "Mia
Bocca" (5:25) later in the fall, but plans to use it in *Purple Rain* were
scrapped. A version containing updated saxophone and orchestration
composed by Clare Fischer (7:21) was eventually released on Jill Jones's
1987 self-titled album. An instrumental version comprised only of the
song's beat and Fischer's orchestration was placed in Prince's second movie,
Under the Cherry Moon, during the party scene when Prince meets Mary and
her mom.

Behind the scenes, Susan Rogers was making efforts to gather all Prince's work
into a vault in Minneapolis:

> When I first went to work for Prince, I set up a task of assembling all his tapes
> from Hollywood Sounds Studios, Sunset Sound, and Warner Bros., to get all of
> his tapes together. We didn't have a vault yet, but what we did have was a com-
> pany that was right up the street, and we stored all of the tapes in their archives.
> That's what the place was called, "The Archives." We had a whole room full
> of shelves and more tapes in plastic and cardboard cartons. We kept the tapes
> there for maybe two or three years. A couple years at least, until Paisley Park
> was built. Their office was only open nine to five, but they had twenty-four hour
> retrieval. So if it was four o'clock in the morning and I needed a tape, I'd call
> and say we need carton such and such, and then they would send them out to
> us. I think they would deliver them or sometimes it was faster for me to just go
> and pick them up. This happened all the time. It wasn't a very efficient system,
> but it was a way to keep all of our tapes at least off-site and safe from tornadoes
> until we had a vault built.[8]

WEDNESDAY, NOVEMBER 23, 1983

The final single from the *1999* album, "Let's Pretend We're Married" (backed with "Irresistible Bitch") is released today. It will stay in the *Billboard* Top 100 for ten weeks, peaking at number 52 on December 17, 1983. The combination of lower-charting singles and the upcoming *Purple Rain* project put an end to promotion of Prince's current album. Despite how the singles performed on the charts, the *1999* album continued to rise up the *Billboard* Top LPs & Tapes list, breaking the top 40 during the second week of December.

DECEMBER 1983

"The Glamorous Life" (basic tracking and saxophone overdubs)
Sunset Sound, Studio 3 | 6:00 p.m.–5:30 a.m. (booked 6:00 p.m.–open)
Producer: Prince | *Artist:* Prince | *Engineer:* Prince | *Assistant Engineer:*
Terry Christian

When you're in the creative process, the first thing you naturally think about is the "bombs," the great ones that you've done before. You want to fill in the slots on your album with the songs that will make everyone the happiest: fans, musicians, writers, and so on. I used to try to fill those gaps first whenever I was trying something new, or wait to challenge myself to do another great one. —Prince[1]

For the first time since September, Prince returned to Los Angeles to record. In many ways L.A. was his adopted home, and whenever he was in town he'd schedule time at Sunset Sound. It was a bond that had been strong since 1981. "The thing with Prince is, as far as the relationship with us goes, is that everybody here was so familiar with him that he felt like part of the family," recalls Sunset Sound general manager Craig Hubler. "He felt secure and comfortable coming here." A great example of how relaxed Prince was at Sunset Sound is how he started making the studio reflect his home. According to Hubler:

He likes to write his lyrics lying on his bed at home, just on top of the bedspread or whatever, just kind of laying there on his stomach with his notepad in front of him. He decided he wanted a bed in the studio, so we somehow arranged a queen-sized bed that we set up in the performance area in the middle of the room. The morning after it was delivered, he hadn't arrived yet, I bought purple sheets, purple bedspread. Here I am in the linen department picking up all this stuff in purple. The clerk looked at me and my purple stuff and I was like, "Don't ask!" I made up his bed, and the bed stayed there for like five or six weeks, making him feel at home.

Before the bed was added, Prince would either take a tape of the instrumental somewhere else overnight to write or find somewhere quiet to compose the lyrics. Susan Rogers remembered that during his time at Sunset Sound, "[he] would just go and sit in his car, he'd take a cassette, a notebook and a pencil, write the lyrics and then come back and do the lead vocal. Or if we were at the warehouse he would go into his bedroom."[2]

"His lyric writing is solid," she continued. "He'd write in pen; he'd usually have the idea fully fleshed out. He'd write on the page and if there was a word or a sentence that he wasn't happy with, he'd take the pen and he'd scratch it out in such a way that it was impossible to see what was written underneath. So all you would really see is the lyric in its finished form."[3]

The bulk of the movie was now in the can. Over the next few weeks, the director and the editor would assemble a rough cut and decide what still needed to be shot. It would be weeks before the first cut was properly assembled and no additional music would be created for the film, so Prince decided to record music that was unrelated to the movie. He had hoped to book his regular engineer, Peggy McCreary, but she and David Leonard were away for a vacation to Mexico. In her place was Terry Christian. Upon arrival, Prince quickly started laying down a melody in E-flat minor, using only the black keys on the piano. The song would eventually be called "The Glamorous Life" and would ultimately be given to someone who had been visiting Prince in the studio recently, Sheila Escovedo (who would later be known professionally as Sheila E.), but at this point it was still listed as a Prince track and not assigned to anyone else. "I'll tell you what I think," Christian reflects on this period. "When he was recording those songs for Sheila, he didn't know he was recording those songs for Sheila. He was looking for ways to get more material out. He made it a point that it should not be reflected on the work orders. Sometimes he would ask to have a title not written down. He didn't want Warner Bros. to know what he was doing."

Prince recorded the basic tracks for the song over the next eleven hours. Christian remembers the consistency of Prince's method: "The way he would work at the time was always the same. He would just put together a drum groove on the LM-1. That was the only thing that was out of the sequencer; everything else he would play. Then usually a bass, or a synth part and then go back and drop in the bass part. First the drum track and then overdub one instrument at a time." Prince would then either work on the lyrics in the studio or take a tape home with him and write the lyrics before the next session.

During the evening, Prince realized that there was an element missing from the song, one he hadn't mastered and couldn't imitate. For the first time in his career he decided to add an outside person on the saxophone. Christian suggested Larry Williams, who had recently been recording in Studio 1. Williams remembers his introduction to Prince: "He comes out and says, 'Hello.' I remember that he had this velvet shirt with ruffles and some kind of hat. To me it was really ridiculous. Other than that, he looked completely comfortable, and there was nobody there! There was no one that he was trying to impress. And as the session went on, it was incredible how focused he was on the music and how there was just no bullshit of any kind. He had a couple of ideas and he threw them out there and then he said, 'What do you hear?' I played a couple of things back and forth, just real in sync. Real easy."

Williams recorded several different saxophone sections, which were stacked up and added to the song. When it came to the solo, Prince pushed him to play something more "free and bizarre":

He just kept pushing me to be as creative as possible. He wanted each track more out of tune, because it was sounding too slick for him. He wanted it to sound more of a street sound, less slick. I'm used to coming in to an R&B situation and I'm used to trying to sneak some hip stuff in, something unusual. It was one of the highlights of my career, not just the way it turned out or the way it sold, but the actual process of it. I had a good feeling about it and I knew it was going to go because he obviously liked it. It was very exciting artistically. There was no wasted time on this, no tripping, no anything . . . there were no frills, except on his shirt!

It was just he and I in the room and that was unusual. He wasn't an engineer and wasn't pretending to be. He just liked the intimacy and having no distractions with anyone else around. He just liked the focus of him being in there by himself, and when he needed something technical, he'd just get on the phone and call.

"Prince dealt very well with Larry," remembers Christian. "Prince had told him what to play and Larry did it for him."

Although Prince hadn't recorded his vocals, he had the title in his mind because it was listed on the nightly work order. Christian explains that Prince "could rely on inspiration. He could come in and it would flow and turn into something great."

After Larry left, Prince and Christian created a rough mix of the track, and two C-60 cassettes were made. Prince left the studio at 5:30 a.m. on December 28.

Status: "The Glamorous Life" (8:12) was considered for placement on albums for Apollonia 6 and Jill Jones before it was given to Sheila E., who added her drums, percussion, and voice to the song. It was released (9:04 as a bonus track and 6:35 as a club edit) as the title track to her 1984 album. An edited version (3:44) was released as a single, climbing to number 7 on the *Billboard* Hot 100, number 9 on the *Billboard* Hot Black Singles chart, and number 1 on the *Billboard* Hot Dance Club Play list.

Sheila's drums would be recorded in early February 1984 and her vocals added in late March.

The "free and bizarre" sax sounds were gaining some notice during that time. Earlier in the year, David Bowie had released his number 1 hit "Let's Dance," containing saxophone parts that sound similar enough to have possibly inspired Prince.

Although Prince was helpful when finding a new stage name for Escovedo, she had been called Sheila E. from her youth. For multiple years, artists like George Duke had referred to her as "E."

WEDNESDAY, DECEMBER 28, 1983*

"The Glamorous Life" (Prince's vocals and Jill Jones's background vocals)
"Next Time Wipe the Lipstick off Your Collar" (basic tracking)
Sunset Sound, Studio 3 | 4:00 p.m.–3:45 a.m. (booked 4:00 p.m.–open)
Producer: Prince | *Artist:* Prince | *Engineer:* Prince | *Assistant Engineer:* Terry Christian

This is my job. This [soundboard] is my desk.—Prince[4]

During this period Prince often rode to the studio on his purple motorcycle. "Prince was someone you noticed," Christian recalls. "But he hadn't enjoyed the popularity that he has now, so back then he could go out on his own." Eventually his status grew so that he'd arrive in a purple limo, but for now he was enjoying playing the role of "the Kid" from *Purple Rain*.

When Prince arrived back to Studio 3, he had the lyrics to "The Glamorous Life" written out on several pages of stationery from Le Parc Hotel in West Hollywood, California. He also had the concept for an additional song. Focusing on "The Glamorous Life," Prince added his vocals to the track in his usual manner. "He would always set up a [Neumann] U 47 microphone over the console," recalls Christian. "You get him assigned to a track and he just runs the machine, punches in, and does the vocal." Prince liked doing this right next to the board, keeping the speakers low enough that the song didn't bleed onto the tape. **"That's how I like to listen to it myself,"** Prince explained in 2010, **"with the music through the speakers and the headphones at the same time."**[5]

Prince enjoyed showing off his latest music to those around him, and he was probably reflecting about how Apollonia inspired this track, so he invited her to attend the day's session. "He brought her in and just played some songs for her to listen to," explains Christian. "They had already done the *Purple Rain* movie. He put in a phone call to her asking her to come by. He said something about how beautiful she was."

After Apollonia left Jill Jones attended the session and sang background vocals, blending her voice with Prince's. Jones was a talented singer who Prince relied on to fill in his sound. "I loved recording with him," she says. "I thought he was probably the most open for trying just about anything."

It seems that Prince wanted to get back in the habit of knocking out a song a day, so he raced through the track, giving "The Glamorous Life" a quick mix before moving on to the second song of the night, "Next Time Wipe the Lipstick off Your Collar."

Christian didn't always agree with the pace at which Prince recorded his tracks: "I thought Prince's records sounded awful, but they have the illusion of sounding good. Prince holds your interest with grooves and parts in the way he produces records. It's an engineer's job to make the record sound good, but he didn't really respect that. Some of the flaws were intended flaws. He would keep things interesting. Sonically they didn't make it for me."

Once Prince announced that he was working on a new track, Christian had to quickly switch around the microphones and repatch the board to be able to record everything: "He was ready to go and I wasn't ready with all the mics. He said, 'Never mind. I don't want this to sound like an L.A. record.' That kind of opened my eyes to a different approach. The main rule was that his records shouldn't sound like everybody else's. The recording flaws maybe weren't intended, but he didn't have the respect for certain recording protocols that other people would."

A simple drum pattern was quickly programmed on the Linn LM-1 and a beat was recorded. Prince added keyboards and piano, but he was looking for something that would create a mood in the song, enlisting help from Christian: "He wanted an accordion on the record. I didn't have a clue where to go, so he just dug up a phone book, and I guess Nick [DeCaro] was the accordion player there." Unfortunately, they weren't able to get DeCaro into the studio for the session, so the addition of accordion to the track would be shelved for a few weeks.

It is unclear if any vocals were placed on "Next Time Wipe the Lipstick off Your Collar" during this session.

Status: "Next Time Wipe the Lipstick off Your Collar" (3:47) was considered for the *Apollonia 6* album, but instead it landed on Sheila E.'s first album, *The Glamorous Life.* The released version contained no major changes or edits except the addition of Sheila's vocals and the elimination of the LM-1 drums that were recorded during this session. Prince removed them from the final mix, creating a song by a drummer that contained no drums.

According to Sheila E.'s book The Beat of My Own Drum: A Memoir, *she and Prince wrote the lyrics to "The Glamorous Life" in March 1984, after most of the rest of her album was complete. Because it has been thirty years since the events occurred, I'm including both versions of the origin of this song, as they all deserve to be heard.*

THURSDAY, DECEMBER 29, 1983*

"She's Always in My Hair" [listed as "Sex Shooter"]
Sunset Sound, Studio 3 | 6:30 p.m.–4:00 a.m. (booked 5:00 p.m.–open)
Producer: Prince | *Artist:* Prince | *Engineer:* Prince | *Assistant Engineer:*
   Bill Jackson

> *I don't plan or anything like that. When I record, I find if I usually just sit down and do something, I'll gradually come up with something. Sometimes it starts with a lyric.* —Prince[6]

Prince was renting a house on Benedict Canyon, but for some reason he was once again writing lyrics on the stationery from Le Parc Hotel. His original draft started with the phrase, "A boy got killed at Disneyland today / Some say he was trying to be Superman," which was supposedly based on a story in the news, but the lyrics were discarded and the focus of the song shifted to a playfully romantic tone. Prince would later use this method of songwriting on "Sign o' the Times."

"She's Always in My Hair" is another amazing track Prince recorded in one day. It is the sort of song that would be a crowning achievement for most musicians, but Prince would relegate it to a B-side. In many respects, the A-sides of Prince's singles were released for the record company and for airplay on the radio, but the B-sides gave him a chance to stretch out and reveal some of his extensive unreleased work that may not have fit the theme of an album. There is also a financial benefit to this, as the B-side of a hit single generates equal sales royalties as the A-side.

The reason Prince listed "Sex Shooter" on the work order can be traced to the influence of the Apollonia 6 song, which was strongly featured in the *Purple Rain* movie. Prince literally sampled himself when he took the lead line from Apollonia 6's "Sex Shooter" (the four-note riff heard at 0:09), slowing it down slightly to create a recognizable sequence that comes between "she's always there" and "telling me how much she cares"[7] at 0:43 of "She's Always in My Hair."

Prince was the only musician on the track, and engineer Bill Jackson remembers how this session began: "He was out at the piano writing a few words, playing some keys, writing a little bit more, and he was out there maybe a little over an hour."

Prince quickly programmed the pattern on the LM-1, nearly replicating the beat and the phasing effect of the drums he'd created on the long version of "Sex Shooter." Jackson says, "He put the two-bar phrase in and within ten minutes, he had the drums. I remember there was a pause in the song [probably at the phrase 'Maybe I'll marry her, maybe I won't?'[8]] and he just stopped it and waited and then started it back up in real time without a click track, and then he went back and erased the kick drum and the snare drum that he didn't want because they were doing the same thing through the song."

Prince then recorded the keyboards on the Oberheim OB-8, a Fender bass, and a guitar, followed by the piano. According to Jackson, "He went out there to the grand piano and recorded the piano with him singing. And I think we went in and fixed a couple of things in the vocals."

When it came time to delegate tasks during the session, Jackson recalls that Prince didn't seem to want to rely on the engineer: "A lot of time he'd just run the tape machine himself. He'd just take his hand off of it and he'd punch in and punch out because a lot of times he was faster than talking to someone about it. Sometimes he'd let me do it. He needed someone to engineer, but he didn't need them to do everything so you were kind of partially an assistant and partially the actual engineer."

Even though Prince hadn't recorded the track before today, he instinctively knew the song. "He'd be listening in his headphones to the tape rewinding and he'd hear it going backwards and say 'Okay, stop there,'" according to Jackson. "He wouldn't tell you to go back to the chorus or anything like that, he'd just say, 'Rewind,' and then, 'Stop there,' and I'd play it and we'd just punch in for the places he wanted to fix. And then he'd do it again. 'Rewind . . . stop,' and he would punch in for a harmony on another track. And he never messed up. It was all there in his head, and he'd just put it down when we'd record it."

The handwritten lyrics contain an additional verse, but because of the length of the track, Prince decided to discard it.

Months later when working on the song in Minneapolis, Prince confirmed the track's muse to his engineer Susan Rogers: "He told me himself that it was inspired by Jill Jones, so I can say that with some authority. Jill was around at that time and he really loved her. He had a lot of affection for her, but as he said, 'She was always in his hair.' She was one of those women who wasn't doing anything wrong. She was always there telling him how much she cared and he said it with a great deal of affection. He really cared for her a lot."[9]

The track's inciting incident supposedly stemmed from Jones leaving food on the counter at his home: "He was really very orderly. Very organized. And he thought I was a complete slob. I was lots of fun, but kind of messy, leaving stuff everywhere. And I was like, 'Well I was going to get it later,' and he was just like, 'But who does that?' I was like, 'Who does what?' 'You leave little bits everywhere you go.' I think Prince sometimes got confused with me. We wanted to do the right thing, but a lot of times he just couldn't. We were all just too young."

Prince offered Jones a cassette of the song as an attempted apology, which was something he'd done for other women in the past. It didn't go over well, especially the line: "Maybe I'll marry her / Maybe I won't." "I asked him 'Who says that?'" remembers Jones. "And he was like, 'Well, I thought you would really like it.' He was really, really sincere and I'm like, going, 'Maybe?' I got really hung up on 'maybe.' I said, 'Everybody knows the woman always decides about marriage. Always. Whether the man knows it or not, it's the woman. The woman can make the man do it.' And I just tore up the house. I didn't really like 'She's Always in My Hair.' I said, 'You can't give me this song and think it's going to make up for everything.'"

Jones never ended up marrying Prince and, reflecting on it years later, she is very philosophical: "I really truly believed that Prince was married to his music. There was no woman who could ever, ever rival that. Or compete. No way. You could try to fit in next to it, but nah, it was his music."

A mix was created at the end of the session that contained a dip in the audio at approximately 6:15, consisting of a brief fade to silence and then a resurface of the last few notes and final sting. Because the song had an obvious Beatles influence, it seemed like a tip of the hat to the Fab Four, who had used this trick on "Helter Skelter." Prince would also revisit this stylistic decision on *The Black Album* with "Rockhard in a Funky Place," and on the 12-inch releases of "Alphabet St." and "Mountains."

Status: "She's Always in My Hair" (6:32) was worked on again in January, adding finger cymbals, creating a new mix, and discarding the false ending. Additional work was done in Minneapolis, but it is unclear if the song was simply overdubbed or completely rerecorded. If it was rerecorded, the newer version was deemed less satisfying and remains unreleased. The version of the song recorded on this date was given the name "She's Always in My Hair (New Mix)" and eventually released on June 19, 1985, as the B-side for the 12-inch of "Raspberry Beret." An edited version (3:27) was released as the B-side to "Raspberry Beret" on May 15, 1985. It was also included on the B-side of the 7-inch and 12-inch of "Paisley Park" in Europe and Australia.

It is possible that this was recorded on January 8, 1984, but documents indicate that this date is accurate. January 8 is probably when it was overdubbed with finger cymbals.

FRIDAY, DECEMBER 30, 1983

Jam session that became **"We Can Fuck/We Can Funk"**
Sunset Sound, Studio 3 | Unknown start time
Producer: Prince | *Artist:* Prince | *Engineer:* Prince | *Assistant Engineer:* Bill Jackson

If you like [him writing on] bass, it's probably something like "We Can Funk" or "Let's Work."—Bobby Z[10]

Work began on a new groove. Prince on bass, Wendy Melvoin on guitar, Lisa Coleman on keyboards, and Bobby Z on drums, were joined by Lisa's brother David in another jam session trying to find a riff. "We started jamming on [what would become] 'We Can Fuck,'" explains David Coleman. "And I was in the isolation booth with the oud [an Arabic type of guitar, similar to the lute] and started doing that riff. Lisa was there, we were all jamming and that's the riff that I was doing, and Prince said, 'I like that riff. Let's do something with it,' so he said, 'When's a good time for you?' and we all agreed that during the [following] day on New Year's Eve would be fine and we could all go our separate ways after that."

They worked on it for about two hours, but at the end of the session the track was just a basic repetitive jam. It wasn't yet a song, but it was a groove that could become a song.

Status: Today's session consisted of a jam, which remains unreleased.

No work order has been found for this session, but it has been discussed in interviews.

SATURDAY, DECEMBER 31, 1983*

"**We Can Fuck**" [listed as "The Dawn"] (basic tracking and overdubs)
Sunset Sound, Studio 3 | 3:00 p.m.–9:00 p.m. (booked 2:00 p.m.–open)
Producer: Prince | *Artist:* Prince | *Engineer:* Prince | *Assistant Engineer:* Terry Christian

He was never prepared. He just came in and got a groove going. Never really knowing what's going to come next is what keeps him fresh. His demos are the masters. —Terry Christian

This was the first year since his debut was released in 1978 that Prince didn't deliver an album. *1999* was a double record and certainly increased his visibility, but he probably realized he needed to create a demand for his music even though he had banked enough to create an album without recording any new music. (In 1985 Prince told *Rolling Stone* magazine: "**I have the follow-up album to *1999*. I could put it all together and play it for you, and you would** go 'Yeah!' And I could put it out, and it would probably sell what *1999* did. But I always try to do something different and conquer new ground.")[11] By not releasing a new record, Prince had created anticipation for his new work. For a workaholic in the studio, this means he was stockpiling his songs, waiting until the proper moment to share them with his fans. The next year was slated to be the biggest in Prince's career, and he wanted people hungry.

The year 1983 had been the sort of year any artist would want. In almost every possible way, Prince was on a creative high note unlike at any other time in his career. Most of the *Purple Rain* movie had been shot and he was on an inspired roll and on the verge of getting the respect he knew he deserved, but directly ahead of him was a lot of work. He'd have to find a way to keep the Time from self-destructing while they finished their third album and create an entire album of new songs for Apollonia 6, but for some reason he ended the year working on a track that wouldn't fit on either album. The song, based on the previous day's jam session, wouldn't be released for another six years, and even then, in a highly censored form.

"I remember that day very well as it was New Year's Eve, and I didn't want to work," recalls Terry Christian. Prince listed the track as "The Dawn" but Christian says it was a fake title because the original was "too sexy to release. The title was 'We Can Fuck.'"

The concept of "The Dawn" was something he'd played with for a while. It is unclear whether he'd recorded a song with that title by that point, but according to those around him "may you live to see the dawn" was a phrase he used quite frequently, and he eventually even used it in his album artwork. "The Dawn" was also the name of a movie project he'd planned several years down the road.

David Coleman recalls that Prince was very excited about getting the song to tape: "I just remember Prince going, 'Come on. Come on, we're going to lose it!' And there was all this repatching everything in and getting us going. And he just said, 'Play that riff' [on the oud] and we'll do it for fifteen minutes and just play it over and over again. Prince counted off and he said, 'Ready, 1, 2, 3 . . .' I remember Prince saying, 'Oh, you're getting a little Italian on it,' because I was going, "Do do do ding ding, do, ding ding, diddle, diddle, diddle."

Prince played drums while Coleman was in the isolation booth playing the oud on the basic tracks. Afterward they added a few additional touches, including Coleman on finger cymbals and Prince likely on synth, keyboards, and bass. "Then we called it a day," Coleman says. "He left unannounced. 'Where's Prince?' 'Oh, he left.' He was the nicest guy, but he would just vanish or something."

The recording of "We Can Fuck" would be a turning point for Prince, as he was always looking for inspiration and found it with the infusion of David Coleman's Middle Eastern vision. "My brother David had a big influence on him," reflected Lisa Coleman. "David [who passed away in March 2004] left an amazing impact on the world and he was quite a musical genius and very worldly. He was quite a character. He taught himself to speak Arabic and French and Spanish, and he was like that with music, too."[12]

"[Prince's] ear was getting more mature and he was hearing things that were not in his tool chest at the time," says Susannah Melvoin, "and he found with Lisa and her family and then Wendy and her family; we brought in an entirely different musical palette that inspired him, to use the finger cymbals and to have David play cello and have him play oud and do all of these things. He didn't know any of it. He knew none of it."

For now, Prince was preparing for additional work on the *Purple Rain* movie, album, and tour, but the seeds had been planted for his follow-up album, *Around the World in a Day*, and Prince was someone who had trouble focusing on only one project at a time.

Status: The name of "We Can Fuck" (10:18) was changed to "We Can Funk," and the track was eventually rerecorded in June 1986 with the Revolution (5:43) during the sessions for the unreleased *Dream Factory* album. According to Eric Leeds, there was a humorous side note during that session. The Revolution referred to it with an alternate title based on the song's initials, W.C.F: "'W.C. Fields' was our working title, our code name for it."[13]

In late 1989 the song was reworked again (5:28), shifting back to the basic recording from this session and adding several elements, including George Clinton's vocals as well as vocals from members of Clinton's band. The track was edited and mixed for release on *Graffiti Bridge* in 1990. "There was a whole new bass part," recalls Sunset Sound engineer Stephen Shelton about the 1989 version. "There are some of the original instruments in the final mix that came from the original date. The drums, I believe, were changed, there were a couple of other things that were overdubbed, but there are bits and pieces of the original mix in there."

It was the only *Purple Rain* era song that was used in the sequel to *Purple Rain*, *Graffiti Bridge*. The song was released as "We Can Fuck" (10:18) on the *Purple Rain Deluxe* (Expanded Edition) CD set in 2017.

JANUARY 1984

"We Can Fuck" [listed as "Moral Majority"] (overdubs)
Sunset Sound, Studio 3 | 2:30 p.m.–4:45 a.m. (booked 2:00 p.m.–open)
Producer: Prince | *Artist:* Prince | *Engineer:* Prince | *Assistant Engineer:*
Terry Christian

*The original version is astonishing. If I were to count five songs
of his that were my favorites, that's right up there. It's one of the
most amazing tracks he has ever done.—*Susan Rogers[1]

New Year's Day occurred on a Sunday and Los Angeles was basically shut
down . . . except Sunset Sound, which opened the studio for Prince.

At a New Year's Eve party, Prince had met a woman named Ashe (who was
associated with the musical group Direct Drive) and invited her down to the
studio. Wally Safford, Prince's friend and one of his bodyguards, was sent to
bring her to Sunset Sound while he continued to overdub the track. When she
arrived, Prince wanted her to hear the track in progress. According to Ashe, the
song was referred to as "Sex" instead of "We Can Fuck." At 5:15 p.m. Prince
took a break and left the studio with Ashe. "We went out for dinner, then Prince
went to do the vocals for 'Sex,'" she said. "He asked me to leave then because
he'd get really embarrassed. I could see why when he played me the song. It
was really rude."[2]

Once Ashe left for the night, Prince had Christian set up his microphone to sing: "I remember a knockout vocal. He was the only one in the studio when he sang it." All of Prince's lyrics are open to interpretation and, as he's stated, they can be based on something happening in his life, so it is easy to imagine why he'd sing "Cause though I just met you, there's this energy between us. . . ."[3]

For the next ten hours, Prince added more vocal overdubs to the song. Wendy Melvoin and Lisa Coleman probably added their vocals to the mix that evening. Jill Jones also recorded a part for the track, but not in her usual capacity. Instead, Prince recorded her in the throes of ecstasy, even though she isn't credited on the track, as she recalls: "I was always little bit adamant about 'We Can Fuck.' I am on that record and not to be descriptive, but yes, I just know I'm on it. And then I guess he expanded on that section because I went out from there and he went in and filled in all the blanks. And I went into the side room and I was just watching TV. (*laughs*)"

Artists' career growth can often be mapped out based on the music they release, but sometimes what they choose not to allow the public to hear can be very illuminating as well. Occasionally with artists as prolific as Prince, a song will surface that can be viewed as a missing link from one era to another. "We Can Fuck" is one of those tracks. Building on the complexity and experimentation of "Computer Blue," he shifted his sound slightly but profoundly with the addition of the new and exotic instruments supplied by David Coleman. Instruments such as finger cymbals, the oud, and the riq (an Arabic tambourine) intrigued Prince, but mastering some of the exotic instruments wasn't easy. "I remember being at Wendy and Susannah's apartment," recalls David Coleman. "And I had the oud and he picked it up and fingered it [like a guitar] for a second and went, 'Ew!' and gave it back to me and he said, and I remember his exact words, 'It sounds so cool, but I can't get used to the feel.' So he really loved the instrument, but he decided that 'I don't play that instrument.'"

These new sounds would dictate the vector of Prince's next album, and this track was a point of entry for the psychedelic vibe of *Around the World in a Day*. David Coleman was a very important person in the charting of Prince's new direction.

"I *know* that my brother inspired Prince, and I am proud of that," reflects Lisa Coleman. "We all loved each other and got so much out of being together. It was all for a common good, so I have never felt competitive in any way. My brother and I were always extremely close, and admired each other greatly. He was a genius in ways I still have never reached, and he would say that I was his idol . . . his older sister! We all influenced each other, and cheered each other on!"

As with the previous day's session, Prince requested that the true title, "We Can Fuck," not be used on the daily work order. Instead, he substituted it with the title of an unreleased Vanity 6 track, "Moral Majority."

No mix was done, more than likely because he knew the session would continue the following day.

MONDAY, JANUARY 2, 1984*

"We Can Fuck" [listed as "Moral Majority"] (overdubs, vocals, and mix)
Sunset Sound, Studio 3 | 3:30 p.m.–4:00 a.m. (booked 3:00 p.m.–open)
Producer: Prince | *Artist:* Prince | *Engineer:* Prince | *Assistant Engineer:* Terry Christian

Prince isn't aware of anything that's going on around him. He told me he hasn't got many friends and I said, "I'm not surprised. You're in this blooming studio all the time!"—Ashe[4]

Prince spent another day working on "We Can Fuck." Because of the pending deadlines for his movie, his album, and music for his protégés, it didn't make sense for him to lose focus recording a track that would basically sit on the shelf for years, but this is part of the reason he was one of the most intriguing performers in pop music. Prince often followed where the music led him: **"I'm happiest making records that tell the truth, and I don't beat around the bush. I have to be what I am and sing what's on my mind."**[5] He also explained that the reason he rushed through projects is the need to "**[get] it all out before another idea comes along.**"[6]

Because Prince seemed to enjoy the process of creating, it is likely that for him, the thrill came with beginning a project. Wrapping up the final details can be boring, and finishing a song or album may be delayed in favor of starting a new and compelling project. Terry Christian believes that Prince followed his urges when it came to creating music: "Everything he does is purely inspired work. As soon as he is bored with something he moves on. He's very impatient. That's why there's so many unfinished projects [in his vault]."

Prince would eventually be forced to focus on what he needed to do, but on days like this one he was focused on what he *wanted* to do. "Prince had a never-ending supply of energy," reveals Christian, "but never any drugs that helped that along. He would order dinner from Martoni's, and he wouldn't eat it because he was afraid of getting tired from it."

Additional work was done on "We Can Fuck," and the final two hours of the session were spent mixing the track.

WEDNESDAY, JANUARY 4, 1984*

"**The Bird**" [live version] (overdub and mix)
Sunset Sound, Studio 3 | 2:30 p.m.–11:00 p.m. (booked 3:00 p.m.–open)
Producer: Morris Day (Prince crossed out) | *Artist:* The Time (Prince crossed out) | *Engineer:* Prince | *Assistant Engineer:* Terry Christian

> *If he was awake, as long as he wasn't on the phone handling business, for the most part, Prince was recording. I've never known anyone else who works like that.*—Susan Rogers[7]

Prince shifted his focus back to some of the projects he needed to complete, and he began working on the live version of "The Bird" from the October 4, 1983, concert by the Time. The original tape captured the band's energy, and if used, would be the first time the entire band would all perform on any of their albums. More importantly, it was the first officially released song by the Time that potentially did not involve Prince controlling the session. However, once he listened to the track, Prince decided that he could do better on some of the instruments. Terry Christian witnessed Prince's need to leave his mark on the track as he selectively replaced various parts with his own performance: "Prince was putting up the tape and going over old guitar parts, him playing guitar instead of Jesse. He made a comment like, 'Jesse can't play that good.' Very arrogant."

"Prince is such an asshole. He's [so] scared of people rising to his level that he always tries to keep you down," Jesse Johnson reflected in 1986. "He played so many mind trips on us—which we had to take or be fired. The stage was our only release. That's why [the Time] were such a treacherous band. When we hit the stage we had a serious mental grudge. Some nights we'd knock on his dressing room door and say, 'We're going to slaughter you!'"[8]

Alan Leeds acknowledged the tension between Johnson and Prince, especially during this period: "You had Jesse, who did not grow up with these guys.

He was the outsider, and probably the most competitive with Prince, because of the fact that they both played guitar, and the reality is Prince is scared to death of how Jesse plays. Prince will tell you that the only guitar player on the planet he's scared of is Jesse, that there are other guitar players who are better, but the only one who can threaten him at what he does is Jesse."[9]

Jellybean Johnson had a different perspective on Prince's way of controlling those around him by pushing them: "He has a way, and it may not be the nicest way. It's almost like he's Bobby Knight or something. It's amazing what you can find yourself doing when you're around him. Because he demands it. He *demands* it. And I admire that. He makes you do things that you think you couldn't do, but you end up doing them. Everybody that's ever been in his band is a lot better musician today than they were before."[10]

The bottom line was that Prince was in control in practically every way, and everyone around him understood that. Accepting his authority was the ante required to stay in the room.

Even on all of his side projects, Prince oversaw every detail and dominated the decisions. The first two albums by the Time were basically recorded by Prince and Morris Day—"Initially Prince did everything," remembered Day. "I played drums and did most of the vocals, but he did most of it. He was sort of opposed to the idea of anybody else doing anything."[11] Every musician in the Time was very talented, but the problem was that Prince could arguably play their instruments as well or better, and since he wrote the majority of their music he didn't need to rely on help from anyone else, and often the members of the Time waited for Prince to invite them to participate in the studio.

"Morris would be around, but I never saw them working together," according to Christian, who engineered several of their sessions. "Whenever the Time was around they would be sitting in the lounge. They were outside the room. It was Prince's show and everybody else was the hired help. I'm sure they did stuff, but not when I was around. When I was around it was them waiting for him to do his thing."

Prince's tight grip unfortunately ended up slowly destroying his own creation. "I was always planning on leaving," Jesse Johnson confessed in 2011. "You really can't fulfill whatever your personal goal is through a group situation. You need something that's just all about you and something that massages your own ego, if you will."[12]

Despite a few technical problems, several instruments were left virtually unchanged, including most of the live drumming, because of the energy of the performance. "Mistakes and everything are left, that's how he is," said Jellybean

Johnson.[13] "I broke a stick right before the last chorus, and I wanted them to use another version because of that, but Prince liked the energy of the live thing."[14]

By the time Prince had finished adding his embellishments to "The Bird," it featured much less of the Time. Prince added new keyboards and completely rerecorded Rocky Harris's bass, then mixed it very low in the final version. It would have been Harris's only part on a song by the Time, as he was in the band for only a brief period. It wasn't uncommon for members of the Time to be on call and just hanging out at Sunset Sound or close by the studio waiting to help out, even though the chance to add to the song often never came. "I sat there for like two or three hours," commented Jellybean Johnson. "But if you say anything, you're wasting your fucking time. It's going to be his way or the highway. He has his ideas and obviously he's had enough hits to know. It must work. Somebody liked it."[15]

Prince had members of the Time add background vocals, and the session ended earlier than usual. A very rough mix was done, leaving a full mix until the following day. Three cassettes were made of the session for review.

Status: The original live version of "The Bird" (7:56) contained three extra callbacks from Day (including another "chili sauce," a squawk, and a "one mo' time"). Prince kept these for today's version but eventually created an edit of the song (7:03) for release on the *Ice Cream Castle* album. An additional thirty seconds of music box sound effects were added to the final album version.

The song was also released in an edited single version (3:41) and a remix (6:25).

THURSDAY, JANUARY 5, 1984*

"**The Bird**" [live version] (mix)
Unnamed track (basic tracking for "Oliver's House")
Sunset Sound, Studio 3 | 1:00 p.m.–5:30 a.m. (booked 1:00 p.m.–open)
Producer: Prince (although he was crossed out) | *Artist:* The Time (Prince crossed out) | *Engineer:* Prince | *Assistant Engineer:* Terry Christian

> *Most keyboard players don't have good rhythm. You have to have an intimate relationship with the beat, and either have it or you don't. You can't learn it.*—Prince[16]

The first four hours of this session were spent mixing "The Bird." Terry Christian noticed that Prince had the same philosophy about mixing a song as he did about tracking one: "He is not a perfectionist at all in technical terms, but if it feels good then for him, it's right. He would be mixing a song and the meters would be pegged. Rather than modifying the levels he would put a track sheet in front of the meters so he wouldn't see them flaming. If it's funky then that's all that matters."

At 5:00 p.m. the mix was done and Prince asked for a fresh 2-inch tape and started working on another song. It would eventually become "Oliver's House" for Sheila E., but for tonight it had no name. "Until it has a lyric, there isn't a title," says Christian. "He would say: 'Put on anything, maybe what we recorded the day before, as the title.'"

The next twelve hours were spent working on the new track. A mix of "The Bird" and of the unnamed instrumental were created and put to tape. Prince took the cassette to write the lyrics before he returned.

The session ended at 5:30 a.m.

FRIDAY, JANUARY 6, 1984*

"Oliver's House" (vocals and various overdubs)
"The Glamorous Life" (cello overdub)
Sunset Sound, Studio 3 | 3:00 p.m.–1:45 a.m. (booked 4:00 p.m.–open)
Producer: Prince | Artist: Prince | Engineer: Prince | Assistant Engineer: Bill Jackson (although Terry Christian was listed)

Prince loved my brother's sense of humor before he had even heard one note of his music, or [his] musical abilities on several instruments. My brother was one of the funniest people I knew and one of the few people that made Prince crack up. Prince would also imitate my brother's hilarious version of someone screaming, "Look out! She's gonna blow!" in a growling adventure hero yarl! That always gave everyone a belly laugh.—Lisa Coleman

"We were working extremely fast," recalls Bill Jackson, who was back in the engineer seat for today's session. "The songs were in his head and he just needed to put it down on tape."

Prince's playful mood shined through in the lyrics and on the page on which they were written. He referred to a neighborhood slut with the absurd name "Glodean," and an examination of the handwritten lyrics shows that he even doodled a castlelike house on the top of the page, complete with stick figures playing in a swimming pool. Once the lyrics were complete, Prince added his vocals to the previous night's instrumental, giving the song a title: "Oliver's House." It is unclear who Oliver was, but he would be revisited a month later on the Apollonia 6 track "In a Spanish Villa," and it is easy to hear how "Oliver's House" could have been placed on the *Apollonia 6* album as well. Additional instruments were overdubbed, and by 8:00 p.m. Prince was looking for someone else to help him find a specific sound.

Over the last few months Prince had seemed to become enamored with the new sounds that were coming from those around him. Sheila E. was gently guiding his music in a new direction, Wendy Melvoin and Lisa Coleman were expanding his emotional range, and Lisa's brother David was bringing a new and yet classic exotic flavor to his music, so Prince asked him to drop by the studio with his cello. He arrived at 10:00 p.m. "He sang what he had in mind and he said, 'Come up with some kind of cheesy melody, what have you got?'" chuckles Coleman. "We both laughed because we both had this thing about cheese: 'Let's have some of that cheese David.' And so I first did pizzicato [plucking] and he said, 'Not that one.' So I did a variation of the *Father Knows Best* theme and that's what that is when the cello drifts out into different keys."

Prince also asked Coleman to add the iconic cello riff to "The Glamorous Life" during this session.

It is likely that Jill Jones was also in attendance and added her background vocals to "Oliver's House" today. According to Jones, she had a very intimate understanding about what he wanted from her: "One interesting thing about recording with him, he wasn't like, 'Can you do it again?' For some reason, you knew, 'I don't think I really nailed that, I'm going to have to do that again!' He's not pushy. He'd just say, 'Can you try something different . . . just do whatever.' He was really good at that."

As the session wound down, Prince created a rough mix of "Oliver's House" and "The Glamorous Life." After making two cassettes, he kept one and gave the other to David Coleman: "He gave me a cassette and I said, 'What about one for the girls?' And he said . . . 'Um, that is for the girls.'"

Status: Sheila E.'s vocals eventually replaced Prince's guide track on "Oliver's House" (6:20) for the version included on her debut album, *The Glamorous*

Life. An edited version (3:14) was released as the B-side of the "Noon Rendez-vous" single.

SUNDAY, JANUARY 8, 1984*

"17 Days" (basic tracking)
"Oliver's House" (overdubs)
"She's Always in My Hair" (probable overdubs and mix)
Sunset Sound, Studio 3 | 2:30 p.m.–4:45 a.m. (booked ?–open)
Producer: Prince | *Artist:* Prince | *Engineer:* Prince | *Assistant Engineer:* Bill Jackson

All of my songs are an extension of me, and any one song couldn't have been written without the other. And just like children, I wouldn't place any above the other.—Prince[17]

Bill Jackson got an early morning phone call saying, "'[Prince is] on his way down. He's got the whole band coming in and you've got to go in and set up the room.' He's on his way and I'm just waking up. I got in like around five [o'clock] and he was calling me in the morning."

The band began arriving around 2:30 p.m., and Wendy Melvoin, Lisa Coleman, and Prince took their places in the room. They were separated by gobo panels (for soundproofing) and amps, which Jackson had mic'd with a Shure SM57 microphone on each one. Bobby Z, David Coleman, and Jonathan Melvoin joined them as well. "Jonathan was in the back in an isolated room playing bongos or something," recalls Jackson. "David was playing cello and there was Lisa on the keyboards, although I think that Prince came over and played something too. Basically they all set up and all played at once, which was nothing like I had expected at all."

Prince and the band worked on the track "17 Days" for the next two hours. They had taken a swing at the song the previous summer—with Brenda Bennett singing the lead—and he decided to give it another try. Probably because the band was just riffing on a familiar track, Prince requested that the tape roll at 15 inches per second (IPS) instead of the usual 30 IPS, giving them thirty minutes of recording space on the tape. Jackson objected but was overruled by Prince: "I said 'That's not aligned. It's not going to sound right,' but he didn't care about that and said, 'Just do it.' He didn't care about that stuff. He just wanted the right vibe. Maybe if he had taken more time to be a little 'hi-fi,' he might have lost the edge."

Although the engineer was not ready to record, Prince started working on the song; Jackson furiously kept plugging the various instruments directly into the mixer, but not everything was being fed to the tape and those tracks that were making it onto the tape did not have the proper EQ (equalization/adjustments to the frequencies of the sound used to smooth out an audio signal): "As they were playing I was adding some EQ and making things sound a little better and getting the levels right and they played until the tape ran out for like thirty minutes." The track would be another of Prince's songs built around a long, repetitive jam similar to other tracks he'd recorded, including "Possessed," "I Would Die 4 U," and "Controversy." Overdubs—including tambourine, additional vocals, and other elements—lasted another four hours.

As midnight got closer, Prince wanted to work on "Oliver's House" again. He asked Jackson to find a harp player, so he grabbed a copy of the local American Federation of Musicians yearly roster, contacted a harpist at random, and booked her for the current session. He remembers:

About an hour later, this woman shows up in this nice, plush van. And she is someone who looks like she'd play harp in the church and not in a rock band. And her husband is in a tie, and she is almost in a gown and I thought, "Oh well, this will be interesting. If she is a good player, this will probably work." So they bring in the harp. Her husband is acting like the roadie and setting it up. I introduce her to Prince. I'm not sure if she knew who he was. Back then, she probably wouldn't have known who he was. So she sits down, and Prince said, "I'm going to play this and I'll just point at you, and I want you to play this [harp type] sound, glisten on the strings." So she sat up and the song went by and she does this very strict kind of glistening and Prince says, "Let's try this one more time. Be fluid." So we do it again and I think he gave her a few shots at it and I remember he walked out there and said, "Well lady, it ain't killing me." She looked at him and asked, "Well, is there something else you'd like me to do?" "No, that's okay. You're done."

Prince paid her for the entire three-hour session despite her harp not making it on the final mix.

"In the meantime," Jackson continues, "[Prince] wanted an accordion, so I had to do the same thing, and called an accordion player, [Nick DeCaro] and he came in, and he let me know that the accordion isn't his main instrument and Prince said, 'That's good,' because he didn't want it to sound really polished.

So he came in and he did his part and Prince knew exactly what he wanted and he got it and sent him on his way."

At the end of the night, three TDK SA C-60 cassettes were used to copy a quick mix that was made of "17 Days" and "Oliver's House." It is probable that a mix for "She's Always in My Hair" was done on this date as well. It is unclear whether any additional was work done on the track, but if there was, it was elements like adding finger cymbals and double and quadruple bass drum over the end. The mix done today also eliminated the false ending from the original version.

Although Prince would remain at Sunset Sound, most of his upcoming sessions would be scheduled exclusively for Studio 2. This would be his last full session in Studio 3 until March.

Status: The new version of "17 Days" (7:25) sat on the shelf for two months before it was worked on again. It was considered for release as an extended B-side, but ultimately only an edited version (3:56) was released as a flip side of "When Doves Cry."

On some releases, the full title was "17 Days (the rain will come down, then U will have 2 choose, if U believe, look 2 the dawn and U shall never lose)." The full version remains unreleased.

"17 Days" was possibly recorded on December 30, 1983, but the work order for today lists it as being tracked during this session. Prince's work orders from this era are notoriously ambiguous on some occasions, but until evidence indicates otherwise, this date will be considered as the session for the released version of "17 Days."

MONDAY, JANUARY 9, 1984*

Untitled jam session with Sheila E.
"Oliver's House" (overdubs)
Sunset Sound, Studio 2 & 3 | 8:30 p.m.–12:30 a.m. (booked 7:00 p.m.–open)
Producer: Prince | *Artist:* Prince | *Engineer:* Prince | *Assistant Engineer:* Bill Jackson

I've come to think of percussion as the last color added that turns a pretty painting into the most beautiful painting in the world.—Sheila E.[18]

During this time Prince maintained a lot of company in the studio. Gone were the days of his ban on visitors. Wendy Melvoin, Lisa Coleman, Apollonia, Jill Jones, and many others were invited to just hang out and watch, but often they'd come in shifts or waves so they weren't in the studio at the same time. Bill Jackson, who had been engineering various recent sessions, remembers his own introduction to one of them:

> There was this woman sitting in the control room beside me not saying a word. She was wearing a T-shirt and jeans being very quiet, coming in for several days, and I'm kind of quiet and working at the same time, and we literally didn't say anything. I'm in the control room and Prince is going in and out of there, and finally when there was kind of a lull, I turned to her and said, 'Are you a musician?' and she said, 'I'm a dancer and percussionist, and I've played with Lionel Richie and Prince had come to a show and invited me down to the studio.' Next thing I realized is that most of the stuff that we'd been working on was actually for [Sheila E.'s] record, regardless of what it said on the work order.

To many around him, there was an unspoken understanding that at any time, inspiration could strike and everything would change. Plans would be canceled, a mix would turn into a recording session, or downtime would turn into a hastily planned studio session. Lisa Coleman reflected on Prince during this period: "All we did was watch movies, eat, and write music. It was incredibly prolific. Everything was a song. Anything we thought of or joked about or felt would be written five minutes later into a song."[19]

This was such a day. Jackson remembers:

> If he came in and he didn't feel like working, he would just leave. He'd go see a movie, go to a concert or go out and play basketball, whatever, and he might come back and he might not. You had to wait there until someone called and said that he wasn't going to come back . . . unless he just absolutely said, 'Nope, I'm going home,' and then you went home and waited for the phone to ring. (*laughs*) But I kind of admired that because he worked fast enough that he still didn't spend any more money than people who worked every day. He worked when he was inspired and he didn't when he wasn't. Outside of that, the mood was very nice and uplifting. Very exciting. Anytime that someone was there that was a friend or a buddy like Morris, it was just a great situation.

Today Prince started out jamming with Sheila E., looking for a groove. This was something that he had done regularly with Morris Day, but Prince was likely expanding his interests and had found a new muse in Sheila, a female drummer who could keep up with him and inspire him on many levels. Although the session was taking place in Studio 2, Sheila's drums were set up in Studio 3 for recording. Once Jackson had her kit properly mic'd, the impromptu jam session began. "I don't think this turned into a song," remembers Jackson. "They were just jamming. He had a formula for making his hits, and this type of drumming wasn't part of that. They were just having fun." For the next groove, Prince picked up the bass and played along. "He would either play one or the other [keyboards or bass] at a time. I never saw him doing both at the same time."

Between 8:30 p.m. and 10:00 p.m., Sheila added drums to "Oliver's House" in Studio 3. Once they were recorded, everyone returned to Studio 2 for overdubs. Sheila's lead vocals were not added on this date.

Although there was no mix and output to tape listed on this work order, it is fairly certain that the addition of Sheila's drums meant Prince would want to create a brief rough mix that he'd dub to cassette for his own personal use.

Status: The only new music recorded on this date were the various studio jams involving Prince and Sheila E., and those recordings remain unreleased, although it is possible that "Shortberry Strawcake" was created on this date.

TUESDAY, JANUARY 10, 1984*

"The Bird" (studio version review and live version overdubs)
Sunset Sound, Studio 2 | 7:00 p.m.–11:00 p.m. (booked 7:00 p.m.–open)
Producer: Prince | *Artist:* the Time (although Prince was listed) | *Engineer:* Prince | *Assistant Engineer:* Bill Jackson

Prince played everything on the studio version of "The Bird" and it's sick!—Jesse Johnson[20]

According to Jackson, it was a hectic time for Prince: "Around this time he was doing several projects at once, and to tell you the truth, I never knew whose record I was working on. I never knew until the end when I was doing some stuff and Morris Day was there that I was doing some stuff for the Time." In fact, the work order lists Prince as the artist and producer, which means that the purpose of the session probably wasn't locked in until arrival.

Prince had finished overdubbing the live version of the "The Bird" for the Time, but he apparently wasn't completely happy with it. Perhaps the live energy stood out from the rest of the album, or perhaps he wanted to add elements from the original track that he'd recorded in April 1983 at his home studio in Minneapolis to the live version. But for whatever reason, Prince decided to spend the first ninety minutes of the session reviewing his studio demo and comparing the two versions to determine which would work best in the context of the album. Jackson remembers that "they had a copy of the live one and would play it and they would listen to the solo, and from what I can remember, this is Prince basically playing everything, and the reason why was because he knew what he wanted to do. It was Prince and Morris. I don't remember the whole band being there. I didn't work with other members of the band. They popped by to listen, but I don't remember them playing."

Although Wendy Melvoin and Lisa Coleman were possibly around for this session, Jackson doesn't remember recording them on this date: "I specifically remember Prince doing the keyboard parts. I remember I was punching in and out for it."

The studio demo started differently than the live version. The first few bars of the drum introduction sounded like a variation of "Little Red Corvette" (from the *1999* album). Prince continued to work on the guitar parts for the song and, as had happened a week earlier, he wasn't completely happy with the outcome. According to Jackson, "[Prince] was a great guitar player and he played this solo and it sounded incredible. He played something that was great and said, 'Erase it' because it was too good. It was just too good to make it work. He wanted it to be believable. It wasn't that it was too good for the Time, it was just that the song didn't demand Jimi Hendrix. And maybe it wasn't right, but for me it was a great solo." In fact, Prince ended up hiding Jesse Johnson's solo, which would have occurred at 4:11 on the album version, by burying it in the mix. A small section can be heard at 4:28, but the solo was practically hidden until it was brought back at 4:55.

The final two hours were spent working on additional overdubs to the track. It is unclear why the session wrapped up at 11:00 p.m., but a quick mix was probably created of the song at this point. It would be put away for a week so Prince could focus on other tracks.

Status: The studio version of "The Bird" (6:29) remains unreleased.

WEDNESDAY, JANUARY 11, 1984*

> **"My Drawers"** (basic tracking)
> Sunset Sound, Studio 2 | 7:00 p.m.–3:45 a.m. (booked 7:00 p.m.–open)
> *Producer:* Prince | *Artist:* the Time (although Prince was listed, Morris
> Day signed the work order) | *Engineer:* Prince | *Assistant Engineer:* Bill
> Jackson

*What I learned from Prince about the studio was there are
absolutely no rules. Stuff people said about spending a million
dollars on equipment and going to recording school, he flushed
all that down the toilet.*—Jesse Johnson[21]

During the *1999* tour Prince focused on creating a dynasty by promoting and
selling his own music as well as music from the Time and Vanity 6. It appeared
that Prince didn't want to just duplicate that success for his film project and
tour—he wanted it to grow. With the *1999* tour he started at a certain level and
expanded, but the movie would give him a forum to prove to everyone that his
last album's success wasn't a fluke. But before any of that, he had to create the
music, so this week Prince was focused on completing the (as yet untitled) third
album by the Time. Today he started another track from scratch: "My Drawers."

Setting up the drums was often the most time-consuming and challenging
task for the engineer, especially during a session for the Time, because left-
handed drummers like Morris Day required a different setup than right-handed
drummers like Prince and Bobby Z. "Morris played drums on 'My Drawers,'"
recalls Jackson. "And if Prince wanted to play drums, I'd have to change everything. Not just the mics, but the whole drum setup had to move around."

The first hour was spent working on the basic tracks, with Day on drums
and Prince on bass. After that, Prince asked Day to start writing the lyrics, so
Day grabbed a pad and a pen and sat down on the couch in the control room.
Jackson recalls that Prince started recording on the Oberheim synth, which was
also set up in the control room, but he kept looking over to see if Day had come
up with any lyrics: "We'd be working for about fifteen or twenty minutes and
then we'd stop the tape and Prince would say, 'Morris, what ya got there?' and
there wouldn't be anything on the pad. Work a little bit more . . . and he'd look
down there and say, 'Morris, what ya got? Got anything?' Nothing. And this
went on for about an hour and a half. Maybe two hours. He didn't write a word.
And Prince was putting the rest of the song together."

Everyone was in a good mood and the recording was going very smoothly, but still no lyrics were being written. Jackson remembers:

[Prince] made some comment about if he got done with the music and Morris didn't have any lyrics, then Prince would have to write them because we were really going fast, and during this time everything was going really fast. So he said something like, "If you don't write any lyrics, you aren't going to make any money off of publishing," so he went over there and got the pen and pad out of Morris's hand and he sat over on the couch and quickly just wrote down the lyrics like he was writing down a grocery list, and about fifteen minutes later he was done. It was probably in his head already and then that was it. And then he went out and started working on the melody of it, working on the singing.

Jesse Johnson has recalled recording the solo, but Jackson has a different recollection: "On this song, Jesse didn't do much. On this solo, I think it is Prince. I'm sure I remember recording that. I would swear that it was Prince playing guitar. I can remember what guitar he was playing. It was his Hohner. Most of what he was playing on this record was on that guitar. He had a rack of Boss pedals and he used them to get that squeezey-swirly sound."

Whoever was actually playing the solo, Prince decided to bury it in the mix, much like he did on "The Bird." In 2016, days after Prince's passing, Jesse Johnson shared his memory of working with his friend: "When Prince did the Time records . . . he wanted total control. The problem was who's going to argue with him about it, because who else knows how to make a record in this room other than him? He should have had total control, he was the only one that was successful, he was the only one who had made records. No one else had made records. He knew what to do so listen, shut up, listen, and learn, and that's what I did."[22]

The lead vocals were recorded and at the end of the session. "My Drawers" was copied to a cassette for Prince's private archival purposes and to play outside the studio, but no real mix was done on this date. The song would become a favorite among many fans as well as those in the band, including Terry Lewis, who had been fired from the group a year earlier but would rejoin later in the decade. In a 2010 interview on KMOJ, he expressed his affection for the track: "I love 'My Drawers.' I don't know why, it's just a fun song to play. That's a really fun song to play."[23]

Status: "My Drawers" (4:04) was released on the Time's *Ice Cream Castle* album. It was edited/faded out early (3:43) for release as the B-side for "The Bird." It was also released as a B-side for "Chocolate" in 1990.

THURSDAY, JANUARY 12, 1984*

"My Drawers" (overdubs)
"Tricky" (not listed)
Sunset Sound, Studio 2 | 7:00 p.m.–4:00 a.m. (7:00 p.m.–open)
Producer: Prince | Artist: the Time (Prince was listed, but Morris Day signed the work order) | Engineer: Prince | Assistant Engineer: Bill Jackson

Morris was the guy who could make him laugh more than anyone on the planet.—Wendy Melvoin[24]

Prince was likely in a great mood, having been nominated for two Grammy Awards earlier in the week for his work on "1999" and "International Lover," and he and Day were probably enjoying the upbeat vibe. Although Day and Prince had some serious disagreements over the last few months, it seems like they shared a friendship (although sometimes strained) and a mutual desire to finish the *Purple Rain* project as well as the third album for the Time. After losing most of the Time, perhaps Prince was working hard to keep the core of the band from leaving. "The four of us—me, Jimmy, Monte, and Terry—were needed," according to Jellybean Johnson, "but Morris and Jesse were the two centerpieces, were his two trophies. Everybody else was interchangeable."[25]

Day may have agreed with that assessment of his role in the band, but although he was vital to the project, he wasn't happy with his input. "I did as much as I was allowed to do," he explained in 1984. "I could have done more. I think that you can actually look at the Time—the whole project—and what you're seeing is me. The songs that I didn't write, if I didn't write them, I inspired the titles. The things that people saw me do is where the lyrics came from. The humor and the attitude, they all came from me. So whether I wrote the songs or not, it all came from me. All the sayings and everything."[26]

Further overdubs, including Prince's addition of drums as well as Day's vocal fixes and pickups, were recorded for "My Drawers" during the evening. Background vocals were recorded with Jill Jones, and she recalls standing around the microphone with Morris Day as they chanted together: "I particularly remember the yelling of the 'My Drawers' part, which was pretty funny. And I would change my voice like (*singing*) 'My Drawers, My Drawers,' just to make it sound like you were all different people."

During a break in the session, Prince and Day took in a concert. It is likely that they went to see Genesis, who were playing a three-night stand at the Forum.

Like "Cloreen Bacon Skin" (recorded on March 27, 1983), "Tricky" was an ad-libbed studio jam involving Prince and Day that contained a similar beat. As with the other song, it was basically a studio exercise to see what groove could be created and probably wasn't initially intended for release on an album, but it fit very well as a B-side for "Ice Cream Castles." Bill Jackson tells the story about the song's origin: "Three or four hours later they come back and they are giggling so hard that they can hardly speak, and they'd been talking about something on the way over and they had an idea and he couldn't even talk because he was laughing so hard, and he said, 'Set up the drums,' because Morris was going to play drums . . . it was set up the other way because Prince was playing drums earlier, so I had to run out there and flip everything back to left-handed. And Prince said, 'Get me that bass' and we had this jazz bass that we rented from SIR [Studio Instrument Rentals] and it was great."

Prince told Jackson, "You've got to get a mic for both of us," so he set up a Neumann U 87 for each of them: "They were both about to bust because they wanted to put this thing on tape for them and I had no idea what was going on, and as soon as I had it set up he said, 'Roll the tape,' and I started the 24-track and he just started going through his thing, and Morris is singing while he is playing drums and Prince is singing little tidbits. They are both kind of laughing in one part and we eventually went back and added a little laughter, so there are three tracks of laughing. They were splitting at the seams when we were done. They were busting out laughing all night."

After the keyboards were overdubbed (including a section of the theme from *The Tonight Show Starring Johnny Carson*), Prince asked for any sound effects of birds. Jackson located a clip containing seagulls, and they were added to the track. Prince also wanted to hear a toilet flushing at the end of the song, so Jackson hooked together multiple cables and dangled a mic above the men's bathroom down the hall. Jill Jones was visiting, so she was stationed nearby and told to wait for a cue. "When we got near the end of the song," Jackson says. "Prince pointed at her and she ran into the bathroom and flushed it. It was perfect and it ran on forever. There were these really old pipes and they hissed. He even said, 'Old pipes!'"

Jackson continues, "[The song] was about George Clinton and his greasy fingers and that old jacket he is always wearing, and it was all done in good fun. It was just like a joke thing, and I don't think there was any reference to him by name so no one would know. I asked him what he wanted to call it, and he said, 'Tricky Dick.'"

The song, which ended up being called "Tricky," contains many of the same elements as "Cloreen Bacon Skin," including variations on some of the lyrics ("When I look in the mirror, I see your ugly face . . .").[27]

At the end of the session, rough mixes for both tracks were completed and copied to two TDK SA 60 tapes, one for Day and one for Prince. In the past, Prince often created several copies of a song that he could give to the Time and tell them to learn it. Although it wasn't yet completely obvious, the need to gather the band to learn songs to perform live was becoming less and less likely.

Status: "Tricky" (3:12) was released as the B-side of "Ice Cream Castles." During live shows in 2015, Day occasionally sat behind the drums and played the track.

It has been suggested that Prince and Day saw George Clinton play on this evening, but there is no record of a performance of Clinton or any of his bands on this date.

FRIDAY, JANUARY 13, 1984*

"**Ice Cream Castles**" [listed as "My Drawers"] (basic tracking)
Sunset Sound, Studio 2 | 8:00 p.m.–6:00 a.m. (7:00 p.m.–open)
Producer: Prince | *Artist:* the Time (Prince crossed out) | *Engineer:* Prince |
Assistant Engineer: Bill Jackson

Me and Prince were so close and we had so much fun and all, and honest to God, when I think of Prince, I think about those days from '81 to '84, and I'm telling you, we did a lot of laughing.—Jesse Johnson[28]

Stories of Morris Day and Prince constantly fighting during this period seem to be exaggerated. They had some major issues, but working together on a project was something that had bonded them since they were young. "It was crazy," reflected Day about their long history of recording together. "He wanted to be in the studio all the time. That's all we did. We started playing music together when we were kids, but he's always been more of a workaholic than I am."[29]

According to Bill Jackson, the mood was good between Prince and Day: "They were laughing a lot and they were getting along great. They were doing a lot of talking. Usually Prince didn't talk a lot in the studio, but when Morris was around, he'd open up and they were talking about all kinds of stuff."

Jesse Johnson, who was also in attendance, agrees: "We did a lot of laughing. 'Cause Morris was really funny, Prince is actually really, really hilarious, and I just had a blast with them. We just had a lot of fun. We had our disagreements and things like that, but I'm telling you, I'm one of those people that I don't really hold onto a lot of negative. I remember the good."[30]

At this point the Time's new album didn't have a title, let alone a title track. Prince dug up a song that Johnson and Day had recorded in Minneapolis called "Old and Ignant" (aka "Old and Ignorant"), reworking and rewriting it to create "Ice Cream Castles." As they had done for their last few collaborations, Prince and Day spent the first hour laying down the basic tracks for the song, but this time Johnson joined them for the recording. The song began with a few seconds of Johnson's riffing before Day's drums kicked in. The rest was fairly sparse, especially for a song by the Time. "I had a lot of creative input. I played the drums and helped craft a lot of the stuff," remembered Day. "I was there every moment of putting the song together. Not to take credit for Prince: it was his vision early on. It was an alter-ego thing, things he felt he couldn't get away with and the direction he was going in."[31]

There are no indications that Prince was planning to use any lyrical content from "Old and Ignant" because no vocals were recorded for this track during today's session. The remainder of Prince's time was spent overdubbing this (still untitled) instrumental, and it is likely that other songs were given embellishments during this session as well.

A quick mix was completed and put to a single cassette so Prince could write the lyrics before the next session.

Status: The untitled instrumental (6:54) was eventually "Ice Cream Castles." Day's vocals were added and the track was released on the Time's *Ice Cream Castle* album (7:31, which contains thirty seconds of music box sounds replacing Johnson's brief guitar warm-up intro). The song was edited for release as a single (3:37) and a music video was made for it. The video was the final promotional tool created by the band for several years. Morris Day quit the Time in late spring or early summer of 1984, weeks before *Purple Rain* premiered.

SATURDAY, JANUARY 14, 1984*

"Ice Cream Castles" (vocals and overdubs)
Sunset Sound, Studio 2 | 3:00 p.m.–4:30 a.m. (booked lock-out)
Producer: Prince | *Artist:* the Time (Prince crossed out) | *Engineer:* Prince |
Assistant Engineer: Terry Christian

*[Prince was] an artist in every sense of the word. A pop vision-
ary. You see a lot of Prince copycats around. He successfully
borrows and combines ideas from other people, and he's probably going to be around for quite a while.* —Terry Christian

Terry Christian was brought back to engineer Day's vocal overdubs of the lyrics
Prince had written earlier in the day. Additional instruments were also added,
including a multilayered keyboard riff that accents Jesse's guitar. At the end of
the shift, a rough mix was completed and copies of "Ice Cream Castles" and
"My Drawers" were sent to the Warner Bros. vault.

The castle in this song was not likely influenced by Darling Nikki's castle/
home, but rather by Joni Mitchell, as Prince borrowed from the opening lines
from her 1969 song "Both Sides Now" (from the album *Clouds*): "Rows and
flows of angel hair and Ice Cream Castles in the air."[32] Prince turned the lyrics
into a laid-back request for better race relations, at least when it comes to dating.

A side note about this session: This was the last new recording of the Time for
several years. Technically, there was additional work done on the album over the
next few days and in early May when a few of the album tracks were edited down,
but for the most part this was the last new song Day recorded with Prince until
they reunited for the unreleased Time album *Corporate World* in 1989.

*During this period, Prince had 24/7 access to the room, and the work orders re-
flected this, listing them as "booked lock-out," which literally means that everyone
else is locked out of the room during the period in which it is reserved. This became
a common practice for Prince when working at Sunset Sound.*

SUNDAY, JANUARY 15, 1984*

"My Drawers" [listed as "Your Drawers"] (overdubs)
"Jungle Love" (overdubs)

Sunset Sound, Studio 2 | 3:30 p.m.–1:30 a.m. (booked lock-out)
Producer: Morris Day (Prince crossed out) | *Artist:* the Time (Prince crossed out) | *Engineer:* Prince | *Assistant Engineer:* "Peggy Mac" McCreary

It was a culmination of all of us being together and with the three different styles. There was just something about it. Especially when you get Prince and Morris, it was really magic. I was just there and fortunate enough to come up with some things and so forth and so on and those guys were magic together.—Jesse Johnson[33]

Prince apparently felt he had enough tracks for the third album by the Time. More than enough were in the can, and this session was the first to start putting them into their final shape. Prince spent ten hours working on another round of overdubs for "My Drawers" and "Jungle Love," which had been recorded the previous March. It is likely that Wendy Melvoin and Lisa Coleman recorded background vocals during this session.

Peggy McCreary returned as Prince's primary engineer on this date. "Whatever motivation he had, [Prince] was quite a pioneer in the use of female engineers," claims Sunset Sound general manager Craig Hubler. "At the time in the mid-'80s, Peggy was probably one of the only female engineers going in this business. Then Susan [Rogers] came along and Prince used her quite a bit. And those two were, for quite some time, his principal engineers. In that way he was quite progressive. We still get calls from people all over America asking to speak to Peggy because they want her to engineer a record for them."

"Women have a very nurturing nature," agreed Rogers, "and Prince thrives in that atmosphere. He likes a studio atmosphere where people are flexible."[34]

"**[I've always] had good relationships with women,**" acknowledged Prince. "**Much better than I have with men.**"[35]

A quick mix was completed and two cassettes were made.

MONDAY, JANUARY 16, 1984*

"**If the Kid Can't Make You Come**" (possible overdubs and mix)
"**My Drawers**" (vocal overdubs and mix)
Sunset Sound, Studio 2 | 2:00 p.m.–6:30 a.m. (booked lock-out)
Producer: Prince | *Artist:* the Time (Prince crossed out) | *Engineer:* Morris Day (Prince crossed out) | *Assistant Engineer:* "Peggy Mac" McCreary

*I think we came out at a time where it was still real music. I
don't think it's fad music, I think it's stuff that [you] can put
on and it still sounds good. It was all baked in the oven like it
was supposed to be—not microwaved! (laughs)*—Morris Day[36]

Prince, Morris Day, and Jesse Johnson continued to whittle the Time album down
to six songs. Left on the cutting room floor were "Tricky," "Chocolate," and "My
Summertime Thang," among others. Tonight's schedule included six hours working on Day's final vocal overdubs and background chants from others, a three-hour
break from 8:00 p.m. until 11:00 p.m., and mixing "If the Kid Can't Make You
Come" and "My Drawers," prepping them for sequencing for the album.

"If the Kid Can't Make You Come" (9:13) was edited (7:33) during an undocumented future session. The edits can be heard at 2:40 and 5:53 in the released
track. It is obvious that not much care was placed in creating smooth edits, so it is
likely that by this point the album was considered "good enough." Although she
wasn't directly involved in these sessions, Susan Rogers was aware that the band
was breaking apart: "Things were pretty much over and *Ice Cream Castle* was just
a sign-off. I don't think anybody had any hopes that it was going to do well. Morris
could put on his best face so they could get through. It was his livelihood, too. He
made money, so he was smart enough to know . . . 'Until I get a better situation I'm
staying here.' So they worked together, but [Morris] was a very unhappy man."

The parts of the songs that were removed consisted of about a minute of
Day and the group of female voices (including Jill Jones and possibly Sharon
Hughes) chanting the track's title and "Holland, France, London, dance," and
forty-five seconds of Day in his sexiest voice saying things like, "As a matter
of fact, let's try another position" and additional repeated chants of "Holland,
France, London, dance." The song comes back in on the last half of that chant,
completely eliminating the "Holland, France" section.

The session ended at 6:30 a.m. and two cassettes were made, including one
containing "If the Kid Can't Make You Come" that was sent to the Warner
Bros. vault.

WEDNESDAY, JANUARY 18, 1984*

"The Bird" (overdubs)
Sunset Sound, Studio 2 | 6:00 p.m.–3:30 a.m. (booked lock-out)
Producer: Prince/Morris Day | *Artist:* the Time (Prince crossed out) | *Engineer:*
blank (Prince crossed out) | *Assistant Engineer:* "Peggy Mac" McCreary

I don't remember any fights in the studio [during the Ice Cream Castle *sessions] because everybody knew to follow Prince. He was "the guy" and you didn't pick on him, he picked on you. It was sometimes very strange because it was sort of a Boys' Club.*—Peggy McCreary

The session was scheduled to begin at 2:00 p.m., but Prince didn't start recording until four hours later. Occasionally on days like this, especially as Prince wrapped up the end of a project and before he was inspired enough to start the next, he wanted to get out of the studio to do something fun. "It was rare that we would sit around and have a conversation," reveals Peggy McCreary, "but there were times that he'd be very chatty and he'd talk about his childhood, and sometimes he'd come in and you'd be ready to work and he'd say, 'Come on, I've got a limo, let's go to a movie.' And I'd say, 'I've got to work' and he'd say, 'No, no, no,' and we'd go down to Santa Monica to see this movie in this huge stretch limo."

Once the session began at 6:00 p.m., Prince spent six hours on additional tweaks to "The Bird." At midnight a more detailed mix was created of the track, and Prince compiled the album for the first time in the order that it would be ultimately released on *Ice Cream Castle*. Five copies were made of this collection. Note that the album is called *Ice Cream Castle*, while the actual title track is called "Ice Cream Castles."

In many ways Prince never understood the power of the Time. Albert Magnoli recalls Prince's reaction when he saw the first edits of the movie: "Prince would look at the footage that I shot of Morris and he would sit there just eyes wide open because he goes, 'They are magnetic.' Now Prince is magnetic, but he's magnetic in a different way. When he saw how I shot them he goes, 'Man, what is it about them? Because the audience goes nuts when they do that. How come?' Well, because they're in unison when they're on stage, they are moving as a pack. When you're on stage you're not moving with the band. It's just a different dynamic."

The ironic part of that dynamic was that Prince would never again find that part of the chemistry in any of his other protégé projects. He could write and record the music on his own and design everything about a band, but the reason it had life was the interaction and brotherhood of the members. The Time was a gang, an exclusive club that was unified in purpose. They wanted to be better than the one pulling the strings, and they fought together to achieve that. The Time was Prince's first real side project, and he allowed them the chance to grow and mature onstage in a way that none of his other protégé groups would ever be permitted.

"We lived fun, we lived cool, we lived wild and loose, but we always respected ourselves and the music," explained Jerome Benton. "We worked hard at it, we rehearsed all the time, and the outcome was what it is."[37]

During this same period in another studio at Sunset Sound (or possibly at Sound Factory, which was also owned by Paul Camarata), Sheena Easton was working with McCreary's fiancé, David Leonard, on her album *A Private Heaven*. Leonard mentioned working with Prince, and this impressed Easton enough to ask Leonard to pass a note to Prince, telling him she was a fan and that she would be appearing on *The Tonight Show with Johnny Carson* that evening. Easton was similar to many of the women Prince mentored: beautiful, with dark hair and a passion for performing. According to Easton, Prince was able to catch her performance of "Hard to Say It's Over" and apparently liked what he saw.

This is two work orders for the same date that have been combined.

THURSDAY, JANUARY 19, 1984*

Ice Cream Castle album compilation including "The Bird" (live version)
Sunset Sound, Studio 2 | 4:00 p.m.–6:00 a.m. (booked lock-out)
Producer: Prince (although Morris Day was listed) | *Artist:* the Time (Prince crossed out) | *Engineer:* blank | *Assistant Engineer:* "Peggy Mac" McCreary

> *Everyone was tired of Prince's control. Everyone was pretty disgruntled by that point. Prince was in control. You did what he said or you were gone. I think Terry and Jimmy were the first to find that out.* —Peggy McCreary

After a review of the first assembly of the Time's *Ice Cream Castle* cassette from the previous session, the album was organized, mixed, edited, and placed on a clean tape for assembly. Five hours of additional overdubs and sound effects were added, blending the songs together.

Five more hours were spent mixing and editing the tracks in order and recording the segues between the songs, including the organ parts at the end of "Ice Cream Castles" that blend into the longer version of "If the Kid Can't Make You Come" as well as the music box sound effects that bookend the album.

The rough assembly consisted of: "Ice Cream Castles" (7:31), "My Drawers" (4:11), "Jungle Love" (5:31), "Chili Sauce" (5:45), "If the Kid Can't Make You Come" (9:13), and "The Bird" (8:13).

Status: The album was later edited down, but this compilation finalized the order of the tracks.

FRIDAY, JANUARY 20, 1984*

"**Sugar Walls**" [listed as "New Song"] (basic tracking)
Sunset Sound, Studio 2 | 6:30 p.m.–2:00 a.m. (booked lock-out)
Producer: Prince (although Morris Day was listed) | *Artist:* Prince (although the Time was listed) | *Engineer:* blank | *Assistant Engineer:* "Peggy Mac" McCreary

He couldn't squeeze it all into just Prince, even extending it into Prince and the Revolution. He needed other outlets. These were ways he could live different lives. His mind is out there, not just on another planet, it's in another galaxy.—Lisa Coleman[38]

Prince had been extremely busy, but according to those around him he was also looking to expand his influence whenever possible. When pop artist Sheena Easton asked him for a track, he saw it as another chance to get his music circulating. "[Prince] wrote and offered songs to whoever it was that wanted one," recalls Peggy McCreary. "Sheena Easton did 'Sugar Walls.' It was a song he was working on and she asked for something and he said . . . 'Here.' That is kind of the way he did things."

Looking at Prince's erratic career, it seems he was easily distracted and followed his musical urges when a new inspiration or a new muse appeared, so he briefly stopped working on music for the Time and dedicated this evening and the next to creating a track for Easton. Prince explained how prolific he was to *Rolling Stone* magazine writer Neal Karlen in 1985: "**I write all the time and cut all the time. I want to show you the archives where all my old stuff is. There's tons of music I've recorded there.**"[39]

Jill Jones witnessed firsthand how much music he was creating and, because of that, how incredibly important it was for Prince to socialize and find new inspiration, but how rare it was for him to have people close enough to actually connect on a deeper level. "I do believe the whole thing about finding different muses to keep inspiring and delivering because it was a monster that needed to be fed," she remembers. "His form of communicating with another person was, at best, being in the studio. You're not going to go take him to a barbeque. (*laughs*) He'd be the husband that you have who is always in the studio."

"He doesn't have normal relationships," agreed Eric Leeds, who later played sax for Prince. "It's not like he's got guys that he hangs out with on Friday night. He's not one for small talk or casual conversation. If he's on a tour bus, he may have some conversation that's relatively casual, but nine times out of ten, even that will be something related to the show or the album or something. Almost everything in the ten years I was with him—save some very specifically allocated leisure time—was somehow about music or the show. He's so strictly defined by his career that there really hasn't been a normal life away from that."[40]

When someone asked Prince to pen a song, he'd often just grab a tape out of his collection at Sunset Sound, dust it off, and hand over a copy. Sunset Sound engineer David Knight remembers where the tracks were stored in the studio: "Studio 3 is in this old, almost derelict apartment building, and if you go upstairs there's these crazy little apartments from back in the twenties. Tiny little places, and two of the apartments had been converted into live echo chambers and then at the end of this dusty old hallway Prince just had shelves and shelves of stuff up there, quarter-inch tapes of rough mixes. On a number of occasions, he would literally just go up there, look through the list of tapes, rough mixes, and literally grab something, yank it and go, 'We'll use this.'"

On future collaborations with Easton (such as in 1985 with the track "Eternity") he would pull something off the shelf, but this first request was different: Prince actually recorded a new song from scratch for Sheena. "'Sugar Walls' was done for Sheena Easton," explains Susan Rogers. "It was never intended for him, it was written after he'd met her. She asked for a song and he wrote that for her."[41]

The instrumentation of the track was sparse and keyboard heavy, containing more or less the same melody as the synth lead line to his unreleased song "Possessed." Prince quickly wrote the lyrics and recorded his temp vocals as he always did, with the microphone dangling over the mixing board. Prince also did a pass with Jill Jones on lead vocals.

The seven-and-a-half-hour session wrapped up at 2:00 a.m., and the master 2-inch tape was sent over to Sound Factory for Easton's vocals.

Easton recalled her vocal session, which took place later that weekend: "[David Leonard] said, 'Prince sent over a track for you. We saw you on *The Tonight*

Show the night before and Prince said "Yeah, I gotta write something for that girl." And so he sent over 'Sugar Walls,' and it was one of those things where it was like, 'Here it is. If you want to do it, here's my number.'"[42]

"Long story short," she continued, "I recorded it on Super Bowl Sunday."[43]

Prince was recording at Sunset Sound at the same time, but it is unclear if he left to attend Easton's vocal sessions at Sound Factory. There are conflicting reports about whether he dropped in on her, but nothing could be confirmed. According to Easton, Prince obviously enjoyed collaborating with her, giving her "Eternity," cowriting "La, La, La, He, He, Hee," and teaming up with her on many tracks, including "U Got The Look," "101," "Cool Love," "Arms of Orion," and the unreleased "Come Back 2 Me." "When we worked in the studio, we got along really well," remembered Easton. "We cracked each other up. We made each other laugh. He really liked my voice and thought we should do more stuff."[44]

Not everyone was happy that the number went to Easton. "'Sugar Walls' was supposed to be my song," remembers Jill Jones. "[When he told me] I remember I was sitting in the bed, and I was just like, 'What? Really? You took me out last night to be able to break this news to me this morning?' We had some words about it. That's all I'm gonna say."

Status: "Sugar Walls" (3:59) was released on Sheena Easton's *A Private Heaven* album. It was entirely Prince's original version, but with his vocals replaced by Easton. Although this ode to a vagina was written and recorded by Prince, it was credited to Alexander Nevermind, his first one-use-only pseudonym. The song eventually became infamous as number 2 on the Parents Music Resource Center's "Filthy 15," a list of tracks that deserved parental labeling. The only song higher on the list was "Darling Nikki," another Prince tune.

Prince later used elements from "Sugar Walls" on the extended remix of "Hot Thing," which was released in 1987.

SUNDAY, JANUARY 22, 1984*

"Take Me with U" [listed as "Sex Shooter"] (basic idea, but not tracking)
Sunset Sound, Studio 2 | 5:00 p.m.–11:30 p.m. (booked lock-out)
Producer: Prince (although Morris Day was listed) | *Artist:* Prince/Apollonia
(only Prince was listed and the Time was crossed out) | *Engineer:* blank |
Assistant Engineer: "Peggy Mac" McCreary

"Take Me with U" has a lot of character to it and works in the framework of Prince and Apollonia because obviously you needed to have some sort of duet with them for the soundtrack.—Matt Fink[45]

With the album by the Time basically done, Prince could start to focus on the next major project: Apollonia 6. So far only one track, "Sex Shooter," had been completed, but Prince was hoping to create an entire album for the group. In many ways this was the first day of work on what was expected to be their album, but more immediately, it would be considered for use in the movie. The Time had two songs ("Jungle Love" and "The Bird") in *Purple Rain*, so there was a need for two songs containing Apollonia 6. This would help promote both groups and, it was hoped, create a demand for their albums. As the movie was being edited, it was obvious to Albert Magnoli that what was missing was Prince sharing a romantic song with his co-star, Apollonia: "I realized I had a place where I could do a musical montage where Prince has been denied Apollonia. She's already said, 'Go to hell,' and he's got that moment where he's thinking through his life, so Prince wrote 'Take Me with U.'"

During the multiple decades Prince spent in the music business, the duets he recorded amount to fewer than ten, and at this stage of his career Prince had never recorded a true duet. The only other co-lead vocals were with Lisa Coleman and Dez Dickerson on the song "1999," but outside of that Prince didn't share the spotlight on the microphone. With "Take Me with U," Prince set out to write a romantic duet in which he was truly the co-lead singer, because half the lyrics were written from Apollonia's point of view. Prince was no stranger to writing from a female perspective nor to singing as such on the scratch tracks, but this is the first time he allowed another person to shine and this seems like a testament to how he felt about Apollonia and her role in the movie.

During this session, Prince likely explored several ideas, hoping to turn them into a song. There was no new 2-inch tape purchased, so it is unlikely that the jamming went any further than recording music to cassette. "Sometimes he'd just want to run the cassette," explains Sunset Sound engineer Stephen Shelton. "And he'd make that quite clear, and there were probably things that would end up being created on cassette and he'd probably review it at some later time and pull from it what he wanted."

It is also unlikely that any vocals were recorded for the track during this session. When lyrics are written and recorded they are often reflected on the work order, but Prince decided to list "Sex Shooter," indicating that he probably had Apollonia on his mind while forming the track.

The session ended early, and at 11:30 p.m. Prince left with a single C-60 cassette of what he'd recorded.

Because the original work order for this track lists it as "Sex Shooter," the details of what was recorded are unclear. The Warner Bros. vault lists "Take Me with U" as having been created today, so it is probable that the genesis of the song began on this date. Although the Time and Morris Day are listed on the daily work order, their participation on this session is doubtful.

Prince flew back to Minneapolis and held a surprise party at a club called Tramps to celebrate Wendy Melvoin's twentieth birthday. She remembered: "At one point during the party, he said, 'Do me a favor and sit down at this table and wait.' So I waited, and then in comes Prince and Joni Mitchell to sit with me, and she gave me three of her lithographs as a present. It was one of my most profound moments."[46]

THURSDAY, JANUARY 26, 1984 (ESTIMATE)

"Take Me with U" (dub to cassette)
Sunset Sound, Studio 2 (assumed)
Producer: Prince | *Artist:* Prince/Apollonia | *Engineer:* "Peggy Mac" McCreary

When I'm writing, sometimes the pen just goes. I'm not in charge and I'm almost listening outside of it. . . . It's like listening to a color and believing that these colors have soulmates and once you get them all together the painting is complete. —Prince[47]

Although the actual studio notes from this session have never surfaced, it is probable that the additional seeds of "Take Me with U" were put to cassette on this day. The studio notes for January 27 detailed that two C-60 cassettes were billed to Prince on this date, but no specific track was listed, and there is no verification that Prince actually attended this session, and if any additional recording took place today.

FRIDAY, JANUARY 27, 1984*

> **"Take Me with U"** (basic tracking and overdubs)
> Sunset Sound, Studio 2 | 7:00 p.m.–1:00 a.m. (booked 8:00 p.m.–open)
> *Producer:* Prince (although Morris Day/Prince was listed) | *Artist:* Prince
> (only Prince was listed and the Time was crossed out) | *Engineer:* Prince |
> *Assistant Engineers:* "Peggy Mac" McCreary and David Leonard

Apollonia was there with us in the studio during that song.
She was there a lot during the recording of a lot of the tracks.
—Peggy McCreary

The daily work order lists this time in the studio as "live," which often means others performed on the track, but that wasn't always the case. "It says, 'Live,' which meant he was cutting tracks or 'tracking,' but he didn't track like normal people," says Peggy McCreary. "He did the piano, he did everything himself, so it depended on what the mood was or what the song needed."

At 7:00 p.m. Prince started fleshing out "Take Me with U," beginning the song by counting in the drums. Although his drummer, Bobby Z, was around the studio during this time, Prince played them for this track. "The Revolution didn't have much to do with this one," explained Matt Fink. "The actual drums on 'Take Me with U' were the Simmons electric kit [Simmons SDS-5] being played. It sounds acoustic, but it's a hybrid set that Bobby would use."[48]

Basic tracks, including Oberheim keyboard, were recorded in the first two hours. The next four hours were spent overdubbing on different sections of the track. Although the actual title is listed, there is no indication that Prince had recorded his lyrics yet; he probably had an idea for the lyrics based on the placement the song would have in the movie, but hadn't fully fleshed them out. They were likely written after the session ended.

Status: "Take Me with U" (5:04) was originally planned for the *Apollonia 6* album, but instead it was trimmed down for release on the *Purple Rain* soundtrack (3:54) and edited for release as the fifth single from the album (3:37). It would make it to number 25 on the *Billboard* Hot 100 chart and number 40 on the *Billboard* Hot Black Singles chart. A 12-inch version of the track was supposedly created (although it was likely just the long version before the edit) but was never released.

SATURDAY, JANUARY 28, 1984*

"**Take Me with U**" (Prince and Apollonia vocals, rough mix)
Sunset Sound, Studio 2 | 6:00 p.m.–3:00 a.m. (booked 8:00 p.m.–open)
Producer: Morris Day/Prince (neither circled) | *Artist:* Prince (only Prince
was listed and the Time was crossed out) | *Engineer:* Prince | *Assistant
Engineers:* "Peggy Mac" McCreary (listed) and David Leonard

*[Prince] has an incredible talent for recognizing strengths and
weaknesses. He has marvelous natural leadership, is very good
at knowing just how to push you to get the best out of you, and
he knew when to stop, in most cases. Singers, musicians, technicians, office people would rise to levels they hadn't thought before.
"Take Me with U" was perfect.*—Susan Rogers[49]

Prince arrived at this session with the lyrics complete, ready to record the
vocals. Tonight's crowd had dwindled down, as Prince didn't enjoy having
people around during this process. Peggy McCreary set up the mic in the usual
position over the console and left a few empty tracks for his lead vocal and
background vocals. Sunset Sound general manager Craig Hubler recalls how
different Prince's techniques were from other singers at the time: "That was
rather unique about him; he may have been one of the first people, at least as far
as major mainstream artists, that actually did his own engineering in a control
room with a live microphone on, dangling over the console. Just sitting there at
the console and doing his singing, the tape machine roaring in the background.
He liked to be alone, just concentrating on his vocals or whatever. If he needed
someone he just popped his head out the door."

Using David Leonard as his engineer, Prince spent the entire nine-hour session working on vocals, first his own and then Apollonia's. The work on this
track were Apollonia's first vocal sessions for new music with Prince. They'd
recorded her vocals for "Sex Shooter" at his home (with his Minneapolis engineer, Susan Rogers), but that was a track originally created for Vanity 6, so this
was Apollonia's first true lead vocal session at Sunset Sound.

Two cassettes were created at the end of the session after a rough mix.

*Prince already knew he'd be calling the track "Take Me with U" instead of "Take
Me with You" because he corrected the work order to reflect the proper title.*

SUNDAY, JANUARY 29, 1984*

"Take Me with U" (strings and various overdubs)
Sunset Sound, Studio 2 | 6:30 p.m.–10:30 p.m. (booked lock-out)
Producer: Prince (Morris Day crossed out) | *Artist:* Prince/Apollonia (only Prince was listed and the Time was crossed out) | *Engineer:* Prince | *Assistant Engineer:* "Peggy Mac" McCreary

I remember Prince asking if I had my finger cymbals and I said, "Yes, I do," and that is when I came in to do "Take Me with U."—David Coleman

After several days of work, "Take Me with U" still wasn't complete, so Prince decided to add strings to tie the music in with some of the other tracks on the album. David Coleman recalls:

[Prince] called me into the studio and Novi [Novog] and I did strings. I don't remember if Suzie [Katayama] is on there or not. I think it is just Novi and I. I don't remember if Lisa was there or if Prince sat down at the piano and gave us notes. He came up with those melodies that the strings did and I kind of jammed a bit of what the cello part would be to harmonize with what Novi was doing.

My recollection was that it was just Novi and I and Prince at the piano, but with my recollection, Lisa did so much arranging, that she might have been there because almost everything we did, she was there.

Novog, who had already recorded the viola and violin for Prince on several tracks, recalls what Prince was like when out of the public spotlight: "Prince was very confident. He always stayed to himself. He was very shy unless he knows you. Always very polite, but very shy, but real nice. Not threatening in any way and no ego trips that I saw."

The track would be the first song he'd release that contained finger cymbals. It is likely that those were added during this session.

MONDAY, JANUARY 30, 1984*

"Take Me with U" (Apollonia and Prince vocal overdubs)
Sunset Sound, Studio 2 | 7:30 p.m.–4:00 a.m. (booked 7:00 p.m.–open)

Producer: Prince (Morris Day was crossed out) | *Artist:* Prince (only Prince was listed and the Time was crossed out) | *Engineer:* Prince | *Assistant Engineers:* "Peggy Mac" McCreary (listed) and David Leonard

"Take Me with U" is just a beautiful song. It's just so great how he got Apollonia in on that, and it's just a beautiful song that really catches you every time.—Bobby Z[50]

For Prince, adding vocals was never simple because he almost always knew what he wanted, and that required translating what was in his head to tape. Recording anyone's vocals often required embellishments, and because it was his first duet, this was no exception. "[Apollonia] was not a singer," explained Lisa Coleman. "She was an actress. So the poor thing was thrown into the studio: 'Here, you have to sing this.' She was like, 'Oh my God, I don't know how to sing.' And she did the best she could. I doubled her vocals on 'Take Me with U' to make it sound a little better."[51]

In fact, you can hear background vocals from Coleman at 1:20 on the album version ("Don't care where we go"[52]) and a variety of other places throughout the track. Jill Jones was also brought in to do additional vocal work, which didn't always sit well with other performers. "He had a guide but I was a ghost vocal," recalls Jones. "I was a ghost vocalist."

If I were another singer, I'd be like, "Goddamn why is she always saying that?" I don't think there was any malice or malicious intent. I always knew that, over a period of time, it instills confidence in the singer. I think that when they think that is them, they go home and they listen to their tapes and they come back and maybe do another vocal on top and they actually get a little bit more cojones if they believe a little bit that it might be themselves.

Even with Apollonia, it wasn't ever to take anything away from her. It was just to strengthen her so she would come back and approach the studio differently. I believe that's how he felt about it, because we saw a difference. Like "Oh wow, she's getting there." And it made for better performances in the studio, and he could discover their style. And that would help Apollonia start to do her Betty Boop–style thing. And on that note, I'd have to say Apollonia created that herself, and that's what happens from that and that's all just because you have the support of somebody behind you.

A total of seven and a half hours were spent adding vocals to the song, with contributions likely from both Prince and Apollonia.

Prince would place this song on a single C-60 tape, but he also transferred something he'd recently recorded to three C-90 tapes. It is possible that he'd been recording potential pieces of the score for the *Purple Rain* movie and was copying this or any incidental music to cassette for the editor and director to consider for placement in the film.

TUESDAY, JANUARY 31, 1984*

"Take Me with U" (mix and edits)
Sunset Sound, Studio 2 | 7:00 p.m.–2:00 a.m. (booked 7:00 p.m.–open)
Producer: Prince | *Artist:* Prince | *Engineer:* Prince | *Assistant Engineer:*
"Peggy Mac" McCreary

One of the things that I think is important is that one learns how to listen. So I never stop being a fan. Even if the music was coming through me. —Prince[53]

Because "Take Me with U" was Prince's first duet and it was to be placed in the movie, five hours were dedicated to getting the mix right. This was different than his usual method. "On things that were really important, we'd set aside time to just mix it," explained Susan Rogers. "But for the most part, we mixed as we went along."[54]

During this session Prince was charged a rental on a Linn drum set (LM-1), so he may have added them to the track, but if he did, they were hidden during the final mix. The distinctive sound of the electronic Simmons SDS-5 drums can be heard clearly in the introductory tom-drum roll that recurs in the break before the end.

At this point, "Take Me with U" was still planned for the *Apollonia 6* album. Now that Prince had completed two songs for their project, the next week would be committed to filling in the remaining spots.

FEBRUARY 1984

> **"Some Kind of Lover"** [listed as "Tricky"] (basic tracking)
> Sunset Sound, Studio 2 | 4:00 p.m.–2:30 a.m. (booked lock-out)
> *Producer:* Prince (although Morris Day was listed) | *Artist:* Apollonia 6
> (although the Time was listed) | *Engineer:* Prince | *Assistant Engineer:*
> "Peggy Mac" McCreary

Each band brings different songs out of you.—Prince[1]

The basic tracks for today's song were recorded by Prince, but the actual idea was inspired by Apollonia 6 singer Brenda Bennett and her relationship with her husband, Roy: "Prince and I both wrote it. I submitted it to him and he kept 99 percent of it. At the time, we had a perfect marriage. The people that knew us knew we had a great marriage. I felt like people put us on a pedestal as an example of working together and being around each other and getting along very well."

No vocals by Prince or by anyone in Apollonia 6 were recorded on this date. A quick mix of the instrumental was created and placed on three cassettes.

Status: "Some Kind of Lover" (4:07) was the sixth track on the *Apollonia 6* album and was attached to a skit involving the three group members. The track was also released as the B-side for "Blue Limousine."

THURSDAY, FEBRUARY 2, 1984*

"**Some Kind of Lover**" (vocals)
Sunset Sound, Studio 2 | 4:00 p.m.–2:30 a.m. (booked lock-out)
Producer: Prince | *Artist:* Apollonia 6 | *Engineer:* Prince | *Assistant Engineer:* "Peggy Mac" McCreary

He had the music done when I recorded the lyrics. And I remember him saying, "Here you go, this is yours."—Brenda Bennett

The session started out with Prince inviting Bennett back to Sunset Sound to record her part. "I remember him playing the track and not having a guide track," she recalls. "He kind of sang it in the studio to give me an idea, melody-wise, for the lyrics. And I said, 'Okay, I can do it. I can do it!'"

While Bennett sang her part, Prince was playing bass. For the end of the track, Prince pushed her to make it even more sensual with her words and moans, and she gave what is probably her sexiest performance, but it is obvious that she was a little shy about it when she added her very honest assessment—"I'm embarrassed"—at the end of the track. "After I got done with my vocals," she remembers, "he got up and was like 'Goddamn, Brenda,' because I put so much of me into this song."

During the seven hours spent recording vocals, Prince and Lisa Coleman added background vocals to the track. Susannah Melvoin was enlisted as well: "He came right out and said, 'You feel like you want to sing?' And of course, it was like, 'Yeah, of course I do.'" The list of people Prince relied on to sing background vocals was short, and Melvoin would quickly become a fixture in the studio, with Prince adding her sounds to many of the tracks on almost every one of his projects for the next several years. She recalls the routine when her phone rang at 3:00 in the morning: "He'd call in the middle of the night and say, 'I'm cutting. What are you doing? I'm cutting.' And you'd say, 'It's three in the morning.' 'I'm cutting. I don't know what you're doing.' And it was always that was literally the sign that you're missing out on all the good stuff and you're a loser if you don't get your ass down here. 'I'm cutting. What are you doing, sleeping? Sleep is for dead people.' And you'd go down to the studio."

Three hours were spent mixing the track, and a single cassette copy was made at the end of the session.

FRIDAY, FEBRUARY 3, 1984*

"A Million Miles (I Love You)" (basic tracking)
"In a Spanish Villa" (basic tracking)
Sunset Sound, Studio 2 | 1:30 p.m.–4:30 a.m. (booked lock-out)
Producer: Prince | *Artist:* Apollonia 6 | *Engineer:* Prince | *Assistant Engineer:* "Peggy Mac" McCreary

Sometimes ideas are coming so fast that I have to stop doing one song to get another. But I don't forget the first one. If it works, it will always be there. It's like the truth: it will find you and lift you up. And if it ain't right, it will dissolve like sand on the beach. —Prince[2]

Creating a new song every day can be draining, so Prince constantly relied on those around him for inspiration. **"I try to let other people influence me . . . other musicians,"** Prince explained in a 2004 interview with CNN. **"Musicians that are in my groups, not ones that are looking to start trends or that I see on TV, but just people that I meet that move me spiritually."**[3]

Today's session began as a jam with Wendy Melvoin, Lisa Coleman, and Sheila E. "Sheila was around a lot," according to Peggy McCreary. "She was a lot of fun. He'd be working on something and she'd be out playing drums, and he'd say, 'Put some tape up to record.'"

As Lisa sat behind the piano, Prince said, "Give me a groove," and she created the signature riff in "A Million Miles" on the spot. When the song was tracked, Prince played the bass while standing at the soundboard, Coleman was on keyboards, Melvoin was on guitar, and Sheila E. was playing drums. Using his falsetto, Prince recorded a scratch track so the singer would have a reference.

"A Million Miles (I Love You)" was another track that was directly influenced by Brenda Bennett: "This was such a hot number. [Prince] gave me the impression that it was written for me. This came from the fact that I always wore my wedding ring. There is a line in there about my 'diamond ring' and there had been a conversation between Prince and I about my ring." At the time Prince wasn't touring and Roy Bennett was on the road with the Scorpions; the song tried to reflect the distance between two lovers.

Apollonia was in the studio for the rehearsals, the initial tracking, and Prince's vocals. The earliest version of the song began with the same drumbeat, followed by Prince purring "Yeah" and some "ooohs" that were later discarded.

Once Prince finished recording the main vocals, he had Apollonia and Brenda Bennett replace his voice with their own for much of the song. "On the chorus, you can hear Prince," remembers Bennett. "If you put your headphones on you can hear him, because he put his voice on there to show Apollonia how he wanted her to do the background vocals."

Another song was tracked on this date: "In a Spanish Villa." In need of inspiration, Prince involved Apollonia once again as his muse, allowing her to create a romantic story line for the track. Prince recorded the Carlos Santana–inspired lead guitar, Melvoin played the rhythm guitar, and, with the studio lights turned down, Apollonia recorded the spoken lyrics. The track was completed in very few takes.

It was the sort of song that Vanity 6 would never have attempted: subtle and slightly romantic, with no danceable groove anywhere to be found. It was different than anything he'd ever recorded, and is a hidden gem that most people would never imagine was Prince.

Six hours were spent mixing and editing the tracks. Sound effects, including waves, were added (it is unclear if that occurred during this session or on a later date), the songs were dubbed to a cassette tape, and the session was over at 4:30 a.m.

Status: "A Million Miles (I Love You)" (5:52) was edited down (3:11) and faded out just before the "Somebody clap your hands" chant, but the shorter version remains unreleased. The complete version was issued as the fourth track on the *Apollonia 6* album. "In a Spanish Villa" (2:15) was the closing track on the album and was also released as the B-side of the "Sex Shooter" single.

SATURDAY, FEBRUARY 4, 1984*

"**Manic Monday**" (basic tracking, Prince vocal)
Sunset Sound, Studio 2 | 1:00 p.m.–1:00 a.m. (booked lock-out)
Producer: Prince | *Artist:* Apollonia 6 | *Engineer:* Prince | *Assistant Engineer:* "Peggy Mac" McCreary

Six o'clock already, I was just in the middle of a dream.
. . .—"Manic Monday"[4]

Few people understand how big a glimpse the opening phrase of today's song exposed Prince's thought process. Peggy McCreary recalls that this track began shortly after the previous day's session ended: "I remember going to bed at six in the morning and he called and said, 'Can you be at the studio at noon?' because he had dreamed a song. He said if he dreamed a chorus he'd call me, and he did, and it was 'Manic Monday.'"

It is easy to see how Prince created this track because he lifts the melody from his earlier track "1999." Compare the opening lines:

Six o'clock already, I was just in the middle of a dream ("Manic Monday")[5]
I was dreaming when I wrote this. Forgive me if it goes astray ("1999")[6]

Even if he ended up being his own muse, Prince was still able to bring something inventive to the song. "That was the secret to his music," reveals McCreary. "He would come in, it was written, it was recorded, and it was done and it was mixed all within the same period. On occasion it was taken down and remixed later, but it was almost always born right there, and that is why it was so fresh. He was so prolific at that time."

In many ways Prince was a master of technique, and he was open to experimenting with technology. For his music, he enjoyed creating new colors with the sounds he discovered, and although he was not truly technical, he enjoyed working with keyboards and preprogrammed keyboard sounds (also referred to as "patches") trying to find something different: "**I don't ever read manuals. I don't want to have a preconception about what a piece of gear should or shouldn't do. I just start using it. I start pushing buttons, and I discover the sounds that I can make with it. Sometimes a particular sound will give me a whole song, like the harpsichord sound on 'Manic Monday.' That sound just dictated the part.**"[7]

"That sounds like Prince, yeah," reflects Mike Kloster, his assistant engineer during this period. "He was really one of those believers who felt that anything that happened was fate. God wanted it to happen that way. Like if he showed up, and we weren't done aligning the tape machine then he'd say, 'Well, that's the way it's supposed to be then, let's record.' He had that attitude."

Although she was very tired, McCreary looks back fondly on this date: "It was actually a great day, and he was in a really great mood. I was exhausted, but it was a fun day, and we went until 1 in the morning. . . . It was a twelve-hour day, just the two of us."

After a quick one-hour mix, the session ended a little early—at least by Prince's usual standards. He wanted the girls to record their vocals that night, but couldn't convince Susan Moonsie and Apollonia to drop by the studio. They told him they were tired but instead went out dancing at a local club called

Voila. Prince eventually tracked them down and spent the rest of the evening dancing with them. He told them about the track and invited them to join him in the studio the following day for vocals.

Status: "Manic Monday" (2:49) was considered for the *Apollonia 6* album and was placed in an early configuration, but it was ultimately removed and replaced by "Happy Birthday, Mr. Christian." The song was later rerecorded by the Bangles, and their cover would hit number 2 on the *Billboard* Pop chart in January 1986. The only song above it on the charts that week was Prince's "Kiss" at number 1.

Aligning a tape deck is a multistep process that involves verifying that anything recorded on this deck will match the specifications of another deck. It can involve adjusting the speed, calibrating the recording tones and playback levels, cleaning the tape heads, and demagnetizing them if necessary, among other things.

SUNDAY, FEBRUARY 5, 1984*

"**Manic Monday**" (various vocal overdubs)
Apollonia 6 album segues/skits
"**Ooo She She Wa Wa**" (basic tracking)
Sunset Sound, Studio 2 | 2:00 p.m.–3:30 a.m. (booked lock-out)
Producer: Prince | *Artist:* Apollonia 6 | *Engineer:* Prince | *Assistant Engineer:* "Peggy Mac" McCreary

Often when he would do those template vocals, guide vocals for someone else to come along and copy them, he would then erase his vocal track, so in many of these cases, the vocals no longer exist on the tapes. He'd permanently erase his vocal pass.—Alan Leeds[8]

The day started with Apollonia and Brenda Bennett recording their vocals, and the mood among them was amazingly optimistic. Even the lyrics reflected the uplifted attitude of the day ("I wish it was Sunday / that's my fun day . . ."[9]) and the studio was filled with the vibe that the song had huge potential to be a hit. The track also took the group in a direction that was different from the overtly sexual music of Vanity 6. "When it came to the studio and the vocal parts on it . . . we did it in a way that was very comfortable and we enjoyed doing it," Bennett explains. "It was something that could be played out there where there wouldn't be any controversy around it, which was something that I wanted us to get away from. We started out as such a controversial thing and we're the stepping stone for a lot of girls that came after us, with any sexual connotations. Madonna, for example. We were so bad, that we couldn't be in the mainstream of stuff."

Not everyone was happy that the track wasn't going to be released by Prince. "I was so upset that he gave that to Apollonia 6," complains McCreary, "because he did it so great with his vocals. He never said why he did things like that, you just did what he told you."

With all the members of the group in the studio, Prince decided to record a few skits for the record, some seemingly based on the previous night's visit to the club, but it didn't go over well with everyone. "[Prince] kept saying that he didn't want *any* filler, but the part with us playing and laughing was filler as far as I was concerned," asserts Bennett. "It was stupid. It was scripted right there on the spot. Prince was saying, 'Think of something!' Apollonia wanted to talk about her rabbit, Smokey, and I came up with the spacemen thing, and he wanted Susan to be sleeping and to have a dream or something."

Work was also done on "Ooo She She Wa Wa." As usual, Prince recorded the basic tracks, but instead of singing it himself he had Moonsie add her vocals. Bennett remembers that Moonsie's songs were different than the other tracks because Prince gave her a lot of room to write her own lyrics. "Her songs never had a guide vocal to it. She was really good at writing. . . . She wrote poetry and she was very, very good but she never wanted to submit anything to him. Maybe once or twice, but not much as she could have."

Bennett also recalls how the mood in the studio had changed from earlier in the day: "Susan and Prince were fighting. You can hear it in the song. Susan didn't really get loud when she got mad; you just knew it."

Bennett also added her vocals for the background.

Once the rest of the group had left, Prince asked Jill Jones to add background vocals to the recently recorded tracks for *Apollonia 6*, including "A Million Miles (I Love You)," "Ooo She She Wa Wa," "Some Kind of Lover," and "Manic Monday." Susannah Melvoin was also recruited for background vocals on some of these tracks as well. As always, each singer was brought in separately to record her part, and all the elements used on any track were at Prince's discretion. "The truth is, none of the girls would've ever really known," according to Jones. "They wouldn't know what he was doing until you got the final mix."

The last four and a half hours of the session were spent on rough mixes and cassette copies.

Status: "Ooo She She Wa Wa" (2:43) was attached to one of the skits they'd recorded, and the song was released on the *Apollonia 6* album.

MONDAY, FEBRUARY 6, 1984*

Apollonia 6 album compiled
"Sex Shooter"
"Take Me with U"
"Manic Monday"
"Some Kind of Lover"
"A Million Miles (I Love You)"
"Ooo She She Wa Wa"
"In a Spanish Villa" (probably included but not verified)
Sunset Sound, Studio 2 | 9:00 p.m.–4:15 a.m. (booked lock-out)
Producer: Prince | *Artist:* Apollonia 6 | *Engineer:* Prince | *Assistant Engineer:* "Peggy Mac" McCreary

Prince loved sequencing albums.—Susan Rogers[10]

Considering the length of many of his recording sessions, tonight's was relatively brief. In five hours he mixed, edited, and assembled the first compilation for the *Apollonia 6* album. During that time, additional mixing was also done on "Sex Shooter" and Prince likely added some of the remaining sound effects, including the sound effect of waves washing up on a beach during "Some Kind of Lover" and the similar sounds on "In a Spanish Villa." It is probable that Prince recorded the keyboards on "A Million Miles" and that he also scored the multiple skits from yesterday's session. From start to finish (with the exception of "Sex Shooter" and "Take Me with U," which were created for the movie), the album was recorded and assembled in less than a week. "I think it was an easier record," says Mc-Creary, "because he had done it before with Vanity 6 and [Brenda and Susan] had done it before and Apollonia, he just slipped her into the mold."

The prospects for a successful album were great, and almost everyone involved agreed that it had at least two hits ("Sex Shooter" and "Manic Monday") as well as an attention-getting duet with Prince ("Take Me with U"). Apollonia had not only replaced Vanity, she'd found a way to create her own identity while blending into Prince's vision of the group. "By the time we recorded it, the whole thing just clicked," according to Susan Rogers. "She sounded like an actress pretending to sing."[11]

This compilation starts with the two movie tracks. Apollonia's lead vocals are on the first three songs, followed by two Brenda Bennett tracks, and one by Susan Moonsie. It is uncertain whether "In a Spanish Villa" was included in this compilation, but if it wasn't, that means that side one was exclusively Apollonia and side two was exclusively Bennett and Moonsie. It is more likely that "In a Spanish Villa" was included to keep the voice of the band's namesake on both sides of the record.

At this point the concept of a bigger version of the *1999* tour—including Prince, the Time, and Apollonia 6 (taking the place of Vanity 6)—was being discussed. A lot would change in the following months.

Status: Two other undated but potential track lists from this era have surfaced:

Take Me with U
Next Time Wipe the Lipstick off Your Collar
A Million Miles (I Love You)
In a Spanish Villa
Some Kind of Lover
Sex Shooter
Velvet Kitty Cat

as well as:

Sex Shooter
Take Me with You
Manic Monday
A Million Miles (I Love You)
Velvet Kitty Cat
Some Kind of Lover
In a Spanish Villa

When Prince was assembling an album, cassettes were created for listening purposes, and for many projects Prince would throw songs together to see how they played in his car. It is unknown whether these track listings were basic assemblies for listening or for serious consideration. "Velvet Kitty Cat" would likely have had Susan Moonsie's vocals on it since she had no other tracks on these compilations. When and if she recorded the vocals for "Velvet Kitty Cat" is not known.

The water sound effects used at the end of "Some Kind of Lover" would be revisited by Prince during his Lovesexy era.

TUESDAY, FEBRUARY 7, 1984*

"**God (Love Theme from** *Purple Rain*)" [listed as "God"] (basic tracking)
"**Father's Song**" [listed as "Piano Jam"]
"**Lisa and Wendy's** *Purple Rain* **Instrumental**" (transferred for movie)
Sunset Sound, Studio 2 | 8:00 p.m.-6:00 a.m. (booked lock-out)
Producer: Prince | *Artist:* Prince | *Engineer:* Prince | *Assistant Engineer:*
   "Peggy Mac" McCreary

*Question: If God came to you right now and asked you to play
one song of yours, what would it be?*
Prince: **God.**[12]

With the *Apollonia 6* album finished, Prince turned his attention to the music
planned for the movie, but tonight's session was delayed for two hours because
of a movie-related meeting. McCreary recalls that the usual flow of the sessions
was being strained: "There were a lot of executives from Warner Bros., the
director and others in the studio. What a time waster! I was not involved in the
movie at all, and didn't want to know about it. I had enough on my plate."

It is likely that Prince watched an early cut of the movie that was missing
some of the music because once he returned to the studio, he quickly recorded
a new version of "Father's Song" that more accurately matched the scene in the
movie when his character's father plays the piano, as well as the music for the
segment containing the version of "Purple Rain" that Wendy and Lisa submitted to the Kid. This music is not considered scoring. "Scoring" can be broadly
defined as background music that helps dramatically underscore a scene and
can create or embellish the mood. Music that features someone performing a
song can also be considered scoring, but these (as well as the performances)
are often labeled as songs and not a score. When it was complete, Prince continued in the same mode and worked on an untitled instrumental that would
eventually be called "God (Love Theme from *Purple Rain*)" and would consist
of keyboards, guitar, piano, Sheila E. on drums, and a few sound effects like
thunder and rain.

"I remember this so well," recalls McCreary. "As I remember it, [Sheila
and Prince] were musically just playing with each other, sort of flirting
with each other. It was midnight, and I was like, 'Okay, can't we just leave?
(*laughs*) Can't you two just get a room?' At the time Sheila just loved to hang
out with him."

The stress of the movie and the rapid pace of recording an album began to take its toll on Apollonia, and she came to Prince for help because she was having difficulty sleeping.

It was common for Prince to look for inspiration by sitting at the piano and just playing whatever came to mind. His engineer would record it to a cassette for him in case there was something worth building into a song or an element that could be added to an existing track. Prince apparently thought some of his piano playing would help Apollonia's insomnia, and he sat down and recorded himself running through a medley of some of his songs including ideas for songs that he had yet to record. Among the songs he played that evening were "Father's Song," "Venus De Milo," "God," "Raspberry Beret," "You're My Love," "Wednesday," "Do Me, Baby," and "Moonbeam Levels."

At 4:30 a.m., while Peggy mixed the instrumental that would become "God," Prince wrote "Poppa's song" on the cassette and left to take it to Apollonia.

Status: "God (Love Theme from *Purple Rain*)" (7:53) was released as the B-side of "Purple Rain." On the UK 12-inch it is listed as "God (Instrumental)" and subtitled "Love Theme from *Purple Rain*." Two minutes of the track can be heard at 41:45 in the movie, soon after the seduction scene when Prince plays the backward crying tape for Apollonia. Lisa and Wendy's "Purple Rain" was placed in the film at 1:21:56, under the scene when the women play the song for Prince. "Father's Song" replaced the previously recorded version in the scene featuring his father (played by Clarence Williams III) at the piano at 57:42 and at 1:19:56 after the Kid's basement tirade.

WEDNESDAY, FEBRUARY 8, 1984*

"The Glamorous Life" (Sheila E. drum overdub)
"Moaning from *Purple Rain* Film" (aka "Backwards Woman")
Sunset Sound, Studio 2 | 6:00 p.m.–2:00 a.m. (booked lock-out)
Producer: Prince | *Artist:* Prince (Apollonia 6 was scheduled but crossed out) | *Engineer:* Prince | *Assistant Engineer:* "Peggy Mac" McCreary

When you're around Prince, you can't help but learn something, because he's so intensely into having everything just the way he wants it. You can't be around that kind of energy and not learn something. —Sheila E.[13]

Prince continued creating music for specific scenes in the movie. Today's music was intended for the scene in which Prince seduces Apollonia in his basement, but it was based on something he'd recorded the previous year and had played for the director of the movie, Albert Magnoli, during preproduction. Magnoli remembers, "I said I needed something really freaking scary, but really sexy and he said, 'Oh, I got that.'"

Prince would collect sounds and find new ways to use them in his recordings. He'd often revisit something he'd previously taped and repurpose it in a way that wasn't expected. Among the elements used in this composition were the sounds of Lisa Coleman and Jill Jones. "He seemed to just have at a tape of me crying," Jones recalls, "and he'd put it in all these weird places like in the movie. That is totally me. He had me and Lisa crying before in 'Automatic' [from his *1999* album]."

At this point "The Glamorous Life" had featured Linn LM-1 machine drums, with no additional percussion from Sheila. During this period it was very common for Prince's music to contain synth drums. Part of the reason was for speed, because when Prince knew what he wanted to record, he didn't want to wait to get the ten mics placed properly on the drum kit. The other part was for space. On a mixing board that only had twenty-four inputs, using up almost half of them on a single instrument limits what else can be recorded. Even on the occasions when he expanded to forty-eight tracks, recording live drums took up a lot of valuable real estate on the tape. But there was still another reason, according to engineer Susan Rogers: "The records that Prince did, his side projects such as Sheila and the Time and stuff, had a narrower range of vision, narrower than his own records did. So he was more reluctant to use a variety of sounds on those. He wanted them to sound smaller and more contained. That was the reason that drum machines made perfect sense for them. Because also Sheila was primarily percussions too, so they'd tape the drum machine and then add a lot of percussion on top of it."[14]

Sheila probably added her drums and percussion to "The Glamorous Life" during this session. It hadn't been placed on the *Apollonia 6* album as planned, so no one was sure where it would reside. If the idea of Sheila having an entire album was in the works, no focus had been given to the project, so this track could have gone to almost anyone, including Jill Jones, who had been told that her album was in the works: "That, ultimately, was supposed to be my record we were doing and I was really a little bit pissed off about that one because Sheila was just showing up at the studio just in her basketball-looking clothes and whatever. And I wasn't quite wise to what that really meant, but that's what that was, and then he took her to my uncle to get her hair and her makeover and all this stuff. And then my project got kicked backwards because of Sheila."

It seemed more and more obvious that Prince was enjoying the new inspiration he had found with Sheila, but it is unlikely that her vocals had been recorded for any track. Rogers noticed a change in Prince during this period. "He had a great deal of affection for Sheila. A great deal," she revealed. "They were not only lovers, but they were friends. He had respect and affection for her."[15]

"We were friends first," Sheila confirmed in a 2012 television interview. "Being that friend, you fall in love with your best friend and that's awesome. We didn't want to fall in love. Music brought us together, but we did."[16] Having found today's muse in Sheila gave Prince a new direction and new priorities. Regardless of where they were emotionally, almost all his projects for the next four years would be affected by this musical partnership.

A FedEx bill was presented for February 8 and 9, 1984, so it is likely that Prince was planning to travel back to Minneapolis soon after and may have shipped some of his music to Minneapolis in case he wanted to record while there. "There wasn't any real concept to where things were recorded; it was a matter of convenience," explained Alan Leeds. "And you can't really make any rhyme or reason. And by the same token, because of overdubbing and so on, you could work five days on one tape in five locations—just take the tape with you. And he would do that. He'd say, 'I've got to go to L.A. for a week, so pack up a box of tapes,' and he'd give us a list of tapes that he wanted to take with him, meaning that 'if I get the urge, I'm going to find a studio and go work on these songs.' And he may come back with tapes as is, they may go with him and he never opens the box, or he may end up going in the studio and working on some of them, and starting ten new songs, or whatever. . . anything!"[17]

THURSDAY, FEBRUARY 9, 1984*

"The Glamorous Life" (mix)
Sunset Sound, Studio 2 | 6:30 p.m.–2:00 a.m. (booked lock-out)
Producer: Prince | Artist: Prince | Engineer: Prince | Assistant Engineer:
"Peggy Mac" McCreary

I think that "The Glamorous Life" is wonderful, I think it is one of Prince's best and catchiest songs. Someone told me once: "Have you ever noticed when you walk through a music store, when you go through the keyboard department it doesn't take

long before somebody starts to go: ta, ta, tata ta, ta, tata?"
What a catchy rhythm that is!—Susan Rogers[18]

Prince spent five and a half hours mixing "The Glamorous Life" and the remainder of the session editing it.

FRIDAY, FEBRUARY 10, 1984

"The Belle of St. Mark" (basic tracking, Prince vocals)
Sunset Sound, Studio 2 (assumed)
Producer: Prince | *Artist:* (unclear) | *Engineer:* Prince (assumed) | *Assistant Engineer:* "Peggy Mac" McCreary or Bill Jackson (assumed)

One of [Prince's] chief strengths was his ability to observe, assimilate and then reinterpret recording techniques. He was also observing and assimilating songwriting techniques and stuff that was freely happening inside the band. And all of that influenced him and he became a shape-shifter. He became great at assimilating these techniques and reinterpreting them in a way people didn't recognize. And that became the genius of Prince.—Dez Dickerson[19]

The spring of 1984 was the busiest time in Prince's recording career to date, at least when considering the scope of his projects. He was creating music for himself, Apollonia 6, and the Time, as well as composing music for the soundtrack to his movie. He was under strict deadlines for all these projects, but that didn't keep him from being inspired to record something outside those projects. "Prince always follows his instincts," according to Steve Fargnoli, his manager during this period. "That's just how he is. I've never seen an artist totally consumed to the level of Prince. It pretty much excludes everything else. He has very little to say about what he's doing other than what's in his music, but he has a clear perception of what he's done and what he wants to be."[20]

According to many people who've spent time with Prince, he was addicted to the creative process. He was constantly looking for something that wasn't familiar to keep him interested. In retrospect, adding Sheila to the mix made complete sense. To keep from becoming bored with one long project and all the arterial side projects, he probably felt an internal desire to expand beyond what was expected. Prince demanded that those around him step up to the plate, which meant leading by example.

But once again Prince needed to continually feed the machine; he was seeking inspiration and at times that came from within his camp. For "The Belle of St. Mark," Prince (consciously or unconsciously) took a part of a song Jesse Johnson had written and made it into his own. Johnson had submitted many tracks to Prince, but only on rare occasions ("The Bird" and "Jungle Love" for the Time and "Bite the Beat" for Vanity 6, for example) were they used. Johnson was in Minneapolis at the time and didn't participate in this session.

Prince recorded his own voice on the demo for this track, and according to Sheila, she helped create the track. In her 2014 autobiography she stated that when she penned the lyrics, she "wrote about Prince."[21]

Status: Prince's vocals were replaced by Sheila E. during a later session. "The Belle of St. Mark" (5:08) was released as the first single from her *The Glamorous Life* album. An edit of the song (3:38) and a "Dance Remix" (7:42) were also released. The bell toll sound effect at the beginning of the track ("Big Ben Strikes Midnight" from the *Authentic Sound Effects* library, vol. 4) was likely added on a later date.

No work order could be located for this session, but the vault at Warner Bros. verified that "The Belle of St. Mark" was recorded on this date. It should be noted that there is evidence that Prince may have traveled to Minneapolis for the weekend of February 10–12. If this is the case, the sessions listed for today and tomorrow were either recorded in Minneapolis or on another date in Los Angeles.

After the movie finished filming, the Time continued to rehearse in Minneapolis, but with one main part of the band missing. "Morris was never there," recalled Paul Peterson. "He barely showed up."[22]

According to Jerry Hubbard, Jesse Johnson was still taking responsibility for the band staying tight:

Jesse was the one saying, "Be at practice at this time. Do this. Here's the songs we're going to work on." But when Prince came to town it was Prince's show. I mean Prince ran the rehearsals. He'd sing Morris's parts. He would tell us what harmonies he wanted us to sing. He would go over to everyone's instrument and say, "I want you to do this," and we rehearsed for a long time and this is when I knew the work ethic of Prince. I thought: "Wow"; he would rehearse with us for fifteen hours or whatever it was. Then he would take a small break in between and wait for the Revolution to come. And then he would rehearse them for another, you know, eight, nine, ten hours. And I was like, "This dude is nonstop."

According to Hubbard, Prince related to the people around him through music, and any chance to jam with others potentially sparked his inspiration:

I remember one time after rehearsal I asked Prince could we hang out, and we jammed for hours with me on the drums and him on the bass. Just me and him. And I'll never forget that day because he was playing the bass with gloves on. It was in the winter and I was thinking to myself, "He's playing that bass with those gloves on. Wow." I remember one rehearsal he played piano for like an hour to me. Just me sitting there listening to him play piano before the Revolution came in and they started rehearsing. And I watched a little bit of the Revolution rehearsing and then I left. It was just special times like that that, I got to hang out with Prince and really witness that genius.

The plan was to have a continuation of the previous tour with Apollonia 6 replacing Vanity 6 as the opening act. The Time would perform their own set, but would once again be responsible for playing behind the curtain for the girl group. "They were talking to us about how we're going to back up Apollonia 6 behind the curtains," recalls Hubbard. "I'll never forget Prince came up to me with an Apollonia 6 song and he says, 'Can you play that?' And it was 'Sex Shooter.' And I said, 'Yeah, I could play that.' And he says, 'Okay.' The whole movie thing was going to go on tour, which would have been crazy."

SATURDAY, FEBRUARY 11, 1984 (ESTIMATE)

"**Shortberry Strawcake**" (basic tracking)
Sunset Sound, Studio 2 (assumed)
Producer: Prince | *Artist:* unclear | *Engineer:* Prince | *Assistant Engineer:* "Peggy Mac" McCreary or Bill Jackson (assumed)

A lot of people say I'm a girl version of Prince because we're so much alike. We like a lot of the same music, the same clothes, some of the same musicians and the same foods, especially spaghetti.—Sheila E.[23]

Prince continued his internal battle between the long-term plans involved with the *Purple Rain* project and his short-term plans in the studio. When Prince was inspired he generally recorded what he was feeling at that time, and he rarely seemed concerned with morality or boundaries. According to Susan Rogers, "I remember him saying that if a woman came along and did what he did she'd rule the world. And I don't know if he had some precognition about Madonna. But when Madonna first came out he called it immediately and he said, 'She's going to be huge.' He knew that a female version of what he was doing would be successful and I think he felt that at this particular stage, and he also was having a strong female side himself. He probably had a pretty vivid imagination about what he could do if he were a woman."[24]

At this point Madonna was still releasing singles from her first album, and it wouldn't be until late 1984—when she released her *Like a Virgin* album—that she showed the world how far she was willing to push the envelope. Prince probably saw that there was no female version of him, so it was very possible that he visualized a way to create that through Sheila, and when inspiration struck Prince everything else took a backseat. In the studio Prince lived in the moment and the outside world often had to wait. Even technical issues had to be put aside. "His focus is what's coming out of the instrument right now," remembers Sunset Sound engineer David Knight. "And can we get this to tape right now? I don't care if it's a little distorted or if it's not EQ'd, we're going to record that anyway. Let me get this down right now because I have to get this out of my head. A very laser-like focus. If I can hear it, if I can get this thing into the song right now, we're good."

Engineer Bill Jackson was often alone in the room with Prince, but even Jackson wasn't sure where these new tracks would be placed: "At the moment that we were recording all of Sheila's tunes, it didn't seem like it was going to be for her. She was there a lot. She could have helped write some of it and then later on they got to working on them for her album."

Like other work with Sheila, "Shortberry Strawcake" started as a jam based around a steady drumbeat. There was a subtle, funky keyboard riff that sounds almost buried, especially when compared to the repeated main riff that begins at 1:05. The rest of the song was Prince jamming on keyboards and guitar above the bed of drums, with Sheila eventually filling it in with percussion and additional drums. Lyrics were written and put to tape (probably through one of Prince's guitar effect pedals to give his voice extra distortion). The track also included Prince singing about a dream he had based on his lover. Ultimately the decision was made to keep the song as an instrumental, and Prince's voice was placed backward in the song, hiding the romantic theme but giving the song a more sensual vibe. Prince had done this earlier in the week while working on music for the *Purple Rain* movie, so the technique was still fresh in his head. Even the title, "Shortberry Strawcake," is a sly acknowledgment of the different parts of the track going in multiple directions.

Prince had borrowed part of a song from Jesse Johnson for "The Belle of St. Mark" on the previous day. So soon after returning to Los Angeles, he reached out to Johnson and offered him a songwriting credit, but not in the usual manner. Johnson was recording with Susan Rogers in Prince's home studio in Minneapolis, and Rogers recalled what happened during that phone call: "Prince asked Jesse if it was okay that he gave Jesse writing credit on one of Sheila's songs. Jesse said, 'Okay, I guess so. What's the name of the song?' Prince said, 'Shortberry Strawcake, bye-bye.' We didn't think any more about it until the record came out. The song 'The Belle of St. Mark' is basically a rhythm track from one of Jesse's songs. . . . So Jesse gets credit for songwriting, but it is not for the song he wrote. Very weird, and Jesse was very offended and he played me the cassette of his song. And I had to agree with him, it was 'The Belle of St. Mark.'"[25]

Elements of this song turned up in the guitar work on "U Just Can't Stop," an instrumental by the Flesh, a jazz-based side project Prince would create in late 1985 that included Sheila E. on drums/percussion.

Status: "Shortberry Strawcake" (4:44) was released on Sheila's *The Glamorous Life* album.

See February 10, 1984, note regarding the uncertainty regarding where and when this was recorded. No documentation for February 12, 1984, has been located, so it is unclear whether Prince spent any time in the studio. It is possible that he was still out of town or traveling back to Los Angeles the following morning.

MONDAY, FEBRUARY 13, 1984*

"Noon Rendezvous" (basic tracking, Prince vocal)
Sunset Sound, Studio 2 | 6:30 p.m.–2:00 a.m. (booked lock-out)
Producer: Prince | *Artist:* Prince/Apollonia (neither was crossed out) |
Engineer: Prince | *Assistant Engineer:* "Peggy Mac" McCreary

*Another song he and I cowrote was "Noon Rendezvous," which
was about our relationship at the time.—Sheila E.*[26]

Prince continued recording, but it was becoming more obvious that he was
working on a new project. Engineer Terry Christian explains his theory:
"Prince always had a big locker of songs he was recording. Some had titles,
some not. He had so much material and he wanted to keep recording, but he
didn't want Warner to know what he was up to."

Something had drastically changed in the last week, and Prince had a new plan
that he kept from practically everyone. Prince had recently spent time with Sheila
and had jammed with her family. She and Prince shared a musical lineage passed
down to them from their fathers, but Sheila's bond with her father probably struck
a chord inside of him and helped him realize that she was someone he could communicate with both musically and emotionally. "It's really the music that brought
us together," Sheila explained in 2004. "The fun part about being his friend was
I think he hadn't met anyone who was as competitive as he was. And being a
woman, he was like 'Oh, I have to beat her!' It was that kind of thing. Growing
up in a family that was very competitive, my mom and all her brothers and sisters
were very athletic. I was very athletic, and so was Prince. We'd play basketball,
we'd play ping-pong, we'd play pool. We did everything besides recording music.
And so I was able to hang with him as a buddy, almost as a friend."[27]

Prince decided to produce an album for Sheila E. and sell the project to Warner Bros., but he would need more music before it could be assembled, so once
again Sheila and Prince recorded together in the studio. "We started writing
'Noon Rendezvous' when I let Prince listen to a ballad I'd written and played
castanets on," she explained in her 2014 autobiography. "We talked about it,
and I told him my dream was to write a song commercial enough to be played
on the radio, which was something totally different for me. Prince was excited
by the idea."[28]

"It was almost as if he could rely on inspiration," states Christian. "He could
come in and it would flow and turn into something great. Sheila E., Jill Jones,
Wendy, and Lisa were around. It was just the women and [his bodyguard]
Chick [Huntsberry]. He was probably as close to a friend as Prince has. He
needs a guy around, and Chick was that guy."

"Noon Rendezvous" was recorded over a six-hour session that included
Prince singing his own vocals. The final two hours were spent creating a mix.

Status: Almost forty seconds of percussion were eventually added to "Noon
Rendezvous" (3:16) at the beginning and end of the track before it was included

on Sheila E.'s *The Glamorous Life* album (3:56). The percussion used for that section was likely inspired by the Linn drum pattern from the backward woman/crying girl scene that was being worked on the previous week. (That part of the *Purple Rain* score can be found at 40:25 in the film.)

An edited version of "Noon Rendezvous" (3:35) was released as the B-side for "Oliver's House."

No documentation of Prince working in the studio on February 14, 1984, has surfaced, so it is likely that he spent Valentine's Day out of the studio.

WEDNESDAY, FEBRUARY 15, 1984*

Multiple scenes for *Purple Rain* movie
Sunset Sound, Studio 2 | Noon–11:30 p.m. (booked lock-out)
Producer: Prince | *Artist:* Prince | *Engineer:* Prince | *Assistant Engineer:* "Peggy Mac" McCreary

> *He saw the movie and he was able to see the movie cut up to that moment. He was actually seeing what the repetition of these images and the colors and what the editing was doing, and he then was inspired to go write music right away.*
> —Albert Magnoli

As *Purple Rain* was being assembled, Prince was given copies to screen. A VHS deck was installed in Studio 2 so Prince could compose music for the finished scenes. After reviewing the movie until 1:30 p.m., Prince took a five-and-a-half-hour break from the studio. He returned around 7:00 p.m. Despite the time Prince spent away, it appears that at least four scenes were scored during today's session, although there is some confusion about what he was doing. Prince might simply have been attempting to create music for multiple scenes, but very little of the music that he recorded during this session was used. According to Magnoli, "At that point he was really invested in the movie, in the relationship he was seeing in the movie, and so he just said, 'I'll just do this thing.' So he gave it to me and if I liked it, I liked it. If I didn't, I didn't. I never got that sense he was coming to me with stuff, he'd usually wait for me to say, 'I could use a song.'" Magnoli would ultimately bring on Michel Colombier to score the movie, leaving Prince more time to work on music for his other projects.

"Michel Colombier worked completely autonomously," says Magnoli. "I think he had one conversation with Prince that was, 'Hello, how are you?' Prince is a lot like Woody Allen when he meets people, which means he hardly wants to meet them. He just sort of . . . 'Meh! Okay,' and then walks away. He's shy. People think it's arrogance, but it's not. It's shyness and he's just being polite. But once Michel came in, I worked with Michel from beginning to end and the music is a result of that work."

Status: Among the scenes that may have been composed during this session were: "Dorito Scene" (Prince eating Doritos in his basement, 47:11–47:23), "Police Scene" (Prince being interviewed by the police, 1:18:32–1:19:17), and "Thought Scene" (it is unclear what scene this is, but possibly when the Kid finds his father's music at 1:20:30). Prince also revisited "Backwards Woman" (39:56–41:45). Of these, only "Backwards Woman" seems to have been used in the final version of the movie.

SATURDAY, FEBRUARY 18, 1984*

"Another Lonely Christmas" (basic tracking)
Sunset Sound, Studio 2 | Noon–11:30 p.m. (booked lock-out)
Producer: Prince | *Artist:* Prince | *Engineer:* Prince | *Assistant Engineer:* "Peggy Mac" McCreary

That song is a work of fiction. —Prince[29]

Prince had never recorded a Christmas song. He enjoyed having his studio decorated with Christmas lights, but a traditional Christmas song wasn't something he ever pursued. Instead he decided to turn the idea of a Christmas song on its head by singing a sad song about the holiday. He wrapped loneliness and depression around a story involving a lover who had died on Christmas Day. With a topic like that, it was unlikely to ever become a holiday/family staple, but to fans it is one of the hidden gems from this period.

There were generally others in the studio during this time, but this is likely a track he worked on exclusively. In an interview for *Uptown* magazine, drummer Bobby Z confirmed that it was recorded by Prince without input from anyone else. The work ended by 10:00 p.m., which was almost unheard of for a Prince session unless he had plans outside the studio. No mix was done, so the song was probably not complete.

Status: "Another Lonely Christmas" (6:47) was released as the 12-inch B-side for "I Would Die 4 U" and edited (4:51) for release on the B-side of the "I Would Die 4 U" single. The edited version also appeared on his *The Hits/ The B-Sides* CD. Another edit (4:20) was apparently completed but remains unreleased.

In 1987 the song was offered to the Special Olympics for the *A Very Special Christmas* project, but it was rejected because it had previously been issued.

SUNDAY, FEBRUARY 19, 1984*

"**Another Lonely Christmas**" (overdubs and mix)
"**Pop Life**" (basic tracking)
Sunset Sound, Studio 2 | 2:30 p.m.–6:15 a.m. (booked lock-out)
Producer: Prince | *Artist:* Prince | *Engineer:* Prince | *Assistant Engineer:* "Peggy Mac" McCreary

> *It's hard to hear this music played complete in my head and not be able to get it out. If I don't get it out, it won't exist on earth. I can't ignore what I hear in my head.*
> —Prince[30]

After spending four hours overdubbing and mixing "Another Lonely Christmas," Prince had Peggy McCreary quickly set up for a live jam session. "I was pretty proud of that drum sound," McCreary fondly remembers. "For the first time, I got a drum sound in about five minutes because he didn't give me any time. People take days or hours to get a drum sound, and I had literally one run-through on 'Pop Life,' so I had less than ten minutes to get all the mics patched in, to get the levels, to make sure it wasn't out of phase, God forbid, and you've got to check that when the tape stops. That was Sheila playing drums on that. I think he was playing bass along with her."

Sheila explained this process to Tavis Smiley in 2003:

What I loved about [Prince] so much is that we'd get in the studio and we wouldn't take two hours to three hours to get a drum sound. That doesn't exist in his world. Actually, you would be done with a record in two or three hours as opposed to getting a drum sound. So it was really cool because the more that things sounded naturally . . . if it was rattling, then bring it on. He didn't want to change tones and make things clean and crisp, and that's why his stuff sounded so full and big. Because everything that you were and what you brought to the table and what your instrument sounded like, he didn't try to change it. He would let you play it like it was. If it was raggedy and old and beat up, then that is what it was going to sound like. And it brought life to the song.[31]

Prince was a little more experimental than usual with his vocals, putting what sounded like a slight delay—but was actually a different take of the vocals—on one of the channels. This surreal audio effect was only on his main vocal; the background vocals were not given the same treatment.

Prince continued looking for new sounds and new inspiration. Many felt that songs like "Pop Life" were shaped by the legacy of the Beatles, but in a 1985 interview with *Rolling Stone* magazine, Prince denied this: "**The influence wasn't the Beatles. They were great for what they did, but I don't know how that would hang today.**"[32] Revolution guitarist Wendy Melvoin agreed with this assessment: "My take on it is that he hated the Beatles, not for the music but for something else. Maybe because of the iconic look of them or there was something about them that didn't ring true for him and his rock stardom. But I always knew if he listened to 'Dig a Pony' and 'Let It Be,' he'd change his mind. Period. I know the guy's taste. And 'Polythene Pam.' If he just sat down and listened to that stuff, he'd get it. But he thinks of 'I Wanna Hold Your Hand' or 'Strawberry Fields Forever' and sees them as too populist."[33]

Lisa Coleman pointed out that there were many sources feeding Prince: "Our brothers were a heavy influence. My brother [David] was a world musician, he played the oud and cello and finger cymbals, darbuka hand drum. When Prince met those guys he was really blown away and impressed. It was our scene that we had going that Prince tuned into."[34]

Prince and Sheila (and probably Wendy Melvoin and Lisa Coleman as well) worked on "Pop Life" for more than ten hours. If Melvoin and Coleman participated in today's session, it is logical to assume that the subject of adding strings to the song came up, and Prince likely asked them to supervise string overdubs on the following day.

Jill Jones was also brought in to add background vocals, but it is unclear whether her parts were recorded on this date.

Today's session lasted almost seventeen hours and wrapped at 6:15 the following morning. No formal mix was completed, and work on "Pop Life" was scheduled to continue during the next session.

Status: In 1985 an edited version of "Pop Life" (3:42) was released on *Around the World in a Day* and was the album's third single. "Pop Life" was the first track completed for the project.

It is likely that Prince's initial recording of "Pop Life" was much longer than what appeared on the album, and some additional overdubbing and remixing were done before it was released in New Zealand, Australia, and the United Kingdom as "Pop Life (Extended Version)" (9:07). Multiple 12-inch mixes of "Pop Life" were created, including Sheila E.'s remix "Pop Life (Fresh Dance Mix)" (6:16), which was released in Europe and the United States, and Kirky J's remix (6:06) in 1994. Many of these remixes added additional sound effects, such as water, found in the *Authentic Sound Effects* library.

Various other remixes from 1984–1985, including a 6:04 version, remain unreleased.

In 1996 Prince proved Wendy correct when he stated, "I think one of the greatest songs ever written, and for the lyrics alone, is Paul McCartney's 'Let It Be', cos, boy, let me tell you, that's what you have to do, you just have to let it be."[35]

MONDAY, FEBRUARY 20, 1984*

"Pop Life" (various overdubs including strings)
Sunset Sound, Studio 2 | 5:30 p.m.–1:30 a.m. (booked lock-out)
Producer: Prince | *Artist:* Prince | *Engineer:* Prince | *Assistant Engineer:* "Peggy Mac" McCreary

It was a lot of fun. Lisa would sit at the keyboard and knock out some notes.—Sid Page

Work resumed on "Pop Life" less than twelve hours later. As he did on several songs from *Purple Rain*, Prince asked Wendy Melvoin and Lisa Coleman to gather local musicians to create an orchestral sound to go with the song. During previous sessions they'd created space for a string solo or a duet, but for the first time they were looking for something larger than they'd ever attempted on a Prince song. Six musicians were brought in: Sid Page and Marcy Dicterow on violin, Denyse Buffum and Laury Woods on viola, and Annette Atkinson and Tim Barr on stand-up bass. "We just kind of made it into a symphony for him," recalls Barr. "That's what I remember. I remember the small string section gave him a symphony on 'Pop Life.'"

Lisa Coleman sat at the piano playing a guide track, but she and Melvoin were very open to hearing the ideas of the musicians, as Sid Page recalls: "[Wendy and Lisa] were very respectful. I remember really liking this session because it was like the old days of working with Sly Stone and Van Morrison because it was a very intuitive session. All the charts weren't laid out and written out, we were just winging it and that was fun. They'd have ideas and I'd sketch them out and reflect them. But there was nothing prescribed when I got there. It was pretty much a stream of consciousness."

The entire string part was finished in just over four hours. The six musicians recorded their parts more than once, slightly tweaking their performances along the way, but the goal was to make the track sound as if they'd recorded a larger ensemble.

The overdub session finished at 10:00 p.m., and three and a half hours were spent creating a rough mix and playing it back before wrapping up around 1:30 a.m. No cassette was made from this session, and Prince didn't sign the work order, so his attendance is uncertain. Page indicated that he doesn't recall seeing Prince, but Barr remembers it differently: "He was always there . . . in the shadows in the back, and the engineer is on the board and I kind of always sensed it and I didn't want to look and peer in, but he was in control. He was listening to everything."

By the end of the session the track may have been edited down and possibly contained many of the elements from the released version, including the sound effects for the "Throw the bum out" section. Contrary to legend, this wasn't the actual recording of Prince getting booed out of the Rolling Stones concert in October 1981; the crowd sounds are actually a blend of two effects from the *Authentic Sound Effects* library, vol. 4: "Barroom Brawl" and "Prize Fight, Large Arena."

Prince would not attend any sessions at Sunset Sound until the following Monday, either because he had left town or because he was involved in shooting pickup scenes required to finish the movie. Any studio work that occurred in Los Angeles over the next few days was probably done without him.

A Linn drum machine was rented on this date, and Bobby Z is listed as playing the drums on the song. There is a strong possibility that the strings were not actually recorded on this date, but instead on February 22, 1984.

TUESDAY, FEBRUARY 21, 1984*

The Glamorous Life album (copied)
"Pop Life" (copied)
"God Instrumental" (copied)
"Another Lonely Christmas" (copied)
Sunset Sound, Studio 2 | 9:00 p.m.–11:00 p.m. (booked lock-out)
Producer: Prince | *Artist:* Prince (listed)/Sheila E. (unlisted) | *Engineer:* Prince | *Assistant Engineer:* "Peggy Mac" McCreary

I have no idea who ["Pop Life"] was written about, but I know in general Prince was aware of the cocaine use in this country; that was something that he thought was absolutely ridiculous. Why would anybody spend money to put that up your nose and get high? I don't know if he was talking about anybody in specific. I really can't say who he might have been inspired by. For all I know it could have been a girlfriend or a date.—Susan Rogers[36]

A safety copy was made of "Pop Life," "God (Instrumental)," and "Another Lonely Christmas" as well as Sheila E.'s album. This was the first time her album was mentioned on any studio document. The track listing is not written on the document but probably consisted of: "The Glamorous Life," "Oliver's House," "Next Time Wipe the Lipstick off Your Collar," "The Belle of St. Mark," "Shortberry Strawcake," "Noon Rendezvous," and possibly "17 Days."

It is likely that Prince was going to take the songs to Warner Bros. to give them a taste of how her album would sound, although it is unlikely any of these tracks contained Sheila's vocals at this point.

Prince was probably not present, as he didn't sign the work order and didn't often attend sessions that only involved making safety copies.

WEDNESDAY, FEBRUARY 22, 1984*

"Wendy and Lisa Song" (no specific track listed)
Sunset Sound, Studio 2 | 6:00 p.m.–11:15 p.m. (booked lock-out)
Producer: Prince | *Artist:* Prince | *Engineer:* "Peggy Mac" McCreary

Prince was by now hungry for influences to take him further, so he relied heavily on Lisa and me to guide him in directions he couldn't think of himself. He knew he needed to go somewhere else, he just didn't know where he was going to go. Lisa and I had the audacity, or sheer stupidity, to try certain things, and he loved it.—Wendy Melvoin[37]

The fact that a work order lists Prince as producer doesn't mean he was involved with that particular session. Peggy McCreary explains: "Sometimes he'd call a 6 o'clock session, and he was going out so he'd say, 'You can have the studio,' and it was still listed as Prince because it was his money. Sometimes he'd say, 'Here, you guys mix such and such and see how you do.' Of course, he'd do it when everyone was fried and he was going out and we wanted to go home if he wasn't there. So sometimes he would do that and I think he did that for Wendy and Lisa. Gave them studio time and said, 'Go for it.' I don't remember. That could have been one of those times; I remember being in the studio with Wendy and Lisa a lot."

Alan Leeds witnessed Prince's growth during this period, noting that he was beginning to allow others to interpret his ideas even though it wasn't necessary: "Unlike Stevie [Wonder], Prince is actually more than 'good' at every instrument he plays. So his recording needs simply never depended on other musicians. That he chose to record with various members of his bands said more about the flavors and individual voices that Wendy Melvoin, Lisa Coleman, Eric Leeds and Sheila E. brought to the table. The caliber of musicianship in his band grew during the *Purple Rain* period and I think it was simply a case of Prince recognizing the elements that these musicians could contribute to his palette."[38]

According to those around him, Prince was beginning to rely on the input of Melvoin and Coleman as collaborators in ways that were unprecedented in his career. Over time he would extend a trust to them that altered the direction of his music. It should be understood that at the end of the day all studio decisions were Prince's, but with the confidence he extended to them, they became a band within the band, creating a circle of trust that allowed him to experiment. "We were absolute musical equals in the sense that Prince respected us, and allowed us to contribute to the music without any interference," Wendy explained in 1997 to *Mojo* magazine. "I think the secret to our working relationship was that we were very non-possessive about our ideas, as opposed to some other people that have worked with him. We didn't hoard stuff, and we were more willing to give him what he needed. Men are very competitive, so if somebody came up with a melody line, they would want credit for it."[39]

According to Susan Rogers, the importance of their role needs to be noted for posterity:

> What I can say is that Prince's music, as interpreted by and played by Wendy and Lisa, fanned out and it was broader in its emotional scope and width and depth it had; more than just the horizontal structure of the composition, they expanded it vertically. They made it higher and lower in its emotional scope, and harmonically, they enriched it. They pulled it further from its source and yet remained true to it. Everything influences you, and Prince is extremely intelligent and so he was obviously influenced by them. They meant so much to him that I can say with 100 percent accuracy that his music wasn't the same after they left. He taught them so much and deliberately placed them in a position where he could learn from them. He obviously wanted to know what they knew about music. He obviously wanted to hear music through their ears, the way they heard it. If they were musicians that he could have just dismissed, he wouldn't have used them to the degree that he did. He so seldom worked with other people in the studio, especially on instruments he could play himself. Obviously he had to work with Eric Leeds because he couldn't play saxophone, but he can play piano and guitar and if he would bring in another piano or guitar player and specifically give his music to that piano or guitar player, he is saying, "You do things I cannot do."

This is one of the few work orders that reflects Peggy McCreary as a full engineer, when in reality she and others were always full engineers in that they ran the session and provided technical support and knowledge. On the daily logs, Prince was listed as engineer, probably because he took over as many tasks as he could, but he always relied on his engineers to set him up and solve any problems. On the albums Prince listed McCreary and David Leonard as full engineers. Susan Rogers noticed her credits:

> I didn't know any other women engineers other than Peggy McCreary and Leslie Ann Jones who worked in San Francisco. When you are a young woman engineer starting up, you really scan records for those credits, because you just want to see it is possible. Can I do this? And not only was Peggy an engineer at very prestigious Sunset Sound, but she was working with Prince. To me she had it all. When I became Prince's employee, we would go out to Sunset Sound where she was an employee, and we would work with her. She would be the other engineer on the project, and we hit it off immediately and I loved working with her. She was wonderful and very, very funny. Her relationship with Prince was quite a

bit different than mine because her personality was quite a bit different, but she really made me laugh and she really knew her stuff and she was a hard worker. And I know that Prince relied on her for many, many years. She just was the right person for him. I think that's part of the reason why he finally found a studio in L.A. that he loved—Sunset Sound—because of working with Peggy. She just had the right personality for him."[40]

Status: It is unclear what was recorded on this date. No song title was listed and there wasn't a new tape reel purchased and used, so it is probable that additional work was done on an existing track, possibly the strings for "Pop Life." Although the strings are listed in this book as being recorded on February 20, there is a very good chance that they were actually recorded during today's session. Unfortunately, no firm evidence tipping the scale to either day has surfaced.

No documentation for February 23–26, 1984, has been located. It is likely that Prince traveled to Minneapolis, but if he remained in Los Angeles it is possible that multiple pickup shots were done for the film.

SATURDAY, FEBRUARY 25, 1984 (ESTIMATE)

"Traffic Jam" (basic tracking)
Kiowa Trail home studio (Chanhassen, Minnesota; assumed)
Producer: Prince | *Artist:* Prince | *Engineer:* Prince | *Assistant Engineer:* Susan Rogers (assumed)

It may sound funny, but there is a real vibe on that board [in his home studio]. Prince recorded 1999, Purple Rain, Vanity, *the* Time *and* Apollonia 6 *albums on it.*—Jesse Johnson[41]

Prince was absent from Sunset Sound from February 21–26, and it is probable that he traveled back to Minneapolis. During trips like this, it was common for Prince to continue his habit of recording whenever the urge hit him, so sessions during this period often happened at his home studio on Kiowa Trail in

Chanhassen, Minnesota. "Traffic Jam" is a Linn drum/keyboard–based instrumental that Prince recorded alone in the studio, likely just as an excuse to get a riff he had in his head on tape. Susan Rogers explains the process from this period: "Prince had reached this point with the record company where he could do whatever he wanted, which is a very rare position to be in. He didn't have to demo anything for anybody. As soon as he thought of it, he worked out the arrangements, he could record it, and it was done."[42]

Considering the quality of the songs that came out of his home studio, it is shocking how plain and inconspicuous it was. "The studio itself was just a regular bedroom," recalled Jesse Johnson, who briefly lived in Prince's house and cut tracks in this studio. "But whenever you walked in, Prince was recording some incredible stuff. He always worked in the middle of the night on some vampire shit. But the dude knew how to make records."[43]

Thanks to some help from Johnson, Rogers learned how to properly engineer a session with Prince:

The most important thing was to never hand Prince an instrument that wasn't in tune. Prince would come downstairs and usually have a lyric sheet written in long hand. And he would tape it up on a stand in front of the drums. I'd hit record and he would play the entire drum track from beginning to end without a click (track) with the song in his head. That's how talented he is. Prince wanted to be able to walk from the drum booth into the control room, pick up the bass and play the bass parts. Next he might do the keyboard or pick up the guitar. He'd get half of the instrumentation done and then by himself he would record his vocals and I would leave the room. He always had to do his vocals alone because he needed that concentration. We could finish an entire song and have it printed and mixed in one day and have copies made. And then a few hours later, the phone would ring again and it's Prince. (*laughs*) And I would come back and do the whole thing again. But that's just so extremely rare. Most people don't or can't work like that.[44]

Status: Although "Traffic Jam" (4:25) remains an unreleased instrumental, its ending was used as the synth-and-drum vamp at the end of "When Doves Cry" on the *Purple Rain* tour.

No documentation regarding this date exists, and evidence that the song was tracked at Sunset Sound has not been located; it was probably recorded away from Sunset Sound/Los Angeles during this week, but the exact date is speculation. It is likely that if he was in Minneapolis, he recorded other songs during this period as well.

MONDAY, FEBRUARY 27, 1984*

> **"Love and Sex"** (basic tracking)
> **"Traffic Jam"** (overdubs)
> Sunset Sound, Studio 2 | 9:15 a.m.–3:45 a.m. (booked lock-out)
> *Producer:* Prince | *Artist:* Prince | *Engineer:* Prince | *Assistant Engineer:* "Peggy Mac" McCreary

James Brown was an inspiration. Was and is.—Prince[45]

Work on *Purple Rain* was still in high gear, but once again Prince followed his urges instead of any pending release schedule. After several days away from Sunset Sound, he jumped back in with a high-energy track that unfortunately ended up having no place in any of his upcoming projects. At the unusually early hour of 9:15 in the morning, work began on "Love and Sex" in Studio 2, and the day was spent fleshing it out, likely with members of the Revolution and possibly Sheila. At midnight Prince began overdubs for the song, ending the session at 3:45 the following morning. All told, Prince and Peggy McCreary spent more than eighteen hours in the studio. "Getting a part right, or being demanding is an art form to get perfection and he's a perfectionist without question and that pushes you and him to find out your limits," explained Revolution drummer Bobby Z. "Nobody worked harder than him. So you were just trying to keep up, and certainly when he was younger it was super, super human. It was amazing to see this go on and to be a part of it, so you rose to the occasion because you felt like you had to."[46]

The song starts off with a count-in by Prince and the girls. A Las Vegas–style vamp, similar to one he would use in his upcoming 1984 birthday show for the song "Possessed," leads into a Prince scream: "YEAH!!!! Come on baby, hurt me!"

"It was very James Brown," recalls McCreary. "You can feel a cockiness in his voice on this song. You can tell that he thinks that he is hot stuff."

The track has the flavor of many songs from that era (such as "17 Days"), and the lyrics question how he'll be treated in heaven by his lover. Will he still be desired or "will he let you hurt me in the upper room?"[47] As with "Irresistible Bitch" when Prince uses the phrase "hurt me," this song continues the theme of the singer enjoying the pain from his lover. It also contains many of Prince's standard comments from his live shows, like "Let me hear you say yeah" and "Hit me." The song ends with Prince saying, "That's right."

Susan Rogers referenced what set his music and attitude apart from other performers:

There's something about him that I think is not well-understood. His generosity of spirit with regard to women. For all of his love of sex and women, Prince never approached women as a conqueror or a predator. The typical Prince song was "Do Me, Baby," from the *Controversy* album. "You do me. You get all the power. I'm taking all this power, giving it to you, and now you do me," is what he sang about. He empowered women. It's what he did. "Take Me with U." In "Darling Nikki" he wakes up and there "was a phone number on the stairs. It said, 'Thank you for a funky time. Call me up, whenever you want to grind.'"[48] She's calling the shots. He brought women to work with him, like Wendy and Lisa, me, and Peggy McCreary, Sylvia [Massy] worked with him. He never treated us like he was doing us a favor. He empowered us and let us do our thing, and he stood out of our way as we did our thing. His imitators talked about, "Baby, I'm going to do this to you," and, "I'm going to do that to you," and how much better they are than their rivals. He empowered women, and I think women loved him for it.[49]

It is likely that some additional work was done on "Traffic Jam," which was probably recorded over the previous weekend in Minneapolis.

A rough mix was created and a single C-60 cassette was made of "Love and Sex" at the end of the session.

Status: Although "Love and Sex" (4:58) was an incredibly passionate homage to James Brown and would have shown off Prince in a completely new light, it didn't have a place on any of his projects from that period, so it remained unreleased during his lifetime, although it was included in the *Purple Rain Deluxe* (Expanded Edition) CD set in 2017. On January 2, 1986, two years after "Love and Sex" was recorded, Sheila E. (with possible help from Prince) recorded a track with the same name (4:17). The two songs have nothing in common except the title.

TUESDAY, FEBRUARY 28, 1984*

"Love and Sex" (mix)
Sunset Sound, Studio 2 | 12:30 p.m.–5:00 p.m. (booked lock-out)
Producer: Prince | *Artist:* Prince | *Engineer:* Prince | *Assistant Engineer:* "Peggy Mac" McCreary

More than my songs have to do with sex, they have to do with one human's love for another . . . the need for love, the need for sexuality, basic freedom, equality. I'm afraid these things don't necessarily come out. I think my problem is that my attitude is so sexual that it overshadows anything else. —Prince[50]

Another relatively early session was held to mix the track and make a safety copy. At some point, Jill Jones added her background vocals to this track during the "Sha-la-la-la" section, but it is unclear if that occurred on this date, or on a later session. Prince left at 5:00 p.m. The Grammy Award ceremonies took place that evening, and he was nominated for Pop Male Vocal for "1999" and R&B Male Vocal Performance for "International Lover." Michael Jackson won in both categories with "Thriller" and "Billie Jean," respectively.

This really was Michael Jackson's year, and it was tough to argue with the success of *Thriller*. Prince wasn't quite in his league just yet, but it was obvious he was gaining momentum. While predicting the Grammy winners, *Los Angeles Times* critic Robert Hilburn accurately noted that Jackson would come out dominant in the Pop Male Vocal category, adding, "Prince will have to wait until next year." Few understood at the time how true that would be.

It is unclear whether Prince actually attended the Grammy Awards that evening as he wasn't seen when his name was announced as a nominee.

WEDNESDAY, FEBRUARY 29, 1984*

Apollonia 6 album compiled
"Take Me with U"
"Sex Shooter"
"Manic Monday"
"A Million Miles (I Love You)"
"Ooo She She Wa Wa"
"Some Kind of Lover"
"In a Spanish Villa"
Sunset Sound, Studio 2 | 5:00 p.m.–7:00 p.m. (booked lock-out)
Producer: Prince (although not listed) | *Artist:* Apollonia 6 (although not listed) | *Engineer:* "Peggy Mac" McCreary

I'm trying to put in that body of work things that I haven't done, so that when I finish, I look at all of it, it represents the whole complete pie as opposed to the same thing over and over.—Prince[51]

Having lost both Grammy Awards to Michael Jackson the previous evening, Prince may not have been in the mood to create a new song. Instead he focused his attention on wrapping up the *Apollonia 6* album. At the beginning of February the album was basically being written in the studio, and now he bookended the month by creating another assembly of the album. (The first took place on February 6.)

The track selections hadn't changed, and this new shuffle would remain the basic sequence for the final release. At this point the album still contained "Take Me with U" and "Manic Monday," but that would change very soon.

Four cassettes were made of the new version of the album.

It is unlikely that Prince attended the actual session, but he would have dropped by to pick up the cassettes. After Prince left the studio he called Apollonia from the limo. She wasn't home, so he hummed the break for a song as a message on her answering machine.

Potentially humbled by the previous night's Grammy loss, it is possible that he was inspired to work on something more introspective, and may have laid the groundwork for what can be argued is the most personal song of his career, "When Doves Cry." That tune would eventually become his first number 1 song, introducing the world to the *Purple Rain* soundtrack and movie as well as to the genius of Prince.

Nothing in his career would ever be the same after that.

SUNSET SOUND
6650 SUNSET BLVD. ● HOLLYWOOD, CALIF. 90028 ●

P.O. NO. LA-14389	SESSION DATE AUG.18,1983	ATTENTION: LYN WEINER	W.O. N 1351

STUDIO USED 3	ARTIST PRINCE	CLIENT: WARNER BROS. RECORDS
PRODUCER PRINCE	ENGINEER PRINCE	3300 WARNER BOULEVARD BURBANK, CALIFORNIA 9
TIME BOOKED 12NOON-OPEN	ASSISTANT ENGINEER PEGGY MC CREARY	

DESCRIPTION OF WORK

TITLES: "Purple Rain" - "Computer Blue"

STUDIO TIME:
MODE OF RCDG: _____ 30IPS _____ 15IPS

		FROM	TO	HRS	@	$
Setup		11:00	12:00	1		
Wait		12:00	3:00	3		
Vocal o/o		3:00	6:00	3		
~~String + Break~~		6:00	6:30	1/2		
String o/o		6:30	2:30	8		
copies/cass -		2:30	5:00	2 1/2		

OUTBOARD EQUIPMENT:

1- Harmonizer 949 @ ___ $ _
1- Lexicon DDL @ ___ $ _
1- LA DA- @ ___ $ _
*2 nd 24 TRK MACH. @ ___ $ _

MATERIALS:

1-C 60 -Cass - @ ___ $ _

ADDITIONAL INFORMATION	SUNSET PERSONNEL	
FROM_____ TO_____	ENGINEER'S SERVICES hrs ___@___	$ _
EXPLANATION:	ENGINEER'S SERVICES OVERTIME hrs ___@___	$ _
*Prince wanted an extra machine kept in studio in case he needed it.	ASSISTANT ENGINEER OVERTIME hrs 10 @___	$ _
	SECURITY SERVICES OVERTIME hrs ___@___	$ _
	hrs ___@___	$ _

CLIENTS SIGNATURE _____

ALL SERVICES ARE SUBJECT TO THE
TERMS OF OUR RATE CARD.

ORIGINAL WORK ORDER

AMOUNT____
SALES TAX .
OTHER____
TOTAL ____

August 18, 1983: Strings for "Purple Rain," "Computer Blue," and "Baby I'm a Star" (uncredited on work sheet) are recorded. It is likely that several of the spoken parts, including the "Wendy . . . is the water warm enough" section, were recorded today. Lisa Coleman recalls that "Prince handed us a piece of paper and said, 'Will you guys go out there and say this?' I didn't think twice." *Used with permission from Paul Camarata/Sunset Sound*

SUNSET SOUND
6650 SUNSET BLVD. ● HOLLYWOOD, CALIF. 90028 ●

J.O. NO.	SESSION DATE	ATTENTION:	W.O.
LA-14556	SEPT. 20, 1983	LYN WEINER	

STUDIO USED 3	ARTIST PRINCE	CLIENT:
PRODUCER PRINCE	ENGINEER PRINCE	WARNER BROS. RECC
TIME BOOKED 12NOON-OPEN	ASSISTANT ENGINEER PEGGY MC CREARY	XRRIXRENTRRXXRKRK 3300 WARNER BOULE BURBANK, CALIFORN

DESCRIPTION OF WORK

TITLES: " The Beautiful Ones "

STUDIO TIME:
MODE OF RCDG: MIXING/OVERDUBS   30IPS   15IPS

		FROM	12:30	TO	1:00	HRS.	1/2	@	$
line		FROM	1:00	TO	5:00	HRS.	4	@	
o/o		FROM	5:00	TO	3:00	HRS.	10	@	
mix		FROM	3:00	TO	4:00	HRS.		@	
Copies		FROM	4:00	TO	5:15	HRS.	1/4	@	
		FROM		TO		HRS.		@	

OUTBOARD EQUIPMENT:
1 - 291RE
1 - 1/2 27rk
2 - LA2A   Built Direct   @
1 - 949 Harmonizer   @ N/C $
1 - Lexicon DDL   @ N/C $

MATERIALS:
1 - 2502"   @
1 - 956 1/2   @ $
2 - CLOCESS   @ $

ADDITIONAL INFORMATION	SUNSET PERSONNEL
FROM_____ TO_____	ENGINEER'S SERVICES hrs ____@____ $
EXPLANATION:	ENGINEER'S SERVICES OVERTIME hrs ____@____ $
	ASSISTANT ENGINEER OVERTIME hrs 83/4 @____ $
	SECURITY SERVICES OVERTIME hrs ____@____ $
	____ hrs ____@____ $

CLIENTS SIGNATURE _____
ALL SERVICES ARE SUBJECT TO THE
TERMS OF OUR RATE CARD.
ORIGINAL WORK ORDER

pour faire
Fed. Express

AMOUNT____
SALES TAX____
OTHER____
TOTAL____

September 20, 1983: Prince records "The Beautiful Ones," which replaced "Electric Intercourse" on the *Purple Rain* soundtrack. "That's what happens when you give Prince 24 hours by himself," observed his drummer, Bobby Z Rivkin. *Used with permission from Paul Camarata/Sunset Sound*

SUNSET SOUND
6650 SUNSET BLVD. ● HOLLYWOOD, CALIF. 90028 ●

O. NO.	SESSION DATE	ATTENTION:	W.O. NC
LA-15164	FEBRUARY 4, 1984	LYN WEINER	085

STUDIO USED 2	ARTIST PRINCE OR THE TIME OR APPOLONIA	CLIENT: WARNER BROS. RECO
PRODUCER PRINCE OR MORRIS	ENGINEER DAY PRINCE	3300 WARNER BOULE' BURBANK, CALIFORN
TIME BOOKED LOCK-OUT	ASSISTANT ENGINEER PEGGY MC CREARY	

DESCRIPTION OF WORK

TITLES: Manic Monday

STUDIO TIME:
MODE OF RCDG: _____ 30IPS 15IPS

Set up FROM _— TO _— HRS _____ @ _____ $ _
Live FROM 1:00 TO 5:00 HRS 4.0 @ _____ $ _
O/D FROM 5:00 TO 12:00 HRS 7.0 @ _____ $ _
Mix FROM 12:00 TO -1:00 HRS 1.0 @ _____ Lockout $ _
FROM _____ TO _____ HRS _____ @ _____ $ _
FROM _____ TO _____ HRS _____ @ _____ $ _

OUTBOARD EQUIPMENT:
2-LA2A
949 Hammer
1-DDL Lexicon

MATERIALS:
1-250 1/2
1-CNS C60
1-250 2"
1-12x12" RMB

ADDITIONAL INFORMATION	SUNSET PERSONNEL		
FROM_____ TO _____	ENGINEER'S SERVICES	hrs _____ @ _____	$ _
EXPLANATION:	ENGINEER'S SERVICES OVERTIME	hrs _____ @ _____	$ _
	ASSISTANT ENGINEER OVERTIME	hrs 4.0 @ _____	$ _
	SECURITY SERVICES OVERTIME	hrs _____ @ _____	$ _
		hrs _____ @ _____	$ _

CLIENTS SIGNATURE _____
ALL SERVICES ARE SUBJECT TO THE
TERMS OF OUR RATE CARD.

ORIGINAL WORK ORDER

AMOUNT _____
SALES TAX _____
OTHER _____
TOTAL _____

February 4, 1984: Prince records "Manic Monday" for Apollonia 6, based on a dream he'd had the night before. According to his engineer Peggy McCreary, "It was actually a great day, and he was in a really great mood." The track was eventually removed from their album and given to the Bangles. *Used with permission from Paul Camarata/Sunset Sound*

SUNSET SOUND
6650 SUNSET BLVD. ● HOLLYWOOD, CALIF. 90028 ●

P.O. NO.		SESSION DATE	ATTENTION:		W.O. NO
LA-15322		MARCH 2, 1984	LYNN WEISS		148
STUDIO USED	ARTIST		CLIENT:		
3	PRINCE		WARNER BROS. RECORDS		
PRODUCER	ENGINEER		3300 WARNER BOULEVARD		
PRINCE	PRINCE		BURBANK, CALIFORNIA		
TIME BOOKED	ASSISTANT ENGINEER				
LOCK-OUT	PEGGY MC CREARY				

DESCRIPTION OF WORK

TITLES: "*When Doves Cry*"

STUDIO TIME:
MODE OF RCDG: ???????????? 30IPS 15IPS

Setup up	FROM 2:30	TO 3:30	HRS 1		@	$	
Live's/od	FROM 3:30 p TO 6:00 A.		HRS 14½	@		$	
Copy.	FROM 6:00 a TO 7:30	s HRS 1½	@			$	
	FROM	TO	HRS	@		$	
	FROM	TO	HRS	*Lockout*		$	
	FROM	TO	HRS	@		$	

OUTBOARD EQUIPMENT:

2-LA2A
1-949 Harmon?
1-DDL Lexicon

	@	$

MATERIALS:

1-250½
1-C4SS-C60

ADDITIONAL INFORMATION | SUNSET PERSONNEL

FROM _____ TO _____

EXPLANATION:

ENGINEER'S SERVICES	hrs	@	$	
ENGINEER'S SERVICES OVERTIME	hrs	@	$	
ASSISTANT ENGINEER OVERTIME	hrs 9.0	@	$	
SECURITY SERVICES OVERTIME	hrs	@	$	
	hrs	@	$	

CLIENTS SIGNATURE _____ *Prince*

ALL SERVICES ARE SUBJECT TO THE
TERMS OF OUR RATE CARD.

ORIGINAL WORK ORDER

AMOUNT _____
SALES TAX _____
OTHER _____
TOTAL _____

March 2, 1984: Prince records the bulk of "When Doves Cry," which would be his first number 1 hit. He'd started it the previous day, but it was on this date that most of the track was put to tape. "He knew exactly what he was doing," remembers Peggy McCreary. "He had a handle on it then, and he just knew he had a hit."
Used with permission from Paul Camarata/Sunset Sound

November 4, 1984: The opening night of the *Purple Rain* tour. This photo is featured on the cover of this book. *Photo copyright Neal Preston*

November 29, 1984: Prince performs a charity show at Gallaudet College (now Gallaudet University), a liberal arts school for the deaf and hard of hearing. The show was free for the students, but Prince paid everyone on the crew one hundred dollars each to put on the private performance. *Courtesy of Gallaudet University*

November 29, 1984: Prince gave his money and time to charitable causes at a rate far beyond what has been generally reported. This was something that he'd continue for his entire career, often without any fanfare or recognition. *Courtesy of Gallaudet University*

November 29, 1984: During the charity concert at Gallaudet College, Prince's lyrics were interpreted via sign language from the stage. According to those around him, this concert meant a lot to Prince, and it was one of the rare times he signed autographs during this tour. *Courtesy of Gallaudet University*

Sunset Sound Studio 2: This is the view of the studio Prince had while recording his vocals for dozens of songs, including "Take Me with U" and "Pop Life." *Photo by Duane Tudahl*

Sunset Sound Studio 2: Among the many songs Prince recorded in this room were "Condition of the Heart," "Jungle Love" (for the Time), and "Manic Monday," which was originally recorded for Apollonia 6 but would ultimately be released by the Bangles. *Photo by Duane Tudahl*

Sunset Sound Studio 3: Although the basic tracks were recorded at First Avenue, Prince spent many sessions adding vocals to "Purple Rain," "Baby I'm a Star," and "I Would Die 4 U" while sitting at this console. *Photo by Duane Tudahl*

Sunset Sound Studio 3: "When Doves Cry," "The Beautiful Ones," and parts of "Computer Blue" were among the multiple songs recorded in this room, many of them using this Yamaha piano. *Photo by Duane Tudahl*

MARCH 1984

> **"When Doves Cry"** [listed as "New Song"]
> Sunset Sound, Studio 3 | 7:30 p.m.–9:30 p.m. (booked lock-out)
> *Producer:* Prince | *Artist:* Prince | *Engineer:* Prince | *Assistant Engineer:*
> "Peggy Mac" McCreary

What is commercial, and what is innovative? One of my
biggest records had no bass—"When Doves Cry."—Prince[1]

A new month, a new song—and back in Studio 3. In many ways Studio 3 was better suited for Prince. Craig Hubler, Sunset Sound's general manager, remembers that Prince kept it busy: "I would say during '84–'85–'86, Prince occupied that room seven to eight months out of the year. He was almost a booking we could depend on, coming in and just camping out. He decorated a bit with candles, and Christmas tree lights dangled around the top of the console."

Prince spent only two hours recording in the studio tonight. The session was probably laying down the basic tracks for "When Doves Cry." No lyrics were written and no title was given to the new song, so it is doubtful Prince made much progress on the track. His time was probably spent creating the right drum sound on the Linn. "Prince was one of the very best drum programmers because he could get very warm sounds out of machines," recalled drummer Bobby Z, "particularly on songs like 'When Doves Cry.' He really liked the sound the Linn gave him, and hung on to it for a long time, even after it was obsolete."[2]

No cassette copies were made from this session.

FRIDAY, MARCH 2, 1984*

"When Doves Cry"
"When Doves Cry" (instrumental)
Sunset Sound, Studio 3 | 3:30 p.m.–7:30 a.m. (booked lock-out)
Producer: Prince | *Artist:* Prince | *Engineer:* Prince | *Assistant Engineer:* "Peggy Mac" McCreary

> *The music, for me, doesn't come on a schedule. I don't know when it's going to come, and when it does, I want it out.* —Prince[3]

When Prince had something to say, he had a singular focus. Today he was completely inspired, and what he created would be his introduction to millions. "When Doves Cry" would claim the number 1 spot for five weeks on the *Billboard* Hot 100, but on this date, it was just a man trying to put a song that only he could hear to tape.

The inspiration for "When Doves Cry" isn't completely clear. According to keyboard player Lisa Coleman, it came from working with her and Wendy Melvoin in the studio: "I think I influenced 'When Doves Cry' to the extent that Prince was engaged in a healthy competition with us. He was always thinking, 'How can I kick their ass?'"[4]

Prince's former guitarist Dez Dickerson is convinced that he knows its genesis: "I wrote a song called 'She Loves 2 Video' that Prince heard my band and I play at a show in L.A. shortly after he finished shooting the film. The rhythm from 'When Doves Cry' is identical to 'She Loves 2 Video.' I'm sure it wasn't intentional on Prince's part. That's what happens when you're in writing mode. But it is unmistakable."[5]

"I suspected for a long time—and I've had hints other people have supported me on this—that 'When Doves Cry' could have been about Susan Moonsie, because that was around the last period, around *Purple Rain*, where he still wanted her around," reasoned Susan Rogers. "But she desperately needed to really just get away and form her own life. She was an adult now. She'd grown up. Now it was time for her to start dating and I think that he kept her around. He caused her a lot of pain by trying to hang on to her, and she loved him. She was willing to stay, but only up to a certain point, and I think she's someone in his life who's gentle, giving, kind, loving, understanding, and she was a little dove and he was reluctant to let her go. But I think 'When Doves Cry' could probably have been inspired by her."[6]

In the lyrics for the track, as well as in the movie, Prince was very honest about the character's complicated history with his father. In a BBC documentary, Matt Fink recalled that Prince had been toying with the subject matter in the song for a long time:

He really opened up with us and discussed a lot of his personal issues with us. You'd be on that tour bus late at night and you'd start talking about the fact that your parents had trouble when you were growing up and they were fighting. His father was very disappointed with Prince when he was around fourteen or so. He decided he wanted to live with his father, but he kept bringing girls into the house and his father said, "You just can't be messin' with women under my roof at this age," and Prince said, "Okay," and Prince didn't obey him and got caught more than once, and finally his father said, "If you can't obey the rules, you're going to have to leave." Prince told me this story, so I know that his father could be difficult, but then again, Prince was no piece of cake either. I don't know for sure how abusive his father could have been. I got to know his father pretty well. I can't picture him being very abusive to Prince.[7]

Regardless of its origin, the track stands out because it was Prince's first number 1 hit on the pop charts, and the collective memory of when and how it was recorded is shared among those around him. Peggy McCreary says the potential for this one was obvious very early on:

I remember that song really well. We were in the studio, and he started the way he always did . . . with the drum machine, then the bass, then the piano, then this and that, and all of a sudden, he knew he had a hit and he got real excited. . . . He knew exactly what he was doing. He had a handle on it then and he just knew he had a hit. You could tell it was going to be a hit. Listen to it, the way he sang, it was incredible. He was the only person on that song. It was a real quiet time, a real personal time in the studio, and I think it was at times like that, that he made his best music, when it was just the two of us.

Prince worked on the full track (including the newly written lyrics) for sixteen hours. When it came time to add the frantic keyboard solo at the end, Prince realized that what he heard in his head would be tricky to re-create, so he and McCreary came up with a plan. Because it would need to be played live, Prince shared the secret with keyboard player Matt Fink: "Prince revealed to me that he took the 24-track 2-inch tape machine and slowed it down to the half speed setting. He played the solo half-time and sped the tape back-up, which made the solo much easier to play. But Prince always handed the football to me when we did 'When Doves Cry' live. It was if he was saying, 'Here, *you* play it dude.' (*laughs*)"[8]

Prince hadn't created a proper mix of the track by the end of the session, but he had McCreary run off a cassette of the song, and before he was finished, he left the studio for a short time. His excitement for the track was obvious because he drove to the homes of several band members and associates to play it for them. According to Lisa, she and Wendy were among the first to hear the track: "He called us at 4 a.m. We were in our jammies, thinking, 'What now?' He came over and we got in his car and drove around L.A. listening to that song. He was so excited about it."[9]

Jill Jones remembers similar behavior: "3 a.m. drop-by? Yeah. That's how he is. And you're half asleep and sitting there listening and then he's like . . . 'Bye' and you are like, 'Thanks for dropping by.'"

In addition to the version of the song that was later released, Prince also created an instrumental on this date to potentially be used in the movie, which was delivered to the Warner Bros. vault.

Status: "When Doves Cry" (5:54) was the lead single from the *Purple Rain* soundtrack and became Prince's first number 1 hit in the United States. It was edited for single release (3:48). An instrumental version (3:49) remains unreleased. Although there has been rumors of an extended 12-inch containing additional lyrics, this has not been confirmed.

"She Loves 2 Video" can be found on Dez Dickerson's 2005 CD, A Retrospective.

SATURDAY, MARCH 3, 1984*

"When Doves Cry" (mix, copies)
Sunset Sound, Studio 3 | 4:30 p.m.–11:30 p.m. (booked lock-out)
Producer: Prince | *Artist:* Prince | *Engineer:* Prince | *Assistant Engineers:* "Peggy Mac" McCreary (listed) and David Leonard (assumed)

*They were almost done editing the movie. "When Doves
Cry" was the last song to be mixed, and it just wasn't
sounding right. . . . Sometimes your brain kind of splits
in two. Your ego tells you one thing, and the rest of you
says something else. You have to go with what you know is
right.* —Prince[10]

Prince continued working with Peggy McCreary and David Leonard trying to
get the proper sound, but he seemed to feel that it wasn't quite there yet. Mc-
Creary remembers that while the track was being mixed, "[Prince] just punched
out the bass. He said something like, 'Nobody would have the balls to do this.
You just wait, they'll be freaking.'"

According to Prince, Jill Jones was also present during the decision. As she
walked in, Prince lifted his head off the console during the rough mix: "**It was
just sounding too conventional, like every other song with drums and bass
and keyboards. So I said, 'If I could have it my way it would sound like this,'
and I pulled the bass out of the mix. She said, 'Why don't you have it your
way?'**"[11]

Leonard has a similar memory of the event: "I remember it had A LOT of
stuff on it, so when it came down to mixing the song, it originally had bass on
it, and he made the decision to remove the bass. I was originally trying to mix
it as it was, but he came in and turned it off, and put reverb on the bass drum
and away you go."[12]

In funk music the bass propels the song and usually adds a heavy dose of sexuality to a track. Removing the instrument completely was practically unheard
of in this genre. Prince explained his thought process best: "**'When Doves Cry'
does have bass in it—the bass is in the kick drum. . . . The bass is in the tone
of the reverb on the kick. Bass is a lot more than that instrument over there.
Bass to me means B-A-S-E. B-A-S-S is a fish.**"[13]

The reverb helped create the sound, but Prince made it deeper by piling
three tracks of bass drum on top of each other.

Regardless of who was there, the most important part of the story remains
the same: Prince decided to remove the bass, which changed everything. He
would do this again a few months later on "Around the World in a Day" and on
"Kiss" in April 1985.

Two C-60 cassettes were made of the mix, and the session ended before
midnight.

SUNDAY, MARCH 4, 1984*

"When Doves Cry" (edit and copy)
Sunset Sound, Studio 3 | 7:30 p.m.–8:30 p.m. (booked lock-out)
Producer: Prince | *Artist:* Prince | *Engineers:* "Peggy Mac" McCreary
(listed) and David Leonard (assumed)

*Do his life experiences inform his art? Of course. How can they
not? I'm not saying that had he never been a celebrity he would
have written the same songs the same way. No, you are who you
are. The music is honest.*—Alan Leeds[14]

Prince probably didn't attend this session but he gave McCreary instructions for
how "When Doves Cry" should be edited. "Peggy was his right arm out there,"
recalled Susan Rogers. "But he worked day and night, long days and long
nights, and Peggy would reach a point when she'd be dropping from exhaustion
and she would call in her boyfriend, David Leonard, to do an edit or something
when she'd been up for twenty-eight hours and was tired. Prince liked and respected David, but he preferred working with women so he preferred to work
with Peggy and at home he'd work with me."[15]

In the credits on the *Purple Rain* album, Leonard was thanked for being
"the blade." Prince enjoyed his editing skills and relied on him to help trim
many songs during this period, but Prince wasn't always present during the
sessions. Sometimes he would conduct sessions over the phone. When this
happened, Prince would pull up to Sunset Sound after the session was over
and wait in his car while the song was recorded to a cassette tape. Someone
would walk out to his car and hand him the cassette. Prince would often roll
up the window and leave without saying a word. He would later tell *Keyboard*
magazine that **"[driving around in my car] is my favorite way to listen to
new music."**[16]

A single C-60 cassette was created of this edit.

After picking up the cassette during one of the sessions this week, Prince invited his drummer, Bobby Z, and his keyboard player, Matt Fink, to ride along
in his white Cadillac to listen to the track. Prince popped in the tape and played
it, to the confusion of his band members. Fink points out that the song had no
bass on it: "Prince said, 'Yeah, I did that on purpose. I didn't want there to be

any bass on it.' He said, 'Because . . . it's different. You'll get used to it.' I said, 'Okay,' and I did! It grew on me afterwards."

"He played 'When Doves Cry' for me," remembered Morris Day. "I got out the car and said, 'Next time play something funky for me,' and slammed the door. Next thing I know, it was one of the biggest hits on radio, so you don't always get it the first listen. Sometimes it takes two or three or four to really hit."[17]

The first listen was confusing to many of those around him. After he left one of the sessions, he brought it back to play for everyone, including Susannah Melvoin, who recalls her initial thoughts: "He comes pulling in in his limousine with his manager, Steve Fargnoli. He pulls in, and you *hear* 'When Doves Cry' and everybody was like, 'Okay, God! What is he doing? This song is awful!' None of us understood: What was that choice about? Like, what?! He heard it. He heard it. And he was right."

MONDAY, MARCH 5, 1984*

"When Doves Cry" (editing and copies)
Sunset Sound, Studio 3 | 8:45 p.m.–11:30 p.m. (booked lock-out)
Producer: Prince | *Artist:* Prince | *Engineer:* Prince | *Assistant Engineers:* "Peggy Mac" McCreary (listed) and David Leonard (assumed)

On the Purple Rain *album he began to realize that he was going to be a big star and sell a lot of records and that they were going to be judged against other people's records, and he began to take a lot of time and care and slow down a little bit in getting some of the songs on tape.—*Susan Rogers[18]

Prince apparently wasn't content with the edit from the previous day and scheduled an additional session to reduce the track for a single (or radio) version, but this time he oversaw the work.

The relatively brief session was over before midnight, but Prince spent almost three hours finding the proper edits for the track and laying it to a single cassette.

WEDNESDAY, MARCH 7, 1984*

"When Doves Cry"
"God (Love Theme to *Purple Rain*)"
Sunset Sound, Studio 3 | 11:00 a.m.–5:00 p.m. (booked lock-out)
Producer: Prince | *Artist:* Prince | *Engineer:* Prince | *Assistant Engineer:*
"Peggy Mac" McCreary

It was written as I was editing the movie. I realized there was an opportunity for a song. I needed to get Prince from one place to another. It wasn't scripted that there would be a song there, but as I was cutting, I realized I needed a song.—Albert Magnoli[19]

Prince and Albert Magnoli had been collaborating very well together, trusting each other's strengths. It was rare that Prince allowed someone to work with him so closely, but as Magnoli explains it, the fact that he was performing a task that Prince couldn't do made it necessary: "The way we worked is I said, 'This is what I need,' and then he supplied the music. He never questioned my need, and I never questioned the music that was sent. And that was just the way we worked because he knew that I was in charge of my division. He was in charge in his. Now, obviously, if I'm getting music from Prince even at that stage I know that it's going to be kinky, niche, and erotic."

Magnoli placed a call to Prince explaining what he was looking for in a song and was invited to meet at the home Prince was renting in Beverly Hills. Prince wanted to audition two tracks: "When Doves Cry" and the instrumental "God." "In those days with Prince," remembers Magnoli, "it was you sitting on the floor with a machine, and so I listened to the two songs, and I said, 'I like that one, what's that called?' And he said, 'When Doves Cry,' and I said, 'Great!'"

A single C-60 tape was made of "When Doves Cry" for placement in the film. Magnoli says, "I went back to the editing room that very day, and I spent the day cutting the whole sequence together. I think I did it in about four hours."

Once it was cut into the movie, Magnoli received a call from the film's producer, Bob Cavallo. The director explained to Cavallo that "When Doves Cry" was already in the movie and that it worked well. Cavallo responded with his doubts about the track. Magnoli remembers:

[Cavallo] goes, "Okay so let's talk about the song for a minute. I heard the song, and you understand there's no bass line. You have to put a bass line on it." And I realize, "Oh yeah, there is no bass. It's just the drum and the groove," and so he goes, "I'm going to call Prince right now and tell him that he needs to add a bass to it." And I go, "Okay, that's your fight." Twenty minutes later, Prince calls me up, and he goes, "You talked to Cavallo?" I go, "Yeah," and he said, "Cavallo told me it's already in the movie and he's asking me for a bass line, what do you think?" And I said, "I think the music works well, the image goes with it like you can't believe, so that's up to you." He said, "I'm not going to do it."

"Both of us were too young to be in charge, right?" laughs Magnoli. "That's the beauty of this. Why is anybody listening to either one of us?"

The raw urgency of the track fit perfectly in the movie as well as on the soundtrack album. The song not only blended with the music he'd already recorded, it elevated the rest of the album, shining a light on Prince as an innovator of sound.

A fresh 2-inch tape was purchased, but no new music was created. It is likely that it was purchased while waiting for the meeting with Magnoli.

Once a rough cut of the movie was pieced together, Prince held a private screening at his Los Angeles home and invited many of the people who were involved in the film. "There was a whole different cut of the movie that he played for us," recalls Time bassist Jerry Hubbard. "And I was thrilled to death because he had me all up in the movie and he had the Time in there more." After the movie premiered, Hubbard got a chance to ask about the final product: "I went up to Prince and I said, 'Hey Prince, what happened in the movie, man? There was a lot of stuff missing. The movie at your house was like three hours long.' And I'll never forget it. He looked at me and he says, 'Well, we had to cut something out. You didn't think we were going to cut *me* out did you?' (*laughs*)"

FRIDAY, MARCH 9, 1984*

"**Paisley Park (Instrumental)**" (basic tracking)
Sunset Sound, Studio 3 | 1:30 p.m.–8:30 p.m. (booked lock-out)
Producer: Prince | *Artist:* Prince | *Engineer:* Prince | *Assistant Engineer:* "Peggy Mac" McCreary

You have to be really fast. He doesn't want to mess around. If you can't get it right he wants to drop it. He says it's an omen and it's not happening. You lose the groove. Five minutes to get a drum sound is pretty unique. —Peggy McCreary[20]

This was the first time the phrase "Paisley Park" appeared in any Prince-related studio document. Although it shares the name of the song eventually released on his *Around the World in a Day* album, the similarities end there. This track is an unrelated instrumental that focuses on a groove created by live drums and bass, accented by some heavily reverbed keyboards and sounding like it was influenced by Gary Numan and Tom Tom Club's 1981 hit "Genius of Love." The overall production gives it a retro feeling that makes it feel very dated. Prince would revisit and update the beat of this song two years later on "Bob George." "Paisley Park (Instrumental)" also contains multiple reverbed sound effects, including children playing in a park, laughter, and whistles. Prince would repeat this theme of children playing in a park when he recorded the version of "Paisley Park" that was released on *Around the World in a Day* as well as in the video.

After presumably taking the previous day off from recording, he requested that Peggy McCreary set up for a session to start at 1:30 p.m. "Sometimes he'd come in and there would be a mix up on the board and you'd think, 'Okay, I'm ready for this,' and he'd tell you to put up some fresh tape because he wanted to record," she recalls. "So you had to re-patch the board from 'mix' to 'live' and EQ everything and you had about twenty minutes to tear it all down and set everything back up, and mic it all. And he would be playing the drums and he would say, 'Come on Peggy, you're blowing the groove. You're losing me here.' The pressure was incredible, but he got some great stuff."

The song is basically a synth workout with no solo, and sounds as if Prince just wanted to lay down a track to see if it went anywhere. He recorded the drums, bass, and keyboards over the next five hours, and sound effects from the Sunset Sound library were used to help create the mood. Instead of strategically placing them (as on "Pop Life" three weeks earlier), he used them as a background bed for the entire "Paisley Park" track. After a quick mix, two C-60 cassettes were made, and the brief session was over by 8:30 p.m. No additional information is known about anyone else participating in this recording.

Prince would not record again at Sunset Sound until March 17, so it is assumed that he either traveled back to Minneapolis or worked on additional scenes for the movie. Any recording he did during this time has not been documented.

Status: "Paisley Park (Instrumental)" (4:16 with sound effects; 3:44 without sound effects) was briefly considered for placement on *The Family* album in 1985, but it remains unreleased to this day.

According to all available sources, the track is called "Paisley Park," but for the purposes of clarity it will be referred to here as "Paisley Park (Instrumental)."

FRIDAY, MARCH 9, 1984, OR SATURDAY, MARCH 10, 1984

The music video for the Time's "Ice Cream Castles" was taped, but outside of this shoot Morris Day had little to do with the band anymore. At the time there was still hope that everything could be worked out, but after the taping, direct communication between Day and Prince became almost nonexistent. Day had basically left Minneapolis behind and moved to Los Angeles, which didn't sit well with Prince. Although they were both in California, Prince and his management felt Day should have been in Minneapolis rehearsing with the Time. "The fact that I moved out here and took the initiative as a grown man to choose my own place of residence seemed to upset certain people," observed Day. "That was the beginning of the end."[21]

Once the Time returned to Minneapolis, Jesse Johnson continued to lead the band during their rehearsals and Prince worked behind the scenes to get Day more involved, including making plans to get the Time onstage again. "Prince was talking about doing a gig with us that never materialized," remembers Jerry Hubbard. "We were going to do First Avenue, and we were all going, 'What are we going to do about Morris? He hasn't even rehearsed with us.' But it never happened."

SATURDAY, MARCH 17, 1984*

"Possessed" (basic tracking)
Sunset Sound, Studio 3 | 1:00 p.m.–5:45 a.m. (booked lock-out)
Producer: Prince | *Artist:* Prince | *Engineer:* Prince | *Assistant Engineer:* "Peggy Mac" McCreary

When I still wrestled with demons, I had moods when I couldn't figure something out and so I ran to vice to sort myself out, like women or too much drink, or working in order to avoid dealing with the problem.—Prince[22]

St. Patrick's Day found Prince back in the studio at Sunset Sound reworking "Possessed," a track he'd originally recorded the previous summer in Minneapolis. Instead of building on the original version, he started from scratch, spending more than six hours alone in the studio laying down the song's basic tracks. "He's excellent on piano and guitar," remembered Peggy McCreary. "He makes me smile when he plays bass; it's impressive. He's good on drums, but I don't think he's as comfortable. He likes to pick up different instruments. One time he said, 'Get me a harp. It wasn't one of those huge harps, but a non-pedal Gothic harp. He picked it right up. He's a natural.'"[23]

Another assistant engineer, Stephen Shelton, was given the task of finding a harp: "I actually called around to several companies to have a harp brought into the studio. And at that point in time he wasn't that inclined to use the sounds that were on the Yamaha DX7, and he went ahead and learned whatever he needed to learn about playing the harp."

Another seven and a half hours were spent overdubbing the harp and recording his vocals, using many of the lyrics from the previous version but making a few minor changes such as switching "Italian lust" in the original to "demonic lust." When Prince had something in his mind, he wanted to give life to the sounds in his head as quickly and as accurately as possible. "Lots of people hear the orchestras in their head," Shelton continues. "Not everybody is capable of pulling that orchestra out of their head, and that's why his multiple-instrument versatility and his ability to adapt to a new instrument he's never touched before is impressive, because he hears a harp part and yet there are times when he would rely on the musical input of other musicians because he wanted their input. Give them a guide, give them structure, but then he'd let them go for it."

Part of the inspiration may have been from the main riff for "Sugar Walls," the Sheena Easton song he had written earlier in 1984. The lead synth of "Possessed" shares the same melody as Easton sings on the intro to "Sugar Walls."

The final seventy-five minutes were spent making a rough mix and a cassette version of the song. The session ended at 5:45 a.m.

Status: "Possessed" (7:56) was not used in *Purple Rain* in this form. Although it was played in many concerts toward the end of the tour, this version remained unreleased during Prince's life, but was included in the *Purple Rain Deluxe*

(Expanded Edition) CD set in 2017. It also appeared on the *Prince & the Revo-lution: Live!* video from the March 30, 1985, concert in Syracuse, New York. The studio version of this track would be revisited the following week.

SUNDAY, MARCH 18, 1984*

"17 Days" (overdubs)
Sunset Sound, Studio 3 | 2:00 p.m.–7:30 p.m. (booked lock-out)
Producer: Prince | *Artist:* Prince | *Engineer:* Prince | *Assistant Engineer:* "Peggy Mac" McCreary

> *Prince always told me, "Brenda, you could be singing in a choir of 200 people and I'd still be able to pick out your voice."*—Brenda Bennett[24]

Susan Rogers remembers the amazing music being created on a daily basis at this time: "That was a great era for B-sides. I loved "17 Days." That was one that he pulled out of the closet a couple of times and reworked. I don't know why he did that but it was probably because he knew that there was something really good there that he just tossed off and he figured he could make it better."

Today's short session consisted of three hours of additional overdubs and two and a half hours of mixing "17 Days." A newly recorded part consisted of Brenda Bennett denouncing a man's "majestic macho attitude" and her ques-tions about when he will finally see how beautiful she is as a person "as well as you can see my vagina."[25] It is likely that this spoken section was recorded at Prince's home studio.

Despite the original intention to have Bennett sing the lead and help shape the lyrics on the song, by this point it was no longer considered to be a track for either Apollonia 6 or even a potential Brenda Bennett solo project. Bennett's husband, Roy, has a theory about why Prince reclaimed the song: "I think the reason why '17 Days' didn't go to the girls was just because he felt it was *too* good for them. He didn't want to waste it on something, that's terrible to say, but on something he didn't feel was going to sell as much as that song could have sold, but then it ended up as a B-side."

Despite the original high-minded goals, it seemed that Prince had been los-ing interest in *Apollonia 6* by this point and he was treating it as an obligatory album, instead of one he wanted to promote.

It is possible that during this session Jill Jones sang background for the track and that Sheila E. added additional drums and percussion as well as tambourine.

MONDAY, MARCH 19, 1984*

"Another Lonely Christmas"
"God (Instrumental)"
"Love and Sex"
"Pop Life"
"Possessed" (with lyrics)
"Traffic Jam"
"We Can Fuck"
"When Doves Cry"
"Paisley Park (Instrumental)"
"17 Days"
Sunset Sound, Studio 3 | 11:00 a.m.–3:00 p.m. (booked lock-out)
Producer: Prince | Artist: Prince | Engineer: "Peggy Mac" McCreary

One thing I ain't going to run out of is music.—Prince[26]

It is unlikely that Prince attended this session, but he requested that Peggy McCreary make two cassette and safety copies of ten songs that he'd created over the last three months. They included "Another Lonely Christmas" (6:45), "God (Instrumental)" (7:53), "Love and Sex" (4:59), "Pop Life" (3:37), "Possessed" (7:56), "Traffic Jam" (4:25), "We Can Fuck" (10:18), "When Doves Cry" (5:52), "Paisley Park (Instrumental)" (4:16), and "17 Days" (7:32).

The purpose of compiling all these songs is unclear, but it was probably for a final review before he started assembling the locked version of the *Purple Rain* album and to decide which album tracks would be released as singles and which B-sides would create the best pairings. Prince also probably wanted to focus on where he could assign some of these songs. "I know that he wrote a lot of songs for the movie soundtrack," recalled Matt Fink. "Of course they only picked eight [*eventually nine—ed.*] out of probably, I don't know, 40? There's a lot of material they went through to pick out those best songs, and he was still writing stuff for the movie as he went along."[27]

Of the tunes assembled during this session, only one track would appear on the *Purple Rain* soundtrack, three would become B-sides, two would appear in some form on his future albums, and four: "Love and Sex," "Possessed,"

"Traffic Jam," and "Paisley Park (Instrumental)," would not be released in this form during his lifetime.
Two C-90 cassettes were created.

WEDNESDAY, MARCH 21, 1984*

"17 Days"
"Computer Blue"
"Darling Nikki"
"Possessed (Instrumental)"
Sunset Sound, Studio 3 | 12:30 p.m.–5:30 a.m. (booked lock-out)
Producer: Prince | *Artist:* Prince | *Engineer:* Prince | *Assistant Engineers:*
"Peggy Mac" McCreary and probably David Leonard

The only thing I have disliked is the late hours. It's not that I like to go to bed early, it's just that when I'm working, it gets pretty weird.—Prince[28]

Prince had chosen the songs that deserved focused attention, and today he and Peggy McCreary (and probably David Leonard as well) began whittling down the tracks for release. The entire session was dedicated to edits, crossfades, and a rough assembly of songs for the album.

"17 Days" was edited from 7:32 to 3:56 by removing much of the repetition as well as Brenda Bennett's speech at the end, and the first lyrics began at 0:42 instead of 1:09. The entire final three minutes of jamming were eliminated.

"Darling Nikki" (which had been merged with "I Am Fine" in September) was edited the least. Prince removed a thirty-second section of drums and guitar at 2:42 to make room for "When Doves Cry" on the album.

Prince went back and forth about keeping the lyrics on "Possessed." During this session he muted the track's vocals, creating an instrumental version, because it was still being considered as a B-side and for use in the movie. He was apparently proud of the song, as he eventually placed the instrumental in the film. The instrumental was also played on the PA before his upcoming First Avenue birthday show later in the year, and the vocal version was played over the PA at the after-party and performed live with the Revolution during the concert.

"Computer Blue" was edited once again, making more room on the album. Work was also done adjusting the segue between "Computer Blue" and

"Darling Nikki." A sixty-minute tape was created for Prince to review on the ride home.

It is unclear which engineers were responsible for the edits on many of his tracks from this era. David Leonard or Peggy McCreary generally took care of them during the actual session, but there is no documentation of this. If an engineer was busy working on a mix, Prince was notorious for just grabbing someone he trusted from the Sunset Sound family and asking for a favor, including Richard McKernan: "He'd sneak things in to me to edit. I cut the 24-track a couple times and then after that he wanted me to edit all of his 24-tracks recordings. I'd be working with other people, and he'd open up the door a little bit and he'd say, 'You've got to edit this, you've got to edit this.' So I'd go out and edit stuff. It was something that wasn't on the work orders. There was no documentation of me doing that. I have no clue what the songs were. He'd just say, 'I want you to cut here and here, and cut that part out and it should work.' And I'd hear it and I would cut it."

THURSDAY, MARCH 22, 1984*

"Computer Blue" (crossfades/edits)
"Darling Nikki"
"Sex Shooter" (edits)
"The Beautiful Ones" (edits)
"Let's Go Crazy" (edits)
Sunset Sound, Studio 3 | 4:00 p.m.–10:30 p.m. (booked lock-out)
Producer: Prince | Artist: Prince | Engineer: Prince | Assistant Engineers: "Peggy Mac" McCreary and probably David Leonard

We edited ["Computer Blue"] down a few times. I can still hear a few problems with the song.—Peggy McCreary

Apparently not satisfied with the previous day's segue work, Prince continued to perfect the crossfade between "Computer Blue" and "Darling Nikki." With songs like "Computer Blue" and "Let's Go Crazy," Prince had produced a more intricate sound. Susan Rogers noticed this while the album was being created: "When you think about it, you hear that guitar, you hear his incredible keyboard skills, and you realize that, at any given moment on that record, he could do that. He could have filled up that record with virtuoso guitar playing, with virtuoso keyboard playing, and with virtuoso singing. Then here's another thing to consider: his lyrics. It's not Leonard Cohen, but think about . . . he's talking about an 'us.' 'I Would Die 4 U.' 'Let's Go Crazy.' 'Take Me with U.' It's a generous record. He's happy to be alive."[29]

Additional edits took place on several of the songs being placed in the movie, including "Sex Shooter," "The Beautiful Ones," and "Let's Go Crazy."

FRIDAY, MARCH 23, 1984*

Purple Rain album compiled (this is the list on the work order, not necessarily the compilation track order)
"When Doves Cry"
"I Would Die 4 U"
"Baby I'm a Star"
"The Beautiful Ones"
"Darling Nikki"
"Purple Rain"
"Let's Go Crazy"
"Computer Blue"
Sunset Sound, Studio 3 | 2:00 p.m.–8:00 p.m. (booked lock-out)
Producer: Prince | *Artist:* Prince | *Engineer:* Prince | *Assistant Engineer:* "Peggy Mac" McCreary

> *Sequencing for the record was a very important part of the process back when the album was the work of art that the consumer was purchasing, not singles. On those earlier records, you hear that unrestrained, unfiltered rawness on some of the tracks, whereas* Purple Rain *was very carefully arranged. It's a masterpiece.—*Susan Rogers[30]

Prince's music had changed and everyone around him noticed the difference. The message of *1999* was that the world was in its final chapter, so you might as well enjoy yourself. In many ways *Purple Rain* was about the arrival of hope. After the apocalyptic tone of *1999*, Prince added the concept of "the dawn" to his work. It wasn't a coincidence that he sang about being the messiah, considering the world was supposed to have stopped in the new millennium. This was

Prince rising from the tomb after three days and strutting his stuff as if to say, "Did you miss me?" to those who were familiar with his work—and an introductory shot across the bow to those who weren't.

"To me, Prince was just finally getting popular and I felt that this was his best time. I thought *1999* and *Purple Rain* were his peak," remembers Peggy McCreary. "I feel that part of that has to do with the chemistry between us. It was a great time. This was raw genius to watch him come in everyday and during this period, he was just on."

For this compilation Prince was still looking for the structure of the album and the flow needed to tell the story of the movie, but it was important that the album stand on its own, so Prince spent five hours editing the tracks together, looking for the proper sequence. Often this is done by trial and error to see how the songs work in context. The track order for this compilation isn't known, but the absence of "Take Me with U" should be noted, as it was still slated to be on the *Apollonia 6* album.

SUNDAY, MARCH 25, 1984*

"Erotic City" [listed as "Electric City"] (basic tracking)
Sunset Sound, Studio 3 | 5:00 p.m.–10:30 p.m. (booked lock-out)
Producer: Prince | *Artist:* Prince | *Engineer:* Prince | *Assistant Engineer:* "Peggy Mac" McCreary

One time [George Clinton] sent me a tape and says, "You pee on it and send it back to me and I'll pee on it, and then we'll see what we got!" I went to see him at the Beverly Theatre and it was frightening. Fourteen people singing "Knee Deep" in unison. That night I went to the studio and recorded "Erotic City."—Prince[31]

The truth about Prince's statement hasn't been verified, but George Clinton's influence on "Erotic City" is impossible to deny. It is dirty, sexy, and layered with fat, greasy funk.

As he often did, Prince started the song with a Linn LM-1 drum track and built it up from there: guitar, bass, and then his vocals, which were processed to change the pitch. Lyrically, Prince revisited the idea of "the dawn," and he also borrowed a phrase from Apollonia 6's "Sex Shooter" (changing "come on boy, let's make some time"[32] to "maybe we can make some time")[33] But Prince had another protégé in mind for this duet, so he asked McCreary to invite Sheila E. down to the studio:

> He'd get a bug up his butt and wanted to have someone on a certain track and he would tell me to call them. It didn't matter what time, just call them. And I would use the list that he gave me: Jill, Sheila, etc. And none of the women could know who else was there at times that they weren't. It became very private and I wasn't allowed to discuss any of it with any of them. Each project had a different list. It all depended on his mood at the time. The funny thing is that they would come, but it was very frustrating living your life knowing that at any moment, someone could call you and you'd have to go into work? It wasn't only these singers and string players that had to do this, it was also me! And that isn't a very fun way to live your life.

"Peggy was probably the most professional in that she kept a really nice arm's length," recalls Jill Jones. "She never ran out and say, 'Oh you know that you just missed the last girl!' (*laughs*)"

"I walked in to find sweet-smelling candles burning and the whole place impeccably clean, as usual," Sheila described in her 2014 autobiography. "Prince had set up the studio like a living room—all comfortable and cozy as if we were at home. It might as well have been—if he wasn't playing live, he was in that studio, so it was 'home.'"[34]

She continued: "I went in to play and I didn't see anything, I just saw a mic and I said, 'Where's the gear?' And he said, 'We don't need any. You're going to sing with me.' And I said, 'I don't like to sing.' He said, 'You've been doing this for a long time. You sing behind everyone, just do it with me.'"[35]

Sheila's vocals were added to tracks 14 and 15 of the song. It was customary for Prince to record two sets of vocals, often adding reverb to one of them and keeping one of them dry (or at least with a lot less reverb).

For the second time this spring Prince sang a duet, which may reveal how open he was to the idea of collaboration—at least on his terms, which meant his collaborators added what he told them to add to a track. He asked her to sing, "We can fuck until the dawn, making love 'til cherry's gone,"[36] but she balked: "There were some words in the song that I thought . . . 'I can't say that.' So I didn't. He said it. I didn't say it, so he kind of ducked [the mix] so it made it sound like maybe you did hear it, maybe you didn't hear it but I didn't say it!"[37]

McCreary remembers Sheila's first time behind the mic: "He pushed people. Maybe he saw talent in people that they really didn't see themselves, and he pushed them to do things that they might not have done without his push. He'd push you in and it was either sink or swim. I remember that she was a little nervous but she could sing. She's a talented girl."

"People still comment on how 'sexy' I sound on that song," remembered Sheila, "which always makes me laugh, because if you had been in the studio with Prince that night, you'd sound sexy too!"[38]

Afterward, Prince discussed his plans for an album with Sheila:

[Prince asked,] "Why don't you do your own album?"
And I said, "Nah."
"Why not?"
"I don't want to."
"Don't you think you have been playing behind other people long enough?"
"But I like it."
"I'm telling you that you need to be out on your own. You can sing, you can play."
I never wanted to sing until Prince asked me to. Lionel Richie had asked me to sing "Endless Love" on tour. I said, "You're crazy. I'm not going to do it." I get kind of scared when I hear my voice. When Prince asked me, though, I just had a feeling that he knew what he was talking about.[39]

The entire session was completed in five and a half hours, another testament to his talent and the speed in which he was recording.

"'Erotic City' was the first song I recorded with Prince," Sheila reflected in 1995 on an AOL Live chat. "And at that time, the person that I was, I was not embarrassed. But I am now."[40]

Status: Today's version of "Erotic City" (7:21) was released as the B-side for "Let's Go Crazy" and edited (3:55) for the 7-inch single release. Other alternate mixes (6:45 and 6:52) remain unreleased. Prince eventually added samples of "Erotic City" to two remixes of "Partyman" in 1989.

According to P-Funk trombonist (and eventual Prince band member) Greg Boyer, "We met briefly at a P-funk concert in '83. It was the night we recorded P-funk live at the Beverly Theatre. He came to check us out a few times over the years, and a couple of times also when I was playing with Maceo."[41] Because the P-funk concert was taped on April 23 and 24, 1983, a year before "Erotic City" was recorded, it is likely that Prince was either incorrect, attended a different show during March 1984, or embellished the story.

MONDAY, MARCH 26, 1984*

Purple Rain album compiled again (same track listing/different order)
"Let's Go Crazy"
"The Beautiful Ones"
"Computer Blue"
"Darling Nikki"
"When Doves Cry"
"I Would Die 4 U"
"Baby I'm a Star"
"Purple Rain"
Sunset Sound, Studio 3 | 1:30 p.m.–3:30 p.m. (booked lock-out)
Producer: Prince | *Artist:* Prince | *Engineer:* "Peggy Mac" McCreary

> *He always regarded albums as having a kernel or a core. For lesser artists, you might consider two or three songs as the heart of your record, and then everything else is really just filler. But for him, five or six songs could be the seeds, the core of the record and, from how much I heard him rehearse these things, he knew that "Beautiful Ones," "Purple Rain," "Computer Blue," those songs were representative of the record to him.*—Susan Rogers[42]

Prince was working very hard to keep *Purple Rain* as focused as possible. His previous album, *1999*, was a two-disc set and there was little interest in doing that again. "We hated the idea of a double album," explains Bob Cavallo. "It was never a great idea."

As with many compilation sessions, this one probably didn't include Prince, but he had decided the structure and Peggy McCreary's job was to assemble it according to his wishes. Unlike the compilation session from March 23, there were no music edits scheduled, so McCreary spent two hours reorganizing and copying the tracks to six C-90 cassettes. The order was now locked—except for "Take Me with U," which was still on the *Apollonia 6* album.

WEDNESDAY, MARCH 28, 1984*

The Glamorous Life album compiled
"The Belle of St. Mark"
"Shortberry Strawcake"
"Noon Rendezvous"
"Oliver's House"
"Next Time Wipe the Lipstick off Your Collar"
"The Glamorous Life"
Sunset Sound, Studio 3 | 3:30 p.m.–5:30 p.m. (booked lock-out)
Producers: Sheila E. and Starr Company (listed for the first time) | *Artist:*
Sheila E. | *Engineer:* "Peggy Mac" McCreary

*He said, "I can make it happen for you if you want to do a
record." I said, "Just like that?" And he said, "Yeah." I said,
"Okay, let's do a record then."—*Sheila E.[43]

In January Prince compiled an early version of *Ice Cream Castle* by the Time,
and by the end of February he had done the same thing for Apollonia 6. Prince
closed out March by compiling an album for his protégée Sheila E. Three new
albums in three months is an amazing pace, especially considering almost every
track was written and recorded without a full band and rehearsals. Now that
Prince had Sheila interested in a solo album, he had the songs that best suited
her voice and style assembled for a demo tape for her to learn. Many of them
didn't contain Sheila's drums yet, but these were the songs that would eventually become her album *The Glamorous Life*.

"I think we influenced each other," Sheila explained to *Time* magazine in
2014:

I influenced him the same way he influenced me. When he came back to the Bay
Area, I introduced him to my family, and he got to see me play with my family,
with my dad, and play Latin jazz music, and he'd never heard it before. He was
like, "This is just crazy. This is amazing." He loved it. We mentored each other,
if you want to look at it that way. That's the good thing about Prince: you can see
how he was influenced by the people around him. I can hear and see it, because
I got to live the influence that I had on him as well as the influence he had on
me—just being around each other, being able to record all the time and play, and
do things that he had never done using live percussion instruments and recording
all the time.[44]

Sheila attended the two-hour session, although it is unclear whether Prince was in the studio for the compilation. Six cassettes were created (probably for Warner Bros. executives, Prince, Sheila, and the Warner Bros. vault). For the first time, the work order listed Sheila E. as the artist and (taking a cue from Prince's anonymous work with the Time) the producers were listed as Sheila E. and the Starr Co.

Status: Sheila E.'s album *The Glamorous Life* contained all of the tracks that were compiled during this session. The album was fast-tracked and released on June 4, 1984, before any of the other albums Prince had created during the spring. The album was certified gold, peaking at number 28 on the *Billboard* Top 200 chart. Sheila was nominated for two American Music Awards for Favorite Soul/R&B Female Artist and Favorite Soul/R&B Female Video Artist as well as two Grammy Awards for Best Pop Vocal Performance and Best New Artist. This was an amazing accomplishment considering many of these tracks were originally recorded without a fully realized concept in place.

THURSDAY, MARCH 29, 1984–SATURDAY, MARCH 31, 1984

The Glamorous Life album (vocals and percussion)
Sunset Sound, Studio 3 (assumed)
Producers: Sheila E. and Starr Company (assumed) | *Artist:* Sheila E. (assumed) | *Engineer:* Prince (assumed) | *Assistant Engineer:* "Peggy Mac" McCreary (assumed)

*It seemed like only five minutes ago that he'd persuaded me to sing a duet with him. Now he'd convinced me that I should be the lead singer in my own band! We worked three days solid without sleep because we were both so excited about the project.—*Sheila E.[45]

No documentation for March 29, 30, and 31 has been located, so the specifics about these sessions are unclear. Fortunately, Sheila E. shed some light on this period in her 2014 autobiography: "In March 1984, I began recording vocals on some songs that Prince and I had chosen for my album. As always, we worked together really well, so it was easy to meet in the middle. The next few days were a mix of writing, recording, singing, playing, and staying up all night."[46]

Additional percussion and Sheila's vocals were added to several of the songs on her album, including "The Glamorous Life," which verified that it was no longer being considered as an album track or even a B-side for the *Apollonia 6* album.

"After rearranging the music and adding other musicians to the song, we were really happy with it," recalled Sheila. "It was very percussive and it had a catchy melody, incorporating all the black keys on the piano so that it almost sounded like a nursery rhyme. And the song was simple. Commercial music—even if it's funky and soulful—sometimes needs to be simplified in order to appeal to a broader audience. Simple melodies and simple rhythms often create hits because they're easy to remember."[47]

Prince also brought Jill Jones into the studio for additional vocal work on several of the tracks from this project, including "Oliver's House," "The Glamorous Life," "Noon Rendezvous," and "Next Time Wipe the Lipstick off Your Collar." The exact date of her new vocal work is not known.

APRIL 1984

"Next Time Wipe the Lipstick off Your Collar" (vocals)
Sunset Sound, Studio 3 | 8:00 p.m.–12:45 a.m. (booked 8:00 p.m.–open)
Producer: Prince | *Artist:* Sheila E. | *Engineer:* Prince | *Assistant Engineer:*
"Peggy Mac" McCreary

> *It seemed like we recorded my album in about a week. . . . I've*
> *never even come close to recording an album in such a short*
> *amount of time since.*—Sheila E.[1]

Prince requested that today's session start at 4:00 p.m., but he was delayed until 8:00. The evening's focus was on the vocals for "Next Time Wipe the Lipstick off Your Collar."

Of all the tracks on Sheila's album, "Next Time Wipe the Lipstick off Your Collar" gave Sheila's voice the best chance to shine, so extra care was taken on her singing. As with the rest of the album, Prince guided her but also relied on her experience to help make her album as powerful as possible. "*The Glamorous Life* [album] came together like magic," detailed Sheila in 1984. "I knew what I wanted and I got it. If it wasn't just right, I wouldn't have let it go. I'm kind of a perfectionist."[2]

Three C-90 cassette tapes were made of this session.

MONDAY, APRIL 2, 1984*

"Next Time Wipe the Lipstick off Your Collar" (vocals, mix)
Sunset Sound, Studio 3 | 7:00 p.m.–midnight (booked lock-out)
Producer: Prince | *Artist:* Sheila E. | *Engineer:* Prince | *Assistant Engineer:*
"Peggy Mac" McCreary

For Prince, making music is the most fun in the world. While we were collaborating, we'd stop to eat. Or we'd play ping-pong or basketball—and I gave him a run for his money, even though he won't admit it. We were like a couple living and working together and enjoying ourselves. It didn't feel like work at all.—Sheila E.[3]

Work continued on Sheila's vocals for "Next Time Wipe the Lipstick off Your Collar," and three hours were spent layering her voice to create the best performance possible. At this point in Sheila's career, her emphasis was on being a musician, not on her voice.

Ironically, Prince decided to draw even more attention to Sheila's vocals, and the drums were basically eliminated in the mix. When the track was originally recorded, the beat was maintained with a Linn LM-1 drumbeat that carried through the entire song. Once they were mixing, it was buried so far that it was basically gone, and the steady beat was replaced by Prince playing piano, which was given a much more prominent role as well. "Next Time Wipe the Lipstick off Your Collar" illustrates that Prince felt so strongly about Sheila's talent that he created a track that contained no drums, even though Sheila's fame at the time was largely based on her drumming and percussion and not her vocal talents. The decision to not include percussion on "Next Time Wipe the Lipstick off Your Collar" was a way to shift attention from her instruments to her voice, which would help introduce the world to a new Sheila E.

WEDNESDAY, APRIL 4, 1984*

Purple Rain album (listen to reference copy)
"Erotic City" [listed as "Electric City"] (vocal overdubs and mix)
Sunset Sound, Studio 3 | 3:30 p.m.–3:30 a.m. (booked lock-out)
Producer: Prince | *Artist:* Prince | *Engineer:* Prince | *Assistant Engineer:*
"Peggy Mac" McCreary

Real artists make albums people love, not just songs.
—Prince[4]

Prince spent the first few hours reviewing the eight-song *Purple Rain* reference LP from the March 26 album assembly. A reference LP is a vinyl version of the album created so it can be played on a turntable before the album goes into mass production. It gives the artist a final chance to preview how the project will sound before money is spent creating a mold for the actual album. A proper listening session can reveal weaknesses in the mix, but it is also the first time an album is heard in the way it was intended, so issues with structure and flow can be addressed before the master copies are pressed. Vinyl reference disks are not made as solidly as albums for release, so usually an artist can't play it more than a dozen times before it starts failing. Although Prince seemed to enjoy the album's eight tracks, it was not complete. "Take Me with U" was still being considered for Apollonia 6, so it had not been included on the record. That would change very soon in a decision that would drastically reduce the potential audience for the *Apollonia 6* album.

Additional vocal overdubs were done on "Erotic City." For some reason it was still listed as "Electric City," but that could be an accident, or he may have been hiding the title from Warner Bros., as he did with "We Can Fuck." No evidence has surfaced that the song was ever recorded as anything other than "Erotic City." Prince enjoyed pushing the envelope with his sexuality. He had decided not to release some of his more blatantly sexual tracks, such as "We Can Fuck," but he had no problem cannibalizing some of the phrases and morphing them into the lyrics of songs like "Erotic City" (*"We can fuck* until the dawn"[5]). In 2004 he was asked if he was embarrassed by some of the "raunchier" songs in his catalog; he responded, **"Embarrassed? I don't know that word. Have you seen my outfits?"**[6]

A mix of "Erotic City" was done at the end of the night and a cassette was created. The session ended at 3:30 a.m. Prince would be away from Sunset Sound for over a week. It is unclear where he went, but it is likely he went to Minneapolis, or possibly to Oakland with Sheila. No documentation for studio sessions during this week has been located.

TUESDAY, APRIL 10, 1984*

Ice Cream Castle album (edited version compiled)
Sunset Sound, Studio 3 | 5:30 p.m.–7:00 p.m. (booked lock-out)
Producer: the Time | *Artist:* the Time | *Engineer:* "Peggy Mac" McCreary

I think Morris was pretty fed up with the whole thing at the time and wanted to do his own thing.—Jesse Johnson[7]

The new version of the Time's *Ice Cream Castle* album was assembled during this session, using two songs that had been edited since the last time they were compiled. "The Bird" was cut from 8:33 to 7:44, losing much of the repeated chanting near the end of the track. The 54-second edit is located just before the seven-minute mark. "If the Kid Can't Make You Come" was reduced from 9:13 to 7:33, with two edits. The first takes place near 2:42; it lasts approximately 58 seconds, eliminating several rounds of Morris Day repeating the title, and rejoins the song at the start of a guitar solo. The second edit occurs around 5:52 and lasts for about 52 seconds. The discarded section contained the female background vocals singing, "Holland, France, London, dance"—which happen to be the final three places Prince visited during his 1981 European trip. Earlier in the track the cities were sung/spoken by Day (as he apparently undresses his girl): "This little hook went to Holland / This little hook went to France / This little hook went to London / and this little hook went to . . . Oh Lawd!"[8] The cities are also sung four times by the background singer, but only the last "France, London, dance" made it into the released version. These poor edits, which don't even bother trying to keep the beats in sync on the track, do not reflect the general quality of work on Prince's music, possibly exposing his lack of interest in this project.

Like many of Prince's album compiling (or comp) sessions, it was doubtful that he was in the studio, since these assemblies occasionally only involved placing the songs in a specific order and putting them on a cassette. Although the Time was listed as the producer of the session, Morris Day did not attend, either.

One cassette copy was created, and a reel was boxed and sent to Bernie Grundman for mastering.

SATURDAY, APRIL 14, 1984*

"**Take Me with U**" (added to *Purple Rain* soundtrack)
"**Computer Blue**" (edit)
Sunset Sound, Studio 3 | 6:00 p.m.–9:30 p.m. (booked 5:00 p.m.–open)
Producer: Prince | *Artist:* Prince | *Engineer:* Prince | *Assistant Engineer:* "Peggy Mac" McCreary

I liked the long version [of "Computer Blue"], but I wasn't sad that he cut it down because he had to for the album purposes.
—Matt Fink

After reviewing the eight-song reference LP of *Purple Rain*, Prince decided to make "Take Me with U" the ninth track on the soundtrack album, removing it from the *Apollonia 6* album. "I'm not upset that it wasn't on the album," explains Brenda Bennett. "It got more exposure on *Purple Rain*."

"He did that occasionally," recalls Peggy McCreary. "He'd give a song away and then take it back. [In 1985] he did it with 'Kiss.' We never knew what anything was for. It was all part of *his* master plan. He probably just felt 'This would fit into my album,' and it was his song, so why not? I mean all of it was his stuff. They were all his songs and he could do what he wanted with them. It was him! The Time was him, Apollonia 6 was him."

To make room for "Take Me with U," Prince had to edit "Computer Blue" once again, this time reducing it to its final length of 3:59. Unfortunately, this final version lost the last part of the song's more complex sections, hiding the richness of the work that went into the track so fans would have to wait until 2017 before the full version was issued on the *Purple Rain Deluxe* (Expanded Edition) CD set.

SUNDAY, APRIL 15, 1984*

"Blue Limousine" (basic tracking and vocals)
Sunset Sound, Studio 3 | Noon–5:45 a.m. (booked lock-out)
Producer: Prince | *Artist:* Apollonia 6 | *Engineer:* Prince | *Assistant Engineer:* "Peggy Mac" McCreary

I think he was very comfortable at Sunset Sound, especially Studio 3, which is kind of its own little fort. It's just got such a vibe. There's a wall behind the engineers, if that wall shook you know you had the right bottom. You could feel it shake. That's how we used to tell if the bass was doing what's right. Sympathetic vibration.—David Z

Because Prince had cannibalized "Take Me with U" from the *Apollonia 6* album, he needed to fill it with another song. Other tracks for their project, such as "The Glamorous Life," "17 Days," and "Moral Majority" as well as the songs from the unreleased second Vanity 6 album, had already been taken out of consideration, so Prince had to create something new to fill the missing spot.

The previous evening's session had ended at 9:30 p.m., and Prince decided to start recording unusually early. Arriving at noon, he quickly began laying down an LM-1 beat (including a countdown that would be edited out when the album was assembled), guitar, bass, synth, and a guide vocal track to follow. Once again Prince borrowed from Joni Mitchell, but this time it was the scenario from "Car on the Hill" (from her 1974 album *Court and Spark*), a song about a woman waiting for her lover to show up for a date. Prince's lyrics were another chance for him to use a car as a metaphor for sex, and he probably hoped to repeat the success he'd had with that formula on "Little Red Corvette."

Although the vocals were recorded by Brenda Bennett and it sounds as if it was tailor-made for her voice, she may not have been his first choice. As the session progressed, Prince contacted Apollonia about dropping by the studio to record the lead, but she was not available, so the song went exclusively to Bennett.

Apollonia wasn't the only person who dealt with situations like this. Jill Jones explains that it happened to her as well: "He would get so hurt over when you finally said, 'No. I'm not doing X, Y, and Z.' He almost looked at you like he didn't understand. He didn't have this cognitive skill of understanding another person's boundaries. And instead of confronting you, he'll just cut it short and move on. He's got an immense amount of charm, if he puts it on. But he can also be like a Dr. Jekyll and Mr. Hyde if you're on his bad side and if he's gunning for you."

Bennett was called in and offered the opportunity to sing the lead on this song. Once she arrived in the studio, he played it for her. "He usually had a work vocal track which you got the chance to listen to once," Bennett remembers. "He didn't expect you to get it, but he wanted that. I had such a good feeling for it and I said, 'Just let me in there and let me get the sound and let's do it.' I ran away with it."

Susan Moonsie was not present that evening, so Bennett was the only member of the group to perform on this track. Susannah Melvoin was also in the studio, so he had her add background vocals. "I wanted Susannah to be on it because we'd sound really good together," remembers Bennett.

Melvoin agrees: "Brenda and I talked about the richness of her voice, and she came to me after I sang on that and said, 'It's so nice to have another deep, rich voice like myself; I'm the only one who can do this.' Oh my God. Brenda was so great."

According to Bennett, "There was a lot of ad-libbing during the middle part of the song. He told me what he wanted Susannah to do and I did my best Susan impression." Their vocals were tracked multiple times and mixed to give a deeper "band feel" to the song. Jill Jones recalls that after Melvoin and Bennett left, she was also brought in to add an additional layer to the vocals. "You have to remember, I never did sessions with these girls. It was always after they weren't there or when he was working on it. So for some reason there was obviously a dynamic. I'm not so sure the girls always knew what was actually going to happen on their project."

Wave after wave of people were coming into the studio, doing their part, and leaving, with Prince overseeing it all and being the only one who understood the overall plan. His stamina seemed unlimited, and he could outlast almost anyone around him.

"He's up at all times at night," recalled Jellybean Johnson. "The man used to sleep only out of exhaustion. And I know I could stay up until five, six o'clock. He could be up two, three days like that."[9]

Jones agrees: "He didn't understand if people would be like, 'I'm tired. We've been here for seven days. I've got to sleep!' It was like, rejection. 'Well you just can't hang.' No, it was like, 'I have a life.' 'What, my life isn't you?' I mean, that's what it always started to be, and sometimes you'd feel sad leaving a studio. You'd feel sad—going out to the car. Because he wasn't willing to go to sleep, so he'd probably call whoever he needed to. I feel like he was lonely."

"I never felt guilty about it. I spent so much time with him, it was just like, 'I'm going to fucking bed,' you know," remembers Susannah. "The thing was, you'd be gone two hours and he'd call you. So there was no sleeping. You'd get to go home and do whatever for two hours and then he was like, 'I'm coming to pick you up.' And you'd be like, 'All right, whatever.' So it was like that all the time."

The session was finished at about 3:00 a.m. McCreary and Prince spent the next two hours and forty-five minutes creating a rough mix. At 5:45 a.m. on April 16, Prince seemed content and left. It would be his last recording session (as opposed to mixing, editing, etc.) at Sunset Sound until October, when he would record "Condition of the Heart."

Sheila E. was credited with writing the music for this song, but that has never been confirmed. The song contains many similarities with "Toy Box," which was recorded nine months later in January 1985 and placed on Sheila's *Romance 1600* album. That track was also credited to Sheila.

Status: "Blue Limousine" (6:19) was released on the *Apollonia 6* album on October 1, 1984, and as an edited single (3:22). It did not enter the *Billboard* charts and was their final release.

In 1986 the S.O.S. Band released a song called "Borrowed Love" (written by former Time members Jimmy Jam and Terry Lewis) that sounds similar to "Blue Limousine," including the singer mentioning the time of day.

TUESDAY, APRIL 17, 1984

Apollonia 6 album compiled
Sunset Sound, Studio 3
Producer: Prince | *Artist:* Apollonia 6 | *Engineer:* Prince | *Assistant Engineer:* "Peggy Mac" McCreary (assumed)

At the risk of sounding contradictory, I would have to say that on one hand, he was the toughest. But, on the other hand, he was the best. Musically, I have never worked with anyone like him and I don't believe I ever will again. I am grateful, proud, and blessed to have had the opportunity to work with him.— Brenda Bennett[10]

The *Apollonia 6* album was assembled with "Blue Limousine" replacing "Take Me with U." The compilation was sent off to make a reference LP. The track listing was:

Side One

"Sex Shooter" (6:46)
"Blue Limousine" (6:23)
"Manic Monday" (2:53)

Side Two

"A Million Miles (I Love You)" (5:50)
"Ooo She She Wa Wa" (4:13)
"Some Kind of Lover" (4:46)
"In a Spanish Villa" (2:22)

At the end of the session, seven C-60 cassettes were created. It is unlikely that Prince attended this session.

Prince's daily schedule was usually in a state of flux. On any day, he could decide to record, remix, or relax, depending on his whim. But his overall month-to-month schedule was slightly more predictable, and once again as the summer approached, Prince left for the Twin Cities. According to McCreary, "You'd come in to work and they'd say, 'Pack it up, he's in Minneapolis,' so it was really bizarre. You never knew, you just always expected 'whatever' was going to happen."

Status: This version of the album was approved, and artwork was created using this rundown. By the end of the month this was considered to be the final version of the album, but there was still one more major shuffle coming before it was locked. Side two would remain the same, but side one would undergo additional changes in order and content.

This work order could not be located, but the date was referenced on other documents; exact times for the session cannot be verified.

THURSDAY, APRIL 19, 1984*

"Pop Life"
"God (Love Theme from *Purple Rain*)"
"Another Lonely Christmas"
"Paisley Park (Instrumental)"
"Traffic Jam"
"Sex Shooter"
Sunset Sound, Studio 3 | 9:00 p.m.–10:45 p.m. (booked 9:00 p.m.–open)
Producer: Prince | *Artist:* Prince | *Engineer:* Prince | *Assistant Engineer:* Terry Christian

I think anybody who is as different as he is—and I don't mean just musically different, I mean someone who tries as hard to be different just for the sake of being different as he does—you know the guy is looking for a certain amount of validation from other people. And the volume of his work could show an unending desire or need for affirmation from people. Again, it could simply be because he is just so prolific. It's hard to know. I mean it goes without saying I think it's both those things. I think the guy is extremely prolific and then people can look at that as a constant need to be validated, and I think both are probably true.—Terry Christian

This short session consisted only of transferring six songs to cassettes with engineer Terry Christian. This collection was similar to the compilation from March 19, except "Sex Shooter" was added to the mix. Although the likely purpose for this was to audition B-sides, the inclusion of the Apollonia 6 song makes it more likely that it was just a tape for listening and possibly for use in the film, which was still in postproduction at this point.

It is unlikely that Prince considered this tape for any protégé project or for any future personal album.

Prince probably wasn't in attendance at this session, so any edits or changes were likely done with instructions from Prince over the phone.

WEDNESDAY, APRIL 25, 1984*

"Possessed" (movie version)
Sunset Sound, Studio 3 | 8:00 p.m.–9:30 p.m. (booked 6:00 p.m.–open)
Producer: Prince | *Artist:* Prince | *Engineer:* Prince | *Assistant Engineer:* "Peggy Mac" McCreary

There was definitely a sense that the Purple Rain *soundtrack and entire project was noteworthy. We had no idea that this thing was going to sell however many millions of copies that it did. But there was a sense that if they hadn't noticed Prince before they would notice him now.*—Susan Rogers[11]

During this time Prince maintained a VCR in the studio to view edited footage, and he continued to find potential spots for his music. A month earlier an instrumental version of "Possessed" had been created by muting all the vocals. This would be copied to another tape, and thirty seconds were edited out for inclusion in the movie. If the edits took place during this session, it is likely that any instructions came from Prince over the phone.

Status: The instrumental of "Possessed" (7:48) was edited (7:16) and placed in the movie during the scene where Morris and Apollonia are having drinks at First Avenue just before Prince and the Revolution perform "The Beautiful Ones" (30:08–32:23 in the film). Although it was part of the movie score, the full instrumental track hasn't been officially released.

MAY 1984

*Sheila has a high, passable voice, but it's the conga line of
Latin rhythms that carries "The Glamorous Life," a winning
dance track about a gold digger who confesses, "Boys with
small talk and small minds really don't impress me in bed."—
Rolling Stone*[1]

Warner Bros. released Sheila E.'s "The Glamorous Life" single as a preview
of her upcoming album of the same name. They had gotten the test printing,
which included her recently recorded vocals, two weeks earlier on April 18.
The speed at which this project went from start to finish shows that Prince was
excited to get his most recent music out into the market. "He saw that some of
his music had an expiration date on it," recalled Alan Leeds to writer Joseph
Stannard, "and that whatever moods and thoughts that went into the new music
were timely enough that he wanted people to hear them as quickly as possible."[2]

Over the course of his career, Prince almost always chose his newest music
instead of his archival works. It is a trait that would both help and haunt him,
causing him to abandon several potentially incredible projects over the course
of his career simply because he couldn't finish and release them quickly enough.
"One day someone will release them," said Prince in 2012. "I don't know that
I'll get to release them. There's just so many, and I like writing new stuff."[3]

In addition to his ego's need to share his latest inspirations, Prince probably
sensed an urgency to get his new music out into the void that was being left by

the Time's likely absence. The timing was crucial, because it could get lost in the potential *Purple Rain* juggernaut, and once the movie was released all his energy would be spent preparing for the fall tour.

The reviews were generally positive, and Sheila E.'s "The Glamorous Life" single would peak at number 7 on the *Billboard* Hot 100 chart.

Although the previous year saw no new albums from Prince or any of his protégés, 1984 was turning into a feast, with Sheila's album leading a year that would include the release of four albums of Prince-penned music along with multiple non-LP B-sides.

The whole experience at that warehouse was a really different thing. It kind of stands out. It was set apart, away from other buildings. Usually we would rehearse in these industrial parks and they were busy. We would have hours where we couldn't play because there were businesses being run there.
—Lisa Coleman[4]

Prince returned to Minneapolis and began working at a new location at 9025 Flying Cloud Drive in Eden Prairie. With the new studio came a new focus: familiarize the Revolution with all the music from *Purple Rain* for the upcoming tour and any upcoming live events. But very quickly he started recording new tracks. As usual, Prince wanted to create, and now that he was in his own studio, he began the process in the same way he did the previous summer: write a song, share it with his band members to flesh it out, then rehearse it for a live debut. The formula had worked very well for *Purple Rain* the previous August and for the Time two months later, but would it work again? And more importantly: Would it be as inspired?

As with Sheila's album, the accelerated timetable for new music was vital because he likely wanted to create something unique and didn't want to be influenced by *Purple Rain*'s success or failure. **"I don't want to make an album like the earlier ones,"** Prince explained when discussing his *Around the World in a Day* album. **"Wouldn't it be cool to be able to put your albums back to back and not get bored? I don't know how many people can play all their albums back to back with each one going to different cities."**[5] It is generally reported that Prince began working on *Around the World in a Day* at this stage, but a different Prince and the Revolution album was being created that would likely rely even more on contributions from the Revolution, especially Wendy Melvoin and Lisa Coleman.

In fact, when Coleman's brother David brought the song "Around the World in a Day" to Prince later that summer, he learned that there was a project planned between 1984's *Purple Rain* and 1985's *Around the World in a Day*: "Prince told me that he was really interested in [the song "Around the World in a Day"] and that this isn't the kind of thing that we would do on the next album, but the album after next, which turned out that he changed his mind."

"'Around the World in a Day' wasn't the title until that song came along," Lisa Coleman explained to author Matt Thorne about that current collection of music, "and that was really far into the project. He was thinking of it as 'Paisley Park.'"[6]

At this point only two tracks that would be placed on *Around the World in a Day* had been recorded: "Pop Life" (February 1984) and an early recording of "Raspberry Beret" (April 1982). "Paisley Park" (March 1984) was the name of an instrumental that had nothing in common with the song that would eventually share the name, so at this stage any new album had no real concept or point of view.

Prince huddled in the warehouse and began rehearsing and recording, but no matter which project was going to be the next album, when it came to collaborating with the entire band, it was still obvious who was boss. "I don't say that we collaborated, as much as the Revolution tried to live out his dream," Brown Mark made clear in 2015. "We got into the mind of Prince. We learned what it was he was trying to accomplish, so I think that was more of the collaboration. Us learning, 'What is it you are looking for?'"[7]

"Believe me, if he had allowed more collaboration, I would have liked to have had more collaboration with him," explained Matt Fink, who cowrote at least six songs with Prince during the twelve years they played together. "In fact, I was always throwing ideas at him in rehearsals and jam sessions."[8]

"Our role in 'Purple Rain' is to fight to get our ideas in there," according to Bobby Z, "and they're in there: You know, Matt's piano part on 'Purple Rain'— or the whole song 'Purple Rain' is the Revolution—or the stop on 'Computer Blue' was a snare drum part. You had to get your little ideas in there. And if he liked it, you felt like a million bucks because it worked in this amazing soup of music that he was creating."[9]

"[Collaboration with Prince] was a reality," according to Wendy Melvoin, "but it didn't pay bills."[10]

No matter who was involved in the actual recordings, Prince made an arrangement so everyone in the band had some financial reward. Each member of the Revolution was granted a percentage, and everyone was given blanket credit for their contributions to the music as part of the business arrangement to keep everything as fair as possible.

With the addition of a movie in the mix, Prince's brand was expanding, and so was his list of employees. "He had personnel around him that he felt confident with; he was very, very happy," recalled Susan Rogers:

I remember . . . at this time he started getting a wardrobe department, Louis [Wells] and Vaughn [Terry] were his wardrobe guys. He was creating a look for himself that was much more finished than how he started with *Dirty Mind* and then continued on *1999*, but now he was getting into exotic fabrics and really refining his look and the look of his band. His whole aesthetic sense was developing. He was becoming a man of wealth and taste. The only time I ever saw him in blue jeans was one day . . . he was wearing blue jeans and a short jean jacket and blue jeans boots. He was at the warehouse, and he was so happy, he was dancing around, and myself and someone else both went to ask him a question at the same time and we both said, "Prince!" at the same time. And he swung around on his heel and he said, "I must be famous!" And I looked in his face and I realized he is famous, and he knows he is famous, and he is delighted to be famous.[11]

LATE APRIL/MAY 1984 (ESTIMATE)

"Roadhouse Garden"
Flying Cloud Drive Warehouse (Eden Prairie, Minnesota)
Producer: Prince | *Artist:* Prince and the Revolution | *Engineer:* Susan Rogers

That was in the warehouse and it happened as just an organic groove. We started a groove.—Wendy Melvoin

Sometime in the late spring, Prince gathered members of the Revolution and began recording a new track called "Roadhouse Garden." The song is a very sparse keyboard-driven number embellished with finger cymbals and sound effects that could be found as standard patches on the Yamaha DX7 (#31 Train, for example). The DX7 was a new toy for Prince and those around him, and their exploration of it would influence the sounds in many of his songs.

The specifics of how "Roadhouse Garden" was initially recorded and what band members were in attendance are unclear, but it is likely the song was created to christen the Flying Cloud Drive warehouse and as a housewarming invite for everyone to join him at the new location. By combining "Roadhouse" (an often rough-looking club generally found on the outskirts of town, featuring loud music, dancing, and partying) with "Garden" (a section of land where vegetables, fruits, and flowers are cultivated often creating feelings of calm) he seemed to be poetically explaining his views on the new venue. The lyrics contain multiple clues about his purpose of the warehouse for playing music, the fact that they recorded day and night, the brown exterior potentially scaring people away, and his fondness for a home to record his music that nurtured creativity and warmth. He even references the twenty-four individual tracks lined up on the recording console: "This is the garden where emotions grow / Twenty-four feelings all in a row."[12]

Lyrics referencing letting emotions grow and opening your soul reflected a more 1960s attitude about nurturing affection, which was counter to some of the angrier themes on *Purple Rain*. The previous year, in a spoken part of "Computer Blue," Prince had touched on the concept of one's home being reflective of one's emotional state, but while that track contained topics like lust, fear, insecurity, hate, and pain, "Roadhouse Garden" was more about a place that fostered hope and bonding with others, perhaps reflecting where he was emotionally at this time. "It reminds me of a sunny day in Minneapolis and things were good," remembered Lisa Coleman. "We were in a good mood. Prince was really happy. It felt like a true story."[13]

"I never asked him about what he meant in certain songs," revealed Fink. "I could usually figure it out, even if it was fairly cryptic. The Beatles did stuff like that all the time, so did Led Zeppelin. It was poetry, so some things didn't always make complete sense, but it all worked, so I just went along with it."[14]

The track came together fairly quickly, and he reached out for additional voices for the chorus, according to Susannah Melvoin: "I remember it being in the new warehouse and everybody was like, 'We've got to go in and sing this vocal with him. You've got to come in there and do this with us.' It was a party basically doing the background vocals."

The final mix of the chorus clearly featured Wendy Melvoin, Lisa Coleman, and Susannah Melvoin, giving it a much lighter ambience than many of the *Purple Rain* tracks. Prince was relying on the sounds they'd bring to him, a practice that unfortunately often left others out of the recording process.

"[Wendy and Lisa] were certainly more involved with Prince's recordings than most of the band members," according to Alan Leeds. "To be very blunt, there wasn't much that either Mark Brown, Matt Fink, or Bobby Z could play on their instruments that Prince couldn't play as well or better. That was not the case with Lisa. And in Wendy's case, it wasn't that she could outplay him, but that she had a distinct kind of sound, and she and Lisa being so close, it's kind of like, you got one, you got the other anyway."[15]

Recording in the new warehouse opened the door for potential technical problems, but thankfully Susan Rogers was once again involved in putting the studio together: "Prince's attitude was: 'Let's go! This is great!' He would make it great by sheer willpower. There was no time for technical perfection. The object was to get it taped as quickly as possible, and that's what we did. He was either happy with the sound I got for him on tape or else he didn't complain if things were bad."[16]

"With Prince, there were no limits and rules," explained Sheila E. "It was basically, 'Let's just set up and play. That's how the [musical] gear should sound—the way that we hear it.' It was genius how he would work these things out."[17]

Once the track was recorded, Prince spent much of May rehearsing this song with every member of the Revolution as they prepared for a potential upcoming birthday show on June 7.

Status: "Roadhouse Garden" debuted at Prince's June 7 birthday celebration. The live version (4:30) and the studio version of the song (3:30) remained unreleased during Prince's lifetime. In 1999 Prince flirted with using this song as a title track for a "new" Prince and the Revolution album. "**It has songs on it that feature the Revolution in a front role, as a band,**" Prince explained to SonicNet Online in 1999.[18] When it was shelved, he went online again to update its status: "*Roadhouse Garden* [the album] got sidelined 4 a sec but it will take at the most—3 weex 2 finish. Most of the trax were cool 2 begin with. They just needed minimal production and a mix."[19]

The studio version of "Roadhouse Garden" was included on the *Purple Rain Deluxe* (Expanded Edition) CD set in 2017. It was combined with "Our Destiny" (6:25) and not issued as a separate track.

LATE APRIL/MAY 1984 (ESTIMATE)

"**Our Destiny**" (basic tracking)
Flying Cloud Drive Warehouse (Eden Prairie, Minnesota)
Producer: Prince | *Artist:* Prince and the Revolution | *Engineer:* Susan Rogers

We'd fool around and play together and a couple times we'd come up with what we thought was a song. Prince would hear

*it and like it—and it would become a "Prince song." There are
still a lot of those songs that we've recorded with Prince on the
shelf. I don't know—they may be used, they may not. But they're
really good songs. . . . Anything we did at the time we figured
was for the band, because we felt it was our band too.*—Lisa
Coleman[20]

Prince had been listening to the music on *Purple Rain* for almost a year, and
although he'd created the songs and they were like children to him, he was
likely very tired of those tracks. Knowing that he was about to conduct a tour
that would consist of playing that soundtrack almost every night for another
year, he was hungry for new inspirations to take him in a different direction and
once again relied on Wendy Melvoin and Lisa Coleman to help him find a new
sound. "It was all of us together," Melvoin recalls about writing "Our Destiny."
"All of us, we all did it together. He's the candle on the cake. We were his line
chef, prep chefs. You know what I mean? A great chef has to have some really
good cooks in his room in order to make that meal and deliver it."

The track itself was a very sparse piece of music that was likely recorded
with only those three in the studio. It is unclear whether Prince recorded the
lead vocals for the studio version of the track during the summer of 1984, but
it is probable because the song was still being considered for the next Revolution album. It was also mentioned as a likely track for the 1999 Prince and the
Revolution *Roadhouse Garden* album, so it is conceivable that he added them
at some point.

The song would be rehearsed by the entire band and performed for Prince's
birthday show at First Avenue on June 7, 1984. Prince would sing the lead on
the track for its only live performance.

Status: "Our Destiny" (3:00) remained unreleased during his lifetime, but it was
edited together with "Roadhouse Garden" and included on the *Purple Rain
Deluxe* (Expanded Edition) CD set in 2017. The edit was done at a later date, as
both tracks were recorded separately and considered two distinct songs. They
were played together during their live debut at Prince's upcoming birthday
show, and that is probably why they were eventually combined.

Strings would be recorded for the track in September 1984 but were repurposed for the beginning of "The Ladder," which was released on Prince's
Around the World in a Day album in 1985.

LATE APRIL/MAY 1984 (ESTIMATE)

"Strange Relationship"
Flying Cloud Drive Warehouse (Eden Prairie, Minnesota)
Producer: Prince | *Artist:* Prince and the Revolution | *Engineer:* Susan Rogers

Q: How did you feel when you heard "Strange Relationship" on Prince's landmark '87 work Sign o' the Times, *stripped of yours and Lisa's contributions?*
Wendy Melvoin: Jealous that our name was not on it and that he took us off.[21]

According to Susan Rogers, Prince revisited another track that he'd been working on the previous year: "'Strange Relationship' was one of those rare examples of when he had a song, and I remember him playing it back at the Flying Cloud Drive warehouse, and he had that one around for a while. We recorded it and set it aside, which was atypical for him to take something he really liked and set it aside." It is unclear how much was done on this song, but Rogers recalls that it would be worked on multiple times in the future before it was released: "I don't know what he was aiming for and I don't know why he was dissatisfied with it. It seemed to be a strong song and always one of my favorites."

Status: "Strange Relationship" ultimately underwent multiple variations, including some that had Prince asking Wendy Melvoin and Lisa Coleman to work on without him. "We got a master tape that had Prince's vocals, piano and drums," according to Melvoin. "He said, 'Take it and finish it.' So Lisa and I went back to Los Angeles and created the other parts to it. The sitar sound came from a sample from the Fairlight."[22]

When "Strange Relationship" was released on *Sign o' the Times* (4:01), the credits omitted their contributions.

Another track recorded during this period was "Most Likely 2." No additional information could be found about this song.

THURSDAY, MAY 10, 1984*

Ice Cream Castle album
Sunset Sound, Studio 1 | 6:30 p.m.–7:15 p.m.
Producer: Morris Day, although he was not present | *Artist:* the Time |
Engineer: "Peggy Mac" McCreary

*I was totally frustrated with everything, and it had been a
great run but I had gotten to a point in my life where I wasn't
really happy with the way shit was going down. . . . And I
started thinking to myself that it's getting to the time for me to
move on.* —Morris Day[23]

A rare session in Studio 1 at Sunset Sound consisted of a final tweak to the *Ice
Cream Castle* album before it was output and sent to Bernie Grundman for mastering. Prince wasn't present. Neither was Morris Day, although he was noted
as the producer. It would be the last time Day was listed on an official studio
document associated with the Time for many years.

It has often been written that Day had basically checked out and left the
Prince camp in the spring, but the reality was that plans were still being discussed by Prince and those around him for the Time—or at least Morris Day
as a solo artist—to continue recording and touring with Prince and potentially
perform on the *Purple Rain* tour. Day had not made up his mind about his
plans. "I waited because I was really trying to be certain," he explained in 1985.
"I don't like to be premature about my decisions."[24]

"I gave Prince's camp the opportunity because they knew I was heading in
the direction of a solo record," according to Day. "[Prince's manager] Steve
Fargnoli came to my house and he's like, 'Yeah, you can do a solo record. Prince
wants you to do a solo record, but Prince wants to be the executive producer.'
So I know what that means. That means the same old shit. So I was like, 'No
thank you.' I said, 'I don't want to do that,' and so that was pretty much it."[25]

With Day no longer living in Minneapolis, the confusion was compounded
because almost all communication had stopped between the two camps. "It
came time for me to break away and build my own castle," confessed Day in the
mid-eighties. "I needed some time to think about it by myself. The phone had
been ringing since May, but I wouldn't talk to anybody. I needed to come up
with my own conclusions. I don't want to sound negative. It just wasn't good
anymore."[26]

Morris Day was an important part of *Purple Rain*, but as of now he no longer pledged his allegiance to the Time. The movie had yet to be released, and plans for the promotion of the film as well as their album were all going to change. A video for the title track had been shot in the spring and there were two "live" performances in the movie, so half of the tracks on the album had potential music videos to release. With this supply of promotional material, no one would know that the Time had come and gone—the exception of course being their obvious absence on Prince's tour.

"Most of the original members are gone," said Day. "I think the Time will go on, but they'll probably change the name. Right now, I have to look out for myself."[27]

Prince's tour manager Alan Leeds recalled the feelings within the band at the time: "Jesse and Jellybean and Jerome wanted to carry on with the band, Morris did not, and there were a lot of internal differences amongst them as to whether or not the band should continue. It was at this point that the future of the Time was being decided, and it had somehow ended up in Jesse Johnson's lap."[28]

As he had done the previous fall, Jesse Johnson took the lead while rehearsing the latest version of the band, which now contained most of the new lineup except Day. "Morris was living in L.A. and promising to come back to rejoin rehearsals at any time," explained Leeds, "and he never did. Prince lost patience and finally said to Jesse, 'What should we do? Do we just disband? Do we give it up? Do we form a new group? Do we call it the Time and get somebody new up front? Do you take over and we rename the band? What do we do?'"[29]

The members of the band remained on the payroll and continued their routine. Band member Mark Cardenas reveals their confusion: "We were still showing up at the rehearsal hall and hanging out and waiting to see what was going on, and nothing was going on and it was really disheartening, because we knew the hype was out there and we're all excited about going on this tour. How come nobody knows where Morris is?"

This left Jesse Johnson as the wild card when it came to continuing the brand and the band name. For now, he would remain the driving force within the band until Day made up his mind.

WEDNESDAY, MAY 16, 1984

"When Doves Cry," the first single from *Purple Rain*, is released to great fanfare. The B-side is "17 Days."

THURSDAY, MAY 17, 1984

A test pressing of *Purple Rain* is made.

"I remember when we saw the album cover for the first time and I kind of remember the scuttlebutt," reflected Rogers. "Just a handful of employees, road crew, and technicians and folks like that, talking about the cover, and everybody's got a complaint and everybody's got an opinion. 'Oh, those flowers look like celery' or 'Why this background and not that?' We didn't recognize what we were looking at. We didn't recognize what this was going to be, but I know we were all aware of the momentum."[30]

MONDAY, MAY 21, 1984

Venue: Carlton Celebrity Room (Bloomington, Minnesota)
4th Annual Minnesota Music Awards

> *It was our thing. It was our home. It was 24 hours a day, seven days a week. It was constant creativity, constant high. It was adventure. You never knew what was going to happen.*
> —Wendy Melvoin[31]

Dez Dickerson was originally scheduled to perform at the Minneapolis Music Awards, but he and his band, the Modernaires, were on tour with Billy Idol and unavailable. Prince was asked to step in, and because he had been rehearsing the Revolution for the upcoming birthday show, they were able to use the performance to stretch their muscles in front of an audience.

Tonight was the live debut of all three songs played: the recently released single "When Doves Cry," the B-side "17 Days," and the unreleased "Possessed." The reaction from the crowd was incredible, but it was only a small taste of how audiences would respond once the movie was released.

Prince was also presented with the awards for Best Producer and Best Songwriter and was inducted into the Minnesota Music Hall of Fame. Although he had just performed, Prince chose not to speak and had someone else accept his awards in his place.

JUNE 1984

*It was my baby. I knew about it before it happened, I knew
what it was going to be. Then it was just like labor, like
giving birth—in '84, it was so much work.* —Prince[1]

MONDAY, JUNE 4, 1984

Sheila E.'s album *The Glamorous Life* is released, and the credits state that the
album was "directed by Sheila E. and the Starr Company." Prince is not mentioned by name, but a special thanks is given to "The Belle of St. Mark." "It
was Prince's idea that his name didn't appear at all," according to Sheila, "even
though he'd co-produced the entire album, co-written most of the songs, and
performed on almost all of them."[2]

TUESDAY, JUNE 5, 1984*

"Let's Go Crazy" (edits/crossfades)
Sunset Sound, Studio 3 | 10:00 a.m.–2:00 p.m. (booked 9:00 a.m.–3:00
p.m.)
Producer: Prince | *Artist:* Prince | *Engineer:* "Peggy Mac" McCreary |
Assistant Engineers: Steve Fargnoli and Suzanne (no last name listed)

He's a pure musician and artist who is so much more prolific than your average rock star. He's constantly frustrated by the environment he's in. He's constantly trying to grasp at new ideas because it's not moving fast enough. There were years when he wrote and recorded four albums. It added up, all that stuff.—Steve Fargnoli[3]

Although Prince had been preparing for his upcoming birthday concert at First Avenue in Minneapolis, he was in Los Angeles during the final days before the event. He didn't attend this editing session at Sunset Sound and sent his manager, Steve Fargnoli, as his surrogate. Once the editing and crossfading were complete, a copy was made and given to Prince. As it might be awhile before Prince recorded in Los Angeles again, some of his studio recordings that were stored at Sunset Sound were shipped to Minneapolis via FedEx.

Later that evening, he met up with Jill Jones and let her hear an early version of "Our Destiny": "He played it for me on June 6 maybe around 2 in the morning. It was just him on a piano. He'd laid it down in the studio and he said, 'I want you to hear this.' I'll be honest with you. I was sitting there going what the hell is this? It didn't sound like the current radio stuff. (*laughs*) And he goes, 'Well, it's going to be part of the show that I'm trying to do.'" Prince went on to explain his next project to her and her part in the production. "He was going to use all of us yet again. He was sort of always like that. Like those movies where Mickey Rooney would say, 'Let's just put on a show!' I mean that really is how he was. He had the spark of a new idea, and he wanted to film it."

Prince flew back to Minneapolis that day to make the final preparations for the upcoming birthday show that was scheduled for June 7.

Status: It is likely that "Let's Go Crazy" was edited down to the single release (3:44) during this session.

Prince was working his band hard to create new songs for the upcoming show. Not content to present a live version of his catalog, he once again pushed to find fresh and hopefully innovative music to share, and everyone was expected to participate in his long jam sessions. Wendy Melvoin found solace in Prince's working methods: "They were like meditations, total meditations. When the groove hit that one plateau . . . it was incredible. It would be one chord progression for hours on end. Prince would be practicing a dance step or coming up with lyrics. He was grooving and playing and soloing. One chord and you'd find your place. It was like a mantra."[4]

Lisa Coleman agreed: "It was an exercise in finding the cogs, especially with funk music, where there's syncopation, so we weren't playing on top of each other. We were experts at getting in synch, two guitar players, two keyboard players. Prince would call for certain people to drop out or come back in. 'Lisa, what have you got?' 'Let's see, I got this.' What chords, things like that. It was an exercise—band yoga, relay racing. It was great training. We became Olympic musicians. It was great."[5]

"All Day, All Night" was created during this period, and Prince wanted it to be heard even before a studio version was finished. "Pretty much every artist is most excited about their most recent work," explains Susan Rogers. "That is the high that exists from recording and releasing music, and you don't get high again until the next song that you write and record and that is the thing you'd like to share."

Prince prepared the band to play First Avenue once again and to overwhelm the hometown crowd one more time. Of course, he wouldn't have it any other way.

THURSDAY, JUNE 7, 1984

"17 Days" (live)
"Our Destiny" (live, debut)
"Roadhouse Garden" (live, debut)
"All Day, All Night" (live, debut)
"Free" (live)
"Noon Rendezvous" (live, debut)
"Erotic City" (live, debut)
"All the Critics Love U in New York" (live)
"Something in the Water Does Not Compute" (live)
"When Doves Cry" (live)
"Irresistible Bitch" (live, debut)
"Possessed" (live)
Venue: First Avenue (Minneapolis, Minnesota)
Producer: Prince | Artist: Prince and the Revolution | Engineer: David Z Rivkin

We've got some stuff you'll recognize and some you won't. —Prince[6]

First Avenue will always be associated with Prince. The odd thing is that to Minneapolis locals, it is just another club that has featured performances ranging from U2 to Soul Asylum to B.B. King and countless other performers of every genre of music, but because it was featured in *Purple Rain* the nightclub will forever be thought of as Prince's house. By June 1984 he'd played there at least five times, but they were all before the career catapult from his film. This birthday show was the last live performance of Prince and the Revolution before the release of the movie, and this was also the first major public event of the super-hype planned for *Purple Rain*. He'd play the club only a handful of times after the *Purple Rain* era, but it would rarely have the intimacy of his early days because he no longer belonged exclusively to the Twin Cities; he was shared by the world. There was a vibe on the street, and everyone knew that Prince was on the cusp of something epic.

The nightclub was decorated with purple napkins, and it was clear that this was not only a birthday party but a chance to celebrate the upcoming single, album, and movie release. The set list (not including the encore) was bookended by the current release ("When Doves Cry") and its B-side ("17 Days"). It is likely he didn't want to push any other tracks from the as yet unreleased *Purple Rain* album because he wanted to focus everyone's attention on his revolutionary single.

"Our Destiny," "Roadhouse Garden," and "All Day, All Night" had been written and rehearsed during the previous several weeks, so they were fresh tracks that Prince wanted to share during the show. As always, Prince continued looking for new influences to add to his music, and because of several shared musical passions, he trusted Wendy Melvoin and Lisa Coleman to add to his lexicon. Coleman recalled the variety of music they enjoyed: "It would be things that you wouldn't necessarily think would have any influence, like [1974 album] *Symbiosis* . . ."

". . . Which was the Bill Evans record with [German composer] Claus Ogerman's orchestra which was a big record that Lisa and I were listening to," added Melvoin. "We also turned him on to a lot of Peter Gabriel. Lisa and I were big *Security* people [Peter Gabriel's 1982 album] and all those records . . ."

"Or Ricki Lee Jones, or Joni Mitchell," replied Coleman, "and we would drive around in my car, which had the biggest and most amazing stereo system in it and we would drive around and listen to Vaughn Williams and [Prince] really got turned on to classical music and got into listening to Mahler and it was really interesting."[7]

Prince respected what Melvoin and Coleman were bringing to him so much that the live version of "Our Destiny" began with a short sample from the beginning of Bill Evans's "Symbiosis 1st Movement (Moderato, Various Tempi)" that was recorded from the actual *Symbiosis* LP, including the static pops and clicks.

It wasn't just those new songs with the Revolution that were important. Nine of twelve songs played were tracks Prince wanted to promote in some way. "Noon Rendezvous" was being released that same week by Sheila E. It makes total sense that he'd be showcasing the track (and "Erotic City," which featured her as well) to promote his new protégée, who was also in attendance that night. Prince eventually introduced her from the stage, but she spent time in the club and in the recording truck as well.

Prince had a lot riding on the success of her album now that it appeared that the Time wasn't going to be a functioning side project anymore. During this period, Prince was still trying to broker something with Morris Day to continue working together, but it wasn't looking hopeful. During "Something in the Water Does Not Compute," a song he had never previously performed live with his full band, Prince started jamming on the guitar and said, "Jesse," as if he's showing him how it was done. It is unclear if Jesse Johnson was in attendance, but the comment was very timely because Johnson would be fronting for the Time for the first time the following night at the Minnesota Black Music Awards.

The encore featured the crowd singing "Happy Birthday" to Prince and ended with the live debut of the recent B-side "Irresistible Bitch" and the unreleased (but potential B-side) "Possessed."

It was obvious Prince was happy, based on his performance. When there was a mistake on a keyboard part in "Something in the Water," he didn't get upset. He simply said, "Eww, that don't compute." He also smiled his way through minor mistakes in "Irresistible Bitch" and "When Doves Cry."

During this show, Prince's performance wasn't about looking too far forward. This wasn't about *Purple Rain*, and it was barely about *1999*. The near future would overshadow everything he'd ever done, and there is no way he wasn't aware of that, but tonight was about this fertile place where he was living at that very moment.

Status: Prince combined "Our Destiny" and "Roadhouse Garden" into one track during the concert, although they were recorded individually. The live versions of both songs remain unreleased.

FRIDAY, JUNE 8, 1984

Review of previous night's concert
"Our Destiny" (live; review and possible mix)
"Roadhouse Garden" (live; review and possible mix)
"All Day, All Night" (live; review and possible mix)
Flying Cloud Drive Warehouse (Eden Prairie, Minnesota)
Producer: Prince | *Artist:* Prince and the Revolution | *Engineer:* Susan Rogers

People really did sit up and take notice. He was different. He was unique and he was turning it upside down on what was normal in this business. I appreciated him in that way. He injected some life into the eighties. (laughs)—Peggy McCreary[8]

As he'd done with his August 3, 1983, show, Prince listened to the live performance so he could decide whether to pursue the tracks as performed and tweak them to maintain their energy or to discard them and start from scratch. He was likely focusing on the performances of "All Day, All Night," "Our Destiny," and "Roadhouse Garden," comparing them to any studio versions as he'd done with other live experiments in the past. "There were songs that the band was working out at the warehouse," according to Rogers. "We did it live and he mixed it with the live mix you heard on those tapes."[9]

It is likely that he worked on additional music, but it is unclear what took place. The sessions occurred earlier than usual because Prince was expected at the Prom Center for the 3rd Annual Minnesota Black Music Awards.

Status: The only track Prince seemed to pursue based on the live performance was "All Day, All Night" (5:27), which was eventually overdubbed and released by Jill Jones. It is uncertain whether it was considered for any Prince and the Revolution projects.

FRIDAY, JUNE 8, 1984

Venue: Prom Center (Saint Paul, Minnesota)
3rd Annual Minnesota Black Music Awards

It was time for me to leave. Things weren't right for me.
—Morris Day[10]

Morris Day wasn't coming back, so Jesse Johnson continued to work with the band as the guitarist and replacement singer. "I decided to hang because there is always a business side to everything you are doing, too," Johnson explained in an interview with Donnie Simpson. "And the business side is to continue to work because you've got to live, and you tried to make that work but Morris was definitely not into it. Morris like disappeared . . . because he didn't want to be a part of it anymore."[11]

Prince was probably still enjoying the excitement from the previous evening's birthday show when he was given another taste of hometown love and presented with the award for Most Valuable Performer in the R&B category at the Minnesota Black Music Awards. At the same event, the new version of the Time was going to be tested with Johnson as the lead, even though they weren't officially scheduled to play. "[Jesse] had been singing in rehearsals with us, so we were cool," remembers Time member Jerry Hubbard. "So this is the funniest thing that happened. Right when Jesse said, 'Ya'll ready to do this?' and the lights were down and people were going crazy, Jellybean drummed tap tap tap and the next thing I know Prince runs up on stage, and we're like, 'What's going on here?' Prince ran up on stage and he grabbed the mic and he sang 'I, I've been watching you.' And he started doing Morris. It was the best thing ever man. Prince turned it out. It was so great. So Prince actually did that performance with us."

It is unclear whether a second song was performed and Johnson took the lead, but this would be their only show with Johnson potentially taking the place of Day.

The following year Prince publicly voiced his disapproval of Johnson in such a prominent role: **"Jesse wanted to be in front all the time. And I just don't think God puts everybody in that particular bag. And sometimes I was blunt enough to say that to people: 'I don't think you should be the frontman. I think Morris should.'"[12]**

Johnson would eventually go on to have a very successful career leading his own group, but at this moment Prince couldn't see his potential; he taunted the remaining members of the Time backstage by complimenting Mazarati, another local group who had performed that evening and was gaining some notoriety. Prince openly discussed the plans he had for them if they signed with him.

"Prince was hyping Mazarati up," recalls Hubbard. "We were thinking 'Why is he doing that?' You know, we want him hyping the Time up. And so he's telling us about how Mazarati's going to do this, and their album's going to be sick and blah, blah, blah and we're like, 'Wow. He's really into Mazarati,' and that's the first time we heard about that. You could feel some tension going on already, but it wasn't to the point where they were fighting or arguing, but Jesse was a little salty, I think, because he was trying to keep the Time going. And it felt like Prince was maybe moving on and getting into Mazarati. And so it was a little tense in the back there."

"Prince needed someone to take the place of the Time, so I think Mazarati was it and he was so excited," recalls Mazarati member Tony Christian. "We played at the Prom Center with the Time and I guess we blew the Time away. I guess there were more Mazarati fans in the audience, and the Time was older and Morris Day didn't show up."

Prince was intrigued enough with Mazarati that he signed them, causing even more chaos within the Time, which by this point was basically the Time in name only. Any long-term plans were up in the air because Johnson wasn't happy and Day wasn't there, which confused everyone. The lack of communication with Day made a tour practically impossible. "I know the guys were wondering why I left," reasoned Day, "especially the new band members who weren't around long enough to understand everything that was involved. I know I disappointed them because they were sounding good in rehearsal. They were anxious to hit the road and have a good time."[13]

It wasn't just the actual band who wanted the Time to tour. Prince had always planned on an epic "battle of the bands" tour to promote the movie, and it is understandable that he was hurt when the plans changed. "**We never got a chance to do the real _Purple Rain_ tour**," Prince confessed in 2004, "**because the Time broke up.**"[14]

Perhaps the Time would eventually get their act together, but Prince couldn't wait on Day any longer, and decisions had to be made about the status of the band—and more immediately, the upcoming tour. Prince gathered the remaining members of the Time and explained it to them, as Hubbard recalls: "He came in and said, 'You guys aren't going to tour with me,' and then we were questioning him: 'What's going on?' And I remember the excuse that he gave us was we could make more money having a Time Tour _and_ a Prince Tour than having a Prince and Time Tour. All I remember is just being crushed. We're not going on the _Purple Rain_ Tour? We're _in Purple Rain_. (_laughs_) How's that going to work?"

Johnson decided it wasn't working for him either, and when he was offered a contract with A&M Records, he followed Day's lead. It was a difficult decision because Prince and Johnson had been through a lot and Prince respected his guitar work and his honesty. **"Jesse is the only one who went away who told what happened, what really went down with the band,"** explained Prince. **"He said there was friction, because he was in a situation that didn't quite suit him."**[15]

When he first moved to Minneapolis, Johnson lived in Prince's house and they became close, so Johnson knew he'd have to discuss his plans with Prince as a friend and as an employee. Before he left, Prince took him for a drive to consider potential long-term plans with a new band he hoped to create that would replace the Time: "Prince gave me the option to stay and be in the Family . . . and I remember asking him if I'd be able to get to write and he said, 'No.' It was really tough for me to understand because this was after me cowriting 'Jungle Love' with him, 'Ice Cream Castles,' 'If the Kid . . .' and all of that stuff, so I just didn't understand because I've more than proved that I'm a capable writer now. And so I turned it down. I didn't yell and scream and curse and go off. I just said, 'Hey man, I'll bring somebody tomorrow to pick up my stuff.'"[16]

Instead of focusing all of his energy on his music, Prince had spent a great deal of time working on the Time, but he was getting diminishing returns on his investment. The previous May he'd replaced Jimmy Jam, Terry Lewis, and Monte Moir. One year later Prince's tight grip was squeezing out additional members, but there was no replacing Morris Day and Jesse Johnson. The Time had finally expired.

They left behind a multi-album legacy as well as an album's worth of material that would have to sit on the shelf. Combined with his other projects, Prince was amassing a vault of material that would either be repurposed or remain unreleased. He needed another outlet, but even more, he needed to prove to those who had left him that he could do it without them. Alan Leeds recalled how quickly the new plans were made: "All I know is, they came back from their drive, Jesse got his things, got in his car and left. Prince grabbed the three guys [Paul Peterson, Jellybean Johnson, and Jerome Benton] and me, took us to his house, and sat down and spontaneously developed an idea for a new band."[17]

According to Peterson, "Prince sat us down and said, 'Those guys are gone and this is what's going to happen. I'm going to form a new band.' Then he pointed at me and said, 'Paul you're the lead singer' and I just about fell out of my chair. He really did take care of his people back in those days." Installing him as the singer for the new band wasn't entirely untested. Peterson (who had just been given the nickname "St. Paul" by Prince) speculated that it dates back to filming *Purple Rain*: "He must have heard me singing. The dressing rooms for the Time and Prince were separated by cloth at First Avenue. Before the shows Morris Day and I would have a little sing off and I would bury him. Again no disrespect to Morris, we were just having fun being boys and Prince must have heard that."[18]

Susannah Melvoin was also asked to join the group. He told her that "these are great players and the Time has disbanded and I want to give these people a place to live. I don't want them out on the street, basically."

Melvoin explained:

> It was Prince's concept to put us together. The reason [the band] was called "the Family" was because we had all been working within the Prince organization: I was the staff singer; [Paul Peterson] was the keyboard player for the Time; [and Jellybean Johnson] was the drummer for the Time. When the Time disbanded, we all felt bad, because they were a bad-ass band. But everybody wanted to play and Prince wanted to hear people play. He was also in a place where he was fertile with music. He said, "We're like a big family here . . . I'm going to get [Peterson], because people don't realize what a bad-ass singer he is. You guys will be the lead singers in the band. We're going to do this, we're going to play together. How about that?"[19]

Once the Time's lead singer and guitarist were gone, Prince decided not to simply re-create the sound and image of the Time. He was looking to take the funk in a new direction, as witnessed by Peterson: "He had a vision for putting people together and I've never seen anything like it in my life. I mean, producers, good producers, do that in the studio, but he not only did it in the studio— he didn't have to actually, he did it all himself—but he was able to do it visually. How do you tell a story with these particular people? Who would be right for the story? And most importantly, what is the story?"[20]

According to many around him, Prince was inspired to oversee more than one group to fill the spot left by the Time. He was forming the Family but was also interested in Mazarati.

JUNE 1984 (ESTIMATE)

"100 MPH"
Flying Cloud Drive Warehouse (Eden Prairie, Minnesota)
Producer: Prince | *Artist:* Prince | *Engineer:* David Z

I think that was a very productive and a very happy time in his life. Unlike many young people who might have reached that stage and just lost it, he had the bull by the horns. He had the reins and he was going to take this as far as he could take it and get as much out of it as he could.—Susan Rogers[21]

It was full speed ahead for Prince, and he pushed to get as much done as possible before the inevitable tour preparations demanded his full attention. Although the movie wasn't out, there was a vibe in every recording session that this was going to be *his* summer. "You did not see fear or trepidation on his part at all," reflected Susan Rogers. "He was confident; he had gotten what he wished for, which was to be huge, and it was coming and he knew it, and he had not one shred of doubt in his personality that it was so."[22]

It is unclear exactly when "100 MPH" was recorded, but it is likely to have been started around this period. The track itself began as a driving but relatively sparse keyboard, guitar, and bass song that was eventually filled in with additional guitar and keyboards. The tune was fairly repetitive and sounds like it was based around a keyboard riff, which was common for Prince. "We play a lot together," Wendy Melvoin told *Musician* magazine in 1984. "When we jam, we'll get caught in a groove and, knowing each other's style so well, we can create a song. That's how a lot of stuff gets created and arranged."[23]

During this period Prince was considering many of his songs for both the Family and Mazarati.

"Right after we signed, '100 MPH' was the first demo we received from him," remembers Tony Christian. "I loved the song. I loved that song so much. [Prince] said, 'I wrote this song especially for Mazarati. "100 MPH" is perfect.' So, I was like, 'Okay.' Now whether he wrote it beforehand or if he just took it out of the vault thinking it would be perfect for us, who knows."

Prince may have had the Time on his mind when working on the track, as right after he says, "Cool, cool, cool" (4:09 in the extended version) there is a bass/synth-line straight from the Time's "Cool."

Jerry Hubbard had been in the Time, but after the split he was asked to stay on as the bass player for the Family, and Prince played a few songs for him from the vault:

One of the songs he played for me blew my mind. I'll never forget, my face was so contorted, I was like, "Oh my God." He played "100 MPH," and he said, "Do you think this would be good for the Family?" And I said, "It would be good for the Family. I would love to have it." (*laughs*) I was like, "Dude that is the most funky thing I ever heard." He was like, "Yeah, it's funky, ain't it?" He played me "100 MPH" and then "Wonderful Ass" and another track. I thought he was going to put together the album from tapes from the vault, and then not too long after that someone start telling me, "He's working on a whole new album." And I went, "Really?"

"He had brought a couple of tracks into it and it was just misguided," agreed Susannah Melvoin. "Prince didn't know at the time once he put me and Eric [Leeds] and Paul together, what it was really going to turn into."

Status: "100 MPH" (7:23) was given to Mazarati for their 1986 debut album. "It was mainly just vocal work and a good mix on it," recalls Brown Mark about working on the song with Mazarati, "and we really didn't do anything on that song."
An edited version (3:09) was also created and released as a single.

According to Susan Rogers, "['100 MPH'] was recorded with temp vocals by Prince at the Eden Prairie warehouse. I don't remember those exact dates, but it was done right around the Around the World in a Day *time period."[24] The album credits state that it was recorded at Sunset and doesn't list any contributions from Rogers, but incomplete credits were common on many of Prince's albums as well as his side projects.*

FRIDAY, JUNE 22, 1984

"**Mazerati**" [working title for "Susannah's Pajamas"] (basic tracking)
Flying Cloud Drive Warehouse (Eden Prairie, Minnesota)
Producer: Prince | *Artist:* the Family | *Engineer:* Susan Rogers

We all came together and Prince designed the record. He didn't give us songs he had in the vault. These were fresh songs designed for us.—Susannah Melvoin[25]

Prince wanted each band to have its own individual look and identity (even though many of them were simply extensions of his own personality). Mazarati was an established band with its own look and sound, so Prince spent some time searching for a unique look and sound for the Family as well.

Today Prince recorded the basic tracks for what would become the Family's first original song, but by the end of the session there was no melody, just a repeating groove that contained a few turns, so it could have gone to any of his potential side projects. "We were supposed to have that one as well," laughs Mazarati member Tony Christian. "I think we turned that one down, or he took it back. Somewhere along the process it didn't work out." It likely consisted mainly of drums, bass, and keyboards, but it had very little distinct personality to it. "'Mazerati' was just an instrumental idea he was fleshing out," recalled Susan Rogers. "Originally it was titled 'Mazerati,' but it became obvious that it was going to sound a lot more like the Family, so he retitled it."[26]

Once it was given to the Family, Prince changed the title as a tribute to Susannah Melvoin, who by this time was his girlfriend as well as the female lead singer in the band. Eric Leeds was credited as the composer of this track, but at this point only Prince was involved in the tune.

If this was the direction of the band, they wouldn't stand out. The song—and in fact, the band itself—needed something to make it different, but at the end of the session the path was still uncertain.

Status: It is unclear if it was a typo, but according to the Warner Bros. vault the song was logged as "Mazerati" (3:56) and not Mazarati (the band) or Maserati (the car). The track was retitled "BMW" and ultimately "Susannah's Pajamas," featuring Eric Leeds—who drastically changed the song—on sax. It was released on August 19, 1985, as the seventh track on the Family's lone album. It would also be the B-side to the band's second single, "High Fashion."

MONDAY, JUNE 25, 1984

There is a correlation between Prince's professional struggle and the movie's storyline. It's a very strong relationship.
—Albert Magnoli

The *Purple Rain* soundtrack is released. The fascinating thing about the music on *Purple Rain* is that, in retrospect, it seems so obvious, but Prince carved his own unique niche. "[*Purple Rain*] was in sync with what was happening in music," reflected Lisa Coleman. "We were trying to mix up the black and white thing. *Purple Rain* was our way of marrying those two worlds. I listen to it now and I say 'No one plays music like that anymore!' It was slammin'."[27]

"Prince worked real hard to create music that appealed to the mainstream which he did with *Purple Rain*," concurred Matt Fink. "It was inclusive to all the ethnic groups in America. At the time, Michael Jackson kind of kicked it off and then MTV picked up on it. So there wasn't the segregation that was prevalent in the industry back then."[28]

Of the album's nine songs, more than half would be released as singles, two of which ("Let's Go Crazy" and "When Doves Cry") reached number 1 on the *Billboard* Hot 100 chart. The title song peaked at number 2, and many of the album tracks still get radio airplay more than thirty years later. Obviously, the music on the soundtrack was created by Prince, and as the album's producer he had final say on the track list, but how did those nine tracks get the nod? Each of the tracks was vital for the movie, and when the music for the film was being decided, Prince conferred with the director, Albert Magnoli, who gave his approval for what would work in the context of the movie. "When people say *Purple Rain*, there's a very good chance that the *Purple Rain* album wouldn't have even had 'Purple Rain' on the album," explains Magnoli. "There's a very good chance that none of those songs in the way they were comprised together would have been there. When I sat down with Prince, Prince goes, 'Here's a hundred songs.' He doesn't know what the music is yet. And then I go, 'I can use some of these, but I don't even know I need that until the narrative is done.' The film shapes the hundred songs. But the film can't exist unless the hundred songs exist. And the hundred songs don't find a life unless the film brings it to life. So the question is, if it was just an album would it be *that* album? Because those songs were selected for a narrative. Would that album have had those songs? There is no way to know, but probably not."

The *Purple Rain* soundtrack doesn't contain music that doesn't fit the story. During the process, songs like "Electric Intercourse" were eliminated because the tone of the story changed. With the exception of the album's end, which features "Purple Rain" instead of "I Would Die 4 U"/"Baby I'm a Star," the release duplicates the order of the tracks in the movie and allows the story to be told in song. The album stands on its own, but when seen in the context of the movie, the links are obvious and it complements instead of confuses the message.

Prince had shared some writing credits in the past, but *Purple Rain* contained his largest publicly recognized collaboration up to this point in his career. The Revolution, as well as Prince's father, John Nelson, are all given credit for their contributions. Coleman explained that this was because of the way the tracks were created: "A lot of those songs came up during rehearsal. We all had a hand in writing."[29]

It wasn't just the writing that was different, it was how many of his bandmates actually played on the album. "The band participated in about three-quarters of the songs on the *Purple Rain* album," declared Matt Fink. "It was a lot of fun doing that album."[30]

Despite the unprecedented help on the soundtrack by the Revolution and Apollonia (who joined him for his first duet), at the core it is a Prince album. *Purple Rain* is very personal, and on at least four of the tracks he expresses his pain through his screams. His lyrics are filled with many of the contradictions Prince seemed to enjoy nurturing. He was strong and yet vulnerable, he craved attention and yet was shy, and he straddled the fine line between raunchy and restrained.

The reviews were almost universally positive. It seemed like Prince had finally hit his stride, and while the curtain may not have been open, we were able to get a brief peek, and Prince came off as accessible and even grateful. The credits for the album recognize those around him, including finally giving people like Peggy McCreary her proper thanks.

Prince worked hard on appearing strong, but that image was mainly for the stage. When he was doing interviews or other appearances, he came off as extremely vulnerable, which often caused fans to instinctively want to protect him and take care of him. How much of it was an act and how much was real can be debated without any real conclusion, but when it came time for the critics to respond to the record, he behaved as if this was his debut album. "**Apollonia and I slept under a hotel table waiting for the reviews [of the album],**" he claimed. "**We were so excited we couldn't sleep. When we saw them, they were all good.**"[31]

The musical alchemy that came from blending the personalities of the band with his vision paid off. The album rocketed to the top of the charts and stayed at number 1 for twenty-four weeks until mid-January, keeping Bruce Springsteen's *Born in the USA* and Madonna's *Like a Virgin* battling for the number 2 and 3 spots for much of the year, and became one of only five albums to top the chart in 1984. (The others were Michael Jackson's *Thriller*, Huey Lewis and the News's *Sports*, the *Footloose* soundtrack, and *Born in the USA*.) It was certified as platinum by the end of the summer, selling nine million copies in the first seven months after its release.

Purple Rain still finds itself near the top of most "Best of" lists, with *Rolling Stone* listing it as the number 2 album of the 1980s. In 2012 the Library of Congress added the album to the National Recording Registry, which only accepts sound recordings that "are culturally, historically, or aesthetically important, and/or inform or reflect life in the United States."

The influence Prince had on culture is difficult to quantify. There have been others who were able to stand on the razor's edge of male/female fashion and be widely accepted. David Bowie and Little Richard did it, but there are very few who carried the quality of music and the crossover sex appeal.

The album was a career-changing triumph, but could the movie duplicate that success?

WEDNESDAY, JUNE 27, 1984

"**Mutiny**" (basic tracking)
"**High Fashion**" (basic tracking)
"**Ecstasy**" [working title for "Desire"] (basic tracking)
Flying Cloud Drive Warehouse (Eden Prairie, Minnesota)
Producer: Prince | *Artist:* the Family | *Engineer:* Susan Rogers

Prince was involved with Susannah at this time and he wrote new basic tracks very, very fast.—Susan Rogers[32]

On an emotional level, Prince was in a difficult spot and the weight of the world was on his shoulders. It is easy to forget that Prince had just turned twenty-six, and multimillion-dollar plans were being drafted based on his talent, or, more accurately, based on how the public would react to his talent. His debut movie, *Purple Rain*, was scheduled to open in a month, and the soundtrack album had just been released to excellent reviews. The first single, "When Doves Cry," had entered the chart on June 2 and was at number 3 on the Hot 100 charts for the week of June 30, just behind Duran Duran's "The Reflex" and Bruce Springsteen's "Dancing in the Dark." By July 7 it would rise two more spots, giving Prince his first number 1 song, where it remained for five weeks.

Arrangements were being made for an epic tour to start in the fall, but only if the movie was a success. If the movie tanked, it could destroy the upward momentum of his career path, and a much more modest tour would take place. As a person who needed to control everything in his life, the prospect was likely both scary and intriguing to Prince. The last year had been one of major changes in his staff and his friendships, and the tighter his grip, the more people were squeezed out. Among the casualties were Jimmy Jam, Terry Lewis, Monte Moir, Dez Dickerson, Don Batts, Vanity, and, most recently, Morris Day and Jesse Johnson. As excited as Prince was about the prospects of his movie, there was a part of him that was angry at those he felt tried to destroy his kingdom, and this would once again be reflected in his music. He'd already lost the Time as the expected opening band for his upcoming tour, and he was in the middle of readjusting his long-term and short-term plans. The short-term plans included recording a song that reflected his need to take back his side project and devote even more passion to the new bands, proving that he could do it without the Time. "It was an outgrowth of the fact that the Time was breaking up," reflected Alan Leeds. "Prince finally threw up his hands and said, 'I'll show those motherfuckers.'"[33]

The process of how and why Prince wrote some of his music is often hidden: **"I don't like to talk about my songs. Let people make up their own minds."**[34]

Leeds agreed: "There's something about his music that is so personal that he just doesn't share with others, meaning the meaning of certain songs. And it's all based on what it means to him, how the song makes him feel, what it reminds him of."[35]

And then there are songs that can be easily understood when looked at in context. "Mutiny" is an example of this, and he poured his frustration into the track.

Borrowing a repeated groove from Prince's 1981 song "Controversy" (which he had already revisited in the song "1999"), "Mutiny" was a pointed jab at Morris Day's departure from Prince's circle of influence. Many of the lyrics included references to the problems with Day over the last few months, including "Maybe you should have called," and he claimed ownership of the new band with the chant "Mutiny! I said I'm takin' over . . ."[36] after explaining that no one gets away with doing him wrong. Prince was throwing insults at Day and Johnson by proxy, using the voice of Paul Peterson, a replacement member of the Time and now the face of the Family. In essence, what Prince was having Peterson say was that Day's time was over because the new man had taken control of that ship. To sharpen the point, Prince (using his Morris Day/Jamie Starr voice) calls out Johnson's name at 1:58 on the original recording and then taunts Day by referencing his onstage insult from the Time's October 4, 1983, show. During that concert, Day asked Prince, "You took, but did you give?" and in response, Prince asked, "Morris? Did you give?"

During this session Prince used the phrase twice more, on "High Fashion": "Donation . . . do you take or do you give?"[37] and at the end with a throwaway "Do you take?"[38] It was obvious that Prince was hurt by what he felt was Day's betrayal, and as usual, music was his weapon of choice to strike back.

"The relationship with these guys was competitive, and in [Prince's] mind it was like, 'There is no competition here, bro, because, I'm the bad, badass one right now,'" reflects Susannah Melvoin. "Part of it would have been a comeback to Morris."

"High Fashion" (or "Hi Fashion," as it is sometimes written in the notes) was not only the name of a song, it was also the concept for the band and for their style, and it would be strongly considered as a name for the album. If the Time was wearing 1950s-style clothing, the Family was going to sport 1920s style in every way. Classy, clean, and funky, but all with high fashion sense. It wasn't a coincidence that both "Mutiny" and "High Fashion" used the phrase "all the way vogue." "The Time was more street urban," explained Jellybean Johnson. "I think he wanted this to be more of a classy, jazzy type of group. He wanted it to be different than the Time. He wanted to feature a great sax player, and do jazz instrumentals, and feature pop songs with Paul, who had the perfect look at the time. He really did."[39]

"He really is a genius when it comes to putting people together and conceptualizing looks," agreed Peterson. "Look at the Time, look at Vanity 6, look at the Family—those are all figments of his imagination, and we bring those characters to life. Very classy, very film noir, and I think it was a brilliant idea."[40]

"Prince went in and was the author of this book," agreed Melvoin. "We were the characters that played out these parts."[41]

Peterson may have been the face of the band, and to those outside it looked like he was calling the shots, but as always, the reality was that only one person was in control, as Peterson explained in 2012: "I had the guy who was The King. . . . He wasn't Prince, he was King, at that time. So I wasn't in any position, nor did I want to be any position, to try to make any musical statement other than translating his stuff, because anything he touched was gold. Musically speaking, it was a 10. Business speaking, not so much."[42]

Much like many of the tracks being recorded by Prince at that time, "High Fashion" was a sparse, driving funk track that was basically drums, guitar, bass, and keyboards, played as if the band was jamming, but as often the case with Prince, he didn't require much input from anyone else. Susan Rogers explained: "It was Prince who did all the tracks by himself. He had a new keyboard at the time, the Yamaha DX7 and you can tell. . . . Prince never bought it to get into programming; he always just used the preset. The whole record is built around the DX7. We did do them very quickly at the warehouse, and Prince put on the guide vocals on each one."[43]

Prince's mind was racing and he was already planning his next movie, which was a variation on *Purple Rain* with the Family replacing the Time. Rogers remembers hearing it discussed during the sessions: "Paul was going to be the pretty white kid from the other side of the tracks, who was going to be Prince's rival in a future movie. He was going to be the kid who had everything that Prince wanted. Unfortunately, Paul wasn't nearly as sexy as Prince."[44]

Mazarati's Tony Christian recalls being told a slight variation of the story for the potential movie plans: "It was going to be a knockoff of *West Side Story* where the Family were like the Jets and Mazarati were like the Sharks. And he told me at the end of the movie I'm going to die. (*laughs*) I said, 'Okay, at least you waited 'til the end of the movie.'"

In the demo for "High Fashion" Prince sang a duet with Peterson, which indicates that for at least part of the movie, the two of them were likely friends.

Prince was once again inspired, and when he was inspired, everything else was pushed aside. "What was so brilliant about it was that the record was coming out of Prince in such an immediate way," explained Melvoin. "He was writing something that was going to last. We were lucky enough to be with him in that period where he was prolific."[45]

This was an incredibly productive day because Prince was able to create a third song. "Desire" (at the time it was still called "Ecstasy") was a bit different from "High Fashion" and "Mutiny" in that it wasn't a groove vamp, but almost a ballad-type track. Built over a simple percussive beat and synth/bass groove, Prince's original version had a snare drum on the two and four that was eventually removed, giving the released version a more laid-back vibe. Its lyrics are somewhat poetic in the sense they ponder the concept of desire rather than talking of desire for another person.

"Those warehouses were incredible breeding grounds for creativity," remembered Wendy Melvoin. "Prince was in the midst of doing *The Family* record. He was really driven, and his moods started getting more serious. He didn't have a lot of time for fun, except he would go outside and play basketball—in the [high] heels. With his heels on, he could run faster than me, and I was wearing tennies."[46]

In 1987 Prince would take the concept of his own recording studio to the next logical step when he opened Paisley Park Studios, but for now the Flying Cloud Drive warehouse was the perfect place, staffed with Susan Rogers as his engineer and providing space to record the entire band in one room and rehearse in another. With all the music that was being created and the influx of band members, singers, and friends, Rogers recalls that Prince also needed a quiet place to work on his music: "Around this time Prince had asked to have a bed in one of the rooms in the warehouse. A bed was brought in—it had a hideous spotted bedspread over it—and he put up some posters on the walls. He was happy about it, because it was a place to go away and write lyrics in. He rarely came in with a song that was finished, lyrically and melodically, in his head; I'd say maybe one out of four or five times he'd walk in with the lyrics done. Often it was started with a groove. I'd get the drum track down, he'd record the basic instrumental part and then he'd go off and write the lyrics."[47]

By the end of this session Prince had laid the groundwork for *The Family* album. Within the next few days, new inspiration would arise and his vision would change once again, radically modifying the band's sound in a direction few around him had considered.

Status: Alterations were made to "High Fashion" (5:08), "Mutiny" (3:47), and "Desire" (5:11), including Paul Peterson and Susannah Melvoin replacing Prince's vocals and Eric Leeds contributing on saxophone. Composer Clare Fischer also added strings to "High Fashion" and "Desire" before they were released on *The Family* album. This was Fischer's first arrangement for a Prince composition and the start of a partnership that would last until Fischer's passing in 2012.

The album version of "High Fashion" (5:07) was edited (3:05) for release as a single, and it peaked at number 34 on the *Billboard* Black Singles chart. It did not chart on the Hot 100 or other US charts. A 12-inch version (7:07) was created but remains unreleased. Elements from the album version were included in Sheila E.'s 1987 song "Hon E. Man," specifically the chant "money man," which can be found at 4:16 on the album version of "High Fashion" and around the 5-minute mark on the unreleased 12-inch.

In 1993, components of "Desire" showed up on the track "Aguadilla" on Eric Leeds's *Things Left Unsaid* album, causing Leeds to co-credit Prince for the song although he had nothing to do with "Aguadilla."

"Mutiny" (3:53) and "Desire" (4:55) were released on *The Family* album but were not issued as singles.

It is possible that "Slow Love" was also recorded during this period (but probably not during this session). The song was later released on Sign o' the Times *in 1987.*

THURSDAY, JUNE 28, 1984 (ESTIMATE)

"Desire" [formerly titled "Ecstasy"] (basic tracking)
Flying Cloud Drive Warehouse (Eden Prairie, Minnesota)
Producer: Prince | *Artist:* the Family | *Engineer:* Susan Rogers

*At first it was an instrumental called "Ecstasy." Then he came
back and finished it so the titled was changed to "Desire."*
—Susan Rogers[48]

Prince was free to push the boundaries of his newest protégé project, and he
was likely inspired by the new flexibility this band brought him as well as his
interest in doing something bigger than the Time. "He wanted to sell records
and he believed this band was going to be the way to do it," Susannah Melvoin
explained. "It wasn't a fly-by-night project. It had weight to him and to us."[49]
   Prince wrote the lyrics and recorded the vocals for the recently tracked instrumental "Ecstasy," changing the title to "Desire."

Status: The date for this vocal session is uncertain, but it more than likely took
place between June 28 and July 1.

FRIDAY, JUNE 29, 1984

Prince attended the opening night of Bruce Springsteen and the E Street Band's
Born in the USA tour at the Civic Center in St. Paul. **"One of my favorite band
leaders is Bruce Springsteen,"** Prince explained in 2012. **"And I've watched
him for many years, and I was backstage one night and I saw him turn
around and give a cue and the band switched on a dime. I used to see James
Brown do that a lot too. You learn from the best."**[50]
   Prince had briefly used saxophone months earlier on "G-Spot" and "The
Glamorous Life," but he hadn't revisited the instrument for further sessions. After spending time with Springsteen and his saxophone player, Clarence Clemons, Prince's concept of how to expand his sound grew: **"Clarence Clemons
don't play funk. There's nothing about Clarence that's funky. He plays old
'50s saxophone that was on those types of records, Frankie Valli and that
type of stuff."**[51] Despite the difference in musical styles, Prince had immense
respect for the "Big Man," referring to Clemons as **"[o]ne of the greatest side-
men in history"** and a **"[b]eautiful dude"** with a huge aura. **"You can't copy
Bruce. I would never mess with somebody whom I respect and who was
actually gigging at the same time."**[52]
   If Prince was going to add sax to his music, he'd have to go in a very different
direction than Springsteen. He wasn't seeking out a rock sideman; he was looking for someone to add funky sax to the Minneapolis sound. Prince very quickly

put out the word that he was looking for a saxophone player for an album he was recording for the Family, and fortunately, the perfect player was closer than almost anyone knew.

Springsteen's time in Minneapolis was historic because it was the debut of guitarist Nils Lofgren as well as Springsteen's future wife Patti Scialfa. It was also where he shot the music video for "Dancing in the Dark" with future Friends *star Courteney Cox.*

JULY 1984

MONDAY, JULY 2, 1984

"Desire" (saxophone overdubs)
"High Fashion" (saxophone overdubs)
"Mutiny" (saxophone overdubs)
"Susannah's Pajamas" (saxophone overdubs)
Flying Cloud Drive Warehouse (Eden Prairie, Minnesota)
Producer: Prince | *Artist:* the Family | *Engineer:* Susan Rogers

> *Prince wanted a vehicle that was not something that was going to be branded as "Prince" but would still be a musical forum for him to do more overtly R&B-influenced music. You had an R&B-influenced band that was going to be fronted by a white guy and a white girl. That was something that was a bit out of the ordinary for that time. Prince said, "We can be funky, and we can be R&B, but let's go get some of that Duran Duran money."*—Eric Leeds[1]

When Prince began seeking a saxophone player, Alan Leeds suggested that his brother Eric would be a great fit and shared examples of his music with Prince. Eric Leeds was quickly invited to fly in from Atlanta, Georgia, to work on a few tracks:

I walked in that day with horn in hand, and Prince was there sitting in the little makeshift recording area of this rehearsal hall, and Alan introduced me to him, and Prince asked me if I wanted to maybe just take a rough cassette of the tunes and listen to them for a day or two, to get familiar with the material or whatever, or did we want to just record? I was a little cocky, and I said, "No, I'm here, let's play, let's record." Apparently he liked that. He just kind of smiled at me funny, and I'd never met Prince—I was not a particular fan of Prince's—so I did not come in with a starry-eyed thing. I certainly respected him, but I did not come in here thinking this was going to be the most exciting day of my life. I figured this was an opportunity that I'm certainly going to take every advantage of that I can. Let's play! Let's play some music![2]

The first track that involved Leeds was "Desire": "Basically I was just soloing. He was constructing solos with me, very much producing and very much looking for a certain kind of vibe. The horn lines, any written lines, I pretty much remember were his. I think he was not really completely sure what he was looking for yet. Because I was playing an instrument that he didn't play . . . I had the opportunity to kind of help define what my role would be along with him."[3]

"High Fashion" was the second track, and it gave Leeds the chance to expand the sound of the band: "My saxophone solo on 'High Fashion' is probably hands-down my favorite solo I've ever played on a Prince song, which doesn't say much for me! I haven't reached that peak yet. I don't know. It just happens to be my favorite."[4]

When they were recording "Mutiny," Prince had an idea for the main sax line. Leeds remembered: "He ran over to the piano for a minute and just kind of came up with a line and said, 'Play that,' and I said, 'Okay, fine,' and we doubled that. But the solos, which were basically what I was doing—it was more solos than anything—that was up to me, and sometimes we'd piece solos together. I might start a solo and get sixteen bars into it and maybe I'd get into something I didn't like or he didn't like, and it would stop there and I'd say, 'Okay, the first eight bars are cool, let's pick it up from there.'"[5]

The final song of the day was the track that would eventually become "Susannah's Pajamas":

> "Susannah's Pajamas" had no melodic idea at all, so what basically ended up being what you could call the melody line was just me. He said, "Well, here" . . . he just played the track and I just went for it. There was a point in time on one of the songs, I'm not sure which one, where I said, "Well, I'm not sure exactly where I'm going with this." I hadn't heard the songs! I didn't hear any one of the songs completely through before we recorded. Literally he just hit the record button, and I was just playing along with it, so if a tune changed keys and went to a bridge at a point, I didn't know whether it was coming up. So I stopped him and said,

"Maybe I could get a little better idea of what I'm going for here if I get a better sense of the structure of the song." And he laughed and he says, "No, you're not going to get that chance!" So I said, "Oh, okay! That's the spirit of the thing." So that's what we did the first day.[6]

"He had used Eric on a couple of things and really liked him right away," recalled Susan Rogers, "and knew that this was going to be a valuable addition to this music."[7]

"I found it very, very easy to work with him, found it very challenging and very enjoyable," Leeds said. "I actually had a ball that day. He was a guy who was serious and knew what he wanted, and I feed off of that. And fortunately, I was giving him something back that he was digging."[8]

A rough mix of the session was completed and recorded to cassettes, which were sent to various band members, including singer Paul Peterson. "Basically, I would get tapes at my mom's house and I'd have to learn his rough vocals as best I could, becoming familiar with them," explained Peterson. "And then David Z would produce them."[9]

"Prince asked David Z, Bobby Z's brother, to be the engineer and producer for the record," explained Susannah Melvoin. "Prince would be the executive producer, but Prince said, 'It's really up to you guys to get this record done.' That made it even more enticing because Prince was like, 'Here's some songs. You guys go!'"[10]

David Z would pack up all of the boxes of tapes and fly back and forth between Los Angeles and Minneapolis to oversee the recording of all the replacement vocals.

"David Z was an old friend, somebody who had a talent for getting the vocal performances together and he would sit there with a singer all day and get their vocals right," recalled Rogers. "Paul was musically extremely gifted, but he had never been a lead singer. It's not the same as doing background singing. You have to have that something extra and that takes years and years to develop. So obviously Paul needed someone extremely experienced."[11]

"At that point [Prince] wanted to delegate some authority," remembered David Z:

So then he wanted me to do Paul and make it sound like Prince singing, so that's what I did. He gave a guide vocal; we had a copy of it to make him sing like that, which was very difficult. Paul is a very good singer, but it is very hard to imitate another singer even if you are a great singer. And all the twists and turns that go into the vocals. . . . I remember the first day we recorded vocals, Paul phoned his girlfriend about an hour into the session and said that he'd be home in about three hours. Twelve hours later we were only about three lines into the song. He was like a melted pool of butter in front of the microphone and his girlfriend kept calling: "Where are you?"[12]

"He had a definite concept, and [Prince] would put down rough vocals, and then I was actually hardly ever in the studio with him," according to Peterson. "It was mostly David Z and myself. We'd go in after Prince had written a song and put the basic tracks down and added a rough vocal, and we used that guide track for attitude and phrasing and different things like that, for sure. At that point in time we were definitely still playing his characters."[13]

"Prince makes his music as if he's a movie director and everyone has a role to play," revealed Eric Leeds. "Prince defines the script and every aspect of it and he chooses the people. Those were the rules, that was it. He knew he was taking the chance on having Paul be the front person, which was a calculated move from a marketing design. He wanted this band to be an R&B band that would serve for him the same purpose that the Time did, but to have the added benefit, hopefully, of being able to cross over to a wider market."[14]

"They billed me as the leader of the group," recalled Peterson, "but I tell you, I certainly wasn't. I was told every move to make by Prince."[15]

"Basically, what he did was bring Paul Peterson in to mimic him," explained Leeds. "And it certainly worked, to Paul's credit. Prince wanted to make us look like these little rich kids who can be funky. The first day we did a photo shoot, I looked at myself in the mirror and said, 'Oh, my God, this is not what I went to music school for.' But it was fun."[16]

The majority of *The Family* album was recorded over the course of the summer by Susan Rogers and David Z. Because of the layout of the warehouse, different methods of recording the tracks were required, according to David Z:

We had to record drums with headphones because there was no control room, just a board in the middle of the room. It was rough, but it came out pretty different. It was hard to do because you couldn't tell what it was going to sound like until you played it back on the system. We couldn't play the speakers while we were recording. We had to record with headphones and had to judge it that way and then kind of throw the cards up in the air and see how they dropped, but records shouldn't sound all like they're done in a studio, because then they all start to sound the same. My theory is that if you use some place that's different, like the one Red Hot Chili Peppers did in a house, it's going to sound different than if you did it in the same room as somebody else did their drums in with the same microphone technique, so that's one of the reasons why it did sound different. That, and the way that we used an orchestra.[17]

SATURDAY, JULY 7, 1984

"When Doves Cry" reaches number 1 on the *Billboard* Top 100 chart, marking the first time that Prince's music sat at the highest position. The B-side was "17 Days." "When Doves Cry" would stay at number 1 for a month, becoming the best-selling single of 1984.

SUNDAY, JULY 8, 1984*

"Erotic City" (mix for 12-inch)
Sunset Sound, Studio 3 | 11:00 a.m.–4:30 p.m. (booked 10:00 a.m.–open)
Producer: Prince | *Artist:* Prince | *Engineer:* Prince (no others listed)

> *I think he was really ahead of what the '80s were about to become.* —Bobby Z[18]

Five hours were spent creating the 12-inch dance version of "Erotic City." Although Prince was listed as the engineer, it is unlikely that he attended this session. If he wasn't present, the engineer did the work for him based on written instructions or over the phone while Prince was in Minneapolis.

Status: The edited version (3:53) was released on the B-side of "Let's Go Crazy" on July 18, 1984, and the extended version (7:24) was released as the B-side for the full-length "Let's Go Crazy" on August 29, 1984.

MONDAY, JULY 9, 1984

The Time's *Ice Cream Castle* album is released.

For an album that was recorded during such turmoil, it has some surprisingly solid content. Songs like "The Bird," "Jungle Love," and "My Drawers" fit well into their musical lexicon, and any future greatest hits compilation would likely feature half of this album. But at the same time, the other half of the album includes "If the Kid Can't Make You Come," which is their obligatory (but weak) slower song; "Ice Cream Castles," which sounds drastically out of place in their catalog; and "Chili Sauce," which is basically filler and might have been better served as a B-side. Multiple songs were left on the shelf including, "My Summertime Thang" and "Chocolate," both of which would come out on their reunion album several years later.

The reviews were generally positive (*Rolling Stone* gave it 3 out of 4 stars[19]), and *Ice Cream Castle* rode the purple wave enough to expand the Time's audience. It was their best-selling album to date, but it lacked the unified sound of their first two efforts. Prince seems to have felt the album was "good enough" and overlooked several flaws, in part because he may have been emotionally disconnected from it, but also it was likely that Prince just ran out of time because of his hectic schedule. Few realized that the Time had broken up. Tensions were so bad that Prince didn't extend an invitation to Morris Day for the upcoming premiere of *Purple Rain*.

MID-JULY 1984

> **"Erotic City"** (remix and edit)
> Kiowa Trail home studio (Chanhassen, Minnesota)
> *Producer:* Prince | *Artist:* Prince | *Engineer:* David Z

> *I remember we did editing at his house on a lake and he had this studio in the basement, and that day was like 100 degrees in Minneapolis. I uncharacteristically wore a Hawaiian shirt. And the machine is under the speakers, and I'm rocking it back and forth to hear where the kick drum is to cut. I said, "I can't really hear the kick drum right here," and he says, "That's because your shirt's too loud."*—David Z

David Z and Prince spent the day remixing "Erotic City" into a dance version. "I wasn't a big remixer. He just wanted me to work on it." Prince knew and trusted David Z; they'd had a long working relationship starting with the demos Prince created for his first album, and Prince felt comfortable enough with him to relax. "[Prince] can be definitely conversationally accessible," he explained. "He can be screaming and yelling in the studio and laughing when he stands on a couch and yelling out things and jokes, and talking and talking and talking. You have to turn around to see if there is anybody else in there. Who the hell is he talking to sometimes? Yes, it just depends on what he wants. Later, when he got successful, he got hit on by a lot of people especially wanting to use his name to escalate their career, so he got really paranoid about that. And he would rarely talk to people, because that's part of his thing, and he learned, I think, earlier on that even in his own family you can't trust everybody."[20]

Status: The long version of "Erotic City" (7:24) was released as "Erotic City ('Make Love Not War Erotic City Come Alive')" on the B-side for "Let's Go Crazy."

SATURDAY, JULY 14, 1984

Prince attended the Jacksons' *Victory* Tour show at Cowboys Stadium in Dallas, Texas. A private plane was chartered for Prince, Alan Leeds, Jerome Benton, Roy Bennett, and several members of Prince's security team. They watched the show from the center of the field at the soundboard tower.

SUNDAY, JULY 15, 1984

"Nothing Compares 2 U" (basic tracking)
Flying Cloud Drive Warehouse (Eden Prairie, Minnesota)
Producer: Prince | *Artist:* the Family | *Engineer:* Susan Rogers

I usually change directions with each record, which is a problem in some respects, but rewarding and fulfilling for me. —Prince[21]

Work resumed on music for the Family. With only his engineer Susan Rogers in attendance, he recorded one of his most emotional tracks, "Nothing Compares 2 U." Rogers remembered:

I was amazed how beautiful it was. He took his notebook and he went off to the bedroom, wrote the lyrics very quickly, came back out and sang it and I was very impressed with it. I was wondering if it was inspired somewhat by Sandy Scipioni. That was his housekeeper who had worked for him for years, and she dealt with the personal side of his life. She was basically maintaining his house. Her father had just died very suddenly, and he never used to get very close to his employees, but I know he must have been feeling something for her. Obviously, they weren't in a romantic relationship, far from that, but I think that he was missing her and I just sort of assumed that that lyric may have come from missing her. When you provide a service for someone like she did, that is love and care. I sort of assumed that it might have been inspired by her absence.[22]

Jerome Benton has told a different and very personal story about the origin of the song: "I was engaged to get married to a girl in Los Angeles. She wanted me to quit music. I was hurting when we broke up. I used to go to Prince with all my problems, so Prince wrote 'Nothing Compares 2 U' about the way I felt."[23] Still others say it was a love song written for Prince's girlfriend, Susannah Melvoin. Melvoin has never been certain of the song's origin and has avoided too much speculation on it. In 2011 she was asked about this and replied: "Maybe . . . yeah, but it's not like he said: 'Babe, I wrote this song for you.' (*laughs*)"[24] Since then, some insiders have quietly suggested that Melvoin was an important inspiration for the track.

Regardless of the original motivation (or, more likely, motivations), many people give the song great praise, including the man who sang it on the album, "St. Paul" Peterson: "It's a classic song, and I think a lot of the songwriting on that record may be some of Prince's best work. Honestly, the whole record was that important. We didn't know, and nor do you ever know, what song's going to take off so you put the same amount of love into every single track. We knew that the meaning and the poetry behind it was special."[25]

Although the album lists Peterson as the song's author, he had nothing to do with the writing: "On the record, it said I wrote 'Nothing Compares 2 U.' I didn't write that song. I had to sign stuff with Prince that said you wrote it but we didn't get paid for it. That's fine; I didn't expect to get paid for something I didn't do. I got paid $250 a week."[26]

"With Prince you never really have creative control," reflected Peterson.[27]

David Z recalls why writing credits were distributed so randomly: "He said, we're going to do this group and that group and do it only on paper. However, he said, 'It's better if there's a lot of people doing the same style, because that way it looks like a movement.' That it didn't just look like just him. He was creating the wave, but he made it seem like there was a lot of people doing that thing in Minneapolis, so it's a movement, which was brilliant. He said, 'I want to have an army going forward that way no one can deny it.'"

"He would never say, 'I'm doing this project.' It was '*We* are doing this project,'" remembers Melvoin. "In everything he ever did, always. I don't know why he did it, because it wasn't always 'We.' As a matter of fact, it almost always wasn't a 'We' doing it; it was an 'I.'"

By the end of today's session, the song still contained Prince's vocals and no saxophone. This version featured a live drumbeat and a basic Yamaha DX7 part on the chords using patch #21 Vibe 1 and probably patch #22 Marimba, as well as another DX7 string patch (#05 Strings 2), a bass guitar, and a few guitar embellishments.

Status: "Nothing Compares 2 U" (4:33) went through several mixes before it was released on the Family's lone album. Prince condensed the beginning of the song, removing almost all the instruments, including the drums, but preserving the moody DX7 synth tones. This sparse mix made the vocals much more heartfelt and haunting, showcasing Peterson and Melvoin's intimate performance. Clare Fischer's orchestra parts were eventually overdubbed to the track, most notably at 1:34, after the line: "It's been so lonely without you here." [28]

Within the next few days of this session, Eric Leeds added his saxophone to the track.

The Family never issued "Nothing Compares 2 U" as a single, and it went largely unnoticed outside of fans of the Family until 1990, when a cover was released by Irish singer Sinéad O'Connor, scoring her a number 1 hit in more than a dozen countries. In the United States her version spent four weeks at the top of the *Billboard* Top 100.

Prince apparently enjoyed the track as well, releasing live versions of the song in 1993 and 2003. It also became a staple on many of his live shows, starting with his 1990 Nude Tour.

MONDAY, JULY 16, 1984

"Feline" (basic tracking, no vocals)
Flying Cloud Drive Warehouse (Eden Prairie, Minnesota)
Producer: Prince | *Artist:* the Family | *Engineer:* Susan Rogers

We did another instrumental that did not go on the album. It was a very hard, aggressive, just ruckus, hard-funk instrumental thing that to this day is one of my favorite things we ever did.—Eric Leeds[29]

Prince began working on a song called "Feline." Although Prince recorded most of the instruments, he invited Bobby Z and Jellybean Johnson to overdub some tom-toms on the track and sent for Eric Leeds to add some sax. "He was still finishing up recording it, and it was like watching a man possessed, because he was deep into this," remembered Leeds:

> It was really great to just sit back and watch someone get lost in something like this. It was a great, great track. At that point he just finished it, and he said, "Here, you got it." And I was really surprised because I figured that this would be just a continuation of what we'd done, where we'd sit there and basically come up with something. He looked at me and said, "You got it!" So I said, "Well, okay!" So I came up with a few lines, and he sat back for a minute, just kind of curious to see where I'd go with it on my own, and after about fifteen or twenty minutes, he said, "You've got it!" and he left, which just let me take it and just roll with it, which I did. And apparently he really dug the final result. The song never made the album, because I think it was just too aggressive.[30]

During a future (undocumented) session, Prince would add his own guide vocals to the track; these would eventually be replaced by Peterson. Prince would also make some changes to the mix, including replacing the loud electronic snare/clap on the 2 and 4 with what sounds like a hard-hit hi-hat, making the vocal version less frantic and edgy. Prince would also add a rap around the 2:50 mark, creating the template for Peterson to copy, even though the lyrics didn't sit well with Peterson: "I did record vocals for 'Feline,' and could actually sing (rap) that song to this day. I thought it was super funky, raw, and a little overly sexual for what I would have done . . . (Mama P wouldn't have approved)."[31]

Susan Rogers explained:

> Paul Peterson's biggest concern, I think, in being the lead singer of the Family was that Paul's mother didn't want him to be with Prince. When it became apparent that Paul was going to be involved to a greater degree, singing his songs, his mother wasn't happy about it at all. Especially the nastier stuff. Therefore, Paul was obligated to tell Prince, "I don't think I can sing this; I think my mother is going to protest." Since Prince is a respectful guy, he respects people's religious beliefs, he respects mothers, and he respects family life even though he didn't have such a good one on his own, so he set the song aside. And I think that's a testament to Prince's respect for religious beliefs and his character in general. Obviously, his beliefs are very . . . most people would say confused, but they are very deep and they are a big part of his worldview and his philosophy, and Prince is going to be the first one to listen when someone says, "My religion doesn't allow me to do this." Those words carry a lot of weight for him.[32]

The lyrics in question involved the size of Peterson's penis, giving a woman knockout pills, and having sex with one hundred different women. The song itself is one of the funkiest and most aggressive tracks Prince recorded for the Family, but the over-the-top rap at the end made the song stand out from the rest of the project, so it is understandable that it didn't make the final cut. Compared to the subtle sensuality of most of the album, the raw and unrefined sexual bravado of "Feline" made it almost impossible to include on the record. "[Prince] never talked to me about what the plan was [for that song]," explained Peterson. "He and I didn't communicate on that level. That was his baby. So, I can't say for sure."[33]

"It was pretty much Prince's choice," according to David Z. "He just said, 'These are the songs we're going to do.' And that was it. We were experimenting the whole time we were doing it. Everything about it was an experiment."[34]

Because of this, Prince gave Jellybean Johnson a chance to break out of his routine behind the drums: "He even let me play a little backwards guitar on the end of it. Yeah, backwards guitar. You play it, and then you flip the tape. He does this shit; he did it all the time. And he did the same shit to me, too. Man, I had this little cheesy solo, he just said, 'Play on the end of this.' Just kind of as a joke, and shit, it actually sounded pretty good. But when I think back, it might not have fit with what we had on there. But yeah, it was some funky shit."[35]

Status: Both the instrumental version (4:11) and the vocal version (3:55) of "Feline" remain unreleased, but several lines from the Feline rap were given to Sheila E. for her 1985 song "Holly Rock."

"Feline" was also taken out of the vault and revisited for a Madhouse project by Eric Leeds. The song didn't make it onto that album either, leaving it as one of the more impressive and elusive outtakes from Prince's vault.

When the Family re-formed almost three decades later as fDeluxe (Prince refused to allow them to use the band's original name), Peterson occasionally sang a few lines from "Feline" during "Mutiny."

There is a possibility that this session occurred on Friday, July 20.

WEDNESDAY, JULY 18, 1984

"**Nothing Compares 2 U**" (saxophone overdubs)
Flying Cloud Drive Warehouse (Eden Prairie, Minnesota)
Producer: Prince | *Artist:* the Family | *Engineer:* Susan Rogers (assumed)

I was one of the first ringers that he brought in. I played an instrument that he didn't play, which of course changed the entire relationship between him and I versus the relationship with other people, because he couldn't pick up a saxophone and humiliate me by saying, "This is how it should be done."
—Eric Leeds[36]

Prince was on fire. Rehearsals for the *Purple Rain* tour were going strong, and the movie was scheduled to open in just over a week. During this incredibly busy time, he continued to focus on music for the Family. Luckily, Eric Leeds was staying in Minneapolis for a longer period, and Prince had Susan Rogers prepare "Nothing Compares 2 U" for sax overdubs, but when he tried to guide Leeds, it didn't go over well: "I remember Prince asking me for a Clarence Clemons kind of solo, which immediately put me in a bad mood. No rock and roll here! So I gave him an Eric Leeds solo, and he dug it."[37]

Although the song was well liked by many in the band, Leeds holds a different view: "'Nothing Compares 2 U' was my absolute least favorite song on the album, and to this day it's not one of my favorite songs of his. A little more rock-and-roll-ish, a little more pop-ish than the other stuff."[38]

Prince was always most interested in his latest songs, so he was excited about the track and seemed very eager to lock it down, according to Susannah Melvoin: "It was newly written when Prince was in Minneapolis, and he called Paul in to do the vocal after he finished that night and it was on a plane to me the next day."

With the addition of Leeds's sax, the Family had taken a very big step away from the sound of the Time. It is obvious that Prince was trying to replace the Time, but not with a sound-alike band playing songs that could have been sung by Morris Day. Instead he boldly relied on sax to distance the two bands. Interestingly, when the Time reformed a few years later, Prince recruited Candy Dulfer to add saxophone to their sound.

Despite all the attention Prince was giving the Family project, no one was sure about what would happen to the group. Prince left many projects in his wake, and he was someone who was generally focused on his current music, so by the time this was released, it would probably be considered outdated music by him. "I don't think he had even really come to terms yet with what he was going to do with the group," explained Leeds:

He knew basically who the people involved were going to be. I think I was kind of a last element, a last thing to be kind of plugged into it. I knew that there was going to be a waiting period, because we were doing these recordings in July of '84. He was already in rehearsals for the *Purple Rain* tour, and I knew that he would not be coming off the road until mid-'85 at the earliest, and only then would this album even be ready to be released. So I know that this was the kind of thing like, "Okay, I'm going to have to be able to pace myself, because if I get too geeked about this, I've got a year before me, and anything can happen in a year." He might decide within a year that maybe this is a project that he's no longer excited about, and the whole thing might just disappear. So I tried to just take it a day at a time.[39]

THURSDAY, JULY 19, 1984

Rehearsal
Flying Cloud Drive Warehouse (Eden Prairie, Minnesota)
Producer: Prince | *Artist:* Prince and the Revolution with Eric Leeds |
Engineer: Susan Rogers (assumed)

I used to go there early every day and just jam. And he would come in we would be just grooving for three hours, and he would yell to Susan to hit the tape machine. So I mean, he's got tons and tons of grooves and stuff that Lisa and Wendy are sort of grooving on, he sort of jumped on top of.—Brown Mark

Prince was spending a great deal of time with his band preparing for the upcoming fall tour. "Prince was on top of his game 24/7 for the 12 years I was his keyboard player," said Matt Fink, "but the amount of discipline he put out there he expected from everyone else and if you couldn't keep up with him, he'd let you know that he was not pleased with that."[40]

"Most of us liked to get our sleep," Fink continued, "but he wasn't sleeping much. Maybe he was doing four hours a night average and when he wasn't sleeping he was either rehearsing the band or writing music or recording it in the studio."[41]

"He was just a force," recalls Susannah Melvoin. "When you get to that sweet spot, you know, when something is running so smoothly and you're so open creatively, you don't get tired, and he had a great, long period there where sleep was unnecessary because the adrenaline of his creative self kept him going."

Now that he'd witnessed what Eric Leeds could add, Prince invited him to several rehearsals, including today's session. According to Leeds, "There were days that he'd just come into rehearsal, dispense with any pleasantries at all and he'd just go right to work, and he'd have something on his mind and we'd all just go on this trip with him. And maybe two or three hours later we'd all come up for air and realize that he'd come up with something really remarkable. But on another given day he might come in with the same attitude, and after several hours he'd just stop and say, 'Boy, this is just a bunch of junk.' And he'd just laugh and say, 'See you tomorrow.' And he'd just leave."[42]

During today's rehearsal, Prince played guitar and ran the band through multiple jams, including an impromptu groove containing parts of at least two James Brown songs, "I Can't Stand Myself (When You Touch Me)" (1967) and "It's Too Funky in Here" (1979). References to hairdresser Earl Jones, "High Fashion" from the Family's music, and a riff from the live version of "Baby I'm a Star" were apparent during the jam.

It was common for Prince to over-rehearse his band, preparing them for any tangent he might decide to follow during a show. The extended jam during "Baby I'm a Star" would give Prince a chance to stretch out a groove, and many of these were based on the groundwork he'd laid and the trust he'd created with the Revolution, remembered Bobby Z: "'Baby I'm a Star' used to go 35 minutes at the end of the *Purple Rain* tour, just before a 30-minute 'Purple Rain,' with Sheila E. and her whole band out there, and 'stop-and-go's' that would make James Brown's band sleepy. Stopping on the one, give me 10, give me 25 horn punches—I still can't sleep at night sometimes, playing Simon Says with that song. But it was epic for the audience, for sure."[43]

With that much rehearsal, the band knew what was going to happen, so even many of the jams that seemed impromptu had probably been worked on in some form ahead of time. "He is a master of making people think it's spontaneous on stage, when they're watching the show, but it isn't," reveals Jill Jones. "It is so rehearsed that he makes the audience feel that he just did this split or did this such-and-such just because he felt like it. But he has this discipline. He is a person who has to have utter, total, complete control on stage. Completely. And if one hair is out of place, it can throw him."

During this rehearsal Prince also played a blues song that has been referred to as either "Sleazy" or "Blues in G," but is actually a cover of B.B. King's "Help I Don't Need," which is about a man finding out that his lover was fooling around with a variety of men. Prince tweaked the lyrics to make the song about Brown Mark and Bobby Z. The track was probably never revisited in the studio.

Additional time was spent working on live versions of "17 Days," "Irresistible Bitch," and "When Doves Cry" for the upcoming movie premiere.

Over the course of his career, when Prince rehearsed the band he was completely focused and in control, but even he had to take some downtime. "There was always a basketball hoop within 10 feet of the front door," recalled Robert "Cubby" Colby, who was an audio tech/live mixer/engineer for Prince from 1980 to 1988. "His favorite thing during rehearsals back then was, he'd tell the band to stop on the one—the old James Brown thing—and he'd say on the microphone, right in the middle of the afternoon, usually on a Friday, 'Who wants to play basketball?' The music would stop, everybody would put their hand up, and he'd disappear into another room and come back with basketball shoes on. Once you were outside, all bets were off."[44]

Even when it seemed like he was taking a break, Prince was still incredibly competitive and worked hard to maintain his control. According to Colby, "He was rough. He would push—'that's all you've got, Rob Colby?' You gave it to him and he took it and still outplayed everybody, always. We'd go back in, he'd come out a half-hour later, all fresh, maybe in a new suit, we'd run the set one more time. If he was going somewhere he'd say, 'See you Monday.' Otherwise, he'd say, 'See you tomorrow at 10.'"[45]

Status: No documentation exists of anything from this jam being recorded in the studio.

Not all rehearsals are documented. Only the ones that have been verified are listed here.

MONDAY, JULY 23, 1984

"America" (basic tracking)
Flying Cloud Drive Warehouse (Eden Prairie, Minnesota)
Producer: Prince | *Artist:* Prince | *Engineer:* Susan Rogers (assumed)

I'm really proud of that song. It's a perfect representation of Prince and the Revolution.—Wendy Melvoin[46]

When Prince jammed with others it often led to new musical discoveries, which helped feed the machine he'd created. While he wasn't always interested in relying on others in the studio, he was open to hearing where a communal jam would take a song. During sessions like these, Prince took advantage of the deep well of talent in the musicians who surrounded him to help expand the scope and range of his music.

Brown Mark remembers that "'America' was one of those songs we jammed on continuously. He basically dished out our parts and he kind of gave us an idea of what he needed it to sound like. It evolved, but I know that was a song that he, himself, came to us with that. He had written that one."

The song had been introduced several days earlier during a rehearsal in which the entire Revolution locked in on a groove that they played for five hours. Prince fleshed it out and brought it back to the band on this date. "Prince came in and did that 'America' solo and started singing and it turned into the song we know," recalled Wendy Melvoin. "To this day, we can put that track on and feel that band's energy and feel what we were like at our best together—a fucking freight train."[47]

Prince would refer to America as **"straightforwardly patriotic"**[48] in an interview on MTV, and Susan Rogers agreed with his assessment about the song and about Prince: "He is very patriotic. He is much more conservative than anybody would guess. Like anybody who is hugely successful in this country, he appreciates his country. You appreciate the mechanism that allows that to happen. He was no different. . . . He is patriotic and he is appreciative of the country in which he lives and he is a firm believer in doing well in school and avoiding drugs. Although he is not preachy by nature, this is something that he is not embarrassed to say."[49]

Prince included almost everyone in the room in the chorus of sound, including his drum tech, Brad Marsh: "When they started, I was sitting behind the console, behind Susan Rogers and he just threw me a tambourine. And I started playing, like, 'Well, it'll be two minutes.' But half an hour goes by and my hand's just about falling off. (*laughs*)"

The song lasted for twenty-one minutes because of the great energy everyone was feeling. According to Rogers, "The only reason why it wasn't longer was because the tape ran out. It's just one of those songs that was so good to play. It sounded great, the band rehearsed it and we were ready to go. We put up tape and pressed record, they played it, he sang it and they just kept playing it until the tape ran out. I think we were actually going to include the sound of the tape running out, but we ended up not doing it, but he decided to just put on all twenty-one minutes of it, because he thought, 'If it feels this good to play, maybe it will feel just as good to listen to.'"[50]

During the spoken part of the song, Prince said, "Why won't you pledge allegiance?,"[51] which was likely an allusion to "The Bird" and the fact that Morris Day had left instead of signing on for the upcoming tour. Prince had been making references like this over the last few weeks in songs by the Family, so it isn't far-fetched that Prince continued to poke at Day.

During the mix, the intro of the song was made to sound like a turntable being slowed down, similar to the scratching sounds being used by artists like Grandmaster Flash and Malcolm McLaren. Herbie Hancock had also demonstrated another variation of the sound at the 1984 Grammy Awards earlier in the year. On "America" the effect was created when the tape was manually slowed down by hand as it passed over the tape heads, while another deck recorded the results.

Status: The long take of "America" (21:46) was released on the 12-inch. An edited version (3:42) was placed on Prince's *Around the World in a Day* album. It was the fourth (third in North America) and final single released from that album, and peaked at number 46 on the *Billboard* Hot 100 chart and number 35 on the *Billboard* R&B chart.

THURSDAY, JULY 26, 1984

Venue: Mann's Chinese Theatre/The Palace (Hollywood, California)
Purple Rain movie premiere and party

> *There were times that he was so personable, and he'd send for me to come to a party in Minneapolis, and then usually what would happen is, I'd get to be a person now, but usually about two days before I'd be getting ready to go, he'd get his road manager, Alan, to tell me that there would be a [recording] truck there, so I did not usually get to participate in many of the parties because I was usually stuck in a truck recording the event, which happens I guess. For example, I didn't get to go to the* Purple Rain *premiere party because I was stuck in a truck with my husband [David Leonard]. Prince liked to have everything like that recorded.—*Peggy McCreary

With the release of *Purple Rain*, Prince had hit the cultural sweet spot. As MTV was gaining in popularity and influence, Prince supplied a movie that in many ways was a series of music videos held together by a compelling story. Almost every song released by Prince, the Time, and Apollonia 6 from this project had a music video ready for air; MTV was hungry for content, so the singles fed the network's appetite, which promoted the movie, which promoted the album, which promoted the upcoming tour, which ultimately promoted the network. This sort of movie/soundtrack/tour synergy was rare, and it would be used as the blueprint for almost every rock-and-roll movie release for years to follow. Most of them would fail, but almost all of them would be compared to *Purple Rain* in the same way *Purple Rain* was compared to the Beatles' *A Hard Day's Night*.

The crowd was filled with celebrities, including Christopher Reeve, Eddie Murphy, Little Richard, Lionel Richie, members of Devo and Talking Heads, Pee Wee Herman, and Steven Spielberg.

To most people, Prince looked like he was in control—and in most cases he was—but on the drive to the premiere as he sat quietly in his limo, clutching a single flower, he wasn't sure what to expect. Alan Leeds, who sat next to him, remembered the mood:

> We all knew this was either going to turn Prince into a major star or be one of the most embarrassing flops of all time. We had carefully plotted a caravan of limos to orchestrate the arrivals of the various figures in the movie. We had pre-arranged a spot a block behind the theatre where we would temporarily park and wait for the cue to pull around and make the "grand entrance." When we reached the appointed spot and parked, [Prince's bodyguard] Chick turned on the walkie-talkie as Prince anxiously asked him, "What's going on there? Can we go yet?" Chick turned around toward us and reported, "The guys say there's a traffic jam two blocks long, more fans than the police can handle and more cameras than a photography store!" At that point Prince suddenly lost it. Just for a flash, but like any mortal human being, he lost it. He suddenly gripped my hand in a desperate vise and his voice broke as he strained to whisper in a tone that sounded like a petrified ten-year-old, "Whhh..aa..tttt d-diid he saayy?" I was stunned too, but instinct took over and I hung onto his hand firmly and said calmly, "He said we're going to have a day to be proud of and it's going to be fun. Now let me get to the theater and I'll meet you there." It was touching and revealing—probably the only moment through the whole, tedious making of the movie that he showed any doubt or vulnerability. And just as quickly, he caught himself . . . probably frustrated that he had let his guard down . . . and said, "Yeah, hurry up over there. And don't let them mess this up!"[52]

Jonathan Takiff of the *Philadelphia Daily News* called Prince the "best thing going in pop today" and a "master of a multi-format, mulatto music that's artistically satisfying, sexually stimulating, and culturally savvy."[53]

The *New Yorker*'s Pauline Kael compared Prince to James Dean, while Roger Ebert called Apollonia "electrifying" and said the movie was "one of the best combinations I've seen of music and drama" and that it was "the best rock film since Pink Floyd's *The Wall*."[54] Although there were some reviewers, such as the *New York Times* and Leonard Maltin, who didn't enjoy it as much, most reviews were fairly positive.

Despite the celebration, Prince was still battling Morris Day, as their mutual friend Pepé Willie remembered:

> It was a very hard time for Morris Day. He called me up and told me that Prince was trying to destroy him and he needed help. So I flew to California to give him my support and help him out as much as I could. We went to Warner Bros. and spoke to Mo Ostin and said that Prince was trying to destroy him. We didn't have tickets for the premiere of *Purple Rain*, which was just about to be released and Morris had no money. Mo Ostin helped us out a lot. He gave us tickets to the premiere of *Purple Rain* so that we could be there and gave us support money so that we could get limos and bodyguards so that we could go in style, just like Prince was going to the premiere in style. Prince was very shocked when he saw us, because he didn't think that Morris had any money or any support from anyone.[55]

With Morris Day and the Time no longer a viable product, Prince decided that Sheila E. should perform at the premiere party. Her band played "Shortberry Strawcake," "The Belle of St. Mark," "Next Time Wipe the Lipstick off Your Collar," and "The Glamorous Life." Prince and the Revolution took the stage to play "17 Days," "Irresistible Bitch," and "When Doves Cry."

FRIDAY, JULY 27, 1984

> *There's a big part of me that doesn't want to see it. Prince and I were so close. I know the effect he still has on me. It hurts. What relationship have you ever been in that didn't hurt? There's a lot of us in that movie.* —Denise "Vanity" Matthews[56]

Purple Rain is released to theaters. Because of the positive word-of-mouth and previews, the movie opened in 917 theaters on its first weekend. The film was so successful that an additional 105 theaters were added the following weekend. It would eventually become the eleventh-highest-grossing movie of the year, earning more than $68 million and ending up on multiple "Best of" movie lists for 1984.

Prince had the number 1 movie, the number 1 single, and the number 1 album, placing him in the category of rock royalty. Susan Rogers summed up Prince's achievement best: "Very rarely has an artist worn the triple crown where they have been in a hit in all three spheres: where the public loves them, where the critics praise them, and where other musicians admire the hell out of them."[57]

Prince—who's gone on record about feeling rejected by those closest to him when he was young—was finally getting unconditional affection and acceptance as an artist, both of which could derail his creative edge if he got complacent.

Los Angeles was hosting the 1984 Summer Olympics, which would begin the following day and last until mid-August, so many people were trying to stay out of the area. Because Prince didn't attend any sessions at Sunset Sound until August 22, it is likely that he traveled to Minneapolis to avoid the predicted traffic.

It has been speculated that Prince may have been introduced to jazz for the first time during this era. It is important to note that Prince's father was a musician in a jazz band so it is likely that Prince was very familiar with that form of music. The recent sessions may have inspired him to write and record in that genre, but they did not introduce him to jazz.

AUGUST 1984

Once it was clear that *Purple Rain* (both the movie and the soundtrack) were launching Prince into the stratosphere, decisions had to be made about the upcoming schedule. Because Morris Day had broken off ties with Prince, the Time (or even Day as a solo artist) would not be performing on the tour, so the original concept of having the three bands from the movie touring together was scrapped. Prince dropped Apollonia 6 from the bill as well, despite the energy they had spent preparing for the tour. In September Apollonia 6 would do a brief series of television performances outside the country to promote their album, but the trio would never participate in a full tour. One possible reason was that Prince wanted to move beyond some of the elements of *Purple Rain*, but an even more likely explanation can be found in the performer who he invited to open the tour for him.

The Family album wasn't finished and the band wasn't ready for a live show, let alone a major tour, and an album for Mazarati was only in the planning stages, so Sheila E. was invited to open for Prince on what would be one of the biggest tours of the year. She had played at the premiere of the movie in July, and her album was doing well, remaining on the *Billboard* 200 Album chart for forty-six weeks (starting July 7, 1984) and the *Billboard* Soul LP chart for forty-two weeks (starting June 30, 1984). The publicity from touring with Prince could help increase the sales of her music, so to get ready, Sheila would venture out in September and October to do some promotion for her album and road-test her new band to prepare them for the upcoming *Purple Rain* tour.

WEDNESDAY, AUGUST 1, 1984*

"Sex Shooter" (safety copy created)
Sunset Sound, Studio 3 | 11:00 a.m.–4:30 p.m.
Producer: none listed | *Artist:* Apollonia 6 | *Engineer:* Coke Johnson |
Assistant Engineer: Mike Kloster

A safety copy (a backup copy of a tape) was made of "Sex Shooter," possibly for editing for the 12-inch, which would likely take place in Minneapolis. Prince was not involved in the session, and no actual recording was done. This copy would be shipped to Prince.

THURSDAY, AUGUST 2, 1984 (ESTIMATE)

"Happy Birthday, Mr. Christian" (basic tracking, Prince vocals)
Flying Cloud Drive Warehouse (Eden Prairie, Minnesota)
Producer: Prince | *Artist:* Apollonia 6 | *Engineer:* Susan Rogers

> *When he came home, we did ["Happy Birthday, Mr. Christian"]. I remember he wrote the lyrics very quickly, and he played all the instruments.*—Susan Rogers

Although Prince had been rehearsing and focusing on his new projects lately, he also needed to put the finishing touches on the *Apollonia 6* album, which by many accounts had become an obligation instead of an inspiration. He had already decided not to have Apollonia 6 perform on the *Purple Rain* tour and had removed many of their best songs, the most painful example being "Manic Monday," which was eventually given to the Bangles and released in 1986.

Wendy Melvoin recalled what influenced Prince to work with them: "Prince's ear was pricked up by The Bangles because he thought Susanna [Hoffs] was cute."[1]

Not everyone was as happy with the decision. "It really disappointed me that it wasn't on the album," Brenda Bennett discloses. "It's a great Top 40 song and I think it would have been great on the *Apollonia 6* album."

Bennett's husband, Roy, fills in the story: "Brenda wasn't one for biting her tongue. She'd speak her mind, and she wasn't afraid to tell Prince what she thought of him, and the same thing with Susan [Moonsie]. She would do it in a sweeter way, but I think one thing that always attracted Prince to Susan was that—not only was she a very beautiful girl, she had a cute personality and she spoke her mind. In some cases, he doesn't like that, but with her it was okay. She could do it in a really sweet way."

It is interesting to note that "Manic Monday" was a harpsichord-based song, and it probably wasn't a coincidence that "Happy Birthday, Mr. Christian," which replaced "Manic Monday," contained harpsichord as well. In fact, it is the only number on the album that used the Yamaha DX7 patch #19 Harpsich 1.

Status: When "Happy Birthday, Mr. Christian" (7:09) replaced "Manic Monday" on the *Apollonia 6* album, it became the lead track, probably because it was the newest song, and Prince usually enjoyed placing his newest music in prominent places.

The Revolution is credited with recording the music, but it is likely a solo track by Prince.

SATURDAY, AUGUST 4, 1984 (ESTIMATE)

"**Happy Birthday, Mr. Christian**" (Apollonia's vocals)
Flying Cloud Drive Warehouse (Eden Prairie, Minnesota)
Producer: Prince | *Artist:* Apollonia 6 | *Engineer:* Susan Rogers (probably)

I remember Apollonia speaking about all the little things that Prince was trying to get out of her, vocal-wise. With inflections, intonations, and little things like not just singing, but all the other little things like the "oohs" and "ahs" and the little ad-libs, and I remember her talking about how she felt embarrassed by it at first and how she felt kind of funny about it, and how it was difficult for her to get that part because she couldn't do it, and he was good about it because he had his little ways to get her to be herself, whether it was to tickle her or make her laugh or one of those kind of things.—Brenda Bennett

Prince invited Apollonia up to Minneapolis for the weekend of her birthday. Prince, dressed in his pajamas and boots, picked her up, drove her to the warehouse, and played her a version of the track that contained his scratch vocals. Although Apollonia wasn't present when the music was recorded, her stamp was all over the song because the lyrics were based on a description of two people who had worked at her school when she was younger. Prince took the innocent information and embellished it for a song.

Once again, Prince had found inspiration from someone close to him giving him the spark necessary to create the number, and he asked for her help fine-tuning the lyrics.

Brenda Bennett helped on the background vocals and added part of the Marilyn Monroe–esque "Happy birthday, Mr. Christian" at 5:54 in the song. Prince also had Apollonia say it in the same breathy tone. "He had this big infatuation with Marilyn Monroe," Bennett relates. "And he was really in the thick of it at that time, and he originally wanted me to do my hair just like her . . . the same color. He wanted me to dye it platinum and wear it kind of like that. Anyway, that's me doing my best Marilyn Monroe at the end."

Susannah Melvoin was eventually called in to sing as well: "It was me and Brenda and Prince (*laughs*), but it was mostly me and Brenda. She was a good singer. She was really one of the great women, and she was married to another great man, Roy, and they were all part of that whole thing. *Purple Rain* isn't *Purple Rain* without Roy and Brenda."

Jill Jones would eventually also add her vocals on a later date at Sunset Sound.

A close listen to the phrasing of the lyrics reveals that this birthday gift could easily have been called "Happy Birthday, Apollonia" instead of "Happy Birthday, Mr. Christian."

This was probably the last official vocal session Apollonia recorded for Prince. With the movie released and the *Apollonia 6* album complete, there was no need for her to spend as much time in Minneapolis.

SUNDAY, AUGUST 5, 1984

"**River Run Dry**" (basic tracking)
"**Lisa**" [working title for "Yes"] (basic tracking)
Flying Cloud Drive Warehouse (Eden Prairie, Minnesota)
Producer: Prince | *Artist:* the Family | *Engineer:* Susan Rogers

He was always open to song writers and songs, but they had to be good. —Bobby Z[2]

Until *Purple Rain*, Prince was very strict about writing almost all his own songs, but on his side projects he welcomed the occasional contribution from band-mates. "If we came together with a musical idea, he was open to listening to it," related Matt Fink, who had cowritten several songs with Prince over his career. "Although after listening to it, then he would reject it if he didn't want to do anything with it which was more often than not. (*laughs*) He had his own vision for his own part of what he wanted to do musically but he was always open to other people's ideas, I'll put it that way."[3]

When it came to filling in *The Family* album, he spoke to his drummer, Bobby Z, about a song he had recorded in late 1983 called "River Run Dry." His original demo had a Gary Numan flavor, which continued into the new version slightly tempered by Prince. Bobby Z played drums, Fink played key-boards, and Prince played the remaining instruments in this early mix. The song continues the bass/keyboard leads from Bobby Z's demo. No saxophone would be recorded for this version of the track.

Prince also recorded "Lisa," an instrumental that shared the title of one of his unreleased tracks from 1980, but the new song contained nothing else in com-mon with the previous number. Once he finished recording the basic rhythm tracks during today's session it was placed on the shelf until early October, when Wendy Melvoin would add guitar and Eric Leeds would overdub sax. The track would be renamed "Yes." "Prince was very, very good at being able to tap in to the specific things that individually we could contribute," explained Leeds. "He knew not to come to me to play on certain kinds of songs, because he knew that that just wasn't my thing. If there was some specific thing that he wanted, I would come in and do that, and he knew he could get that well done, but he knew basically the kind of songs that I was going to want to sink my teeth into."[4]

It is also possible that "Jerk Out," which was originally intended for the Time, was taken out of the vault and considered for the Family. During this period Prince reportedly considered "I Don't Wanna Stop" and "Rough" (also known as "Too Rough" and "2 Rough") for either the Family or Mazarati projects. It seems these were only reviewed and not actually updated for either group. "'Rough' was an old track that we brought out of the vault," according to Susan Rogers. "I remember it was just kind of one of those macho funk things. Something that he didn't spend that much time on, I guess. It wasn't one of his better ideas."[5]

Status: Bobby Z's demo of "River Run Dry" remains unreleased. Eventually, Paul Peterson and Susannah Melvoin added their vocals to the version (5:08) that was worked on during this session, but most of it would also be shelved once Prince decided to rerecord the music later in the fall. The updated version of the track was placed on the Family's only album.

The longer version of "Lisa"/"Yes" (6:48) remains unreleased, but it was eventually edited (4:25) and included on *The Family* album. Another shorter edit (3:22) was created (probably for release on a single or a B-side), but that also remains unreleased.

"Rough" (5:34) would be offered to Joyce Kennedy as well as Jill Jones (who would record lead vocals on the track in 1986), but it remains unreleased.

SUNDAY, AUGUST 5, 1984*

"Sex Shooter" (12-inch mix)
"Belle of St. Mark" (12-inch mix)
"Jungle Love" (12-inch mix or 7-inch edit)
"Let's Go Crazy" (12-inch mix)
"Happy Birthday, Mr. Christian" (12-inch mix)
"America" (12-inch mix)
Sunset Sound, Studio 3 | Noon–3:15 a.m. (booked lock-out)
Producer: Prince (not present for the session) | *Artist:* Prince (listed, but also Apollonia 6, the Time, and Sheila E.) | *Engineers:* Coke Johnson and David Leonard

He had a desire and maybe a need to have continuous projects that he could express himself musically, but through the persona of different people.—Eric Leeds[6]

Prince requested that every upcoming single from the four most recent projects (*Purple Rain*, as well as albums by the Time, Apollonia 6, and Sheila E.) be collected, and had David Leonard and Coke Johnson edit and mix them for release. "I would make a copy of the master," according to Johnson, "then we would take that and pretty much destroy it by cutting it to little pieces. We were doing crossfades between three different machines. That's why we ended up blowing through so much tape down there. We went through eight reels of half inch. We were making the extended versions."

Prince rarely brought new people in to assist on his sessions. Luckily, Johnson was a familiar face around Sunset, and they knew each other from outside the actual studio:

The way I got to know him was from playing basketball and ping-pong with him. There were times when I first started there, when I was assisting, that I didn't have to spend all the time in the control room. So I would have time to shoot baskets with him and he thought Coke was a crazy name to have, and I thought Prince was a ridiculous name to have. So we called each other "cuddin"/"cousin." We got to be comfortable around each other in another environment, which is weird because Prince doesn't have another environment besides the studio. He lives it, and breathes it. That's all he does.

Three C-60 tapes were made from this session.

Status: It is interesting to note that Prince was already working on the 12-inch version of "America" at this stage. It is unclear whether that was being considered as a B-side for an upcoming single release, or if he just wanted to get the longer version finished before he went on tour. He'd just recorded it a month earlier and probably hadn't placed it on a project yet. This long version of the song (21:46) was released in October 1985.

The edited single of "Let's Go Crazy" (3:46) had been out since July 18, 1984, and peaked at number 1 on the *Billboard* 100. A "Special Dance Mix" (7:37) was finessed on this date to capitalize on the success of the track. A mix of this track had likely been created previously, as sections of the longer version were used in the opening scene of the movie. The "Special Dance Mix" was released on August 29, 1984.

A "Dance Remix" of "The Belle of St. Mark" (7:42) was constructed during this session and released on November 16, 1984, in the Netherlands. It was released in the United States in December 1984 and in the United Kingdom in January 1985. An edit for the 7-inch (3:38) may have also been fashioned on this date for release later in 1984.

A "Dance Version" of "Sex Shooter" (6:52) was mixed for release on August 31, 1984.

No remix of "Jungle Love" has been released, so it is possible that the edited version (3:24) was made on this date. The single was released in December 1984.

No remix of "Happy Birthday, Mr. Christian" was ever released, and the song was never issued as a single, so Prince may have just wanted to have a potential third single if needed. It is very possible that this longer version ended up on the *Apollonia 6* album (7:09).

TUESDAY, AUGUST 7, 1984

> **"Computer Blue Jam"** (rehearsal of "work out" section)
> Flying Cloud Drive Warehouse (Eden Prairie, Minnesota)
> *Producer:* Prince | *Artist:* Prince and the Revolution | *Engineer:* Susan Rogers

We would jam all night and then he would be like, "Susan Rogers, roll tape."—Brown Mark[7]

Prince continued to prepare the Revolution for the tour, but as they were practicing, he would experiment with new sounds, potentially for performing during the tour or for finding a new riff to expand into a song. Many of Prince's tracks are based on finding a groove and riding it. "I think Prince's genius was that he was able to take a funk group and make pop songs out of it," notes Susan Rogers. "I have never considered him as a great lyricist; I don't think he has ever really approached, with the same depth, the universal truth that perhaps Brian Wilson did, or John Lennon, Paul McCartney or Stevie Wonder. I wouldn't rate him on that level. I think his genius is in record making and in rhythm, dance grooves. I think he is funkier than anyone I know and he is a genius with rhythm. He has a wonderful sense of melody."

During this rehearsal the band worked on various tracks for the tour, including riffing during the "workout" part of "Computer Blue" and additional work on the live version of "Darling Nikki." It is unclear whether Eric Leeds was invited to participate in today's rehearsal, but according to Alan Leeds, it was getting more common to include him:

He actually sat in at the tail end of a couple of rehearsals when the band was rehearsing for the *Purple Rain* tour, much like he did on the tour, after a while. At the end of rehearsal, they'd be jamming on "America" in the warehouse, the band, Prince and the Revolution. And Eric would be conveniently hanging around and Prince would say, "Do you have your horn?" And he'd say, "Sure," and he'd get a ten-minute solo on a rehearsal version of "America," much to the confusion of the members of the Revolution, who were like, "Why are we rehearsing for the biggest tour in our lives, and we've got this poacher, this invader, with this horn instrument hanging out with us? Why?" I mean, they were just a little confused, I think, because it was unusual. I think Eric was confused, too.[8]

THURSDAY, AUGUST 9, 1984

"Purple Rain" (edit)
Unknown studio, but probably Sunset Sound
Producer: Prince | *Artist:* Prince and the Revolution | *Engineer:* David Z (probably)

You couldn't get radio play as a black artist on mainstream rock radio in America—Matt Fink[9]

With the incredible success of the album and the movie, multiple singles from the *Purple Rain* soundtrack album were prepped for an upcoming release. In retrospect, "Purple Rain" was an obvious choice for a single, but it wouldn't be easy to convince rock-and-roll radio stations to play a seven-minute track from a black artist known for funk music, so the song was edited. With a successful movie and soundtrack raising awareness of Prince, "Purple Rain" ended up being a perfect crossover success for him. "The song 'Purple Rain' for me was his masterpiece in terms of marrying commerciality and emotion," said Dez Dickerson. "It's one of those songs that you remember where you were the first time you heard it. It causes your endorphins and the serotonin to be released in your brain. And it was a real step forward for him in terms of his evolution as a commercial artist, but yet a distinct artist. You know that it's him, but at the same time it's a classic song. You'll hear it twenty years from now and it will still be classic."[10]

This wasn't the first time the song had been edited. One verse that referenced buying someone's love had been eliminated before the movie was shot because it stood out from the rest of the track. "The funny thing," explained Lisa Coleman, "is the third verse that he took out, when you listen to it you don't understand what the song is about, but you understand that that verse doesn't fit."[11]

Status: Multiple versions of "Purple Rain" were created, including an edit (4:02), a radio edit (4:19), a 7-inch edit (4:30), a long radio edit (5:37), and a long version (7:05). These were all released in some form when the single hit the market and the track peaked at number 2 on the *Billboard* 100.

FRIDAY, AUGUST 10, 1984

"Miss Understood" (basic tracking, Prince's vocals)
Flying Cloud Drive Warehouse (Eden Prairie, Minnesota)
Producer: Prince | *Artist:* the Family | *Engineer:* Susan Rogers (assumed)

This one song, "Miss Understood," that I did for him was sup-posed to be on that first Family record. I just could not have him put it on the record. I hate the fucking song.—Susannah Melvoin

Prince was still adding new songs to *The Family* album. So far they'd all been tracks that would eventually contain Paul Peterson's lead vocals, so today he recorded "Miss Understood," a song that would favor Susannah Melvoin. "Miss Understood" was a pop song that could have been offered to any of his protégées and seemed completely out of place when placed next to the other numbers planned for this project. The basic tracks were recorded at the warehouse on this date, including Prince's vocals. Soon afterward (on an undocumented date), Prince brought the tape with him to Los Angeles to record Melvoin's vocals.

"We had the multitrack out at Sunset Sound in Los Angeles," recalled Susan Rogers:

Susannah was there, it was time to rehearse it, and she just didn't like the song. She didn't like the lyrics. She didn't like to say those words. She didn't like it. She was his girlfriend at the time, so they had an argument about it. I remember we found her in the courtyard and she was saying: "I hate it! I just don't like it. It's not me!"

[Susannah] was strong-willed musically because she was raised in a musical family and she went back in and told him that she didn't like it. She didn't want to do it. She didn't think that she should sing those words. And he just said, "Look, this is your vehicle to make money and I'm providing you this vehicle and if you are not going to sing it, I'll get someone else who will, but this is a song that I wrote for you."[12]

Melvoin explains how she confronted Prince: "He flew out to L.A., came to the studio, and I said, 'Can I talk to you for a minute?' And we went out to the courtyard and I said, 'I don't really feel great about telling you this, but I can't do this song. I can't live with it. I'm just terrible on it. I couldn't stand my vocal, it was too contrived, and I can't have you put this on the record,' and he said, 'Okay.' He said, "We'll work on it for the next record. I want you to sing more leads on the next record anyway."'

Melvoin was correct. The song seemed more like an outtake from Vanity 6 than the new sound Prince was debuting with the Family.

"I think we all got a taste of that song, every single one of us," recalls Jill Jones. "And it was slated to be on my record too. I think something was happening because psychologically, the relationships that were going on with Prince interpersonally would affect the song. If he gave you a song, you were like, 'Ugh, really? Is this what you think a woman should be singing about at this point?' I even thought he had Wendy sing on it at one point because I remember there was a track at the beginning where it was her voice."

Status: "Miss Understood" (5:23) was offered to several other artists, but it remains unreleased.

It is possible that "Yes" (aka "Lisa") was originally tracked on this day instead of August 5.

TUESDAY, AUGUST 14, 1984

Venue: First Avenue (Minneapolis, Minnesota)
Capacity: 1,558 (sold out)

Prince and the Revolution played their second show of the summer at First Avenue, but this time they were debuting two more of the tracks from *Purple Rain*, outlining an early version of a typical *Purple Rain* tour set list: "Controversy," "Let's Go Crazy," "Delirious," "1999," "Little Red Corvette," "Computer Blue," "Darling Nikki," "The Beautiful Ones," "When Doves Cry," "Baby I'm a Star," and "Purple Rain." Parts of the "Baby I'm a Star" jam are very similar to the recently recorded "America," specifically around the 11-minute mark, which contains elements of the "America" 12-inch.

WEDNESDAY, AUGUST 15, 1984 (ESTIMATE)

"She's Always in My Hair" (basic tracking, mixing)
Flying Cloud Drive Warehouse (Eden Prairie, Minnesota)
Producer: Prince | *Artist:* Prince | *Engineer:* Susan Rogers

It was done at the Flying Cloud Drive warehouse. When we first started it I thought it might be for Mazarati. —Susan Rogers[13]

The scramble to get ready for yesterday's First Avenue show had everyone working overtime, so today a more casual day was scheduled for the crew as well as the band. Because of the pending tour, there were crew members working around the warehouse, but the atmosphere was a little slower than usual. Prince decided to take a fresh pass at "She's Always in My Hair," a track he'd originally recorded in late December 1983. According to Rogers, "He got this incredible guitar tone, played the lead line and we all flipped for it. When he would really dig in on guitar and really get a great rock sound and play a great line it's amazing. The band wasn't in, just he and I recording."[14]

Unlike many of the tracks for *Purple Rain*, which took days and even weeks to complete, Prince once again seemed to want to get his ideas to tape immediately. This is probably because he had a very limited amount of time to finish his current projects before the bigger rehearsals and staging for his tour would demand all his time. "He was recording day and night during that period," Rogers explained to author Jake Brown, "and songs tended to get done very quickly. 'Nothing Compares 2 U,' 'America,' 'Condition of the Heart,' 'God,' and 'She's Always in My Hair' were recorded then. We would sometimes start them at the warehouse and finish them in his home studio."[15]

Bobby Z remembered "She's Always in My Hair" being recorded completely at Prince's home, but Rogers recalls it differently: "I can tell you that we mixed it at the warehouse on Flying Cloud Drive, and the reason I know that is because he and I were sitting there and Prince was wearing a scarf over his head. We were both tired, and I finally said to him, 'Can you hear any high end with that scarf over your head? I mean, what are we doing?' We were so tired and working so hard, and I think it suffered because of that."

Status: Prince decided he preferred the original version of "She's Always in My Hair," and today's recording remains unreleased.

THURSDAY, AUGUST 16, 1984

"Around the World in a Day" (basic tracking)
Flying Cloud Drive Warehouse (Eden Prairie, Minnesota)
Producer: Prince | *Artist:* Prince and the Revolution | *Engineer:* Susan
Rogers

*We're pretty much a unit now. Prince has allowed all of us to express ourselves with our instruments. He hasn't tried to tame us down at all and he's more willing to accept ideas from each of us.—*Wendy Melvoin[16]

Although "Around the World in a Day" was tracked on this date, the song can be traced back to a birthday gift Prince gave to Lisa Coleman's brother David, who remembers: "His management company called me in early June and said, 'We're calling representing Prince. And he's calling to wish you a happy birthday and he's giving you two days of "lock-out" [twenty-four-hour a day access] at Sunset Sound.'"

David Coleman recruited Wendy Melvoin's brother Jonathan to help on the tracks—including a song Jonathan wrote called "B.B.," which contained a beautiful jazz solo by his father, Mike Melvoin—but the song that stood out was "Around the World in a Day." "We worked it up as a nice kind of demo thing," recalls engineer Bill Jackson. "They redid it for Prince's next record, and it was a song that David had written and it was almost exactly the same as the released version."

Prince kept the music but decided to rewrite the words, retaining only the "around the world in a day" refrain.

According to David, the song was inspired by someone very close to him: "I wrote the song based on a close friend of mine, but to me she was a high school sweetheart, a young girl from Beirut, Lebanon, named Christine Maalouf. We were very good friends and we just lost touch."

Prince had explained that the sessions were a gift and he didn't expect anything in return, but David wanted to share what he and Jonathan had created, and they gave a copy to their sisters. Lisa Coleman remembers: "David and Jonathan had sent us a cassette of two new songs. I had my pink [salmon] Mercury Montclair with a badass stereo cassette deck, and to make a long story short, Wendy and I *loved* the new songs and we pulled into the parking lot playing the tape. We called Prince out to come listen. When it got to the chorus of

'Around the World in a Day,' Prince got a look on his face like he'd seen a ghost. The song ended and I think he ejected the tape and took it, saying, 'Can your brother come out here?'"

"He was floored by it," according to Wendy Melvoin. "That's how [the album] kind of kick-started."[17]

Susannah Melvoin also recalls Prince's enthusiasm for the track: "It was really exciting to hear him say, 'I want to do this song of David and Jonathan's. Let's do this and have David go out there and play on it' and it was the beginning of that. It was beautiful."

Hearing this song altered Prince's plans for the next Revolution project, pointing him in a different direction. After the August 14 concert, Prince conveyed to David how much he enjoyed his song—but, as mentioned earlier in the book, it wasn't going to be his next project: "He must have changed his mind, and management or something called me and said that Prince wanted to work on 'Around the World in a Day.'" Almost immediately, Prince scheduled time to record the track with the Revolution, but also with the members of Wendy and Lisa's extended family who worked on the demo. "Prince was very excited about the song," according to Susan Rogers. "At this time, the Colemans and the Melvoins were a big part of his life."[18] He asked Jonathan and David to bring their instruments and join him in the studio. In addition to tracking the song during this session, the band spent time rehearsing, which helped the track evolve.

Early in the process, the song began with just the sound of drums programmed by Bobby Z. A ten-minute rhythm track was recorded, with David playing darbuka while Prince pointed at Jonathan to play a tambourine pattern. Additional elements were added, including a police whistle, cello, finger cymbals, and an oud. Prince expressed interest in adding some of these new sounds to his music. He may have had the song in his head, but he was willing to try to build it with elements from outside influences. "That was another moment that he was so charming and unassuming," David explains. "He was standing up on the drum set hitting the cymbal with a police whistle in his mouth going dee-dee-dee-dee. He never used that track, but that's just a moment I remember fondly."

Prince expressed his desire for the chorus to sound like the demo, so he had the Colemans and Melvoins replicate their singing as closely as possible. "He was going to call my eldest sister [Cole Ynda] out," remembers David. "But I couldn't get a hold of her. The Revolution included in the vocals were Matt and Bobby, and Lisa with Susannah and Jonathan. I'm a little happier with his version of the background vocals. My demo background vocals are a little darkish and his are a little more flowery, so it was for the good."

Wendy confirmed that the final call was always Prince's when it came to who was invited to participate in the session: "Our involvement was obviously important, but you have to remember that when he hires you, he hires you as part of a band, not as a solo artist. Whatever Prince saw as the direction to go in, we'd follow him and hopefully be able to contribute something as it evolved."[19]

"For me that was so exciting," added Rogers, "because it just seemed like there wasn't anything that couldn't be done. We could do everything! He's got a position to see whatever there is out there for him to see. It was the right, right, right situation for all of us. None of us had any money, but he had made a lot of money, so anything he wanted to do he could afford to do."[20]

Wendy saw how things were changing for Prince and recognized the level of comfort that she and Lisa brought to him:

> I believe that it was a sense of freedom and a complete tolerance and acceptance that we had for everything that he stood for and wanted in his life, and it became his moment where he didn't feel slightly apologetic for what he wanted in life. And prior to that he had a "punk" attitude about it. He was like, "I don't care if I shock the shit out of you. I'm going to because I want it," but once we were there, he solidified into this less, "Fuck you, I'm going to fuck you because this is who I am and I'm not going to apologize for it," and it became, "Oh my God, I feel good about being vulnerable and wanting what I want because I'm surrounded by people who accept it." And I think that's what made him become the flower that he became at that very moment.

Several versions of the song were recorded, ranging from three and a half minutes to six minutes in length. The multiple performances shared most elements, the main change being the addition of the synth flute at the beginning of the track. "The flute sounds utilized on that song specifically were all DX7 flutes," according to Matt Fink. "He added the delay in the studio. There weren't any synthesizers that had on-board effects in those days, you had to have outboard pieces running on them, so we would use standard boss pedals for those effects."[21] The bass would also be very prominent in at least one of the versions, but not in the released mix of the song, where it was muted, much like it was done for "When Doves Cry."

A quick mix was done at the end of the session with Rogers, who says there is a misconception about the work an engineer puts into creating his mixes after it is recorded: "I have heard from so many people in the music industry that Prince does it himself. He didn't do it himself. I was there, and the stuff that he mixed with me sounds definitely different than the stuff he mixed with anybody else."[22]

Prince likely understood the impact this track would have on his next album and had the opening lyrics reproduced in his *Purple Rain* tour book, which was being designed during this period. This addition to the tour book was typical of Prince, who had a habit of presenting enigmatic riddles and then deciding if and when the meaning would eventually be revealed. When he did this, Prince seemed to be writing his career as a mystery novel and inviting others to look for the answers in cryptic clues that would hopefully make sense when viewed backward.

Susan Rogers felt that Prince saw the song as "a cornerstone for his record."[23] He seemed so taken with this new sound and direction that he would eventually remix it with her and during separate sessions with David Leonard.

Status: "Around the World in a Day" (3:29) was the title track for Prince's next album. The alternate versions remain unreleased.

Various sources have contradicted the actual recording date for "Around the World in a Day," but August 16, 1984, seems the most likely based on interviews and personal notes from those involved. The other possible date is September 16, 1984.

FRIDAY, AUGUST 17, 1984

"The Dance Electric" (basic tracking)
Flying Cloud Drive Warehouse (Eden Prairie, Minnesota)
Producer: Prince | *Artist:* Prince | *Engineer:* Susan Rogers

This is a guy who sits in a recording studio, and his creative muse happens so fast that the only way that he can do it and get what he wants done is just to do it himself, and since he can, why not?—Eric Leeds[24]

Prince was everywhere, and everyone wanted to know more about the man behind the music. Newspapers, magazines, and television shows were praising *Purple Rain* as a masterpiece, and invitations were coming from everywhere to talk about the movie and the album, but Prince seemed to be more interested in surrounding himself with people he trusted, creating new music instead of reflecting on what he'd already recorded. Many of the songs on *Purple Rain* had been around for years, so what was "new" music to the public had grown stale to him, and he seemed eager to show the world that *Purple Rain* wasn't a fluke. Prince had the world's ear, and he was making plans to take advantage of that.

"The Dance Electric" was another in a series of tracks that was created by Prince and the Revolution playing over a repetitive groove. Parts of it had been worked on while preparing for the August 14 show. "We jammed all the time at sound checks," says Matt Fink. "And at rehearsals there was always a warm-up period where the band would just flow with ideas and stuff. And every once in a while something would just hit Prince, and he'd take it and do something with it."

Bass player Brown Mark recalls it as well: "I remember jamming on that, and then I think what happened was he took the reel into the studio and edited it, and added to it and made it what it was. That's how a lot of that stuff came about."

The track itself is another apocalyptic song about the end of times—in the spirit of "1999"—about how we've got to get ourselves in balance as the end draws near. There is even a reference to the year 1999 when Prince sings, "We've got fourteen years . . ."[25] (if the track was to be released in 1985). Prince had been dropping references to a rebirth over the last year, both in the movie and on the soundtrack album, with the phrase "May U live 2 see the dawn," which also appeared on the sleeve for "17 Days (The Rain Will Come Down, Then U Will Have 2 Choose If U Believe. Look 2 The Dawn And U Shall Never Lose").[26]

Prince didn't just revisit concepts, he had a habit of reusing phrases in his songs, which sometimes helped chronicle his mood or his attitude about a topic during certain focused periods in the studio. For example, on "The Dance Electric" Prince started the song with "Good morning children."[27] The day before, during the recording of "Around the World in a Day," he sang, "All the little babies sing around the world."[28] It is as if he were putting himself in a position to instruct those he felt were looking to learn.

The entire band worked on the music for the song, but it appears that Prince may have done the studio work by himself and then invited Wendy Melvoin and Lisa Coleman as well as Jill Jones to add their distinct background vocals to the track. It is unclear whether the entire band participated in the actual recording, but the Revolution were actively involved in creating the groove.

Coleman (who celebrated her twenty-fourth birthday on this date) posted on WendyandLisa.com that the song was "one of my favs,"[29] and Eric Leeds glowingly told his brother Alan how impressed he was when he'd heard the track: "[Eric] came home from the session raving about this new jam they had done. . . . 'Man, this is the shit!' And he played me the tune and I went, 'What? Oh, my God!' In retrospect, maybe it wasn't the greatest tune they ever did, but at the time, it was smoking!"[30]

Within a few days, Alan Leeds was talking to Prince about how this song would show everyone how funky he could be when it was finally released. Prince responded, **"I can't do that song."** Leeds was in shock, and when he asked about it, Prince confided, **"That's not for me. I can't do a song like that."**

"To this day," Leeds confessed, "I don't understand what he meant."[31]

Although Prince had decided it wouldn't fit on one of his own albums, he apparently liked "The Dance Electric" so much that he found a spot for elements of it during the *Purple Rain* tour. A segue containing material lifted from "The Dance Electric" was created to bridge "Darling Nikki" and "The Beautiful Ones." Wendy Melvoin's singing on the chorus was played backward and then overdubbed with Prince saying, "I'm so confused. / Don't be confused, there's only one lord, Jesus. . I'm so confused . . . I'm sorry. I'll be good / I–I promise . . . / If you believe, he'll forgive you . . . / I'm so confused, so confused. . . . / the beautiful ones you always seem to lose. (2x)"[32]

Status: An approximately twelve-minute version of "The Dance Electric" was given to Prince's childhood friend André Cymone, and they worked on it the following year for release on Cymone's *A.C.* album. It was edited down (5:44), but otherwise the track basically stayed the same, with Cymone adding his vocals at Ocean Way Studios in Hollywood.

Several versions of the song were mixed. Some were released—the single version (3:59), long version (5:31), and extended version (10:24)—while multiple versions were created (11:32, 11:41, and 12:03) that remain unreleased.

The song peaked at number 10 on the *Billboard* Black Singles chart and number 8 on the *Billboard* Hot Dance/Disco Club Play chart for André Cymone. It did not chart on the *Billboard* Hot 100.

An early version of "The Dance Electric" with Prince's lead vocals (11:30) was also released on the *Purple Rain Deluxe* (Expanded Edition) CD set in 2017.

Prince would continue to write about the approach of the year 1999 in his music, including his 1991 song "Horny Pony," which proclaimed itself as "a new dance for the next 8 years."[33]

374

SATURDAY, AUGUST 18, 1984

"The Screams of Passion" (basic tracking)
"The Dance Electric" (overdubs)
Flying Cloud Drive Warehouse (Eden Prairie, Minnesota)
Producer: Prince | *Artist:* the Family/Prince | *Engineer:* Susan Rogers
(assumed)

Prince wrote some of his best funky/pop stuff and his lyrics on "Screams of Passion"; they're beautiful poetry. That's his stuff. I think that's where he was best. Some of his best Prince songs are on the Family record. —Paul Peterson[34]

The Family project was a chance to showcase Prince's new sound, but when "Screams of Passion" was recorded, it was one of only two tracks on the final version of the album that didn't feature Eric Leeds on sax (the other being "River Run Dry"). When Prince recorded alone in the studio his routine was fairly simple, and often it started by contacting Susan Rogers: "He would call me in the morning of the day we were going to record and say what he needed set up, whether it was live drums or drum machine, whether he wanted all his stuff in the control room or out in the studio, and sometimes he would just call and say, 'Can we record?'"[35]

In the first version of the track, Prince didn't have an ending for the song, so he stopped it with his comment, "Oh baby, don't do that!," which Peterson would eventually duplicate while replacing the vocals. When the song was mixed (at a later undocumented session), it was faded earlier, eliminating that section.

It is likely that this track was started during the evening of August 18, but the session went past midnight so it was probably finished sometime in the morning on August 19.

Additional overdubs were likely done to "The Dance Electric" during this session with others, including Jill Jones and possibly Susan Moonsie, adding background vocals.

Status: "The Screams of Passion" (5:26) was edited for release as a single (3:10) in 1985. Clare Fischer wrote an orchestral part for the track later in the fall. An extended version (6:45) was created as well, and Fischer's additions can be heard at the beginning of the track.

The released version peaked at number 63 on the *Billboard* Hot 100 chart.

SUNDAY, AUGUST 19, 1984

"God" (vocal version; basic tracking)
Flying Cloud Drive Warehouse (Eden Prairie, Minnesota)
Producer: Prince | *Artist:* Prince | *Engineer:* Susan Rogers

> *There were certain songs that I remember were saved for Sundays or inspired on Sundays . . . and "God" was one of those Sunday songs.*—Susan Rogers[36]

Prince set the mood for today's session by lighting a candle and turning the lights off in the warehouse. He sat at the piano ready to play, but unfortunately, every time he began the equipment would fail. Susan Rogers described the mood: "It was really, really difficult and he was getting very frustrated. He was in one of his uncommunicative moods where he just wasn't speaking to me at all. I don't think he was mad at anything, other than that technically the equipment wasn't working right and it was my responsibility to get it fixed, but I was doing the best I could, and he really wanted to record this song."[37]

It was after midnight before she was able to get the equipment working, and this time when she pressed "record" the tape machine kept recording and the tape kept rolling. He tracked the piano and vocals for "God" in one take, closed the lid on the piano, and walked out without a word, ending the session.

"I had no idea what was going on in his head," confesses Rogers. "It was just one of those days—and we had plenty of days like that—when he would come into the studio in a certain mood, when you knew he would so much rather be alone but he needed somebody there, and I would try to make myself as invisible as possible just to facilitate getting whatever it was down on tape."

Rogers later explained to Minnesota Public Radio that at times like this "[h]e could be really difficult to work with because he was under a lot of pressure. Unlike a lot of celebrities or other artists, he didn't relieve that pressure by taking drugs or engaging in bad behavior. He was able to take that pressure and let it be released slowly over time, rather than one impulsive, angry burst, and we had to just let it pass. When it did pass, he was cheerful and funny and in his heart of hearts he was a warm and loving human being. That was always there. We could rely on that."[38]

For most of his career, Prince mixed both the profound and perverse into his own views, which often confused even those closest to him. "I felt it was showbiz for me," Wendy Melvoin admitted to author Matt Thorne. "I did not relate personally. But part of the beauty of it back then is that there were Jews, Mexicans, blacks, whites, gays and straights in his band. Everyone had their own opinions and they were tolerated and embraced."[39]

Status: This is the second time Prince recorded a song with the title "God." This version (4:03) is technically the same number but sounds very different than the instrumental track that was recorded on February 7, 1984. Both songs contain identical chords/chord progression (Fsus2 || G/F || Em7 || Am7/E || Em7/sus4 || Gsus4/D || C).

In the lyrics for today's version of "God," Prince says, "Wake up children . . . dance the dance electric"[40] (at 3:34 in the released version), a reference to the track he'd recorded earlier that week. The vocal version of "God" would be released as the B-side of "Purple Rain" in all territories except the United Kingdom, which contained both the instrumental and vocal versions of "God."

WEDNESDAY, AUGUST 22, 1984*

"**God**" (vocal version)
"**Purple Rain**"
"**God (Love Theme from** *Purple Rain*)"
Sunset Sound, Studio 3 | 7:00 p.m.–2:00 a.m. (booked 7:00 p.m.–open)
Producer: Prince | *Artist:* Prince | *Engineer:* Prince | *Assistant Engineer:* Terry Christian

Inspiration comes from God. That's the original source. And so to use your gift in a creative fashion, that's the best thing you can do. —Prince[41]

It appears that plans were in place for the next single, and Prince traveled back to Los Angeles and scheduled some work at Sunset Sound to complete "God." "After *Purple Rain* he got a lot more elaborate with the things he would bring down to the studio," remembers engineer Terry Christian. "After the movie he would fill the room with all sorts of things; there were Mardi Gras masks and stuff hanging around, candles. He got really into bringing his home to the studio." With the assistance of Christian, Prince added sound effects, keyboards, and some additional vocals to the track that was recorded on August 19. Two C-60 cassettes were created from this session.

Terry Christian cites a story regarding Prince's spirituality: "I was working with a Christian artist named Steve Camp, and Steve told me he ran into Prince at the Westwood Marquis, where they were both staying. And I remember [hearing about] Steve getting into an elevator with Prince, and Steve told me about the conversation. Steve said, 'Hey, I'm familiar with your work. We're working out of the same studio,' and Prince said, 'Oh really? What kind of stuff do you do?' Steve said, 'I'm a contemporary Christian artist,' and Prince paused for a moment and said, 'I'm into God.' And that is all he said, 'I'm into God.'"

According to Susan Rogers, people asked her about Prince's spirituality and beliefs on occasion:

> I remember an incident when Prince had finished at Sunset Sound and he was flying home, and I had stayed behind an extra day to pack up all his tapes. The next client who was coming into Studio 3 was a Christian act, and they were in the lobby and they saw tapes with song titles like "God" and "We Can Fuck," which threw them for a loop and launched a conversation. I was always very kind when I was talking to these people, and I tried to emphasize to them that what Prince was doing was no different than what they were doing, respecting his beliefs and living the best life that he thought he could and being respectful of other people and being true to a belief system that he had engrained in him, and that involved discipline, self-sacrifice, doubt, and questions just like theirs did, and I saw no difference. They kept drilling me and wanting to know, "Well, what would your parents think about you working for this man?" And I said, "Naturally, they're very proud."[42]

Tapes were sent to Bernie Grundman for mastering. The elements for the UK 12-inch of "Purple Rain" were collected during this session.

Status: This UK 12-inch was released on September 10, 1984, and contained an exclusively edited version of "Purple Rain (Long Version)" (7:05), the instrumental of "God" (7:54), and the recent vocal version of "God" (3:59). In the United States, an edited version of "Purple Rain" (4:05) was released as a single on September 26, with the vocal take of "God" (3:59). It peaked at number 2 on the *Billboard* Hot 100 and at number 4 on the *Billboard* Black Singles chart.

THURSDAY, AUGUST 23, 1984

"Too Sexy" (basic tracks/vocals)
Unknown studio, but probably Sunset Sound
Producer: unknown, but likely Sheila E. | *Artist:* Sheila E. | *Engineer:*
unknown

*Those first couple of years with Prince felt to me like the kind
of physical and mental training that an Olympic athlete must
have to put herself through.*—Sheila E.[43]

Sheila E. recorded "Too Sexy" during this session. Prince's participation is
unlikely. There has been a lot of speculation about his involvement in the recording of the track, and there are many who feel this was a Prince song that
he simply gave to Sheila to mix, but the reality is that there may have been very
minimal, if any, involvement by Prince.

Although parts of this song sound like a faster version of Prince's 1981 track
"Controversy," it is listed as being composed by Sheila E., Michael (Miko)
Weaver, Stephan (Steph) Birnbaum, and Benjamin (Benny) Rietveld. Birn-
baum played guitar, Rietveld played bass, Weaver was on rhythm guitar, and
Sheila was on drums and percussion.

Weaver came up with the title of the song (if Prince had been involved,
it would have likely been named "2 Sexy"). Rather than being featured on
one of her albums, the track would be relegated to a B-side for Sheila E.; this
is another indication that Prince had very little to do with the number. Any
sales from the A-side would be mirrored on the flip side, so if Prince wasn't
involved, all the sales for this composition went directly to those involved in
writing the track. This was a way that Prince kept those around him making
a little extra money.

"Too Sexy" is basically an instrumental that features Sheila repeating
the title phrase in the most seductive way possible. It also contains several
stabs and multi-hit sequences that were common for Prince, so the track was
likely inspired by rehearsals for jams on songs like "Baby I'm a Star" while
prepping for the *Purple Rain* tour. The song ends with the sound of the
record stuck in the run-out groove at the end of a vinyl 45. This is similar to
a discarded ending that Prince had considered for the 12-inch of "America"

a month earlier, except in that case it would have been the sound of the tape running out instead of the record.

Status: "Too Sexy" (5:07) was released as the B-side of "The Belle of St. Mark."

THURSDAY, AUGUST 30, 1984*

"Too Sexy" (mix)
Sunset Sound, Studio 3 | 12:30 p.m.–7:00 p.m. (booked lock-out)
Producer: Sheila E. | *Artist:* Sheila E. | *Engineer:* "Peggy Mac" Leonard

> *I consider myself a musician much more than I consider myself a female pop vocalist or whatever it is they call me.—* Sheila E.[44]

It is unclear whether Prince attended this session. His name/signature is absent on the daily work order for this mixing session, and there has been no verification that he participated, although any mix for one of his artists would eventually have to be approved by him, so even if he didn't attend the session, he would have been given a cassette tape for review and for his notes. Sheila E. was listed as producer, and she signed her name at the bottom of the sheet exercising another of her talents by writing her signature backward as if she was signing her name in the reflection of a mirror.

Two C-60 tapes were created from the session.

Peggy McCreary was married earlier in the month and is credited as Peggy Mc-Creary, Peggy Mac, and Peggy Leonard interchangeably on studio documents. They are all the same engineer.

FRIDAY, AUGUST 31, 1984

"Sex Shooter" is released as the first single from the *Apollonia 6* album. It would peak at number 85 on the *Billboard* 100 chart and number 19 on the *Billboard* Black Singles chart.

SEPTEMBER 1984

MONDAY, SEPTEMBER 3, 1984*

"The Belle of St. Mark" (remix of 12-inch single)
"Too Sexy" (likely mix)
Sunset Sound, Studio 3 | 7:30 p.m.–4:00 a.m. (7:00 p.m.–open)
Producer: Sheila E. | *Artist:* Sheila E. | *Engineer:* "Peggy Mac" Leonard

> *Prince is a nice guy. He just knows what he wants and that's the way he wants it. If he hires you for something, he expects you to deliver. One of the main things I've learned from him is that you have to follow your heart musically. You can't just do what everyone else does. Follow your heart.*—Sheila E.[1]

Although the track had been remixed a month earlier, an additional eight and a half hours were set aside to mix the 12-inch of "The Belle of St. Mark" during this session. Prince's involvement is unclear, but it was probably only with suggestions over the phone or after reviewing a cassette tape, as he had done in the past.

Any changes that Prince noted after reviewing a cassette of "Too Sexy" were likely made during this session.

Status: A remix of "The Belle of St. Mark" (7:42) was released (with "Too Sexy" as the B-side) later in the year.

The 7-inch single was released in the United States on December 7, 1984.

WEDNESDAY, SEPTEMBER 5, 1984

Venue: the Agora (Cleveland, Ohio)
Capacity: 1,000 (attendance unknown)

Prince joined Sheila E. onstage at the Agora in Cleveland, Ohio, where they performed a duet on "Erotic City." He also performed "The Bird" with Jerome Benton and ended the show with "When Doves Cry."

FRIDAY, SEPTEMBER 7, 1984

Sheena Easton's album *A Private Heaven* is released, containing the Prince-penned "Sugar Walls," which would be released as a single later in the year.

FRIDAY, SEPTEMBER 7, 1984 (ESTIMATE)

"Raspberry Beret" (basic tracking)
Flying Cloud Drive Warehouse (Eden Prairie, Minnesota)
Producer: Prince | *Artist:* Prince and the Revolution | *Engineer:* Susan Rogers

One of the little-known facts is that this song was written while I was still in the band, and I have very, very clear memories of being in the back of the tour bus with guitars and these portable little guitar amps, working the chord changes and the vocals and the elements of that song while we were touring. So that song, for me, had a special place because I was there in its early stages. I was there in its prototype stage, and to hear the final version and to see it be one of those hits that's very much connected with him as an icon, that's kind of a cool thing.—Dez Dickerson[2]

"Raspberry Beret" was originally recorded on April 27, 1982, in Studio 2 at Sunset Sound. However, on this date Prince began creating a new version from scratch, ignoring the version he had recorded more than two years earlier. The history of the song is shrouded in mystery, but considering how Prince worked, that isn't a surprise. "This is the first I've heard of there being a prior version," recalled Susan Rogers. "There is no tape that existed that was called 'Raspberry Beret.' I know because I saw him do it. I saw him writing the lyrics for that, so I know that there was no lyric before. I know that the lyrics to 'Raspberry Beret' were done when he was sitting there. And I also know that when I came to work for him, one of the first things I did was to gather up all the tapes, and there was nothing called 'Raspberry Beret.'"[3]

"It could be maybe a song that he wrote down in April of '82 and called it 'Raspberry Beret,'" Rogers continued, "and then later changed the title to it later on the tape box. It may say something else. That's really a mystery."[4]

According to Sunset Sound studio documents, there is some evidence that the song existed at the time, but it is unclear how complete it was and how different any lyrics may have been; no matter how complete it was, it was placed on the shelf along with many other songs that were written but deemed unready for release. "He would pull stuff out from the vaults that would fit his album," relates engineer Peggy Leonard. "For example, 'Raspberry Beret' was old, old, old. That was one of his songs from a long time ago. He has vaults of material."

The full contents of the vault are not publicly documented, and an entire book could be created focusing solely on what it contains. **"There are over 1,000 songs in the vault,"** proclaimed Prince in 1996. **"They're fully realized, though some aren't ready. The time's not right for them to come out yet."**[5]

"Prince was always talking about how he was capable of creating music faster than the industry could absorb it. It's always been a big issue," explains Albert Magnoli. "This goes to the heart of Prince."

Sensing how well "Raspberry Beret" would fit in with the vibe of the new album he'd been creating, Prince gathered several members of the Revolution to help him rerecord the track. After a few rehearsals to work out any issues, Prince asked Rogers if she was ready to record, and Prince and the band began the song.

During a concert in 2016, Prince explained a bit about how the song got its signature opening line: **"I'd write music and I'd let them both [Wendy and Lisa] in the studio and just mess around and see what they'd come up with, and Lisa wrote this harpsichord part.** (plays the opening riff) **It's the whole song, right?"**[6]

A clue to Prince's cryptic lyrics (such as "she walked in through the out door"[7]) can be found in the music he may have been listening to at that time: *In Through the Out Door* was the title of Led Zeppelin's 1979 album. "I remember playing a Led Zeppelin record, and he was saying, 'Oh, this is terrible, this is awful," Susannah Melvoin told author Matt Thorne, "and I just kind of rolled my eyes and thought, 'One day.' He just couldn't stand it at the time. He thought it was crap."[8]

"Prince's lyrics were often autobiographical," observed Rogers. "They often came about as an encounter with somebody or if he had a specific person in mind. 'Raspberry Beret' is pure storytelling; there was no one with a raspberry beret. It was a story that he was telling. I think a lot of times his listeners and fans could be confused as to what was real and what was imaginary. It was something that he made up, and I think the imagery is amazing. I think 'the horses wonder who you are'[9] is visual and so beautiful. I think some of his best lyric writing is stuff that is not autobiographical, stuff that was narrative where he was storytelling. When he did that he frequently wrote better songs."[10]

The lyrics in that section discussed making love in a barn, which was based on a deleted scene from *Purple Rain* that included Prince making love with Apollonia. The farm was owned by "old man Johnson," which was a subtle swipe at Jesse Johnson, the former guitarist for the Time who had quit four months earlier. "Prince told me this himself, so I know it's true," remembered Rogers. "He said that 'down by old man Johnson's farm,' that was a stab at Jesse Johnson. He was mad that Jesse had left. . . . I remember Prince laughing about it: 'Ha, ha I'll get back at Jesse—old man Johnson.'"[11]

If Prince did write the lyrics late in the recording, as Susan Rogers recalls, the references to Led Zeppelin and Jesse Johnson make complete sense. But there are other elements he recorded that seem to make no sense at all. Peggy Leonard explains what may have happened during overdubs on a later date: "I have no idea why he is coughing during the beginning of the song. I do remember he used to tell me to never stop the tape and I remember, I think it was this song, I stopped it and he just flipped out at me because he wanted certain things on the tape, so we would have to go back and fix things. He always had Vicks cough drops around because his throat would get kind of funky."

As the *Around the World in a Day* album progressed, Prince spent more time working either on his own or with the help of Wendy and Lisa. Days like this, when he used the entire band, were becoming more rare, and the unity they'd had recording *Purple Rain* was dissolving.

Status: An edited version of "Raspberry Beret" (3:33) was included on *Around the World in a Day*. In May 1985, four weeks after it appeared on the album, it was released in the United States as the album's first single. In many other territories "Paisley Park" was released first (also in May), with "Raspberry Beret" following a month later as the second single. It peaked at number 2 in the *Billboard* Hot 100.

The full-length version of "Raspberry Beret" (6:36) would be released on a 12-inch.

MONDAY, SEPTEMBER 10, 1984 (ESTIMATE)

"Paisley Park" (basic tracking)
Flying Cloud Drive Warehouse (Eden Prairie, Minnesota)
Producer: Prince | *Artist:* Prince and the Revolution | *Engineer:* Susan Rogers

Paisley Park is the place one should find in oneself; where one can go when one is alone. It's a feeling someone knows when they get it. That's all I can really say. —Prince[12]

The concept for the new album was clearly beginning to coalesce for Prince, and he was revealing it to those around him. The tour was scheduled to start in November and rehearsals were in full swing, but Prince was still looking for new music and continued to steamroll everyone on his quest. "The closer you get to that specific gig or tour, then the rehearsals might go to midnight. He'd want to jam all night. Then all of a sudden he'd start playing 'Body Heat' and vamp on it for like an hour. Everybody was on retainer," Alan Leeds explained during an interview with Questlove, "so they knew better than to make plans. You just didn't dare make plans."[13]

"We really didn't have a personal life. Personal life was Prince and that was it," explains drum tech Brad Marsh. "Here we are, eleven o'clock and we're still jamming on those same three fucking chords we started at four o'clock this afternoon, and you're sitting there thinking, 'God. Wish I could fucking leave. I could really stand to use the time to work on this or that.' He's just got all this music and all these ideas that he wanted to use or experiment with. Like 'Raspberry Beret' turning up on an album, and all these other songs started out as jams on a sound check."

"I can't say it was fun all the time," reveals Susannah Melvoin, "because it was grueling. But we all knew that the work ethic that we have is because of him. So we all knew, even at the time, as difficult as it was and we had no outside lives, per se, it was just part of the gig."

Susan Rogers remembered how Prince's vision was unfolding during this particular session: "I think 'Around the World in a Day' gave him a sense of direction. I think if 'Around the World in a Day' was the head of the project, I think 'Paisley Park' was the tail of the project. I think 'Paisley Park' was a summary of what he intended to say."[14]

Taking the title of an instrumental he had recorded at Sunset Sound in March, Prince recruited Wendy Melvoin and Lisa Coleman to help create a new and unrelated song. "*Around the World in a Day* was a lot of the three of us sitting down and saying, 'Let's write this,'" observed Melvoin. "He'd have the two of us go in and do arrangements—string arrangements, vocal arrangements—and the guitar and keyboard parts. That's where it really started—our writing a lot together."[15]

"We were there to help create and facilitate and put the right frame around or give him the right choices or make him feel good about his choices," she adds. "He got it when we were there. It was like, 'Okay, we're here to help. Let's go!'"

Eric Leeds addressed Prince's shifting musical focus: "I think Prince got an idea early on that *Around the World in a Day* was not going to appeal to as many people. I don't think that particularly concerned him. It was going to be what it was going to be."[16] Prince agreed: "**I sorta had an F-you attitude, meaning that I was making something for myself and my fans. And the people who supported me through the years—I wanted to give them something and it was like my mental letter.**"[17]

Susan Rogers was with him for the entire fall and sheds some light on this statement: "I think that a 'fuck you' attitude sounds way too harsh. I think he was at the happiest time in his life, and I think that was important. He was in power. He was determined that he wasn't going to make "*Purple Rain II.*" He was in a position where he could test his creative strength. He was smart enough to know what he had to do; *Around the World in a Day* was the record he absolutely had to make."[18]

"Prince just couldn't wait to get *Around the World in a Day* out," insisted Bobby Z. "He was fed up with *Purple Rain*. You make the album, you record it, you mix it, you promote it and tour with it—you are sick of the music. It's a tedious process."[19] Prince continued feeling that the music of *Purple Rain* was dated and he unrelentingly recorded as much new music as time would allow and pushed to have it released as quickly as possible.

"Paisley Park" was an infectious way to introduce an idea that Prince wanted to share with everyone. "**I've heard some people say I'm not talking about anything on this record,**" Prince told *Rolling Stone* in 1985. "**And what a lot of other people get wrong about the record is that I'm not trying** to be this great visionary wizard. Paisley Park is in everybody's heart. It's not just something that I have the keys to. I was trying to say something about looking inside oneself to find perfection."[20] This concept was placed over a nearly flawless pop song that reflected a good time at a park. The song even included a calliope sound, normally found in parks and circuses, slightly buried in the mix.

"For songs where the band was used to record the basic tracks, he usually had the lyrics and melody before working out parts with the Revolution," explained Rogers. "There was never any pre-production as it is typically defined—a rough audio sketch of what the finished product might sound like. Prince was remarkable in his ability to make the appropriate artistic decisions while a song was taking shape. I am not saying that he never second guessed or revisited his process, because he did. He was like any great producer: critical, skeptical, and honest."[21]

"The basic track was done with the band at the warehouse," she recalled. "But it was heavily overdubbed by Prince, who may have replaced some of the parts that the band members played. I don't remember specifically which ones, but he took a long time with that."[22]

Lisa Coleman, Wendy Melvoin, and Susannah Melvoin added their vocals on the track, but not everyone in the Revolution felt they were being included with songs recorded during this era. "I was perturbed about that record," says Matt Fink, "because he did most of it, and utilized Wendy and Lisa a lot. He was totally favoring them. He just started vibing off of them, their writing and their production work and everything else. I was going to get married, and he didn't like it when you were committed to a woman; he wanted you committed to him. So you'd kind of get cut out of the picture when that happens. I could have been around a lot more if I'd hung out, but I was hanging out with my girlfriend and that is probably why I wasn't being utilized creatively." In a 1997 interview with *Mojo* magazine, Wendy agreed with Fink's perception that Prince favored the girls in the band over the men: "We had a very private, very deep relationship with him that no one else had at the time."[23]

Although this date has come up multiple times in the research, there is a small possibility "Paisley Park" was recorded in May 1984.

It is also worth noting that the Flying Cloud Drive warehouse was referred to as "Paisley Park" on his Around the World in a Day *album, even though Paisley Park Studios didn't open until September 1987.*

Jimmy Jam has gone on record stating that the track sounds like a retread of the slow version of the Beatles song "Revolution."

WEDNESDAY, SEPTEMBER 12, 1984

> **"Paisley Park"** (strings)
> Flying Cloud Drive Warehouse (Eden Prairie, Minnesota) | 9:00 a.m.–8:00 p.m.
> *Producers:* Wendy and Lisa | *Artist:* the Revolution/Prince | *Engineer:* "Peggy Mac" Leonard and Susan Rogers

Prince said to Lisa, "This is your baby; you write the string part, you hire the string players, you do it." And she was delighted because that's something that she did well. So she wrote a part for two cellos and a viola.—Susan Rogers[24]

Prince seemed to understand that Lisa Coleman could bring something to the tracks that expanded his sound, and three days were scheduled for the string arrangements on his most recent songs, including "Raspberry Beret" and "Paisley Park." Prince once again allowed her to conduct the strings with great autonomy. "Lisa sat down at the piano and played us our notes," remembers her brother David Coleman. "Lisa would come up with the arrangements and Prince would or would not have input and casually play something and I'd learn it and sometimes I'd write my own line in what we were all doing. But Lisa was mainly the string arranger."

Susan Rogers oversaw the string sessions for both songs: "We recorded the strings as an overdub in the warehouse, using no isolation between the control room and recording space. Prince's home studio was too small to accommodate a lot of musicians at once."[25]

Although the personal memories of those involved place the string sessions from September 12–14 at the Flying Cloud Drive warehouse in Eden Prairie, the official paperwork for the American Federation of Musicians lists them as having taken place at Sunset Sound. This is likely an accidental oversight on the union paperwork.

THURSDAY, SEPTEMBER 13, 1984

> **"Raspberry Beret"** (strings, vocals)
> Flying Cloud Drive Warehouse (Eden Prairie, Minnesota) | 9:00 a.m.–4:00 p.m.

Producers: Wendy Melvoin and Lisa Coleman | *Artist:* the Revolution/ Prince | *Engineer:* Susan Rogers

He wasn't afraid to grow, he wasn't afraid to mature, he didn't insist on remaining true to his roots or singing like a teenager when he was no longer a teenager, or singing about teenage things. He allowed himself to grow up and mature publicly; I think Susannah was helpful towards that, because she was mature, but I don't think that she was the only one. Lisa was someone who probably contributed to that just as much as anyone, Prince was like a sponge; he was absorbing from Steve Fargnoli, from Alan Leeds—anybody who had been around—the qualities that he wanted to nurture in himself, and a lot of those qualities were the qualities of a little bit more worldliness and sophistication, and I think a better understanding of art and politics and religion and things like that.—Susan Rogers[26]

"Raspberry Beret" had such an emotional connection to the Revolution that it was one of seven songs played in their 2003 reunion show for Sheila E.'s Family Jamm. "Mostly we wanted to pick songs that were 'band-oriented,'" Lisa Coleman explained at the time to *Uptown* magazine. "They were songs from a period when we wrote in the rehearsal hall and then sometimes did strings there with my brother David (cello), Suzie (cello), and Novi (viola) on 'Raspberry Beret.' So we felt very connected to them."[27]

Prince didn't attend the session, and the vibe was often very different when he wasn't around. Rogers remembers:

I remember how stilted our behaviors could be in his presence because he was so controlling and because of how constrained your options are. You've got Prince watching you, and you must meet his standards. And what that forces you to do is throw your standard out. I don't want to say you become a puppet, but part of your psyche does. Like you have to compromise your notion of what is the appropriate way of singing or dancing or playing or acting or behaving or even talking to what is acceptable. Was it different with him not there? Yeah it was different! Casual Friday when he wasn't there. It was more relaxed. But at the same time his being there applied a kind of pressure to the situation that brought out the best in us.

According to Rogers, Wendy and Lisa recorded their background vocals on this same day. Although Prince didn't attend the sessions, he was reportedly "delighted" with the results.[28]

THURSDAY, SEPTEMBER 13, 1984

Venue: the Ritz (New York, New York)
Capacity: 1,500 (sold out)

Prince came onstage and we played side by side. The crowd was going wild. You couldn't squeeze a fly into that room. It felt like 120 degrees, and everyone was soaked from the funkiness and the heat. —Sheila E.[29]

Prince flew to New York City to perform with Sheila E. at the Ritz, a club he'd played in 1980 and 1981, joining her for "Erotic City" and "When Doves Cry."

Sheila was on the road promoting her album *The Glamorous Life*, and she would soon join Prince for the upcoming *Purple Rain* tour. After the show, Prince flew back to Minneapolis to continue rehearsing and working on new music.

FRIDAY, SEPTEMBER 14, 1984

"High Fashion" (strings)
Flying Cloud Drive Warehouse (Eden Prairie, Minnesota) | 9:00 a.m.–8:00 p.m.
Producers: Wendy Melvoin and Lisa Coleman | *Artist:* the Family | *Engineer:* Susan Rogers

Prince and I were listening to a bunch of Rufus records back in the day—and this was before we thought about doing strings on [The Family album]. We were talking about how brilliant the strings were on those albums. I had also been listening to a lot of Claus Ogerman and Bill Evans. There's one record they did called Symbiosis *and it's just one of the most beautifully arranged records. Ogerman's string arrangement, and Evans playing the piano over it, is some of the most beautiful music I have ever heard.*—Susannah Melvoin[30]

This session was the first attempt to add strings to a song by the Family. Prince had been very happy with the strings Lisa Coleman was overseeing for his own tracks, so Suzie Katayama and Novi Novog were brought back in for the recording. The results are unclear, but further work was required for this particular track. It is likely he may have been looking for another, more unique sound signature for the Family, and after hearing the results of this session he spoke to Susannah Melvoin about finding something completely different than he'd ever done. She remembers: "We had been listening, and listening to a lot of Clare Fischer stuff. I told him that my favorite string arrangements were Clare Fischer because we had been listening to all of the *Rufusized* record [by Rufus featuring Chaka Khan]. And I said to him, 'You know, my father knows Clare, let me ask. What do you think?' And he was like, 'Yes.' That's how Clare came into the picture."

"One of the good features at the beginning was that [Prince] allowed me freedom and space to make value judgments," recalled Fischer, who would work with Prince for several decades. "He left me completely free. It is a wise man who after he hires someone, does not interfere with his product. Prince was very open in this area."[31]

It was decided to send several tracks to Fischer for his scoring (starting with "River Run Dry"), and by October, Clare added strings to five of the songs for the Family.

SUNDAY, SEPTEMBER 16, 1984

"Around the World in a Day" (mix)
Flying Cloud Drive Warehouse (Eden Prairie, Minnesota)
Producer: Prince | *Artist:* Prince | *Engineer:* Susan Rogers

"Around the World in a Day" was going to be his new statement, in other words: "No longer purple, no longer 'Purple Rain.' We've got a new look now. We've got a new vision."
—Susan Rogers[32]

Prince may have decided to leave "purple" behind, but he hadn't completely let go. The lyrics to "Around the World in a Day" mention the color ("the former is red, white and blue. The latter/ladder is purple, come on and climb"),[33] but he seemed to be trying to create an overall vibe that was very different from the *Purple Rain* album. Because of his upcoming tour and other commitments to promote that project, Prince couldn't completely let go of *Purple Rain* yet, but as the new album began to gel it was getting more of his attention.

According to many of his engineers, Prince preferred to mix songs while recording them, and then he'd spend a little time on a brief mix at the end of a session for any final tweaks. Occasionally, when the song was extra important to him, he'd take it back out for a mix at a later time. On this date Prince decided to have some additional mixing done on "Around the World in a Day" with David Leonard. "Prince had him come in and do a mix on 'Around the World in a Day,'" remembered Susan Rogers, "which for David Leonard was very difficult because he was in the middle of this warehouse with no isolation. He wasn't in the studio environment."[34]

"David did a couple of mixes," continued Rogers. "It was a difficult song to mix because it was long and pretty orchestral. He did a couple of beautiful mixes, probably better than the one we did, because Prince just like grabbed the knobs and cranked them. Technically David was a much better, more experienced mixer, so his mix would have had more polish. Prince doesn't like *too* much polish. He used to always say that he didn't want to sound like 'those engineers out in L.A.' He wanted to have his own sound. He didn't care if it was worse as long as it was his sound. That's what excited him. So we didn't go for high fidelity, we went for low fidelity."[35]

One of the mixes contained a male voice (likely David Coleman) detailing people traveling from countries like Afghanistan, Tibet, Iraq, Egypt, and other areas of the world who were all going to a small village to meet a certain woman. This speech was played backward and buried in the mix, but it was not on the released version. This monologue is likely from Coleman's original version of the song.

Because of the layout of the warehouse, an engineer creating a mix was stuck working in the middle of a large rehearsal space, which exposed many flaws in the process because the room wasn't built for this type of work. According to Rogers, Prince soon realized he wasn't going to use any of Leonard's mixes; he would take the track back out in October for follow-up work.

Now that there was a title track to his next project, the *Around the World in a Day* album was taking shape. Up until now, he had been thinking of the project as "Paisley Park," but the new song brought in a renewed energy, and any other plans were scrapped.

Status: The mixes of "Around the World in a Day" from today's session remain unreleased.

This song was supposedly originally tracked on August 16, 1984, but it is possible that it was actually recorded during today's session.

SUNDAY, SEPTEMBER 23, 1984

Venue: Bogart's (Cincinnati, Ohio)
Capacity: 1,300 (sold out)

Prince was recording the bulk of his next album, but his focus was also on a fire much closer: the pending tour. For the first time Prince would be touring as a superstar, and every move would be watched. Instead of waiting until the tour's premiere in November, he scheduled a dress rehearsal of the show in front of an audience at Bogart's in Cincinnati, Ohio, a small club he'd played four years earlier. They were discreetly billed as "Red, White and Blue" (likely inspired by lyrics from the recently recorded "Around the World in a Day"), but word quickly spread and the show sold out immediately. Prince and the Revolution performed eight of the nine songs on the album and the reaction was exactly what was expected, providing a harsh reality check for Prince that shaped the remainder of the year for him: **"In some ways, [*Purple Rain*] was more detrimental than good. People's perception of me changed after that, and it pigeonholed me. I saw kids coming to concerts who screamed just because that's where the audience screamed in the movie. That's why I did** *Around the World in a Day*, **to totally change that. I wanted not to be pigeonholed."** [36]

Additional shows were scheduled for Denver and Chicago, but they were canceled when word leaked out.

WEDNESDAY, SEPTEMBER 26, 1984

"Purple Rain" is released as a single with "God" (vocal version) as the B-side.

THURSDAY, SEPTEMBER 27, 1984

"Tamborine"
Flying Cloud Drive Warehouse (Eden Prairie, Minnesota)
Producer: Prince | *Artist:* Prince | *Engineer:* Susan Rogers

If you like "Tamborine" on Around the World in a Day, *that's him writing on the drums.*—Bobby Z[37]

The band had a few down days after the Cincinnati show. Wendy and Lisa were in Los Angeles, and Prince decided to record a track by himself in the warehouse. The previous year, Cyndi Lauper had released a cover of the Prince-penned "When You Were Mine," and Prince seemed to take inspiration from her recent single about masturbation, "She Bop."

Susan Rogers recalled Prince's mood: "It was just Prince and me and it was the first time that I had ever recorded him playing drums. He probably didn't intend to be a drummer, but he is so competitive. When he first started to hang out with Sheila and saw how she played drums, I know that that fired him up. He wanted to play drums as well as Sheila, and so he began playing drums a lot more. He played the drums on 'Tamborine' with such exuberance."[38]

"Prince was really good on drums," affirms drum tech Brad Marsh. "He's not trained. He's just naturally funky. He once said, 'Brad you got to know where to leave the holes. Leave the empty spaces. It's not all supposed to be one barrage of music.' He drew from everything. In sound checks, whatever, he'd be just noodling around and he'd go into an Aerosmith something or other, or Led Zeppelin."

The track came together very quickly and, according to Rogers, Prince seemed ecstatic with the outcome: "As a producer you can tell or remind the band that when they are about to play a song in the studio, that to the listener it is going to sound like what it felt like to play it. Prince was gleeful that day; it was just happy days for him. He loved the song, he was in a great mood, he pounded the hell out of the drums, and that's what it sounds like. You can hear his joy and his enthusiasm on that song. Technically it isn't perfect, but to me it sounds great. It is a pleasure to listen to it."[39]

The energy and the lyrics make this song stand out. Prince playfully uses the idea of referencing a tambourine as a sexual metaphor, and it is impossible not to smile as he continues to find ways to sing about pleasuring himself without actually spelling it out. It wouldn't be the first time he sang about masturbation, nor would it be the last, but it was one of his most joyful songs about the topic. The differences in Prince's attitude can be understood when listening to a song he recorded several years later called "Me Touch Myself," which, as the title implies, doesn't bother to hide it at all. Perhaps by then the art of teasing about the topic seemed to have lost its importance. "Me Touch Myself" remains unreleased.

Interestingly, this was another song about masturbation that Prince played alone in the studio. He had also performed solo on "Darling Nikki," another track that contained lyrics about masturbation. Maybe there was a pattern when it came to this topic.

Status: Some additional work was done on the track during the fall, and "Tamborine" (2:48) was released on Prince's *Around the World in a Day* album in 1985. It was never played regularly on any tour.

THURSDAY, SEPTEMBER 27, 1984*

"**Our Destiny**" [listed as "Love-Our Destiny"] (overdubs, vocals)
"**Roadhouse Garden**" (not listed, but possible overdubs)
"**Wonderful Ass**" (not listed, but possible overdubs)
Sunset Sound, Studio 2 | 10:00 a.m.—11:00 p.m. (booked 10:00 a.m.–open)
Producer: Wendy Melvoin and Lisa Coleman | *Artist:* the Revolution/Prince | *Engineer:* "Peggy Mac" Leonard | *Assistant Engineer:* Coke Johnson

It got to the point where he'd be somewhere else on the planet and he'd say, "Here is the master of the idea I have; finish the track."—Wendy Melvoin

Prince often referred to Wendy Melvoin and Lisa Coleman as "the girls" in a way that showed how happy he was with their contributions and with their relationship to him. "Prince has traditionally been more comfortable with women," revealed Alan Leeds. "The majority of his collaborations have been with female artists. That's what inspires him. His creative juices—that's an interesting choice of words!—His creative juices flow better with women."[40]

While Prince was recording in Minneapolis, he asked the girls to add layers to "Our Destiny," a track performed live for his 1984 birthday show and demoed in

Minneapolis. Because Melvoin and Coleman were very involved with the recording, it was natural to have them finish the song. "This was one of the first times I had worked with Wendy and Lisa," remembers Coke Johnson, who assisted during these sessions. "On 'Our Destiny' Prince wasn't there at all, it was strictly Wendy and Lisa."

According to Johnson, the session consisted of work on "three tunes on that 24-track reel they brought. None of them, I think, were dance tunes, more acoustic guitar oriented, melodic tunes."

It is unclear what the other songs were, but it is likely that they were "Roadhouse Garden" from his birthday show and possibly either "All Day, All Night" or "Wonderful Ass."

Melvoin and Coleman would lend their voices to the track, with Coleman taking lead. Susannah Melvoin recalls their mood about the track, specifically a part that required Coleman to compliment the song's love interest in a way that was awkward for anyone but Prince: "I remember when she was finished and Wendy and Lisa came back, and they were like, 'I cannot believe what I had to sing.' I think that at one point the lyric says, 'You're the finest specimen I've ever seen.' (*laughs*) It's completely *not* Lisa. It's completely anathema to Lisa's personality. And she *had* to sing it. So it was really interesting. This sort of lead vocal was *so* not her."

It should be noted that "the Revolution" was listed as the artist, which shows the respect Prince had for Melvoin and Coleman, allowing them to represent the Revolution in the studio even without Prince in attendance.

"Wonderful Ass" had originally been recorded in early 1983. It is probable that Melvoin and Coleman added their vocals, and possibly additional overdubs to the original track sometime during this three-day period at Sunset Sound. Considering the session was credited to "the Revolution," it makes sense to hear Melvoin and Coleman chanting "the Revolution will be heard."

Status: The updated version of "Wonderful Ass" (6:24) from these sessions was included on the *Purple Rain Deluxe* (Expanded Edition) CD set in 2017.

FRIDAY, SEPTEMBER 28, 1984*

"**Our Destiny**" [listed as "Love-Our Destiny"] (string overdubs)
Sunset Sound, Studio 2 | 11:00 a.m.–9:30 p.m. (booked 10:00 a.m.–open)
Producers: Wendy Melvoin and Lisa Coleman | *Artist:* the Revolution |
Engineer: "Peggy Mac" Leonard | *Assistant Engineer:* Coke Johnson

I don't feel like we're just hired musicians taking orders. He's always asking for our ideas. —Lisa Coleman[41]

"The Revolution" was once again listed as the artist for this session, which was run by Wendy Melvoin and Lisa Coleman without Prince or any other members of the band. Today's focus was bringing in outside players for "Our Destiny." The first batch included Suzie Katayama (violin), Sid Page (violin), Marcy Dicterow (violin), Denyse Buffum (viola), David Coleman (cello), Tim Barr (double bass), Annette Atkinson (double bass), and Laury Woods (viola). "I remember it wasn't really well structured," recalls Woods. "It was a really loose session. Suzie [Katayama] was doing a lot of taking down the arrangements at the sessions. Prince wasn't there as I recall. Suzie was running the session and the three of them [Wendy, Lisa, and Suzie] were working together. There were no egos involved in the session."

We were thinking in terms of what would suit him, what would fit in with what he was doing," explained Melvoin. "Everything was focused on what he would want. We couldn't just throw in a ukulele."[42]

Unlike some of the other efforts with arranging the orchestration, it was decided to have the strings follow the vocals, creating a duet with the lead voice. After six hours working on the strings, the union musicians were released. According to the union session notes, four horn players were brought in, including John James Liotine (trumpet), who was the leader, Brad Warnaar (french horn), Steven Madaio (trumpet), and Dick Mitchell (alto sax, tenor sax, or flute) who would record from 7:00 p.m. until the end of the shift. If they actually played on this track, their contributions were drastically muted in the final mix.

According to the union documents, no other songs were recorded during this session.

The newly recorded string intro to "Our Destiny" replaced the sample of Bill Evans's "Symbiosis," which was briefly played during the June 7, 1984, birthday show.

FRIDAY, SEPTEMBER 28, 1984*

"**Sex Shooter**" (7-inch edit of the extended version)
Sunset Sound, Studio 3 | 6:00 p.m.–6:30 p.m.
Producer: Prince | *Artist:* Apollonia 6 | *Engineer:* Coke Johnson

Sex is always the most interesting thing to write about. It's the one subject people can't talk about without losing their cool. Have you ever noticed people can talk about Iran, they can talk about JFK being shot, but as soon as you bring up their sex life, they start stuttering? My family, my father and my mother, life and death, are far more personal to me than sex. —Prince[43]

Coke Johnson briefly left the session in Studio 2 so he could make a quick 2-track edit of "Sex Shooter." A copy was sent to Prince.

Status: "Sex Shooter" had already been edited as a single (3:39) for a promo copy to radio stations (3:00), and both had been released in August, so neither of these were done today. It is unclear why this edit was scheduled a month after they were on the market, but it is possible that today's version was created as an additional radio/promo edit, or as an edit of the "Dance Version" if needed. No edit of "Sex Shooter (Dance Version)" has been released.

SATURDAY, SEPTEMBER 29, 1984*

"Our Destiny" (Jill Jones vocals)
Sunset Sound, Studio 3 | 11:00 a.m.–11:00 p.m. (lock-out)
Producer: Wendy Melvoin and Lisa Coleman | *Artist:* the Revolution (and Jill Jones) | *Engineer:* "Peggy Mac" Leonard | *Assistant Engineer:* Coke Johnson

We were really young. I was twenty or twenty-one then and we were like, is this selling millions or not? We didn't really care. We just thought it was selling to the right people. —Wendy Melvoin[44]

Once again Prince (or perhaps Warner Bros.) listed "the Revolution" as the artist on the daily studio log, so it wasn't a one-time mistake. Wendy and Lisa were representing the band in Prince's absence.

Jill Jones recorded the lead vocals during this session. When Prince had played her a version of the track several months earlier, it was a much more stripped-down demo. "When he sang it originally, it was just him and a piano," remembers Jones. "He had a concept of a play at one point, so when I went in to do that song it was with Lisa on that session and I kind of did a very stagey performance, like musical theatre. Then at one point Prince wanted it for my album, and then it was like, I don't think it's going to go in the direction for an album. Thankfully, Steve Fargnoli intervened on that one, saying to Prince, 'Uh, what kind of record are you trying to make with Jill?'"

Lyrically, the main difference Jones brought to the song was that she dropped part of the spoken word section. Apart from that—and the two different voices—any musical differences were trivial. Once the vocals were complete, Melvoin, Coleman, and Peggy Leonard mixed the track. As with the previous sessions, Prince had no direct involvement.

Status: Jill Jones's version of "Our Destiny" (3:04) remains unreleased.

OCTOBER 1984

OCTOBER 1, 1984

The *Apollonia 6* album is released.

The reviews reflected the beginning of a Prince backlash, and many pointed out that Prince didn't seem interested in the project. While some claimed that the album wasn't deep, it has many moments of fun that were overlooked and overshadowed by *Purple Rain*. Unfortunately, because of Prince's decision to remove songs like "Manic Monday" and "Take Me with U," the album didn't make a huge mark, and by the end of the year it had fallen off the charts completely.

Because MTV had such a huge impact on music, a video album was planned but never completed, as Brenda Bennett explained: "The project was a concept of doing an extended EP, only in a video format as opposed to an audio EP: take one of the songs from the album ('Happy Birthday, Mr. Christian'), write a story line around the subject of that song and incorporate other songs from the album into the story to create a mini movie. The project was dubbed 'Mr. Christian's Birthday.'"[1] Ricky Nelson was cast as Mr. Christian in what was one of his last roles, as he was killed in a plane crash two months later. Bennett continued, "Unfortunately, Prince never liked the 'Mr. Christian' project and it never got any further than the first edits. Such a waste of time and money. The other project we did was a semi-nude photo session using live doves. There were a dozen or more cages of all these white doves that were set free once we got on the set and began to start posing. The photo session was to produce a poster. I never saw the finished product, but I do know it got out there finally."[2]

Apollonia 6 had kept a media presence through the early fall, especially in Europe, but soon after the album was released the entire project ended. Although Apollonia was not officially slated to perform on the *Purple Rain* tour, she would occasionally guest onstage and even made an appearance in the *Prince and the Revolution: Live* concert video that was taped on March 30, 1985. She would remain friends with Prince until his passing in 2016.

"Prince and I had planned on working on a solo record—a project away from what I was doing with Apollonia 6," recalled Bennett, "but it never seemed to get off the ground. There was so much going on at that time: *The Family* coming out; Prince working on more film projects; Apollonia resuming her acting career. With all the changes going on, I started looking in different directions to do a solo project on my own."[3]

Susan Moonsie also parted ways with Prince. According to Jill Jones, Prince had considered extending the group without Apollonia, creating a revolving-door opportunity for a third lead singer in the group. The next version was to be called "Pandora 6," but Prince didn't cast the role of Pandora and the project never materialized.

Status: Apollonia 6 peaked at number 62 on the *Billboard* 200 Chart. It was their only album.

TUESDAY, OCTOBER 2, 1984

"The Dance Electric" (mix)
Sunset Sound, Studio 3 (assumed)
Producer: Wendy Melvoin (assumed) | *Artist:* Prince | *Engineer:* "Peggy Mac" Leonard

He totally cared. He cared so much that he second guessed himself all the time. We did two songs a day for a long, long time. A lot of times I'd said, "Prince, that's a hit," and he goes, "Well that's what they expect from me. I'm not going to give it to them." "But it's a great song!" And he'd say, "I'm going to do something else."—David Z

Prince had asked Peggy Leonard to mix "The Dance Electric," but the results weren't what he'd hoped: "Prince just handed it to me and told me to mix it.

I used every track he recorded, but Prince didn't like what I had done with it. Wendy and I did a mix together, but we had a hard time agreeing about what we liked."

Although many in the Prince camp enjoyed the track, Peggy Leonard felt the song was "kind of boring" and that it was "obvious that his heart wasn't in it." Susan Rogers agreed and was also unimpressed by the song: "'The Dance Electric' was a kind of funk-jam that he could turn around in his sleep. As good as other people might think it is (that's why the *Black Album* came about), those kinds of funk-jams were the sort of things that he did so easily and well. He did it for fun and he did it because he enjoyed it. The band enjoyed playing it."[4]

It is unlikely that Prince attended this session, and it is unclear whether any of these mixes of "The Dance Electric" were ever released.

THURSDAY, OCTOBER 4, 1984

Rehearsal
Venue: Met Center (Minneapolis, Minnesota) | 10:00 a.m.–10:00 p.m.

> *I remember the first day we went in for full-on production, and that was astonishing to see it. That's when I realized it, "Holy shit, this is massive. We're in a stadium right now in production rehearsals." I know it doesn't sound like much right now, but back then it was like, "Oh, my God."*—Wendy Melvoin[5]

Most of October was spent shaping the *Purple Rain* tour. Demand for the concerts was unlike anything Prince had ever experienced. Multiple-night shows in cities like Washington, DC, were selling out within two hours and additional performances were selling out even faster. Basic band rehearsals had been going on at the warehouse since the summer, but on October 4, full stage rehearsals shifted to the Met Center in Minneapolis.

Prince took great pride in creating a tight band. As someone who not only loved music but also loved performing, he worked hard so there were no mistakes, and he drilled it into the sound crew, the lighting crew, and into the band with his famous all-day rehearsals. "We'd jam so much," bassist Brown Mark declared in 2015. "We'd jam from 10 o'clock in the morning until 10 o'clock at night. And I remember times that I was eating lunch while I was still playing. I walked to the lunch room with my bass, on a wireless rig, and I'd go in the refrigerator and grab food and come back and still be playing one handed while eating. That's how intense we were. It was a very interesting time period, but I think a lot of his music, came from that type of grooving, jamming together."[6]

"He'd have us not move for four hours, and he'd be practicing dance moves," remembered Wendy Melvoin. "He became mature and he felt very comfortable in his body, and the band that was behind him was relentlessly in tune to every move he made, and that was the countless hours of not moving and giving him as much confidence and safety in that environment to perfect that thing."[7]

When he wasn't front and center, Prince directed the show from the soundboard and had changes for the staging and lighting as well as for the band. It was run like a tight ship, remembers Susannah Melvoin: "If you were five minutes late, he would say, 'Your pay has been docked.' You could not be late. If he was there before you, you were late."

Matt Fink explained that the rehearsals sounded fun, but they sometimes got a little stressful:

> They were tense if you showed up and didn't know your stuff when you got there, which happened rarely, but there were a few moments that I recall when I was unprepared, whether it was due to some lack of time because something got in the way, and that happened a couple of times, and when it did, he was not a happy camper. And then you would get in trouble, and he would scold you in front of everybody, he'd say, "Okay everybody, take a break, Fink has got to learn his parts." And then everybody would take a break, I would feel sheepish and embarrassed, and I would have to sit there and work on my stuff, and that happened to several people over the years.
>
> [Prince] usually knew his stuff, because it was his music, he was usually very well prepared. But he made mistakes, he even made mistakes during shows on rare occasions. Yeah, he made a few, but nothing severe where the audience would know or say he really screwed that up, nothing to that extent.[8]

"I remember when Prince used to forget his words on stage, it was the funniest thing because he would start scratching his head, and he would pace back and forth," recalled Brown Mark on his podcast in 2016. "And then me and Bobby, would look at each other and say, 'He forgot the words,' and then sure enough, he'd walk up to the microphone and say, 'You know the words, sing!'"[9]

FRIDAY, OCTOBER 5, 1984

Rehearsal
Venue: Met Center (Minneapolis, Minnesota) | 10:00 a.m.–10:00 p.m.

SUNDAY, OCTOBER 7, 1984

Rehearsal
Venue: Minneapolis Auditorium (Minneapolis, Minnesota) | 10:00 a.m.–
10:00 p.m.

MONDAY, OCTOBER 8, 1984

Rehearsal
Venue: Minneapolis Auditorium (Minneapolis, Minnesota) | 10:00 a.m.–
10:00 p.m.

What Prince was really good at was pushing people beyond their limits. He saw that they could do it and he would force it out of them.—Roy Bennett

Prince was scheduled to leave town, but rehearsals for everyone else would continue in his absence. "When Prince wasn't around, we'd go in and play without him," remembered Bobby Z. "Then he'd come back and change everything. Rehearsal to Prince is not 'work.' He lives to play and plays to live. I enjoyed the process, where you just got totally focused on playing. It was an exciting, exciting time."[10]

Even though he was prepping for the biggest tour of his life, Prince continued to record new music. While he was away, videotapes of the rehearsals he missed were made for him to review.

TUESDAY, OCTOBER 9, 1984

"Lisa" [working title for "Yes"] (Wendy Melvoin guitar overdubs and saxophone overdubs)
Flying Cloud Drive Warehouse (Eden Prairie, Minnesota)
Producer: Prince | *Artist:* the Family | *Engineer:* Susan Rogers (assumed)

*Prince had recorded the rhythm tracks for ["Yes"] and
actually—this wasn't credited on the album, but if I remember
correctly, Wendy Melvoin was the guitar player on the
song—and once the track was done. I got a call from Prince
to come in and listen to it.*—Eric Leeds[11]

Prince decided that the unfinished track (likely recorded in August) would fit
well on *The Family* album if given the proper treatment, so he contacted Eric
Leeds, with whom he'd rapidly built a very trusting musical relationship: "He
just said, 'Here's the track. You got it. Send me a tape when you're done.' I
spent an evening in the studio messing around with it, and that's kind of what
I came up with."[12]

Prince left for Los Angeles, allowing Leeds to create the melody by adding flute
and overdubbing multiple sax lines: "Once again I had an opportunity to just take
something that he had done and go in and just completely do whatever I wanted
to do with it, and fortunately, he really dug it. So that was the end of that."[13]

Unfortunately, when the final mix was complete, some of Leeds's contributions were hidden or completely removed, and Leeds wasn't happy with the
result: "To be honest, I never cared for the mix or the edit, as it didn't make
much sense to me musically. Also, several of the harmony lines were, shall we
say, underrepresented. So the final mix doesn't really reflect what I had in mind
when I recorded it. Obviously Prince heard it a bit differently."[14]

The date on this session was listed in the Warner Bros. archives as October
8, but Eric Leeds recalls listening to the World Series (which was played on
October 9), which indicates that either it was a two-day session or it occurred
on Tuesday.

*It is possible that Wendy's guitar part was recorded in August during the initial
tracking session.*

OCTOBER 1984 (ESTIMATE)

"**The Screams of Passion**" (orchestral overdubs)
"**River Run Dry**" (orchestral overdubs)
"**Nothing Compares 2 U**" (orchestral overdubs)
"**High Fashion**" (orchestral overdubs)
"**Desire**" (orchestral overdubs)
Monterey Studios (Glendale, California) | Unknown time
Producer: Clare Fischer | *Artist:* Prince (although he didn't attend) |
  Engineer: Arne Frager

> *The first Prince session we did, actually, wasn't for Prince, it was for the Family, and we did five songs: "The Screams of Passion," "River Run Dry," "Nothing Compares 2 U," "High Fashion," and a song called "Desire."*—Arne Frager

For the first time, Prince allowed someone to add an element to his music without overseeing any of his work. "One of the problems in the recording studio is the money to pay musicians," explained composer and arranger Clare Fischer, "so people are given such low budgets that you can't hire a large string section. Prince spends money and so I was able to write string sections as opposed to writing for a small string ensemble."[15]

"When we had the string date and went in with Clare Fischer, Prince wasn't actually there—it was all of us as a band and [David Z]," according to Susannah Melvoin. "It felt really great and we knew that we were doing something really special, but no one really knew what was going to happen with it. Eric [Leeds] said that Prince wanted to write a hit record, that was his intention period. But Paul and I were not aware of any of that. We were just doing it."[16]

Once the session was over, tapes were shipped to Prince to review, but Arne Frager mixed them in a way that wouldn't sound like the final product: "The point of these mixes is not to mix them the way the song will be mixed for the record, but for Prince to hear Clare's orchestrations."

"We were so excited to put up the multitrack at the warehouse," remembered Rogers about their first listen once it was delivered to Minneapolis. "We listened to the strings and I said I thought it sounded as if someone had left the TV on in the next room. To me the strings sounded disjointed, but the more I listened to it the more I realized it was the perfect complement to Prince. It had so much movement and so much melody, and it was so unpredictable. I thought it was incredible, and Prince really enjoyed it. He was delighted. He just couldn't be happier. This was his first experience of really letting one of his babies go to somebody else and have it come back with something recorded on it."[17]

"When Prince first started sending me songs," recalled Fischer after working with Prince on multiple tracks the following year, "I thought maybe that by the time I had done four arrangements that I would have started getting some sort of a repetitive something or other. I have been extremely surprised to find that each one is as different from the last as the next one is going to be different."[18]

Although Prince and Fischer eventually worked together on dozens of songs, they had never attended any sessions with each other, which impressed Fischer: "Prince is a very smart man. And now when I say smart, it takes a man—I don't care how big somebody's ego is—a man who can come to a realization like that and know that his ego will get in the way of somebody else's doing well and stays out of it for that reason, that is a smart man. That's just one of the many ways that I think he is a smart man."

Not only did Prince never attend a recording session with Fischer, they never met in person and throughout their years working together (Fischer passed away in 2012), Prince had no idea what Fischer looked like, although he did have at least one close call: "I sent him this album that had a picture on the cover of me, with my seven singers around me. I've heard from somebody that was there at the time that he held the album away from his eyes so he would not see the picture on the front, took the disk out, and played it. And his comment? 'I don't want to see what he looks like, I have this image and this has been working beautifully.'"

"I just send him a tape, we talk on the phone and he sends me the finished orchestra tracks. I wouldn't want to jinx it by meeting him," explained Prince in 1999.[19]

According to Paul Peterson, these new additions would cause Prince to remix the songs: "Prince pulled instruments out and made [the orchestration] such a prominent feature of that record." Once the new mixes were complete, the Family had a sound that was unlike anything Prince had ever attempted. Peterson summed up the secret behind their brand: "So you have the classy orchestration of Clare with the nasty, one-chord funk underneath and the beautiful poetry of Prince, and that was the concept. With a white kid singing up front."[20]

Prince and Fischer had one more close encounter when they both worked on the 2004 Grammy Awards show. They practically stood next to each other, but the only person who recognized the situation was Fischer's son Brent, and he decided it was best to respect Prince's wishes and not reach out to introduce them, especially since Prince and Brent Fischer were getting ready to perform that evening with Beyoncé.

TUESDAY, OCTOBER 9, 1984*

"Condition of the Heart" (basic tracking)
Sunset Sound, Studio 2 | 6:30 p.m.–9:30 p.m. (booked 7:00 p.m.–open)
Producer: Prince | *Artist:* Prince | *Engineer:* Prince | *Assistant Engineer:* "Peggy Mac" Leonard

If you listen to that album [Around the World in a Day], it's experimental sounding to me. Pretty complicated, technically. He was literally playing exactly what he heard in his head in one take, like Mozart used to write symphonies down that he had in his head and he'd just write it out on paper.—Matt Fink[21]

Prince no longer maintained a studio in his home now that he'd sold his Soundcraft console to former Time guitarist Jesse Johnson, so while the band continued to rehearse in Minneapolis, Prince spent a few days alone in Los Angeles recording at Sunset Sound. It is unclear why he didn't record at his warehouse, but it may have been in use by the Family or Mazarati, or he just may have wanted to spend a little time in Los Angeles before the tour. Although Prince was able to work on his own, he continued to seek out new inspiration from others for his music, but because of his private nature, the origins are often lost or simply never understood. Then there are songs like "Condition of the Heart," which was a direct result of his continued relationship with Susannah Melvoin. "I can say with some assurance that I think it was inspired by Susannah," revealed Susan Rogers. "He wrote it when it was unsure whether or not he and Susannah would be a couple. When he says in the lyrics: 'There was a woman who made funny faces just like Clara Bow,'[22] I know he is referring to Wendy, because he used to talk about how Wendy reminded him of Clara Bow. The next line in the song is: 'How was I to know that she would wear the same cologne as you and do the same giggle that you do.'[23] He had no idea that this person he admired so much, Wendy, would have a twin sister and that he would be absolutely in love."[24]

"I think what attracted Prince to Susannah largely would have been the personality," continued Rogers. "The two women, Wendy and Susannah . . . I think the vivaciousness, the intelligence, the worldliness, coupled with being down-to-earth. Both girls loved a good laugh, and because they straddled the worlds of the everyday with the world of celebrityhood, I think that made Susannah very appealing. She was a very normal girl in so many ways, and yet had the star quality that Prince himself had."[25]

The track was started on this date during a relatively short session at Sunset Sound. Prince recorded the basic piano and some of the vocals, but it is unclear how much further he got before he ended the session unusually early. No mix was done and no cassettes were made of the number.

Although the song would be credited to Prince and the Revolution, no other members of the band were involved; this was typical of Prince, who had the ability to play almost anything in the studio. "I don't think you know how he operates, because if you could do everything yourself, you would be doing it," declares Albert Magnoli. "Do you know how easy it is to do it yourself? You just get up in the morning and do it. So he doesn't have to talk to anybody."

Status: "Condition of the Heart" (6:48) was released on April 22, 1985, when it was included on Prince's *Around the World in a Day* album. The song was never issued as a single, but it did make its live debut during a concert in Rosemont, Illinois, on December 9, 1984. Only a part of the song was played, and it was never a regular feature on the *Purple Rain* tour.

WEDNESDAY, OCTOBER 10, 1984*

"Condition of the Heart" (overdub/mix)
Sunset Sound, Studio 2 | Noon–12:30 a.m. (booked lock-out)
Producer: Prince | *Artist:* Prince | *Engineer:* Prince | *Assistant Engineer:* "Peggy Mac" Leonard

I would love to listen to him on the piano, but he fancied himself a better guitar player. I think he was also great on the bass and the guitar, but it's too easy to just goof off on the guitar, and I always felt that he played the piano beautifully.—Peggy Leonard

"Condition of the Heart" wasn't complete, and Prince continued working on it during this session. During the eleven and a half hours he spent overdubbing with light guitar, finger cymbals, keyboards, and synth strings (although it is possible that much of this was actually from the DX7), Prince began searching for an instrument that would mimic a human heartbeat, so he asked Sunset Sound staff member Stephen Shelton to find a kettledrum. According to Shelton, once the drum arrived in Studio 2, Prince recorded it very quickly.

In many ways "Condition of the Heart" was similar to "God," which he'd recorded in Minneapolis in mid-August. Both tracks prominently feature Prince's vocal gymnastics and distinct piano playing, with a variety of ethereal overdubs. Each of these tracks is also best heard while sitting in a darkened room, which is the way he recorded them. "'Condition of The Heart' was done similar to 'God'—in the dark with one candle on the piano," remembered Susan Rogers. "Most of the work on that one is done at night. I remember just being wacked out by the lyrics. I really thought it was great and I think it really represented a vulnerability in him that he didn't get close to too often. To me it is a similar song to 'The Beautiful Ones,' but it's even better. It's one of his masterpieces."[26]

THURSDAY, OCTOBER 11, 1984*

"Paisley Park" (mix)
"Condition of the Heart" (possible mix)
Sunset Sound, Studio 3 | Noon–2:15 a.m. (booked lock-out)
Producer: Prince | *Artist:* Prince | *Engineer:* Prince | *Assistant Engineers:* "Peggy Mac" Leonard and David Leonard

I've been recording almost every day of my life, working on a vast number of styles. —Prince[27]

By this time Prince was very specific about the sound he was seeking for his post-*Purple Rain* career, and "Paisley Park" was given another mix, which likely expanded the prominence of the work of the women around him. "Sometimes it would be Wendy and Lisa, or he would have Susannah and Wendy sing together to create a sound," explained Bobby Z. "You can hear the way the separation is. He liked to keep them pretty clear, not double them or anything. So you can hear Wendy and Lisa over there, then there's Susannah mixed in there. If there was anything, it's his music and their singing."[28]

It is possible that another mix was done for "Condition of the Heart" as well. As the fall went on, Prince spent more time working on the next phase of his career. Because of the newly expanded fan base and its anticipation, the *Purple Rain* tour would be his biggest, its size and scope dwarfing almost anything else on the road that year. As the final tour rehearsals were taking place, Prince found himself surrounded by a small army of people, and both his status and career path were changing. "In the beginning it was great, because there usually wasn't anyone around, because people didn't seem to give two shits about him," remembers Peggy Leonard, who had been recording with him since 1981. "But as soon as he started selling, people came around like flies and everything changed. He changed. He had a hard time being diplomatic, and sometimes there would be three or four engineers around and you don't need that. Susan [Rogers] and I worked together fine, but there were occasional problems with some of the other engineers being competitive with each other. And that was the beginning of the end. There were no clearly defined roles anymore and nobody knew what was going on, and he kept everyone guessing."

Prince pushed himself hard. He was racing against the clock before the tour began, but he was also filled with the energy of youth focused on creating as much new music as possible, refusing to fall into the stereotypical role of the rock star who needed to get away from the pressure. "I never saw him do anything," says David Z. "I mean, maybe a glass of wine or a drink, but that's it. I never saw him take a drug. Ever. His eyes were always clear. If you worked for Prince you had to be on point, dressed and ready to go at all times. And you couldn't be drunk."

Susan Rogers also recalled that Prince refused to do anything that would dull his edge: "He didn't get into drugs. He didn't get into scandalous lifestyles. He was smart enough to know, 'I'm going to do my work and I'm going to approach this as work,' and that's what he did, like a great filmmaker or a great painter would do. He created his art. Works that would survive him."[29]

This was Prince's last session at Sunset Sound in 1984. He returned to Minneapolis to continue working with the Revolution for the final rehearsals of the tour.

FRIDAY, OCTOBER 12, 1984

Rehearsal
Venue: Minneapolis Auditorium (Minneapolis, Minnesota) | 10:00 a.m.–
   10:00 p.m.

We spent more time in rehearsal than we had ever done before. It was almost like we did a tour of Minneapolis because we kept changing venues once a week, or once a week and half.—Roy Bennett[30]

After today, everything was moved to the St. Paul Civic Center. Three different venues would be used for dress rehearsals this month (Minneapolis Auditorium being the third) as every part of the show was tested over and over, including verifying that breaking down the elaborate stage, loading up and moving the trucks, and setting everything back up went smoothly. "There was a lot to do with loading it in and loading it out," explains Roy Bennett, who was once again designing the stage and lights. "It was a very complex show. It was the first super-theatrical show that we had done, so it just took time to put together. I think he was overwhelmed a bit. Just because of the magnitude of what this thing was. There was pressure on him, and we delivered."

SATURDAY, OCTOBER 13, 1984

Rehearsal
Venue: Saint Paul Civic Center (Saint Paul, Minnesota) | 10:00 a.m.–10:00 p.m.

SATURDAY, OCTOBER 13, 1984

Live Performance
Venue: First Avenue/7th Street Entry (Minneapolis, Minnesota)
Capacity: unknown

According to Eric Lindbom, writing for the *Twin Cities Nightbeat*, Prince performed a quick set at First Avenue/7th Street Entry on this evening. Lindbom wrote that Prince "graced 7th Street Entry's intimate confines with a mini-set performed before a 'captive' audience, which was locked into the tiny room. A lengthy, almost heavy metal treatment of 'When Doves Cry' was the reported highlight."[31]

There has not been any independent verification of this show, so either it was an unscheduled surprise gig or the information is incorrect.

SUNDAY, OCTOBER 14, 1984

Rehearsal
Venue: Saint Paul Civic Center (Saint Paul, Minnesota) | 10:00 a.m.–12:00 a.m.

SUNDAY, OCTOBER 14, 1984 (ESTIMATE)

"Around the World in a Day" (mix)
Flying Cloud Drive Warehouse (Eden Prairie, Minnesota)
Producer: Prince | *Artist:* Prince | *Engineer:* Susan Rogers (assumed)

As I was coming into my own persona and understanding of who I was, I never talked down to my audience. And when you don't talk down to your audience, they can grow with you, and I give them a lot of credit to be able to hang with me this long, because I've gone through a lot of changes, but they've allowed me to grow, and thus we can tackle some serious subjects and try to just be better human beings, all of us. —Prince[32]

Prince continued to place a great deal of energy into artistic growth, and part of that was getting his next album done properly. He continued to work on mixing the title track for his next album, working hard to make it the anti–*Purple Rain* and hopefully keep people guessing about where he'd go next. "I think there was a part of him that was beginning to fear that his artistic integrity would be compromised," explained Alan Leeds:

And some critics were even beginning to say, "Hey man, you've got an entourage now, you're up there with Elvis. I suppose we've heard the end of your art, Mr. Rock Star." So it was his way of telling people, "I'm not turning my back on the music; I didn't sell out. I'm going to do something that I consider artistically honest, that is not contrived to fit a format. I'm not writing for a movie, I'm not writing to try to duplicate a hit song and say I want another song like "Purple Rain," or another song like "Little Red Corvette." I'm just going to let the music flow, be totally honest, and if it's this weird record, hopefully the fans I've assembled in the last two years with *Purple Rain* and *1999* will follow me on this weird little path while we go explore these crazy little songs that struck my fancy." And I don't really think it's any more than that.[33]

Once again Prince had Susan Rogers set up for an additional mix for "Around the World in a Day." "That was the mix that ended up on the record," she explained. "Because we were used to sitting in the warehouse and going quickly and flying by the seat of our pants. When I say we mixed it together, I'll be specific. Prince would often say, 'I'm going to mix such and such; get it started for me and I'll come in.' Which meant that I would EQ the individual instruments, I would do processing on them, any limiters, any gates. I'll get sounds on the basic instruments, which he may or may not change later, but I would get the basic sounds. He would come in and do the blend."[34]

Prince seemed very happy with the new mix, but not everyone around him shared the sentiment. Once again, sax player Eric Leeds disagreed with the new sound: "I said that I always missed the fact that the rhythm section wasn't there on the released version. And I kind of said it in a challenging way, and he just said, 'Hey, that's how I heard the song then.' And I know how that is."[35]

No official documentation has surfaced to verify when this session occurred, but it has been referenced by other sources as a probable date for mixing of "Around the World in a Day." There is a possibility that it was mixed on the afternoon of Saturday, October 20.

MONDAY, OCTOBER 15, 1984

Rehearsal
Venue: Saint Paul Civic Center (Saint Paul, Minnesota) | 10:00 a.m.–12:00 a.m.

TUESDAY, OCTOBER 16, 1984

Rehearsal
Venue: Saint Paul Civic Center (Saint Paul, Minnesota) | 10:00 a.m.–12:00 a.m.

WEDNESDAY, OCTOBER 17, 1984

Rehearsal
Venue: Saint Paul Civic Center (Saint Paul, Minnesota) | 10:00 a.m.–12:00 a.m.

THURSDAY, OCTOBER 18, 1984

Rehearsal
Venue: Saint Paul Civic Center (Saint Paul, Minnesota) | 10:00 a.m.–12:00 a.m.

FRIDAY, OCTOBER 19, 1984

Rehearsal
Venue: Saint Paul Civic Center (Saint Paul, Minnesota) | 10:00 a.m.–10:00 p.m.

Some of the funniest moments we had were at rehearsal. During some breaks we would joke around and make up skits and silly songs. Lisa is the perfect Olive Oyl to my Popeye. While we were on tour we would all go out to dinner together, take in an occasional movie or go to after-show parties. By the way,

Prince never cooked and served us pancakes after playing basketball with him.—Matt Fink[36]

After this rehearsal, the entire *Purple Rain* stage was taken down, loaded on the trucks, and moved from Saint Paul Civic Center back to the Met Center in Bloomington.

SATURDAY, OCTOBER 20, 1984

Rehearsal
Venue: Met Center (Bloomington, Minnesota) | 7:00 p.m.–12:00 a.m.

SUNDAY, OCTOBER 21, 1984

Rehearsal
Venue: Met Center (Bloomington, Minnesota) | 10:00 a.m.–12:00 a.m.

MONDAY, OCTOBER 22, 1984

Rehearsal
Venue: Met Center (Bloomington, Minnesota) | 10:00 a.m.–12:00 a.m.

TUESDAY, OCTOBER 23, 1984

After almost three weeks without a day off, the Revolution was not scheduled for rehearsal. The crew, however, did not have the day off, and moved the equipment to the Minneapolis Auditorium.

The rehearsals began shifting to the evenings to reflect the upcoming concert schedule.

WEDNESDAY, OCTOBER 24, 1984

Rehearsal
Venue: Minneapolis Auditorium (Minneapolis, Minnesota) | 7:00 p.m.–
12:00 a.m.

THURSDAY, OCTOBER 25, 1984

"I Would Die 4 U" (recording of 12-inch)
Rehearsal
Venue: Minneapolis Auditorium (Minneapolis, Minnesota) | 7:00 p.m.–
12:00 a.m.
Producer: Prince | *Artist:* Prince and the Revolution | *Engineer:* Susan
Rogers (assumed)

*I think that my greatest memories of my musical career are of
rehearsals that were spectacular, not shows. It was an exciting,
exciting time.*—Bobby Z[37]

This was a very busy day.

According to those around him, Prince wasn't going to leave anything to
chance. The twenty-six-year-old discovered that the tour would sell out regardless of its quality, but because this was the first time many fans would see
him play live, he decided to give them everything they wanted—and what they
wanted was to revisit the movie. To accommodate that, it was decided to play
every track from the soundtrack album. (Although "Take Me with U" wasn't
regularly played by the band until January 1985, it was in rotation as part of
the piano set beginning two weeks into the tour.) *Purple Rain* had created a
steamroller that had the potential to crush everything in its path—including
Prince if he stood still for too long. By buying into the idea of re-creating the
movie and taking on the persona of its lead character, he was taking a gamble
that could derail his image as a musical rebel, and Prince realized that his
major success could also bring major consequences, which caused him to
actively work against the direction of the purple tidal wave. In 1984 Prince

had achieved a level of fame that few entertainers would match, but that success threatened to permanently brand him as "the Kid" from *Purple Rain* and could haunt the rest of his career. Years later, he'd admit: **"My own competition is myself in the past."**[38]

Prince worked very hard to make the entire *Purple Rain* project a success, but he had spent the fall working just as hard to distance himself from it. He always wanted to release as much new music as possible, but *Purple Rain* was still at the top of the charts, and Warner Bros. was trying to get as much out of their investment in the album as possible. Prince needed to be part of that machine, but he wanted to do it on his terms. On every single, he'd released a "new" B-side, but the extended versions of his tracks were only variations on the album versions, which was arguably frustrating him, so he continued to create more new music. **"Music is a part of my DNA,"** Prince would later reflect. **"And the weird thing is: if I don't get the things I come up with out of my head, I'm unable to function."**[39]

Not only did Prince want to get them out of his head, he wanted his creations to be heard by others. "With someone with a mind that is as fertile and creative as Prince, he would have been bored," reflects Susan Rogers. "His fertile brain was constantly wanting to record new material."

"He has a vault of shit. And he probably wanted to put it out, and they're like, 'Shit. Slow down,'" laughed Jellybean Johnson. "But [what] you've got to realize is, he writes all the fucking time. Anything comes to him, he's going to do it. And that's how he was back then."[40]

Several Warner Bros. Records executives were frustrated by this. "His attitude was, 'I have a lot to say musically and I want to say it right now,'" remembered senior PR exec Bob Merlis. "While we were working on [promoting] the second single from the current album, he'd already recorded the next album and wanted us to put it out."[41]

Alan Leeds saw this up close as he managed the *Purple Rain* tour:

He didn't really care about the needs of a record label to mount the campaign to successfully and fully exploit an album. He was someone who saw his songs like newspapers. They were timely things, so that if he went into the studio tonight and made a new record, in his mind it was something to be listened to quickly because it was of the moment. If there were a way for him to release a new song every day, he would do that. Much like you'd go to the stoop and get the newspaper, you'd start your day with a Prince song-of-the-day. By the time a record got released, it was all old news to him, and he'd written—and in some cases even performed—dozens and dozens and dozens of newer songs that were more relevant to who he was at that particular time. He didn't choose to understand the concept of spacing out singles and gradually retaining interest in an album so it could continue to sell, and meanwhile the label is just up and running working on that latest album and wondering why he isn't there to support it, so it was a recipe for disaster.[42]

In many ways Prince was looking to satisfy his fans as well as his critics, who may have seen his success as a fluke. When the time came to release an extended version of "I Would Die 4 U," Prince decided to forgo a simple remix of the track as well as the actual live version from the August 3, 1983, show, which was only slightly longer. Instead he'd chosen to record a new version that was an expansion of how it would be played on the *Purple Rain* tour, which was scheduled to start in just over a week. This updated rendition was only played in late November at the Capital Center in Landover, Maryland, when they were recording the videos for "I Would Die 4 U" and "Baby I'm a Star."

Taking a quick break from the tour's final dress rehearsals, Prince gathered the Revolution and Sheila E.'s band and put their long jam to tape. Susan Rogers recalled that period and the method for getting it done properly: "This was one month of renting these places out. By the end of this month the *Purple Rain* tour was pretty much ready to go—all the bugs had been worked out—and the band would jam for a few hours, and that's when we recorded the long version of 'I Would Die 4 U.' It was recorded on 24-tracks remote in the mobile truck, and that's how it was done."[43]

The song included all the members of both bands, with Wendy Melvoin, Lisa Coleman, Eddie "Eddie M." Mininfield, Miko Weaver, and others called out by name. Very few of the lyrics were actually used, and because it was such a loose jam, Prince actually had to say "verse" and "song" to let them know when he'd start singing. It was obvious that Prince was still working out details of the jam, most of which would be edited out.

The track was brought back to the warehouse for additional overdubs. The beginning of the tape included Prince's instructions to his engineers: "You guys mix this down to a cassette or a 2-track or something so I can listen to the cassette. Okay, let's jam."

Status: The lengthy performance of "I Would Die 4 U" (30:55) that was recorded today was eventually edited down (10:20) and released as the song's 12-inch. The unedited version remains unreleased.

THURSDAY, OCTOBER 25, 1984

Live Performance
Venue: First Avenue/ 7th Street Entry (Minneapolis, Minnesota)
Capacity: unknown

Oh, he's a workaholic, no question. We'll end up going to a club and playing for another three hours. It's that much fun. —Sheila E.[44]

After recording the long version of "I Would Die 4 U," Sheila E. performed her final pre-tour concert at First Avenue, where Prince joined her onstage during her second encore to play guitar on "Too Sexy." Subsequently, Prince, Brown Mark, and Bobby Z borrowed some instruments and took over the stage next door at the 7th Street Entry. "All the rehearsals made us a tight machine," remembers Brown Mark. "We would walk into anybody's bar, get on the equipment, and we would throw down. We challenged everybody; we weren't afraid. We all kind of developed very unique techniques. We mixed all that together, especially the back end with the drums and the bass. It was rocking! And people hadn't ever seen anything like that before. It was massive. We could hit jazz. . . . It didn't matter what. We hit it all."

The power trio performed a five-song impromptu jam featuring Prince's own songs ("Mutiny" and "Erotic City") and compositions by Sly & the Family Stone ("Africa Talks to You" and "The Asphalt Jungle") and James Brown ("Give It Up or Turnit A Loose"). Prince also included a track he introduced as "Blues in G," but it was actually the B.B. King/Dave Clark song "I Got Some Help That I Don't Need," which had been rehearsed by Prince and the Revolution in mid-July. It was fairly obvious that this set was not a formal show but more like an unrehearsed free-form jam to blow off some steam, with Prince cueing the others with various songs' keys. The show wrapped around 1:00 a.m.

A rehearsal, a jam recorded for release, a guest appearance with Sheila E., and a twenty-five-minute concert performance. It was a big day and proof that Prince had more energy than almost anyone. "**In the past, a lot of [friends] said I was a maniac, a workaholic,**" Prince would reflect in 1997. "**But I take that as a compliment. Coltrane played sax 12 hours a day. Can you imagine a spirit that would drive a body that hard? I wanna play 15 hours at a time!**"[45]

FRIDAY, OCTOBER 26, 1984

Rehearsal
Venue: Minneapolis Auditorium (Minneapolis, Minnesota) | 10:00 a.m.–
10:00 p.m.

Prince rehearsed the band at the Minneapolis Auditorium for three more days then switched once again to the St. Paul Civic Center for the last batch of rehearsals until November 1, when the trucks left for Detroit, Michigan, to begin the tour.

Prince had also wanted to play at 7th Street Entry on October 30, but the Hoodoo Gurus were scheduled to perform and refused to give up their slot.

WEDNESDAY, OCTOBER 31, 1984

"Strange Relationship" (basic tracking)
"The Ladder" (basic tracking, vocal overdubs, mix, and possible edit)
"Do Me Baby" (instrumental rehearsal)
Venue: Saint Paul Civic Center (Saint Paul, Minnesota) and Flying Cloud
Drive Warehouse (Eden Prairie, Minnesota)
Producer: Prince | *Artist:* Prince and the Revolution | *Engineers:* David
Tickle, Rob "Cubby" Colby, and Susan Rogers

He was in and out of the studio constantly, and it seemed like more than any other time in his career, brilliant music was just passing through him. It was as if this huge flower had just blossomed.—Alan Leeds[46]

As the opening of the *Purple Rain* tour got closer, the band was functioning beautifully. Everyone knew their parts, and once Prince locked in on that, he expanded the way the band performed together. Part of his trust with the Revolution went to creating new music based on finding a groove that felt right. Brown Mark sheds some light into how this worked: "Our rehearsals weren't really rehearsing the show. We'd do a lot of jamming and creating a sound, and that's where a lot of that came from. And he would have the tapes rolling."

As he'd done in the past, Prince ran through "Strange Relationship," but it was abandoned yet again. On "The Ladder," Prince showed the various members of the band what he expected them to play. Some were more complicated and some were more basic, including the music for Matt Fink: "I played on that, but it was a pretty easy part. Something he just handed to me: 'Here's the chords, play it on the organ.' Pretty simple. Nothing challenging."

Sheila E.'s saxophone player Eddie Mininfield (aka Eddie M.) takes up the story: "We were in production getting ready to go on the *Purple Rain* tour, and we were in Minneapolis and he had a mobile recording unit set up, and I had no idea that I was going to be on the record. They were calling me to be on the stage and play, and I played. I was so green. I didn't know what I was doing. The next thing you know, Jerome Benton said, 'Eddie, come here come here,' and he drags me out to the mobile recording unit, and I was like, 'What is this?' (*laughs*) And they played it back and I was like, 'Oh my goodness, I'm on a record!'"

Several takes of the song were attempted before Prince seemed content with the results. During the first verse on one of the final takes, Eddie M. added some improvisational horn lines that were ultimately omitted from the final mix. The song ends with another sax solo followed by Prince singing the chorus, both of which were also eliminated.

"We brought it back to the warehouse afterwards," Susan Rogers continues the story, "and Wendy and Lisa did the vocals with Taja Sevelle [credited as "Taj," but her real name is Nancy Richardson]. Prince brought her in because she was around at the time and he was curious about working with her in the future, so she joined us." Susannah Melvoin also joined them for the vocal overdubs. Prince replaced some of his lead vocals as well.

"He was really happy with that song," recalled Melvoin. "He loved it. I think he had fully realized a concept that he had been spiritually feeling. I think it was one of those songs that he could say, 'I nailed it. This is what I wanted to do, this is what I wanted to say and this is how I said it, and all the music is right and I'm right on it and I'm fully realized on this track.' I do believe that."

Status: "The Ladder" (7:10) was edited down (5:29) for release on Prince's *Around the World in a Day* album. Today's attempt at "Strange Relationship" also remains unreleased.

"I think it was at the Civic Center in preproduction for the tour for four to five days," emphasizes Eddie M. "We hadn't taken off yet. I don't know what day it was on, but it was kind of the middle of that rehearsal, and we took off right after that. But that definitely went down in preproduction, we weren't on the road yet."

NOVEMBER 1984

Prince's studio work was temporarily put on hold as he focused on the first month of the *Purple Rain* tour. As the tour progressed he found ways to spend time in the studio, but for the next few weeks his priority was making sure the tour went smoothly. To offset the monotony of the live shows, Prince would hold long rehearsal jams with the Revolution, often reworking a track enough to give Prince room to improvise when it was played live, but that required strict attention from the band, Matt Fink explained: "You had to watch him like a hawk . . . you had to watch the hand signals for the cues that were worked out in advance to go to those sections because if Prince was at a certain section onstage and you had a bad angle on his hand you could miss a cue. It almost became a running joke during the shows that if you missed the horn punches or didn't count them right and you were off Prince could hear that, especially if Bobby missed one. As a joke Prince would kick you off your instrument and take over like, 'Okay. That's it . . . you screwed up. You are done.' It happened to everybody in the band at one time or another."[1]

Everyone was ready for the tour.

SUNDAY, NOVEMBER 4, 1984

Venue: Joe Louis Arena (Detroit, Michigan)
Capacity: 18,533 (sold out)

Detroit! My name is Prince and I've come to play with you.
—Prince[2]

"The tension the first night was astronomical," remembered Lisa Coleman. "But after the first chord, everything was okay."[3] As he had with his last two tours, Prince decided to launch it in November, and this time he stacked the cards in his favor and premiered with a seven-night series at the Joe Louis Arena in Detroit. To give some perspective, Prince had played the same venue the previous year and sold out a single performance. Prince had always had a very personal relationship with Detroit, on occasion referring to it as a "second home."[4] The show was a tremendous success, overshadowing everything he'd done so far in his career.

"When they turned the lights off and you'd stand by the side of the stage and hear, 'Ladies and gentlemen . . . ,' it was deafening," detailed Wendy Melvoin. "To this day, I have never heard anything like that. It was so loud that my ears became distorted at one point."[5]

"Opening night in Detroit. It was chaos!" declares lighting director Roy Bennett. "I remember 'Let's Go Crazy,' the first song, and dropping thousands and thousands and thousands of dollars' worth of live flowers along with all the silk flowers. It seemed like it rained flowers for an hour. It seemed like it just didn't stop coming down. It was unbelievable. The audience was just going berserk. It was seriously a hair-raising feeling, where the hair just stood up on your arms. It was just a constant level of excitement around everywhere."

The flowers made such a mess that the concept had to be changed: instead of real flowers raining down from the stage, flowers made out of fabric were used. Everyone on the crew was busy working on these changes, including drum tech Brad Marsh: "From then on we carried around half a truck of fake flowers and half a truck of purple tambourines, because we used to hand out one hundred purple tambourines a night. And before we got the purple tambourines actually purple, I'd have to go and get some cans of purple spray paint every fucking night and spray paint one hundred tambourines in some distant room whatever venue we were at. *(laughs)*"

The fans were enjoying the show and the reviews were generally flattering, but many exposed a painful flaw in the show. The *USA Today* review started by saying, "The biggest surprise about Prince's *Purple Rain* sellout show, which opened Sunday, is that there aren't any big surprises."[6] The tour was highly choreographed, with a song list that would eventually contain every track off the *Purple Rain* album as well as several of the *Purple Rain*–era B-sides, including "17 Days," "God," and "Another Lonely Christmas," as well as Sheila E. performing "Erotic City." Ultimately Prince seemed to focus on his *1999*-era and his B-sides more than any music from his first four albums, likely indicating his preference to more recent music.

A review of the Detroit shows by Nelson George notes that Prince was "obedient to the images of *Purple Rain*,"[7] which is very accurate and probably wasn't lost on Prince.

Prince was a forward thinker and loved to create new art, but he was also an amazing performer and recharged his internal batteries from the energy from a cheering crowd. The huge contradiction was that at the end of the day, a stage show is at its core a retrospective package, so although Prince did as much as he could to add new elements to the show, because the show was so structured it left Prince unable to be as spontaneous as he might enjoy. The lights, the confetti, and the length of the show all had to fall within a certain parameter, which ended up limiting him. In 2012 Prince admitted how difficult it was for him: "**I nearly had a nervous breakdown on the *Purple Rain* tour [in 1984] because it was the same every night. It's work to play the same songs the same way for 70 shows.**"[8]

In another interview Prince confided that he preferred a less structured show: "**I think that's cool for the circus. The trapeze artist has to catch the person right on cue, but music is not like that. It should be organic and unexpected.**"[9]

The size of the spectacle also affected Prince. "It was so big, Prince didn't like it," Fink recalled. "He said, 'This isn't intimate enough. It's too large for the band.' Everybody was spread out from each other too much, so he had them rein it in."[10]

Although this was the peak of Prince's popularity, this feeling of creative claustrophobia would haunt the *Purple Rain* tour. The irony was that although Prince had exposed more about himself with the movie, he seemed to run in the other direction on a personal level, erecting additional barriers around himself, even to those who were in his inner circle. "I think because he became so popular, he started putting walls around himself because actually going out was really a problem," suggests Jill Jones.

"The amount of security at that time was over the top," agrees Roy Bennett:

It was embarrassing and unnecessary. This was the beginning of the negative side, because up to that point there was always this interrelationship between the band and the crew. Although the band still associated, it was just between Prince and everybody, all of a sudden a wall came up. It was just the security was over the top. It just slowed me down getting in to see him sometimes. I would go on in there, but suddenly you felt like you had to make an appointment with the king, and it was never like that before. It was still me and it was still him, so it changed. He retreated quickly because he saw what was happening. It was everything against what he believed in. You know, the stardom and all that stuff. He's a complex man.

The list of non-*Purple Rain* album songs regularly featured on the tour included "Irresistible Bitch" and "Possessed," which were not played at the beginning of the tour but were performed in December and into 1985 quite regularly. As the tour progressed, additional tracks were also added, including "Let's Pretend We're Married," which was done briefly; a coda of "International Lover"; and "Do Me, Baby," which predated *1999.* "Free" and "How Come U Don't Call Me Anymore?" (both *1999*-era tracks) were often played as part of his piano set.

MONDAY, NOVEMBER 5, 1984

Venue: Joe Louis Arena (Detroit, Michigan)
Capacity: 18,533 (sold out)

> *I don't know many artists who have the patience to sit there and watch everything unless they have a goal—and his goal was always to modify. Modify, modify, modify.—*Jill Jones

After practically every performance, Prince would gather various band members and others in the crew to watch a videotape of the evening's show. "I think he gets bored," explains Jill Jones. "He's a Gemini. I think he got bored just singing it all the time, and that's probably where that obsession comes with watching a show after you've completed it."

Prince would alter the show during the piano solo. It gave him the chance to stretch out and play some songs that were inspiring him at that moment. During the tour he'd use this section of the concert to debut songs from future projects and dip into his more obscure catalog to play some of his non-LP B-sides.

The three members of Apollonia 6 (Brenda Bennett, Apollonia, and Susan Moonsie) guested onstage during this performance.

WEDNESDAY, NOVEMBER 7, 1984

Venue: Joe Louis Arena (Detroit, Michigan)
Capacity: 18,533 (sold out)

THURSDAY, NOVEMBER 8, 1984

Venue: Joe Louis Arena (Detroit, Michigan)
Capacity: 18,533 (sold out)

FRIDAY, NOVEMBER 9, 1984

Venue: Joe Louis Arena (Detroit, Michigan)
Capacity: 18,533 (sold out)

SUNDAY, NOVEMBER 11, 1984

Venue: Joe Louis Arena (Detroit, Michigan)
Capacity: 18,533 (sold out)

MONDAY, NOVEMBER 12, 1984

Venue: Joe Louis Arena (Detroit, Michigan)
Capacity: 18,533 (sold out)

WEDNESDAY, NOVEMBER 14, 1984

Venue: Greensboro Coliseum (Greensboro, North Carolina)
Capacity: 14,877 (sold out)

THURSDAY, NOVEMBER 15, 1984

Venue: Greensboro Coliseum (Greensboro, North Carolina)
Capacity: 14,877 (sold out)

Alan Leeds invited his brother Eric to attend this show and bring his horn. Prince lent Eric one of his fur coats to wear onstage and invited him to play on "Baby I'm a Star." Eric remembered:

> I asked him what key it was in, and it was a good thing I did, because as many years as I'd been playing clubs, this was one of the first experiences I'd ever had in that kind of a situation, and just the immensity of the sound. It was just one big wash conglomerate. This huge glob of sound that was coming out of the sidefills and I would not even have been able to determine what key it was in, because it was just too much information to try to figure it out. So I knew we were in D, so, he said, "You got it!" And of course, he gave me my trial by fire, because he completely cut the whole band off at one point and just left me hanging, completely in front of fifteen thousand people, entirely acapella, and I loved it. It was great![11]

FRIDAY, NOVEMBER 16, 1984

Venue: Greensboro Coliseum (Greensboro, North Carolina)
Capacity: 14,877 (sold out)

A show in Richmond, Virginia, was canceled to add this extra show in Greensboro.

SUNDAY, NOVEMBER 18, 1984

Venue: Capital Centre (Landover, Maryland)
Capacity: 19,026 (sold out)

MONDAY, NOVEMBER 19, 1984

Venue: Capital Centre (Landover, Maryland)
Capacity: 19,026 (sold out)

TUESDAY, NOVEMBER 20, 1984

Venue: Capital Centre (Landover, Maryland)
Capacity: 19,026 (sold out)

"I Would Die 4 U" was scheduled to be released as a single, so a promotional video had to be created. Because Prince was on tour and had little time to create a new video, it was decided to tape part of his live show at the Capital Centre. This worked well because Warner Bros. had shifted from promoting the film to promoting the album (which had been at number 1 on the charts for fifteen weeks since entering at the top of the *Billboard* listings on August 4), the tour, and the *Purple Rain* home video, which had been released the previous day on VHS and Betamax. A music video featuring Prince's live performance covered all of those bases. The song had been played the previous night but the band missed several cues. The recording from this evening was used to create the music video.

THURSDAY, NOVEMBER 22, 1984

Venue: the Spectrum (Philadelphia, Pennsylvania)
Capacity: 18,639 (sold out)

During the sound check for this concert, Prince spent some time teaching the band how he wanted to add a spoken section in which he discussed sexual temptation. The spoken parts of this were eventually included in "Temptation," a track he would record in December.

The spoken section would be performed during this concert before "Let's Pretend We're Married."

FRIDAY, NOVEMBER 23, 1984

Venue: the Spectrum (Philadelphia, Pennsylvania)
Capacity: 18,639 (sold out)

SATURDAY, NOVEMBER 24, 1984

Venue: the Spectrum (Philadelphia, Pennsylvania)
Capacity: 18,639 (sold out)

MONDAY, NOVEMBER 26, 1984

Venue: Capital Centre (Landover, Maryland)
Capacity: 19,026 (sold out)

The tour headed back to Washington, DC—Landover is just outside the city—for four more sold-out shows.

WEDNESDAY, NOVEMBER 28, 1984

"I Would Die 4 U" is released as a single, backed with "Another Lonely Christmas." It would peak at number 8 on the *Billboard* charts.

WEDNESDAY, NOVEMBER 28, 1984

Venue: Capital Centre (Landover, Maryland)
Capacity: 19,026 (sold out)

THURSDAY, NOVEMBER 29, 1984 (MORNING)

Venue: Gallaudet College Field House, Washington, DC
Capacity: 3,100 (full house)

One of the students there had made a cutout cardboard guitar for him. I heard that when Prince left, he was reduced to tears.—Brad Marsh

A surprise concert was scheduled for the morning at Gallaudet College (now Gallaudet University), a school for the deaf and hard of hearing in Washington, DC. During the show, Prince's lyrics were interpreted via sign language from the stage. "I remember we went to Gallaudet, the school for the deaf [in Washington, DC] and did the entire show in their auditorium, and it was incredible," reflected Wendy Melvoin. "There were huge monitors on the floor in the audience so the kids could feel the bottom end. I remember at least 25 signers in the audience who were watching us and signing all the words to every song. The kids loved it."[12]

Throughout his lifetime Prince was always dedicated to charity. On this tour, special $50 "Purple Circle" seats were made available for practically every show, with the money earmarked for the Marva Collins Preparatory School. It has been reported that Prince donated $500,000 to the school, in addition to the money collected for the Purple Circle tickets. This was something he'd do for his entire career, often without any fanfare or recognition. It was in Prince's nature to help those he felt truly needed the help, and he gave his money and time to charity work at a rate far beyond what has been reported.

Today's show was free for the students, but Prince paid everyone on the crew $100 each to put on the private performance. The show meant a lot to everyone involved, especially Prince; it was one of the few times he signed autographs. Once the show was over, everyone went back to the Capital Centre to prepare for the evening concert.

THURSDAY, NOVEMBER 29, 1984 (EVENING)

Venue: Capital Centre (Landover, Maryland)
Capacity: 19,026 (sold out)

FRIDAY, NOVEMBER 30, 1984

Venue: Capital Centre (Landover, Maryland)
Capacity: 19,026 (sold out)

My favorite time frame? With him, working with him, I'd say the Purple Rain *era, just because it was the most collaborative point with the band and I enjoyed that side of it. And then of course the massive success of it all, but there were trade-offs at that point, because you became very famous but at the same time you couldn't go in public without being recognized all the time, and people maybe bugging you in public places, so there's a trade-off then.* —Matt Fink[13]

Prince and the Revolution began this show by playing his 1981 track "Controversy" from behind the curtain. Because it didn't require choreographed lights or effects, this was likely Prince's way to stretch outside the straitjacket of the meticulously designed tour, and it was often the final song for his afternoon jam session/sound checks. It was also one of the rare instances that the full band played something from earlier than 1983.

In the first month of the tour, Prince and the Revolution had sold more than 363,000 tickets but had played in only four cities. The tour was incredibly successful, but it was moving very slowly through the country.

DECEMBER 1984

Venue: Maple Leaf Gardens (Toronto, Ontario, Canada)
Capacity: 17,500 (sold out)

It was always his decision to make show changes, and then if something had to change, we would rehearse it.—Matt Fink[1]

Prince played the first of two shows at Maple Leaf Gardens in Toronto, Ontario. This was the first time he'd performed outside the United States since 1981, and these were the only dates he performed outside the country during the *Purple Rain* tour. During the concert, he dipped into his archive by once again, adding songs like "I Wanna Be Your Lover" and "Dirty Mind" to his solo piano set, but he also looked ahead to the future when he performed an instrumental portion of the as yet unreleased "Under the Cherry Moon."

MONDAY, DECEMBER 3, 1984

Venue: Maple Leaf Gardens (Toronto, Ontario, Canada)
Capacity: 17,500 (sold out)

WEDNESDAY, DECEMBER 5, 1984

Venue: Richfield Coliseum (Richfield, Ohio)
Capacity: 18,200 (sold out)

This was the first of two performances in Richfield, Ohio, just outside of Cleveland.

THURSDAY, DECEMBER 6, 1984

"Temptation" (sound check, basic tracking)
Venue: Richfield Coliseum (Richfield, Ohio) (afternoon)
Producer: Prince | *Artist:* Prince | *Engineers:* David Tickle, Rob "Cubby" Colby, and Susan Rogers

> *[Prince] would write a song a day and we would record just about every day. When we were on the road, when we were playing places that we'd stay for a week at a time. The first day we'd set up, and then every other day we'd record the sound check. We had a recording truck with us all the time.*—David Tickle

With the tour in its second month, Prince was once again focused on creating new music, and the sound checks were fertile ground for him, as Susan Rogers recalled: "If we were in the same city, recording was always his priority. He'd come on stage at two o'clock in the afternoon as soon as the lines were plugged in. Before they had finished hanging the lighting and all that stuff and testing everything, he'd be on stage and he'd be rehearsing with the band."[2]

"He'd give everyone parts and start playing and we'd record stuff," adds the tour's sound engineer David Tickle. "Then it'd be time to do the show. We'd get ready to do the show, and after the show we'd go back into the studio to record the vocals on whatever we recorded in the afternoon and then basically mix it. I'd going to bed at like, eleven in the morning, back up by two in the afternoon. It was that kind of intensity."

For a few weeks, Prince had been teasing the audience with talk about "sexual temptation" at the beginning of "Let's Pretend We're Married," and he decided to fold those nonmusical comments into a new song called "Temptation."

The full song was rehearsed and recorded with the band on this afternoon, but Prince got frustrated and changed his mind after hearing it filtered through others. "Originally he was planning to have the Revolution record it because he rehearsed it at a sound check in Ohio," observes Sheila E.'s saxophone player, Eddie M., "but after the sound check, Alan Leeds comes up and says, 'Eddie, pack your bags. We're leaving after the show tonight.' Prince had a change of heart I guess, because we went to L.A. and he just tracked everything there."

"You're dealing with a situation where the guy can play all the instruments," explained Bobby Z. "He can do it fast. He hears it in his head. If he can teach you a part and you have a feel to it that he didn't have, then he'll use it. Otherwise, he can complete the entire work without saying a word to anybody. It's convenience."[3]

A show in Buffalo, New York, originally scheduled for the following day, had been rescheduled for December 17, leaving a small gap in Prince's itinerary. Because of the complexity and stress of a tour, the band usually enjoyed the days off that were scheduled so they could recharge. Prince was fed by music, and creating new music was something that renewed him. **"That's my life," Prince told Tavis Smiley in 1998. "I got into the music business because I loved playing so much. You don't really get into the business to be a star; at least I didn't. I didn't get into it to make a whole bunch of money or meet a whole bunch of women. Just so happens those are the things that came along with it. But I was always playing a lot."[4]**

Status: Today's faster version of "Temptation" was never completed and remains unreleased.

THURSDAY, DECEMBER 6, 1984

Venue: Richfield Coliseum (Richfield, Ohio) (evening)
Capacity: 18,200 (sold out)

FRIDAY, DECEMBER 7, 1984

"Temptation" (basic tracking and mix)
"I Would Die 4 U" (12-inch mix, additional vocals assumed)
Capitol Studios, Los Angeles, California | 11:00 a.m.–open (assumed)
Producer: Prince | *Artist:* Prince | *Engineer:* David Leonard

I feel if I can please myself musically, then I can please others, too.—Prince[5]

December 7 and 8 were days off scheduled for rest and travel, but Prince dedicated them to creating new music. It appears he wanted to finish his next album—which would let the world know that *Purple Rain* wasn't his only artistic statement—before the end of the year.

Many times Prince used the Revolution to help flesh out songs. Most of them were jam-based tracks that were built by having everyone contribute a part and noting what worked and what didn't. There were also times Prince preferred to record by himself. When asked in 1995 what trait Prince most deplored about himself, he replied: **"My inability to communicate my music. I hear it, but it has to go through someone else. That person may have had a bad day or may not think the same way I do."**[6]

"He was having some existential crisis going on at this time," recalls Susannah Melvoin. "He wanted a record that represented a bigger part of him, but I think he was frustrated because he couldn't access it well, and all of that became frustrating. He'd get belligerent, he'd be dismissive, he could be really, really, really tough. And you could tell by when he was in the studio and what he was doing."

With this in mind, Prince took "Temptation" into the studio and recorded it on his own—or at least mostly on his own. Eddie M. explains: "We recorded 'Temptation' because he had some really deep thoughts going on. He had a serious concept in his brain and I think that is why he didn't want the Revolution to record it."

Because of the gap in the schedule, Prince was able to travel to Los Angeles. He wanted to see one of the final shows of the Jacksons' Victory Tour at Dodger Stadium, and he brought Sheila E., Jerome Benton, and Eddie M., who remembers the reaction of Prince's unannounced arrival at the Jacksons' show: "The crowd was going crazy because [Prince] was walking down the middle and everyone's noticing him! It was kind of a tricky thing because I think Prince wanted to go and have his presence just rile Michael's fans."

The session began much earlier than usual so that Prince could attend the concert, and for the first time in several years, Prince booked a facility other than Sunset Sound in Los Angeles. He requested David Leonard to engineer the session at Capital Studios.

Since the basics for "Temptation" had been developed during the previous day's sound check, Prince easily recorded the entire song, with two exceptions: the final conversation between God and Prince, and Eddie M.'s sax work: "I came in at the end of the day and put saxophone on it and then went home. He had a lot of ideas: I think in certain parts of the song he had me start recording from the back of the room and recording while I was walking to the mic, and he had me just play something really wild and crazy. It was just like a musical. It was really interesting because when I finally saw it come together, I was like . . . 'Dude, I don't know what you are thinking!' (*laughs*) It was interesting because I went from this wild player in the beginning of the song, and ending giving it closure." Eddie recorded his parts from 2:00 p.m. to 4:00 p.m.

"I was glad I was able to play something that he wasn't able to play," continues Eddie. "He was always willing to help and give people opportunities, but no one knows the music better than him. He was the one who taught me that there are no such thing as mistakes. Don't fear mistakes, don't worry about bad notes. And that was a lesson well taught because you always grow up not wanting to squeak here and you don't want that, and that isn't how he records, and I really admired that. That becomes part of the song, like the old jazz cats or Motown stuff. It keeps it close to what it really is. He just puts it down. Too much time for him is not good."

The thirty-minute version of "I Would Die 4 U" was likely edited down for the 12-inch release during this session by David Leonard while Prince attended the Jacksons' concert, and vocal overdubs were probably added upon his return.

Status: "Temptation" (8:19) was released as the final song on *Around the World in a Day* in 1985. An acetate for the 12-inch version of "I Would Die 4 U" (10:20) was completed by Bernie Grundman Mastering on December 10, and the extended version was released on December 19, 1984, in the United States.

After his time at Capitol Studios, Prince left Los Angeles to rejoin the tour. He shared "Temptation" with the Revolution during their five-day stay in Illinois and explained to the band that once the album was released, he was going to retire for two years and spend his time "looking for the ladder."

Some members of the Revolution weren't happy with this decision. "We could have kept touring with *Purple Rain* for another six months in America, really milked it," reasoned Matt Fink. "We just did a six-month tour. We didn't do Europe or Japan or Australia, because Prince didn't want to go. He said, 'I'm tired of the road—that's it guys, we're taking two years off.' He said we'd be on the payroll, don't worry, you can all do whatever you want."[7]

Despite the success of the tour, Prince saw that there were problems. In a 1999 interview he opened up about his internal conflict and why he knew he had to change direction: **"We looked around and I knew we were lost. There was no place to go but down. You can never satisfy the need after that."**[8]

In a French documentary, Wendy Melvoin shared her thoughts about the way the world saw Prince, and more importantly, the way success had changed Prince: "We knew now that Prince wasn't only a musician, he was also an entertainment phenomenon, a star. We couldn't just hang out together anymore. . . . So it started to change then."[9]

"Things got a little more separate," agreed Fink. "We became more of an employee relationship to the boss. The friendship that we had maybe earlier on in the band sort of changed a bit."[10]

Prince was now a superstar, with constant headlines about the tour; the album still number 1 on the charts; the fourth single, "I Would Die 4 U," about to start its way toward the top 10; and the movie among the highest grossing films of the year. Prince was in a place he'd never been before, and everyone wanted a piece of him. He was constantly bombarded with requests for interviews, and he turned them all down.

"In order to write that much, and be that prolific, you must protect your psyche, because you go to this dangerous place, really easily and often," explained Susan Rogers. "You put up a wall, and you tell your management, 'Don't let anyone approach me. I've got my system. Here's the system that allows me to create. These are my people who I'm familiar with. These are my places. This is a system where, within this circle, I can create.' That allows you to have a very long career, because you've figured out an armor to protect yourself. Prince was smart enough, as a young man, to know what he'd need to do that if he wanted to have a long career, so he did it. But, to the outside world, he appeared as a big enigma."[11]

Prince limited access to anyone hoping to solve the mystery. He was a master of illusion, and any light shined on him as a person could potentially expose the secrets he'd hidden. It worked perfectly, but in his quest for secrecy and control, various members of his inner circle got hurt. "He just kind of shut himself off," recalls Roy Bennett:

He became a different person at that point. His whole personality, as far as being approachable, changed. Prior to that, he was pretty insular only to people outside, but he would always talk to us. Suddenly he became a lot more closed off, although I can't say, it just seemed it was the beginnings of it. At that point, I'd be up in the middle of the night because I knew that he'd call me at four in the morning to come and sit up in his room with him to watch some videos [of that evening's show] and stuff. It still was the interaction, but it started kind of drifting away a lot more. And I'm sure the pressure suddenly dropped on him a lot more. As soon as you get to the top there's a lot more pressure to perform and come up with more stuff.

[The band] all started to feel the distance when he started to break away from us. The difference between *1999* and *Purple Rain* was his ego.

Prince was still working with his band on new—or at least unreleased—music. During the sound checks in Chicago, he had the Revolution jam on songs like "Feline," which was now officially removed from *The Family* album. He would later reuse elements of it in "Holly Rock," released by Sheila E. in 1986.

Prince's focus had changed, and with the new album he was getting closer to a light at the end of the tunnel. He was obviously ecstatic about the upcoming project, and he began playing sections of "Condition of the Heart" during his piano set on the first night in Chicago. The rest of the tour would feature tastes and teases of the next chapter in his musical career.

SUNDAY, DECEMBER 9, 1984

Venue: Rosemont Horizon (Rosemont, Illinois)
Capacity: 18,138 (sold out)

This was the start of five concerts in Rosemont, Illinois, just outside of Chicago.

MONDAY, DECEMBER 10, 1984

Venue: Rosemont Horizon (Rosemont, Illinois)
Capacity: 18,138 (sold out)

TUESDAY, DECEMBER 11, 1984

Venue: Rosemont Horizon (Rosemont, Illinois)
Capacity: 18,138 (sold out)

THURSDAY, DECEMBER 13, 1984

Venue: Rosemont Horizon (Rosemont, Illinois)
Capacity: 18,138 (sold out)

FRIDAY, DECEMBER 14, 1984

Venue: Rosemont Horizon (Rosemont, Illinois)
Capacity: 18,138 (sold out)

This date was originally scheduled for a performance in Indianapolis, Indiana, but the popularity of the tour created a demand for a fifth show at the Rosemont Horizon. The Indianapolis concert was postponed until April 1, 1985.

SATURDAY, DECEMBER 15, 1984

Venue: Rupp Arena (Lexington, Kentucky)
Capacity: 22,347 (sold out)

MONDAY, DECEMBER 17, 1984

Venue: Memorial Auditorium (Buffalo, New York)
Capacity: 13,418 (likely sold out)

This show in Buffalo had been originally slated for December 7, but was postponed until this evening as the tour schedule shifted to accommodate the high ticket demand. December 17 and 18 were originally scheduled for performances at the Pittsburgh Civic Arena in Pittsburgh, Pennsylvania, but due to this rescheduling, both were canceled.

During the concert, a variation of "Ice Cream Castles" was added to the "Baby I'm a Star" jam. The chanted lyrics were "we are young / we're not old and we are funky," possibly a playful variation of the original lyrics from Jesse Johnson and Morris Day's "Old and Ignant," on which the song "Ice Cream Castles" was based.

TUESDAY, DECEMBER 18, 1984

Venue: Memorial Auditorium (Buffalo, New York)
Capacity: 13,418 (likely sold out)

WEDNESDAY, DECEMBER 19, 1984

The 12-inch single of "I Would Die 4 U" (10:15) is released, backed by a long version of "Another Lonely Christmas" (6:47). The 12-inch would chart on the *Billboard* Hot Dance/Disco list, peaking at number 50 on February 9, 1985.

THURSDAY, DECEMBER 20, 1984

Venue: St. Louis Arena (St. Louis, Missouri)
Capacity: 17,000 (likely sold out)

FRIDAY, DECEMBER 21, 1984

Venue: St. Louis Arena (St. Louis, Missouri)
Capacity: 17,000 (likely sold out)

SUNDAY, DECEMBER 23, 1984

Venue: Saint Paul Civic Center (Saint Paul, Minnesota)
Capacity: 17,516 (sold out)

Prince was back home, playing in the arena that had housed the final rehearsals for the tour. The performance was a sold-out series of concerts for those who'd known him longest and the number of tickets sold in this unprecedented five-night run of shows in the Twin Cities dwarfed that of any other artist.

MONDAY, DECEMBER 24, 1984 (MATINEE SHOW)

Venue: Saint Paul Civic Center, Saint Paul, Minnesota
Capacity: 17,516 (sold out)

An important insight about this era involves Prince's choice of which songs made the set list. For the most part Prince showcased music that largely ignored his past beyond the last two years. With only minor exceptions, Prince played songs that had been in the spotlight since January 1983, and to the newer fans there was little indication that he'd released any music before the *1999/Purple Rain* era. It was almost as if he'd drawn a line in the sand after *Controversy* and wanted everyone to focus on his current music only. "The interesting thing is when you have a massive hit record you get to start over," explained Susan Rogers. "This is what artists do. So when you have a record that totally says you've arrived, after you arrive, you get to start a new journey. You can think of *Purple Rain* as being a singular point, the apex of where Prince was. So now that he's shown the depth of what he can do, that he's hugely talented and very creative, now he has to show the breadth of it and how far he can go stylistically."[12]

In other words, Prince seemed to understand that his career would be seen in two very distinct phases—the era leading up to *1999/Purple Rain* and the era that was created by the releases of *1999/Purple Rain*—and the path he would forge was now completely uncharted. *Purple Rain* was his most intimate project and his most successful, and it is no coincidence that he never revealed as much about himself again; by seeking shelter, he never reached the same level of popularity. The price of exposing himself was very high and he was making plans to pull the curtain closed to regain control.

MONDAY, DECEMBER 24, 1984

"Temptation" (spoken part by Prince)
"Tamborine" (overdubs)

> "The Ladder" (edit)
> *Around the World in a Day* album compiled
> Mobile truck at Saint Paul Civic Center (Saint Paul, Minnesota) and at
>   Kiowa Trail home (Chanhassen, Minnesota) driveway | 11:00 p.m.–
>   5:00 a.m. (assumed)
> *Producer:* Prince | *Artist:* Prince | *Engineer:* Susan Rogers

When you're trying to change, you have to divorce yourself from the past. —Prince[13]

The matinee show was scheduled for Christmas Eve so it wouldn't interfere with anyone's Christmas plans—at least just about anyone's. For Prince and Susan Rogers, the concert was just the prelude to a very long day.

As usual, Prince recorded the show with the mobile unit. After the concert Prince asked Rogers to prepare for the final session for the album. She went back to the warehouse, gathered all the reels, and took them to her hotel room: "I was sitting alone with all those tapes, looking at all those boxes and I was thinking, 'There it is. I'm sitting in this room with the next Prince record. The last one sold eleven million; I have no idea how this will be received—maybe it will be the biggest-selling record he has ever had, maybe people will hate it, maybe his fans will be disappointed, maybe they'll love it and think it's genius. I'm sitting here looking at it.' To me it was such a profound moment, because there it was. These metal reels with oxide dust on it were his next record. You realized how many hopes, thoughts, genius, inspiration had gone into that."[14]

During this period Prince didn't maintain his home studio. He'd sold his console to Jesse Johnson and had to record outside of his home. Prince called Rogers to his house, and when she arrived the mobile unit was waiting in his driveway. He joined her in the truck, and they began the session with some voice work: "We did the very end of the record on 'Temptation,' where he has this conversation with God. Just the two of us. We set up a mic in the mobile truck and recorded that little bit."[15]

Although it is impossible to get inside Prince's mind, it is insightful that the final speech he recorded for his next project was a conversation with God, in which he humbly said, "Goodbye." It was as if he was expressing how tired he was and how overwhelmed he felt, putting the words he'd told his band into a song. Once again his music was reflecting his mood.

Minor overdubs, including vocals and probably a few finger cymbals, were added to other songs, including "Tamborine," until Prince decided that the tracks were complete. Now he had to structure the album. Rogers was cutting the tape with a razor, shuffling the numbers so that there was a flow to the album. In 1984, CDs were just starting to gain popularity, so the ultimate medium for sale was still the cassette or vinyl record. Compiling for those was a different task because, unlike today, the album/cassette had two sides and needed to build and crescendo on side one, then launch with a big song on side two and build again to the final track.

At some point during the compilation stage, the string interlude from "Our Destiny" was lifted and used prior to "The Ladder." The distant drums from "Our Destiny" can still be heard bleeding through when listening to "The Ladder" on a good pair of headphones.

"I think we finished around four or five in the morning on Christmas morning," recalled Rogers. "I know that Prince had a Christmas tree inside, but he had nobody over there at Christmas. He had some presents under the tree that people had given him, but I don't think he was too interested in them. He was mainly interested in getting his record cut together."[16]

The finished album was recorded to cassettes, and Rogers went back to her hotel room. This was the final documented recording session of the year. Because of the urgency to create this album and the speed in which it came together, it is the perfect snapshot of where Prince was at this very moment in his life. Like the album itself, he seemed filled with joy, with regret, with new love, and with conflicts both external and internal. Once again, his music spoke for him.

The tour would resume on the day after Christmas.

Prince explained to Eric Leeds (after seeing the faces of some industry people who weren't happy with the album): "Well, sometimes you know right away that maybe it just doesn't reach some people, but that's okay. It still was where I was at at the time. It was what I wanted to do and this is the way I want to hear the music."[17]

WEDNESDAY, DECEMBER 26, 1984

Venue: Saint Paul Civic Center (Saint Paul, Minnesota)
Capacity: 17,516 (sold out)

Prince performed "Another Lonely Christmas" at the December 26 show. It would be the only time it was ever played live, and its inclusion probably conveyed more about Prince's state of mind than anyone understood at the time.

THURSDAY, DECEMBER 27, 1984

Venue: Saint Paul Civic Center (Saint Paul, Minnesota)
Capacity: 17,516 (sold out)

FRIDAY, DECEMBER 28, 1984

Venue: Saint Paul Civic Center (Saint Paul, Minnesota)
Capacity: 17,516 (sold out)

SUNDAY, DECEMBER 30, 1984

Venue: Reunion Arena (Dallas, Texas)
Capacity: 18,276 (approximately 17,758 tickets sold based on three-show average)

The tour shifted to Dallas, Texas, for a three-night stay.

MONDAY, DECEMBER 31, 1984

Venue: Reunion Arena (Dallas, Texas)
Capacity: 18,276 (approximately 17,758 tickets sold based on three-show average)

I am energized by music. Music is my reason for existence.
Writing it, playing it, listening to it.—Prince[18]

To the casual observer, Prince seemed happy to have achieved all his dreams, but as an artist—at least according to those close to him—his passion for *Purple Rain* had diminished. "He was bored," Wendy Melvoin later revealed to Alan Light. "He gave it everything onstage, and he was always in that. But he was gone, he was uninterested, and he had moved on."[19]

For a man whose entire life appeared to be focused on creating new music, the prospect of having to repeat the same songs over and over for the rest of his career must have been like a prison sentence.

Prince seemed to be concentrating on his next move and how it would be received, and he was focused on advancing beyond *Purple Rain* as quickly as possible. **"I'm about the present and moving forward. New joke, new anecdote, new lesson to be discovered,"** Prince told *Entertainment Weekly* in 2004. **"You know that old lady in *Sunset Boulevard*, trapped in her mansion and past glories? Getting ready for her close-up? I don't run with that."**[20] He would have to cut the cord to this era at some point. He could either allow the industry to pressure him into changing or do it on his own terms, so he made the choice to control his own destiny. History has shown that Prince preferred to make his own mistakes rather than follow anyone else's advice. "He told me when I first joined the band, 'Don't ever argue with me,'" recalled Brown Mark. "'Even if I'm wrong, I'm right.' Those were his exact words."[21]

Having achieved what he desired with *Purple Rain*, Prince was growing impatient now that his next project was complete. The "three-year obligation" he'd originally presented to members of the Revolution was being cut almost in half. It was obvious to practically anyone around him that he wanted to get the new album out quickly, but he had to finish his responsibilities, so he begrudgingly continued. Prince seemed eager to put "the Kid" aside and release more music from Prince. Before this show Prince played the completed *Around the World in a Day* album to his band and to those close enough to be in his inner circle, confirming that he was wrapping up this phase and moving past *Purple Rain* after he fulfilled his current obligations.

Prince had opened his heart and his mind to the influence of others in a way he never had before, and *Around the World in a Day* was the product of that. No one expected this seismic shift when he started working in the direction that David Coleman had presented to him. Lisa Coleman explains how her brother altered the direction of Prince's career: "Prince was inspired by David and the creative flow we all had together, and that was why the *Purple Rain* tour ended after only six months."

Over the last two years Prince had appeared onstage at least 118 times and sold more than 11 million albums, not including more than 1.5 million in sales for his associate artists. He'd written and recorded between 100 and 150 songs, many of which would be divided among albums by Sheila E., the Family, the Time, and Apollonia 6, and singles for the Bangles, Stevie Nicks and Sheena Easton. The music he recorded during this time found its way onto two full Prince albums (and tracks for various future albums) and multiple B-sides, and included more than an album's worth of unreleased songs. Each of these projects had been influenced by someone or something around him. Prince was the musical architect, but he was always somewhat dependent on the world being filtered through those closest to him. "I think everyone contributed to the sound and to the feeling in the music," explains Peggy Leonard, who participated in the majority of tracks he'd recorded over the last two years. "He couldn't have done it alone. Not entirely. There were a lot of good people involved."

"I think it was the combination of who and what Prince is as a unique and once-in-a-lifetime artist, with the particular time period, and the bands that he surrounded himself with through that period," noted Dez Dickerson. "I don't know if anyone will ever reproduce that."[22]

Along the road from cult hero to international superstar, he had selectively invited a small circle of people into his life who shared his vision and helped him achieve his goals, but more than a few were left behind in the wake of his new success. Many of them had known him as far back as high school and felt able to voice their opinions to him, but as his fame grew he distanced himself from several of those who were influential to him, including Vanity, Morris Day, Jimmy Jam, Terry Lewis, Monte Moir, Jesse Johnson, Dez Dickerson, André Cymone, and Don Batts. Susan Moonsie, Brenda Bennett, and Apollonia were all on their way out as well, and he would be drawn closer to the shrinking group of people he had chosen to know him intimately—not just physically but emotionally, which was the hardest thing for him to share.

Prince has stated, "**I miss nothing and no one. Attachment is stagnation.**"[23] The reality was that once those who had been close to him were gone and contact between Prince and the outside world became limited, he would have to be even more selective about those who helped him create his songs. "He became a little more paranoid with newer people coming in," acknowledges Jill Jones. "He didn't really understand who to really trust. And as it progressed on, I think he had a harder time. He wanted you to be there because you loved him. Even the men. He wanted them to love *him*, not just because he could make them money. And as he got more successful, I think he started to realize people were coming because he could make them money."

"He was incredibly suspicious and paranoid," explains Susannah Melvoin. "Always. That's why he never paid you. He wouldn't pay you. Because if he didn't pay you and you stuck around, you were loyal. If he paid you and you threatened, in any way, it'd be like this person is only here for the money."

What Prince didn't seem to comprehend was that those around him *did* love him. Almost without exception, each of those in his inner circle blocked for him, shielded him from harm, and preserved his legacy and his image, and they still do to this day. Those who were close enough to him to call him their friend could separate the superstar image from the insecure artist who needed reassurance, finding ways to make sure he was safe and protected from those who would take advantage of him.

Once those friends and coworkers were gone, he would rely on new people, new influences, new stories, and new experiences to feed his insatiable demand for new music, and as always, those around him would be reflected in his songs. "I think if you listen to his records you learn a lot about him," explained Jimmy Jam in a 2003 BBC documentary. "That he's a very complex guy with a lot of different sides, as many people are. But I think that he is able to express that through his music, and that's the one thing that he's always been able to do."[24]

As Prince himself said, "**All my life is in my records.**"[25]

EPILOGUE

His competition at that time was Michael Jackson, Bruce Springsteen and Madonna. Now there have been other artists since that have seemingly done it all in the studio, but they don't really do it all. They are not writing, producing and arranging all of their material, and playing every instrument and writing music for movies at the same time and writing for other artists. Prince was doing all this and designing every aspect of his live show. He even designed his own clothes. To do all this and be on top for as long as he was and to have that many hit records and exercising that much control and power. . . over that many aspects of your music, there's no precedent for that. —Susan Rogers[1]

The next few months of 1985 would include the release of his recently finished *Around the World in a Day* album, the recording of a second album for Sheila E. (*Romance 1600*) during the current tour, and the debut of the lone album by the Family. The only common link between these projects—besides being created and overseen by Prince—was that none of them involved *Purple Rain.* He would receive many awards in the spring for *Purple Rain*, including an Academy Award for Best Original Song Score, but he was quickly moving away from almost everything that anchored him to this era. In fact, he would only do one more tour with the Revolution before permanently disbanding them. After the 1984–1985 tour, Prince shelved most of the *Purple Rain*–era songs from his live performances for years: "Take Me with U" and "Baby I'm a Star" for five years, "The Beautiful Ones" for eight years, "Darling Nikki" and "I Would Die 4 U" for twelve years, and "Computer Blue" for fifteen years, although it was never performed as a full-blown song again after 1985. It was reduced to a coda in "When Doves Cry" when he toured in 2000–2001. "I think he had fears of being typecast as Mr. Purple Rain," suggested Alan Leeds. "By the time that tour was over, he was so sick of that music and that whole concept."[2]

Purple Rain was Prince's greatest success, but it set the bar so high that he seemed resigned not to attempt to duplicate it. **"In some ways *Purple Rain* scared me,"** he explained to the Electrifying Mojo in 1986. **"It was too successful, and no matter what I do, I'll never top it."** He admitted that **"it'll be hanging around my neck as long as I'm making music."**[3] In retrospect, it is easy to see the signs that he was feeling career stagnation, and his reflex was to hastily proceed beyond *Purple Rain*.

"From the moment I met him to when I stopped working with him, he never really changed, except that he became a powerful mogul, which was probably hard for him," confides engineer Peggy Leonard. "He was a little bit nicer when he came here and didn't have a car, and then when he rented limos his attitude certainly changed, but he was always Prince. He knew who he was and he knew where he was going."

In the two years detailed in this book, Prince went from a darling of the critics to one of the biggest rock stars on the planet. He had achieved almost everything he'd wanted, but the price he was being asked to pay was higher than he imagined. He was a man who seemed to enjoy being able to say anything and try anything because he was under the radar, but once his ability to blend into a crowd was destroyed by the harsh spotlight *Purple Rain* shined on him, he would never again enjoy the freedom of being the underdog; from that point on, everything he did and everything he said would be dissected and studied, and with that, his career path was in danger of being hijacked.

Unfortunately, what started as a revolution had turned into routine. Prince's eccentricity was not only accepted, it was expected, as if everyone had figured him out. He had built a career out of mystery and remaining one step ahead of his fans and the critics. He seemed to revel in the controversy regarding whether he was black or white, straight or gay. And now, with *Purple Rain*, everyone was putting the clues together. He became accessible in a way he'd never experienced, and he ran the risk of becoming boring. Pop music is littered with the forgotten careers of one-trick ponies, because very few artists can survive the public's extreme adoration because in most cases the fans burn out and migrate to the next rising star. Prince probably sensed that the knives were being sharpened, even from those who praised him earlier.

He was "the Kid" to many of his new fans, and because they'd seen his (supposedly autobiographical) movie, many of them felt they knew him and that there were no more secrets to be revealed, but the reality was the Kid was just another character he'd created. It's no coincidence that he was the only musician in the movie who didn't use his actual name. The Kid was no more real than Jamie Starr, Alexander Nevermind, or any of the other alternate identities he'd manufactured, and now he was ready to shed that character and move on to the next.

Few others in popular music have experienced the epic heights Prince reached during 1984. Now that he was loved by the masses, he had to choose to either continue to serve them, responding to what they wanted while enjoying the undeniable riches, or turn his back on what he'd created and trust himself to rebuild it again by his own rules. This synchronicity of product and popularity made him financially wealthy, and it also made a large deposit into his artistic bank, giving him the freedom to decide his path. Prince probably instinctively knew that if he decided to allow his career to simply coast, it would destroy him creatively. As usual, he looked for a new direction. Externally, he would continue this tour, but as it neared the end in the coming months, he would change his iconic hair and the style of his clothing. Internally, Prince was going through a "great spiritual revelation."[4] In 1995 he explained to *Q* magazine that this sort of thing happened occasionally in his life, clarifying that it was similar to the spiritual changes he went through when creating his 1988 album *Lovesexy* as well as when he changed his name to a symbol in 1993.

On New Year's Eve exactly two years earlier, Prince played to a sold-out crowd for one night at the Reunion Arena in Dallas, Texas, but a second show the following night was canceled for unknown reasons. At that time his *1999* tour was selling modestly, but with the album already sliding back down the charts, a month off the road was scheduled to allow him time to regroup. On this night in 1984 Prince and the Revolution had the number 1 album on the charts, and they were in the middle of a sold-out three-night stand at the very same Dallas arena.

That stage in Dallas may have been the same, but the stage of his career was completely different. As Prince stood there and the last chords of "Purple Rain" and "Auld Lang Syne" echoed in the halls, he was saying good-bye to more than the previous year; he was celebrating the passing of something he'd created. The last of the purple confetti was still in the air when Prince left the stage, and the crowd was cheering for more, as if it would never end. Although few people outside his circle knew what was happening at the time, Prince was trusting his gut and resetting his internal compass, having faith that the world would find him and join him again. He voluntarily lit the match that would burn down practically everything he'd spent the last two years building.

Once again Prince, the twenty-six-year-old musical genius, was at a crossroads . . . but that's a story for another book.

NOTE ON RESEARCH

This book has been a gigantic, meticulous puzzle, and to understand it, it is important to explain how the research was done. Sunset Sound supplied their daily work orders for Prince's studio sessions (as well as those for all of his protégé projects). There are a few sessions that are missing, but when there was doubt, I've tried to fill in the blanks with the information supplied by Warner Bros. about the contents of their vault, and many of the dates that are listed as "assumed" are based on their dating system. When there is no specific date mentioned in the research from those sources, I've relied on data from the Library of Congress, personal logs of those who worked on the music, newspaper articles, session notes from multiple unions, and various other sources. For those sessions that couldn't be confirmed, I listed the most likely date as an estimate. I did the same when there was no indication of who worked on the sessions behind the scenes; I referred to them as assumed if the information was likely. Personal details were filled in using quotes from the people who were in the recording studio with Prince during the sessions.

I've gone to great lengths to confirm the running times to any tracks mentioned. The timing for the released songs were relatively easy to confirm, but the unreleased tracks and alternate versions are more problematic. Some of these are ballpark figures supported by information from the Warner Bros. vault or studio notes, but many of them were verified by actually listening to the songs whenever possible. Please understand that any sources that exist are thirty years old, and tape speed, drift, and wear may cause the timing to be off by a few seconds. There are likely additional edits and mixes that I was not able to locate.

The quotes used in this book were obtained by me, unless otherwise noted.

My personal research involved more than three hundred hours of interviews with the people involved. I am eternally grateful to those who have opened up their memories to me. I've tried my best to honor each and every one of them by fact-checking and verifying as much as I could. My intent has been to create a fair and nuanced account of everyone's involvement in Prince's history, and I've relied on the information thoughtfully provided by each of them. I also conducted brief follow-up interviews to check the facts as additional information was unearthed. When the subjects weren't available, I relied on the extensive library of interviews in the public record, including more than two thousand articles, multiple books, and numerous podcasts and radio shows from around the world.

For the interviews I conducted for this project, I generally refer to the conversations in the present tense ("She remembers"), and quotes I use from outside sources are referred to in the past tense ("She remembered").

NOTES

PREFACE

1. Spike Lee, "The Artist," *Interview*, May 1997, accessed March 5, 2017, http://www.interviewmagazine.com/music/new-again-prince.
2. Bobby Z Rivkin, in Marc Weingarten, "Prince: The Purple Gang," *Mojo*, February 1997, 48.
3. Eric Leeds, interview by Alan Freed for *Uptown* magazine/Per Nilsen, Los Angeles, CA, October 15, 1993.
4. Prince on 3RDEYEGIRL Twitter account, November 22, 2013. Account now deleted.
5. Leeds, interview by Freed, October 15, 1993.
6. Will Hodgkinson, "All the Critics Love U In . . . London!?" *Mojo*, April 2014, 84.

JANUARY 1983

1. Prince, interview by Larry King, *Larry King Live*, CNN, December 10, 1999, accessed April 21, 2016, https://www.youtube.com/watch?v=m8mg7CxAYUM.
2. Alan Leeds, interview by Alan Freed for *Uptown* magazine/Per Nilsen, Minneapolis, MN, January 20, 1994.
3. Brian Raftery, "Prince: The Oral History of *Purple Rain*," *Spin*, July 2009, 59.
4. Michael Goldberg, "*Purple Rain* Star Morris Day Goes It Alone," *Rolling Stone*, September 13, 1984, 41.
5. "Jesse Johnson on *Video Soul*," 1986, accessed March 8, 2017, https://www.youtube.com/watch?v=gIy6eB0C350.

6. Ronin Ro, *Prince: Inside the Music and the Masks* (New York: St. Martin's, 2011).

7. Pamela Littlejohn, review of *1999*, *Los Angeles Sentinel*, January 20, 1983.

8. Mike Ragogna, "Chatting with Cobra Starship's Ryland Blackinton, Plus Jimmy Jam and Jason Reeves, and the Real Tuesday Weld Video Exclusive," *Huffington Post*, November 15, 2011, accessed March 5, 2017, http://www.huffingtonpost.com/mike-ragogna/chatting-with-cobra-stars_b_1094086.html.

9. Monte Moir, interview by Leo Sidran, *The Third Story Podcast with Leo Sidran*, podcast audio, May 5, 2016, accessed August 6, 2016, http://www.third-story.com/listen/on-prince.

10. Anthony DeCurtis, "Burning Down the House," *Rolling Stone,* May 27, 2004, 58.

11. Robert Hilburn, "Mixed Emotions: Prince on the Music," *Musician*, September 1983, 58.

12. Priya Elan, "Purple Reign," *Guardian*, September 20, 2008, accessed March 6, 2017, https://www.theguardian.com/music/2008/sep/20/1.

13. Jake Brown, *Prince in the Studio (1975–1995)* (Phoenix: Amber Communications Group, 2010).

14. Prince, interview by Stephen Fargnoli, MTV, November 15, 1985, accessed August 18, 2016, http://www.dailymotion.com/video/x49h7vy.

15. Dean Van Nguyen, "Big Time Morris Day," *Wax Poetics*, winter 2012, 50.

16. Jimmy Jam, "Soul Corner," *P3 Soul*, date unknown, accessed June 23, 2017, https://www.youtube.com/watch?v=OScQ3unXnWY&feature=youtu.be.

17. Jellybean Johnson, interview by Alan Freed for *Uptown* Magazine/Per Nilsen, Minneapolis, MN, February 2, 1995.

18. Miles Marshall Lewis, "Prince Hits N Runs N Talks!" *Ebony*, December 22, 2015, accessed March 2, 2016, https://www.facebook.com/notes/housequake/prince-hits-n-runs-n-talks-ebony-interview-dec-22-2015/916986788385046.

19. "Jesse Johnson on the Power of Penetration," *Ebony*, August 8, 2011, accessed March 11, 2017, http://prince.org/msg/5/364813.

20. Morris Day, interview by Tom Neeham, *The Sounds of Film*, WUSB, April 28, 2016, accessed June 23, 2017, https://www.youtube.com/edit?o=U&video_id=t7ceI27JPSI.

21. Michael A. Gonzales, "Rock Star Jesse Johnson," *Wax Poetics*, winter 2012, 44.

22. Morris Day, in *The Original 7ven*, directed by Lee Librado (Los Angeles, CA: Chronology Entertainment and Flyte Tyme Productions, 2011), DVD.

23. Margena A. Christian, "The Time," *Ebony*, July 2012, 126.

24. Morris Day, interview by Amy Scott, VH1 Classic, June 19, 2004.

25. Chaz Lipp, "An Interview with Jimmy Jam of The Original 7ven," *Morton Report*, April 13, 2012, accessed March 4, 2017, http://www.themortonreport.com/entertainment/music/an-interview-with-jimmy-jam-of-the-original-7ven.

26. Christian, "The Time," 127.

27. Dave Hill, *Prince: A Pop Life* (New York: Harmony Books, 1989), 102.

28. "Jerome Benton of the Funk group 'The TIME' interview w/TheFunkcenter," *Funk Chronicles with Dr. Turk Logan*, April 16, 2015, accessed September 27, 2015, https://www.youtube.com/watch?v=_yfnvX8yF9o.

29. Morris Day, in Michael Patrick Welch, "Interview with Morris Day of the Time (OffBeat, Sept. 2012)," michaelpatrickwelch.org, October, 2, 2012, accessed March 1, 2017, https://michaelpatrickwelch.org/2012/10/02/interview-with-morris-day-of-the -time-offbeat-sept-2012.

30. Debby Miller, "The Secret Life of America's Sexiest One-Man Band," *Rolling Stone*, April 28, 1983, 23.

31. James Hunter, "Soul Survivors," *Vibe*, April 1995, 61.

32. Morris Day, in *The Original 7ven*, directed by Lee Librado (Los Angeles, CA: Chronology Entertainment and Flyte Tyme Productions, 2011), DVD.

33. Steve Perry, "Prince: The Purple Decade," *Musician*, November 1988, 85.

34. "Jellybean! The Time's Jellybean Johnson Talks about Prince, the Minneapolis Sound and the Blues (Part 1)," *Beldon's Blues Point* (blog), March 11, 2013, accessed March 3, 2017, http://beldonsbluespoint.blogspot.com/2013/03/in-2007-or-2008-i -saw-jellybean-johnson.html.

35. Prince, interview by the Electrifying Mojo, *The Electrifying Mojo*, WHYT, June 7, 1986, accessed February 14, 2016, https://www.youtube.com/ watch?v=NJZCoxZ5COY.

36. Jellybean Johnson, interview with Alan Freed for *Uptown* magazine/Per Nilsen, Minneapolis, MN, February 16, 1995.

37. Moir, interview with Leo Sidran.

38. Hill, *Prince*, 119.

39. Hill, *Prince*, 118.

40. Prince, interview by the Electrifying Mojo.

41. Leeds, interview by Freed, January 20, 1994.

42. Leeds, interview by Freed, January 20, 1994.

43. Lynn Van Matre, "'I'm Out and Everything Is Cool,' Says Morris Day," *Chicago Tribune*, September 9, 1984.

44. Mobeen Azhar, *Hunting for Prince's Vault*, BBC Radio, March 21, 2015, ac- cessed March 5, 2016, https://www.mixcloud.com/Emancipatio/hunting-for-princes -vault-bbc-documentary-by-mobeen-azhar-march-2015.

45. Mary Aloe, "Clothes of Passion Vanity," *Rock*, February 1985, 29.

46. Aloe, "Clothes of Passion Vanity," 29.

47. Jellybean Johnson, interview by Freed, February 16, 1995.

48. Geoffrey Himes, "Prince Sustains Dramatic Opening with Music That Obliter- ates Rules," *Baltimore Evening Sun*, March 7, 1983.

49. Pete Bishop, "Was Prince Worth Waiting For?" *Pittsburgh Press*, March 1, 1983.

50. Miller, "The Secret Life of America's Sexiest One-Man Band," 73.

51. Jellybean Johnson, interview by Freed, February 2, 1995.

52. Brown, *Prince in the Studio.*

53. "Vanity 6 Lives Out Daring Fantasies on Stage," *Jet*, January 1983, 60.

54. Susan Rogers, interview by Alan Freed for *Uptown* magazine/Per Nilsen, Los Angeles, CA, March 26, 1995.

55. Jon Bream and Chris Riemenschneider, "Prince: An Oral History," *Minneapolis Star Tribune*, March 14, 2004.

56. Rogers, interview by Freed, March 26, 1995.

57. Brown, *Prince in the Studio.*

58. Elysa Gardner, "Prince: 'If I Knew the Things I Know Now Before, I Wouldn't Be in the Music Industry,'" *Los Angeles Times*, July 14, 1996, accessed March 7, 2017, http://www.latimes.com/entertainment/music/la-et-ms-prince-archive-19960714-story .html.

59. Jellybean Johnson, interview by Freed, February 16, 1995.

60. Prince, lyrics to "The Dance Electric," performed by Prince and the Revolution, *Purple Rain Deluxe* (Expanded Edition), NPG Records/Warner Bros., 547374-2, 2017, compact disc.

61. Susan Rogers, interview by Alan Freed for *Uptown* magazine/Per Nilsen, Los Angeles, CA, December 1994.

62. Rogers, interview by Freed, December 1994.

63. Prince, lyrics to "The Dance Electric."

64. Dez Dickerson, interview by Joe Kelley, *Upper Room with Joe Kelley*, WVOF, March 19, 2004, accessed March 1, 2017, http://www.upperroomwithjoekelley.com/ mpls.html.

65. Ro, *Prince.*

66. Dez Dickerson, interview, WTVF, April 21, 2016, accessed March 1, 2017, https://www.youtube.com/watch?v=epQZ_izbdcc.

67. Martin Townsend, "Puppet Master Prince by His Right Hand Man, Dez Dickerson," *No. 1*, February 2, 1985, 11.

68. Townsend, "Puppet Master Prince," 11.

69. Townsend, "Puppet Master Prince," 11.

70. Dez Dickerson, interview with Michael Dean, *The Prince Podcast*, podcast audio, January 2, 2013, accessed June 25, 2017, http://podcastjuice.net/30-days-of -podcasting-day-9-dez-dickerson.

71. Dickerson, *Upper Room with Joe Kelley.*

72. Hill, *Prince*, 122.

73. Jim Maloney, "Wendy & Lisa: After the Revolution Comes the Challenge," *Music Connection*, February 22–March 6, 1987, 13.

74. Lisa Coleman, interview by Jim DeRogatis and Greg Kot, *Sound Opinions*, WBEZ, July 24, 2009, accessed March 5, 2016, http://www.soundopinions.org/topic/ wendyandlisa.

75. Elan, "Purple Reign."

76. Jem Aswad, "The Revolution Remembers Their Last Moments with Prince—and the First Time They Heard *Purple Rain*," *Billboard*, December 12, 2016, accessed March 6, 2017, http://www.billboard.com/articles/events/year-in-music-2016/7604454/the-revolution-prince-final-moments.

77. Craig Marks and Rob Tannenbaum, *I Want My MTV: The Uncensored Story of the Music Video Revolution* (New York: Dutton, 2011).

78. Moir, interview with Leo Sidran.

FEBRUARY 1983

1. Margena A. Christian, "The Time," *Ebony*, July 2012, 127.

2. Jellybean Johnson, interview by Alan Freed for *Uptown* magazine/Per Nilsen, Minneapolis, MN, February 16, 1995.

3. "Jesse Johnson on *Video Soul*," 1986, accessed March 8, 2017, https://www.youtube.com/watch?v=gIy6eB0C350.

4. Mark Brown, interview by Questlove, *Questlove Supreme*, Pandora, September 28, 2016, accessed October 4, 2016, https://www.pandora.com/station/play/3642532478040643917.

5. Karen Glover, "Morris Day," *Black Beat*, April 1985, 43.

6. Timothy White, *Rock Lives: Profiles & Interviews* (London: Ombibus, 1991), 622.

7. Rya Backer, "Stevie Nicks Wants to Work with Timbaland, Opens Up about Collaborating with Prince," *MTV News*, April 2, 2009, accessed February 14, 2016, http://www.mtv.com/news/articles/1608437/20090402/fleetwood_mac.jhtm.

8. Backer, "Stevie Nicks."

9. Jon Bream, "Stevie Nicks' New Whirl," *Minneapolis Star Tribune*, August 23, 2011, accessed March 7, 2017, http://www.startribune.com/stevie-nicks-new-whirl/128097743.

10. Prince, interview with Cubby and Cindy, WKTU, December 13, 2010, accessed January 17, 2012, http://ktu.iheart.com/iplaylist/artist/5182.

11. Stevie Nicks, *VH1 Storytellers*, VH1, August 18, 1998, accessed March 6, 2017, http://rockalittle.com/storytellerstranscript.htm.

12. White, *Rock Lives*, 622.

13. Stevie Nicks, *Timespace* tourbook, 1991, accessed March 12, 2017, http://www.buckinghamnicks.info/words-wildheart.

14. Stevie Nicks, interview, *Mark and Brian Radio Show*, KLOS, Los Angeles, CA, December 1994, http://www.buckinghamnicks.info/words-wildheart.

15. Alex Hahn, *Possessed* (New York: Billboards Books, 2003), 48.

16. Jesse Johnson, interview by Tomi Jenkins, February 1, 2014, accessed June 23, 2017, https://www.youtube.com/watch?v=suk5yjlmJoQ.

17. Jellybean Johnson, interview by Freed, February 16, 1995.

18. Michael A. Gonzales, "Rock Star Jesse Johnson," *Wax Poetics*, winter 2012, 44.

19. "Jellybean! The Time's Jellybean Johnson Talks about Prince, the Minneapolis Sound and the Blues (part 1)," *Beldon's Blues Point* (blog), March 11, 2013, accessed January 7, 2016, http://beldonsbluespoint.blogspot.com/2013/03/in-2007-or-2008-i-saw-jellybean-johnson.html.

20. Jimmy Jam, "Soul Corner," *P3 Soul*, date unknown, accessed June 23, 2017, https://www.youtube.com/watch?v=OScQ3unXnWY.

MARCH 1983

1. Ronin Ro, *Prince: Inside the Music and the Masks* (New York: St. Martin's, 2011).

2. Dez Dickerson, in *Prince: The Glory Years*, produced by Rob Johnstone for Prism Entertainment (New Malden, Surrey, UK: Chrome Dreams Media, April 2004), DVD; also available at https://www.youtube.com/watch?v=dRNYiFxR2Ps, accessed June 17, 2017.

3. Jellybean Johnson, interview by Alan Freed for *Uptown* magazine/Per Nilsen, Minneapolis, MN, February 16, 1995.

4. Lisa Coleman, "Questions for Wendy & Lisa," *WendyandLisa.com*, November 25, 2009, accessed June 25, 2017, https://web.archive.org/web/20100917211952/http://www.wendyandlisa.com/forum/qa-wendy-lisa/hello-ladies-i-have-question-yall.

5. Jellybean Johnson, interview by Freed for *Uptown* Magazine/Per Nilsen, Minneapolis, MN, February 2, 1995.

6. "Dez Dickerson," *Those City Nights* (blog), February 8, 2011, accessed March 7, 2017, https://citinite.wordpress.com/2011/02/08/dez-dickerson-2.

7. Jon Bream, "'Purple' Afterglow: 25 Years Ago, Film and Soundtrack Turned Prince into a Megastar," *Pantagraph*, August 1, 2009, accessed March 12, 2017, http://www.pantagraph.com/entertainment/movies/purple-afterglow-years-ago-film-and-soundtrack-turned-prince-into/article_d1b4d342-7e05-11de-acec-001cc4c03286.html.

8. Monte Moir, interview by Leo Sidran, *The Third Story Podcast with Leo Sidran*, podcast audio, May 5, 2016, accessed June 20, 2016, http://www.third-story.com/listen/on-prince.

9. Denise "Vanity" Matthews, interview, *Omega Man Radio Show*, April 3, 2013, http://www.blogtalkradio.com/omegamanradio/2013/04/03/episode-957-fasting-will-dynamite-the-kingdom-of-darkness--denise-matthews.

10. "From *Purple Rain* to the Blues: Part 2 of Our Interview with the Time's Jellybean Johnson," *Beldon's Blues Point* (blog), March 13, 2013, accessed January 7, 2016, http://beldonsbluespoint.blogspot.com/2013/03/from-purple-rain-to-blues-part-2-of-our.html.

11. Steve Polopoli, "Summer Fest Preview: Morris Day & the Time," *Activate*, August 8, 2012, accessed March 12, 2017, http://activate.metroactive.com/2012/08/summer-fest-preview-morris-day-the-time.

12. Steve Perry, "Prince: The Purple Decade," *Musician*, November 1988, 85.

13. Jellybean Johnson, interview by Freed, February 16, 1995.

14. Jimmy Jam, in *The Original 7ven*, directed by Lee Librado (Los Angeles, CA: Chronology Entertainment and Flyte Tyme Productions, 2011), DVD.

15. Jimmy Jam, in The Time, *Words & Music Reunion Show*, 1990, Paisley Park/Reprise Records, pro-cd-4378, compact disc.

16. Jimmy Jam, in The Time, *Words & Music Reunion Show*.

17. Alan Leeds, interview by Alan Freed for *Uptown* magazine/Per Nilsen, Minneapolis, MN, January 20, 1994.

18. Jellybean Johnson, interview by Freed, February 16, 1995

19. Margena A. Christian, "The Time," *Ebony*, July 2012, 127.

20. R. Marshall-Greene, "Prince Devours S.A. with Soul-Funk," *San Antonio Express-News*, March 26, 1983.

21. Rob Tannenbaum, "Producer Jimmy Jam Pays Tribute to 'Ultra Sharp, Ultra Witty' Prince: 'His Talent Was Singular, Second to Nobody,'" *Billboard*, April 26, 2016, accessed April 29, 2016, http://www.billboard.com/articles/columns/pop/7348342/jimmy-jam-remembers-prince.

22. Charley Crespo, "Prince: Intimate Relations," *Rock & Soul*, August 1986, 19.

23. Jon Bream and Chris Riemenschneider, "Prince: An Oral History," *Minneapolis Star Tribune*, March 14, 2004.

24. Michael A. Gonzales, "Rock Star Jesse Johnson," *Wax Poetics*, winter 2012, 44.

25. Prince, interview on AOL Live, July 22, 1997, accessed February 17, 2014, http://prince.org/msg/7/404685.

26. Terry Lewis, in *Purple Rain: Backstage Pass*, produced by New Wave Entertainment (Burbank, CA: Warner Home Video, 2004), DVD.

27. Susan Rogers, interview by Alan Freed for *Uptown* magazine/Per Nilsen, Los Angeles, CA, August 4, 1997.

28. Liner notes from Prince, *Crystal Ball*, NPG Records, B000006CHF, 1998, compact disc.

29. Prince, lyrics to "Cloreen Bacon Skin," performed by Prince, *Crystal Ball*, NPG Records, 1997, compact disc.

30. Susan Rogers, interview by Alan Freed for *Uptown* magazine/Per Nilsen, Los Angeles, CA, March 25, 1995.

31. Rogers, interview by Freed, March 25, 1995.

32. Chaz Lipp, "An Interview with Jimmy Jam of the Original 7ven," *The Morton Report*, April 19, 2012, accessed March 4, 2017, http://www.themortonreport.com/entertainment/music/an-interview-with-jimmy-jam-of-the-original-7ven-part-two.

33. Michael Patrick Welch, "St Aug's Hamp Fest: Interview with Prince's Arch Rival, Morris Day", September 26, 2012, accessed June 12, 2017, http://www.offbeat.com/news/st-aug's-hamp-fest-interview-prince's-arch-rival-morris-day.

34. "Jellybean! The Time's Jellybean Johnson Talks about Prince, the Minneapolis Sound and the Blues (Part 1)," *Beldon's Blues Point* (blog), March 11, 2013, accessed January 7, 2016, http://beldonsbluespoint.blogspot.com/2013/03/in-2007-or-2008-i-saw-jellybean-johnson.html.

35. Margena A. Christian, "The Time," *Ebony*, July 2012, 127.

36. Mike Ragogna, "Chatting with Cobra Starship's Ryland Blackinton, Plus Jimmy Jam and Jason Reeves, and the Real Tuesday Weld Video Exclusive," *Huffington Post*, November 15, 2011, accessed March 5, 2017, http://www.huffingtonpost.com/mike-ragogna/chatting-with-cobra-stars_b_1094086.html.

37. Prince, interview by Larry King, *Larry King Live*, CNN, December 10, 1999, accessed April 21, 2016, https://www.youtube.com/watch?v=m8mg7CxAYUM.

38. "The Five Count's Sixth Annual Princemas Celebration—An Evening with Prince & the Revolution's Brown Mark," *The Five Count*, January 31, 2015, accessed March 8, 2017, http://thefivecount.com/interviews/the-five-counts-sixth-annual-princemas-celebration-an-evening-with-prince-the-revolutions-brown-mark.

39. Matt Fink, "Real Rube Radio Matt Fink," *Real Rube Radio*, podcast audio, May 20, 2006, https://archive.org/details/SteelersDrummer38_0/Real_Rube_Radio_Matt_Fink_Part_1.mp3.

40. Colin Dangaard, "The Magnificent Prince of Purple Rain," *Photoplay*, November 1984, 30.

41. Kurt Loder, "Prince Reigns," *Rolling Stone*, August 30, 1984, 47.

42. Loder, "Prince Reigns," 21.

43. Charley Crespo, "Minneapolis Update: Jesse Johnson," *Rock & Soul*, February 1985, 32.

44. Dave Hill, *Prince: A Pop Life* (New York: Harmony Books, 1989), 119.

45. Jellybean Johnson, interview by Freed, February 16, 1995.

46. Susan Rogers, interview by Alan Freed for *Uptown* magazine/Per Nilsen, Los Angeles, CA, March 26, 1995.

47. Alan Leeds, interview by Alan Freed for *Uptown* magazine/Per Nilsen, Minneapolis, MN, February 18, 1994.

48. Alan Leeds and Gwen Leeds, "Behind the Purple Ropes: Prince and the Revolution," *Wax Poetics*, winter 2012, accessed March 3, 2017, http://www.waxpoetics.com/blog/features/behind-the-purple-ropes-prince-and-the-revolution2.

49. Leeds and Leeds, "Behind the Purple Ropes."

50. Alan Leeds, interview by Alan Freed for *Uptown* magazine/Per Nilsen, Minneapolis, MN, January 27, 1994.

51. Evan Sawdey, "Inside Prince's Revolution," *PopMatters*, June 4, 2009, accessed March 7, 2017, http://www.popmatters.com/feature/94061-inside-the-revolution/P0.

52. Leeds, interview by Freed, January 27, 1994.

53. Dorian Lynskey, "Prince: 'I'm a Musician. And I Am Music,'" *Guardian*, June 23, 2011, accessed March 6, 2017, https://www.theguardian.com/music/2011/jun/23/prince-interview-adele-internet.

54. Morris Day, interview by Tavis Smiley, *Tavis Smiley Show*, PBS, June 18, 2004, transcript, accessed June 17, 2017, http://www.purplemusic.mynetcologne.de/the_time.html?2004-06-18.html.

55. Jellybean Johnson, interview by Alan Freed for *Uptown* magazine/Per Nilsen, Los Angeles, CA, March 2, 1995.

APRIL 1983

1. Jimmy Jam, "Soul Corner," *P3 Soul*, date unknown, accessed June 23, 2017, https://www.youtube.com/watch?v=OScQ3unXnWY.

2. Alan Leeds, interview by Alan Freed for *Uptown* magazine/Per Nilsen, Minneapolis, MN, November 1993.

3. Jimmy Jam, interviewed in *Purple Reign: The Story of Prince*, documentary, BBC Radio, January 18, 2003, accessed April 25, 2004, http://www.bbc.co.uk/programmes/b00snwb4.

4. Dez Dickerson, interview with Michael Dean, *The Prince Podcast*, podcast audio, January 2, 2013, accessed June 25, 2017, http://podcastjuice.net/30-days-of-podcasting-day-9-dez-dickerson.

5. Per Nilsen, *DanceMusicSexRomance* (London: Firefly, 1999), 123.

6. Harold Lewis, Tony Melodia, and Stefan van Poucke, "Take This Beat: An Exclusive Interview with Bobby Z Rivkin—Part 2," *Uptown* 43 (fall 2000): 18.

7. Jesse Johnson, Facebook post, March 1, 2014.

8. Jesse Johnson, Facebook post, August 31, 2014.

9. Wendy Melvoin, "Questions for Wendy & Lisa," *WendyandLisa.com*, June 5, 2009, accessed September 27, 2010, https://web.archive.org/web/20110722202344/http://www.wendyandlisa.com:80/forum/qa-wendy-lisa/chili-sauce.

10. Steve Appleford, "Jimmy Jam and Terry Lewis: Our Life in 15 Songs," *Rolling Stone*, October 9, 2015, accessed March 12, 2017, http://www.rollingstone.com/music/lists/jimmy-jam-and-terry-lewis-our-life-in-15-songs-20151009/the-time-get-it-up-1981-20151008.

11. Bilge Ebiri, "Prince: The Y-Life Interview," *Yahoo! Internet Life*, June 2001, accessed March 12, 2017, https://sites.google.com/site/prninterviews/home/yahoo-internet-life-june-2001.

12. Jimmy Jam, interviewed in *Being: The Original 7ven*, directed by L. D. Holland, Centric TV (December 10, 2011).

13. Serge Simonart, "The Artist," *Guitar World*, October 1998, accessed March 4, 2017, http://princetext.tripod.com/i_gw98.html.

14. Neal Karlen, "Prince Talks," *Rolling Stone*, September 12, 1985, 86.

15. Greg Kot, "Twin Cities Tycoon," *Details*, November 1998, accessed March 2, 2016, https://sites.google.com/site/prninterviews/home/details-november-1998.

16. "Prince and Chris Rock Talk about Performing in 1997," *MTV News*, January 11, 1997, accessed March 13, 2017, http://www.mtv.com/video-clips/wcdlyb/mtvnews-series-prince-and-chris-rock-talk-about-performing-in-1997.

17. Paul Mathur, "Revolt into Style," *Melody Maker*, August 15, 1987, 21.

18. Kim Allegrezza, "Interview: The Revolution Reminisce about the Secret Sides of Prince," *AXS.com*, March 4, 2017, accessed March 14, 2017, http://www.axs.com/interview-the-revolution-reminisce-about-the-secret-sides-of-prince-115577.

19. K Nicola Dyes, "Feel Better, Feel Good, Feel Wonderful: Dr. Fink Talks 2 Beautiful Nights," *The Beautiful Nights* (blog), March 24, 2013, accessed March 26, 2013, http://beautifulnightschitown.blogspot.com/2013/03/feel-better-feel-good-feel-wonderful-dr.html.

20. Jellybean Johnson, interview by Alan Freed for *Uptown* magazine/Per Nilsen, Minneapolis, MN, February 16, 1995.

21. "Jimmy Jam on Prince: 'Everything That Drove Him Was the Music,'" *Access Hollywood*, April 22, 2016, accessed June 13, 2017, https://www.youtube.com/watch?v=5iozb_8DanQ.

22. Jellybean Johnson, interview by Freed, February 16, 1995.

23. Prince, lyrics to "Chocolate" (demo), unreleased version, 1983; released version performed by the Time, *Pandemonium*, Paisley Park/Warner Bros./Reprise Records, 27490-2, 1990, compact disc.

24. Jam, "Soul Corner."

25. Jesse Johnson, in *The Original 7ven*, directed by Lee Librado (Los Angeles, CA: Chronology Entertainment and Flyte Tyme Productions, 2011), DVD.

26. Margena A. Christian, "The Time," *Ebony*, July 2012, 127.

27. Neal Karlen, "Prince Talks," *Rolling Stone*, October 18, 1990, 59.

28. Christian, "The Time," 127.

29. Ed Masley, "Q&A: Morris Day on New Time Album, Prince," *Arizona Republic*, August 23, 2011, accessed March 11, 2017, http://archive.azcentral.com/thingstodo/music/articles/20110823morris-day-interview-time-prince-purple-rain-new-album.html.

30. Johnson, in *The Original 7ven*.

31. Jimmy Jam, onstage at T. J. Martell Foundation benefit, Lincoln Center, June 13, 1996.

32. Edna Gundersen, "New Interview with the Time," *USA Today*, June 22, 2008, accessed March 11, 2017, http://usatoday30.usatoday.com/life/music/news/2008-06-22-time-main_N.htm.

33. Brian Raftery, "Prince: The Oral History of Purple Rain," *Spin*, July 2009, 59.

34. Jerome Benton, in *The Original 7ven*, directed by Lee Librado (Los Angeles, CA: Chronology Entertainment and Flyte Tyme Productions, 2011), DVD.

35. "From *Purple Rain* to the Blues: Part 2 of Our Interview with the Time's Jelbean Johnson," *Beldon's Blues Point* (blog), March 13, 2013, accessed June 13, 2017, http://beldonsbluespoint.blogspot.com/2013/03/from-purple-rain-to-blues-part-2-of -our.html.

36. Prince, lyrics to "Velvet Kitty Cat," performed by Prince and the Revolution, *Purple Rain Deluxe* (Expanded Edition), NPG Records/Warner Bros., 547374-2, 2017, compact disc.

37. Karlen, "Prince Talks," 85.

38. Spike Lee, "The Artist," *Interview*, May 1997, accessed March 5, 2017, http:// www.interviewmagazine.com/music/new-again-prince.

39. Matt Fink, interview by Michael Dean, *The Prince Podcast*, podcast audio, July 20, 2015, http://podcastjuice.net/the-prince-podcast-dr-fink-interview.

MAY 1983

1. Elahe Izadi et al., "Prince Autopsy Completed, 'No Obvious Signs of Trauma,' Sheriff Says," *Washington Post*, April 22, 2016, accessed March 12, 2017, https:// www.washingtonpost.com/news/arts-and-entertainment/wp/2016/04/21/authorities -investigating-death-at-princes-paisley-park.

2. Ronin Ro, *Prince: Inside the Music and the Masks* (New York: St. Martin's, 2011).

3. Barry Walters, "The Revolution Will Be Harmonized," *Out*, April 16, 2009, accessed March 11, 2017, http://www.out.com/entertainment/2009/04/16/revolution -will-be-harmonized.

4. Neal Karlen, "Prince Talks," *Rolling Stone*, September 12, 1985, 86.

5. Jem Aswad, "The Revolution Remembers Their Last Moments with Prince— and the First Time They Heard 'Purple Rain,'" *Billboard*, December 12, 2016, accessed March 6, 2017, http://www.billboard.com/articles/events/year-in-music -2016/7604454/the-revolution-prince-final-moments.

6. Matt Fink, in Marc Weingarten, "Prince: The Purple Gang," *Mojo*, February 1997, 45.

7. " Dez Dickerson," Those City Nights (blog), February 8, 2011, accessed March 7, 2017, https://citinite.wordpress.com/2011/02/08/dez-dickerson-2.

8. "Dez Dickerson."

9. Dez Dickerson, interview with Michael Dean, *The Prince Podcast*, podcast audio, January 2, 2013, http://podcastjuice.net/30-days-of-podcasting-day-9-dez-dickerson.

10. Aswad, "The Revolution Remembers Their Last Moments with Prince."

11. Bobby Z Rivkin, in Annie Zaleski, "Prince's genius, through the Revolution's ears: "He took the best bits of Beethoven, the Beatles and James Brown," *Salon*, April 24, 2017, accessed June 18, 2017, http://www.salon.com/2017/04/24/princes-ge nius-through-the-revolutions-ears-he-took-the-best-bits-of-beethoven-the-beatles-and -james-brown/.

12. Dez Dickerson, *My Time with Prince* (Nashville, TN: Pavilion Press, 2003), 238.

13. Matt Fink, in Annie Zaleski, "Prince's genius, through the Revolution's ears: "He took the best bits of Beethoven, the Beatles and James Brown," *Salon*, April 24, 2017, accessed June 18, 2017, http://www.salon.com/2017/04/24/princes-genius-through-the-revolutions-ears-he-took-the-best-bits-of-beethoven-the-beatles-and-james-brown/.

14. Harold Lewis, Tony Melodia, and Stefan van Poucke, "Take This Beat: An Exclusive Interview with Bobby Z Rivkin—Part 2," *Uptown* 43 (fall 2000): 19.

15. Lewis, Melodia, and van Poucke, "Take This Beat," 19.

16. Bilge Ebiri, "Prince: The Y-Life Interview," Yahoo! Internet Life, June 2001, accessed March 12, 2017, https://sites.google.com/site/prninterviews/home/yahoo-internet-life-june-2001.

17. Susan Rogers, interview by Alan Freed for *Uptown* magazine/Per Nilsen, Los Angeles, CA, March 26, 1995.

JUNE 1983

1. Rick Bellaire, "Hold Me Closer: The Story of Brenda Bennett," *Rhode Island Music Hall of Fame Historical Archive*, 2015, accessed March 10, 2017, http://www.ripopmusic.org/musical-artists/musicians/brenda-bennettbrenda-mosher.

2. Jellybean Johnson, interview by Alan Freed for *Uptown* magazine/Per Nilsen, Los Angeles, CA, March 2, 1995.

3. Alan Light, *Let's Go Crazy: Prince and the Making of* Purple Rain (New York: Atria Books, 2014).

4. Charley Crespo, "Minneapolis Update: Jesse Johnson," *Rock & Soul*, February 1985, 32.

5. Monte Moir, interview by Mike Mauren, "Mike Interviews Monte Moir of The Time #2," January 23, 2017, accessed February 2, 2017, https://www.youtube.com/watch?v=zWccue24_H0.

6. Jellybean Johnson, interview by Freed, March 2, 1995.

7. Andrea Swensson, "fDeluxe's St. Paul Peterson Talks about the Minneapolis Sound, Working with Prince, and the Rebirth of the Family," *City Pages*, September 14, 2011, accessed March 12, 2017, http://www.citypages.com/music/fdeluxes-st-paul-peterson-talks-about-the-minneapolis-sound-working-with-prince-and-the-rebirth-of-the-family-6628206.

8. K Nicola Dyes, "Every Day Is a Winding Road: St. Paul Peterson Talks 2 Beautiful Nights," *The Beautiful Nights* (blog), August 18, 2013, accessed August 18, 2013, http://beautifulnightschitown.blogspot.com/2013/08/everyday-is-winding-road-st-paul.html.

9. Eddie "Stats" Houghton, "A Death in the Family: St. Paul of the Family Remembers Prince, the Teacher," *Okayplayer*, June 7, 2016, accessed March 11, 2017, http://www.okayplayer.com/news/prince-the-family-st-paul-prince-day-interview.html/2.

10. Jesse Johnson, interview by Donnie Simpson, "The Time Interview with Donnie Simpson Part 1," 1990, accessed June 15, 2017, http://www.youtube.com/watch?v=DDfeYqQR1Vs.

11. Paul Peterson, interview by Leo Sidran, *The Third Story Podcast with Leo Sidran*, podcast audio, May 5, 2016, http://www.third-story.com/listen/on-prince.

12. Jellybean Johnson, interview by Alan Freed for *Uptown* Magazine/Per Nilsen, Los Angeles, CA, February 16, 1995.

13. Peterson, interview by Leo Sidran.

14. Jellybean Johnson, interview by Freed, February 16, 1995.

15. Morris Day, interview by Donnie Simpson, "The Time Interview with Donnie Simpson Part 1," 1990, accessed June 15, 2017, http://www.youtube.com/watch?v=DDfeYqQR1Vs.

16. Steve Harvey with Strother Bullins, "Remembering Prince: Engineer 'Cubby' Colby," *ProSound Network*, April 28, 2017, accessed June 9, 2017, http://www.prosoundnetwork.com/business/remembering-prince-engineer-cubby-colby/46040.

17. Keith Murphy, "Purple Rain Turns 30: The Revolution's Dr. Fink Breaks Down Prince's Classic Track-by-Track," *Vibe*, June 25, 2014, accessed June 15, 2017, http://www.vibe.com/2014/06/purple-rain-turns-30-revolutions-dr-fink-breaks-down-princes-classic-track-track/dr-fink-breaks-down-prince-purple-rain-track-by-track-5.

18. Harvey with Bullins, "Remembering Prince."

19. Bobby Z Rivkin, interview by Questlove, *Questlove Supreme*, Pandora, September 28, 2016, accessed October 4, 2016, https://www.pandora.com/station/play/3642532478040643917.

20. Alan Leeds, "Jesse Johnson and Miguel on Prince," April 22, 2016, accessed May 17, 2016, https://www.youtube.com/watch?v=9Xlq1pvvBdw.

JULY 1983

1. Prince, interview by Sway Calloway, *MTV*, 2004, accessed May 19, 2017, http://prince.org/msg/7/91779?pr.

2. Per Nilsen, *DanceMusicSexRomance* (London: Firefly, 1999), 129.

3. Jon Bream, "Revolution Keyboardist Shares Untold Stories from Prince's Soon-to-Be-Reissued 'Purple Rain,'" *Minneapolis Star Tribune*, June 17, 2017, accessed June 18, 2017, http://startribune.com/revolution-keyboardist-shares-untold-stories-from-prince-s-soon-to-be-reissued-purple-rain/428738003.

4. Harold Lewis, Tony Melodia, and Stefan van Poucke, "Take This Beat: An Exclusive Interview with Bobby Z Rivkin—Part 2," *Uptown* 43 (fall 2000): 19.

5. Prince, lyrics to "Vibrator," performed by Vanity 6, unreleased.

6. Prince, interview by Calloway, 2004.

7. Stevie Nicks, *Mojo*, December 2013, quoted on Buckingham Nicks Info, accessed June 15, 2017, http://buckinghamnicksinfo.tumblr.com/post/143214286071/so-prince-id-dead-wasnt-he-at-1-stage-in-love.

8. Kurt Loder, "Prince Reigns," *Rolling Stone*, August 30, 1984, 46.

9. K Nicola Dyes, "Feel Better, Feel Good, Feel Wonderful: Dr. Fink Talks 2 Beautiful Nights," *The Beautiful Nights* (blog), March 24, 2013, accessed March 26, 2013, http://beautifulnightschitown.blogspot.com/2013/03/feel-better-feel-good-feel-wonderful-dr.html.

10. Prince, interview by Love4OneAnother.com, November 17, 1997, accessed June 15, 2017, https://sites.google.com/site/prninterviews/home/love4oneanother-com-17-november-1997.

11. Alan Leeds, interview by Alan Freed for *Uptown* magazine/Per Nilsen, Minneapolis, MN, January 27, 1994.

12. Dez Dickerson, interview by Housequake.com, January 16, 2004, accessed March 6, 2017, https://web.archive.org/web/20070421211256/http://www.housequake.com/showthread.php?s=&threadid=12453.

13. Wendy Melvoin, in *Purple Rain: Backstage Pass*, produced by New Wave Entertainment (Burbank, CA: Warner Home Video, 2004), DVD.

14. Gary Graff, "Why Prince Asked for Journey's Blessing Before Releasing 'Purple Rain,'" *Billboard*, April 26, 2016, accessed March 10, 2017, http://www.billboard.com/articles/news/7348372/prince-purple-rain-journey-faithfully-interviews.

15. Graff, "Why Prince Asked for Journey's Blessing."

16. Keith Murphy, "Purple Rain Turns 30: The Revolution's Dr. Fink Breaks Down Prince's Classic Track-by-Track," *Vibe*, June 25, 2014, accessed June 15, 2017, http://www.vibe.com/2014/06/purple-rain-turns-30-revolutions-dr-fink-breaks-down-princes-classic-track-track/dr-fink-breaks-down-prince-purple-rain-track-by-track-9.

17. Lisa Coleman, interview by Jim DeRogatis and Greg Kot, *Sound Opinions*, WBEZ, July 24, 2009, accessed January 10, 2010, http://www.soundopinions.org/topic/wendyandlisa.

18. Melvoin, in *Purple Rain: Backstage Pass*.

19. Lisa Coleman, in *Purple Rain: Backstage Pass*, produced by New Wave Entertainment. (Burbank, CA: Warner Home Video, 2004), DVD.

20. "Exclusive! Prince Reaches Out to Former Revolution Member after Heart Attack," *Dr. Funk* (blog), February 18, 2001, accessed June 15, 2017, http://www.drfunkenberry.com/2011/02/18/exclusive-prince-reaches-out-to-former-revolution-member-after-heart-attack.

21. Jon Bream and Chris Riemenschneider, "Prince: An Oral History," *Minneapolis Star Tribune*, March 14, 2004.

22. Matt Fink, in *Prince, A Purple Reign*, produced by BBC, documentary, 2011, accessed June 15, 2017, https://www.youtube.com/watch?v=LlTwe9LxZ8w.

23. Melvoin, in *Purple Rain: Backstage Pass*.

24. Lucy Jones, "Stevie Nicks: 'Prince Wanted a Romance with Me,'" *NME*, November 3, 2013, accessed June 15, 2017, http://www.nme.com/news/music/stevie-nicks -11-1234690#gIYDeObimmHw3bH1.99.

25. David Sinclair, "The Man with No Label Has No Name," *London Times*, July 6, 1996, accessed March 12, 2017, https://sites.google.com/site/prninterviews/home/london-times-6-july-1996.

26. Jem Aswad, "The Revolution Remembers Their Last Moments with Prince—and the First Time They Heard 'Purple Rain,'" *Billboard*, December 12, 2016, accessed March 6, 2017, http://www.billboard.com/articles/events/year-in-music-2016/7604454/the-revolution-prince-final-moments. Wendy Melvoin—*Billboard* Magazine (December 12, 2016).

27. Prince, interview on *The Biz*, CNN, July 16, 2004, accessed June 15, 2017, https://www.youtube.com/watch?v=CVk5c2DY3Zw.

28. Lorraine Ali, "Party Like It's 2004," *Newsweek*, April 11, 2004, accessed March 5, 2017, http://www.newsweek.com/party-its-2004-124875.

29. Leeds, interview by Freed, January 27, 1994.

30. Nick Caren, "Here Comes #1—Delirious Rock & Soul Readers Vote Prince Best Artist of 1983," *Rock & Soul*, February 1984, 12.

31. Coleman, in *Purple Rain: Backstage Pass*.

32. Melvoin, in *Purple Rain: Backstage Pass*.

33. Neal Karlen, "Prince Talks," *Rolling Stone*, October 18, 1990, 60.

34. "Biggest Regret in 2008: Not Publishing This Wendy and Lisa Interview," *Tampa Bay Times*, December 30, 2008, accessed March 5, 2017, http://www.tampabay.com/blogs/media/content/biggest-regret-2008-not-publishing-wendy-and-lisa -interview/2095624.

35. "Biggest Regret in 2008."

36. Miles Davis, *Miles: The Autobiography* (New York: Simon & Schuster, 1989), 385.

37. Prince, interview by Tavis Smiley, *Tavis Smiley Show*, PBS, February 20, 2004, accessed June 15, 2017, http://prince.org/msg/12/81402.

38. Harold Lewis, Tony Melodia, and Stefan van Poucke, "Take This Beat: An Exclusive Interview with Bobby Z Rivkin—Part 2," *Uptown* 43 (fall 2000): 19.

39. Nilsen, *DanceMusicSexRomance*, 130.

40. Montrose Cunningham, "Celebrating Black Music Month: The 25th Anniversary of Prince's Sign o' the Times (Part 2)," *Soultrain.com*, June 22, 2012, accessed March 5, 2017, http://soultrain.com/2012/06/22/celebrating-black-music-month -the-25th-anniversary-of-princes-sign-o-the-times-part-2.

41. Susan Rogers, interview by Alan Freed for *Uptown* magazine/Per Nilsen, Los Angeles, CA, December 21, 1995.

42. Susan Rogers, interview by Lesley Mahoney, *Inside Berklee–Susan Rogers*, podcast audio, August 26, 2011, accessed June 15, 2017, https://www.berklee.edu/news/3651/podcast-inside-berklee-susan-rogers.

43. Susan Rogers, interview by Alan Freed for *Uptown* magazine/Per Nilsen. Los Angeles, CA, December 1994.

44. Rogers, interview by Freed, December 1994.

45. Rogers, interview by Freed, December 1994.

46. Rogers, interview by Freed, December 1994.

47. Rogers, interview by Freed, December 1994.

48. Coleman, interview by DeRogatis and Kot, July 24, 2009.

49. Rogers, interview by Freed, December 1994.

50. Susan Rogers, in *Purple Reign: The Story of Prince*, part 2, documentary, BBC Radio, January 25, 2003, accessed June 29, 2004, http://www.bbc.co.uk/programmes/ b00svtj7.

51. Prince, interview on *The Biz*.

52. Michael A. Gonzales, "Rock Star Jesse Johnson," *Wax Poetics*, winter 2012, 46.

AUGUST 1983

1. Debby Miller, "The Secret Life of America's Sexiest One-Man Band," *Rolling Stone*, April 28, 1983, 23.

2. Jon Bream, "'Purple' Afterglow: 25 Years Ago, Film and Soundtrack Turned Prince into a Megastar," *Pantagraph*, August 1, 2009, accessed March 12, 2017, http://www.pantagraph.com/entertainment/movies/purple-afterglow-years -ago-film-and-soundtrack-turned-prince-into/article_d1b4d342-7e05-11de-acec -001cc4c03286.html.

3. Alan Leeds, interview by Alan Freed for *Uptown* magazine/Per Nilsen, Minneapolis, MN, January 20, 1994.

4. Matt Fink interview by Julie Nelson and producer Tacy Mangan, "'Purple Rain' Highlights Influence on Local Music Scene," *KARE*, May 20, 2014, accessed June 17, 2017, http://www.kare11.com/entertainment/movies/purple-rain-highlights-influence -on-local-music-scene/107185711.

5. Prince, interview by Larry King, *Larry King Live*, CNN, December 10, 1999, accessed April 21, 2016, https://www.youtube.com/watch?v=m8mg7CxAYUM.

6. Matt Fink, interview by Girl Bros., *Girl Bros. Network*, podcast audio, September 2006, accessed September 28, 2004, http://www.myspace.com/girlbrosnetwork.

7. Jon Bream and Chris Riemenschneider, "Prince: An Oral History," *Minneapolis Star Tribune*, March 14, 2004.

8. Prince, lyrics to "Let's Go Crazy," performed by Prince and the Revolution, *Purple Rain*, Warner Bros., 1984, compact disc.

9. Robert Hilburn, "From Fellow Artists, a Case of Respect," *Los Angeles Times*, February 27, 2005, accessed June 17, 2017, http://articles.latimes.com/2005/feb/27/ entertainment/ca-joni27; reprinted from the liner notes from the CD *Joni Mitchell: Songs Chosen by Her Friends & Fellow Musicians*.

10. Ethan Brown, "Influences: Joni Mitchell," *New York*, May 9, 2005, accessed March 13, 2017, http://nymag.com/nymetro/arts/music/pop/11888/.

11. Keith Murphy, "Purple Rain Turns 30: The Revolution's Dr. Fink Breaks Down Prince's Classic Track-by-Track," *Vibe*, June 25, 2014, accessed June 17, 2017, http://www.vibe.com/2014/06/purple-rain-turns-30-revolutions-dr-fink -breaks-down-princes-classic-track-track/dr-fink-breaks-down-prince-purple-rain -track-by-track-8.

12. Marc Weingarten, "Prince: The Purple Gang," *Mojo*, February 1997, 45.

13. Susan Rogers, interview by Alan Freed for *Uptown* Magazine/Per Nilsen, Los Angeles, CA, December 1994.

14. Jake Brown, *Prince in the Studio (1975–1995)* (Phoenix: Amber Communications Group, 2010).

15. Rogers, interview by Freed, December 1994.

16. Brown, *Prince in the Studio.*

17. Brown, *Prince in the Studio.*

18. Robert I. Doerschuk, "Portrait of the Artist," *Musician*, April 1997, 32–33.

19. Brown, *Prince in the Studio.*

20. Jon Bream, "Dez Dickerson and André Cymone: Why These Early Prince Collaborators Joined the Revolution's Tribute Concerts," *Minneapolis Star Tribune*, August 26, 2016, accessed March 11, 2017, http://www.startribune.com/dez-dicker son-and-andr-xe9-cymone-why-these-early-prince-collaborators-joined-the-revolution -s-tribute-concerts/391345571.

21. Brown, *Prince in the Studio.*

22. John Bream, "Revolution Keyboardist Shares Untold Stories from Prince's Soon-to-Be Reissued 'Purple Rain,'" *Minneapolis Star Tribune*, June 17, 2017, accessed June 18, 2017, http://startribune.com/revolution-keyboardist-shares-untold -stories-from-prince-s-soon-to-be-reissued-purple-rain/428738003.

23. Brown, *Prince in the Studio.*

24. Keith Murphy, "Purple Rain Turns 30: The Revolution's Dr. Fink Breaks Down Prince's Classic Track-by-Track," *Vibe*, June 25, 2014, accessed June 20, 2017, http://www.vibe.com/2014/06/purple-rain-turns-30-revolutions-dr-fink -breaks-down-princes-classic-track-track/dr-fink-breaks-down-prince-purple-rain -track-by-track-10.

25. Matt Fink, interview by Michael Dean, *The Prince Podcast*, podcast audio, July 20, 2015, http://podcastjuice.net/the-prince-podcast-dr-fink-interview.

26. Susan Rogers, interview by Alan Freed for *Uptown* magazine/Per Nilsen, Los Angeles, CA, March 25, 1995.

27. Rogers, interview by Freed, March 25, 1995.

28. Rogers, interview by Freed, March 25, 1995.

29. Weingarten, "Prince: The Purple Gang," 45.

30. Evan Sawdey, "Inside Prince's Revolution," *PopMatters*, June 4, 2009, accessed March 7, 2017, http://www.popmatters.com/feature/94061-inside-the-revolution/P0.

31. Prince, interview by Stephen Fargnoli, MTV, November 15, 1985, accessed June 19, 2017, http://www.dailymotion.com/video/x49h7vy.

32. Susan Rogers, interview by Alan Freed for *Uptown* magazine/Per Nilsen, Los Angeles, CA, December 21, 1995.

33. Wendy Melvoin in "Wendy & Lisa," *BAM*, October 23, 1998, reprinted in *Prince Family Newsletter*, Vol. 6, no. 23, 138.

34. Leeds, interview by Freed, January 20, 1994.

35. Sawdey, "Inside Prince's Revolution."

36. Ronin Ro, *Prince: Inside the Music and the Masks* (New York: St. Martin's, 2011), Kindle.

37. Denise "Vanity" Matthews, interview, *Omega Man Radio Show*, April 3, 2013, http://www.blogtalkradio.com/omegamanradio/2013/04/03/episode-957-fasting-will -dynamite-the-kingdom-of-darkness--denise-matthews.

38. Lynn Van Matre, "'I Don't Have Any Regrets about Leaving,' Says Vanity," *Chicago Tribune*, September 9, 1984, accessed June 17, 2017, http://archives.chi cagotribune.com/1984/09/09/page/293/article/i-dont-have-regrets-about-leaving -says-vanity.

39. Rogers, interview by Alan Freed, December 21, 1995.

40. Dennis Wilen, "Prince Explains His Royal Secrets," *Los Angeles Herald-Examiner*, March 27, 1981, accessed May 21, 2017, http://voidmstr.blogspot .com/2010/07/prince-explains-his-royal-secrets.html.

41. Rogers, interview by Freed, March 25, 1995.

42. Matt Thorne, *Prince* (London: Faber & Faber, 2012).

43. Thorne, *Prince*.

44. Rogers, interview by Freed, March 25, 1995.

45. K Nicola Dyes, "The Voice: Brenda Bennett Talks 2 Beautiful Nights," The *Beautiful Nights* (blog), April 5, 2014, accessed March 12, 2017, http://beautifulnights chitown.blogspot.com/2014/04/the-voice-brenda-bennett-talks-2.html.

46. Bobby Z, in *Purple Rain: Backstage Pass*, produced by New Wave Entertainment (Burbank, CA: Warner Home Video, 2004), DVD.

47. Brown, *Prince in the Studio*.

48. Scott Isler, "Prince in Exile," *Musician*, October 1984, 46.

49. Brown, *Prince in the Studio*.

50. Isler, "Prince in Exile," 46.

51. Jim Maloney, "Wendy & Lisa: After the Revolution Comes the Challenge," *Music Connection*, February 22–March 6, 1987, 16.

52. Jill Jones, in *Prince, A Purple Reign*, produced by BBC, documentary, 2011, accessed June 15, 2017, https://www.youtube.com/watch?v=LlTwe9LxZ8w.

53. Jorge Hernandez, "Gary Numan, Still Electric after All These Years," *Vibe*, March 20, 1014, accessed June 15, 2017, http://www.vibe.com/2014/03/gary-numan -still-electric-after-all-these-years.

54. Lisa Coleman and Wendy Melvoin, interview by Jim DeRogatis and Greg Kot, *Sound Opinions*, WBEZ, July 24, 2009, accessed April 10, 2011, http://www.sound opinions.org/topic/wendyandlisa.

55. Ernie Rideout, "Produced by Prince," *Keyboard*, December 1999, 40.

56. Handwritten lyric sheet, Prince, John L. Nelson, Lisa Coleman, and Wendy Melvoin, lyrics to "Computer Blue," performed by Prince and the Revolution, *Purple Rain Deluxe* (Expanded Edition), NPG Records/Warner Bros., 547374-2, 2017, compact disc.

57. Dialogue of Wendy Melvoin and Lisa Coleman on "Computer Blue," *Purple Rain Deluxe* (Expanded Edition), NPG Records/Warner Bros., 547374-2, 2017, compact disc.

58. Brian Raftery, "Prince: The Oral History of Purple Rain," *Spin*, July 2009, 58.

59. Raftery, "Prince," 58.

60. Raftery, "Prince," 58.

61. Barry Walters, "The Revolution Will Be Harmonized," *Out*, April 16, 2009, accessed March 11, 2017, http://www.out.com/entertainment/2009/04/16/revolution -will-be-harmonized.

62. Novi Novog, in *Prince: The Glory Years*, produced by Rob Johnstone for Prism Entertainment (New Malden, Surrey, UK: Chrome Dreams Media, April 2004), DVD; also available at https://www.youtube.com/watch?v=dRNYiFxR2Ps, accessed June 17, 2017.

63. Rogers, interview by Freed, March 26, 1995.

64. Rideout, "Produced by Prince," 37.

65. Serge Simonart, "The Artist," *Guitar World*, October 1998, accessed March 4, 2017, http://princetext.tripod.com/i_gw98.html.

66. Prince, interview with Fargnoli, November 15, 1985.

67. James Brown with Bruce Tucker, *James Brown: The Godfather of Soul* (New York: Macmillan, 1986), 264.

68. Prince, interview by Chris Rock, January 11, 1997, accessed March 13, 2017, https://www.youtube.com/watch?v=l6M0WjGyC-E.

69. Jill Jones, interview by Mr. Chris, *The Soul Brother Show*, KPFT, October 10, 2016, accessed June 1, 2017, http://player.fm/series/the-soul-brother-show/for-love-a -conversation-with-jill-jones.

70. Alan Light, *Let's Go Crazy: Prince and the Making of Purple Rain* (New York: Atria Books, 2014).

71. Prince, interview by the Electrifying Mojo, *The Electrifying Mojo*, WHYT, June 7, 1986, accessed February 14, 2016, https://www.youtube.com/ watch?v=NJZCoxZ5COY.

72. Jon Pareles, "A Re-Inventor of His World and Himself," *New York Times*, November 17, 1996, accessed March 4, 2017, http://www.nytimes.com/1996/11/17/ arts/a-re-inventor-of-his-world-and-himself.html.

73. Murphy, "Purple Rain Turns 30."

74. Prince, interview by Sway Calloway, MTV, 2004, accessed May 19, 2017, http://prince.org/msg/7/91779?pr.

SEPTEMBER 1983

1. "The Time, Voted #8 in Rock & Soul's Reader's Poll," *Rock & Soul Special*, spring 1985, 32.

2. Andrea Swensson, "fDeluxe's St. Paul Peterson Talks about the Minneapolis Sound, Working with Prince, and the Rebirth of the Family," *City Pages*, September 14, 2011, accessed March 12, 2017, http://www.citypages.com/music/fdeluxes-st-paul -peterson-talks-about-the-minneapolis-sound-working-with-prince-and-the-rebirth-of -the-family-6628206.

3. Pepé Willie, interview by Kristie Lazenberry for *Uptown* magazine/Per Nilsen, Minneapolis, MN, Summer 1995.

4. Charley Crespo, "Minneapolis Update: Morris Day," *Rock & Soul*, February 1985, 31.

5. Crespo, "Minneapolis Update: Jesse Johnson," 32.

6. Brian Raftery, "Prince: The Oral History of Purple Rain," *Spin*, July 2009, 57.

7. Simon Witter and the New Power Generation Fan Club, "Sex on a Stick," *Sky*, July 1990, 12.

8. Susan Rogers, interview by Alan Freed for *Uptown* magazine/Per Nilsen, Los Angeles, CA, March 26, 1995.

9. Robert Hilburn, "Mixed Emotions: Prince on the Music," *Musician*, September 1983, 58.

10. Witter and the New Power Generation Fan Club, "Sex on a Stick," 12.

11. Rogers, interview by Freed, March 26, 1995.

12. Joshua Levine, "Prince Speaks," *Forbes*, September 23, 1996, 180.

13. Scott Isler, "Prince in Exile," *Musician*, October 1984, 42.

14. Prince, lyrics to "Baby I'm a Star," performed by Prince and the Revolution, Warner Bros., W2-25110, 1984, compact disc.

15. Prince, lyrics to "Baby I'm a Star."

16. G. Brown, "Pop Star Doing Away with Middleman," *Denver Post*, October 4, 1997, accessed March 12, 2017, https://sites.google.com/site/prninterviews/home/ denver-post-4-october-1997.

17. Neal Karlen, "Prince Talks," *Rolling Stone*, October 18, 1990, 59.

18. André Cymone, interview with Michael Dean, *The Prince Podcast*, podcast audio, April 23, 2016, http://podcastjuice.net/andre-cymone-interview.

19. Prince, interview with Tavis Smiley, *Tavis Smiley Show*, PBS, July 19, 2009, accessed March 12, 2017, http://www.pbs.org/video/1189739252.

20. Robert I. Doerschuk, "Portrait of the Artist," *Musician*, April 1997, 75.

21. David Stubbs, "Jimmy Jam and Terry Lewis: The Super-Producers That Shaped Modern Pop," *Guardian*, March 22, 2016, accessed March 6, 2017, https://www.theguardian.com/music/2016/mar/22/janet-jackson-superproducers-jimmy-jam-and-terry-lewis.

22. Susan Rogers, Red Bull Music Academy lecture, hosted by Torsten Schmidt, Montreal, QC, December 8, 2016, accessed June 19, 2017, http://www.redbullmusicacademy.com/lectures/susan-rogers-lecture.

23. Wendy Melvoin, in *Dr. Prince & Mr. Jackson*, directed by Philip Priestley (Paris: Arte France, 2009), broadcast July 9, 2009.

24. Jim Maloney, "Wendy & Lisa: After the Revolution Comes the Challenge," *Music Connection*, February 22–March 6, 1987, 25.

25. Lisa Coleman, liner notes for *Purple Rain Deluxe* (Expanded Edition), NPG Records/Warner Bros., 547374-2, 2017.

26. Maloney, "Wendy & Lisa," 25.

27. Jake Brown, *Prince in the Studio (1975–1995)* (Phoenix: Amber Communications Group, 2010).

28. Hilburn, "Mixed Emotions," 58.

29. Neal Karlen, "Prince Talks," *Rolling Stone*, September 12, 1985, 86.

30. Joe Gore, "Prince's Guitarists Past + Present," *Guitar Player*, February 1992, 36.

31. Isler, "Prince in Exile," 42.

32. Ronin Ro, *Prince: Inside the Music and the Masks* (New York: St. Martin's, 2011).

33. Alex Hahn, *Possessed* (New York: Billboards Books, 2003), 60.

34. Ernie Rideout, "Produced by Prince," *Keyboard,* December 1999, 40.

35. Brown, *Prince in the Studio.*

36. Marc Weingarten, "Shoot-out at the Fantasy Factory," *Mojo*, February 1997, 42.

37. Matt Fink, interview on *Real Rube Radio*, pocast audio, May 20, 2006, https://archive.org/details/SteelersDrummer38_0/Real_Rube_Radio_Matt_Fink_Part_1.mp3.

38. Brown, *Prince in the Studio.*

39. Joni Mitchell, interview on Dutch National TV, May 28, 1988, accessed March 13, 2017, https://www.youtube.com/watch?v=GBfXuiv9XOg.

40. Prince, interview by Stephen Fargnoli, MTV, November 15, 1985, accessed June 17, 2017, http://www.dailymotion.com/video/x49h7vy.

41. Isler, "Prince in Exile," 46.

42. Hilburn, "Mixed Emotions," 58.

43. Brown, *Prince in the Studio.*

44. Debby Miller, "The Secret Life of America's Sexiest One-Man Band," *Rolling Stone*, April 28, 1983, 20.

45. Tom Mann, "An Oral History of Prince's 'Purple Rain,'" *FasterLouder*, August 21, 2014, accessed March 7, 2017, http://fasterlouder.junkee.com/an-oral-history-of-princes-purple-rain/839367.

46. Evan Sawdey, "Inside Prince's Revolution," *PopMatters*, June 4, 2009, accessed March 7, 2017, http://www.popmatters.com/feature/94061-inside-the-revolution/P0.

47. Steve Perry, "Prince: The Purple Decade," *Musician*, November 1988, 84–85.

48. Jon Bream, "A Star Is Reborn: With His Musicology Tour, Prince Again Proves He's the Most Complete Rock Star," *Cleveland Free Times*, March 2004, accessed June 20, 2017, https://web.archive.org/web/20040820100051/http://www.freetimes.com/modules.php?op=modload&name=News&file=article&sid=1324.

49. Brown, *Prince in the Studio*.

50. Alan Leeds, interview by Alan Freed for *Uptown* magazine/Per Nilsen, Minneapolis, MN, November 1993.

51. Andrea Swensson, "Bobby Z Shares His *Purple Rain* Memories on the Album's 30th Anniversary," *The Current*, June 25, 2014, accessed June 18, 2017, http://blog.thecurrent.org/2014/06/bobby-z-shares-his-purple-rain-memories-on-the-albums-30th-anniversary.

52. Marc Weingarten, "Prince: The Purple Gang," *Mojo*, February 1997, 46.

53. Parts of this quote have been used in other books and incorrectly credited to David Leonard. It is originally from an interview conducted by the author with Peggy McCreary in February 1996.

54. "He Has No Name, and Not Much of a Credit Rating Either," *Philadelphia Inquirer*, February 7, 1995, 50.

55. Liner notes from Prince, *Crystal Ball*, NPG Records, B000006CHF, 1998, CD.

56. Billy Amendola, "Morris Day, Funky Time on Drums," *Modern Drummer*, January 2005, 43.

57. Prince, lyrics to "Let's Pretend We're Married," performed by Prince, Warner Bros., 9 23720-2, 1982, compact disc.

58. Harold Lewis, Tony Melodia, and Stefan van Poucke, "Take This Beat: An Exclusive Interview with Bobby Z Rivkin—Part 2," *Uptown* 43 (fall 2000): 19.

59. Brown, *Prince in the Studio*.

60. Bream, "A Star Is Reborn."

61. Jim Bickal, "The Revolution Reunites to Benefit Heart Health," MPR News, February 19, 2012, accessed June 18, 2017, https://www.mprnews.org/story/2012/02/16/revolution_reunion.

62. Prince, in *Purple Reign: The Story of Prince*, part 2, documentary, BBC Radio, January 25, 2003, accessed June 29, 2004, http://www.bbc.co.uk/programmes/b00svtj7.

63. Brown, *Prince in the Studio*.

64. Susan Rogers, in *Purple Reign: The Story of Prince*, part 2, documentary, BBC Radio, January 25, 2003, accessed June 29, 2004, http://www.bbc.co.uk/programmes/b00svtj7.

65. Larry Crane, "Susan Rogers: From Prince to Ph.D.," *Tape Op*, January/February 2017, accessed February 20, 2017, http://tapeop.com/interviews/117/susan-rogers.

66. Prince, interviewed by Love4OneAnother.com, November 17, 1997, accessed June 18, 2017, https://sites.google.com/site/prninterviews/home/love4oneanother -com-17-november-1997.

67. Rogers, interview by Freed, March 26, 1995.

68. Matt Thorne, *Prince* (London: Faber & Faber, 2012).

69. Miles Marshall Lewis, "Prince Hits N Runs N Talks!" *Ebony*, December 22, 2015, accessed June 18, 2017, https://www.facebook.com/notes/housequake/prince -hits-n-runs-n-talks-ebony-interview-dec-22-2015/916986788385046.

70. Swensson, "Bobby Z Shares His *Purple Rain* Memories on the Album's 30th Anniversary."

71. Keith Murphy, "Purple Rain Turns 30: The Revolution's Dr. Fink Breaks Down Prince's Classic Track-by-Track," *Vibe*, June 25, 2014, accessed June 18, 2017, http://www.vibe.com/2014/06/purple-rain-turns-30-revolutions-dr-fink-breaks-down-princes -classic-track-track/dr-fink-breaks-down-prince-purple-rain-track-by-track-7.

72. Wendy Melvoin, in *Purple Rain: Backstage Pass*, produced by New Wave Entertainment (Burbank, CA: Warner Home Video, 2004), DVD.

73. Keith Murphy, "Purple Rain Turns 30: Prince's Engineer Shares Majestic (and Maddening) Studio Stories," *Vibe*, June 25, 2014, accessed June 22, 2017, https://web .archive.org/web/20151101151644/http://www.vibe.com/2014/06/purple-rain-turns -30-princes-engineer-shares-majestic-and-maddening-studio-stories/susan-rogers-talks -prince-purple-rain-2.

74. Brown, *Prince in the Studio*.

OCTOBER 1983

1. Margena A. Christian, "The Time," *Ebony*, July 2012, 127.

2. Morris Day, interview by Amy Scott, VH1 Classic, June 19, 2004.

3. Susan Rogers, interview by Alan Freed for *Uptown* magazine/Per Nilsen, Los Angeles, CA, December 1994.

4. Jake Brown, *Prince in the Studio (1975–1995)* (Phoenix: Amber Communications Group, 2010).

5. Lynn Norment, "*Ebony* Interview with Prince," *Ebony*, July 1986, 30.

6. Charley Crespo, "Behind the Scenes at Purple Rain," *Rock & Soul*, November 1984, 29.

7. Rogers, interview by Freed, December 1994.

8. Susan Rogers, interview on Housequake.com, May 9, 2006, accessed March 6, 2016, https://web.archive.org/web/20060624184248/http://www.housequake.com/ showthread.php?s=&threadid=65388.

9. Rogers, interview by Freed, December 1994.

10. Rogers, interview by Freed, December 1994.

11. Prince, lyrics to "Wednesday," performed by Prince and Jill Jones, unreleased.

12. Prince, lyrics to "Wednesday."

13. Denise "Vanity" Matthews, diary from October 25, 1983, posted on eBay, http://www.ebay.com/itm/VANITY-DENISE-MATTHEWS-PERSONAL-JOURNAL -RARE-RARE-Prince-Barry-Gordy-1983-/281941999298?hash=item41a50d7ec2%3Ag %3AcHsAAOSwe7BWyjHg, accessed March 1, 2016, and Prince.org, http://prince.org/ msg/5/421861/RIP-Vanity-Denise-Matthews?&pg=16, accessed May 20, 2016.

14. Evan Sawdey, "Inside Prince's Revolution," *PopMatters*, June 4, 2009, accessed March 7, 2017, http://www.popmatters.com/feature/94061-inside-the-revolution/P1.

15. Jon Bream, "Revolution Keyboardist Shares Untold Stories from Prince's Soon -to-Be-Reissued 'Purple Rain,'" *Minneapolis Star Tribune*, June 17, 2017, accessed June 18, 2017, http://startribune.com/revolution-keyboardist-shares-untold-stories -from-prince-s-soon-to-be-reissued-purple-rain/428738003.

NOVEMBER 1983

1. Charley Crespo, "Behind the Scenes at Purple Rain," *Rock & Soul*, November 1984, 29.

2. Susan Rogers, interview by Alan Freed for *Uptown* magazine/Per Nilsen, Los Angeles, CA, December 26, 1994.

3. Marc Weingarten, "Prince: The Purple Gang," *Mojo*, February 1997, 45.

4. Akbar Cojoe, "Brenda Bennett of Vanity 6 Talks Prince & Her New CD," *Examiner.com*, May 18, 2011, accessed March 5, 2017, http://prince.org/msg/5/358836.

5. Susan Rogers, interview by Troy L. Foreman, *PC Principle Podcast*, podcast audio, May 18, 2016, http://thepcprinciple.com/?p=9145.

6. Susan Rogers, interview by Alan Freed for *Uptown* magazine/Per Nilsen, Los Angeles, CA, March 25, 1995.

7. Susan Rogers, interview by Alan Freed for *Uptown* /Per Nilsen, Los Angeles, CA, August 4, 1997.

8. Rogers, interview by Freed, March 25, 1995.

DECEMBER 1983

1. Robert I. Doerschuk, "Portrait of the Artist," *Musician*, April 1997, 32.

2. Susan Rogers, interview by Alan Freed for *Uptown* magazine/Per Nilsen, Los Angeles, CA, February 1995.

3. Rogers, interview by Freed, February 1995.

4. Jim Walsh, "TAFKAP Speaks," *St. Paul Pioneer Press*, November 18, 1996, accessed March 5, 2017, http://princetext.tripod.com/i_sppp96.html.

5. Hans-Maarten Post, "Prince 'Ik Word steeds beter,'" *Het Nieuwsblad*, June 24, 2010, accessed June 27, 2010, http://qmusic.be/blog/wimoosterlinckshowtime/hans maartenontmoetteprince.

6. Robert Hilburn, "Mixed Emotions: Prince on the Music," *Musician*, September 1983, 58.

7. Prince, lyrics to "She's Always in My Hair," performed by Prince and the Revolution, Warner Bros., 7-28972, 1985, vinyl record.

8. Prince, lyrics to "She's Always in my Hair."

9. Susan Rogers, interview by Alan Freed for *Uptown* magazine/Per Nilsen, Los Angeles, CA, February 1995.

10. Harold Lewis, Tony Melodia, and Stefan van Poucke, "Take This Beat: An Exclusive Interview with Bobby Z Rivkin—Part 2," *Uptown* 43 (fall 2000): 22.

11. Neal Karlen, "Prince Talks," *Rolling Stone*, September 12, 1985, 86.

12. "Biggest Regret in 2008: Not Publishing This Wendy and Lisa Interview," *Tampa Bay Times*, December 30, 2008, accessed March 5, 2017, http://www.tam pabay.com/blogs/media/content/biggest-regret-2008-not-publishing-wendy-and-lisa -interview/2095624.

13. Eric Leeds, interview by Alan Freed for *Uptown* magazine/Per Nilsen, Los Angeles, CA, November 11, 1994.

JANUARY 1984

1. Susan Rogers, interview by Alan Freed for *Uptown* magazine/Per Nilsen, Los Angeles, CA, March 25, 1995.

2. Paul "Scoop" Simper, "Princess for Ten Days," *No. 1*, June 29, 1985, 27.

3. Prince, lyrics to "We Can F**k," performed by Prince and the Revolution, *Purple Rain Deluxe* (Expanded Edition), NPG Records/Warner Bros., 547374-2, 2017, compact disc.

4. Simper, "Princess for Ten Days," 27.

5. Barbara Graustark, "Strange Tales from Andre's Basement," *Musician*, September 1983, 63.

6. Adrian Deevoy, "I Am Normal!," *Q*, July 1994, 94.

7. Mobeen Azhar, *Hunting for Prince's Vault*, BBC Radio, March 21, 2015, accessed March 5, 2016, https://www.mixcloud.com/Emancipatio/hunting-for-princes-vault-bbc-documentary-by-mobeen-azhar-march-2015.

8. Simon Witter and the New Power Generation Fan Club, "Sex on a Stick," *Sky*, July 1990, 12.

9. Alan Leeds, interview by Alan Freed for *Uptown* magazine/Per Nilsen, Minneapolis, MN, January 27, 1994.

10. Jellybean Johnson, interview by Alan Freed for *Uptown* magazine/Per Nilsen, Minneapolis, MN, February 2, 1995.

11. Michael Patrick Welch, "Interview with Morris Day of the Time (OffBeat, Sept. 2012)," michaelpatrickwelch.org, October 2, 2012, accessed June 18, 2017, https://michaelpatrickwelch.org/2012/10/02/interview-with-morris-day-of-the-time-offbeat-sept-2012.

12. "Jesse Johnson on the Power of Penetration," *Ebony*, August 8, 2011, accessed March 11, 2017, http://prince.org/msg/5/364813.

13. Jellybean Johnson, interview by Alan Freed for *Uptown* magazine/Per Nilsen, Minneapolis, MN, March 2, 1995.

14. Eric Deggans, "Funk Drumming Forefathers," *Modern Drummer*, March 1997, 110, accessed June 18, 2017, https://moderndrummer.com/wp-content/uploads/2016/05/md208.pdf.

15. Jellybean Johnson, interview by Freed, March 2, 1995.

16. Ernie Rideout, "Produced by Prince," *Keyboard*, December 1999, 40.

17. Tony Norman, "Former Prince Gives the Fax on His Career, Motivation," *Pittsburgh Post Gazette*, September 21, 1997, accessed March 12, 2017, https://sites.google.com/site/prninterviews/home/pittsburgh-post-gazette-ap-21-september-1997.

18. Sheila E., *The Beat of My Own Drum: A Memoir by Sheila E.* (New York: Atria Books, 2014).

19. Lisa Coleman, interview by Jesse Esparza, 2008, published on MySpace but sent to the author by Jesse Esparza via Facebook message on March 8, 2017.

20. Jesse Johnson, Facebook post, March 1, 2014.

21. Michael A. Gonzales, "Rock Star Jesse Johnson," *Wax Poetics*, winter 2012, 46.

22. Jesse Johnson, "Jesse Johnson and Miguel on Prince," April 22, 2016, accessed June 18, 2017, https://www.youtube.com/watch?v=9Xlq1pvvBdw.

23. Terry Lewis, interview by Big Sy, KMOJ, June 14, 2010.

24. Brian Raftery, "Prince: The Oral History of Purple Rain," *Spin*, July 2009, 59.

25. Jellybean Johnson, interview by Alan Freed for *Uptown* magazine/Per Nilsen, Minneapolis, MN, February 16, 1995.

26. Michael Goldberg, "*Purple Rain* Star Morris Day Goes It Alone," *Rolling Stone*, September 13, 1984, 41.

27. Prince, lyrics to "Tricky," performed by the Time, Warner Bros., B001J4N954, 1982, vinyl.

28. Johnson, "Jesse Johnson and Miguel on Prince."

29. Steve Palopoli, "Summer Fest Preview: Morris Day & the Time," *Activate*, August 8, 2012, accessed March 12, 2017, http://activate.metroactive.com/2012/08/summer-fest-preview-morris-day-the-time.

30. Johnson, "Jesse Johnson and Miguel on Prince."

31. Dean Van Nguyen, "Big Time Morris Day," *Wax Poetics*, winter 2012, 53.

32. Joni Mitchell, lyrics to "Both Sides Now," performed by Joni Mitchell, Reprise Records, 1975, compact disc.

33. Jesse Johnson, interview by Tomi Jenkins, February 1, 2014, accessed June 25, 2017, https://www.youtube.com/watch?v=suk5yjlmJoQ.

34. Marc Weingarten, "Prince: The Purple Gang," *Mojo*, February 1997, 44.

35. Elysa Gardner, "Prince: 'If I Knew the Things I Know Now Before, I Wouldn't Be in the Music Industry,'" *Los Angeles Times*, July 14, 1996, accessed March 7, 2017, http://www.latimes.com/entertainment/music/la-et-ms-prince-archive -19960714-story.html.

36. Craig Belcher, "Some Quality Time with Morris Day," *Style Weekly*, October 1, 2013, accessed March 12, 2017, http://www.styleweekly.com/richmond/interview -with-morris-day/Content?oid=1961357.

37. "Jerome Benton of the Funk Group 'The TIME' interview w/TheFunkcenter," *Funk Chronicles with Dr. Turk Logan*, April 16, 2015, accessed June 18, 2017, https:// www.youtube.com/watch?v=_yfnvX8yF9o.

38. Liz Jones, *Slave to the Rhythm* (London: Little, Brown, 1997), 65.

39. Neal Karlen, "Prince Talks," *Rolling Stone*, September 12, 1985, 86.

40. Touré, "The Artist," *Icon*, October 1998, accessed March 4, 2017, https://sites. google.com/site/themusicinterviewarchive/prince/prince-1998-icon-magazine-interview.

41. Susan Rogers, interview by Alan Freed for *Uptown* magazine/Per Nilsen, Los Angeles, CA, March 26, 1995.

42. Marc "Moose" Moder, "Sheena Easton: Looking Back at Her Musical History," *Windy City Times*, August 8, 2012, accessed March 4, 2017, http://www.windycityme diagroup.com/lgbt/Sheena-Easton-Looking-back-at-her-musical-history-/38975.html.

43. Sheena Easton, interview by RuPaul, WKTU, October 18, 1996, accessed June 22, 2017, http://www.sheenaeaston.co.uk/sewebchatrupaulint.html.

44. Moder, "Sheena Easton: Looking Back at Her Musical History."

45. Keith Murphy, "Purple Rain Turns 30: The Revolution's Dr. Fink Breaks Down Prince's Classic Track-by-Track," *Vibe*, June 25, 2014, accessed June 18, 2017, http:// www.vibe.com/2014/06/purple-rain-turns-30-revolutions-dr-fink-breaks-down-princ es-classic-track-track/dr-fink-breaks-down-prince-purple-rain-track-by-track-1.

46. David Marchese, "Members of the Revolution Share Their 5 Favorite Prince Stories," *Vulture*, March 20, 2017, accessed March 20, 2017, http://www.vulture .com/2017/03/prince-revolution-best-stories.html?mid=facebook_vulture.

47. Spike Lee, "The Artist," *Interview*, May 1997, accessed on March 5, 2017, http://www.interviewmagazine.com/music/new-again-prince.

48. Murphy, "Purple Rain Turns 30."

49. Jones, *Slave to the Rhythm*, 65.

50. Andrea Swensson, "Bobby Z Shares His *Purple Rain* Memories on the Album's 30th Anniversary," *The Current*, June 25, 2014, accessed June 19, 2017, http://blog.thecurrent.org/2014/06/bobby-z-shares-his-purple-rain-memories-on-the -albums-30th-anniversary.

51. Raftery, "Prince," 57.

52. Prince, lyrics to "Take Me with U," performed by Prince and the Revolution, Warner Bros., W2-25110, 1984, compact disc.

53. Prince, interview by Sway Calloway, MTV, 2004, accessed May 19, 2017, http://prince.org/msg/7/91779?pr.

54. Susan Rogers, interview by Alan Freed for *Uptown* magazine/Per Nilsen, Los Angeles, CA, August 4, 1997.

FEBRUARY 1984

1. Dorian Lynskey, "Prince: 'I'm a Musician. And I Am Music,'" *Guardian*, June 23, 2011, accessed March 6, 2017, https://www.theguardian.com/music/2011/jun/23/prince-interview-adele-internet.

2. Jon Pareles, "A Re-Inventor of His World and Himself," *New York Times*, November 17, 1996, accessed March 4, 2017, http://www.nytimes.com/1996/11/17/arts/a-re-inventor-of-his-world-and-himself.html.

3. Prince, interview on *The Biz*, CNN, July 16, 2004, accessed June 19, 2017, https://www.youtube.com/watch?v=CVk5c2DY3Zw.

4. Prince, lyrics to "Manic Monday," performed by the Bangles, Sony BMG Music, B00137IDLC, 1986, compact disc.

5. Prince, lyrics to "Manic Monday."

6. Prince, lyrics to "1999," performed by Prince, Warner Bros., 9 23720-2, 1982, compact disc.

7. Ernie Rideout, "Produced by Prince," *Keyboard*, December 1999, 40.

8. Mobeen Azhar, *Hunting for Prince's Vault*, BBC Radio, March 21, 2015, accessed June 19, 2017, https://www.mixcloud.com/Emancipatio/hunting-for-princes-vault-bbc-documentary-by-mobeen-azhar-march-2015/.

9. Prince, lyrics to "Manic Monday."

10. Susan Rogers, Red Bull Music Academy lecture, hosted by Torsten Schmidt, Montreal, QC, December 8, 2016, accessed June 19, 2017, http://www.redbullmusicacademy.com/lectures/susan-rogers-lecture.

11. Marc Weingarten, "Prince: The Purple Gang," *Mojo*, February 1997, 45.

12. Brian McCollum, "Detroit Asks the Questions, and the Artist Reveals Himself as a Prince of Mystery," *Detroit Free Press*, December 26, 1997.

13. Brandon Turner, "Sheila E.," *Black Beat*, April 1985, 58.

14. Susan Rogers, interview by Alan Freed for *Uptown* magazine/Per Nilsen, Los Angeles, CA, March 26, 1995.

15. Rogers, interview by Freed, March 26, 1995.

16. Sheila E., interview in *Unsung: Sheila E.*, A. Smith & Co. Productions, TV One, February 27, 2012.

17. Alan Leeds, interview by Alan Freed for *Uptown* magazine/Per Nilsen, Minneapolis, MN, February 18, 1994.

18. Susan Rogers, interview by Alan Freed for *Uptown* magazine/Per Nilsen, Los Angeles, CA, August 4, 1997.

19. Abby Borovitz, "Touré on Why Prince Became an Icon," *MSNBC*, March 18, 2013, accessed March 4, 2017, http://www.msnbc.com/the-cycle/toure-why-prince-became-icon.

20. Nick Caren, "Here Comes #1—Delirious *Rock & Soul* Readers Vote Prince Best Artist of 1983," *Rock & Soul*, February 1984, 13.

21. Sheila E., *The Beat of My Own Drum: A Memoir by Sheila E.* (New York: Atria Books, 2014).

22. Paul Peterson, interview by Leo Sidran, *The Third Story Podcast with Leo Sidran*, podcast audio, May 5, 2016, accessed June 19, 2017, http://www.third-story.com/listen/on-prince.

23. Lee Hildebrand, "Minneapolis Update: Sheila E.," *Rock & Soul*, February 1985, 28.

24. Susan Rogers, interview by Alan Freed for *Uptown* magazine/Per Nilsen, Los Angeles, CA, March 25, 1995.

25. Rogers, interview by Freed, August 4, 1997.

26. Sheila E., *The Beat of My Own Drum*.

27. Sheila E., interview, *The Fuze*, August 2004, accessed June 19, 2017, https://web.archive.org/web/20040616220909/http://www.the-fuze.com/sheilae.html.

28. Sheila E., *The Beat of My Own Drum*.

29. Prince, interview by Love4OneAnother.com, November 17, 1997, accessed June 19, 2017, https://sites.google.com/site/prninterviews/home/love4oneanother-com-17-november-1997.

30. Edna Gunderson, "Emancipation Conversation," MSN Music Central, December 1996, accessed June 19, 2017, https://sites.google.com/site/prninterviews/home/msn-music-central-december-1996.

31. "A Conversation with Sheila E.," *Tavis Smiley Show*, NPR, December 10, 2003, accessed February 18, 2004, http://www.npr.org/templates/story/story.php?storyId=1540501.

32. Neal Karlen, "Prince Talks: The Silence Is Broken," *Rolling Stone*, September 12, 1985, accessed June 23, 2017, http://www.rollingstone.com/music/news/prince-talks-the-silence-is-broken-19850912.

33. Matt Thorne, *Prince* (London: Faber & Faber, 2012).

34. Thorne, *Prince*.

35. Sylvia Patterson, "'I Feel Like This Is My Last Time on Earth . . .,'" *NME*, December 14, 1996, accessed June 19, 2017, https://sites.google.com/site/prninterviews/home/new-musical-express-nme-14-december-1996.

36. Susan Rogers, interview by Alan Freed for *Uptown* magazine/Per Nilsen, Los Angeles, CA, December 1994.

37. Liz Jones, *Slave to the Rhythm* (London: Little, Brown, 1997), 85.

38. Evan Sawdey, "Inside Prince's Revolution," *PopMatters*, June 4, 2009, accessed March 7, 2017, http://www.popmatters.com/feature/94061-inside-the-revolution/P2.

39. Weingarten, "Prince: The Purple Gang," 44.

40. Susan Rogers, interview by Alan Freed for *Uptown* magazine/Per Nilsen, Los Angeles, CA, February 1995.

41. "Jesse Johnson: Time's Up," *Fresh*, May 1985, 23.

42. Rogers, interview by Freed, February 1995.

43. Michael A. Gonzales, "30 Years Post-'Purple Rain,' Prince Upholds the Funk," *Ebony*, March 7, 2014, accessed March 11, 2017, http://www.ebony.com/ entertainment-culture/vintage-vision-30-years-post-purple-rain-prince-319#ax zz4b43vlus9.

44. Keith Murphy, "Purple Rain Turns 30: Prince's Engineer Shares Majestic (and Maddening) Studio Stories," *Vibe*, June 25, 2014, accessed June 25, 2017, https://web .archive.org/web/20151101151644/http://www.vibe.com/2014/06/purple-rain-turns -30-princes-engineer-shares-majestic-and-maddening-studio-stories/susan-rogers-talks -prince-purple-rain-2/.

45. Serge Simonart, "The Artist," *Guitar World*, October 1998, accessed March 4, 2017, http://princetext.tripod.com/i_gw98.html.

46. "The Five Count's Fifth Annual Princemas Celebration—An Evening with Prince & the Revolution's Bobby Z. & André Cymone," *The Five Count*, January 25, 2014, accessed March 7, 2017, http://thefivecount.com/interviews/the-five-counts -fifth-annual-princemas-celebration-an-evening-with-prince-the-revolutions-bobby-z -andr-cymone.

47. Prince, lyrics to "Love And Sex," performed by Prince and the Revolution, *Purple Rain Deluxe* (Expanded Edition), NPG Records/Warner Bros., 547374-2, 2017, compact disc.

48. Prince, lyrics to "Darling Nikki," performed by Prince and the Revolution, *Purple Rain Deluxe* (Expanded Edition), NPG Records/Warner Bros., 547374-2, 2017, compact disc.

49. Larry Crane, "Susan Rogers: From Prince to Ph.D.," *Tape Op*, January/February 2017, accessed February 20, 2017, http://tapeop.com/interviews/117/susan-rogers.

50. Steve Perry, "Prince: The Purple Decade," *Musician*, November 1988, 99.

51. Prince, interview by Tavis Smiley, *Tavis Smiley Show*, PBS, February 20, 2004, transcript accessed June 19, 2017, http://prince.org/msg/12/81402.

MARCH 1984

1. Brian McCollum, "Detroit Asks the Questions, and the Artist Reveals Himself as a Prince of Mystery," *Detroit Free Press*, December 26, 1997.

2. Marc Weingarten, "Prince: The Purple Gang," *Mojo*, February 1997, 46.

3. Jon Pareles, "A Re-Inventor of His World and Himself," *New York Times*, November 17, 1996, accessed March 4, 2017, http://www.nytimes.com/1996/11/17/ arts/a-re-inventor-of-his-world-and-himself.html.

4. Weingarten, "Prince: The Purple Gang," 44.

5. Dez Dickerson, interview on Housequake.com, January 16, 2004, accessed March 6, 2017, https://web.archive.org/web/20070421211256/http://www.house quake.com/showthread.php?s=&threadid=12453.

6. Susan Rogers, interview by Alan Freed for *Uptown* magazine/Per Nilsen, Los Angeles, CA, March 26, 1995.

7. Matt Fink, interviewed in *Purple Reign: The Story of Prince*, part 2, BBC Radio, documentary, January 25, 2003, accessed June 29, 2004, http://www.bbc.co.uk/pro grammes/b00svtj7.

8. Keith Murphy, "Purple Rain Turns 30: The Revolution's Dr. Fink Breaks Down Prince's Classic Track-by-Track," *Vibe*, June 25, 2014, accessed June 19, 2017, http://www. vibe.com/2014/06/purple-rain-turns-30-revolutions-dr-fink-breaks-down-princes -classic-track-track/dr-fink-breaks-down-prince-purple-rain-track-by-track-2.

9. "Best Selling Albums of All Time," *Entertainment Weekly*, May 3, 1996; reprinted in *Prince Family Newsletter*, May 11, 1996, 56.

10. Karl Coryat, "His Highness Gets Down!," *Bass Player*, November 1999, accessed June 19, 2017, http://www.bassplayer.com/news/1174/remembering-prince -his-highness-gets-down-cover-story/57724.

11. Coryat, "His Highness Gets Down!," accessed June 19, 2017, http://www .bassplayer.com/news/1174/remembering-prince-his-highness-gets-down-cover- story/57724.

12. Jake Brown, *Prince in the Studio (1975–1995)* (Phoenix: Amber Communications Group, 2010).

13. Coryat, "His Highness Gets Down!"

14. Alan Leeds, interview by Alan Freed for *Uptown* Magazine/Per Nilsen, Minneapolis, MN, November 1993.

15. Susan Rogers, interview by Alan Freed for *Uptown* magazine/Per Nilsen, Los Angeles, CA, December 1994.

16. Ernie Rideout, "Produced by Prince," *Keyboard*, December 1999, 40.

17. Morris Day, interview by Tom Neeham, *The Sounds of Film*, WUSB, April 28, 2016, accessed June 23, 2017, https://www.youtube.com/edit?o=U&video_ id=t7ceI27JPSI.

18. Rogers, interview by Freed, December 1994.

19. John Kenneth Muir, *Music on Film: Purple Rain* (Milwaukee, WI: Limelight, (2012), 78.

20. Scott Isler, "Prince in Exile," *Musician*, October 1984, 42.

21. Michael Goldberg, "Purple Rain Star Morris Day Goes It Alone," *Rolling Stone*, September 13, 1984, 41.

22. Serge Simonart, "The Artist," *Guitar World*, October 1998, accessed March 4, 2017, http://princetext.tripod.com/i_gw98.html.

23. Isler, "Prince in Exile," 43.

24. K Nicola Dyes, "The Voice: Brenda Bennett Talks 2 Beautiful Nights," *The Beautiful Nights* (blog), April 5, 2014, accessed March 12, 2017, http://beautifulnights chitown.blogspot.com/2014/04/the-voice-brenda-bennett-talks-2.html.

25. Prince, lyrics to "17 Days," performed by Prince and the Revolution, Warner Bros., B002CA4YDU, 1993, compact disc (spoken section of unreleased extended version).

26. Greg Kot, "Twin Cities Tycoon," *Details*, November 1998, accessed June 19, 2017, https://sites.google.com/site/prninterviews/home/details-november-1998.

27. Tom Mann, "An Oral History of Prince's 'Purple Rain,'" *FasterLouder*, August 21, 2014, accessed March 7, 2017, http://fasterlouder.junkee.com/an-oral-history-of-princes-purple-rain/839367.

28. Cynthia Horner, "A Special Interview 'For You,'" *Right On!* Super Special Presents Prince 1, no. 4 (1985): 9.

29. Larry Crane, "Susan Rogers: From Prince to Ph.D.," *Tape Op*, January/February 2017, accessed February 20, 2017, http://tapeop.com/interviews/117/susan-rogers.

30. Alan Light, *Let's Go Crazy: Prince and the Making of Purple Rain* (New York: Atria Books, 2014).

31. Prince, remarks during the Rock and Roll Hall of Fame Induction of Parliament/Funkadelic, Cleveland, OH, May 6, 1997.

32. Prince, lyrics to "Sex Shooter," performed by Apollonia 6, Warner Bros., WPCP-3701, 1984, compact disc.

33. Prince, lyrics to "Erotic City," performed by Prince and the Revolution, *Purple Rain Deluxe* (Expanded Edition), NPG Records/Warner Bros., 547374-2, 2017, compact disc.

34. Sheila E., *The Beat of My Own Drum: A Memoir by Sheila E.* (New York: Atria Books, 2014).

35. Sheila E., interview in *Unsung: Sheila E.*, A. Smith & Co. Productions, TV One, February 27, 2012.

36. Prince, "Erotic City."

37. Sheila E., interview in *Unsung*.

38. Sheila E., *The Beat of My Own Drum*.

39. Per Nilsen, "The Sheila E. Story," *Uptown* 20 (fall 1995): 14.

40. Sheila E., interview on AOL Live, December 13, 1995, accessed June 20, 2017, http://web.archive.org/web/19961231052851/http://www.mcs.net:80/~nation/home/cpn/sheila.htm.

41. Greg Boyer, interview on Housequake.com, February 28, 2004, accessed March 5, 2017, https://web.archive.org/web/20070623035352/http://www.housequake.com/showthread.php?s=&threadid=14508.

42. Light, *Let's Go Crazy*.

43. Sheila E., interview in *Unsung*.

44. Melissa Locker, "Sheila E Reflects on Her 'Glamorous Life': 'It's Hard to Be That Popular,'" *Time*, September 19, 2014, accessed March 4, 2017, http://time.com/3387754/sheila-e-glamorous-life-interview-book.

45. Sheila E., *The Beat of My Own Drum*.

46. Sheila E., *The Beat of My Own Drum*.

47. Sheila E., *The Beat of My Own Drum*.

APRIL 1984

1. Sheila E., *The Beat of My Own Drum: A Memoir by Sheila E.* (New York: Atria Books, 2014).

2. "Who Is the Real Sheila E.?," *Black Beat*, October 1984, 52.

3. Sheila E., *The Beat of My Own Drum.*

4. Will Hodgkinson, "I'm A Giver . . ." *Mojo*, April 2014, 85.

5. Prince, lyrics to "Erotic City," performed by Prince and the Revolution, *Purple Rain Deluxe* (Expanded Edition), NPG Records/Warner Bros., 547374-2, 2017, compact disc.

6. Jon Pareles, "For Prince, a Resurgence Accompanied by Spirituality," *New York Times*, July 12, 2004, accessed March 4, 2017, http://www.nytimes.com/2004/07/12/arts/for-prince-a-resurgence-accompanied-by-spirituality.html.

7. Jesse Johnson, interview by Tomi Jenkins, February 1, 2014, accessed June 23, 2017, https://www.youtube.com/watch?v=suk5yjlmJoQ&feature=youtu.be.

8. Prince, lyrics to "If the Kid Can't Make You Come," performed by the Time, unreleased section.

9. Jellybean Johnson, interview by Alan Freed for *Uptown* magazine/Per Nilsen, Minneapolis, MN, February 16, 1995.

10. Akbar Cojoe, "Brenda Bennett of Vanity 6 Talks Prince & Her New CD," *Examiner.com*, May 18, 2011, accessed March 5, 2017, http://prince.org/msg/5/358836.

11. Keith Murphy, "Purple Rain Turns 30: Prince's Engineer Shares Majestic (and Maddening) Studio Stories," *Vibe*, June 25, 2014, accessed July 10, 2014, http://www.vibe.com/2014/06/purple-rain-turns-30-princes-engineer-shares-majestic-and-maddening-studio-stories/susan-rogers-talks-prince-purple-rain-2; archived at https://web.archive.org/web/20151101151644/http://www.vibe.com/2014/06/purple-rain-turns-30-princes-engineer-shares-majestic-and-maddening-studio-stories/susan-rogers-talks-prince-purple-rain-2/.

MAY 1984

1. Debby Miller, review of "The Glamorous Life," *Rolling Stone*, September 13, 1984, 50.

2. Joseph Stannard, "Prince's *Around the World in a Day*: A Reappraisal," *Red Bull Music Academy Daily*, May 28, 2015, accessed June 19, 2017, http://daily.redbullmusicacademy.com/2015/05/prince-around-the-world-in-a-day.

3. Prince, interviewed on *The View*, ABC, September 17, 2012, accessed June 19, 2017, https://www.youtube.com/watch?v=TW_S6PuePKM.

4. Alan Light, *Let's Go Crazy: Prince and the Making of* Purple Rain (New York: Atria Books, 2014).

5. Neal Karlen, "Prince Talks," *Rolling Stone*, September 12, 1985, 30.

6. Matt Thorne, *Prince* (London: Faber & Faber, 2012).

7. "The Five Count's Sixth Annual Princemas Celebration—An Evening with Prince & the Revolution's Brown Mark," *The Five Count*, January 31, 2015, accessed March 8, 2017, http://thefivecount.com/interviews/the-five-counts-sixth-annual-prince mas-celebration-an-evening-with-prince-the-revolutions-brown-mark.

8. Matt Fink, interview by Michael Dean, *The Prince Podcast*, podcast audio, July 20, 2015, http://podcastjuice.net/the-prince-podcast-dr-fink-interview.

9. Annie Zaleski, "Prince's Genius, through the Revolution's Ears: "He Took the Best Bits of Beethoven, the Beatles and James Brown," *Salon*, April 24, 2017, accessed June 18, 2017, http://www.salon.com/2017/04/24/princes-genius-through-the-revolu tions-ears-he-took-the-best-bits-of-beethoven-the-beatles-and-james-brown.

10. Wendy Melvoin, interview by Jim DeRogatis and Greg Kot, *Sound Opinions*, WBEZ, July 24, 2009, accessed June 19, 2017, http://www.soundopinions.org/topic/wendyandlisa.

11. Susan Rogers, interview by Alan Freed for *Uptown* magazine/Per Nilsen, Los Angeles, CA, February 1995.

12. Prince, lyrics to "Roadhouse Garden," performed by Prince and the Revolution, *Purple Rain Deluxe* (Expanded Edition), NPG Records/Warner Bros., 547374-2, 2017, compact disc.

13. Jon Bream, "Revolution Keyboardist Shares Untold Stories from Prince's Soon-to-Be-Reissued 'Purple Rain,'" *Minneapolis Star Tribune*, June 17, 2017, accessed June 18, 2017, http://startribune.com/revolution-keyboardist-shares-untold-stories-from -prince-s-soon-to-be-reissued-purple-rain/428738003.

14. Fink, interview by Dean, July 20, 2015.

15. Alan Leeds, interview by Alan Freed for *Uptown* magazine/Per Nilsen, Minneapolis, MN, November 1993.

16. Rogers, interview by Freed, February 1995.

17. Sheila E., as told to Eric Renner Brown, "Late Greats: Stars Pay Tribute to Those We Lost in 2016," *Entertainment Weekly*, December 28, 2016, http://ew.com/news/late-greats-stars-we-lost-2016/sheila-e-on-prince.

18. Chris Nelson, "Exclusive: The Artist Portrays Music's Future," SonicNet Online, March 3, 1999, accessed March 12, 2017, https://sites.google.com/site/prninter views/home/sonicnet-3-march-1999.

19. Prince, interview by Love4OneAnother.com, January 19, 1999, accessed June 19, 2017, http://prince.org/msg/7/248584.

20. Jim Maloney, "Wendy & Lisa: After the Revolution Comes the Challenge," *Music Connection*, February 22–March 6, 1987, 13.

21. "The Revolution Duo on Prince's Lost Dream," *Vibe*, March 2009, accessed June 7, 2009, http://www.vibe.com/news/online_exclusives/2009/03/what_had_hap pened_was_lisa_coleman_and_wendy_melvoin.

22. "The Revolution Duo on Prince's Lost Dream."

23. Morris Day, *The Original 7ven*, directed by Lee Librado (Los Angeles, CA: Chronology Entertainment and Flyte Tyme Productions, 2011), DVD.

24. April Eugene, "Morris Day Goes Solo," *Black Beat*, January 1985, 43.

25. Day, in *The Original 7ven*.

26. Charley Crespo, "Minneapolis Update: Morris Day," *Rock & Soul*, February 1985, 30.

27. Eugene, "Morris Day Goes Solo," 44.

28. Alan Leeds, interview by Alan Freed for *Uptown* magazine/Per Nilsen, Minneapolis, MN, November 1993.

29. Leeds, interview by Freed, November 1993.

30. Susan Rogers, interview by Troy L. Foreman, *PC Principle Podcast*, podcast audio, May 18, 2016, http://thepcprinciple.com/?p=9145.

31. Dennis Hunt, "Revolution Frees Lisa and Wendy," *Los Angeles Times*, September 13, 1987, accessed March 12, 2017, http://articles.latimes.com/1987-09-13/entertainment/ca-7727_1_lisa-coleman.

JUNE 1984

1. Alan Light, "Body & Soul," *Tracks*, September 2004, 76.

2. Sheila E., *The Beat of My Own Drum: A Memoir by Sheila E.* (New York: Atria Books, 2014).

3. Bruce Orwall, "Purple Drain," *St. Paul Pioneer Press*, January 15, 1995, accessed June 19, 2017, http://princetext.tripod.com/n_1995.html.

4. Matt Thorne, *Prince* (London: Faber & Faber, 2012).

5. Thorne, *Prince*.

6. Prince, remarks in concert, First Avenue, Minneapolis, MN, June 7, 1984, accessed June 19, 2017, https://www.mixcloud.com/GINOFOXY/prince-the-revolution-1984-birthday-show.

7. Lisa Coleman and Wendy Melvoin, interview by Jim DeRogatis and Greg Kot, *Sound Opinions*, WBEZ, July 24, 2009, accessed June 19, 2017, http://www.soundopinions.org/topic/wendyandlisa.

8. Peggy McCreary, in *Prince: The Glory Years*, produced by Rob Johnstone for Prism Entertainment (New Malden, Surrey, UK: Chrome Dreams Media, April 2004), DVD; also available at https://www.youtube.com/watch?v=dRNYiFxR2Ps, accessed June 17, 2017.

9. Susan Rogers, interview by Alan Freed for *Uptown* magazine/Per Nilsen, Los Angeles, CA, March 25, 1995.

10. April Eugene, "Morris Day Goes Solo," *Black Beat*, January 1985, 43.

11. "Jesse Johnson on *Video Soul*," 1986, accessed June 19, 2017, https://www.youtube.com/watch?v=gIy6eB0C350.

12. Neal Karlen, "Prince Talks," *Rolling Stone*, September 12, 1985, 86.

13. "The Time, Voted #8 in *Rock & Soul*'s Reader's Poll," *Rock & Soul Special*, spring 1985, 32.

14. Light, "Body & Soul," 76.

15. Karlen, "Prince Talks," 86.

16. Jesse Johnson, interview with Teddy Bear, *LOTL Radio*, podcast audio, March 20, 2012, accessed June 1, 2017, http://www.blogtalkradio.com/reginald ford/2013/01/01/lotl-welcomes-jesse-johnson-orig-aired-march-19th-2012.

17. Alan Leeds, interview by Alan Freed for *Uptown* magazine/Per Nilsen, Minneapolis, MN, November 1993.

18. Keith Valcourt, "fDeluxe: The Family Reunion," *Rockerzine.com*, May 5, 2013, accessed March 7, 2017, https://www.rockerzine.com/2013/05/f-deluxe-the-family -reunion.

19. K Nicola Dyes, "Miss Understood: An In-Depth Interview with Susannah Melvoin," *The Beautiful Nights* (blog), April 18, 2013, accessed April 19, 2013, http:// beautifulnightschitown.blogspot.com/2013/04/miss-understood-in-depth-interview -with.html.

20. Paul Peterson, interview by Leo Sidran, *The Third Story Podcast with Leo Sidran*, podcast audio, May 5, 2016, http://www.third-story.com/listen/on-prince.

21. Rogers, interview by Freed, March 25, 1995.

22. Rogers, interview by Freed, March 25, 1995.

23. Scott Isler, "Prince in Exile," *Musician*, October 1984, 46.

24. Rogers, interview by Freed, March 25, 1995.

25. Charles Waring, "Family Values . . . fDeluxe's Susannah Melvoin talks to SJF," *Soulandjazzandfunk.com*, November 9, 2011, accessed March 10, 2017, http://soul andjazzandfunk.com/interviews/1541-family-values-fdeluxes-susannah-melvoin-talks -to-sjf-.html?showall=1.

26. Susan Rogers, interview by Alan Freed for *Uptown* magazine/Per Nilsen, Los Angeles, CA, December 1994.

27. "Best Selling Albums of All Time," *Entertainment Weekly*, May 3, 1996, reprinted in *Prince Family Newsletter*, May 11, 1996, 56.

28. "Interview with Matt Fink of the World's Greatest Prince Tribute: THE PURPLE XPERIENCE," *MotorCityBlog* (blog), July 21, 2014, accessed March 12, 2017, http://motorcityblog.blogspot.com/2014/07/interview-with-matt-fink-of-worlds.html.

29. Isler, "Prince in Exile," 46.

30. Robert L. Doerschuk, "The View from Graffiti Bridge," *Keyboard*, January 1991, 96.

31. Beth Coleman, "Prince and the Revelation," *Paper*, April 21, 2016, accessed June 17, 2017, http://www.papermag.com/prince-1999-cover-story-1744672669.html.

32. Rogers, interview by Freed, December 1994.

33. Miles Marshall Lewis, "Prince and Reed Man Eric Leeds Teamed Up to Create Two Albums under the Monkier Madhouse," *Wax Poetics*, winter 2012, accessed June 19, 2017, http://www.waxpoetics.com/blog/features/articles/prince-madhouse -jazz-band-eric-leeds.

34. Mick Brown, "Prince Interview: 'I Didn't Let Fame Rule Me,'" *Telegraph*, December 6, 2004, accessed March 4, 2017, http://www.telegraph.co.uk/music/inter views/prince-interview-the-act-didnt-finish-when-he-stepped-off-stage.

35. Leeds, interview by Freed, November 1993.

36. Prince, lyrics to "Mutiny," performed by the Family, Warner Bros. Records, 7599-25322-2, 1985, compact disc.

37. Prince, lyrics to "High Fashion," performed by the Family, Warner Bros. Records, 7599-25322-2, 1985, compact disc.

38. Prince, lyrics to "High Fashion."

39. Jellybean Johnson, interview by Alan Freed for *Uptown* magazine/Per Nilsen, Los Angeles, CA, March 2, 1995.

40. Rico "Superbizzee" Washington, "fDeluxe 2011 Soulmusic.com Interview—Pt. 1: Paul Peterson," *SoulMusic.com*, September 26, 2011, accessed March 17, 2012, http://www.soulmusic.info/index.asp?S=80&T=80&ART=702.

41. Rico "Superbizzee" Washington, "fDeluxe 2011 Soulmusic.com Interview—Pt. 2: Susannah Melvoin," *SoulMusic.com*, September 26, 2011, accessed March 4, 2017, http://www.soulmusic.info/index.asp?S=80&T=80&ART=703.

42. Rohan Williams, "fDeluxe: The Prince and I," *Scene*, June 7, 2012, accessed June 19, 2017, http://scenemagazine.com.au/music/pop-electro/fdeluxe-the-prince-and-i.

43. Rogers, interview by Freed, December 1994.

44. Rogers, interview by Freed, December 1994.

45. Keith Valcourt, "Prince's fDeluxe Proteges Still Have 'Fire' in Their Blood after Making 30 Years of Funky Music," *Washington Times*, May 5, 2015, accessed May 17, 2015, http://www.washingtontimes.com/news/2015/may/5/interview-with-fdeluxe-the -family-behind-prince-ma.

46. Jon Bream and Chris Riemenschneider, "Prince: An Oral History," *Minneapolis Star Tribune*, March 14, 2004.

47. Rogers, interview by Freed, December 1994.

48. Rogers, interview by Freed, December 1994.

49. Dyes, "Miss Understood."

50. Prince, interviewed on *The View*, ABC, September 17, 2012, accessed June 19, 2017, https://www.youtube.com/watch?v=JQQVpSDHq-M.

51. Miles Marshall Lewis, "Prince Hits N Runs N Talks!" *Ebony*, December 22, 2015, accessed June 19, 2017, https://www.facebook.com/notes/housequake/prince -hits-n-runs-n-talks-ebony-interview-dec-22-2015/916986788385046.

52. Lewis, "Prince Hits N Runs N Talks!,"

JULY 1984

1. Kenneth Partridge, "Prince Protégés the Family Return as fDeluxe, Talk Purple One's Peculiarities," *Spinner.com*, November 18, 2011, accessed June 19, 2017, http:// prince.org/msg/5/371066.

2. Eric Leeds, interview by Alan Freed for *Uptown* magazine/Per Nilsen, Los Angeles, CA, October 15, 1993.

3. Leeds, interview by Freed, October 15, 1993.

4. Leeds, interview by Freed, October 15, 1993.

5. Leeds, interview by Freed, October 15, 1993.

6. Leeds, interview by Freed, October 15, 1993.

7. Susan Rogers, interview by Alan Freed for *Uptown* magazine/Per Nilsen, Los Angeles, CA, December 1994.

8. Leeds, interview by Freed, October 15, 1993.

9. Paul Peterson, interview by Leo Sidran, *The Third Story Podcast with Leo Sidran*, podcast audio, May 5, 2016, http://www.third-story.com/listen/on-prince.

10. Keith Valcourt, "fDeluxe: The Family Reunion," *Rockerzine.com*, May 5, 2013, accessed March 7, 2017, https://www.rockerzine.com/2013/05/f-deluxe-the-family-reunion.

11. Rogers, interview by Freed, December 1994.

12. David Z Rivkin, interview by Alan Freed for *Uptown* magazine/Per Nilsen, May 13, 1995, via telephone.

13. Rico "Superbizzee" Washington, "fDeluxe 2011 Soulmusic.com Interview—Pt. 1: Paul Peterson," *SoulMusic.com*, September 26, 2011, accessed March 17, 2012, http://www.soulmusic.info/index.asp?S=80&T=80&ART=702.

14. Eric Leeds, interview by Alan Freed for *Uptown* magazine/Per Nilsen, Los Angeles, CA, November 11, 1994.

15. Dave Hill, *Prince: A Pop Life* (New York: Harmony Books, 1989), 182.

16. Jon Bream and Chris Riemenschneider, "Prince: An Oral History," *Minneapolis Star Tribune*, March 14, 2004.

17. David Z, interview by Alan Freed for *Uptown* magazine/Per Nilsen, March 4, 1995.

18. Andrea Swensson, "Bobby Z Shares His *Purple Rain* Memories on the Album's 30th Anniversary," *The Current*, June 25, 2014, accessed June 18, 2017, http://blog.thecurrent.org/2014/06/bobby-z-shares-his-purple-rain-memories-on-the -albums-30th-anniversary.

19. Christopher Connelly, "*Ice Cream Castle*: The Time (review)," *Rolling Stone*, August 30, 1984, 43.

20. David Z, interview by Freed, March 4, 1995.

21. Robert Hilburn, "Mixed Emotions: Prince on the Music," *Musician*, September 1983, 58.

22. Susan Rogers, interview by Alan Freed for *Uptown* magazine/Per Nilsen, Los Angeles, CA, February 1995.

23. Charley Crespo, "Prince: Intimate Relations," *Rock & Soul*, August 1986, 18.

24. Charles Waring, "Family Values . . . fDeluxe's Susannah Melvoin talks to SJF," *Soulandjazzandfunk.com*, November 9, 2011, accessed March 10, 2017, http://soul andjazzandfunk.com/interviews/1541-family-values-fdeluxes-susannah-melvoin-talks -to-sjf-.html?showall=1.

25. Washington, "fDeluxe 2011 Soulmusic.com Interview—Pt. 1: Paul Peterson."

26. Bream and Riemenschneider, "Prince."

27. Liz Jones, *Slave to the Rhythm* (London: Little, Brown, 1997), 81.

28. Prince, lyrics to "Nothing Compares 2 U," performed by the Family, Warner Bros. Records, 7599-25322-2, 1985, compact disc.

29. Leeds, interview by Freed, October 15, 1993.

30. Leeds, interview by Freed, October 15, 1993.

31. Paul Peterson, e-mail to the author, July 2, 2014.

32. Rogers, interview by Freed, February 1995.

33. K Nicola Dyes, "Every Day is a Winding Road: St. Paul Peterson Talks 2 Beautiful Nights," *The Beautiful Nights* (blog), August 18, 2013, accessed August 18, 2013, http://beautifulnightschitown.blogspot.com/2013/08/everyday-is-winding-road -st-paul.html.

34. David Z Rivkin, interview by Freed, March 4, 1995.

35. Jellybean Johnson, interview by Alan Freed for *Uptown* magazine/Per Nilsen, Los Angeles, CA, March 2, 1995.

36. Leeds, interview by Freed, October 15, 1993.

37. Leeds, interview by Freed, October 15, 1993.

38. Leeds, interview by Freed, October 15, 1993.

39. Leeds, interview by Freed, October 15, 1993.

40. "The Five Count's Fourth Annual Princemas Celebration—An Evening with Prince & the Revolution's Doctor Fink," *The Five Count*, January 26, 2013, accessed March 7, 2017, http://thefivecount.com/interviews/the-five-counts-fourth-annual -princemas-celebration-an-evening-with-prince-the-revolutions-doctor-fink.

41. "The Five Count's Fourth Annual Princemas Celebration."

42. Eric Leeds, interviewed in *Purple Reign: The Story of Prince*, BBC Radio, documentary, January 18, 2003, accessed June 29, 2004, http://www.bbc.co.uk/pro grammes/b00snwb4.

43. Swensson, "Bobby Z Shares his *Purple Rain* Memories."

44. Steve Harvey with Strother Bullins, "Remembering Prince: Engineer 'Cubby' Colby," *ProSound Network*, April 28, 2017, accessed June 19, 2017, http://www.pro soundnetwork.com/business/remembering-prince-engineer-cubby-colby/46040.

45. Harvey with Bullins, "Remembering Prince."

46. Matt Thorne, *Prince* (London: Faber & Faber, 2012).

47. Thorne, *Prince*.

48. Prince, interview by Stephen Fargnoli, MTV, November 15, 1985, accessed June 19, 2017, http://www.dailymotion.com/video/x49h7vy.

49. Rogers, interview by Freed, February 1995.

50. Rogers, interview by Freed, February 1995.

51. Prince, lyrics to "America," performed by Prince and the Revolution, *Around the World in a Day*, Paisley Park Records/Warner Bros., 25286, 1985, compact disc.

52. "Alan Leeds: The Questions, the Answers & More Besides," *Prince.org*, December 24, 2005, accessed March 13, 2017, http://prince.org/msg/7/171968/ALAN -LEEDS-THE-QUESTIONS-THE-ANSWERS-MORE-BESIDES.

53. Jonathan Takiff, "The Flamboyant Prince of Pop," *Philadelphia Daily News*, July 31, 1984.

54. Roger Ebert, *At the Movies with Gene Siskel and Roger Ebert*, accessed June 26, 2017, http://www.mediaite.com/online/roger-ebert-loved-purple-rain-as-for-princes -other-movies.

55. Pepé Willie, interview by Kristie Lazenberry for *Uptown* magazine/Per Nilsen, Minneapolis, MN, [1995].

56. Mary Aloe, "Clothes of Passion Vanity," *Rock*, February 1985, 29.

57. Mobeen Azhar, *Hunting for Prince's Vault*, BBC Radio, March 21, 2015, accessed March 5, 2016, https://www.mixcloud.com/Emancipatio/hunting-for-princes -vault-bbc-documentary-by-mobeen-azhar-march-2015/.

AUGUST 1984

1. Matt Thorne, *Prince* (London: Faber & Faber, 2012).

2. Bobby Z Rivkin, interview by Joe Kelley, *Upper Room with Joe Kelley*, WVOF, February 2012, http://www.upperroomwithjoekelley.com/mpls.html.

3. Tom Mann, "An Oral History of Prince's 'Purple Rain,'" *FasterLouder*, August 21, 2014, accessed March 7, 2017, http://fasterlouder.junkee.com/an-oral-history-of -princes-purple-rain/839367.

4. Eric Leeds, interview by Alan Freed for *Uptown* magazine/Per Nilsen, Los Angeles, CA, November 11, 1994.

5. Susan Rogers, interview by Alan Freed for *Uptown* magazine/Per Nilsen, Los Angeles, CA, March 25, 1995.

6. Mobeen Azhar, *Hunting for Prince's Vault*, BBC Radio, March 21, 2015, accessed March 5, 2016, https://www.mixcloud.com/Emancipatio/hunting-for-princes -vault-bbc-documentary-by-mobeen-azhar-march-2015.

7. Mark Brown, interview by Questlove, Questlove Supreme, Pandora, September 28, 2016, accessed October 4, 2016, https://www.pandora.com/station/ play/3642532478040643917.

8. Alan Leeds, interview by Alan Freed for *Uptown* magazine/Per Nilsen, Minneapolis, MN, January 20, 1994.

9. Mann, "An Oral History of Prince's 'Purple Rain.'"

10. Dez Dickerson, in *Prince: The Glory Years*, produced by Rob Johnstone for Prism Entertainment (New Malden, Surrey, UK: Chrome Dreams Media, April 2004), DVD; also available at https://www.youtube.com/watch?v=dRNYiFxR2Ps, accessed June 17, 2017.

11. Jem Aswad, "The Revolution Remembers Their Last Moments with Prince—and the First Time They Heard 'Purple Rain,'" *Billboard*, December 12, 2016, accessed March 6, 2017, http://www.billboard.com/articles/events/year-in-music-2016/7604454/the-revolution-prince-final-moments.

12. Susan Rogers, interview by Alan Freed for *Uptown* magazine/Per Nilsen, Los Angeles, CA, February 1995.

13. Rogers, interview by Freed, February 1995.

14. Rogers, interview by Freed, February 1995.

15. Jake Brown, *Prince in the Studio (1975–1995)* (Phoenix: Amber Communications Group, 2010).

16. Scott Isler, "Prince in Exile," *Musician*, October 1984, 42.

17. Jon Bream and Chris Riemenschneider, "Prince: An Oral History," *Minneapolis Star Tribune*, March 14, 2004.

18. Rogers, interview by Freed, February 1995.

19. Paul Mathur, "Revolt into Style," *Melody Maker*, August 15, 1987, 21.

20. Rogers, interview by Freed, February 1995.

21. Brown, *Prince in the Studio*.

22. Rogers, interview by Freed, February 1995.

23. Rogers, interview by Freed, February 1995.

24. Eric Leeds, interview by Alan Freed for *Uptown* magazine/Per Nilsen, Los Angeles, CA, October 15, 1993.

25. Prince, lyrics to "The Dance Electric," performed by Prince and the Revolution, *Purple Rain Deluxe* (Expanded Edition), NPG Records/Warner Bros., 547374-2, 2017, compact disc.

26. Title on sleeve for "17 Days," performed by Prince and the Revolution, B-side to "Purple Rain," Warner Bros., 0-20228, 1984, vinyl record.

27. Prince, lyrics to "The Dance Electric."

28. Prince, lyrics to "Around the World in a Day," performed by Prince and the Revolution, *Around the World in a Day*, Paisley Park Records/Warner Bros., 25286, 1985, compact disc.

29. Lisa Coleman, "Questions for Wendy & Lisa," *WendyandLisa.com*, November 25, 2009, accessed January 17, 2010, http://www.wendyandlisa.com/forum/qa-wendy-lisa/hello-ladies-i-have-question-yall.

30. Leeds, interview by Freed, January 20, 1994.

31. Leeds, interview by Freed, January 20, 1994.

32. Prince, on the *Purple Rain* tour, November 4, 1984, Detroit, MI.

33. Prince, lyrics to "Horny Pony," performed by Prince and the New Power Generation, *Diamonds and Pearls*, Paisley Park Records/Warner Bros., 25379-2, 1991, compact disc.

34. Paul Peterson, interview by Leo Sidran, *The Third Story Podcast with Leo Sidran*, podcast audio, May 5, 2016, http://www.third-story.com/listen/on-prince.

35. Susan Rogers, interview by Alan Freed for *Uptown* magazine/Per Nilsen, Los Angeles, CA, August 4, 1997.

36. Rogers, interview by Freed, August 4, 1997.

37. Rogers, interview by Freed, August 4, 1997.

38. Cathy Wurzer, "Prince Sound Engineer Reflects on Recording Some of His Biggest Hits," *MPR News*, April 22, 2016, http://www.mprnews.org/story/2016/04/22/sound-engineer-on-working-with-prince.

39. Thorne, *Prince*.

40. Prince, lyrics to "God," performed by Prince and the Revolution, *Purple Rain Deluxe* (Expanded Edition), NPG Records/Warner Bros., 547374-2, 2017, compact disc.

41. Prince, interview by Larry King, *Larry King Live*, CNN, December 10, 1999, accessed April 21, 2016, https://www.youtube.com/watch?v=m8mg7CxAYUM.

42. Duane Tudahl, "Sunset in My Heart," *Uptown* 27 (spring 1997): 21.

43. Sheila E., *The Beat of My Own Drum: A Memoir by Sheila E.* (New York: Atria Books, 2014).

44. Robert Santelli, "Sheila E.," *Modern Drummer*, July 1991, 21, accessed March 8, 2017, https://moderndrummer.com/wp-content/uploads/2016/05/md140.pdf.

SEPTEMBER 1984

1. Brandon Turner, "Sheila E.," *Black Beat*, April 1985, 58.

2. Dez Dickerson, in *Prince: The Glory Years*, DVD, produced by Rog Johnstone (East London, UK: Prism Films, 2007); also available at https://www.youtube.com/watch?v=dRNYiFxR2Ps, accessed March 6, 2017.

3. Susan Rogers, interview by Alan Freed for *Uptown* magazine/Per Nilsen, Los Angeles, CA, February 1995.

4. Rogers, interview by Freed, February 1995.

5. Jim Walsh, "Former Prince's Coming Out Bash Is Unforgettable," *St. Paul Pioneer Press*, November 14, 1996; based on a press conference at Studio B in Paisley Park on November 13, 1996.

6. Prince, remarks in concert, Piano & A Microphone show, Paisley Park, Chanhassen, MN, January 21, 2016.

7. Prince, lyrics to "Raspberry Beret," performed by Prince and the Revolution, *Around the World in a Day*, Paisley Park Records/Warner Bros., 25286, 1985, compact disc.

8. Matt Thorne, *Prince* (London: Faber & Faber, 2012).

9. Prince, lyrics to "Raspberry Beret."

10. Rogers, interview by Freed, February 1995.

11. Rogers, interview by Freed, February 1995.

12. Neal Karlen, "Prince Talks," *Rolling Stone*, September 12, 1985, 30.

13. Alan Leeds, interview by Questlove, *Questlove Supreme*, Pandora, October 11, 2016, accessed October 16, 2016, https://www.pandora.com/station/play/3642532478040643917.

14. Susan Rogers, interview by Alan Freed for *Uptown* magazine/Per Nilsen, Los Angeles, CA, August 4, 1997.

15. Jim Maloney, "Wendy & Lisa: After the Revolution Comes the Challenge," *Music Connection*, February 22–March 6, 1987, 13.

16. Eric Leeds, interview by Alan Freed for *Uptown* magazine/Per Nilsen, Los Angeles, CA, November 11, 1994.

17. Prince, interview by the Electrifying Mojo, *The Electrifying Mojo*, WHYT, June 7, 1986, accessed March 2, 2017, https://www.youtube.com/watch?v=NJZCoxZ5COY.

18. Rogers, interview by Freed, February 1995.

19. Liz Jones, *Slave to the Rhythm* (London: Little, Brown, 1997), 79.

20. Karlen, "Prince Talks," 30.

21. Jake Brown, *Prince in the Studio (1975–1995)* (Phoenix: Amber Communications Group, 2010).

22. Rogers, interview by Freed, February 1995.

23. Marc Weingarten, "Sisters of the Revolution," *Mojo*, February 1997, 47.

24. Rogers, interview by Freed, February 1995.

25. Brown, *Prince in the Studio*.

26. Rogers, interview by Freed, August 4, 1997.

27. Duane Tudahl, "The Revolution Will Be Heard," *Uptown* 60 (March 2004): 103.

28. Rogers, interview by Freed, August 4, 1997.

29. Sheila E., *The Beat of My Own Drum: A Memoir by Sheila E.* (New York: Atria Books, 2014).

30. K Nicola Dyes, "Miss Understood: An In-Depth Interview with Susannah Melvoin," *The Beautiful Nights* (blog), April 18, 2013, accessed April 19, 2013, http://beautifulnightschitown.blogspot.com/2013/04/miss-understood-in-depth-interview-with.html.

31. Clare Fischer, interview on Housequake.com, April 2006, accessed March 12, 2107, http://web.archive.org/web/20060526102515/http://www.housequake.com/showthread.php?s=&threadid=63884.

32. Rogers, interview by Freed, August 4, 1997.

33. Prince, lyrics to "The Ladder," performed by Prince and the Revolution, Paisley Park/Warner Bros. Records, 25286, 1985, compact disc.

34. Rogers, interview by Freed, August 4, 1997.

35. Rogers, interview by Freed, August 4, 1997.

36. "Interview with The Artist," *Entertainment Weekly*, May 28, 1999, accessed March 11, 2017, https://sites.google.com/site/themusicinterviewarchive/prince/prince-1999-entertainment-weekly-interview.

37. Harold Lewis, Tony Melodia, and Stefan van Poucke, "Take This Beat: An Exclusive Interview with Bobby Z Rivkin—Part 2," *Uptown* 43 (fall 2000): 22.

38. Rogers, interview by Freed, August 4, 1997.

39. Rogers, interview by Freed, August 4, 1997.

40. Alan Leeds, interview by Alan Freed for *Uptown* magazine/Per Nilsen, Minneapolis, MN, November 1993.

41. Neal Karlen, "Ladies in Waiting," *Rolling Stone*, April 24, 1986, 44.

42. Duane Tudahl, "Daughters of the Revolution," *Uptown*, summer 1998, 24.

43. Ed Ochs, "Mom's Favorite Freak," *Rock & Soul*, June 1981, 35.

44. Jones, *Slave to the Rhythm*, 84.

OCTOBER 1984

1. K Nicola Dyes, "The Voice: Brenda Bennett Talks 2 Beautiful Nights," *The Beautiful Nights* (blog), April 5, 2014, accessed March 12, 2017, http://beautifulnights chitown.blogspot.com/2014/04/the-voice-brenda-bennett-talks-2.html.

2. Rick Bellaire, "Hold Me Closer: The Story of Brenda Bennett," *Rhode Island Music Hall of Fame Historical Archive*, 2015, accessed March 10, 2017, http://www .ripopmusic.org/musical-artists/musicians/brenda-bennettbrenda-mosher.

3. Dyes, "The Voice."

4. Susan Rogers, interview by Alan Freed for *Uptown* magazine/Per Nilsen, Los Angeles, CA, January 19, 1996.

5. David Browne, "Prince's Epic 'Purple Rain' Tour: An Oral History," *Rolling Stone*, June 22, 2017, accessed June 27, 2017, http://www.rollingstone.com/music/ features/princes-epic-purple-rain-tour-an-oral-history-w476429.

6. "The Five Count's Sixth Annual Princemas Celebration—An Evening with Prince & the Revolution's Brown Mark," *The Five Count*, January 31, 2015, accessed March 8, 2017, http://thefivecount.com/interviews/the-five-counts-sixth-annual-prince mas-celebration-an-evening-with-prince-the-revolutions-brown-mark.

7. Wendy Melvoin, interview by Questlove, *Questlove Supreme*, Pandora, September 28, 2016, accessed October 4, 2016, https://www.pandora.com/station/ play/3642532478040643917.

8. Matt Fink, interview with Michael Dean, *The Prince Podcast*, podcast audio, July 20, 2015, http://podcastjuice.net/the-prince-podcast-dr-fink-interview.

9. Mark Brown (aka BrownMark), "BrownMark Made Prince Pancakes," *The BrownMark Podcast*, podcast audio, September 2016, http://thebrownmarkshow.lib syn.com/2016/09.

10. Harold Lewis, Tony Melodia, and Stefan van Poucke, "Take This Beat: An Exclusive Interview with Bobby Z Rivkin—Part 2," *Uptown* 43 (fall 2000): 19.

11. Eric Leeds, interview with Gary "G-Spot" Baca, KPFA, January 31, 1998, *Prince Family Newsletter* 6, no. 5 (February 28, 1998): 27.

12. Leeds, interview with Baca.

13. Eric Leeds, interview by Alan Freed for *Uptown* magazine/Per Nilsen, Los Angeles, CA, October 15, 1993.

14. Miles Marshall Lewis, "Prince and Reed Man Eric Leeds Teamed Up to Create Two Albums under the Moniker Madhouse," *Wax Poetics*, winter 2012, accessed June 17, 2017, http://www.waxpoetics.com/blog/features/articles/prince-madhouse -jazz-band-eric-leeds.

15. Clare Fischer, interview on Housequake.com, April 2006, accessed March 12, 2107, http://web.archive.org/web/20060526102515/http://www.housequake.com/ showthread.php?s=&threadid=63884.

16. Charles Waring, "Family Values . . . fDeluxe's Susannah Melvoin talks to SJF," Soulandjazzandfunk.com, November 9, 2011, accessed March 10, 2017, http://soul andjazzandfunk.com/interviews/1541-family-values-fdeluxes-susannah-melvoin-talks -to-sjf-.html?showall=1.

17. Susan Rogers, interview by Alan Freed for *Uptown* magazine/Per Nilsen, Los Angeles, CA, August 4, 1997.

18. Clare Fischer, interview by Ben Sidran, circa 1985, as quoted in *Talking Jazz with Ben Sidran*, Volume 1: The Rhythm Section (Shoreditch, East London, UK: Unlimited Media, 2014), accessed March 12, 2017, https://books.google.com/books?id= O3hZDQAAQBAJ&pg=PT456#v=onepage&q&f=false.

19. Ernie Rideout, "Produced by Prince," *Keyboard*, December 1999, 40.

20. Rico "Superbizzee" Washington, "fDeluxe 2011 Soulmusic.com Interview—Pt. 1: Paul Peterson," *SoulMusic.com*, September 26, 2011, accessed March 17, 2012, http://www.soulmusic.info/index.asp?S=80&T=80&ART=702.

21. Matt Fink, in *Prince, A Purple Reign*, produced by BBC, documentary, 2011, accessed June 15, 2017, https://www.youtube.com/watch?v=LlTwe9LxZ8w.

22. Prince, lyrics to "Condition of the Heart," performed by Prince and the Revolution, *Around the World in a Day*, Paisley Park Records/Warner Bros., 25286, 1985, compact disc.

23. Prince, lyrics to "Condition of the Heart."

24. Rogers, interview by Freed, August 4, 1997.

25. Rogers, interview by Freed, August 4, 1997.

26. Rogers, interviewed by Freed, August 4, 1997.

27. Anthony DeCurtis, "In the Studio: Prince Records 3 Hours of 'Emancipation,'" *Rolling Stone*, October 1996, accessed March 12, 2017, https://sites.google.com/site/ prninterviews/home/rolling-stone-745-17-october-1996.

28. Lewis, Melodia, and van Poucke, "Take This Beat," 20.

29. Susan Rogers, interview with Troy L. Foreman, *PC Principle Podcast*, podcast audio, May 18, 2016, http://thepcprinciple.com/?p=9145.

30. Browne, "Prince's Epic 'Purple Rain' Tour: An Oral History."

31. Eric Lindbom, "Sheila E.: Actual Talent," *Twin Cities Nightbeat*, October 29, 1984.

32. Prince, interview by Tavis Smiley, *Tavis Smiley Show*, PBS, February 20, 2004, transcript accessed June 17, 2017, http://prince.org/msg/12/81402.

33. Alan Leeds, interview by Alan Freed for *Uptown* magazine/Per Nilsen, Minneapolis, MN, November 11, 1994.

34. Susan Rogers, interview by Alan Freed for *Uptown* magazine/Per Nilsen, Los Angeles, CA, December 1994.

35. Leeds, interview by Freed, November 11, 1994.

36. Matt Fink, interview by Girl Bros., *Girl Bros. Network*, podcast audio, September 2006, http://www.myspace.com/girlbrosnetwork.

37. Alex Hahn, *Possessed* (New York: Billboards Books, 2003), 99.

38. Robert I. Doerschuk, "Portrait of the Artist," *Musician*, April 1997, 89.

39. Hans-Maarten Post, "Prince 'Ik Word steeds beter,'" *Het Nieuwsblad* (Antwerpen, Belgium), June 24, 2010, 9.

40. Jellybean Johnson, interview by Alan Freed for *Uptown* magazine/Per Nilsen, Minneapolis, MN, February 2, 1995.

41. Cynthia Littleton, "Warner Bros. Records Exec on Prince: 'It Was Not in Our Interest to Be Confrontational with Him,'" *Variety*, April 21, 2016, accessed March 10, 2017, http://variety.com/2016/music/news/prince-dead-warner-bros-records-bob -merlis-1201758543.

42. Alan Leeds, in *Purple Reign: The Story of Prince*, part 2, documentary, BBC Radio, January 25, 2003, accessed June 29, 2004, http://www.bbc.co.uk/programmes/ b00svtj7.

43. Rogers, interview by Freed, August 4, 1997.

44. Steve Dougherty, "Sex and God and Rock and Roll," *People*, November 14, 1988, accessed March 12, 2017, http://people.com/archive/sex-and-god-and-rock-and -roll-vol-30-no-20.

45. Ekow Eshun, "Purple Pain," *Face*, March 1997, 92.

46. Alan Leeds, in *Prince, A Purple Reign*, produced by BBC, documentary, 2011, accessed June 15, 2017, https://www.youtube.com/watch?v=LlTwe9LxZ8w.

NOVEMBER 1984

1. Keith Murphy, "Purple Rain Turns 30: The Revolution's Dr. Fink Breaks Down Prince's Classic Track-by-Track," *Vibe*, June 25, 2014, accessed June 17, 2017, http://www.vibe.com/2014/06/purple-rain-turns-30-revolutions-dr-fink-breaks-down -princes-classic-track-track/dr-fink-breaks-down-prince-purple-rain-track-by-track-1.

2. Prince, on the Purple Rain tour, November 4, 1984, Detroit, MI.

3. Tim Blanks, "Lisa Coleman and Wendy: Prince's Revolutionaries," *Graffiti* 1, no. 2 (February 1985).

4. Prince, interview by the Electrifying Mojo, *The Electrifying Mojo*, WHYT, June 7, 1986, accessed March 2, 2017, https://www.youtube.com/watch?v=NJZCoxZ5COY.

5. David Browne, "Prince's Epic 'Purple Rain' Tour: An Oral History," *Rolling Stone*, June 22, 2017, accessed June 27, 2017, http://www.rollingstone.com/music/features/princes-epic-purple-rain-tour-an-oral-history-w476429.

6. Miles White, "Prince in Concert: Playful, Powerful," *USA Today*, November 6, 1984.

7. Nelson George, "Too Much Rain Clouds Prince Show," *Billboard*, November 17, 1984, 36.

8. Greg Kot, "Tribune Archive: A Peek into Prince's Mind," *Chicago Tribune*, September 20, 2012, accessed March 12, 2017, http://www.chicagotribune.com/entertainment/music/chi-prince-interview-music-chicago-20120920-column.html.

9. Prince, interview on *The Biz*, CNN, July 16, 2004, accessed June 17, 2017, https://www.youtube.com/watch?v=CVk5c2DY3Zw.

10. Alan Light, *Let's Go Crazy: Prince and the Making of* Purple Rain (New York: Atria Books, 2014).

11. Eric Leeds, interview by Alan Freed for *Uptown* magazine/Per Nilsen, Los Angeles, CA, October 15, 1993.

12. Browne, "Prince's Epic 'Purple Rain' Tour."

13. Matt Fink, interview with Michael Dean, *The Prince Podcast*, podcast audio, July 20, 2015, http://podcastjuice.net/the-prince-podcast-dr-fink-interview.

DECEMBER 1984

1. Matt Fink, interview by Michael Dean, *The Prince Podcast*, podcast audio, July 20, 2015, http://podcastjuice.net/the-prince-podcast-dr-fink-interview.

2. Susan Rogers, interview by Troy L. Foreman, *PC Principle Podcast*, podcast audio, May 18, 2016, http://thepcprinciple.com/?p=9145.

3. Jake Brown, *Prince in the Studio (1975–1995)* (Phoenix: Amber Communications Group, 2010).

4. Prince, interview by Tavis Smiley, *BET Tonight*, BET, October 27, 1998, accessed March 8, 2017, https://www.youtube.com/watch?v=pqyjwhFiQqg.

5. Neal Karlen, "Prince Talks," *Rolling Stone*, October 18, 1990, 59.

6. Dan Glaister, "The Singer vs. the Record Company," *Guardian*, March 3, 1995, *Prince Family Newsletter 3*, no. 6 (March 18, 1995): 32.

7. Liz Jones, *Slave to the Rhythm* (London: Little, Brown, 1997), 78.

8. Beth Coleman, "Prince and the Revelation," *Paper*, April 21, 2016, accessed June 17, 2017, http://www.papermag.com/prince-1999-cover-story-1744672669.html.

9. Wendy Melvoin, in *Dr. Prince & Mr. Jackson*, directed by Philip Priestley (Paris: Arte France, 2009), broadcast July 9, 2009.

10. Tom Mann, "An Oral History of Prince's 'Purple Rain,'" *FasterLouder*, August 21, 2014, accessed March 7, 2017, http://fasterlouder.junkee.com/an-oral-history-of-princes-purple-rain/839367.

11. Larry Crane, "Susan Rogers: From Prince to Ph.D.," *Tape Op*, January/February 2017, accessed February 20, 2017, http://tapeop.com/interviews/117/susan-rogers.

12. Montrose Cunningham, "Celebrating Black Music Month: The 25th Anniversary of Prince's *Sign o' the Times* (Part 1)," *Soultrain.com*, June 22, 2012, accessed March 5, 2017, http://soultrain.com/2012/06/20/celebrating-black-music-month-the-25th-anniversary-of-princes-sign-o-the-times-part-1.

13. Vickie Gilmer, "A Portrait of the Artist: Healthy, Happy, Ready to Play," *Minneapolis Star Tribune*, September 3, 1999, accessed March 6, 2017, http://princetext.tripod.com/i_startrib99.html.

14. Susan Rogers, interview by Alan Freed for *Uptown* magazine/Per Nilsen, Los Angeles, CA, December 1994.

15. Rogers, interview by Freed, December 1994.

16. Rogers, interview by Freed, December 1994.

17. Eric Leeds, interview by Alan Freed for *Uptown* magazine/Per Nilsen, Los Angeles, CA, October 15, 1993.

18. David Sinclair, "The Man with No Label Has No Name," *London Times*, July 6, 1996, accessed March 12, 2017, https://sites.google.com/site/prninterviews/home/london-times-6-july-1996.

19. Alan Light, *Let's Go Crazy: Prince and the Making of* Purple Rain (New York: Atria Books, 2014).

20. Nolan Feeney, "Prince: EW Remembers the Music Icon's Life and Legacy," *Entertainment Weekly*, April 27, 2016, accessed June 20, 2017, http://ew.com/article/2016/04/27/prince-ew-cover.

21. Dave Hill, *Prince: A Pop Life* (New York: Harmony Books 1989), 189.

22. Dez Dickerson, in *Prince: The Glory Years*, produced by Rob Johnstone for Prism Entertainment (New Malden, Surrey, UK: Chrome Dreams Media, April 2004), DVD; also available at https://www.youtube.com/watch?v=dRNYiFxR2Ps, accessed June 17, 2017.

23. Michael Gray, "Former Prince Holds Court by Fax," *Nashville Banner*, August 22, 1997, D3.

24. Jimmy Jam, in *Purple Reign: The Story of Prince*, documentary, BBC Radio, January 18, 2003, accessed June 29, 2004, http://www.bbc.co.uk/programmes/b00snwb4.

25. Bruno Galindo, "Interview with Prince," *El Pais* (Madrid, Spain), December 15, 1996, 94.

EPILOGUE

1. Keith Murphy, "*Purple Rain* Turns 30: Prince's Engineer Shares Majestic (and Maddening) Studio Stories, *Vibe*, June 25, 2014, accessed June 25, 2017, http://web.archive.org/web/20151101151644/http://www.vibe.com/2014/06/purple-rain-turns

-30-princes-engineer-shares-majestic-and-maddening-studio-stories/susan-rogers-talks
-prince-purple-rain-2.

2. Alan Leeds, interview by Alan Freed for *Uptown* magazine/Per Nilsen, Minneapolis, MN, January 20, 1994.

3. Prince, interview by the Electrifying Mojo, *The Electrifying Mojo*, WHYT, June 7, 1986, accessed March 2, 2017, https://www.youtube.com/watch?v=NJZCoxZ5COY.

4. David Cavanagh, "Sign Here . . . ," *Q*, May 1995, accessed June 10, 2017, https://sites.google.com/site/prninterviews/home/q-may-1995.

ACKNOWLEDGMENTS

First off, for the record, I was never fortunate enough to interview Prince, so I turned to those who knew him best.

Sadly, with his passing on April 21, 2016, I will never get the chance to interview him. The loss of such a talented individual will be felt for generations. His premature death devastated the world, and millions mourned his loss, understanding that his story wasn't ready to be over. With Prince, there was always the promise of something amazing just around the corner. One more incredible song. One more mind-blowing tour. One more album. With his passing, the focus of his career shifts from what he'll do to what he'd done.

I finished this book in March of 2016, one month before his passing, so most of the interviews were conducted while he was still alive. Because of that, in the interviews, Prince is more often than not referred to in the present tense. I chose not to change this, as each interview is a snapshot in time and should reflect the thoughts at that moment. The most difficult thing for me was to go back and change the tense of the narrative to reflect that he was gone. His part in telling his story, sadly, was over. I have interviewed so many people for this project, and I can tell you that they all loved him in some way, and many of them teared up when I reached out to offer my condolences. It is easy to forget that these are all real people who lost someone they love, and no matter how much we hurt because we mourn Prince the icon, missing Prince the friend, brother, partner, husband, and mentor is almost inconceivable.

There were times I thought this book would never be completed and that all the research I'd done was simply for an elaborate hobby, but what you are holding in your hand (or reading electronically) is the culmination of more than twenty-three years of research. This started out as a crazy conversation I had with Per Nilsen while writing for *Uptown* magazine (in my opinion, still the best Prince magazine) and researching his books *DanceMusicSexRomance* and *The Vault* (still two of the best Prince books ever released), and we deemed it practically impossible and shelved it . . . until I decided to dive in head first a few years ago. Once the project became a reality, Per supplied all the interviews conducted for *Uptown*/DMSR/The Vault for this project. Those interviews included: Susan Rogers, David Z Rivkin, Jellybean Johnson, Eric Leeds, Alan Leeds, Pepé Willie, and Tony Christian, among others. Thank you, Per, for believing in this project and working hard to maintain our long-term friendship, even though I've never met you in person despite knowing you for almost half my life.

A huge leap in my research began in 1994, when I reached out to Peggy McCreary (aka Peggy Mac), who opened up to me over the course of multiple sessions that totaled more than eighteen hours. Her insights into Prince's time in the studio were invaluable, and she deserves so much praise. Peggy, you were *the* pioneer, and you opened so many doors for woman engineers. So many female engineers that I know have asked me to thank you—so thank you, from them and from me. Likewise with Susan Rogers, who is one of the people who followed in your footsteps. Susan, you are the face of Prince's studio sessions, even though by definition studio engineers are rarely recognized because all of their work is done behind a closed door. You have done so much to educate the public on the boundless energy and creative whirlwind known as Prince. Your knowledge of his time in the studio and of the science of sound is unrivaled. Thank you for being so patient with me with my seemingly endless follow-up questions.

For this particular book (1983–1984), I have been fortunate to personally interview Lisa Coleman, Wendy Melvoin, Matt Fink (Dr. Fink), Mark Brown (Brown Mark), Susannah Melvoin, Albert Magnoli, Peggy McCreary Blum (Peggy Mac), Alan Leeds, Susan Rogers, Jesse Johnson, Jill Jones, David Z Rivkin, David Coleman, Brenda Bennett, Bob Cavallo, Arne Frager, David Tickle, Tim Barr, Bill Jackson, Mark Cardenas, Coke Johnson, Craig Hubler, Paul Camarata, Eddie Mininfield (Eddie M.), Jerry Hubbard, Larry Williams, Laury Woods, Mike Kloster, David Knight, Brad Marsh, Novi Novog, Richard McKernan, Sid Page, Stephen Shelton, Murielle Hamilton, Terry Christian, Tony Christian, LeRoy "Roy" Bennett, Brent Fischer, and Clare Fischer, as well as several others who wished to remain anonymous but supplied valuable information. Also, thank you, William Blinn, for providing me with a copy of the original draft of "Dreams" many years ago.

A few people I did not interview extensively agreed to clear up a handful of contradictions for this book, including Jellybean Johnson, Paul Peterson, Benny Rietveld, Rick "Hawkeye" Henriksen, Miko Weaver, and Robbie Paster. Thank you to each of you for providing some clarity and giving me another point of view.

I reached out to several additional people for full interviews, but had to rely on public comments/interviews they've given in the past to other sources. Each of them had a hand in the musical legacy chronicled in this book, and their voices deserved to be heard.

It is difficult to sum up the people who helped machete the vines out of the way on this book for the last two decades, but here I go. For the research, the first wave of people included Brian Charrell (one of my closest friends; sadly, he didn't live long enough to see this book finally come to life), Alan Freed (who supplied countless hours of interviews he'd done, several dinners and connections, as well as a great friendship), Alex Hahn (for nearly daily questions and encouragement), Laura Tiebert, David Wild, Alan Light, Marc Roberty, Jose Álvarez, Roger Cabezas, Sylvia M. Burch, Florent Bidaud, Susan Lane, Chambers Stevens, Stacey Castro, Katherine Copeland Anderson, André Cymone, Terry Jackson, Miles Marshall Lewis, Mathieu Bitton, Kna Lo Venge, David Dubow, Ken Caillat, Cat Glover, Femi Jiya, Christine Elise McCarthy, Craig Mortimer-Zhika, Adele Burchi, Wendy Pardike, CC, Michael Van Huffel, Jill Willis, Steve Parke, Marc Weingarten, De Angela Duff, Elle Richardson, Craig Rice, Neversin, Steve Wask, John Greenewald, and the entire *Uptown* magazine staff. Also, big thanks to Ted Springman and Steve Lang at Warner Bros., Clare Zupetz and Tom Baskerville at Twin Cities Musicians Union, and Gordon Grayson and Andrew Morris at American Federation of Musicians Local 47, and to the clerks at the Library of Congress during my repeated visits. A *ginormous* thank-you to Jesse Esparza for believing in this and getting me in contact with Wendy and Susannah Melvoin, who were insanely cool and open with me and even funnier than I'd hoped. Thank you to the transcribers (including John Warehand, Jessica Pucci Winter, Kat Johnson, John Parlier, Rocio Sevilla, Jasmine Orlandini, Devon Bartholomew, Charli Transue, Chandra Wicke, Jeff Downing, Luis Hernandez, Liana Kleinman, Seema Pejman, and Unique Mills, among others), Tim D'Aquino, Scott Ramsey, Carol McGovney, Jamie Shoop, Trudy Frederick, Michael Kaliski, Ken Meyer, Anne Beringer, Gavin McLaughlin, Stephen Fredricks, Jason Draper, Tony Melodia, Harold Lewis, Jesse and Sheila Johnson, Geoffrey Himes, Paul Stojanovich (for getting me a meeting at William Morris), and all of the members of the PRINCE: The Complete Studio Sessions Book Series Facebook group (all 4,511 of you as

I type this). There are probably more, and if I've accidentally overlooked your contribution, I apologize.

And, of course, to my acquisitions editor, Natalie Mandziuk: Thank you for holding my hand on this beast and maintaining a smile and good cheer throughout. To Katie O'Brien, Jessica McCleary, and Meghann French: Thank you for getting this closer to the goal line. To Linda Ganster and Michael Ganster: Thank you for your faith in this book and in me. I owe you both more than you realize (and your nickname for me cracks me up).

Most of my research was primary, but there were many secondary sources. Several books were valuable resources for this project, including *DanceMusic-SexRomance* by Per Nilsen, *The Vault* by Per Nilsen and *Uptown* magazine, *Prince: A Pop Life* by Dave Hill, *Prince: Inside the Purple Reign* by Jon Bream, *Possessed: The Rise and Fall of Prince* by Alex Hahn, *Let's Go Crazy: Prince and the Making of Purple Rain* by Alan Light, *The Beat of My Own Drum: A Memoir* by Sheila E., *My Time with Prince* by Dez Dickerson, *Prince in the Studio* by Jake Brown, *Prince: Inside the Music and the Masks* by Ronin Ro, *Music on Film: Purple Rain* by John Kenneth Muir, *Prince* by Matt Thorne, *Slave to the Rhythm* by Liz Jones, and *Spin* magazine's article "Prince: An Oral History" and *Wax Poetic*'s Prince issue (winter 2012). I'd also like to personally thank everyone working on PrinceVault.com. I've had a small part in their research so I know many of them and I can tell you that everyone involved with PV seeks out the truth and dedicates their time and money to honoring Prince's legacy. This site really is the (pre-fire) Library of Alexandria of Prince information on the Internet, and I can guarantee you that they are a primary source on virtually every book that has come out about Prince (including mine), and they really are the unsung heroes when it comes to chronicling Prince's legacy. Many members of Prince.org and other sites in the Prince community have become my friends outside of the cold indifference of the Internet.

It is important to call out a group of friends who are my Algonquin Roundtable of Prince scholars: jooZt Mattheij, Camron Gilreath, Scott Bogen, and Thomas de Bruin. Without their daily (even hourly) help, this book wouldn't have been nearly as informative and fun to write. They understood this book early on and devoted a lot of time to getting the facts right.

Thank you to Paul Camarata and Craig Hubler at Sunset Sound for opening the doors of your studio to me and understanding when I've made multiple follow-ups over the last two decades. Thank you for doing it with a smile and encouragement. Without your help, this book wouldn't have been possible.

Thank you to Neal Preston for the incredible cover shot. I still can't believe I was able to get the art of one of the most famous rock photographers on my book cover. Please find his art and enjoy it. I've included the original shot inside the book without the Photoshop elements so people can see his incredible talent.

An epic thank-you is also due to Phil "Rev" Hodgkiss for creating the cover art. You have brought what I had in my head to the page. There is no way to describe my appreciation in words. You'll have to trust me: I can't wipe this grin off my mug! Thank you for being so generous and helpful with my infinite suggestions and questions.

Thank you to Michael Olson from Gallaudet University for supplying the photos of Prince from his November 29, 1984, concert.

Questlove, thank you for the foreword. You are truly the most well-known and respected Prince scholar out there, and it was important for me to have you read this before almost anyone. I knew you'd relate to it, and you have no idea how honored and humbled I was to read what you wrote. You rock!

Albert Magnoli, you have been so incredibly forthcoming and have become a great friend. Thank you for opening so many doors for me on this project; I look forward to working with you again.

Hucky Austin and Jacqui Thompson, my research went into the stratosphere after we started talking, and I cannot thank you enough. I am lucky to call both of you my friends and I look forward to the next project down the road.

Obviously this book wouldn't have been possible without the legacy of Prince and the Revolution. Thank you to Wendy Melvoin, Lisa Coleman, Matt Fink, Brown Mark, and Bobby Z, as well as future Revolution members Eric Leeds and Susannah Melvoin. I hope this book honors the work all of you have done. Your music is the soundtrack to my life, and I hope I have helped remind people of the contributions you've made to modern culture as well as to the history of rock and roll. Thank you for getting our asses off the chairs and making us dance. Because you helped create Prince's music, each of you know it from the stage. What you don't understand is what your work does to the people in the audience. You've heard the applause and seen our smiles, but you don't understand the life-changing experience of putting on the headphones and hearing the music you gave to us for the first time. That is something that bonds those of us in the arena, and we are eternally grateful.

There are several podcasts, radio shows, blogs, and hosts that deserve notice because of their incredible source material and their dedication to finding the truth: *The Soul Brother Show* with Mr. Chris, *The Third Story Podcast* with Leo Sidran, *The Electrifying Mojo* on WHYT, Podcastjuice.net with Michael Dean and Big Sexy, *Inside Berklee, PC Principle Podcast, Hunting for Prince's Vault* with Mobeen Azhar (BBC), Dr. Funkenberry, *The Upper Room with Joe*

Kelley, Boomer Movement Network, *Sound Opinions* on Chicago Public Radio, *Tomi Jenkins Radio Show*, *Omega Man Radio Show*, Red Bull Music Academy Lectures, Real Rube Radio, *Purple Reign: The Story of Prince* (BBC), Swedish Radio P3, LOTL Radio, Rico "Superbizzee" Washington, The Five Count, The Current, Funk Chronicles with Dr. Turk Logan, Bobby Z's radio show on 96.3 K-TWIN, *The BrownMark Podcast* and The Beautiful Nights blog by K Nicola Dyes, among others. I hope they get as many people from Prince's past telling their stories. This is history, and as we've learned with the passing of so many talented people, sometimes a story ends in midsentence. Thank you for documenting these for the sake of Prince's legacy.

In the decades since I started this, several of the people I interviewed have passed away. When I hear the voices of David Coleman, Denise "Vanity" Matthews, and Clare Fischer, I am saddened that these creative artists are no longer with us. Thank you to Donna Fischer and Gary Coleman for the permission to share their stories. I hope books like this can help extend their amazing legacies.

Thank you also to Leslie and Milton, my mom and dad, who taught me to read and encouraged me to write. I love you both very much, and without the two of you showing me how important it is to enjoy art, a book like this would have never taken form.

Finally, I need to thank the two most important people in my life, my wife, Monique, and my daughter, Zoe. I love you both more than you realize and thank you for understanding the countless evenings, weekends, and vacations that I spent parked in front of the computer breathing life into this project. This book is dedicated to the two of you.

If you love the music of Prince and those who helped create it, please support the PRN Alumni Foundation (http://www.prnalumni.com), a philanthropic organization consisting of former employees of Prince who have kept his legacy alive by raising money and contributing to many of the charitable causes that Prince championed.

This is the first in a series of books about Prince's studio sessions. If you worked with Prince in the studio and would like to be a part of the upcoming volumes, please visit my website (DuaneTudahl.com) or reach out to me at DuaneT@ MarinerPointProds.tv.

Thank you very much.

INDEX

ABOUT THE AUTHOR

Duane Tudahl is a documentary filmmaker who has produced and/or directed programming for the History Channel, CBS, GTV, Fox, Discovery, Pax, the Gospel Music Channel, the Food Channel, Tru-TV, and HGTV. He was an executive producer for a documentary about the Special Olympics that was hosted by former Miss America Vanessa L. Williams and featured Stevie Wonder, Bono, Jordin Sparks, Run DMC, and Jimmy Iovine.

A Baltimore native, Tudahl got his start as a medical photographer for Johns Hopkins Hospital. He is a former stand-up comic and has spoken at conventions around the country about the documentaries he produced for the History Channel. He has also been an editor on multiple Emmy-nominated programs, including *Intervention*, *Unsolved Mysteries*, and *Cops*, as well as music videos for Coolio, Krayzie Bone, and various others.

He has been writing about Prince and the Minneapolis music scene for more than twenty-five years and has researched and contributed to several books about the subject as well as moderated multiple panels of Prince's former employees put together by the PRN Alumni Foundation. This is his first book and is the introductory volume of his series about Prince's studio sessions.

FRANKFORT FREE LIBRARY
123 Frankfort St.
Frankfort, NY 13340
(315) 894-9611